A Friend to God's Poor

A Friend to God's Poor

Edward Parmelee Smith

By William H. Armstrong

The University of Georgia Press

Athens & London

© 1993 by the University of Georgia Press
Athens, Georgia 30602
All rights reserved
Designed by Kathi L. Dailey
Set in Ehrhardt by Tseng Information Systems, Inc.
Printed and bound by Maple-Vail
Book Manufacturing Group
The paper in this book meets the guidelines for
permanence and durability of the Committee on
Production Guidelines for Book Longevity of the
Council on Library Resources.

Printed in the United States of America

97   96   95   94   93   C   5   4   3   2   1

Library of Congress Cataloging in Publication Data

Armstrong, William H. (William Howard), 1932–
    A friend to God's poor : Edward Parmelee Smith /
William H. Armstrong.
        p.   cm.
    Includes bibliographical references and index.
    ISBN 0-8203-1493-5 (alk. paper)
    1. Smith, Edward Parmelee, 1827–1876.
    2. Social reformers—United States—Biography.
    3. Congregational Churches—United States—
Clergy—Biography.   4. Howard University—
Presidents—Biography.
    I. Title.
    E664.S638A76   1993
    973.8'092—dc20
    [B]   92-17663

British Library Cataloging in Publication Data available

Frontispiece: Edward Parmelee Smith (1827–76) when he
was United States agent for the Chippewa Indians in
Minnesota (1871–73). Courtesy of the Amistad Research
Center, New Orleans, Louisiana.

To
Lonson
Elaine, Erick, Conner, and Cara
Lester, Ellen, Louisa, and Graham
and
Bill

Contents

Illustrations

Preface

And there's a nice youngster of excellent pith,—
Fate tried to conceal him by naming him Smith.

Oliver Wendell Holmes, "The Boys"

On a winter Sunday in 1863, in the quiet town of Pepperell, Massachusetts, the members of the Congregational Church gathered to hear a request from their pastor. The United States Christian Commission was asking ministers to volunteer their services among the Union soldiers, and the church's thirty-five-year-old minister, Edward Parmelee Smith, was eager to go. The members gave their permission for him to take one month's leave, and the next morning their pastor left for Virginia and the Army of the Potomac.

Smith never returned to his pulpit. The Christian Commission soon recognized that this New England minister had uncommon business and organizational abilities, that he was a man of action as well as of faith. He was asked to stay with the commission as one of its paid agents and sent west to organize its work in the Army of the Cumberland. He worked among the western soldiers for almost two years, ministering to them himself and directing the work of others, and then was called to Philadelphia as field secretary in the commission's headquarters.

During the war the Christian Commission cooperated with the American Missionary Association, one of the largest of the many agencies engaged in relief and educational work among the freed slaves, and in 1866 Smith went to work for the association. He began as district secretary in Cincinnati, but within a year he was moved to New York City as the association's general field agent. There he supervised hundreds of teachers who went south to teach the freedmen and helped organize scores of schools among the blacks, including Fisk and Atlanta universities, Hampton Institute, and Tougaloo and Talladega colleges.

In 1870 the Grant administration, in an attempt to deal more justly with the Indians, appealed to the churches to provide agents for them. Smith offered his services and was appointed United States Indian agent for the Chippewa Indians in Minnesota. His next two years were spent traveling among the

Chippewa reservations in northern Minnesota, with the exception of three months devoted to a trip to Arizona on a peace-seeking mission to the Apache Indians with General Oliver Otis Howard.

The success of his work among the Chippewas led to Smith's appointment in 1873 as United States commissioner of Indian affairs. His selection as commissioner came at a time when almost the entire field service of the Office of Indian Affairs had been provided by churches and mission societies, and the appointment of a Protestant minister as commissioner was the culmination of President Ulysses S. Grant's peace policy toward the Indians. But Smith's appointment came also at a time of greatly increased migration to the West with its inevitable resistance by the Indians, and his two and a half years as commissioner were filled with conflict and the threat of conflict throughout the West and with conflict over the means and purposes of the peace policy itself.

When he resigned his position as Indian commissioner, Smith was elected president of Howard University in Washington, D.C. But he had barely begun his work at Howard when the American Missionary Association sent him to Africa to investigate the possibilities of future work there, and a few months later he lay dead in an African grave, the victim of malaria.

Smith's story weaves together some of the main threads running through American church history in the mid-nineteenth century: the massive response of the churches to the Civil War and its suffering; their work with the freed slaves, especially in the field of education; and the assistance the churches gave to President Grant's Indian policy. Many clergy and lay workers like Smith labored in each of those movements; few were involved in all of them. His story is both typical of the times and fascinating in itself.

To write a biography about a little-known minister with the common name of Smith is to make a statement about the significance of lesser-known people in our history. A familiar passage from the ancient book of Ecclesiasticus speaks of the famous persons of the past: "Let us now praise famous men, and our fathers that begat us. . . . All these were honoured in their generations, and were the glory of their times" (Ecclus. 44:1, 7). But the passage also recognizes that some people well-known in their own time are unknown to later generations. "There be of them, that have left a name behind them, that their praises might be reported. And some there be, which have no memorial; who are perished, as though they had never been; and are become as though they had never been born; and their children after them. But these were merciful men, whose righteousness hath not been forgotten" (Ecclus. 44:8–10).

Edward Parmelee Smith is among those who have had no memorial. But he and his associates in the Christian Commission, the American Missionary Association, and the peace policy of President Grant played a significant role in their generation and deserve at least a modest memorial in ours. "Famous men" appear in these pages too—Ulysses S. Grant and William T. Sherman, Red Cloud and Frederick Douglass—but the focus is on those who have not left a name behind them, on persons like Annie Wittenmyer and Hannah Cleaveland Smith, George Hay Stuart, George Whipple, Henry Whipple, and John Mercer Langston. If this book is a memorial to Edward Smith, it is one on which many other names are inscribed, to keep them from perishing.[1]

Whether these were "merciful men," persons of "righteousness," is a question that bears examination. Most of them were religious persons who thought of themselves as merciful and who were thought by many to be righteous. Yet Smith's brief service as commissioner of Indian affairs was the subject of six official investigations, and he was frequently accused of immoral and illegal activities. Those who observe his life from today's perspective may also ask whether the quality of his mercy toward blacks and Indians was not somewhat strained. But at least his actions were significant enough to warrant answers to the questions raised about them, and in the asking and the answering unfolds a story worth retelling.

A study like this can be accomplished only with the help of many people. I owe a special debt of thanks to the Amistad Research Center for its award of the Edward Parmelee Smith Fellowship, which enabled me to gather materials and to do the traveling necessary to research Smith's life; the members of the Burton Congregational Church (United Church of Christ) for their generous sabbatical policy, which gave me the time to conduct the study; Clifton H. Johnson, the former executive director of the Amistad Research Center, for his encouragement and guidance; the late Ruth Crawford Mitchell, Smith's granddaughter, for her generosity in sharing her family papers and memories; Ludwig F. Schaefer and John K. Tsui, who with Clifton Johnson and Ruth Mitchell met as the Edward P. Smith biography committee in the early stages of my study; Clifton Johnson, John Y. Simon, and Robert H. Keller, Jr., who read the book in manuscript and offered helpful suggestions for improving it; the University of Georgia Press for its care in preparing the book for publication; and my wife, Gloria, for her assistance with the research and for her constant support, from the day I first encountered E. P. Smith to the day the book was finally done.

Let us read old letters awhile,
Let us try to hear
The thin, forgotten voices of men forgotten
Crying out of torn scraps of paper. . . .

Stephen Vincent Benét,
John Brown's Body

A Friend to God's Poor

1

A Stammering Priest

> I am glad that I grew up under these wholesome Puritanic influences, as
> glad as I am that I was born a New Englander; and I surely should have
> chosen New England for my birthplace before any region under the sun.
>
> Lucy Larcom, *A New England Girlhood*

It was a solemn congregation that gathered in the meetinghouse of the
Congregational Church in South Britain, Connecticut, on an October day
in 1830. They came to mourn the untimely death of their pastor, Noah Smith,
dead of typhus fever at the age of thirty-six.

The preacher at the funeral adhered to the ancient advice to speak well of
the dead. He spoke of Smith's extraordinary powers of mind, his attachment
to his parishioners, his purity of motive, his devotion to duty, his humility,
and his piety. As on many such occasions, a good deal was left unsaid. Apart
from the erection of a fine new meetinghouse and the adoption of a new confession and covenant, Smith's eight-year ministry had not been particularly
successful or happy. And there was the unspoken question of the future of
his widow, Laura, and the four children born to them in the parsonage at
South Britain: Sarah, Martha, Mary, and Edward Parmelee.[1]

Noah Smith's life had been deeply rooted in New England and its Congregational religion. He was born on March 8, 1794, in Hanover, New Hampshire, one of eleven children born to Edward and Hannah Smith. Hannah
was determined to give her children the education she had not received, and
she succeeded in sending three of her sons to college before she learned
to read herself. Noah prepared for college at Moor's Indian Charity School
(studying Cicero and the Greek New Testament) and then progressed to
Dartmouth College. He graduated from Dartmouth in 1818, the same year
Daniel Webster made his impassioned plea for the college before the United
States Supreme Court. Both Moor's school and Dartmouth College were
located in the village of Hanover, a few miles south of the Smith home. Before
he began his college work, Noah had made a public profession of his religious

Noah Smith (1794–1830),
the father of Edward Smith.
Courtesy of the Amistad
Research Center, New Orleans,
Louisiana.

beliefs at Albany, New York, and after his graduation he entered Andover
Theological Seminary, a Congregational school in Andover, Massachusetts,
to study for the ministry.[2]

Noah did well in his studies at Andover. His "Translation & commentary
of Psalm 16th.10. with a discussion of the question, whether this Ps[alm] re-
lates to the Messiah" and an essay on "the influence of emotion on delivery"
show a clear thinker and writer. His election as vice-president of the Society
of Inquiry and as the chairman of a delegation sent by his class to tell the
faculty about the students' dissatisfaction with one of their professors show
him succeeding with his peers. Considerable comment, however, was made
about his marriage to Laura Parmelee while he was still a student. His sister
Hannah said that "Noah was caught by a pair of black eyes," and others indicated enough displeasure with the marriage to cause Noah "severe trials"
on the subject. Because of Laura's ill health, and perhaps also because of the
oddity of a married student of theology, Noah's wife stayed in New Haven in
what Noah called "a kind of widowhood" while he completed his education.[3]

While still a student, Noah took an interest in revivals occurring in various parts of New England, traveling to some of the centers of the revivals to
attend meetings and to visit from house to house as an evangelist, while observing the methods of other evangelists. "It is a good time to study divinity,"

he wrote, "when the spirit of God is operating on the hearts of men." On his graduation from Andover in 1821, he was ordained as an evangelist and was commissioned by the Missionary Society of Connecticut for work in the western and southwestern states.[4]

In the fall of 1821, Noah set out for Ohio with two other missionaries. When the three arrived in Geneva, New York, several of the local ministers asked that one of them remain there "and supply the destitute congregations or preach as missionaries." The novice missionaries agreed, and "as there were some circumstances in [Noah's] case a little peculiar" (namely, his wife and his desire to find a congregation in a place where he could "settle"), he was selected to stay in New York. Noah accepted a commission from a local missionary society and began to work in Sodus and Williamson on Lake Ontario while waiting to hear whether the Connecticut society would agree to a change in his commission. In December the society issued a new commission for one year's work in the western counties of New York.

Noah's service as a missionary lasted thirty-one weeks and took him across western New York. He preached 153 sermons, administered the Lord's Supper six times, baptized two adults and nine children, and visited almost daily in homes. He found the tour pleasant and was well received by settlers eager to see a minister. Meetings were crowded. On Thanksgiving, both men and women ventured out in a snowstorm to hear him preach. "Oh," he wrote, "it is pleasant to lead the inquiring and to see the pious eye glisten with tears of joy at the arrival of a missionary." He stayed longer in some places than he thought acceptable to the society, but he was persuaded that "a sermon here and there from one always on the wing does but little good."[5]

The end of his tour found him in the extreme western part of New York, only a day's ride from his original destination of Ohio. He used the opportunity to visit the Seneca Indians there, "called on their missionary, Mr. Harris, and attended a meeting of the chiefs with him." In May 1822, he was back home, convinced of the need for more good ministers to visit the western settlements with their small congregations and their "vast multitude who have no faith and no concern in religion." Baptist, Methodist, and Universalist ministers were at work in the new communities, as well as a variety of sectarians, but too few settled Congregationalists or Presbyterians, with whom the Congregationalists had made common cause on the mission field since 1801.[6]

In March 1822, the pulpit of the Congregational Church of South Britain, Connecticut, became vacant with the resignation of the pastor, Bennet Tyler. That summer Noah Smith preached in the church as a candidate for the ministry, received a call, and on October 9 was installed as pastor. The local consociation of churches met to examine the candidate the day before the installation. After Noah was approved, seven of the visiting ministers participated in the installation service, including Lyman Beecher of nearby Litchfield and the newly appointed professor of theology at Yale, Nathaniel Taylor.[7]

It may have been a mistake for the young Noah Smith to follow the pastorate of Bennet Tyler. Tyler had been in South Britain for fourteen years, during which time "the church had enjoyed great peace and prosperity," and 108 members had been added to the congregation. So successful had Tyler's ministry been that he was elected president of Dartmouth College, going directly from South Britain to the school at Hanover. During Noah's ministry at South Britain, only eighteen members were added, and dissatisfaction was expressed about the young man's work. Toward the end of his pastorate, some of the members withdrew from the congregation and began to hold separate meetings in the schoolhouse, one of them stating that he did not wish to be considered a member of the church "so long as Rev. Noah Smith remains a minister in said Society."[8]

One difficulty was that Noah Smith was not a good speaker. Both his father, Edward Smith, Jr., and his grandfather, Edward Smith, Sr., stuttered badly. When Noah's father prayed in public, his words came "with perfect ease," but when he attempted to speak in public he broke down completely. Because of his stuttering he refused the office of deacon when it was offered to him, an office Edward, Sr., had held despite his difficulty in speaking. A member of the family said that Noah's mother "would not allow one of the 11 children to stammer, though they all tried it. She would pounce down on them with 'Say that over again!' and the child would not dare stutter again. Her husband would try to intercede, & say the child could not help it, but poor man never a word could he get out, while she exclaimed, 'He *can* help it. Don't you interfere with me about my children.'" The effect on Noah was not what his mother intended. "Being slow and hesitating of speech his preaching was uninteresting to some and without notes he could do nothing." Sermons welcomed by settlers on brief visits in New York were not always welcomed by his parishioners in Connecticut. When the new meetinghouse erected during his pastorate was dedicated, an unfriendly neighbor ridiculed the building, the minister, and the congregation by writing

> A small church with a tall steeple
> A stammering priest and a wicked people.[9]

Despite the criticism, the building was a notable achievement. At first the congregation intended only to complete and repair the old building, which had stood unfinished since 1770, but finally decided to erect an entirely new building in the style established by a Connecticut architect, David Hoadley. The church was distinguished by a large steeple of two octagonal stages, crowned with an octagonal spire, by a large circular dome that filled the ceiling of the audience room, and by the pulpit's location near the church doors—perhaps placed there to discourage latecomers, who had to enter the church facing the congregation. When the building was completed, Noah's brother Chandler was invited to sing at the dedication.[10]

Another achievement to which Noah Smith could point was the adoption of a new confession of faith and a new covenant of membership. Both placed the congregation squarely in the Calvinist tradition, distinguishing it from the churches involved in New England's new Unitarian movement. The confession stressed the trinity and the sovereignty of God in its opening statement:

> You believe in the one only living and true God, the Father, the Son, and the Holy Ghost, who is a spirit, infinite, eternal, and unchangeable in his being and perfections, that it is the duty of all his intelligent creatures to worship him in spirit and in truth, that he created all things, preserves and governs all his creatures, and overrules all their actions for his own glory, and that in whatsoever comes to pass he is accomplishing his eternal purposes according to the council of his own will, in such a way that man is a free agent, and accountable for all his actions.

The covenant prescribed the commitment required of new members and the way of life they were expected to follow:

> You do now in the presence of God and this assembly, solemnly, and as you hope, with sincerity of soul, dedicate yourself to God in Christ, humbly confessing and repenting of all your sins.
>
> You solemnly avouch the Lord Jehovah to be your God, the Lord Jesus your Redeemer, the eternal Spirit your Sanctifier.
>
> You covenant and promise, that by the strength of Divine grace, you will make it your endeavor to walk worthy of the Christian vocation.
>
> You also covenant with the church that you will walk with it in Christian fellowship, and in a due attendance on all the Institutions of Christ.
>
> Thus in the presence of God you solemnly covenant and promise.[11]

Besides the satisfaction Noah Smith found in the erection of the new meetinghouse and the adoption of a new confession and covenant, he also found satisfaction in his home and growing family. When Noah came to South Britain, he had bought the Wheeler House, which was previously owned by his predecessor, Bennet Tyler. The house had been the home of

South Britain's first physician, Dr. [Lemuel?] Wheeler, in prerevolutionary days. The two-story, center-chimney, saltbox house with clapboard siding had seven rooms. In addition to a large fireplace and oven in the kitchen, two rooms downstairs and two upstairs also had fireplaces. Here Noah and Laura Smith's children were born: Sarah Matilda on August 14, 1823; Martha Miranda on April 29, 1825; Edward Parmelee on June 3, 1827; and Mary Shipman on May 9, 1830.[12]

Noah's sister Hannah married a resident of South Britain and moved there early in 1829. After visiting Noah and his family, she wrote to the rest of the family that "little Ed goes to school some. He says he wants to see Grandpa Smith way up in New Hampshire. . . . He is a very smart boy for one of his age." She also wrote that "the difficulty in Noah's Church and society is subsiding in some measure. It has affected his health very materially. . . . At times . . . neither man or beast could suit him. Hard study, family affairs, troubles in his Parish have been a great injury to his health." A young nephew also visited Noah and later remembered him as "a tall, slim man with a long and pleasant face [who] wore side whiskers."[13]

The Wheeler House, the home of Noah and Laura Smith in South Britain, Connecticut. Courtesy of Evangeline Cassidy, the present owner of the house, and South Britain Congregational Church.

Laura Parmelee Smith (1796–1857), the mother of Edward Smith. Courtesy of the Amistad Research Center, New Orleans, Louisiana.

In May 1830 Noah wrote to his father to tell him about Mary's birth, adding that the other children were attending school and that Edward, soon to celebrate his third birthday, "can read very well in the Testament." His own health, he said, was better than usual. But his good health did not last. At times both his health and his spirits were so depressed that he thought he might have to abandon the ministry. His last illness was brief and at first was not thought serious. He was able to preach up to two weeks before his death. "His mind was singularly calm and unruffled to the last," but he said little during his illness, leaving no memorable last words for his family and friends to remember. He died on October 10, 1830.[14]

Laura Smith was not prepared to raise four small children by herself, and the decision was made to distribute them among members of the Smith family. Having inherited more debts than assets from her husband, Laura left South Britain to live with her mother, taking only the baby, Mary, with her. Noah's sister Hannah took the oldest girl, Sarah; his brother Chandler took Martha. Noah's brother Ashbel and his wife, Lucinda, were visiting in South Britain when Noah died, and three-year-old Edward accompanied them on their return to the Smith homestead in Hanover, New Hampshire.[15]

Ashbel Smith was working the family farm in Hanover, his parents having retired to a little red house Ashbel had built for them a short distance from the farmhouse. To that red house, with his grandparents, sixty-year-old Edward Smith, Jr., and fifty-nine-year-old Hannah Chandler Smith, Edward came to live.

THE SMITH FAMILY had been in New England for almost two hundred years when Edward Smith was brought to Hanover. His ancestor Samuel Smith had sailed from Ipswich, England, to Watertown, Massachusetts, in 1634. The family had lived in Hanover since 1767—just two years after its settlement—when Samuel Smith's great-grandson, Timothy Smith, moved there from Connecticut at the age of sixty-five. The sale of his property in Connecticut enabled Timothy to give his children land in New Hampshire, one hundred acres to each son and sixty acres to each daughter, enough to induce his whole family to follow him into what was then an unbroken wilderness, covered with white pines four and five feet in diameter, their first limbs one hundred feet above the ground. Timothy Smith settled on the river road about three miles north of the present site of Dartmouth College. When the college was founded, he gave one hundred acres of his land to the new school. Timothy was a large, athletic man, who, while chopping wood at the age of seventy-five, was blinded by a splinter, after which he ran a ferryboat on the Connecticut River, using a small boy to give directions for guiding the boat.[16]

One of Timothy Smith's sons was Deacon Edward Smith, a carpenter, who was forty-one when he and his family moved with Timothy to Hanover. There, two years after the move from Connecticut, Edward Smith, Jr., was born, and there he lived his entire life. "Ward," as Edward, Jr., was known, was married in 1791 to Hannah Chandler. Hannah was born in Portsmouth, New Hampshire, and was orphaned there at the age of seven when her parents drowned in the harbor. She and her brother were sent to a poor farm, where her brother also died. After working in various homes, Hannah went to work in the home of Deacon Edward Smith, where she met and married his son Ward. Ward and Hannah Smith raised the eight of their eleven children who survived infancy—Asahel, Noah, Ashbel, Cyrus Porter, Russell, Chandler, Irene, and Hannah—and were retired on the farm Ashbel had taken over. When Ashbel returned from Connecticut with their grandson Edward, Ward and Hannah welcomed him into their home as though he were their own son.

Edward's new home, the little red house on the family farm some five miles north of Dartmouth College, consisted of two rooms and a loft. A large chimney occupied the center of the house with one fireplace facing the kitchen and another facing the living room. Edward was given a room in the loft just big enough for a bed, one chair, and his trunk. The mistress of the house was a strong-willed woman who made a lasting impression on Edward. He said in later years that he could never see a boiled tongue without seeing his grandmother's black eyes as she pointed to a tongue hanging in the buttery and said, "Edward, there's a tongue that never told a lie; can you say as much for yours?" Later, when his future was to be decided, Edward's uncle and grandfather urged him to stay on the farm and promised him ample land for farming, but Hannah would hear nothing of it. "Edward, don't you stay on the farm, you get an education." And that settled the matter. His grandparents also had a great influence on Edward's religious life. Lying in his trundle bed one night, he heard them saying that they wanted him "to grow up a good Christian man." Although he did not know just what that meant, he said to himself, "I certainly will if they want me to." It was also said that his grandmother, in particular, was determined from his early years that he be trained for the ministry.[17]

Living with his grandparents did not isolate Edward from the rest of the family. His uncle Ashbel and aunt Lucinda lived next door on the same farm. Edward later called Ashbel "one of the best of New England men, not wealthy and not poor and very kind," and said that on his uncle's farm he had been a "happy and a very useful boy." Ashbel and Lucinda eventually became the parents of eleven children (Ashbel wanted to call the eleventh Omega, "the last"), and their house was a hive of activity. One of the children, especially, was a frequent visitor to his grandparents' home and came to regard Edward as his cousin-brother. This was Roswell T. Smith, and his recollections of his boyhood in Hanover provide a clear picture of Edward's boyhood as well.[18]

Two years before Edward's arrival in Hanover, Roswell had become paralyzed in a confrontation with a "fierce and untamable hog" on the farm. He lost the use of his legs and for a time did not grow, but his mind was active. Carried about in a small chair, he became a great pet of his grandmother Smith, spending hours in her home. As he grew older, he learned to use crutches, and his brothers and sisters pulled him to school in a wagon, even though he was not a regular student. On one occasion, a thoughtless hired man donned a "hideous mask" and frightened the children on their way home from school. The children fled, as did the teacher who was accompanying the group, leaving Roswell helpless in the street. Only Roswell's "cousin-brother" Edward was willing to place himself between Roswell and the masked man and to "show fight," until the man realized his mistake and unmasked.[19]

Ashbel Smith's house—Roswell's home and Edward's second home—was a one-story building with a large living and working room and a huge fire-place and oven, where all the cooking, baking, brewing, and washing were done. The less-used parlor had a "stiff and uncomfortable air and repre-sented the dignity of the family." A shop in the house contained "a large loom, two large spinning wheels, a linen wheel and conveniences for winding and spooling yarn. . . . It also contained a shoemaker's bench and kit with a goodly show of leather." Roswell Smith said proudly that growing up in that house he "was fourteen years old before I ever saw a drunken man, heard an oath, or knew the meaning of the word dishonest, and I never in that house heard a word of disapprobation of any man because of religious or political belief."[20]

The Smith farm had four small barns and was large enough to require hired help. "In the winter the farmer with a sled load of produce made a trip to Boston or Salem and exchanged it for sugar, salt, codfish &c for family use, bringing not only supplies for the table but marvellous stories of Boston and the haps & mishaps of the journey." Edward did his share of the work on the farm. Years later he remembered how he "used to drive the cows[,] pick potatoes & apples & stones & cut & pile wood" with his many uncles and cousins.[21]

When Edward was eight years old, his uncle Ashbel sold his interest in the farm and moved across the Connecticut River to Thetford, Vermont, to allow his growing family to attend the Thetford Academy. Roswell was per-mitted to attend classes with the others, a special "student that did not study" but learned "by absorption." Ashbel's family lived in Thetford for five years before moving back to Hanover, and it was probably during that time that Edward, too, began his studies at the Thetford Academy. He had, however, been to school before he entered the academy. When he first went to school, Edward was asked if he had come to learn to read. "Oh! no," he replied. "I can read now, I want to study arithmetic."[22]

The principal of the Thetford Academy was "a man of parts, a thorough teacher and a good wise man." The students were eager to learn, the boys with ambitions for college and professional life, the girls for teaching and missionary work. The academy was known as a place that sent out "students who were thoroughly imbued with the necessity and spirit of *work*, students who somehow had acquired the use of their faculties, and liked to use them; it was a kind of education which fitted one to *accomplish* something."[23]

The people of New England had a passion for learning and an absolute faith in the power of education. As Henry Adams described it, "Education was divine, and man needed only a correct knowledge of facts to reach per-fection." The first priority in every New England town, after building the

church, was to establish a school. Not only were common schools and acade-
mies available for formal education, but it was not unusual for a girl to have
a book at her spinning wheel or for a housewife to have one at her kitchen
table. Every home had a large family Bible, which was faithfully read at family
gatherings by the man of the house, reading "regularly through in course . . .
without note, comment, or explanation," in the same manner the Bible was
read again by the children as a reading book in the common schools. Hanover
also had the influence of Dartmouth College, both the students who

> Sang songs, and told us what befalls
> In classic Dartmouth's college halls,

and the school's collection of books. "There was seldom a time," Roswell
Smith said, "when there was not one or more books from [the college]
Libraries in the home and they were always books selected by men who read
to learn; not for amusement." The community was tied to the larger world
by subscriptions to weekly publications such as the *New Hampshire Statesman*
and the *New York Evangelist.* [24]

Central to the life of the community was the church. Roswell said that
"every one in the parish went to church every Sunday. The very horses knew
when Sunday came and would go upon that day to the church without guidance. The congregations were large, the preaching excellent, and the singing
was of the best. . . . The old meeting house was very large and was really a
fine house. It had the most graceful spire I ever saw." [25]

The people "went to meeting" both in the morning and the afternoon.
Edward Everett Hale, the Unitarian minister and author, said of his New
England boyhood that "any person who had been seen driving out of town
on Sunday, either in the morning or in the afternoon, would have lost credit
in the community." The children went too, and though they may not have
understood much of what was said in the meeting, they began to learn, as
another New Englander put it, "that the heavens and earth stood upon firm
foundations—upon the Moral Law as taught in the Old Testament and confirmed by the New. Whatever else we did not understand, we believed that to
disobey our parents, to lie or steal, had been forbidden by a Voice which was
not to be gainsaid." They also learned to serve God by resisting the evils they
found in the world. Henry Adams said that "for numberless generations his
predecessors had viewed the world chiefly as a thing to be reformed, filled
with evil forces to be abolished." [26]

The Smith family had participated in the Hanover Center Church of
Christ (Congregational) since its beginning. Timothy Smith and his wife,
Esther, were signers of the original covenant in 1771, and the first meeting-

house was built next to their home. Each succeeding generation found Smiths on the church rolls. Edward became a church member in May 1842 at the age of fourteen. He had been baptized by his father shortly after his birth, but church membership required also what Harriet Beecher Stowe called a "conviction of some spiritual experience gained, of some familiar communion with the Great Invisible," or as it was expressed in the confession of faith at Noah Smith's church: "Without a special interest in [Christ's] atonement there is no salvation . . . without a change of heart wrought in the unregenerate by the special Divine agency of the Holy Spirit, (who is truly God,) no one can be an heir of eternal life." That change of heart was often acquired during one of the frequent revivals of religion. The revivals, so important to Edward's father, were described by Stowe as times when "that deep spiritual undercurrent of thought and emotion with regard to the future life, which was always flowing quietly under [New England's] intense material industries, exhaled and steamed up into an atmosphere which pervaded all things, and made itself for a few weeks the only thought of every person in some town or village or city. It was the always-existing spiritual becoming visible and tangible." But it was tangible usually in quieter ways in New England than the shouting, convulsive revivals of the frontier. Edward said simply— years later—"the night I began to love Jesus & try to do as He wants me to" he read the first chapter of the New Testament book of James "and then I learned it by heart that week." [27]

The minister of the church was expected not only to preach and pray in the public services but "to bring every one in his flock to a living, conscious union with God; to a life whose source and purposes were above this earth and tending heavenward." The minister was the first citizen of the parish. The author Lucy Larcom, looking back on her New England girlhood, remembered finding it hard to "sit still through the 'ninthlies,' and 'tenthlies,' and 'finallys' of the sermon," yet she also remembered that her reverence for the minister took "the form of idolatry." She realized later that her "graven-image worship of him was only a childish exaggeration of the general feeling of grown people around me," who universally held the ministerial office in "deep reverence." [28]

Alongside the New Englander's devotion to God was a devotion to work. "We were taught to work," Lucy Larcom said, "almost as if it were a religion; to keep at work, expecting nothing else. It was our inheritance, handed down from the outcasts of Eden." Harriet Beecher Stowe's description of one New Englander would have applied to many: "a do-something,—an early-rising, bustling, driving, neat, efficient, capable little body." Growing up in New England, one inherited an awful sense of responsibility to use one's life and one's time well. [29]

But growing up in New England also had its joys. Roswell Smith remembered with fondness the daily coaches that came up the river road in Hanover, pulled by "six splendid horses" that "seldom broke their trot except as they passed over the crest of a hill down which and across the valley they would go upon the run ... one can almost hear the thunder of their crossing Slate brook bridge and see the leaders as they shake their manes at the top of the hill and change their run into a trot." On the morning of the Dartmouth commencement, a noisy public holiday, when, one visitor said, "that quiet little place is like a box of toys shook up by a great hand," an almost continuous line of carriages would pass up the road. Edward Everett Hale remembered that when carriages met a group of children in the country, the children would line up on the side of the road and "make their manners," bowing as the carriages passed, "good-naturedly, with no sign of deference, but rather ... as a pleasant recognition of human brotherhood in a lonely region."[30]

Young New Englanders knew other joys too: the training days of the militia—social as well as military occasions—in which Colonel Ashbel Smith played his part; Independence Day, "the only really secular fete known to the Yankee mind"; Thanksgiving, "the king and high priest of all festivals," with its turkey in a "tin-kitchen" turning on the spit; sleigh rides, with hot bricks to keep the feet warm, the runners "squeaking and crunching over the frozen road, and the lively jingle of bells"; Saturday afternoons, "a sort of child's Paradise," when "even household disciplinarians recognized a reasonably well-behaved child's right to a Saturday afternoon play-spell"; and exciting stories told at the firesides by people who had witnessed attacks by Indians when Hanover was still young. In this serious but pleasant setting Edward Smith enjoyed life as a "happy and a very useful boy."[31]

2

Cleavie

We count them good soldiers, devout church-goers, prim, virtuous, but rather ascetic; seldom mirthful, never freakish or gamesome, doing even their courting in solemn Scriptural phraseology. Fie upon you, narrow-minded modern! Our fathers and mothers, nay, even our great-great grandfathers and grandmothers were young men and women in their day, who ate and drank, and made merry, who sang and danced, and—shall we say it?—flirted as outrageously as you do.

Gail Hamilton, *Twelve Miles from a Lemon*

With Dartmouth College close enough that he could walk to the school, it was natural that Edward chose to study there. Dartmouth was also the school to which his grandmother had sent three of her sons. Noah graduated from the college in 1818. Cyrus Porter graduated in 1824, after which he read law and then began to practice law in Brooklyn, New York. He served as clerk and attorney of the city corporation, as the city's counsel, and then from 1839 to 1842 as mayor. Chandler graduated from Dartmouth Medical School in 1831 and served both as a physician and a minister before his death in 1843. Following the family tradition, Edward "fitted for college at Hanover" and then entered Dartmouth in the fall of 1844.[1]

His cousin Roswell, who had taken up portrait painting, commemorated Edward's status as a student by painting his portrait with Dartmouth Hall in the background. During his second year at Dartmouth, Edward wrote to his sister Mary, "I like college life very well." He discovered, however, that the townspeople did not like the students nearly as well because of their frequent pranks. The summer before, his uncle Russell had become a victim of students who put his carriage on the college roof.[2]

The education Dartmouth offered Edward was little different from what it had offered his father thirty years before. Mathematics and the classics were the basic subjects; philosophy and rhetoric were also stressed. Some attention was given to the natural sciences but little to the social sciences, and modern languages were offered only by private teachers. Moral and religious training was the school's highest priority. The schedule included chapel exercises each morning and evening, biblical exercises each Monday, and church services twice each Sunday. The faculty, most of whom were theologically trained, promoted an orthodox theology, a position encouraged by the trustees because of the school's dependence on the Congregational churches for its financial survival.[3]

Most of Edward's immediate family was living in Connecticut. His sister Sarah had become a teacher and then had married George Thacher, a young minister who was serving a church in Derby; Mary was both studying and teaching in New Haven, and their mother was living with her. Edward decided to move to Connecticut, too, to complete his college work at Yale. His decision to leave Dartmouth may have been influenced by doubts about that school's future. In five years Dartmouth's enrollment had dropped by nearly one-half, and the resulting financial crisis was obvious to everyone.

Edward planned to pay for his move to New Haven by teaching school. He had already taught at Hartford, Vermont, during winter vacations, and after he completed two school years at Dartmouth, he taught for a full year to raise the money he needed to enter the junior class at Yale. The district schools in New England were often taught by students who "boarded round" among the families in the school district. Walt Whitman, who had also "boarded round," considered it "one of my best experiences and deepest lessons in human nature." Classes were typically held in one-room schoolhouses, modest buildings surrounded by a trampled playground, with a flagpole outside and a privy in the back.

> In that smoked and dingy room,
> Where the district gave thee rule
> O'er its ragged winter school,
> Thou didst teach the mysteries
> Of those weary ABC's,—

and along with the ABC's, writing, numbers, grammar, spelling, Bible reading, geography, declamation, and even a little Latin.[4]

The family tradition is that Edward walked to New Haven in the fall of 1847, carrying a small trunk with his belongings on his shoulder. He may well have walked at least part of the way, only to be disappointed when he could not pass the oral examination in Latin that was a prerequisite to entering Yale. With only three weeks until the opening of the term, Edward appealed for help to his sister Mary, who was teaching in New Haven. After three weeks of tutoring, night and day, he insisted that he be given another opportunity to take the test, and when he had passed it, he proudly gave the credit to his sister. His sisters continued to help him while he was in New Haven, making his shirts and doing his laundry and mending, while he worked at odd jobs to pay his school expenses.[5]

Life at Yale was similar to life at Dartmouth: early morning chapel services followed by recitations before breakfast, evening prayers, and worship services twice each Sunday. The curriculum was designed to "give that furniture, and discipline, and elevation to the mind" necessary as a preparation for later life, and especially for the ministry, the law, and medicine, the professions that claimed most of Yale's graduates. Edward's friend and classmate Timothy Dwight thought their studies in mathematics and the classics useful for mental discipline but "not very stimulating, or calculated greatly to awaken enthusiasm." The offerings of the senior year were somewhat broader: mental philosophy, history, chemistry, and oratory. Electives, chiefly modern languages, were offered only in the third term of the junior year and the second term of the senior year, and even then little time was allowed for them. Despite the dullness of the curriculum, the class of 1849 developed strong ties with the university, "the kind Mother who had given us her benediction."[6]

Little remains of Edward's two years at Yale apart from his autograph album full of fond greetings to "E.P." and recollections of times spent together in German classes, "in the prayer circle & in the crowded church." "Though he became a member of [the class of] '49 at a late hour," one of his friends wrote, "[he] succeeded in gaining the respect and esteem of his classmates," who came to value his "presence of mind," his "ceaseless activity," his "un*quench*able fund of humor," and his "unblemished Christian character."[7]

Although many of Edward's classmates expected him to follow his "sainted father" into the ministry, it was teaching that first claimed his attention. On October 17, 1849, he sailed on the bark *St. Marys* from New York City for Mobile, Alabama, where he had accepted a position as a teacher in the Barton Academy. Four of the eight passengers on the ship were women, two of them teachers who were also going to teach at the academy and who were traveling under Smith's charge. With no steward aboard, Smith felt obliged to attend the women in their seasickness, playing "the part of nurse and *general physician*." One of the women had consumption and vomited blood for three days. "I have heard of the pleasure of *sitting up* with ladies," he wrote after their first night's illness. "But if that night's experience is a *fair* trial, deliver me from such sweets."[8]

On Saturday, November 3, the ship reached Mobile Bay. The passengers were unable to charter a schooner to get to land until the next day, which raised the question of the morality of employing persons to take them into town "and have all the bustle of landing: finding our places of residence: meeting with friends, &c &c" on the Sabbath day. Keeping the Sabbath was a primary article of faith with nineteenth-century Christians, and "the question was discussed some what warmly," with appeals to the relevant passages in the Bible. "All *disapproved* of Sabbath breaking. But then—Circumstances. Necessity in the case of the disciples gathering corn. The sheep in the pit. Christ's miracles. The *hypocritical* Pharisees. &c &c all came up, and had their due weight upon minds unconvinced." In the morning the fog lifted and they could see the city, the academy, and the church "and almost hear the silver notes of the Sabbath bell calling us to worship"—and the debate resumed. Smith argued against breaking the Sabbath for any reason and suffered the abuse of some of the other travelers for taking that position. Finally, an opportunity arose to go ashore, and all except Smith took it, including the two teachers in his charge. He was sure he was right in letting the women go alone. "In my own mind, to go or stay was a question between gallantry and duty: and I trust was decided cheerfully and with no hesitation." Smith was not able to reach shore until Tuesday, classes at the academy having begun without him. He moved into a room in the academy and began teaching a class of fifty students the next day.[9]

Mobile was then, in the value of its exports, the third largest seaport in the United States, its most important export being cotton. A British traveler described it as "a pleasant cotton city . . . where the people live in cotton houses and ride in cotton carriages." It was, however, more cosmopolitan than many southern cities and had strong ties to the northern states and to Europe. One-fifth of the free adult males had been born in the North; almost one-half were foreign-born. Still, it was clearly a southern city: one-third of the population were slaves. After Smith's death, it was said that "during his sojourn at Mobile, he frequently preached to the colored people. His sympathy was greatly aroused in their behalf, and he spoke his mind freely and boldly at all times respecting their condition," something that was still possible in the moderate political climate that prevailed in Mobile at the time.[10]

The Barton Academy had been built in 1836 as a public school by the Mobile County Board of School Commissioners. A Connecticut-born citizen, Henry Hitchcock, a grandson of Ethan Allen, played a major part in the founding of the school. The impressive three-story Greek Revival building was at first leased to various private and denominational schools, which were subsidized with tax money to educate the city's poor. Not until a few months after Smith left Mobile did the academy become a truly public school. Smith probably taught for the Presbyterians who conducted free schools for the poor and private schools for those who could afford them, as well as "Creole schools" for the children of the free blacks of Mobile. During part of his three years in Mobile, Smith also taught in a school at Cottage Hill, a suburban community where he could escape the yellow fever that frequently threatened the city's residents.[11]

On March 10, 1852, Smith became a member of the Second Presbyterian Church in Mobile. The South had few Congregational churches, but it did have a good number of Presbyterian churches, in which Congregationalists felt at home. Both churches were Calvinistic in theology and differed mainly in their form of government, the Congregationalists stressing the authority of the local congregation and the Presbyterians the authority of the presbytery. The Presbyterians received Smith as a member on the presentation of a certificate of membership in the Congregational Church at Hanover.[12]

It was in the Presbyterian church that Smith responded to the call to become a minister. The Alabama Presbyterians were in need of ministers. The Synod of Alabama had only forty-eight ministers to serve ninety-seven churches and only four men preparing for the ministry. At the urging of his pastor, Robert Nall, and with his father's example before him, Smith decided to put himself under the care of the presbytery as a candidate for the ministry. Even before he applied for membership in the church in Mobile, Smith traveled to Cahaba, near Selma, to attend a meeting of the Presbytery of South Alabama to "be examined and put upon a prescribed course of study and at the next session if I pass a satisfactory examination, receive a license to preach." Finding that the meeting at Cahaba had adjourned before his arrival, Smith accompanied some ministers to Selma, where the Presbyterian synod was meeting, and then returned to Mobile.[13]

His steamboat trip up the Alabama River allowed Smith to see some of rural Alabama (including the first hill of any size he had seen since he left Connecticut). "The whole country and all the crops were new to me, and you may judge that it was a strange as well as pleasing sight to a New Hampshire farmer boy like me to see a field of cotton extending over 300 acres without a hill, tree, fence, or stump to mar the prospect. Field hands, men and women, were busy picking the white bolls. It is a beautiful sight[,] a cotton field white for picking."[14]

Several deaths occurred in Smith's family while he was in Mobile. Both Ward and Hannah Smith died at their home in Hanover. Smith's sister Sarah, who was married to George Thacher, also died. A year later, Thacher married Mary Smith, Edward's youngest sister. Smith was especially close to Mary and not close to Thacher, and he would have preferred that she marry some-one else, but he resigned himself to the marriage and to the inevitable loss of intimacy with the sister he called "my own confiding, affectionate Mollie."[15]

That loss was made up for in his newfound love for one of the teachers in Mobile, Hannah Cleaveland Bush, whom he described in a letter to Mary.

> Miss B., as might be surmised, is a fellow-*teacher*, the 2nd daughter of Mr. Levi Bush of Westfield Mass., at the present time engaged in a sort of missionary school in Mobile. She came to board with Mr. Merrill last winter & taught part of the time in his school. I saw her every day and often during the day, had every opportunity to study her habits and disposition, was satisfied[,] fell in love, and the result is as you see (or hear). Miss B. is one year younger than myself (23 *June 4*). About the height of my sister Mary . . . blue eyes, chestnut hair, round face &c, &c, for at least *two pages*. Her five *leading* traits are piety, energy, amia-bility, cheerfulness & industry. Sings well, of good native mind, fair education, refinement & taste, and so on to the end of another chapter.

So far removed from his family, Smith could not ask their advice in the selec-tion of his future wife, but he was confident he had been led to the right choice. "I believe that, that kind, all wise Providence, Who has guided my steps thus far, has also led me to this choice; and that He will bless our union by making us each a help to the other in promoting His glory on earth."[16]

Hannah Bush was born June 4, 1828, in Whately, Massachusetts, where her father, Levi, kept a variety store and later a "temperance hotel." Her mother, Ann, died when Hannah was nine years old. Levi marked his wife's grave in the Whately cemetery with a monument to commemorate "one whose amiable disposition, meekness, christian benevolence, and ardent piety rendered her an ornament to the social circle, and community, and to the church of Christ." After her death, Levi remarried and moved to Westfield, Massachusetts. The father of seven daughters, Levi Bush was said to be "a strong temperance advocate," "opposed to the use of tobacco as well as spiri-tous liquors," and a Congregationalist who "was always in the harness in the service of the Master."[17]

In addition to attending public schools and the Westfield Normal School, Hannah attended Mount Holyoke Female Seminary in South Hadley, Mas-sachusetts. Her days there began at five o'clock when she rang the bell that awakened the other students, who took turns at the various household chores. Hannah's life at Mount Holyoke was stamped by the strong character of the principal, Mary Lyon. Even in the domestic hall, Hannah found Mary Lyon "at the head of it all. She stands ready to assist in any place where her *kind* of

work is needed, that is talking[.] She makes every thing fly where she is. We
have lectures every day, by Miss Lyon, some, most splendid ones. . . . She
gives us the best of *advice*, and in the most winning way possible." [18]

Hannah, too, demonstrated strength of character while at Mount Holyoke.
She was a niece of Parker Cleaveland, a well-known professor of mathematics and natural philosophy at Bowdoin College, who was known in his time
as "the father of American minerology." Henry Wadsworth Longfellow later
honored Cleaveland's memory with a poem that begins

> Among the many lives that I have known,
>   None I remember more serene and sweet,
>   More rounded in itself and more complete,
>   Than his, who lies beneath this funeral stone.

At Cleaveland's suggestion, Hannah began to call herself "H. Cleaveland
Bush" and gave her name in that form to be printed in the school catalog.
When the proofs appeared, however, the name had been changed back to its
original form, and Hannah was told that "Miss Lyon does not like to have
names put in this manner, because she thinks it does not look natural." One of
the teachers also objected, saying people would not know whether the name
was "*Jack*, or *Joe*." After the teacher learned about Hannah's relationship to
Professor Cleaveland, she was willing to change the name in the catalog to
the form Hannah preferred, but Hannah thought it should be changed because of *her* wish to have it changed and not because of her relationship to
the professor. Her "Bush temper" had been aroused, and she later admitted
to her uncle that she had spoken "*rather* independent" to the teacher. The
school's resistance to her change of name was soon forgotten, and thereafter,
at least to her friends and eventually to Edward Smith, she was always known
as Cleavie.[19]

Cleavie left Mount Holyoke in 1848 after studying only two of the three
years required for graduation, and then, like Smith, went south as a teacher.
During her stay in Alabama, she taught in several schools. Smith said that
she was teaching in "a sort of missionary school in Mobile" and that she had
boarded with "Mr. Merrill" the previous winter and "taught part of the time
in his school." William Merrill was at that time principal of the Presbyterian
Female Seminary, for which he had leased the Barton Academy. The school
had preparatory and academic departments and offered all the major subjects
as well as music, drawing, ornamental needlework, Latin, Greek, Spanish,
German, Italian, and French, but it was first of all a religious school, "religious instruction being at the foundation of all good education." Prayer, the
Bible, and the catechism were part of each day's schedule. Later, Cleavie

moved to a school in Uniontown, Alabama, where, like Smith, she transferred her membership to the Presbyterian church, becoming the thirtieth member of the small congregation in Uniontown on December 3, 1854.[20]

Now that Cleavie was part of his life, Smith began to make plans for the future. He thought he would return to the North and enter a theological seminary, either at Yale or Andover, study for two years, and then return to Alabama or go west "to settle for life, expecting to have Mother with me." But his mother's needs claimed his attention earlier than he thought. She had been staying with his oldest sister, Martha, who was married to Elisha Woodbridge Cook, a Congregational minister serving a church in Haddam, Connecticut. Cook, however, was moving to New York City, and he informed Smith that his mother would no longer be able to stay with them, news that Smith said "unsettled me entirely." He could find no fault with Cook, who had done more than was asked of him in helping the family. But Smith said he had "often felt as if mother's dependence upon him [Cook] reflected severely upon me, as an unnatural son, who was throwing off his first obligations, filial duty. My preparation for future usefulness may have drawn me from present duty. Now the order must be reversed, mother's comfort & happiness first, myself last." Some in the family thought he, as his mother's only son, should take her as soon as possible. His aunt said he should "give up all idea of the ministry," settle where he was, and take his mother to live with him "immediately," saying he could do as much good as a teacher or in some other profession as in the ministry.[21]

But it was the ministry that called him. A revival was then in progress in the Presbyterian churches in Mobile. Meetings for prayer and preaching had been held every day for nearly three weeks, and about twenty conversions had been experienced. "O how it rejoices the heart of God's servants to find such a harvest season after so many years of toil," he wrote. "It makes me long to be a minister more than ever." He determined to do his part for his mother by providing the money Martha and her husband needed to care for her or paying for her board elsewhere until the time he could take her into his own home. In the meantime, he would study for the ministry.[22]

After saying his good-byes to Cleavie, who remained at her school in Uniontown, Smith left Mobile in August 1852 and traveled to New Haven, Connecticut, to enroll as a student in the Yale Divinity School. His decision to study at Yale may have been merely a result of his familiarity with the school from his college days, but he may also have been influenced in his decision by his two brothers-in-law, George Thacher and Elisha Cook, both graduates of the Yale Divinity School. Smith easily met the requirements for admission: a "hopeful piety and a liberal education at some College."

The requirements of the first year of the three-year course of study were more forbidding: Hebrew grammar, Hebrew exercises and readings, principles of sacred criticism and hermeneutics, critical and exegetical study of the Hebrew and Greek scriptures, critical and exegetical dissertations, lectures on some topics in introduction to theology and in exegetical theology, and lectures on mental philosophy, including the will. Free rooms were provided for the students, and all the costs of their education were absorbed by the school; apart from a fee of $3.50 for incidental expenses, there were no charges to the students.[23]

Among the faculty of five, the best-known teacher was Nathaniel William Taylor, who had participated in Noah Smith's installation at South Britain, Connecticut, thirty years before. Taylor was the leading spokesman for the New Haven Theology, a development within New England Calvinism that allowed for a person's own choice in his religious destiny, a teaching that fit in well with the revivals and appeals for conversions that were so important to the churches at that time. The older New England theologians had taught that humans had lost freedom of the will with Adam's fall and could contribute nothing to their salvation, but Taylor disagreed. Sin is a universal certainty, Taylor taught, but humans nevertheless have a "power to the contrary" to which ministers could make their appeal.

Taylor impressed his students not only with his conclusions but also with his method. "He makes you feel a few important truths strongly," one of them wrote. "He makes you think for yourself." Even though classes met in "an old building with loose and rattling windows which were often broken" and in rooms sometimes so cold that Taylor lectured in his overcoat, the students' affection for him could not be chilled.[24]

Smith did not remain for the second year at Yale when he could have had greater exposure to Taylor's teaching. Instead, he transferred to Union Theological Seminary in New York City, entering in the fall of 1853. Again his decision may have been influenced by his two minister brothers-in-law. George Thacher had begun a ministry at the Allen Street Presbyterian Church in New York City in 1850, and Elisha Cook had left his church in Haddam, Connecticut, in 1852 to begin two years of missionary work, also in New York City. Smith may have been influenced even more by his uncle Cyrus Porter Smith—Noah's brother—who had long been a prominent resident of Brooklyn and was an honorary member of Union Seminary's board of directors.

Union Seminary was founded in 1836 by a group of ecumenically minded Presbyterians as a place where "all men, of moderate views and feelings, who desire to live free from party strife, and to stand aloof from all the extremes of doctrinal speculation, practical radicalism, and ecclesiastical domination may cordially and affectionately rally." The faculty and directors of the school were Presbyterians, but the school was open to students of "every denomination of evangelical Christians." With the thirty other members of the middle class, Smith was required to study a doctrinal course in theology, selected books of the Bible in Hebrew and Greek, the history of the church in apostolic times, church government, and the planning of sermons. The seven members of the faculty included the prominent biblical scholar Edward Robinson and the musician and composer George F. Root, who was the school's instructor in sacred music.[25]

Union had been deliberately located in New York City, the founders "believing that large cities furnish many peculiar facilities and advantages for conducting theological education." One of the advantages of the school's location was the opportunity of giving the students a practical education, of "adding to piety and solid learning the teachings of experience." Smith took full advantage of that opportunity, involving himself in the work of the Five Points Mission and the new Children's Aid Society so deeply that that work completely overshadows his studies at Union Seminary.[26]

3

The Children's Aid Society

Ragged young girls who had nowhere to lay their heads; children driven
from drunkards' homes; orphans who slept where they could find a box or
a stairway; boys cast out by step-mothers or step-fathers; newsboys, whose
incessant answer to our question "Where do you live?" rung in our ears,
"*Don't live nowhere!*" little bootblacks, young peddlars, "canawl-boys," . . .
pickpockets and petty thieves . . . ; child beggars and flower-sellers . . . all
this motley throng of infantile misery and childish guilt passed through our
doors, telling their simple stories of suffering, and loneliness, and temp-
tation.

Charles Loring Brace, *The Dangerous Classes of New York*

New York was a bustling city of 520,000 in 1853. Its wharves were
crowded with full-rigged ships and barks, creating a "forest of masts"
along the riverfront. The city contained 272 churches, thirteen parks and
squares, and elaborate places of entertainment such as Barnum's American
Museum with its theater and four floors of exhibits, Franconi's Hippodrome
with seats for 10,000 people, and the celebrated Crystal Palace. The city
also contained increasingly large numbers of immigrants. More than one and
a half million immigrants had arrived at the port of New York in the decade from 1840 to 1850—largely Irish and German—and many of them had
remained in the city. The crowding had created appalling poverty and increasing disorder. According to the chief of police, there were nearly 10,000
vagrant children in the city, girls as well as boys. The diarist George Templeton Strong complained that "no one can walk the length of Broadway without
meeting some hideous troop of ragged girls, from twelve years old down,
brutalized already almost beyond redemption by premature vice, clad in the
filthy refuse of the rag-picker's collections, obscene of speech, the stamp of
childhood gone from their faces."[1]

The most scandalous section of the city was the Five Points, where Little-
Water, Cross, Anthony, Orange, and Mulberry streets came together. Charles
Dickens had visited the Five Points a decade earlier and described its "lanes

and alleys, paved with mud knee-deep, underground chambers, where they dance and game . . . ruined houses, open to the street . . . hideous tenements which take their name from robbery and murder: all that is loathsome, drooping, and decayed is here." The area had not improved in the decade following Dickens's visit. There were still "miserable-looking buildings, liquor-stores innumerable, neglected children by scores, playing in rags and dirt, squalid-looking women, [and] brutal men with black eyes and disfigured faces, proclaiming drunken brawls and fearful violence." It was to New York City's Five Points that Edward Smith came to work in March 1853, before entering Union Seminary.[2]

Smith worked with two men who were pioneer missionaries in the New York slums: Louis Morris Pease and Charles Loring Brace. Pease conducted the Five Points Mission, begun by members of the Ladies' Home Missionary Society of the Methodist Episcopal church. The group had bought a "large, yellow-colored, dilapidated, old house called the Old Brewery," which "during the last twenty years had been the haunt of murderers and robbers," razed the building, and in the spring of 1853 erected a five-story mission house in its place. Pease also founded the Five Points House of Industry to provide employment in the area and soon left the Five Points Mission to devote all his time to the House of Industry. Smith worked for a time with Pease, but more of his work was done with Charles Brace.[3]

Brace was one year older than Smith and had also graduated from Yale. Like Smith, he had taught in country schools and studied one year at Yale Divinity School and a second year at Union Seminary. But the condition of the urban poor had drawn him away from theology. Brace worked with Pease for a time and said of him that "no one whom we have ever known was so qualified for this desperate work, or was so successful at it. Still it was but one man against a sea of crime." Brace became discouraged working with adults and determined to work instead with the city's children. After first attempting to work through boys' meetings, he helped organize the Children's Aid Society, assumed the full-time position of secretary, and in March 1853 issued the society's first circular. In it Brace appealed to the public for the means to "meet the increasing crime and poverty among the destitute children of New York." The work was motivated by a feeling of a "responsibility to God" for the children. "We remember that they have the same capacities, the same need of kind and good influences, and the same immortality, as the little ones in our own homes. We bear in mind that One died for them, even as for the children of the rich and the happy."[4]

An equally important motive for the new work was a desire to protect society from a growing class of dangerous citizens. "These boys and girls,

Charles Loring Brace
(1826–90). Courtesy of the
Children's Aid Society, New
York, New York.

it should be remembered, will soon form the great lower class of our city.
They will influence elections; they may shape the policy of the city; they will,
assuredly, if unreclaimed, poison society all around them. They will help to
form the great multitude of robbers, thieves, and vagrants who are now such
a burden upon the law-respecting community."[5]

Brace realized that new methods were needed to deal with the problems
of the city's children, that, in James Russell Lowell's words, "New occasions
teach new duties." "We would not breathe a word," he wrote, "against the
absolute necessity of Christianity in any scheme of thorough social reform."
But the old methods of "distributing tracts, and holding prayer meetings,
and scattering Bibles" were no longer adequate. In their place Brace proposed the creation of industrial schools, lodging houses, and reading rooms,
while at the same time not neglecting the importance of religious influences.[6]

The new Children's Aid Society employed an agent or visitor for each district of the city as a means of reaching out to the children. Edward Smith
was the first visitor employed, beginning his work with the Children's Aid
Society in the first months of its existence. The visitors went

> from house to house, searching every shanty, and every poor tenant lodging-
> house. They become familiar with the families, and induce the parents to send

their children to the Public Schools, or to the Industrial Schools. They find the homeless and neglected children, and take them to the Central Office, to be sent, after the approval of parents, to farms, or shops, or families in the country. They search out the cells of the Prison and the Police Station, and even rescue some just falling into houses of crime. The poor wandering boy, and the begging girl of the garret, come soon to know them. They feel that in these gentlemen they will always find a friend; and when hunger and bitter desperation have been urging them on to crime or to ruin, these Visitors have not unfrequently been able to put in the saving hand. Their business and occupation is to be *the friends of the children of the poor.* [7]

Growing up in rural New England, Smith had not been exposed to the poverty he found in New York. Lucy Larcom said that "a ragged, half-clothed child, or one that could really be called poor, in the extreme sense of the word, was the rarest of all sights in a thrifty New England town." But Smith adjusted easily to the work. Brace said of him that

he spent his time in going among the garretts and cellars of the poorest tenements of this city, seeking out the destitute or forsaken children. He showed in these efforts a profound sympathy for the unfortunate, and an unusual tact in dealing with the lowest classes. He was inspired by a deep enthusiasm, and to his mind the poorest child of the streets was an object of respect and sympathy, because Christ had lived and died for such as he. In these efforts he was without difficulty impressed with the ideas and principles which lay at the basis of our work; he sought every where to discourage pauperism and to encourage self-help; he saw at once the importance of individual influence over the poor compared with institutional influence, and he early appreciated the value of our great object—the transplanting of homeless children to good homes in the country. . . . In all his labors for this Association he showed remarkable tact, energy, and the most tender sympathy for the poor and unhappy.

During the society's second year, Smith, working on the city's west side, near Twenty-eighth Street, made 1,615 visits to the children of the poor.[8]

The society made frequent appeals to the public for assistance with its work, using sermons and lectures, "incessant writing for the daily papers," and especially anecdotes or "incidents" of the work. Smith proved to be particularly useful in these efforts, demonstrating an unusual ability to capture the nature of his work in words, as a published excerpt from his diary shows.

April 25th.—A cold, raw, wet day, passing up Second street, near First Avenue, I saw a pair of heavy boots half exposed under a cart box. Bending down I looked in. A boy of about twelve years, well formed, a good head, with a large beautiful eye, was making himself ready for breakfast. From a deep pocket of his long coat he brought up a dry crust, from the other he pulled out a dirty package and began unwrapping a bit of paper, then a rag, and so on for several layers till he came to a bone, which he gnawed like a dog. When I spoke he started, hid his bone under his coat, and looked up, trembling with fright. It required patience and kindness to draw him from his hiding place and coax out his story. "Hai'nt got no father." How long has he been dead? "He ain[']t dead, sir; but I don't know where he is. He breaks up mother, sir, and we can't live anywhere. Now, mother don't live; she works out, sir." But where do you stay? "I don't know." Where did you stay last night? "A woman in Sixth Street took me in this week."

Smith went with the boy to Sixth Street and found the woman who had taken him in. She was married to a drunken man and was burdened with five small children.

Why did you take in this street boy? "I couldn't help it, sir; I should be sorry for the mother that could shut the door in such a face as that. No, my husband kicked him down stairs, but I called him up when C—— had gone to sleep, and in the morning I wake up the boy and send him out with his breakfast before my husband is up. No, sir, John is nothing to me, but I have seen his drunken mother, and I know the boy has no home. . . . Yes, I *am* poor. God knows I have little to spare; but I hope never to be so poor that I can't help all that are poorer than we are."[9]

The boy was later sent to Pennsylvania through the society's program for "placing-out" city children in homes in rural areas. Brace had studied such systems in Europe, saw the advantages they offered over institutional care, and spoke in the society's first circular of its plans for being "the means of draining the city of these children, by communicating with farmers, manufacturers, or families in the country, who may have need of such for employment." Circulars describing the program were sent to rural newspapers, and applications for children began to flow in. No formal contracts were made with the families; the society or the parents retained guardianship over the children in case the placements were not satisfactory.[10]

Many of the children who migrated were homeless; "I don't live no where!" they would say when asked about their homes. Some had parents who could not support them. Some were from prisons. At first the children were sent out individually to families in neighboring states. Soon, however, plans were made for sending "little companies of emigrants." The first group went to Pennsylvania in March 1854. The first group to go to the West, forty-six boys and girls under the leadership of Edward Smith, left for Dowagiac, Michigan, on September 20, 1854. Many of the children were those Smith had known on the streets. He personally gathered them for the trip, raised some of the expense money by his own efforts, and accompanied them unassisted. His account of the trip has the sound of the great adventure it must have been for the children from the streets and alleys of New York.

On Wednesday evening, with emigrant tickets to Detroit, we started on the Isaac Newton for Albany. . . . [The children] were between the ages of 7 and 15—most of them from 10 to 12. The majority of them orphans, dressed in uniform—as bright, sharp, bold, racy a crowd of little fellows as can be grown nowhere out of the streets of New York. . . .

As we steamed off from the wharf, the boys gave three cheers for New York, and three more for "Michigan." All seemed as careless at leaving home for ever, as if they were on a target excursion to Hoboken. . . .

In the morning [Friday], we were in the vicinity of Rochester; and you can hardly imagine the delight of the children as they looked, many of them for the first time, upon country scenery. Each one must see everything we passed, find its name, and make his own comments. "What's that mister!" "A corn-field." "Oh yes, them's what makes buckwheaters." "Look at them cows," (oxen plowing,) "my mother used to milk cows." . . .

The boys were in good spirits, sung songs, told New-York yarns, and made friends generally among the passengers. Occasionally some one more knowing than wise would attempt to poke fun at them, whereupon the boys would "pitch in," and open such a sluice of Bowery slang as made Mr. Would-be-funny beat a retreat in double quick time. No one attempted that game twice.

After various adventures, the group reached Dowagiac, "a smart little town," at three o'clock Sunday morning. "With apparent misgiving," the depot master allowed the children to sleep on the floor until morning.

At day-break they began to inquire, "Where be we?" and, finding that they were really in Michigan, scattered in all directions, each one for himself, and in five minutes there was not a boy in sight of the depot. When I had negotiated for our stay at the American House . . . and had breakfast nearly ready, they began to straggle back from every quarter; each boy loaded down—caps, shoes, coat-sleeves, and shirts full of every green thing they could lay hands upon—apples, ears of corn, peaches, pieces of pumpkins, etc. "Look at the Michi*gan* filberts!" cried a little fellow, running up, holding with both hands upon his shirt bosom, which was bursting out with *acorns*. Little Mag, (and she is one of the prettiest, sweetest little things you ever set eyes upon,) brought in a "nosegay," which she insisted upon sticking in my coat—a mullen-stock and corn-leaf, twisted with grass!

Later that morning the "ragged regiment" filed into the schoolhouse where the Presbyterian congregation was meeting. After the service, Smith explained the purpose of the visit, and on Monday he began to receive applications and recommendations from the local families. Before the week was over, all the children had been placed except nine of the smallest whom Smith took to Chicago and then sent on to Iowa City. Smith often said that the successful placement of just two of the children, who later became useful citizens, was in itself worth the entire cost of the trip. In his report to the society, he said that "on the whole, the first experiment of sending children West is a very happy one, and I am sure there are places enough with good families in Michigan, Illinois, Iowa, and Wisconsin, to give every poor boy and girl in New York a permanent home." His estimate of the trip was correct. The pattern of that first trip west was followed again and again; by 1890 more than ninety thousand children had been placed in homes by the Children's Aid Society.[11]

Despite Smith's immersion in his new work, Cleavie was not forgotten. Smith wrote to her about his life in New York City: "Children's Aid goes on. Now & then there are misunderstandings & unpleasant things, with those whom we seek to benefit, but in the main we are prospering." The Know-Nothing movement, with its violent opposition to immigrants, was at its height, and Smith admitted that "the Know Nothing excitement has created some predjudice against us. Two nights since three balls were fired thro' our office window from the Romish church opposite." Cholera had also broken out in New York, but Smith seemed not to be concerned about the dangers of gunshot or disease. Instead he changed the subject to a recent "surgical operation" that had laid his chin "bare & smooth, for the first time in three years."[12]

What did concern him was Cleavie's poor relationship with her father. Her father had objected to her leaving Mount Holyoke without graduating and her going to Alabama and had recently written her a letter that Smith found most uncharitable. "In those four closely written pages from Chicago I cannot find one line of parental affection & tenderness. . . . The religion of Jesus was *love,* love to God & love to man & there is no love to God which does not *include* love to man & often is best shown *by* love to man, and nowhere can that love be cherished so deeply & exhibited so beautifully as in the family circle. . . . I *do* think, & I cannot help it, that this letter is *unforgiving, unrelenting*[,] *unkind* & *unfatherly.*"[13]

Smith was tempted to write to Cleavie's father and tell him what he had told her, but he realized that it might only make the matter worse and that "it is Christlike to forgive & forget & love as if there had been no injury." He attempted to comfort Cleavie: "I hope you are happy in the conscious love of God and the desire to make others happy. May Our Savior help in every moment of doubt & enable you to glorify Him under all circumstances. I believe you may get good out of the trials of home & perhaps by an example of patience & affection do good to the family." [14]

His association with the Children's Aid Society was drawing to a close. In June 1854 Charles Brace sailed to Belfast, Ireland, where he was married to Letitia Neill. During his absence, Smith took charge of the society as its assistant secretary. After Brace's return in September, Smith left New York for Andover, Massachusetts, to begin his third and final year of theological studies at Andover Theological Seminary.[15]

Andover Seminary stood for strict Calvinistic orthodoxy. It was founded in 1808 by Congregationalists as a bulwark against the new Unitarian theology. Calvinists who had formerly disagreed among themselves banded together to create a school where traditional Calvinism would be taught and defended. "Andover Seminary," wrote a Congregational historian, "began at once to be a source of strength to the orthodox churches, a center around which the defenders of the faith of the fathers gathered with renewed courage." [16] One suspects that candidates for the ministry who hoped for calls to orthodox churches found it useful to have studied at Andover. For Smith, it also had the appeal of being the school from which his father had graduated.

The largest groups of students at Andover were from traditional Congregational colleges: Dartmouth, Amherst, Yale, and Middlebury. The course of study for the third-year students was directed toward the needs of the parish pastor. There were lectures on rhetoric, English style, sermons, and the general qualifications of a preacher; public and private criticism of sermons and sermon plans; critical examination of English and American preachers; lectures and recitations on ecclesiastical history; and lectures on pastoral theology and pastoral visiting.[17]

Smith described his studies at Andover to Cleavie, who, though she was still teaching in Alabama, had become "the center & end" of Smith's "earthly affections."

> I am getting deeply interested in my studies here. Am laying out my time into divisions, so as to give each duty its allotted portion. I don't know as I shall be able to carry out my plan. The fact is, Cleavie, I am only half a man, or perhaps more truly, only just a *quarter*. I undertake but half what I ought & accomplish but half I undertake. So you see, if you would have matters go right in *our Parish*, you must be the minister's wife, & three quarters of the minister.
>
> Ought you not to spend a few years in the Sem[inar]y? . . .
>
> I shall love the ministry Cleavie, if I can only love mental application. If I can bring my mind to work close four consecutive hours & *love* it, I shall have some hope of knowing something & being able to teach others.[18]

In February 1855, the Andover Association licensed Smith to preach, recommending him "as a preacher of the Gospel to the churches of our Lord Jesus Christ, wherever God, in his Providence, may call him." Although a Congregational association licensed ministers, it had no authority to place them in churches. A minister had to wait for a call from a local congregation and usually was not ordained until a call came. So when Smith graduated from Andover in August 1855, he was not guaranteed a call to a church and, in fact, preached for almost a year before he received and accepted a call. From August to December, he preached in the manufacturing village of Rockville, Connecticut, probably in First Congregational Church, which had lost its minister and was in a time of "general confusion. The church was compelled to secure a loan of $2500, the bass viol of the society was lost, many members withdrew, and were very emphatic about their withdrawal." From Rockville, Smith went to the First Congregational Church at Pompey, New York—in Onondaga County, near the Onondaga Indian Reservation—and remained there for six months, leaving behind him "the reputation of a Godly and earnest minister." So highly was he thought of at Pompey that he received a call to the church, but he declined it and accepted instead a call to become the minister of the Congregational Church at Pepperell, Massachusetts.[19]

4

Pepperell

As the hart longeth for the water brooks, my soul longeth for the green hills of Pepperell—and its shady retirement.

William Hickling Prescott, August 29, 1842

The historian William Hickling Prescott, author of histories of the conquests of Mexico and Peru, was drawn by his own history to the town of Pepperell, Massachusetts. His grandfather, Colonel William Prescott, who commanded the American troops at the Battle of Bunker Hill, made his home some two miles north of the village of Pepperell. There on the ancestral farm, the Highlands, the grandson retired each spring and fall to pursue his studies, relishing "the quiet—uninterrupted occupation of the country," "the delicious stillness of the fields." "How sweet the mountain air—the green fields," he wrote, "how sweet the solitude." [1]

It was to that quiet town—a world away from Mobile's cotton wharves and the Five Points of New York—that Edward Smith was called in 1856. Sydney Smith, the English cleric and wit, said that his parish in Yorkshire was so far out of the way that it was "twelve miles from a lemon." Pepperell was nearly that far. [2]

The town was on the Worcester and Nashua Railroad, about midway between Groton Junction and Nashua, New Hampshire, and some thirty-five miles from Boston. It had fewer than two thousand residents, most of them born in Massachusetts and most of them farmers, living in simple frame farmhouses and working small farms on which much of the plowing was still done with oxen as it had been two hundred years before. Some manufacturing was carried on in Pepperell, notably in the paper mills and shoe factories, and the factories and mills had begun to draw immigrants to the town, especially workers from Ireland. The town also had a sprinkling of the tradesmen likely to be found in any New England community, butchers and carpenters, millers and masons, and with them schoolteachers, physicians, and the clergy. Ten of the residents were black, one of whom was married to a white man and had six children by him. The town boasted a boarding school and the Pepperell Academy, which stood next to the parsonage of the Congregational Church and in which the church's new minister took a special interest.[3]

Pepperell originally had one church, the Congregational church common to New England towns, but in 1831 the congregation had divided. When some church members, influenced by the Unitarians, became dissatisfied with their minister, the minister and a majority of the congregation withdrew, formed the Evangelical Congregational Church of Pepperell, and built a meeting-house of their own. It was this second parish of Pepperell that called Edward Smith to be its minister, the Evangelical Congregational Church, so called to stress its orthodox, trinitarian beliefs in contrast to the beliefs of the original church, which had become Unitarian.

At a meeting in May 1856, the members of the church voted unanimously to call Smith as their minister. They had previously invited him to preach a trial sermon, and for anyone but Smith the experience might have been a disaster. "On his first visit to Pepperell, to preach as a candidate, he lost his valise, which contained his sermons and a change of raiment. Nothing daunted, however, he went into the pulpit in his traveling suit, and preached an extempore sermon, so fraught with freedom, fervency and zeal that he aroused the enthusiasm of the congregation, and received a call from them directly." Smith was never troubled by such emergencies. As one of his later associates, Gustavus Pike, said, emergencies brought out "one of his marked characteristics—that of doing his best when under some severe pressure."[4]

Having a call to "settle over" a congregation gave Smith and Cleavie the opportunity to marry. They were married in Cleavie's hometown, Westfield, Massachusetts, on June 3, 1856, with Smith's brother-in-law Elisha Cook performing the service. Eight days later, Smith was ordained and installed as pastor of the church in Pepperell. An ecclesiastical council, composed of representatives from neighboring Congregational churches, met first to examine him. Finding his papers in order, "the council then proceeded to examine the candidate in relation to his theological views, his religious experience & his purpose in entering the ministry." When the council was satisfied in these matters, it assigned the parts of the "public exercises" to the various ministers who were present, and with Elisha Cook preaching, Smith was "ordained Pastor over the said ch[urch] in Pepperell." Now that the Smiths were settled in their own home, Smith could finally bring his mother to live with them, but she lived less than a year after coming to Pepperell, dying on March 14, 1857.[5]

The new pastor and the parish were a good match. One of his deacons said that Smith demonstrated a "peculiar . . . adaptedness to this part of his mas-

Edward and Hannah Cleaveland Smith. Courtesy of the Amistad Research
Center, New Orleans, Louisiana.

ter[']s vin[e]yard." And the people generally were pleased with their minister.
The church's standing committee expressed its pleasure in one of its annual
reports: "Our Spiritual teacher has been in & out before us, uninterruptedly
ministering at the altar, & unwearied in his offices has *faithfully* divided the
word of truth to the various classes of his hearers, giving to each a portion,
according to his state, character & circumstances in life. As one that must
give account, he has watched for souls by cautioning us against the errors and
sins to which we have been exposed, exhorted, comforted & charged every
one of us as a father doth his children, that we would walk worthy of God."[6]

The church was particularly pleased at the good rapport Smith developed
with the children, the "lambs" of his flock, who responded with "commendable promptness, by being present at the times appointed for their meetings,
& giving an attentive ear to the exercises." Children's sermons were coming
into fashion, and Smith spoke to the children with good effect. The Sabbath school, "the nursery of the church," prospered. Teachers' classes were
begun, and Cleavie taught a large class of infants. Children's periodicals
were distributed, including *Child at Home* and the antislavery *Well-Spring.*
The children gathered with children of other churches for Sabbath school
festivals with "long processions . . . gaily trimmed vehicles, flying banners,
and music." In 1857 Smith attended a state convention of Sabbath schools
where he urged the adoption of hymns and tunes "such as would touch the
hearts of little children." Smith himself touched the hearts of the children of
Pepperell, who were captivated by their new minister.[7]

Smith had, in addition, the usual pastoral duties: marriages, burials, a
Tuesday evening prayer meeting, administering the sacraments, and conducting worship services, both for Sunday congregations and occasionally for
smaller congregations assembled in the district schoolhouses in various parts
of the town. Smith was as concerned about adults singing in their services
as he was about the children singing. In 1859 he spoke at a conference of
churches at Groton. His address, "Public Praise," was described as "an earnest plea for congregational singing, by one competent both as a musician and
pastor, to hold a decided opinion." There were other conferences to attend as
well, especially the frequent councils called to discuss pastoral relationships
and other matters affecting neighboring Congregational churches. Smith also
served as the church's clerk and left a plea to his successors to "keep full &
accurate accounts," noting "matters that are in any way unusual in the passing affairs of the ch[urch]. They seem of slight value now but like wine they
are the better for age. 'Distance lends enchantment.'"[8]

Finances were a constant concern both to the minister and to the congregation. The Congregational churches had once been the established churches

in Massachusetts, supported by taxes, but the establishment was ended in 1833. The only remnant of the establishment in Smith's time was a peculiar dual system of church government, with the "church" on one hand, the professing members who made decisions about spiritual matters, and the "parish" or "society" on the other, the voters of the community convened "in the name of the Commonwealth of Massachusetts" to look after the material concerns of religion in the parish. But even though the community at large still had a voice in the temporal concerns of the parish, it was no longer required to provide funds; all fund-raising was voluntary.[9]

Early in Smith's ministry, the Pepperell church attempted to raise its funds by "apportionment," requesting specific amounts from the members, determined by what a committee thought they could pay. Most members were willing to pay what was asked, but "a few were opposed to the arrangement & refused to pay what the assessors had named as their proportion." John Greenleaf Whittier had met similar reluctant contributors in other New England churches.

> Church-goers, fearful of the unseen Powers,
> But grumbling over pulpit-tax and pew-rent,
> Saving, as shrewd economists, their souls
> And winter pork with the least possible outlay
> Of salt and sanctity. . . .[10]

The assessors, however, were instructed "not to receive *unwillingness* on the part of any member to pay" as an excuse to reduce the amount owed, and a committee was appointed to meet with "delinquent members." Those who would not pay were to be charged with "palpable unchristian conduct in refusing to do their part in support of the gospel."[11]

It was not long before one church member, Daniel F. Dow, was formally charged with refusing to pay his apportionment. Dow said in his defense that the society's expenses were too high, the "tax" on him was more than he could pay, and the only Christian way to support the gospel was by voluntary contributions. "It is better to give a *little willingly*," he said, "than a *great amt* grudgingly." He refused to change his position and said that the church "might as well undertake to remove the Rocky Mountains" as to move him from what he considered his duty. As a result, the charge of contempt was also brought against him. In the end Dow agreed to pay what was asked of him, but he then asked to be dismissed to the Congregational Church in nearby Hollis, New Hampshire.[12]

Similar charges were brought against Nathaniel Shattuck and his wife, Zoa. Shattuck requested that the amount asked of him be reduced because of an annual gift of twenty dollars he was making to his "aged and infirm mother." The church found his request "not satisfactory." The Shattucks grudgingly paid what was asked of them but then asked to be dismissed from the church. But because they had not named another church with which they would unite, their request was ruled out of order. The Shattucks then stopped attending services and as a result were charged with "breach of cov[enan]t in refusing to walk in fellowship with us in the sab[bath] worship & in the ordinances of the Lord's house." Shattuck in turn charged that the church had treated him unfairly "and that the pastor had meddled with the business of the church & in a church meeting had declared that he (the pastor) could not walk in fellowship with him," a statement Smith said misinterpreted his remarks. When the charges and the countercharges were ended, the Shattucks were excommunicated, an action the church called "a rare & painful duty." At one point during these proceedings, it was proposed that the church "raise money for the support of the gospel by an assessment on ch[urch] members according to the plan adopted last year. This motion called out a protracted & warm discussion & was finally lost."[13]

The church was more successful in raising money by pew rent. The pews were numbered, appraised according to their desirability, and rented to the members for various amounts, payable semiannually. The pews were quickly rented, and Smith's own name was on the list of pew holders. The members were pleased with the new system, believing that "the matter which has heretofore been a source of trouble is now dissipated, & we have established a system of finance for which we shall have no occa[s]ion to regret. Every pew in the house is now rented & [there is] a demand for more."[14]

Nevertheless, finances continued to be a concern, and the church's deficit mounted throughout Smith's ministry. Smith himself tried to assist by offering to relinquish $100 of his $800 annual salary. He also tried to add to his uncertain income by bidding for the job of sexton, the church custodian, which was, however, given to a lower bidder.[15]

The church prospered in other ways, if not financially. At one point the attendance at worship services ranged from 300 to 425 and the Sabbath school attendance averaged nearly 200. Nationally, a celebrated series of revivals had begun in 1857, and the church officers felt obliged to explain that even though there had been no revival locally, the church had experienced a quiet growth. "During the year there has been no so-called *Revival of Religion* in connection with our church. But there has been a more than usual religious interest on the part of many of God[']s people here, & a more than usual concern on the part of those out of Christ. . . . We have been blest by the constant, quiet, genial influences of the Spirit;—He has come gently & noiseles[s]ly, as come the *dews* of evening, & not in *showers*, & as the *rushing*,

New Evangelical Congregational Church building, Pepperell,
Massachusetts, erected during the pastorate of Edward Smith.
Courtesy of Beatrice B. Parker.

Mary Gertrude Smith (1859–1930) (*left*), and Clarke Smith (1860–64) (*right*), children of Edward and Hannah Smith. Courtesy of the Amistad Research Center, New Orleans, Louisiana.

mighty, wind." New members were added during most years, persons who were first examined by the standing committee as to their "personal religious experience & present purpose to live a new life" or who presented letters of dismissal from other churches—as the Smiths did from their churches in Alabama—and who afterward were received as members by the vote of the entire congregation.[16]

The Smiths also added to the congregation with the birth of a daughter, Mary Gertrude, always known as Gerty, on February 9, 1859.[17]

On July 27, 1859, Smith was in New Haven, Connecticut, to celebrate the tenth anniversary of his graduation from Yale. Members of the various classes gathered "to smoke the pipe of peace in the old council chambers"; so many graduates appeared that a reporter said "even the hotel-keepers were fain to cry, Hold. Enough!" That night the church building in Pepperell burned to the ground. The fire started in Luther Tarbell's tavern and store next door. The heat of the fire was so intense that it melted the church bell. The tower clock and the organ were also destroyed. The insurance on the building covered only $3,000 of the $8,500 loss, which added to the church's financial burden.[18]

The loss of the vestry was particularly painful. Complaints about the basement room's low ceiling, poor ventilation, and unsightly square posts had earlier prompted the people to agree to renovate the vestry. Six hundred dollars was raised, the work was completed, and the "neat & commodious rooms" would have been consecrated on the Sunday following the fire. Instead, "the villagers, aroused by the midnight alarm, hastened from their homes to behold their finished work, & the work of their fathers, & older brethren, devoured by the flames."[19]

Accepting an offer by the Unitarians, the congregation met the next Sunday in the Unitarian Church, where Smith preached on the text "Our holy and our beautiful house, where our fathers praised thee, is burned up with fire" (Isa. 64:11). Ten days after the fire, the decision was made to rebuild. Smith proposed a building large enough to seat six hundred people in partially circular pews, with a church tower containing the entrance starting from the ground, a singers' gallery behind the pulpit, and at "some convenient place a privy with water trap and drain." After some disagreement about the site of the new building, work was begun on the site of the old one.[20]

During the building of the church, another addition was made to the Smith family. Their second child was born on July 14, 1860, "a little Pilgrim from the unknown land," his father called him, "a boy with *nine pounds* in his bundle," who remained nameless for weeks but was finally named Clarke.[21]

On January 29, 1861, the 114th anniversary of the founding of the original church in Pepperell, the new church building was dedicated. A reporter wrote that "its capacity which is that of almost 500 sittings, was fully tested at the dedication services, by a crowded congregation, who heard with evident interest, an appropriate and eloquent sermon by the Pastor, Rev. Edward P. Smith, from Luke iv:16, 'As his custom was, he went into the synagogue on the Sabbath day.' "[22]

The previous year had been difficult for the congregation in its "unsettled state," without a building. "A feeling of depression, if not of discouragement was apparent." During the early part of the year, the members had met in Parker's Hall in East Pepperell; later they met in the vestry of the uncompleted church. "Twice in the year we have celebrated the Lord[']s supper in a dancing Hall, once within the rough walls of the unfinished" church. But as the new building went up, "confidence & unanimity prevailed." Once the building was occupied, the congregation again flourished.[23]

Immersed as it was in its own parochial concerns, the Pepperell congregation was nevertheless affected by the larger issues of American church life. American Protestants were full of optimism and anticipation during the years before the Civil War. It seemed to many as though the millennium was not far off, "the great millennial day, when wars should cease and the whole world, released from the thraldom of evil, should rejoice in the light of the Lord." The words Stephen Foster set to music spoke for an entire generation:

> There's a good time coming, boys,
> A good time coming,
> A good time coming;
> We may not live to see the day,
> But earth shall glisten in the ray,
> Of the good time coming.

Some believers pored over the biblical prophecies to determine the time of the millennium's coming. But many others took a more active role, banding together to reform society to prepare the way for the millennium. A great number of voluntary benevolent organizations were formed, each with its own publications, its well-known philanthropic officials, and its agents who organized local branches and collected funds. Massachusetts churches became familiar not only with national organizations concerned with issues like temperance and slavery but with a variety of regional organizations: the Massachusetts Bible Society, the Massachusetts Home Missionary Society, the Massachusetts Colonization Society, the Boston Seaman's Friend Society, and the New England Female Moral Reform Society, among others.[24]

The Pepperell church made contributions to the antislavery American Missionary Association and, because of its pastor's interest, to the Children's Aid Society, but its giving to benevolent causes was low—the lowest of all but one of the churches in its conference during one year. As good as the causes were, church members acquired a resistance to the constant appeals of the agents of the societies. "Rapidly and statistically they unfold the origin and operation of their plans," said one New Englander, "and cheerfully we listen, quite well knowing we are masters of the situation, and shall present a firm front to the foe. . . . Still, if it pleases you to come to us in appeal, come. You little know the invincibility and the invisibility of our defenses; but come." One New England pastor was reported to have said that "if the Angel Gabriel should call on his congregation for a contribution they wd give just $33.00 & no more or less." The Middlesex North Conference, to which the Pepperell church belonged, voted to dispense with the services of the agents and assigned each of the principal societies to one of its own pastors, who was to make the appeals for the society, a plan "regarded with an evident preference by the people" and officially approved by the Pepperell church. Under the plan, Edward Smith became the spokesman for the American Congregational

Union, which published information about the Congregational churches, assisted churches in building meetinghouses and parsonages, and sought to further good relationships among Congregational churches and ministers.[25]

THE QUIET PAROCHIALISM of Pepperell was quickly shattered by the beginning of the Civil War. Four days after the bombardment of Fort Sumter, the Sixth Regiment of Massachusetts Volunteers, which included twenty-two men from Pepperell, was ordered to Washington. Only four days after that the regiment was assaulted and four men were killed by southern sympathizers as the soldiers passed through Baltimore. Before the rebellion was over, 134 men from Pepperell had gone to war.

Pepperell entered the war with a long history of patriotism. A local historian said it was one of the first places in revolutionary days to have a liberty pole, "and there was not a single Tory within its limits." The town voted unanimously in 1770 to boycott British goods. Colonel William Prescott of Pepperell commanded a regiment of minutemen from Pepperell, Groton, and Hollis, New Hampshire, who responded to the call for assistance after the first skirmish of the Revolution at Lexington. The men from Pepperell later served under Prescott at the Battle of Bunker Hill, where eight Pepperell soldiers were killed and eight more wounded. The Reverend Joseph Emerson, minister of the church in Pepperell and an ardent patriot, visited his parishioners among the troops at Cambridge during the summer of 1775. The local tradition is that he offered the first public prayer in the American camps at Cambridge.

Pepperell's patriotic and military spirit continued to thrive after the Revolution. A volunteer militia company, known as the Prescott Guards, was organized there about 1819. A local regiment of militia, the "Old Sixth," was the unit called into the service of the United States and assaulted in Baltimore on its way to Washington. The Reverend Charles Babbidge, the minister of the First Parish in Pepperell (Unitarian), was the chaplain of the Old Sixth and left with the regiment on April 15, 1861, the first graduate of Harvard and the first minister in the nation to take the field during the Civil War, according to the people of Pepperell. In Joseph Emerson and Charles Babbidge the townspeople believed their town had furnished the first chaplains of both the Revolution and the rebellion. After serving three months with the Old Sixth, Babbidge reenlisted in the Twenty-sixth Massachusetts Regiment and served as its chaplain for three more years.[26]

The Massachusetts General Association of Congregational Churches met at Ware, Massachusetts, in late June 1861 with Edward Smith attending as a delegate from the Middlesex Union Conference. The Massachusetts association unanimously adopted resolutions supporting the actions of the Lincoln administration and making clear the association's hope that the war would result in the end of slavery.

> *Resolved,* that we cordially approve the vigorous measures of the Government for the maintenance of the Constitution, and that we are ready to devote our property, our influence, and if need be, our lives to its vindication and support.
>
> *Resolved,* that while we earnestly desire the speedy return of peace to our divided country, we deprecate any concession or compromise which shall not secure the loyalty and obedience of all the States of the Union to the Federal Government. . . .
>
> *Resolved,* that believing the institution of slavery to have been the fruitful source of the great trouble which is now upon us, we cannot but pray and hope that the present war may be overruled by Divine Providence for the ultimate removal of human bondage from our land.[27]

The response of Pepperell's Evangelical Congregational Church to the war was also unanimous. The report of the church's standing committee for 1861 said with pride: "We are thankful to be able to report a patriotism so unanimous & fervent as that which animates the ch[urc]h of Christ in Pepperell. Our country has made her appeal in our pulpit, in our Prayer meeting, in the Benevolent circle, & in the sabbath school, & never in vain." Eight men from the church had already enlisted, having gone "bearing spiritual as well as carnal weapons." Some of them, who went into the Twenty-sixth Massachusetts Regiment, took "with them the Thursday evening prayer meeting from Oak Hill District" and established it in the regiment.[28]

The members of the Old Sixth Regiment returned home in August, their three-month tour of duty completed. As the three-month regiments were mustered out, three-year regiments were organized, and Governor John Andrew made an appeal for men to fill them. Twenty-five thousand men were needed to fill Massachusetts's share of the half million soldiers the nation required.[29]

No less patriotic than the other citizens of Pepperell, Edward Smith threw himself into recruiting, with the goal of raising a regiment of Christian soldiers. In September he addressed his plan directly to Governor Andrew. "I tried two days since to get an interview with you respecting a plan for a *Cromwell Regt* to be raised in Mass. My observations as pastor of a country church lead me to the belief that such a Regt is entirely feasible." He was confident that the members of his church would enlist in such a regiment and that the regiment when formed would be valuable in bringing "the importance and duty of volunteering right home to a large class of men that stand aloof from putting their own hands to bloody work."

> I have thot over the matter till I am fully committed to it & prepared to bear a hand in the ranks. I have no practical acquaintance with these matters, but have been *thinking* & venture to suggest a word as to [the] mode of recruiting the "Roundheads."
>
> Organize the Regt appointing a Col. thoroughly furnished for his work & in entire *personal sympathy* with *praying, psalm-singing* men, *as such.*
>
> Have for a chaplain a clergyman of some note in the religious community.

He suggested appealing for recruits through religious newspapers and through the use of agents who would speak to Sunday congregations and weekday religious meetings and recruit men after the meetings. "Religious minds," he said, "are as susceptible to an *esprit de corps* as any class of men, Firemen, N. York Roughs or Sharpshooters. Cannot Mass, under her strong Governor, lead off with the first Regt. of Ironsides?"[30]

Andrew suggested that Smith attempt to raise a company of "Cromwellians" rather than a regiment, and Smith personally began the recruiting. With the help of Joseph Stedman of Medfield, "a young man of high Christian character & a graduate of the military school at Norwich Vt." whom he had convinced to take command of the company, nearly fifty men were recruited. The men were, however, not immediately called into service, and it is not clear whether they did in fact serve.[31]

Although all the Pepperell men in the Sixth Massachusetts Regiment survived the assault in Baltimore, death soon brought the reality of war to Pepperell. The first man from the town to die was Thomas H. Bailey, a soldier in the Thirty-second Massachusetts Regiment, who died of measles at Harrison's Landing, Virginia, at the age of nineteen. His body was brought back to Pepperell, where services were conducted by Edward Smith in the second parish church. Bailey had been a member of Pepperell's Engine Company No. 1, which draped its engine and the engine house with flowers and other signs of mourning. Members of the company provided an escort for the body, and as the procession passed the engine house on the way to the church, "the bell on the machine was tolled, telling that one of the Company, the first soldier from this town to fall, had passed from the scenes of strife and war to the peaceful streets of that city where flames cannot devour, where battles all are fought." Bailey's funeral was but the first of many Smith was to conduct as he personally became involved in the agony of the war as a delegate of the United States Christian Commission.[32]

5

The Christian Commission

The labors of the Christian Commission are undoubtedly one of the brightest, if not *the* brightest chapter in the history of the civil war.

Philip Schaff, January 10, 1866

Despite the first part of its name, the United States Christian Commission had no official relationship to the federal government. It was a voluntary organization, which grew out of the Young Men's Christian Association (YMCA). Through it nearly five thousand evangelical Christians ministered to the Union forces during the Civil War.

In the early days of the war, representatives of the YMCA in several cities made efforts to serve the soldiers. Vincent Colyer, a prominent New York artist, was one of the first to serve, leaving his business to visit the camps around New York City. (His first visit was to the men of the Sixth Massachusetts Regiment, when they stopped in New York on their way to Baltimore and Washington.) Reflecting the evangelical concerns of the YMCA, Colyer organized worship services and distributed tracts, hymnbooks, Bibles, and New Testaments. After the first Battle of Bull Run, he went to Washington and ministered to the wounded in the hospitals there. Colyer soon realized that a national organization was needed to conduct such work, and he proposed that a national convention of YMCAs be called to create a unified agency for soldiers' aid.

Thirty-six delegates from seven states and the District of Columbia convened at the YMCA offices in New York City November 14 and 15, 1861. Under the chairmanship of George Hay Stuart, a forty-five-year-old immigrant from County Down, Ireland, who had become a successful merchant in Philadelphia, the convention created the United States Christian Commission "to promote the spiritual and temporal welfare of the soldiers in the army and the sailors and marines in the navy, in co-operation with the chaplains and others." The commission's primary goal was to meet the spiritual needs of the soldiers and sailors, but their material needs were never ignored; as

Stuart said, "There is a good deal of religion in a warm shirt and a good beef-steak." The day after the convention, a circular was sent to all the YMCAs in the country appealing for contributions of money and for "articles for the comfort of the soldiers."[1]

A commission of at first twelve and later fifty prominent evangelical ministers and laymen was appointed, with Stuart as chairman. It was an ecumenical group; by the end of the war, thirteen different denominations had been represented on the commission. The commission established an office in New York, but for the first eight or nine months little was accomplished. This initial period of "feebleness, hesitancy, and inactivity" ended in the summer of 1862, when the office was moved to Philadelphia and the work of the commission came "directly under the personal supervision of its energetic President," George Hay Stuart. Stuart offered the use of his firm's large warehouse for the commission's stores and the counting rooms for its secretaries and clerks. He remained at the head of the commission throughout the war, and his fellow workers gave him the credit for its success. One of the original organizers said Stuart was "from first to last the great power that guided and controlled it," giving the commission his energy, "his wonderful administrative ability, his powerful influences over business men, and his magnetic style of oratory."[2]

The commission also strengthened its work by employing William E. Boardman, a gifted organizer, as general agent and secretary. Boardman was a Presbyterian minister who had previously served as secretary of the American Sunday School Union. He was also widely known for his book *The Higher Christian Life*, a popular statement of the possibility of a second conversion to "entire sanctification" or "Christian holiness." Stuart and Boardman provided the efficiency and good management the Christian Commission sorely needed.[3]

High-ranking officials of the government were asked to endorse the commission, and their endorsements were published with the commission's appeals to the public. Abraham Lincoln responded by saying, "Your christian and benevolent undertaking for the benefit of the soldiers, is too obviously proper, and praise-worthy, to admit any difference of opinion," and Simon Cameron, the secretary of war, said his department would "cheerfully give its aid to the benevolent and patriotic of the land, who desire to improve the condition of our troops." As the war went on, more and more officials, generals, and admirals responded to the commission's appeal for endorsements, and the commission gave the endorsements wide publicity.[4]

At the center of the Christian Commission's work were the delegates, largely clergymen and students of theology but laymen as well. They were

George Hay Stuart (1816–90), the chairman of the United States Christian Commission. Courtesy of the Historical Society of Pennsylvania, Philadelphia, Pennsylvania.

unpaid volunteers, valued for their "home ties," who came to the soldiers as representatives of the churches, and when they had completed their service, represented the soldiers and the commission to the churches. Each delegate was, in theory at least, a member of an evangelical church. The commission sought delegates of three classes: "1st. Preachers who have head, heart, and lungs to command audience in the open air. 2d. Workers who can distribute wisely, help dress wounds, wash and dress helpless men, make soup and give it, speak to soldiers about salvation, pray with the dying, write letters for them, or do anything the varying circumstances demand. 3d. Business men to manage affairs, at offices and stations, obtain facilities and papers and direct the work as field agents." Every delegate was expected to have four indispensable qualities: "piety and patriotism, good common sense and energy."[5]

At first, the commission allowed delegates to serve at their convenience, but later it required a commitment of six weeks' service. Some were assigned to army camps, some to hospitals, and some served as "minute-men" who were prepared to leave on short notice for the battlefield. All the delegates were cautioned to avoid interfering in any way with the military authorities. Most of the leading railroad, steamship, telegraph, and express companies furnished their facilities to the delegates without charge or at reduced rates.

Among the first delegates to go to the battlefield was a group of fourteen led by James Grant, the secretary of the central committee of the YMCA, who went to Bull Run after the second battle there. When the delegates arrived at the battlefield, they ministered to the wounded with the "few stimulants, and what other stores and conveniences we could carry for immediate use. . . . With a candle in one hand, and a bucket of water or coffee in the other, we wended our several ways among the heroic masses of bleeding humanity." The commission's delegates performed similar battlefield service throughout the war, personally ministering to the wounded in a way the army was not prepared to. Walt Whitman, who, despite his unorthodox opinions, was in January 1863 given a commission as a delegate, said he had "seen many battles, their results, but never one where there was not, during the first few days, an unaccountable and almost total deficiency of everything for the wounded—appropriate sustenance, nursing, cleaning, medicines, stores, etc. . . . Scores, hundreds, of the noblest young men on earth, uncomplaining, lie helpless, mangled, faint, alone, and so bleed to death or die from exhaustion, either actually untouched at all, or with merely the laying of them down and leaving them, when there ought to be means provided to save them." The Christian Commission provided delegates who were willing to roll up their sleeves and minister to the wounded wherever they were needed.[6]

Christian Commission delegates in the field. Courtesy of the National Archives.

Their work forced the delegates to adjust to new circumstances. Travel on the Sabbath was one of them. The group led by James Grant left Philadelphia at midnight on a Saturday and arrived in Washington early on Sunday morning. Grant believed that none of the delegates had ever traveled on the Sabbath before. He justified the travel by saying that "our mission was considered to be one of necessity and emergency." Similarly, J. R. Miller, one of the paid agents of the commission, said of a Sunday train ride: "At home, there is generally no excuse for the performance of such journeys on the Sabbath, but, in the army, Sabbath work often becomes a work of mercy." Even when such travel was not required, the delegates had to adjust to Sabbaths entirely different from what they were accustomed to. One of the ministerial delegates conducted five services one Sunday and reflected afterward that he "had preached from strange pulpits,—three stumps, an old Virginia harrow, and a tired horse's back." "This is a strange Sabbath to me," another delegate wrote. "I have spent many in the western wilds, but none before in a military camp. The jargon is intense. Bugles and drums, and mules and men, all contribute to disturb the hallowed stillness which should prevail." There were enough men in the army with the same feeling about the sanctity of the Sabbath to convince President Lincoln as commander in chief to enjoin "the orderly observance of the Sabbath by the officers and men in the military and naval service." But the war had a logic of its own that defied the desires of both the president and the Christian Commission delegates for a peaceful Sabbath.[7]

The delegates also had to adjust to the use of alcoholic beverages as medicines in the army. Many of them were strict "temperance men," total abstainers from alcohol, and yet they found themselves dispensing whiskey, brandy, and wine cordials as "stimulants" and blackberry cordials as a remedy for diarrhea. They quoted the Bible to defend their actions, using the verse that said: "Give strong drink unto him that is ready to perish" (Prov. 31:6). One delegate was pleased to be able to report that "in no case has any complaint been whispered that any of the cordials . . . go down the wrong throats."[8]

The besetting sins of army life—swearing, gambling, drinking, stealing— also required adjustments by the delegates. "Great noise, terrible profanity, & drunkenness," one young Congregational minister reported on his first day away from home. Some of the delegates confronted the sinners, berating them for their actions and calling for repentance. Others challenged them indirectly. Two delegates who found themselves in the midst of a coarse gambling session on a Mississippi riverboat began to sing the hymn "All Hail the Power of Jesus' Name." "If a thunderbolt had fallen into their midst," one of the delegates said later, "the astonishment could not have been greater. For a moment every man stopped and looked at us in perfect amazement." The delegates seized the opportunity to speak to the officers at the gambling tables about the example they were setting for their men.[9]

Still other delegates came to accept the realities of army life with good humor. A story popular among delegates concerned General Clinton B. Fisk, a member of the commission. At the suggestion of a visiting preacher, the men of Fisk's regiment had agreed to let the nonswearing Fisk "do all the swearing for the thirty-third Missouri." Later, when Fisk heard one of the teamsters swearing at his mules and asked him about it, the soldier admitted that he had agreed to let Fisk do his swearing for him, but said, "But then you were not there to do it, *and it had to be done right off!*" Fisk himself repeated the story at the last anniversary meeting of the commission in Washington, and its frequent retelling indicates the good humor of the delegates in the presence of evils they could not change.[10]

The appeal for volunteers to serve as delegates was made not only by the national organization but by auxiliaries or "army committees" in major cities. New England was served by the Boston Army Committee, which in turn organized local committees in the principal towns. The Boston committee appealed for delegates and contributions through circulars and newspapers and through returned delegates who spoke about their experiences. "Almost every community was reached; in many churches the fourth Sunday evening of each month was observed as a concert of prayer for the army; and the supply of resources was continuous and large." [11]

The Christian Commission was just what Edward Smith was looking for, the perfect vehicle for involving himself in the war. In January 1863, he wrote a letter asking his church to release him for service as a delegate, and on Sunday, January 25, after the morning service, his letter was read to the congregation.

> Dear Brethren & friends of this church and congregation.
>
> You have known somewhat of my desire for the past two years, to bear a personal part in the life & death struggle of the nation.
>
> My strong desire has been, to go as a messenger of the Gospel to the army, but I would gladly have enlisted in the ranks to do a humble soldier[']s duty. Now, an opportunity opens by which I can *volunteer* as a minister of the Gospel.
>
> The Christian Commission . . . send men to the Hospitals, camps & battle-fields, to carry help & comforts, & instruction to the soldiers.
>
> Their delegates work without pay, & the Rail Roads carry them & their supplies without charge. Thus a wide field is occupied at comparatively little expense, if laborers can be found on such terms. It is my desire, with your permission, to enter this service for one month, fulfilling my duties in the pulpit meanwhile by proxy.
>
> I am aware that I am not giving *my* time & strength to the country, but yours,—but I trust I shall go with your hearty approbation, & continued prayers for the grace I need.

The church and the society readily gave their permission, and in the evening service Smith spoke about the Christian Commission, after which "prayer was offered by the brethren, imploring the divine blessing on the Pastor & the enterprise[,] & warm parting words were given." The next morning Smith left for Virginia and the Army of the Potomac.[12]

The Boston Army Committee furnished delegates with blankets, haversacks, and badges. It advised the delegates to "wear a suit of clothes they are willing to have spoiled, an old one is quite as good as any; thick boots; flannel shirts, such as soldiers wear, no linen being worn in camp." They were to take only such baggage as they could carry—a light bag or valise would serve— and to "take a little red pepper and a few ounces of tea, the first as a remedy in bowel troubles, the latter to chew for refreshment." Smith also carried with him his commission as a delegate, the 266th commission issued.[13]

The Army of the Potomac had gone into winter quarters on the north bank of the Rappahannock River, opposite the city of Fredericksburg, Virginia. The condition of the camps reflected the low morale in the army following its defeat at Fredericksburg on December 13, 1862, and an unsuccessful attempt to recross the Rappahannock in late January. A soldier described the camps, "with their canvas roofs discolored by various kinds of dirt stains, and with their gaping rents caused by storms or black margined holes burned by sparks from their own chimneys, in some cases patched with stray bits of old rubber blankets, or odd pieces of discarded tent cloth of almost every hue. . . . A nearer view disclosed mud everywhere, banked up against the houses and plastered between the logs to keep out the cold." Another soldier described the depressing sounds of the camps: "All night long the sounds go up of men coughing, breathing heavy and hoarse with half choked throats, and groaning with acute pain." Even the weather was dismal, the entire winter being "terribly severe, raining and freezing most of the time." The Army of the Potomac was, in Stephen Vincent Benét's words, a "sullen army . . . licking its wounds" in a "cold winter of doubt and grief." [14]

Various civilians had come to provide relief for the troops. Volunteers from the Ladies' Aid Society of Philadelphia established a rest station in the Lacy House, a mansion taken over by the army. Walt Whitman had worked in the mansion in December, following the battle, and described "a heap of amputated feet, legs, arms, hands, etc.—a full load for a one-horse cart," piled outside the mansion—"human fragments, cut, bloody, black and blue, swelled and sickening." "Several dead bodies lie near, each covered with its brown woolen blanket. . . . Death is nothing here," he said. "No one makes an ado." [15]

The Christian Commission had established two stations for its work: one at Falmouth Station, the railroad terminal opposite Fredericksburg, where a tent fourteen feet square held a sign identifying it as the "Christian Commission"; and the other at "the shanty village of Aquia," at the other end of the railroad, a major supply point on Aquia Creek near the Potomac River. Here the commission had a rough board building, fifteen by twenty feet, "its front door opening upon the marsh." In these two shelters the delegates of the commission lived and slept, surrounded by shelves and boxes containing the supplies for their work: Bibles, hymnbooks, tracts, fruits and wines, warm shirts, socks, mittens, drawers, lint, bandages, lanterns, pails, brandy, soup. "Here in the day was a constant stream of chaplains, and surgeons, and soldiers, coming for the weekly supply of reading for the regiment, some hospital luxuries for the sick, or for the little 'housewife,' with its needles and thread and much-prized letter." And here each evening the delegates gathered to conduct a prayer meeting for the soldiers. [16]

About ten Christian Commission delegates were working in the Army of the Potomac when Smith arrived. He was assigned work at both Falmouth and Aquia and later at Belle Plain, another of the army's supply points, on the Potomac Creek near the Potomac River, nine miles from Fredericksburg. He and the other delegates were furnished passes by the provost marshal general, which gave them access to the entire army and allowed them free transportation on government trains and boats. They also had free use of the government's telegraph lines and the right to purchase supplies at the army's commissary. Much of Smith's work was devoted to the distribution of religious publications: soldiers' hymnbooks, flexible-covered "knapsack books," periodicals, tracts, and portions of the Scriptures. The Christian Commission had determined to furnish every regiment in the army with New Testaments. On March 23 Smith reported on the work to the American Bible Society:

> We have canvassed this first army corps, some twenty-five or thirty thousand troops, pretty thoroughly, and are working in the sixth corps. If the army of the Potomac lies still one week more, and the supplies do not fail us, there will be comparatively few men in the army that will not have had the opportunity to furnish themselves with a Testament and paper. I found one regiment (121st Penn. Vols.) where there were thirty men (Germans) in one company who came from home without the Word of God, and they had become hungry for it. A squad of them in a tent promised the chaplain that they would give him their cards and play no more, if he would get them a Testament. In another company of this regiment, an English Testament had circulated for the winter among *five tents* (some thirty readers), and had seldom lain an hour by daylight unused. . . .
>
> How often an inquiry, "Would you like a Testament?" is answered, "Yes I should very much; I lost mine, that I had from home, at Antietam," or "South Mountain," or "Fredericksburg!" Our prayer-meetings are full and solemn. This is a serious time with these armed hosts. They know from the antecedents of their general that there is sharp work before them, and these warm days and spring voices are perpetual reminders of coming battle, wounds, and death; and they feel that something must be done to get ready for these realities.[17]

Smith also worked among the sick. The army had established a large field hospital at Windmill Point, a few miles below Aquia Creek. A city of tents was laid out on what had been a cultivated field, but long before the hospital was ready, the sick began to arrive from all parts of the army. "The rain fell almost incessantly, and the whole camp presented a scene wretched in the extreme. Thousands of pale, weak, disease-stricken men lay for days in the fireless tents, on the muddy floors, or on beds of poles or boughs, suffering from cold and from hunger. Many died daily, and the mounds of sand in the lone 'God's acre' told a sad story of the cruel necessities of war." Here Smith visited the sick and buried the dead. He had wanted badly to come to the war;

now, as the soldiers said, he had "seen the elephant." He had discovered the underside of war: suffering and death.[18]

The delegates preached and conducted prayer meetings for groups of soldiers, but much of their work was done in conversations with individuals. There was an urgency about conversations that might be interrupted at any time by transfers or death, and the delegates inquired freely about the spiritual life of the soldiers. Smith wrote about one conversation he had with a young soldier detailed for fatigue duty at the First Division Hospital at Belle Plain.

> Giving him some reading-matter from my haversack, I asked him about his personal salvation. He gave me an interesting account of his early life and orphanage, of his education in the family of a kind Christian man, who had given him a home, and of the subsequent death of his foster-father. He told me of an only surviving friend, his Sabbath-school teacher, who occasionally had remembered his pupil in the army by a letter. He showed me one of these letters, full of kindness and tender solicitude for his conversion. I said—
> "Then you are not a Christian?"
> "No, but I wish I was. I have been thinking and talking about it so long."
> "Do you know that you can become a Christian to-day?"
> "You don't mean so soon as that?"
> "Yes; I mean that you can begin a new life and a true life,—and that's a Christian life, to-day. Wouldn't you like to try?"
> "Yes, I would."
> "Well, just over that hill, near the run, is a place where you will be entirely by yourself. Go and kneel down by that tree and tell your Saviour that you want to be a Christian *now*, and are going from this time to try and do His will. . . . Will you do it? I don't mean, 'Will you *think* about it?' but, 'Will you *do* it,' and begin now over by the tree?"
> "I will try, sir." . . .
> Three days after, just as I was leaving that army, in a battalion drill, I saw my soldier on the extreme left. As the line swung past me, I had only time to step alongside and ask, "Did you do it?" and to get the answer, quick and firm—
> "Yes, sir, I did it." [19]

Some soldiers had no use for the delegates. Oliver Wendell Holmes, Jr., said, "It's very well to recommend theoretical porings over Bible and Homer —One's time is better spent with Regulations & the like." Colonel Charles L. Peirson of the Thirty-ninth Massachusetts Volunteers said that when he lay wounded in a hospital at City Point, he was visited "by some well meaning but clumsy Christians, whose mission it was to supply the patients with testaments and tracts. They, seeing me, stopped to urge me, since I was so soon to meet my Creator, to turn from my evil ways while there was yet time, and to read the instructive words with which they burdened my couch. One of my friends afterwards said . . . that I had only strength enough to reply, 'Go to blazes.'" The delegates were sometimes jeered. A group of delegates moving to the front, carpetbags in hand, was asked by a veteran soldier if they had any lemons to sell. One of them answered gravely, "No, my friend, we belong to the army of the Lord," to which the soldier called back, "Oh, ye—es; stragglers! stragglers!" Even when Christian officers arranged for church services, the preachers were not guaranteed a good reception. "We had Sunday morning inspection," one soldier wrote, "went to church, sit on the ground, most of the boys played Mumly Meg instead of listening to the sermon." [20]

But many other soldiers received the delegates gladly. Frank H. Snow, who went from Andover Theological Seminary as a delegate, reported afterward that all the soldiers he had met "seemed willing, and many anxious, to converse on religious subjects. I did not meet with a single rebuff during the whole term of my service." The Reverend David Weston, who worked among the wounded at Fredericksburg in the spring of 1864, washing and dressing wounds, giving food and medicine, writing letters, and praying with the soldiers, said he had "heard no sneer at religion, Christians, or the church." The work of the delegates "had demonstrated to them that religion was not all emptiness." A surgeon attached to the headquarters of the Army of the Potomac said he had "never attended a meeting held by the Christian Commission that was only half full. As a rule they are overflowing, even where they are held every evening in the week." [21]

Most of the soldiers were young and impressionable; half of all the volunteers were under the age of twenty-three and a half; nearly a third were under twenty-one. A good many of them came from Christian homes and were either church members or members of a Sabbath school. Many of them had been influenced by the revivals that swept the nation after the fall of 1857 and were genuinely interested in the Bible. Major Thomas C. Thoburn wrote about a Bible class that met "in one of the shanties of Co. F," and he recorded how he had himself spent a Sunday during the Atlanta campaign "lying in the rifle pits reading my testament." The members of Company C in the 125th Pennsylvania Volunteer Infantry each carried a pocket Bible and were known as the Bible Company. The Seventh Regiment, Ohio Volunteer Infantry, included a Bible class of forty from the college and theological seminary at Oberlin, Ohio, half of whom studied the New Testament in Greek. Walt Whitman said that in his visits to soldiers he found himself naturally led to reading "passages from the Bible, expounding them, prayer at the bedside, explanations of doctrine, etc. (I think I see my friends smiling at this confession, but I was never more in earnest in my life.)" Whatever interest the men had in religion was heightened by the dangers they faced. Eighteen-year-old Private William McKinley confided to his diary before a march, "It may be I will never see the light of another day." If he should be killed, McKinley wanted it recorded "that I not only fell as a soldier for my Country, but also a Soldier of Jesus." The delegates were often aware that they were "preaching to men in their graveclothes." The men were aware of it, too, and listened carefully to the preaching, and the preachers generally came away feeling that their time among the soldiers was well spent.[22]

IN THE MIDST OF HIS WORK, Smith began a series of letters to his four-year-old daughter, Gerty, describing the war in terms a child could understand. One typical letter was written from a boat on the Potomac River.

My dear little Gerty:

Papa is riding on a steamboat this morning from Belle Plain to Aquia. He has only this bit of paper to write Gerty a letter.

Last night papa slept on his blanket in a white cloth house, and when he woke up this morning the birds were singing beautifully. A little red bird sat up in a high tree, and opened his mouth and sang, oh, so *sweetly!* Then a large brown mocking-bird jumped up over red bird's head and sang just like him. Then red bird sang again. And mocking-bird sang again, when red bird flew away. I suppose he thought mocking-bird was saucy.

When the birds were gone, papa went into one of the white houses, where there were a great many sick men—more than Gerty's fingers on both hands. One boy was trying to read a book with a red cover. His hand trembled, his head ached, and his lips were all sore and dry. He was very pale, and tired and sick. Papa looked into his book. It was a little Bible. His sister Jane gave it to him. Papa asked him if he loved his Bible.

"Very much."

"Do you love Jesus, too?"

"Oh, yes, yes, and I want to hear you pray."

So papa kneeled down on the ground and asked God to bless this poor sick soldier, and make him very patient, and help him to get well, so that he could go home and see his sister and his mother.

The other sick soldiers listened, and some of them got out of bed and kneeled down. Some of them cried, and asked me to come again.

Now, Gerty, are you not glad that you are not a sick soldier, away out in Virginia?

From your dear
Papa.[23]

Smith's letters to Gerty did not gloss over suffering or death, and yet they were playful and charming. On one occasion he wrote to Gerty as though she were with him to see a trainload of convalescent soldiers.

> There, Gerty, don't you hear? One of the convalescents speaks to you. He is coming down. Never mind now; he will not hurt you: no soldier, who takes a little girl in his arms that way, is going to hurt her. Do you know why he wanted to take you? He has a little girl, you may depend upon it, way up in Michigan; and when he saw you it made him think of his little Susy or Nelly, and he couldn't stay up on the cars. Do you feel that little wet spot up on your cheek, close to where he kissed you? I wonder if it can be a tear? Do papas ever cry when they think of their little girls?[24]

The letters to Gerty were meant not only for her but for all the children in Pepperell. The letters were Smith's way of sharing with them his new experiences and the things he had seen: the steamboats and railroads, the drummers and buglers, the captains and generals. He had the letters sent to Asa Bullard, the editor of the *Well-Spring*, a magazine published for children by the Massachusetts Sabbath School Society. Bullard published them in the *Well-Spring*, where they introduced thousands of children to the Civil War and the work the Christian Commission was doing for the soldiers.[25]

In one of the letters published in the *Well-Spring*, Smith appealed to the children to send what he called "housewives" or "comfort bags," small sewing kits, to the soldiers. The children responded by sending thousands of comfort bags, often with tracts and personal letters enclosed, which the Christian Commission delegates distributed to the soldiers. The children continued to support the commission throughout the war. They collected clothing and conducted fairs to raise money, while their parents contributed hospital stores, food, and reading matter as well as money. The churches spurred them on by asking the question Moses had asked: "Shall your brethren go to war, and shall ye sit here?" (Num. 32:6). By the end of the war the general public had contributed nearly $5,500,000 in cash and goods for the work of the Christian Commission.[26]

About the time Smith went to the army, the Christian Commission decided to appoint a general field agent in each of the federal armies, a salaried representative who would plan the commission's work and supervise both the activities of the delegates and the distribution of supplies. Station agents would serve under them, one in each army corps. John A. Cole, a twenty-four-year-old civil engineer from Medway, Massachusetts, who had served as a delegate since August 1862, was appointed general field agent in the Army of the Potomac. Cole, in turn, recommended that Edward Smith, "tried as a delegate," be appointed general field agent in the Army of the Cumberland, then operating in Tennessee. The executive committee made the appointment, and at the end of March 1863, after serving two months in the Army of the Potomac, Smith left Virginia to assume his new duties in the West.[27]

6

The Army of the Cumberland

[At Murfreesboro, Tennessee,] we found a field for Christian effort such
as is rarely presented. Hospitals crowded with sick and wounded soldiers;
whole brigades without a chaplain, and a vast army almost destitute of the
Scriptures, or any religious reading.

John H. Boggs, *United Presbyterian*, August 29, 1863

The Christian Commission needed a person with field experience to
establish its work in the West, someone who also had organizational
ability and the ability to act decisively in a part of the country far removed
from the oversight of the commission's officers. Edward Smith met the commission's requirements. One of Smith's associates in Pepperell said of him
that "he was a man of remarkable executive ability; with him to think was to
act; so much so that he was liable to hastily follow his first impulse, rather
than wait for the sober second thought." That trait may have been a liability
in a quiet country pastorate, but it was a decided asset in a fast-moving war.[1]

On March 30, 1863, Smith was at the commission's headquarters in Philadelphia, making arrangements for his new work and for the supply of his pulpit and the care of his family. That night he left Philadelphia with three delegates and traveled to Cincinnati. On April 2 he was at the office of the United
States Sanitary Commission in Louisville, Kentucky, with seven boxes of
stores and publications, taking advantage of the Sanitary Commission's offer
to ship his supplies to Nashville. On April 6 he was in Nashville, "waiting on
officials," and two days later he telegraphed from Murfreesboro, Tennessee:
"Commission working under Rosecrans."[2]

Major General William S. Rosecrans commanded the Department of the
Cumberland. As soon as Smith arrived at Murfreesboro, he went to Rosecrans's headquarters and obtained "an interview under favorable circumstances" with the general. Several days later he made a formal application
for government transportation from Louisville for delegates and permission
for the delegates to make purchases for their own use from the army's com-

missaries. Rosecrans gave his approval—at least for the purchases. Later, the medical director in the Army of the Cumberland authorized the shipment of the commission's hospital stores and reading materials. One month after Smith's arrival, it was reported that "the United States Christian Commission has received from Gen. Rosecrans all needful facilities for carrying on their work in the Army of the Cumberland" and that twenty delegates were already at work. Smith had also been directed by the Christian Commission's executive committee to "organize and commence" work in the Army of the Ohio. Major General Ambrose E. Burnside, who commanded the Department of the Ohio, also welcomed the presence of the commission, and later that year a field agent was assigned to supervise its work in that army.[3]

Within a week of his arrival in the West, Smith described the situation he found there in a letter to Charles Demond, a member of the Christian Commission's executive committee. "We are in good working order, after manifold trials, under Rosecrans. Great want here of just what the Christian Commission furnishes—sick men hungry for something from home and wanting to hear of Jesus." He had also discovered many soldiers, especially from East Tennessee, Kentucky, and southern Illinois, who wanted to learn to read. "Contrabands," too, black refugees serving as officers' servants, were eager to begin reading. Smith was convinced that there were at least five thousand suitable books "lying in Boston publishing houses, out of date and out of sale," which could be purchased at cost or obtained without cost, and he urged the commission to send a supply to him by express. He wrote also about a war of a different intensity from that in the East. "The war is very bitter here. The Army of the Potomac is at play, compared with the work here by these soldiers. There is a personal animosity,—a hate between families and neighbors, which makes this a war terribly in earnest." But he was confident that the Union soldiers were equal to the task. "Start Hooker on the Rappahannock, and we will take care of Middle Tennessee, and shortly hurry on to carry deliverance to those hunted, oppressed families in East Tennessee. Then the rebellion will be over. God hasten it. Meanwhile we will keep our hands and hearts open for the suffering, dying men."[4]

Among the "manifold trials" Smith encountered in establishing the commission's work in the West was the conviction some people had that the commission was interfering with the work of the army chaplains. Early in the war, the Christian Commission had issued an unfortunate circular proposing to place a volunteer chaplain in each army brigade, a proposal that was resented by the regular chaplains. General Oliver Otis Howard, a firm supporter of the Christian Commission, had also contributed to the ill feeling by saying in a speech early in 1863 that the chaplaincy had proved almost a total failure and suggesting that the Christian Commission should have an agency in each division of the army.[5]

Although the Christian Commission had been tactless in presenting the issue, there were problems with the chaplaincy: a shortage of chaplains and the incompetency of too many men serving as chaplains. Brigadier General David Bell Birney complained about the scarcity of chaplains in his command and about the "wretched broken-down men that often seek refuge in an army chaplaincy." Major Thomas C. Thoburn said of his chaplain, "He is a man of very little mental ability, and might have a great deal more grace without being injured thereby. I think however that he means well." Later, in the Atlanta campaign, Thoburn said he had not seen the chaplain in over four months. More than two years of military experience had led him to the conclusion that chaplains were "a useless appendage in the army." Many of the common soldiers agreed. A private wrote from Fredericksburg in 1862 that he had lost all confidence in his chaplain. "He lied to me about carrying the mail & does nothing at all but hang around his tent & sort the mail. He never goes around any amongst the men & I think he is nothing but a confounded humbug & nuisance." A Hoosier soldier thought chaplains were of little use in the army. "I suppose the reason is that the most worthless pre[a]chers, those who can not make a good living at home, are the ones who strive to secure the position for the money."[6]

In Ohio, a committee of the Presbyterian Synod of the Western Reserve issued a report on the military chaplains. While acknowledging that there were many "excellent and faithful and self-denying" men in the chaplaincy, the committee nevertheless reported that "the uniform testimony of men, who have had the best opportunities of forming a correct opinion, is, that a majority of the Chaplains are unworthy of the place they hold; that by their incompetency, or the gross neglect of their duties, they prove themselves faithless servants of the State, and do incalculable injury to the profession of the ministry and to the Christian religion." Even at its best, the chaplaincy suffered from the fact that the law under which chaplains were appointed did not define their rank or authority or even their duties. The position of chaplain, one Christian Commission official concluded, was a "most difficult and discouraging one."[7]

After its initial blunder, the Christian Commission was careful not to criticize the chaplaincy or to interfere with the work of the chaplains. "A chaplain's regiment," the delegates were told, "is his peculiar parish, and there should be no intrusion upon it." The commission offered to support the chaplains in their work by supplying them with reading materials and chapel tents. But the commission did insist that there was a need for delegates because of the shortage of chaplains. Many of the army regiments had no chaplain; at one time in the Army of the Potomac thirty-seven regiments in the Fifth Corps and thirty-eight regiments in the Second Corps were without chaplains. Moreover, soldiers in hospitals were often located where they could not be visited by their chaplains even if they had them. Artillery batteries were not assigned chaplains, nor were field hospitals, ambulance trains, wagon trains, headquarter units, regular army regiments, and, in the navy, the entire blockading squadron. Smith said that more than two-thirds of the soldiers in the Army of the Cumberland had no chaplains. But even though he criticized the shortage of chaplains, Smith was careful to establish good relations with the chaplains that were serving in the army, and his efforts bore good results. In May he met in a deserted church at Murfreesboro with twenty-two chaplains serving in the Army of the Cumberland who unanimously passed a resolution welcoming the delegates of the Christian Commission: "*Resolved*, that we hail with gratitude to God, the advent of the Delegates of the U.S. Christian Commission among us; that they have our thanks for the supply of religious reading furnished us; and that we assure them that we shall be happy to cooperate with them in sowing the good seed in this vast field of labor." Smith said later that the delegates and the chaplains worked together "like brothers, and the Master honors the united effort."[8]

The Christian Commission delegates had an advantage over the chaplains in coming to the army directly from home. "They carried to the brave boys words of kindness and tokens of sympathy from mothers, wives, sisters, and daughters. . . . Home and its associations rose before the young men" at the appearance of the delegates. The chaplains were in uniform ("plain black frock coat with standing collar and one row of black buttons, plain black pantaloons, and a black felt hat or army forage cap"), but the delegates came in civilian clothes with only a small, silver, Christian Commission badge to

identify them. The badge, Smith said, "became an invitation to the soldier to tell all his troubles even to a stranger, and oftentimes to commit his watch and purse to that stranger's care without taking a receipt or asking his name." The soldiers uniformly called the delegates "chaplain," but they received them not as part of the military establishment but as representatives of the churches at home.[9]

When Smith arrived in Tennessee, the Army of the Cumberland was at Murfreesboro, thirty miles southeast of Nashville on the railroad to Chattanooga. The Battle of Murfreesboro or Stones River had been fought there from December 31, 1862, to January 2, 1863, and the army remained at Murfreesboro for the first half of the year, rebuilding its strength. One-fourth of the 43,400 men Rosecrans had before the battle had been wounded, captured, or killed.[10]

The Christian Commission had done little work in the Army of the Cumberland before the Battle of Stones River. News of the battle, however, brought an immediate response. Two bands of delegates, one from Philadelphia and one from Chicago, hurried to the battlefield and ministered to the wounded. Smith arrived after their work was done, with the commission's directive to create a permanent organization in the Army of the Cumberland.

After securing Rosecrans's permission for the work, Smith opened stations in Nashville and Murfreesboro. For the first four months, the delegates in Nashville lived in a large storeroom on Cherry Street, "sleeping on dry goods shelves and boxes, partaking the scanty fare served up by a disabled soldier, who volunteered to cook for our mess." As the work grew, the delegates moved to other quarters, and the storeroom became a reading and writing room for the soldiers. Newspapers, New Testaments, hymnbooks, and other religious publications were available to them, as were stationery and writing tables. A card said: "If you are in trouble, speak to any agent in the room; you are the one he wants to see." Dwight L. Moody, who had helped form the Chicago Army Committee and had been its first delegate in the field, opened a daily prayer meeting in the basement of the Second Presbyterian Church, then being used by the army as a chapel. Work was also begun in Nashville's six hospitals, in the Convalescent Camp, and in Maxwell Barracks, across the street from the commission's reading room.[11]

At Murfreesboro, the commission soon had as many as thirty delegates working in the "ragged little village of wooden houses, surrounded by an immense city or cluster of cities of tents." In the month of May alone, twenty-five thousand copies of Scripture and thirty thousand hymnbooks were distributed. The delegates also preached, visited in the hospitals, held prayer meetings, and opened a reading room similar to the one in Nashville. Their work among men "made thoughtful in the Battle of Stone River" resulted in a celebrated revival, a "remarkable work of grace." At one meeting alone more than five hundred men rose to ask for prayers. "There is heard everywhere," a reporter wrote, "the sound of prayer, or the voice of song and Christian exhortation."[12]

A Christian Commission chapel and reading room (*above*) and the interior of one of the commission's chapels (*left*). Courtesy of the Amistad Research Center, New Orleans, Louisiana.

Smith not only supervised the work of the delegates, he too participated in the revival. He wrote about one of his experiences near Murfreesboro.

> On a Sunday morning in May, I was on my way to fill an appointment for service with a regiment, when I came upon a group of soldiers, sitting on logs in a hollow square, under an oak tree. I found it was a Bible-class of the First Michigan Engineers, with a Corporal for teacher. I took my place as a scholar and went through with the morning's lesson,—the first chapter of St. James. There were no Commentaries in the soldiers' knapsacks; some of them had reference Bibles: the teachings of the hour were from the men's hearts, aided by such knowledge as they had stored away in early life.

After the Bible class, the soldiers held a meeting of the regiment's Christian Association. Two men were admitted into the association who had never been members of a church.

> They desired baptism by immersion. At the close of the afternoon service, we marched to the banks of Stone River, where we went down into the water. The comrades of the men stood near the side of the stream, singing—
>   "Am I a soldier of the cross?"
> It was a strange and beautiful scene. Those scarred veterans on the bank, cheering their two comrades who were dedicating themselves to God, in the very stream which, a few months before, had run red with the blood of their fellow-soldiers and enemies.[13]

Smith's work required supplies, not only religious publications to feed the spirit but food for the body as well: delicacies for distribution in the hospitals, coffee for men on the march, and onions and pickles for the soldiers to prevent scurvy. Medicines were also needed and bandages, slings, and crutches. Support for the commission's work in the Army of the Cumberland came from the army committees in Indianapolis and Louisville and especially from the committees in Cincinnati and Pittsburgh. Stores of all kinds were collected, along with cash contributions, and Smith made constant appeals for additional supplies. "One-half of the children of Ohio," he wrote on one occasion, "should now be at work pe[e]ling onions and putting them in vessels of vinegar, the other half preparing small fruits. Would it not be well to send a circular to every Sabbath School in Ohio, urging the children thus to go to work for our soldiers[?]" The army committees responded to Smith's appeals with support not only for the soldiers but for Smith himself. The Cincinnati committee reported that "the General Field Agent of our Department—Reverend Edward P. Smith—is eminently the right man in the right place; he is fortunate, too, in having secured the services of an excellent, efficient corps of subordinate agents."[14]

Smith appealed to the army committees for men as well as supplies. In a letter published in the Methodist *Pittsburgh Christian Advocate*, he described the kind of ministers he needed.

> Our experience in the army has proved the desirableness of age and minis-
> terial experience in delegates. . . . One main work is holding meetings in hospi-
> tals and camps, and a delegate should be able to stand before a body of men, and
> by his words and general bearing make himself acceptable. . . . The best preach-
> ers in Pennsylvania will find here a field in this army such as rarely offers to a
> minister of the gospel—an opportunity to preach to men by the hundred and
> sometimes by the thousand. Can you not entreat some of our first class preach-
> ers to come this way? A good old fashioned, camp meeting Methodist preacher
> would be welcomed by hundreds and hundreds of men here. Send us down half
> a dozen, but let them be men of age and experience, if possible.[15]

Smith had decided that his own preaching would be done in the army as long as the war lasted. Soon after he arrived in Tennessee, he submit-ted his resignation to the church in Pepperell. "An intended absence of four weeks," he wrote, "has grown almost to three months. Obligations & oppor-tunities for good have multiplied with every day[']s increased experience in this christian army work, till I have come to feel that I ought to give myself altogether to the comfort & spiritual welfare of the soldiers for life or for the war." He said he had come to his decision to resign "with hestitation & pain," but he felt strongly that the church needed regular pastoral leadership: "You need a shepherd, the dear lambs of the flock must be constantly folded." The church, however, would not accept his resignation. The members preferred to wait and see how the war developed, hoping that Smith would be able to return to them. A motion to file his letter for six months, without action, was adopted by a vote of thirty to two (the two perhaps being the same two members who preferred to table the matter "for the war"). As a courtesy, the women of the church were invited to vote informally on the question and voted fifty for and none against. The church was in full sympathy with the work Smith was doing. "We love our pastor," they said, "and feel the need of his labors with us, but we love our country, and yield to its call." [16]

With the Christian Commission successfully established in the armies of the Cumberland and the Ohio, the executive committee directed Smith to visit General Ulysses S. Grant's Army of the Tennessee, which was then engaged in the campaign against Vicksburg. George Hay Stuart, the com-mission's chairman, wrote to Grant to explain the work of the commission, noting the endorsements it had received from the president and other offi-cials. The pressure of other work and the remote location of the Army of the Tennessee, he said, had prevented the commission from carrying on any systematic work among Grant's men. "We have however now sent forward Rev[d] E P Smith of Massachuset[t]s, Rev W W Harshaw[,] Messrs Underwood, Ferrier, Marsh, & Morse, of Chicago, and hope to send others on Monday; and would commend them to your kindness, & request for them such facilities in the various divisions of your army as have been afforded us in the other armies, including passes, transportation for themselves & stores, and tents." [17]

Grant, however, had closed his lines to any civilians except the agents of the United States Sanitary Commission, which enjoyed a privileged status as a creation of the War Department. At the urging of prominent citizens concerned for the health of the army, the secretary of war had appointed the commission in June 1861. The Sanitary Commission provided advice and material support to the army's Medical Department, employing paid agents rather than volunteers for its work.

Earlier in the war, Grant had permitted delegates from the Chicago Army Committee—the Christian Commission's branch in that city—to work among his troops and on one occasion had written their passes himself. But representatives of various relief organizations had descended on the army and in Grant's opinion had "led to great abuse and much trouble. Many persons desiring to visit the Army take advantage of this to get here, free, and are the most importunate persons for free passages to their homes, and for other favors. In some instances they bring a few articles to sell." Grant had confidence in the Sanitary Commission and ordered a steamboat put at its disposal to transport its stores but with the proviso that no one could travel on the boat except military officers, discharged soldiers, and the officials of the Sanitary Commission. [18]

Smith traveled to Louisville and then to Cairo, Illinois, on his way to Vicksburg and the Army of the Tennessee. At Cairo he learned about Grant's restrictions. Two of the Christian Commission delegates had arrived in Cairo before him and, believing they would not be able to reach Vicksburg, had left for Memphis instead, where no passes were required. The other delegates had taken positions as nurses with the Sanitary Commission in order to get to Vicksburg. Smith was able to persuade Dr. John Strong Newberry, the secretary of the western department of the Sanitary Commission, to authorize free transportation on the Sanitary Commission's boat for him and for the supply of hymnbooks, soldiers' books, New Testaments, and tracts he had with him. [19]

The trip to Vicksburg was made in early June. Smith landed on the Yazoo River and then rode a mule nine miles over the bluffs General William Tecumseh Sherman's soldiers had fought for during the winter. When he reached the Army of the Tennessee, he observed the "trenches which our soldiers were then digging,—running zi[g]zag lines till they should get close up to the rebel works" and the "fevers and dysentery" the men in the trenches were suffering. The task of organizing the commission's work in the Army of the Tennessee was soon accomplished. By July 4, when Vicksburg fell, arrangements had been made for the work of the delegates, and a station had been opened, with a library, reading room, writing table, and supplies for distribution.[20]

Smith himself, however, was not able to see the work completed. He said he had been in Grant's army only a few days when he was taken

> sick with the malarial fever, and carried to a division hospital. It was my first experience of sickness in camp. I said to myself, when they had carried me into the tent and left me alone, without even a sick comrade—
>
> "Now you will have an opportunity to try the efficacy of the counsels you have so often given to soldiers in like circumstances." . . .
>
> But I found it far easier to preach than to practice. I knew that God does all things right and well, but I could not help the feeling that a change in my present prospects would be an improvement. . . . My theology said, "It is right and well for me to be sick among strangers, if God wills;" and my heart always added, "Yes, but it would be better to be sick at home."

He said that he was made well by the faith of a black laundress, who despite losing her family during slavery told him that she was always able to see the bright side of things. "Well, Nanny," he had said to her, "if you can do that, I think I ought to?" " 'Pears like ye ought to, massa, an' you's a preacher of de Word of Jesus."

> She went away. I turned myself on my blanket and said in my heart, " 'The Lord is my Shepherd.' It *is* all right and well. Now, come fever or health, come death or life, come burial on the Yazoo Bluff or in the churchyard at home,— 'the Lord *is* my Shepherd.' "
>
> With this sweet peace of rest, God's care and love became very precious to me. I fell asleep. When I woke I was in a perspiration; my fever was broken. "Old Nanny's" faith had made me whole.[21]

After regaining his health and returning to Nashville, Smith addressed a public letter to Dr. Newberry of the Sanitary Commission expressing appreciation for the assistance the commission had given him in his work, not only on the trip to Vicksburg but during the entire time he had been in the West.

> I desire, on behalf of the Christian Commission, to render grateful acknowledgment for the uniform, generous and cordial co-operation of yourself and the agents of your Commission in our work of bringing spiritual comforts and

blessings to the soldiers. But for your assistance at the first, and its continuance all along, our work would have been greatly impeded in the Army of the Cumberland.

Also, in my recent trip to Vicksburg, in the service of the Christian Commission, I was at all points kindly received and materially aided by the Sanitary Commission. My own feelings that the work of both Commissions, though wrought in different departments, should be entirely co-operative, were fully reciprocated by your agents at Cairo, Memphis, and on the Barge on Yazoo River. . . .

Every week's experience in my army work, bringing me among the camps and through the hospitals, and giving an opportunity, which I always improve, to look in at the different quarters of your Commission, leads me to a continually higher estimate of the work you have in hand. I am satisfied that your system of distributing hospital stores is the correct one. Such large contributions as the people are making, cannot be handed over to the army on any volunteer system, unless it be for a few days, amid the emergencies of a severe battle. A business involving such expenditures, would be entrusted by a business man only to permanent and responsible agents. . . .

Let me close this letter of thanks, my dear brother, with my daily prayer, a prayer which I *learned* in the "Soldier's Home" in Louisville, and have often repeated since in the "Soldier's Rest," at Memphis, on the "Barge" in Yazoo River, in the division hospitals under the guns of Vicksburg, in the Nashville "Home" and storeroom, and in the camps and hospitals at Murfreesboro—a prayer fresh on my lips, as I have just come from seeing wounded and typhoid patients at Tullahoma and Winchester, lifted from rough blankets, and undressed from the soiled clothes of march and battle, and laid in your clean sheets and shirts, upon your comfortable quilts and pillows—a prayer in which every Christian heart in the land will yet join—"God bless the Sanitary Commission!"[22]

Despite its eloquence, Smith's letter to Newberry offended some supporters of the Christian Commission and nearly caused his dismissal from the commission's service.

7

The Two Commissions

The town is one vast hospital. . . . The agents of the Sanitary and Christian Commissions are seen everywhere with the green ribbon of the former or the metal badge of the latter, ministering to the bodies and souls of wounded and dying men.

Report from Fredericksburg, Virginia, May 1864

The Christian Commission and the Sanitary Commission were to some degree rivals. Although in theory their tasks differed, in practice they overlapped. The Christian Commission emphasized its spiritual ministry, but it also served the material needs of the soldiers, especially in the hospitals and through its reading and writing rooms. The Sanitary Commission emphasized the assistance it gave to the army's Medical Department, but the commission's Auxiliary Relief Corps, composed primarily of theological students, provided reading materials, wrote letters for soldiers, visited the sick, and buried the dead—work that could hardly be distinguished from that of the Christian Commission's delegates. Representatives of the two commissions worked side by side on the battlefields, doing whatever was needed at the time.[1]

The two commissions competed in their appeals for public support. The Sanitary Commission, despite its official status, relied on voluntary contributions just as the Christian Commission did, and the public did not always discriminate between the appeals of the two. The Sanitary Commission held a series of successful sanitary fairs in various cities, and the Christian Commission published notices to inform the public that it received no benefit from the fairs. It also criticized the Sanitary Commission for using balls and raffles to raise funds. The Sanitary Commission objected to the sentiment and emotion in the "incidents" the Christian Commission used in its appeals to the public, taking pride in its own sober, factual appeals. And it objected to the encouragement the Christian Commission gave the public to send packages for personal distribution to the soldiers. The Sanitary Commission preferred that packages be sent to its offices to be opened and the contents distributed as needed, a method much less popular with the public.[2]

Underlying the rivalry between the two commissions was a difference in theology and spirit. The Christian Commission was the creation of evangelical Christians; the Sanitary Commission was more the creation of scientists and physicians and included members of a variety of religious persuasions from Catholicism to Unitarianism. The heads of the two commissions typified the differences. George Hay Stuart, the chairman of the Christian Commission, was a ruling elder and the superintendent of the Sunday school at the First Reformed Presbyterian Church in Philadelphia, a church of a denomination regarded by some as "a little exclusive." He was also a member of national boards for temperance, Sunday schools, foreign missions, and Bible distribution and, in later life, a promoter of the evangelist Dwight L. Moody. Stuart was a man who could conclude a letter to General Grant by saying he was praying that God would "long preserve you to lead our armies to victory, bless you with the guidance of his grace, and in the last great conflict make you more than a conqueror through the merits of our Saviour[']s death."[3]

The president of the Sanitary Commission was the Reverend Dr. Henry Whitney Bellows, the minister of the First Unitarian Church (All Souls Church) in New York City. It was said of Bellows that "he left the port of supernaturalism far behind him, and neared the port of rational religion faster and faster as the busy years went by." Bellows was satisfied with "essential goodness" as the only necessary part of religion. "Of all the old Puritanic and Calvinistic creed," he wrote, "the only article in New England that survives in its original splendor, or that deserved to survive, is the profound sentiment of duty,—and of goodness, essential goodness, as the end of duty and its guide." A man of the world, Bellows shocked religious people in 1857 by a public defense of the theater; he said he did not believe in concealing his unorthodox opinions just "because they might shock the unthinking." Bellows could imagine himself touring the country, "blowing a long trumpet against the dogmas which scare & stultify the public mind."[4]

The differences in the two commissions and their leaders resulted in suspicions and hostility. George Templeton Strong, the treasurer of the Sanitary Commission and an Episcopal vestryman, confided his feelings about the Christian Commission to his diary. "There is an undercurrent of cant, unreality, or something else, I do not know what, in all their talk, that repels and offends me. This association, calling itself a 'commission' when it is no more a commission than it is a corporation, or a hose company, or a chess-club, or a quadratic equation, and thus setting out under false colors and with a lie on its forehead, seems to me one of the many forms in which the shallowness, fussiness, and humbug of our popular religionism are constantly embodying themselves."[5]

After President Lincoln's assassination, both commissions sent delegations to the funeral service in Washington. Strong had a disapproving eye on the Christian Commission delegation throughout the ceremonies. "We went in a body to the office of the Secretary of the Treasury in the Treasury building. A delegation of our 'Christian' friends reported at the same place, including that evangelical mountebank and philanthrope, Mr. G. H. Stuart of Philadelphia. They were an ugly-looking set, mostly of the Maw-worm and Chadband type. Some were unctuous to behold, and others vinegary; a bad lot." Strong thought the service itself "vile and vulgar" and the "whining, oratorical" prayer of Bishop Matthew Simpson, a member of the executive committee of the Christian Commission, "most nauseous."[6]

Supporters of the Christian Commission were no less scathing in their comments on the Sanitary Commission. Walt Whitman wrote to his mother about the agents of the Sanitary Commission, who were not volunteers but salaried workers. "As to the Sanitary Commissions & the like, I am sick of them all, & would not accept any of their berths—you ought to see the way the men as they lie helpless in bed turn away their faces from the sight of these Agents, Chaplains &c. (*hirelings* as Elias Hicks would call them—they seem to me always a set of foxes & wolves)—they get well paid, & are always incompetent & disagreeable—As I told you before the only good fellows I have met are the Christian Commissioners—they go everywhere & receive no pay—"[7]

Not surprisingly, Smith's letter praising the Sanitary Commission raised protests from supporters of the Christian Commission. "I have heard no indistinct rumblings from the East respecting my former letter to you," Smith wrote to Dr. Newberry. "It seems to have been taken up in cities like Buffalo, where I am sorry to know, a fierce rivalry between the two Commissions has grown up, as a damaging blow to [the] Ch^r Commission. A Buffalo clergyman complains to Head Quarters most mournfully of the effect of the letter there. I am called to account for it by the Sec'y & have just now in connection with a brief defense sent in my resignation."[8]

The Sanitary Commission agent in Nashville found the response of the Christian Commission officials to Smith's offending letter "a matter of surprise and regret." When he learned of Smith's resignation, he immediately offered Smith the office of hospital visitor and relief agent with the Sanitary Commission, if his resignation was accepted. But it was not accepted. Smith visited the Philadelphia headquarters of the commission, expecting to conclude his service with it, only to find, to his surprise, that the executive committee had declined to receive his resignation. Although the committee's reasons are not known, it must have helped Smith's case that the army committee in Cincinnati, which was close to the situation in the West, endorsed Smith's position and that the treasurer of the Pittsburgh committee, Joseph Albree, said he was glad to see the letter that offended others.[9]

"I hope," Smith wrote, "this little conflict between a subordinate & his superiors has not been without good effects. . . . I think it will result to some degree at least in defining our work more definitely & our relations to the Sanitary Commission." The rivalries between the two commissions persisted on the national level, but in the West the two groups continued to work in harmony. Privately, the western officials of the two commissions expressed their differences, but they also shared information and supplies and were careful in public always to speak well of each other. Dr. Newberry assured Smith that "every expression of partisan feeling emanating from the representatives of the Sanitary Commission has been received with sincere disapprobation. . . . I have been determined not to tolerate anything which should peril the harmony and cordiality which upon every consideration I felt should prevail between the two great benevolent organizations which we represent." William A. Lawrence, a Christian Commission agent in Nashville, expressed the feeling of the Christian Commission to Newberry: "I believe that our commission will be most efficient for good as a Sanitary *Christian* Commission[,] yours (though both are ours & yours) as a Christian *Sanitary*, & as such I am ever at the service of both alike." [10]

LATE IN JUNE 1863, before Smith returned from Vicksburg, the Army of the Cumberland began its offensive against General Braxton Bragg's army. Rosecrans, with an army of 80,000 men, accompanied by 4,200 wagons and 600 ambulances, 22,000 artillery horses, 3,000 private horses, and 36,000 mules, advanced along the railroad toward Chattanooga as Bragg's army fell back before the Union assault.[11]

As the army advanced, the Christian Commission delegates—soon joined by Smith—moved with it. They established stations at Tullahoma, Winchester, and Cowan in Tennessee, Stevenson and Bridgeport in Alabama, and then at Chattanooga, Tennessee. The delegates conducted the usual religious services, but, especially after the Battle of Chickamauga, they also attended the wounded and became involved in the suffering themselves. Three of the delegates died of illness; another was captured at Crawfish Spring Hospital and taken to Libby Prison in Richmond, Virginia. Seven government wagons loaded with hospital stores supplied by the Christian Commission were captured and burned by Confederate cavalry.[12]

Smith's task was to organize the work of the delegates. One of them wrote that on a Saturday evening at Winchester "the efficient" Smith sent notices to the army brigades about the services the delegates would conduct on Sunday. "Our packages of papers, tracts, hymn books and testaments," the delegate said, "are all done up and ready." On Sunday evening, Smith himself spoke in a service for the soldiers held in one of the local churches. On another Sunday, Smith arranged for the Lord's Supper to be administered at two churches, and after distributing handbills announcing the services, he personally conducted the one at the Presbyterian Church.[13]

He also continued his appeals for supplies. He wrote to George Stuart to request books for the Anderson Cavalry (the Fifteenth Pennsylvania Cavalry, composed largely of Philadelphians). "They are reading men. All their lives they have, until now, had abundance of books. The want, therefore, is now the more keenly felt." On another occasion, he sent a Confederate buckshot from the battlefield at Murfreesboro to the editor of the *Well-Spring* with an appeal for books: "Who will give good for evil—a loyal soldier's library for a rebel soldier's buck-shot?" In another letter to the *Well-Spring,* he asked the editor, "What right have we to be indifferent and comfortable, and growing rich, while our brothers are in the field struggling, suffering and dying, without the many comforts and consolations of the gospel which we can send them?"[14]

Smith was skilled at writing such appeals, mixing fact, sentiment, practicality, and flattery in good proportions. In July he wrote a long letter to the American Bible Society, which had supplied him with New Testaments for the Army of the Cumberland. He said that not far from thirty thousand copies had been distributed and over six hundred Bibles. After the army moved from Murfreesboro, he had "looked over the old camp grounds for Testaments thrown away by soldiers packing for the march, and to my surprise and gratification I found none. I did not go over all the camp sites, but was satisfied that there had been no reckless waste of the Word of God." But when he reached Tullahoma and Winchester, he found that two-thirds of the New Testaments had been lost in the heavy rains the army had encountered and in "those fights from Murfreesboro' to Tullahoma." "I have seen stout men brush off a tear with their rough hands, while they told me how they lost their all, and very often among the lost articles you would hear of—'The Bible mother gave me'—'My Sabbath school teacher told me not to let the Testament go, and I meant to carry it back'—'It was the Testament your chairman of the committee gave me.'" The supply of Bibles was running low. The commission did not propose to distribute them as widely as before because the army would be moving again soon. "But to men who *want* a Testament we intend to give one, even if he is to begin his march in twenty-four hours."

> Personally I owe a debt of gratitude to the American Bible Society. It has cheered us beyond measure to open your full boxes—1,370 strong—and fill the requisitions of chaplains and privates who were waiting for the Bread of Life. Sometimes from difficulty in transportation we would be days without a Testament at Murfreesboro', and obliged to say, "Not a Testament," to many a poor fellow who had come two or three times, only to be disappointed. Often I would have been willing to buy at a dollar a piece for special cases. Then when the boxes came, and we were able to say, as we do over and over, "This is a gift, without a penny cost, from the American Bible Society to the soldiers," it would do you good to hear the expressions of admiration and gratitude from the chaplains, and the equally hearty and grateful, "Bully for the Bible Society," from the privates. . . .
>
> I said at a county Bible society meeting in Keokuk, Iowa, not long since, that when I reached home the first collection I should ask from my church would be, not for the Christian Commission but for the American Bible Society.[15]

Smith was not present at the Battle of Chickamauga in September, where almost sixteen thousand Union soldiers were killed, wounded, or missing. On September 4 he was in Philadelphia, at the headquarters of the Christian Commission, consulting with officials about his relations with the Sanitary Commission. On Sunday, September 6, he was in the pulpit at Pepperell, where he had gone on a brief leave. He apparently used the time at home to recruit his townsmen for work in the Christian Commission, for that month William A. Lawrence went from Pepperell to Chattanooga, and later Pepperell residents John E. Blood, Charles P. Shattuck, and Deacon Charles Crosby served with the commission. The question of Smith's returning to his pulpit was also undoubtedly discussed during his visit.[16]

The Army of the Cumberland fought the Battle of Chickamauga on September 19 and 20, and on September 22 the treasurer of the Cincinnati Army Committee telegraphed George Stuart: "Send us E. P. Smith as soon as possible." Smith had, however, left Pepperell the night before, the news of the battle making him "impatient of delay." On October 1 he was back with the army at Stevenson, Alabama.[17]

As soon as Smith returned to the army, he wrote to the church at Pepperell, noting that the six-month delay in acting on his resignation, which the church had agreed to, was over, "while the work which I came to do, is still upon my hands, & every day growing more important & pressing." Saying that personal feelings, "yours for me & mine for you," should be put aside, and "the interests of Christ's Church" should be considered, he renewed his request that the church accept his resignation and call another pastor who could serve its needs. The church and the society, however, would not accept the resignation and made arrangements to supply the pulpit until Smith's return.[18]

On October 17, Smith wrote from Chattanooga, Tennessee, to "The Tuesday Evening Prayer Meeting At Home." He described a soldiers' prayer meeting held in Chattanooga a few days earlier, when sixty men gathered during a storm at the commission's chapel in the Baptist church. He said he had told the soldiers how people were praying for them "in a little praying circle in North Eastern Mass." The men at Chattanooga "talked of a soldier's trials, of the blessings they used to have at home, of praying wives & sisters & mothers, of their desire to hold out true thro' this fearful struggle. They prayed most touchingly for their comrades in hospital wasting of wounds, and for loved ones at home & for God's blessing on the country." At the end of the meeting, eight men rose for prayers, and six stayed "for inquiry." Such prayer meetings and preaching services, Smith said, were held every night. Every seat was filled before the services began, and the aisles were crowded with soldiers standing.[19]

In another letter to the Pepperell prayer meeting, he described a visit to a hospital in Chattanooga. He had entered a ward where forty of the most severe cases were kept. "Thirty men of those forty are going to die, according to all army experience with their disease." Because there was not time to visit each one, the ward master suggested he stand in the center of the ward and speak to all the men. Smith sang Isaac Watts's hymn "Heavenly Joy on Earth," which begins "Come, We That Love the Lord."

> None are indifferent. It is getting too dark to read easily. So I make the hymn my text. My dear Brothers, that song is true, every word. You need not die to go to heaven. Glory begins below. . . . Jesus wants to come here tonight. He is here. Some of you know it. He wants to bless you all. So I talk & then we pray. . . . As I pass out[,] their hands stretch up from the blankets beckoning me. Some want to thank me. Some want me to pray for them. But I must hasten to other duties & am obliged to pass by many an uplifted hand.[20]

Obtaining and transporting supplies was a continuing concern to Smith. After the Battle of Chickamauga, Dr. Newberry authorized Christian Commission delegates to draw on Sanitary Commission stores at any of its depots to care for the wounded. But the army was not as cooperative. In August,

George Stuart had asked the War Department for facilities to distribute read-ing matter in the Army of the Cumberland. The department replied that it was disposed to act favorably but asked for more details about the privileges desired. Stuart referred the letter to Smith, who specified his requests: trans-portation for delegates and stores; authority for the agents to make purchases from the quartermasters and to obtain forage for their animals; permission to have disabled privates detailed to serve in the commission's libraries and in similar positions; and whatever other facilities might be required. The War Department's reply to his requests was so bureaucratic as to be useless in the field: "In each case where the transportation of delegates or stores is sought, a specific statement, giving the names of delegates and the objects they have in view, lists of stores desired to be sent, etc. be forwarded to this Department, when it will be promptly submitted to the Secretary of War for his consideration and orders in the case." [21]

In the Army of the Cumberland relations with the military were deteriorat-ing. Dr. Glover Perin, the army's medical director, who had earlier approved transportation for Christian Commission supplies, began to refuse to trans-port its sanitary stores. In October, General George H. Thomas replaced Rosecrans in the Army of the Cumberland, and the agent of the Sanitary Commission at Nashville reported that "Gen. Thomas directs Gen. Granger in command here to grant papers to Sanitary Commission agents but to treat agents [of the] Christian Commission as other citizens and they are all refused papers at this time." [22]

Another change in army commands in the West gave Smith an opportunity to make a new appeal for government facilities for the Christian Commission. When General Thomas replaced Rosecrans in the Army of the Cumberland, that army was also combined with the armies of the Ohio and the Tennes-see to form the Military Division of the Mississippi under the command of Ulysses Grant.

Smith took his appeal directly to Grant. Despite the many visitors who came to Grant's headquarters—doctors, lawyers, state officials, congress-men, and the "delegations from the Almighty," as Lincoln referred to the clergy (or "busybodies" as others referred to them)—Smith was well re-ceived. He had put his requests in writing, explaining the work of the com-mission and describing its delegates as "the representatives of home affection & solicitude, urging men to a better life & animating them to duty to God & country. In this way there can be little doubt we are bringing daily a moral reinforcement to your army." Smith said that although he went to Grant's headquarters "with fear and trembling," Grant received him "easily; read my papers with attention; said an order should be issued, covering the points made, as soon as he had leisure to prepare it; laid my paper on the Adjutant's desk, saying, 'There is a paper to which I wish to give attention.' " Grant then directed the adjutant to give Smith a pass and transportation to any part of his command and signed the pass himself. "I came back all the way to our quarters," Smith said, "with my heart full of the first line of the 'Doxology in Long Metre.' [Praise God from whom all blessings flow.]"[23]

Grant issued his order concerning the Christian Commission—Special Field Orders No. 32—on December 12, 1863. It gave Smith everything he had asked. The officers in Grant's command were ordered to aid the delegates in every way possible, to give them passes to all points within the lines, to sell stores to delegates on the same terms as officers, to transmit telegrams over the government's lines at the delegates' expense, and to furnish free transportation within the division for delegates and their stores on all government steamers and trains. These were all matters that had caused difficulties to some degree since the commission was formed, and Grant had settled them once and for all in one of the Union's largest armies. The commission published the order over and again to call attention to Grant's acceptance of the commission and its work. And Smith, who had organized the commission's work in all three departments under Grant's command, was able to report: "General Grant's facilities have given us a new footing entirely."[24]

Less than a week after Smith's interview with Grant, the Battle of Chattanooga was fought. This time Smith was present. On November 25 the Army of the Cumberland charged the rifle pits at the foot of Missionary Ridge and then stormed the five-hundred-foot-high ridge itself, scrambling up its "broken and crumbling face" under fire from the top and dislodging the panic-stricken Confederates from what had seemed an insurmountable position. Smith and a group of delegates were there, watching the "climbing columns, or rather climbing mass, for every man was stretching away for himself, fired with the single purpose of gaining the top." Soon the wounded began to return "supporting a disabled arm or limping on a musket, or borne on a blanket by their comrades." The delegates opened a hospital in an abandoned farmhouse at the foot of the ridge, ripped open some cotton bales to make beds and pillows, and fed the men with soup, coffee, and cornmeal mush.[25]

"The enthusiasm of the men over their victory," Smith said, "was unbounded."

> The soldier forgot he was wounded while telling of the fight, and while a ball was being cut out of an arm or leg with a Delegate's pocket-knife, would occupy the time telling how he came to be hit, or "pegged," as they called it. During the charge up the ridge, four soldiers were seen bearing back a comrade on a blanket. . . . The men halted when they saw us, and laid down their burden,

asking if we would see whether the Color-sergeant was badly wounded. I knelt down by him and said—

"Sergeant, where did they hit you?"

"Most up the ridge, sir."

"I mean, Sergeant, where did the ball strike you?"

"Within twenty yards of the top,—almost up."

"No, no, Sergeant; think of yourself for a moment; tell me where you are wounded;" and throwing back the blanket, I found his upper arm and shoulder mashed and mangled with a shell. Turning his eye to look for the first time upon his wound, the Sergeant said—

"That is what did it. I was hugging the standard to my blouse, and making for the top. I was almost up when that ugly shell knocked me over. If they had let me alone a little longer,—two minutes longer,—I should have planted the colors on the top. Almost up; almost up!" [26]

The delegates went out with the stretcher-bearers to search for others who were wounded. Then, when all the wounded in their makeshift hospital had been sent to the town by ambulance, the delegates loaded themselves with crackers, kettles of soup, and canteens full of stimulants and climbed to the top of the ridge. There they found a one-story log house filled with Union and Confederate wounded and surrounded by Confederate dead, who had been carried from the house to make room for the living. It was a frosty night, and the men had no fire or food. "There was no Surgeon or nurse, and the men were lying in clothes stiff with blood from undressed wounds." In the cellar were the women and children of the house, who refused to help the wounded, saying, "You'uns brought 'em all here, and you'uns mought take care on 'em." The delegates spent the night at the house, dressing wounds, giving stimulants, serving soup and coffee, and taking notes for letters they offered to write for the soldiers. They also found small groups of men gathered around fires for a mile along the top of the ridge, and they ministered to the wounded among them. Then they went among the dead, searching their pockets for letters or other identification so they could write to their families about their deaths. When the battlefield work was done, the delegates continued their work in the Chattanooga hospitals until the railroad to Bridgeport was rebuilt and the patients who could be moved were transferred to Nashville and Louisville.[27]

With the rout of Bragg's army at Chattanooga and the repulse of General James Longstreet's army at Knoxville, the Union campaign was ended, and Grant's army rested for the winter. Early in the new year Grant moved his headquarters to Nashville. Smith too moved to Nashville, making the Christian Commission station there his own headquarters.

On the last day of 1863, Cleavie Smith was commissioned as a Christian Commission delegate, and she prepared to leave Pepperell, with her two children, to join her husband in Nashville. The members of the church in Pepperell gave their sad and "unwilling assent" to the departure of one "whose presence made the Pastor[']s absence, already greatly prolonged, more tolerable." The instructions printed on Cleavie's commission directed her to report to the agent of the Christian Commission in charge of the field to which she was sent. The general field agent at Nashville, whom she had been with only on one brief visit during the past year, was just the man she wanted to see.[28]

8

Nashville

In this once beautiful and proud city almost everything bears the impress
of war. Churches, Masonic halls, school buildings, Court House, and many
other fine edifices are occupied as barracks or hospitals.

Evangelist, June 23, 1864

The streets are literally crowded with Government wagons engaged in the
transportation of stores. Soldiers meet you at almost every step; and the
stirring strains of martial music fall upon the ear.

Presbyterian Banner, February 17, 1864

Society in this city is very much demoralized; assassinations are almost
nightly and brawls daily occurrences.

Pittsburgh United Presbyterian, September 21, 1864

Nashville had been occupied by Union forces since its surrender on
February 25, 1862. Soon after the surrender, Andrew Johnson was
appointed military governor of Tennessee and commissioned as a brigadier
general, with his headquarters in Nashville. The city was, in effect, under
martial law for the rest of the war, with the army involved in regulating prices,
protecting against fires, policing the streets, and looking after the city's sanitation. The army also strongly fortified the city, which was often threatened
by Confederate troops and by the guerrillas who were constantly attacking
the roads, railroads, and waterways leading into Nashville.[1]

An important city with thirty thousand inhabitants before the war, Nashville grew to seventy-five thousand by the war's end, not including the large
number of Union soldiers stationed there. At the same time, it became the
center of communications, supplies, and transportation for the entire western theater of the war. Almost every Union soldier who served in the West
passed through the city at one time or another, and it was continually con-
gested with troops. As many as twenty-two hundred soldiers a day stayed at
Barracks Number 2, near the Nashville and Chattanooga Railroad depot. On

one occasion the barracks porch was so crowded that it collapsed, seriously injuring twelve veterans of the Twenty-ninth Ohio Regiment. Confederate prisoners, too, filled the city. In September 1863, so many of them were confined on the fourth and fifth floors of the Convalescent Barracks in the Maxwell House Hotel building across the street from the Christian Commission office that the stairway gave way. Six men were killed and ninety-six injured, fifteen of them seriously.

Black refugees flocked to the city—about the time Smith arrived in the West, fifty wagonloads of contrabands arrived in Nashville in one week—and the army created a large contraband camp for them. In September 1863, Major George Luther Stearns began to recruit blacks for the Army of the Cumberland. Soldiers for ten black regiments were recruited in the vicinity of Nashville, and black regiments from other places frequently passed through the city, attracting much attention. White refugees—mostly women and children—from East Tennessee, Georgia, Mississippi, and Alabama also came into the city, driven from their homes by hunger and the persecution they suffered because of their loyalty to the Union. They lived in makeshift tents, crowded into depots, or were gathered into shelters. Many fell ill, and some died of exposure or diseases such as measles and smallpox.

The city streets were crowded with soldiers, prisoners, citizens, refugees, and "immense trains" of government wagons and teams; they were also filled with disorder: robberies, shootings, and drunken brawls. So frequent were the shootings that the *Nashville Daily Union* once reported as a "singular fact" that "we heard of no one being shot" the day before. The army tried in its own way to keep order, and the newspapers recorded its efforts. A guard bayoneted a bounty jumper near the Chattanooga depot. Two soldiers lay dead at the corner of Cherry and Union streets, "lying within thirty steps of each other, each killed by the guard within half an hour." Two Confederate prisoners were shot by guards in two days at the Convalescent Barracks. A bystander was killed at Cherry and Cedar streets when a patrol fired at a fleeing soldier. A deserter was executed near the city, in the presence of a large number of soldiers and other spectators. Five "rebel bushwhackers," condemned to death by a military commission, were hanged at one time at the state prison.[2]

Prostitution was rampant; one Union surgeon called Nashville "a city of whores." Riots and thievery were common in the red-light district known as Smoky Row. But the disorder was not confined to the brothels. On one occasion, one of the women drove up Cherry Street—past the Christian Commission reading room—exhibiting herself "entirely nude from her waist heavenward," while the soldiers at the Convalescent Barracks across the street cheered her on. At first, the army, concerned about the men disabled by venereal diseases, banished the prostitutes, sending them north on the steamer *Idaho,* but at Cincinnati the boat was ordered back to Nashville by the secretary of war. The army Medical Department was then ordered to examine the women and to establish a hospital to treat those who were diseased. The women were ordered to report for examination or face a thirty-day jail sentence. Those who were free of disease were given a certificate and licensed "to practice their profession in this city," after which they were required to be reexamined every ten days. By January 31, 1865, 393 prostitutes had been licensed, 109 had reported but failed to receive a license, and 207 had been treated for venereal diseases. When the licensing began, many of the prostitutes were reported to be "exceedingly filthy in their persons and apparel and obscene and coarse in their language," but, the report continued, "this soon gave place to cleanliness and propriety."[3]

Twenty-five military hospitals were established in Nashville, housed in churches, schools, factories, hotels, and other buildings commandeered by the army. The army's Cumberland Field Hospital alone covered thirty acres and contained 2,304 beds. In addition to general hospitals and two hospitals for prostitutes, there was a venereal hospital for soldiers, a prison hospital, a smallpox hospital, and hospitals for officers, convalescents, government employees, white refugee women and children, and contrabands. From April 2, 1862, to December 12, 1864, 212,143 admissions were recorded in the Nashville hospitals. The number of deaths was staggering. From March 3, 1862, to December 12, 1864, 10,203 soldiers and civilians died. The newspapers regularly carried information about the services of the government undertaker, W. R. Cornelius, who was "always supplied with metallic burial cases and wooden coffins of every description" and whose embalming process was "unrivalled, both for durability and economy." Soldiers' bodies, once buried, could be disinterred on a request made to the government undertaker, who would ship the bodies "securely packed, by express. Hundreds of persons have availed themselves of his services." The coffins etched themselves into soldiers' memories. Thirty-seven years later one soldier could still picture them. "Coffins stood up on end, empty and hungry. They seem to petition you to get in and be composed. Here and there may be seen oblong, unpainted boxes, awaiting shipment, with the word *head* written on one end."[4]

To serve the hospitals in Nashville, the army had, on one occasion at least, only eight hospital chaplains. The city itself had no post chaplains, because Nashville was not a military post. The local citizens offered their help to the Confederate prisoners but were not usually sympathetic to the Union sol-

Edward Smith as an official of the
Christian Commission. Courtesy of the
National Archives.

diers. The local clergy appear to have had other concerns. In October 1863, when almost six thousand men wounded at Chickamauga had been brought to hospitals in Nashville, the Reverend Dr. Robert B. C. Howell of the First Baptist Church, an outspoken supporter of the Confederacy, was engaged in preaching a series of sermons titled "The Christology of the Pentateuch" and continued the series even when his own church building was taken for a hospital and the congregation was forced to meet in a theater.[5]

The Christian Commission delegates helped fill the gap in ministries to the soldiers. All the delegates for Grant's army came through Nashville, where Smith assigned them work either in the city or at the other stations in the army. In Nashville the delegates served in the commission's reading and writing room at 6 North Cherry Street (formerly the residence of William L. Boyd, Jr., "general agent and dealer in slaves"), in the storeroom at Maxwell Barracks, in the camps and hospitals, and among the fifteen thousand quartermaster's men in Nashville, "most of them hardened men," Smith said, "and ungodly to excess." The delegates found that they needed no countersign or pass to reach the soldiers; their Christian Commission badges were recognized and accepted by everyone.[6]

The delegates spoke well of Smith's direction of their work. "I cannot but admire," one of them said, "the good management of Rev. E. P. Smith, the General Agent at Nashville. While willing and anxious to gratify the wishes of the delegates, he never loses sight of the interests of the Commission, and so controls the work as to accomplish the greatest amount of good." Another delegate said that Smith "knows how to do a thing well and at the same time so quietly that no noise or din arises." Still another delegate said that anyone going to Nashville would find Smith to be "a *true Christian gentleman,* with a calm, firm, far seeing and comprehensive mind, a good general, and a *good bishop*—though a Congregationalist."[7]

But not everyone was pleased with Smith's performance. James Russell Miller had been appointed the commission's general field agent in the Department of the Ohio, which had formerly been under Smith's direction. Miller was convinced that Smith was withholding supplies for his work, and, finding his position untenable, Miller asked to be relieved. "I feel convinced that the work will not be allowed to enlarge to its just proportions while the Department is nominally separate—that Mr. (Rev.) Smith will not support me—and that he will not support any one unless he himself controls the work, and has the honor to himself." Miller left his post and recommended that Smith be given the authority to appoint an assistant field agent to work under his direction in the Department of the Ohio.[8]

In March the commission obtained the use of the large private residence of southern sympathizer William Berry at 14 South Spruce Street, which the secretary of war had previously assigned to the Philadelphia Ladies' Aid Society. The residence served as the delegates' home, and Smith put Cleavie in charge of it. One of the delegates estimated that the residence had cost at least $20,000 and said that the furniture alone was worth a "snug fortune." Another delegate, who said he had come to the war expecting hardship, found himself living in what he called "the palatial residence of some Southern Nabob," which, "under the superintendence of Mrs. Smith, . . . is a complete home." A newspaper correspondent was critical of the commission's use of the mansion; he thought it should be made available for the needy. He also criticized the commission for distributing too many tracts and too little food to the hungry.[9]

At any time from twenty to fifty delegates could be found in the commission's home, "representing as many towns and all the evangelical denominations." Each morning and evening the residents knelt together for prayer, ignoring their theological differences and rivalries in their common work. "The Rev. and Mrs. Smith," wrote one of the delegates, "make a very cheerful and pleasant home in Nashville for the delegates, and the question of denomination is never thought of."[10]

The spirit of Christian unity that prevailed in the Christian Commission was a surprise to the delegates. One man, stationed in the East, was curious about the denominational affiliation of the other delegates and asked them to note their denominations in his autograph book. The general agent there chided him gently for asking, saying "we [know] no denomination here except the *Christian Commission.*" A returned Methodist delegate urged the Methodists to do their share for the commission but added that "a sectarian bigot should be the last man *sent,* for he is the last man *wanted* there." [11]

Other civilians might be found at the Nashville residence too, often family members seeking soldiers or soldiers themselves, "pale-faced boys tottering up from the hospitals, and making constant applications for personal relief out of Mrs. Smith's large store-room, which came to be famous for its numberless little comforts, such as only a home and a mother's care afford." [12]

A few women had served as delegates earlier, but now greater numbers of women began to come to Nashville to serve in the commission's newly created special diet kitchens. The diet kitchens were the creation of Annie Wittenmyer, a widow from Keokuk, Iowa, who came to Nashville originally as an Iowa state sanitary agent. Observing the need of special diets in the hospitals and the army's inability to provide them, she developed a plan for special diet kitchens to supplement the general hospital kitchens. The kitchens would be supplied by the government but staffed by women from the Christian Commission, with disabled soldiers detailed to assist them, their goal being to bring "to the bedside of every patient, in homelike preparation, such delicate food as might be prescribed or allowed by his surgeon." [13]

When the diet kitchens were formed, the women worked under the general superintendence of the Christian Commission but with the consent of army medical officers and under their control. Surgeons were presented with a daily list of food available, from which they could prescribe diets just as they prescribed medicines. The Christian Commission provided furniture and utensils for the work when necessary and the foods the government did not supply: "delicacies and cordials." The commission described the diet kitchen as "a home kitchen enlarged." "When the surgeon is baffled, he calls in the aid of the ladies, and thus saves many a veteran to the ranks." One surgeon testified to the value of such food in the treatment of gangrene. "Without good food properly prepared, hospital gangrene cannot be successfully treated. With good food, and rigid hygienic measures there is good success even in extremely bad cases." Army officials generally agreed on the worth of the kitchens and gave them their full support. Nationally, between fifty and sixty diet kitchens were established and over one hundred women engaged in managing them. In addition to preparing food, the women visited the patients, read to them, wrote letters for them, and performed "any other office of kindness and trust that their condition might require." [14]

Annie Wittenmyer said that Smith was the first to encourage her in her plan for diet kitchens and "to him more than to any other co-laborer am I indebted for its success." It was on Smith's recommendation that the Christian Commission's executive committee approved the plan in January 1864. The first diet kitchen was organized in the Cumberland Hospital in Nashville, where from a thousand to fifteen hundred patients were fed under the direction of Mary E. Moorhead of Pittsburgh, the daughter of Congressman James K. Moorhead. When Annie Wittenmyer left to organize diet kitchens in the other armies as the Christian Commission's general superintendent of diet kitchens, Cleavie Smith was made superintendent of the kitchens in the Department of the Cumberland, which, by August 1864, numbered eleven, serving five thousand "of the worst sick and wounded men." In addition to her other duties, Cleavie made personal visits to the hospital wards, wending her way among the cots with "her pails and tubs and baskets" full of specially prepared foods. For her services as superintendent of diet kitchens for the Cumberland Department, the Christian Commission's executive committee voted unanimously to pay Cleavie $200 a year.[15]

Edward Smith continued to remain close to the diet kitchen work, corresponding frequently with Annie Wittenmyer, especially about assignments of delegates and their transportation, and stressing the need for "personal piety" in the delegates. In one of his letters to Wittenmyer, Smith signed himself as "Yr's for another year of solid work for the Master & his suffering children." [16]

Another Christian Commission program that originated in the West was the provision of magazines and lending libraries for the soldiers. The creator of that program was the chaplain of the Eighty-eighth Regiment of Illinois Volunteer Infantry, Joseph Conable Thomas. Smith said of Thomas that "he likes three things in the following order[:] His Master whom he serves, the souls of men especially soldiers[,] & *reading matter*, the latter chiefly by way of getting it in the reach of men." Thomas was concerned that the soldiers were paying exorbitant prices for worthless literature, and he determined to find a way to provide good, cheap reading material for them. An energetic man— Gerty Smith called him "the bright eyed man who used to fly round & be in a hurry"—he appealed to publishers to provide newspapers and magazines, both secular and religious, at half price and convinced the Adams Express Company to ship them free of charge. General George H. Thomas was sufficiently impressed by the chaplain's efforts to detail him as general reading agent for the Army of the Cumberland.[17]

Chaplain Thomas urged the Christian Commission to support his work to give it greater scope. At first the commission was reluctant, in part because it involved selling publications to the soldiers (even though they were sold at cost) and in part because it involved secular as well as religious literature. But at the request of General Thomas and with the endorsements of Generals Grant and Howard and the strong recommendation of Smith, the commission agreed to sponsor the project.

In cooperation with the Christian Commission, Chaplain Thomas also developed a system of "loan libraries." He selected a small number of religious and secular books, using the rule "None but the best works." He then convinced the publishers to furnish the books at half price. The books were packed in compact wooden cases, each case containing either 75 or 125 books, and were then placed as lending libraries in military hospitals. Thomas eventually became the Christian Commission's general library agent.

Chaplain Thomas's work, like Annie Wittenmyer's, began in the West, with Smith's encouragement, and then spread through the entire army and navy. Thomas's books, newspapers, and magazines met a need among the soldiers, well expressed by Major Thomas Thoburn: "We are living a monotonous life. . . . The terrible dearth of news continues. We have read everything even to the Almanac. . . . O for a march, even if among the snow and ice again and short rations too, rather than this." [18]

With the coming of spring, it became clear that the army was planning for a major offensive. "Gigantic preparations" were made for the army's move. Vast amounts of food, grain, hay, saddles, and uniforms were purchased. Nashville became "one vast storehouse—warehouses covering city blocks, one a quarter of a mile long—stables by the ten and twenty acres, repair shops by the fieldful." The railroads were at the center of the army's attention. All the railroads south of Louisville had been taken over by the army, and technicians, engines, and cars were gathered to supply the army in the field. As early as February, twenty-four freight trains a day were running from Nashville to Chattanooga, and stores were rapidly accumulating there as well as in Nashville.[19]

The Army of the Cumberland waited for the spring offensive at Ringgold, Georgia, in an area near Chattanooga that had formerly been the home of the Cherokee Indians. Of what once had been a "handsome town of about 1,000 inhabitants," nothing but a few scattered houses and "shapeless piles of brick and lone chimneys" remained. In April, while the army waited, "a remarkable religious revival began among the veteran troops, who knew very well what it meant to be at the front, waiting marching orders, with the enemy lying in full force before them." The church at Ringgold was crowded every night, "not a foot of standing-room unoccupied. The doors and windows were filled, and the crowds extended out into the street. . . . Sometimes hundreds of persons would go away unable to get within hearing distance." The morning meetings for inquirers were also crowded, and the soldiers formed prayer meetings in their huts and on the picket lines. Forty-four men were baptized in the Chickamauga Creek on one Sunday afternoon (twenty-four choosing to be baptized by immersion, eighteen by sprinkling, and two by pouring), after which about four hundred men received communion, celebrated with commissary bread and currant wine in tin plates and cups. The following Sunday forty-eight men were baptized and on the Sunday after that fifty-seven more. Altogether, Smith said, more than three hundred men were "added to the Lord" in about three weeks. General Howard's Fourth Corps, stationed at Cleveland, Tennessee, experienced a similar revival while it waited for the spring offensive.[20]

Some of the Christian Commission delegates were astonished by the revivals. Smith told of one "sober Old School Presbyterian minister, who probably has not been excited since his conversion," who came on a Saturday and on the following evening said that he wanted to have a word with Smith. "He said, with preliminary remarks as to the importance of his communication, 'Mr. Smith, I have discovered that this army is in a revival state, and I thought you ought to know it.' And that good slow brother," Smith said, "had seen nothing but what he might have seen at almost any of our meetings for the past year."[21]

In March, Ulysses Grant was called to Washington, commissioned as lieutenant general, and placed in command of all the federal armies. William Sherman replaced Grant in the Military Division of the Mississippi. One of Sherman's first orders was to prohibit all civilian use of the railroads, except on his own express order or the order of the commander of one of the three departments in his army. "The railroads," he said, "are purely for army purposes." Citizens and sutlers would have to use wagons. Even troops were not to travel by railroad if they could march. Nothing would be allowed to interfere with the transportation of the army and its supplies.[22]

Sherman's order threatened to cripple the work of the Christian Commission. The railroad was the only effective way for delegates and their supplies to reach the commission's stations south of Nashville and the only way to reach the army once it began its offensive. Perplexed by the actions of the new commander, Smith turned for help to General Oliver Otis Howard.

Howard, like Smith, was a New Englander, a committed Christian, a Congregationalist, and a strong supporter of the Christian Commission. After proving himself in the East—and losing his right arm at the Battle of Fair Oaks—Howard and his corps had been ordered to reinforce the Army of the Cumberland in September 1863. Then, in the spring of 1864, Sherman gave Howard command of the Fourth Corps in the Army of the Cumberland. It was in that army that Smith came to know Howard, and the two men formed a close friendship that lasted until Smith's death. Smith asked Howard to give him an introduction to Sherman, saying:

> Gen. Sherman has never met the Christian Com[n] as an organized effort in the army & consequently holds our request for so much passing and transportation as a presumption to be denied & rebuked. . . .
>
> This, of course, will make a speedy end of all our present plans of working in this Mil. Division. These plans require the passing, on an average, of one delegate per day from Nashville front. . . .
>
> I am waiting a suitable opportunity to lay before the General Commanding a statement of the object and plan of the Commission & ask his permission to go on.
>
> A note of introduction and y'r endorsement of the twofold purpose of the Commission[,] bodily relief & moral reinforcement[,] would be of great weight in our favor.
>
> My full conviction after a year's experience is that an average delegate in his volunteer service reinforces the *fighting* ability of the army by as much as one able bodied veteran.

Howard wrote a letter of introduction to Sherman, outlining the work of the commission and saying he believed Smith to be "a good and faithful man." Then he advised Smith to "go right to him, and in a brief and manly way, tell him the object and operation of the Commission . . . and just as soon as transportation will admit of it, I doubt not he will give you every facility."[23]

Sherman, however, had no use for the Christian Commission and would not budge from his position. His reply to Smith has not survived, but a letter to Assistant Secretary of War Charles A. Dana makes his position clear. "To make war we must and will harden our hearts. Therefore when preachers clamor and sanitaries wail, don't join in. . . . In the time allotted to me for preparation I must and will be selfish in making those preparations which I know to be necessary." Sherman boasted of the dispatch with which he dealt with "the insidious cotton speculator, camp follower, & hypercritical humanity seeker. . . . A citizen cannot understand that an officer who has to see to the wants and necessities of an army has no time to listen to the usual long perorations & I must confess I have little patience with this class of men."[24]

In the midst of these activities, the Smith family was struck by tragedy. In late March, a "rapid increase in sickness" was reported in Nashville, more sickness than for many years previously, according to the city's physicians. Officials blamed the lack of proper sanitation: "foul and fetid accumulations of decomposing matter have increased." A Michigan soldier put it it more bluntly, saying that Nashville was "the filthiest place" he ever saw. The military authorities stepped in and began to clean the city, removing "vast piles of dirt and rubbish." The practice of "depositing the carcasses of dead horses and mules within the city limits" was prohibited by the army, which began to collect the dead animals and throw them into the river. But sickness and deaths from sickness continued to increase. In March, 792 soldiers and civilians were buried in the city cemeteries; in April there were 817 deaths of soldiers and civilians in the military hospitals alone. One of the victims of the sickness was Clarke Smith.[25]

Clarke had been ill earlier but was thought to be recovering. "My pet boy slowly improving," Smith wrote to Annie Wittenmyer on March 5. But on May 3, two months before his fourth birthday, Clarke died. The morning after his death, Smith, struggling bravely to look at the death as a minister rather than a father, shared the news with his sister Mary.

> Clarke is entirely well. He recovered last night at eleven. The threads of his little life have been breaking steadily for two months, till the last gave way & the unfettered boy went straight home. He has been asking to go to "Pepel" for some days whenever he felt weary, but he has not stopped there.
>
> I wish you could look upon the sweet face lying before me this mor'g. You would say he has found his best friend. . . .
>
> We shall send home our boy embalmed & prepared for burial by tomorrow's express. Mrs. Wallace & Mrs. Case will take care of him there.
>
> Cleavie is comforted, Gerty is prattling away about the hearse, casket, heaven & her little brother. Just as I was writing this she came up & said she was tired & has gone & laid down on our bed by the side of Clarke to sleep. There they are, how much alike! . . . Both sleeping[,] only one sleeps deeper & sweeter[,] both here only one is *there* too. There comes over me as I stop & look at them, a strange suspicion that perhaps this difference between the two is not for a long time & then, Mollie, that *other* feeling not of tumultuous grief, as I expected, but of delightful acquiesence. It is a miracle of grace. I can stand looking on the dead and the living, with that dark shadow flitting before me, & say "Let my Father do as seemeth him best"!
>
> The death was very gentle & his sickness has had but little of acute pain. He has not cried once, but has only said "Oh dear! I'm tired[.] Draw me, mama," & then when he felt the motion of his carriage he would lie back on his pillow with a look of sweet satisfaction that went far to stay the [weariness?] of watching him.[26]

The funeral service was held in the Christian Commission home on Spruce Street, "with the Delegates for mourners, when [the] mother and the father closed the coffin lid upon the face of their little boy of four years, and committed his casket to the express company, to be carried home for burial by his Sabbath-school class, in Massachusetts." In Pepperell, the Sabbath school and the congregation gathered in large numbers for the services held there and, after the burial in the Pepperell cemetery, erected a monument to the child of their pastor and his wife, who had chosen not to leave their work in Nashville even for the burial of their son. But despite their heroism and the rush of events that swept them up soon after Clarke's death, Smith admitted later that he "carried the burden of the dreadful loss all the way on the march to Atlanta." [27]

9

Marching Through Georgia

Bearing the bandages, water and sponge,
Straight and swift to my wounded I go,
Where they lie on the ground after the battle brought in,
Where their priceless blood reddens the grass the ground,
Or to the rows of the hospital tent, or under the roof'd hospital,
To the long rows of cots up and down each side I return,
To each and all one after another I draw near, not one do I miss,
An attendant follows holding a tray, he carries a refuse pail,
Soon to be fill'd with clotted rags and blood, emptied, and fill'd again.

Walt Whitman, "The Wound Dresser"

The day after Clarke Smith's death, Grant's army crossed the Rapidan River in Virginia to begin its advance toward Richmond. Over the next three days, Sherman, with an army of almost one hundred thousand men, began his advance from Chattanooga toward Atlanta. The Christian Commission found it extremely difficult to reach the western army. Sherman would allow no civilians to pass over the railroad beyond Nashville except by his own order. When the commission requested a pass for two delegates to Chattanooga, Sherman replied: "Certainly not. There is more need of gunpowder and oats than any moral or religious instruction. Every regiment at the front has a chaplain." (Smith disagreed, saying the army had no more than eighty chaplains to serve 150 regiments and forty batteries, and no more than half the chaplains were at the front—but there was no opportunity to debate the matter, and in any case Sherman's mind was made up.)[1]

Some of the commission's agents and delegates who were with the army when the campaign began marched alongside the soldiers. In General Howard's Fourth Corps, agent J. F. Loyd and one delegate, equipped with canteen, blanket, gum coat, haversack, tent, and five days' rations, set out on foot with the army. Other agents and delegates accompanied the Twentieth and Twenty-third corps. They had neither teams nor saddle horses but marched with the men or with the ambulance trains, assisted the wounded, wrote letters for the soldiers, and ministered to the sick and dying wherever they could.[2]

There were ample opportunities to be of service. One of the delegates described the scene he encountered in the hospital tents at Resaca, Georgia, on Sunday, May 15.

> Men lying in scores, upon their hurried beds of straw, with bleeding or ghastly wounds, awaiting the Surgeon's care; others brought in at intervals upon stretchers from the field; here a group of six corpses ready for burial, there a heap of limbs and members marking the operating tent, where the knife of the Surgeon was always busy.
>
> Strange sights and scenes and labors for the Sabbath; yet somehow the Master seemed nearer than ever before. . . . And to do some little kindness in His name, to give the cup of cold water, the timely nutriment, the fragrant orange; to adjust a bandage, to soothe a weary head, to write a message for the loved ones at the soldier's home, to speak some brief word of hope and cheer—was not this doing *His* work?[3]

Soon after the campaign began, Sherman modified his prohibition of passes to allow delegates to go to the front "whenever by requisition of a medical officer at the front they were shown to be needed for the distribution of hospital stores." This was the opening the commission needed. The medical officers were generally cooperative, and with the exception of one period during the summer when Sherman prohibited personnel of either the Christian Commission or the Sanitary Commission from going to the front, the Christian Commission was usually successful in sending delegates forward.[4]

Sherman, however, had in no way mellowed in his attitude toward the commission. In July, in refusing a request to pass state recruiting officers, he showed his attitude by saying: "I cannot permit it here, and I will not have a set of fellows here hanging about on any such pretenses. We have no means to transport and feed them. The Sanitary and Christian Commissions are enough to eradicate all traces of Christianity out of our minds, much less a set of unscrupulous State agents in search of recruits."[5]

It was only after the war, in response to a letter from George Stuart asking his opinion of the commission's work, that Sherman showed any appreciation of the commission's efforts. "At times," he wrote, "I may have displayed an impatience when the agents manifested an excess of zeal in pushing forward their persons and stores when we had no means to make use of their charities. But they could hardly be expected to measure the importance of other interests, and I have always given them credit for good & pure motives." With the war's end and the opportunity to "look back on the past with composure," he was "not only willing but pleased with the opportunity to express my belief that your charity was noble in its conception, and applied with as much zeal, kindness, and discretion as the times permitted."[6]

Smith himself was soon at the front. Sherman arrived at Kingston, Georgia, on May 19, and Smith and a group of delegates followed him into town, having walked to Kingston from Resaca. They made their headquarters in a large hotel near the railroad depot. Soon every room in the hotel was filled with sick soldiers, waiting to be sent to hospitals in Chattanooga. Smith and his delegates nursed and fed the soldiers and then assisted in loading them into the boxcars that would take them to Chattanooga.

When it became apparent that the army would remain at Kingston over Sunday, May 22, Smith gave each delegate preaching assignments and assigned himself to the Baptist Church in the morning and to General Howard's headquarters in the afternoon. The morning's activities provided one of the few light moments of the campaign and a story about Smith that Howard liked to tell in later years and that Smith told about himself. The Baptist Church, Smith said, had been used as a Confederate hospital and was not cleaned after the soldiers left. Smith asked the sexton to clean it, but he failed to do so, and only an hour before the service, Smith discovered that another man, whom he had hired to clean it, had also failed to do it.

> It was too late now to look for help. I took off my ministerial coat, and for one hour, with the mercury at ninety degrees, worked with might and main. When I had swept out the straw, cleared the rubbish from the pulpit, thrown the bunks out the window, pitched the old seats down from the loft, arranged them in order on the floor, and dusted the whole house over twice, it was time for service. I sprang up into the belfry (the rope had been cut away), and, with some pretty vigorous strokes by the bell tongue, told the people around that the hour for worship had arrived. Dropping down again, through the scuttle upon the vestibule floor, a treacherous nail carried away an important part of one leg of my pantaloons. It was my only suit at the front, and while I was pondering how I should present myself before the congregation, a corporal and two bayonets from General Sherman's headquarters, not twenty yards away, came to help me in the decision. "Did you ring the bell?" "I did." "I am ordered to arrest you." "For what?" "To bring you to General Sherman's headquarters." "But, Corporal, I can't see the General in this plight. I am an agent of the Christian Commission, and am to preach here this morning, and was ringing the bell for service. If you will tell the General how it is, it will be all right." "That's not the order, sir." "Well, Corporal, send a guard with me to my quarters, till I can wash up and pin together this rent." "That's not the order, sir;—fall in." Without hat or coat, and with gaping wardrobe, preceded by the corporal and followed by the bayonets, I called at headquarters. General Corse, chief of staff, standing

by the side of General Sherman, received me. Without waiting for charges or questions, I said, "General, I belong to the Christian Commission. We are to have service in the church across the way, and I was ringing the bell." "Is it Sunday? Some mischievous soldiers had alarmed the people by ringing the bell, and an order was issued against it; but we were not aware this was Sunday. There is no harm done. At what hour is the service?"—and, bowing me out, he discharged my guard. As I entered, General Sherman was drumming with thumb and finger on the window-sill, and when the corporal announced his prisoner, the General commanding fixed his cold gray eye on me for a moment, motioned to his chief to attend to the case, and, without moving a muscle of his face, resumed his drumming and his Sabbath problem,—how to flank Johnston out of the Allatoona Mountains.[7]

Having missed the morning service, Smith rode to General Howard's headquarters in a woods four miles away, where he preached on the theme "The safety of those who do their duty, trusting in God." Howard spoke, too, in what Smith called "the most effective sermon of the day." "The General spoke of the Saviour, his love for Him and his peace in His service, as freely and simply as he could have spoken in his own family circle." Two of Howard's division commanders were present, as was Brigadier General Charles Harker. Howard told how he had personally ministered to a dying soldier after the Battle of Resaca and then asked Smith and his generals if what he had done was not "right and beautiful." "And so," Smith said, "under the pressure unconsciously applied by their superior officer, with lips all unused to such confession, [the generals] acknowledged the power and grace of God."[8]

When the army moved from Kingston, Smith returned to Chattanooga. But when he learned that the commission's delegates had also moved with the army and that neither of the two hospitals in Kingston had chaplains, Smith decided to return to the hospitals. The men hospitalized in Kingston were those wounded too badly to be moved, and Smith said he "knew it must be the time for many of the wounded to die; and they must not die alone." He returned to Kingston, visited the dying, prayed and sang hymns with them, wrote letters for them, and spoke with them about home.[9]

After one of the battles in the Atlanta campaign, Smith conducted a communion service for the survivors. "At four o'clock, we spread the table of our Lord, in our chapel, and the Christian soldiers filled the house. It was a touching scene—those battle-scarred men, each one feeling, 'I only have escaped of my many comrades'—sitting down in the communion of saints and of Christ, consecrating anew the life spared, and girding themselves for the coming strife."[10]

In June, Smith was back in Chattanooga, where he attended the deathbed of Joseph Bancroft Hill, a delegate from Temple, New Hampshire. Hill
was a sixty-seven-year-old minister who, despite his age and the fact that
his time as a delegate had expired, had marched with the army to Acworth,
Georgia, within thirty miles of Atlanta. He returned to Chattanooga with a
trainload of the wounded and there fell under the wheel of a railroad car. His
arm was crushed and was amputated, and he died soon after. Smith wrote to
Hill's widow to describe his death and then said, "Would I could say something to mitigate your grief and your burden of heart, but I know very well,
from a personal experience in bereavement, that words on such occasions are
empty things,—that the wound can only be bound up by a Saviour's hand;
that the only possible relief and peace are to be found in the abiding, controlling conviction, 'the Lord hath done it.'" Later that summer, Frances
Hosford, a delegate who managed one of the commission's diet kitchens, died
in Hospital Number 3 at Lookout Mountain. Altogether, forty-three Christian Commission delegates—including two other women—died during the
war or from illnesses contracted during their service.[11]

In June, also, Smith and the Reverend Alfred Emerson of Fitchburg,
Massachusetts, prepared a "pastoral letter" that was read at the meeting of
the Massachusetts General Association of Congregational Churches held in
Springfield. The letter was an appeal to the churches to support the soldiers
because the ones who returned home, Smith and Emerson said, would "tone
and shape society, for at least two generations." Two opposite reports had
come from the army: one about "recklessness" among the soldiers and the
other about an openness to religious influence. Both were true, they said.
At first, a soldier often was reckless and wicked. "But, after a few months
in the field, amid its narrow escapes, the graves of his comrades, its wounds
and sickness, not unfrequently in utter disgust at the extreme wickedness of
others, he begins to feel his loss of character, and to hunger and thirst for
something better. Speak kindly to that man, of Christ and of eternity, bring
him in at a soldiers' prayer-meeting, and none so eager as he to listen, or so
ready to obey." The army was a mission field such as had never been seen
and one that required an immediate response from the churches. The authors
appealed to the churches for prayers and letters for the soldiers, for reading materials, and for support of the Christian Commission. "Give it a large
place in your heart and in your contributions. . . . If possible, send your pastor
as a delegate, and fill his hands with gifts for the soldiers, your token of love
and gratitude to men who are enduring and perilling every thing for you."[12]

Smith also wrote again to the church in Pepperell about his position as its
pastor. The officers had asked him about the prospects of his return, and in

response Smith again appealed to the church to put sentiment aside and, for the good of the church, to accept his resignation. "Personal considerations & feelings, would bring me to Pepperell Station by the next train of cars;—but I cannot leave my present position & work, without turning away from duty. God, in his Providence seems to have enlisted me 'for the war, unless sooner discharged.'" This time, in August 1864—sixteen months after his resignation was submitted—both the church and the society reluctantly voted to accept it, and two months later a new pastor was called. The church adopted a set of resolutions to explain its action in dismissing Smith and to express its gratitude for the work of the pastor "and his companion" and especially for Smith's work among the children and youth. The members felt honored to be able to give to the Christian Commission "one who is becoming known throughout the loyal North, as a man of a great & benevolent heart." [13]

By late June, Smith was back in Nashville, where he spent the summer obtaining supplies for the delegates and the soldiers: a span of horses for the station at Chattanooga, fresh berries for distribution in the hospitals in Nashville, books for the hospitals, stamps and stationery for the writing rooms. He appealed to the army committee in Pittsburgh for crutches and dramatized his appeal by sending a package of the homemade crutches the soldiers had exchanged for crutches the committee had sent earlier. Five hundred dollars worth of butter and eggs were shipped to Nashville every week for the sixteen diet kitchens in the Department of the Cumberland. Smith reported that he was forwarding one and a half carloads of stores a week to Chattanooga and the front besides those distributed in Nashville and along the line to Chattanooga.[14]

On September 1, Atlanta fell to Sherman's army, and on November 16, Sherman began his march to the sea, "cutting loose," as Smith put it, "from all loyal creation." Two Christian Commission agents, William A. Lawrence, whom Smith had recruited from Pepperell, and Arthur Lawrence from Boston, accompanied Sherman's army on the march to the sea. As the army moved farther from Nashville, Smith's work became less urgent. In October 1864, he visited Philadelphia, where both he and John A. Cole, the general field agent for the armies operating against Richmond, reported on their work to the commission's executive committee. Later that month, Smith made a brief visit to Cole's headquarters at City Point, Virginia. After returning to Philadelphia, where he again met with the executive committee, he went back to Nashville by way of Pittsburgh, Cincinnati, Columbus, and Louisville.[15]

The executive committee asked Smith to visit areas west of his own field, down to the Gulf Department, to improve and extend the commission's work in the West. He was also authorized to visit the army committees in St. Louis

John A. Cole (1838–1932), a civil engineer from Medway, Massachusetts, who, after repeated rejections by the army because of his poor eyesight, entered Christian Commission work. One Union soldier said that "what Grant was to the military forces, John A. Cole was to the Christian Commission. To his energy and skill is due in great measure the efficiency and success of the work." Courtesy of the National Archives.

and Peoria. Military activities, however, interfered with the visits. With Sherman on his way to the sea, Confederate Lieutenant General John Bell Hood brought his army into Tennessee and laid siege to Nashville. After some delay, Major General George H. Thomas attacked and routed Hood's army at the Battle of Nashville on December 15 and 16.[16]

The Christian Commission was well represented at the fighting at Columbia, Spring Hill, and Franklin that preceded the battle at Nashville. "The Delegates dressed wounds till midnight at Spring Hill, then marched on foot with the ambulance train to Franklin, dressed wounds again till dark, and came into Nashville at twelve o'clock of the second night, with ten box-cars filled with wounded, who, before daylight, were all lifted and loaded into the ambulances, for the hospitals." The delegates were the sole attendants of the wounded soldiers, caring for them without the help even of stretcher-bearers.[17]

Smith, who was present at the Battle of Nashville and wrote an account of it, said that at the battle Hood brought the front "within two miles of our door." After a hurried breakfast on the morning of the battle, Smith gathered the Christian Commission agents and delegates—between twenty-five and forty of them—for devotions. "How that prayer of Brother Smith will linger in memory," one of them wrote. "It was so simple, so direct, so heartfelt,— so full of earnestness, faith, and power. Its burden was, first for victory, and then, if achieved, that it might be at small cost." The delegates were soon in the midst of the battle, "dressing wounds, comforting sufferers, and taking home addresses, memoranda for home letters, and the last message of the dying." The night after the first day's fight, they searched the battlefield for soldiers missed by the stretcher-bearers and gathered up the dead. At a house taken for a hospital, Smith said "all the rooms below, and the piazza on the three sides of the house, were laid thick with officers and privates. Some were sleeping under the power of an opiate, some were already sleeping in death, others were writhing in mortal agony." The next day, the delegates fed the wounded and then took them in ambulances into the city. "We found the planter's spades, and dug graves in his garden for our dead, while the shells of hostile batteries were screaming across from two opposite hills almost in line over our heads." [18]

During the first night of the battle, one of the delegates, twenty-one-year-old James S. Kimball of Boston, lay dying of "congestion and brain fever" in the commission's home. "As his chamber windows shook with the guns from Fort Negley, multiplied into a hundred batteries along the line, his zeal for saving men kindled anew. He was passing in spirit through the barracks and hospital wards, gathering imagined congregations, leading them in song and prayer, and exhorting them most earnestly to a new life. So he continued to the last." After the second day's fighting, the delegates divided the field into sections and went over it to search for the wounded and to mark the dead who could be identified. That night they worked among the wounded in five hospitals. For the following three days they fed the wounded, no other provision having been made for feeding them.[19]

The Christian Commission delegates were conspicuous on the battle-field. One of them admitted that he was "a strange-looking figure." "Two great haversacks, distended with crackers, tea, dried toast, whisky, bandages, brandy, sponges, etc., were over my shoulders; a three-gallon coffee-pot was in one hand; a big twelve-quart tin pail with fresh water in the other, while a bundle of tin-cups hung on my arms and over my back and shoulders." The delegates made an impression too by offering their services not only to the white soldiers but also to the two brigades of black soldiers that fought at Nashville. On the second day of the battle, the *Nashville Daily Union* commented: "These good Samaritans are no respecters of persons. They minister alike to the white and the colored soldier. . . . In no other country has such a spectacle of disinterested benevolence been witnessed." General Hood was said to have had so much admiration for the work of the commission at Nash-ville that he invited it to send delegates to minister to the Confederate army as well.[20]

With the defeat of Hood's army, the work of the Christian Commission in the West diminished rapidly, and Smith's future role with the commission came under discussion. Since Smith's visit to Philadelphia in October, there had been talk of placing him in charge of all the field work of the commis-sion. Smith was not eager for the position. He told Annie Wittenmyer, "I do not want the larger field spoken of. But I hope the position will be created & a competent man found to put into it." A. E. Chamberlain, the president of the Cincinnati branch of the commission, asked George Stuart not to take Smith away from Nashville, saying he could not think of sparing him.[21]

Late in January 1865, "unexpectedly" and "without previous arrange-ment," Smith appeared at the commission's headquarters in Philadelphia. The officers of the western branches of the commission were also there to celebrate the commission's third anniversary. Smith attended the celebra-tion at the American Academy of Music and sat on the platform, where Benjamin Chidlaw, after mentioning Smith and his work, turned to him and said, "There he is! . . . And he is our Captain-General in the Army of the Cumberland, and thousands of soldiers will rise up to call him blessed!"[22]

The unplanned gathering in Philadelphia became an opportunity to re-solve the question of Smith's future. Because most of the soldiers had left

Smith's field of work, and because certain unspecified "entanglements" in the commission's work in the East had convinced the executive committee that a change in leadership there was necessary, the committee voted unanimously to give John A. Cole's position as general field agent for the armies operating against Richmond to Smith. It also asked Cole to remain with Smith as long as that arrangement was agreeable to them both. Smith was also to retain his position in the West, which he would manage through the agents there. Even though Smith was to be nominally in charge in the West, the Cincinnati branch of the commission considered his removal from Nashville "a severe loss. From the beginning he had superintended the work in the West with a sagacity, discrimination and zeal worthy of the highest praise. His self-denying labors, amid suffering and personal dangers, in behalf of his country, in all the dark days and months of the great rebellion, should endear him to the hearts of his countrymen." [23]

The meeting of the executive committee that gave Cole's position to Smith was held on February 3. A few days later, Smith was at his new post at City Point, Grant's headquarters in Virginia. On February 8, George Stuart wrote letters of introduction for Smith to Generals Edward Ord, George Meade, Marsena Patrick, and Grant. On that same day, however, Smith sent a telegram from City Point saying he was returning to Philadelphia and wanted to meet again with the executive committee. At that meeting on February 11, Smith proposed to the committee that instead of replacing Cole, he serve as Cole's assistant, replacing Samuel Ashley, a Congregational minister from Northboro, Massachusetts. The committee agreed, and on February 16, Smith was back at City Point as assistant field agent. [24]

When he first went to City Point, Smith had encountered resentment about the directive the executive committee had given him to replace John Cole. Cole, though only twenty-six years old and a layman, had served as a delegate since August 20, 1862, five months before Smith began his service. Cole had directed Smith's work as a delegate in the Army of the Potomac early in 1863 and recommended Smith for his position in the West. Edward Williams, a Congregational minister who was the commission's field agent in the Army of the James, reacted strongly to Smith's appointment: "Cole is relieved! The most *unjust* piece of business I ever heard of. E. P. Smith takes his place, a good [fellow?], but not Cole." Williams found no fault with Smith but placed the blame for the action on the executive committee. [25]

Smith quickly realized that it would be a mistake to try to replace Cole, and he offered to come instead as Cole's assistant, replacing Ashley and thus doubly pleasing Williams, who did not care for Ashley. "Ashley goes home tomorrow," Williams wrote in his diary. "The biter has bitten himself. Mr. Cole has come out triumphant in the matter. Mr. Smith has shown great magnanimity." Smith's self-effacement in the affair calmed a troublesome situation, and Smith, Cole, and Williams worked harmoniously from that time on. Cole, in fact, thought so highly of Smith that, a few years later, he named his only son Edward Smith Cole.[26]

Cleavie Smith and Gerty did not accompany Smith to City Point but remained in Nashville, where the Christian Commission home had become their home and where Cleavie still had work to do among the men she called her "boys in blue."[27]

10

Field Secretary

It is proper to return our grateful acknowledgments to the officers who have conducted the affairs of the Commission. . . . Diligence, system, economy, earnestness, and deep devotedness have marked their varied movements. . . . Immense stores have been issued, and vast labor has been performed, without confusion and without ostentation.

Bishop Matthew Simpson, Fourth and closing anniversary of the Christian Commission held in the House of Representatives, Washington, D.C., February 11, 1866

City Point, which General Grant had made his headquarters, was also the headquarters of the Christian Commission. A hospital had been established there on a broad plain above the Appomattox River, about one mile from the James River. The hospital grew until it comprised five separate hospitals, containing from four thousand to ten thousand men. "Forty acres of hospital!" visitors remarked. One soldier noted with amazement the arrival in one day of eighty wagonloads of wounded soldiers. The hospitals were at first merely canvas tents pitched on wide streets, and in the summer of 1864 the dust from the streets was suffocating. At the suggestion of one of the Christian Commission delegates, a steam fire engine was brought from Baltimore with 2,200 feet of hose to bring water from the river to keep the dust down and supply water for the hospital.

The Christian Commission established its headquarters next to the hospital. A large chapel tent was erected, where services were held each evening. There were also a reading room with writing tables and a circulating library, an office, a warehouse, and accommodations for the ten to twenty delegates stationed there. The entire Christian Commission establishment was at first contained in fifteen tents, but when winter came, frame buildings were erected. A second chapel, for black soldiers, was also built.

The commission had a similar establishment at Point of Rocks, the base of the Army of the James, about five miles away. Stations were also estab-

105

lished in strategic positions in each army corps, sixteen of them in the armies of the Potomac and the James, each staffed by five to ten delegates, ready to move with the army at any time. Altogether some seventy-five delegates were stationed at City Point and along the fifty miles of federal lines around Petersburg and Richmond.

The commission also furnished canvas roofs, stoves, and lamps for seventy-five regimental chapels. The Twenty-fifth Corps in the Army of the James was made up entirely of black troops, and the chapels there were also used as schools, the commission furnishing both teachers and supplies.[1]

Smith's arrival at City Point enabled him to observe the second of the two main fields in which the Christian Commission had been working. A few days after his arrival, he drew on his experiences to write a long letter to George Stuart, stating the case for "volunteer aid to soldiers outside the military channels." Strictly speaking, he said, outside aid was not needed in the army. Soldiers may suffer and die, but the war will go on. But outside aid could prevent suffering and deaths among the soldiers without interrupting military movements. Outside aid was not made necessary by the government's poverty or indifference but by its procedures. "There is no arm of the service as essential to its very life as red tape." Officials were held strictly accountable for supplies and were given no discretion in issuing them. "The official must have a voucher, and the shiver and hunger of a soldier will not make one."[2]

The volunteer, Smith said, could distribute supplies to individuals at his own discretion, without red tape. Also, in the time of battle, volunteers could fill the gap when a military unit suffered more casualties than it was prepared to care for. "Just here comes our supply wagon, which is foot-loose, and can go from one division to another, wherever the call is, and if necessary all the wagons we have in the army can be brought up, and all the force of a hundred delegates given to that division. The Government cannot do that, without having just such men, and a dozen hospital wagons to follow with each army division, and then it will be obliged to violate a fundamental rule, and give discretionary power to those in charge of stores." The aid the volunteers rendered not only relieved suffering but "very often it is a relief applied at the point where life and death are in the scale for decision."[3]

During January and February, rumors of impending attacks circulated at City Point, and the troops began to move from their winter quarters. In March it became clear that military operations would soon be resumed, and both the army and the Christian Commission supplied themselves for the coming battles. In the midst of the preparations, illness forced John Cole to return to his home, leaving Smith in charge. On March 8, one of the delegates wrote to Edward Williams that "Mr. Cole is used up—worn & sick—&

goes North this morning." On his way back to Massachusetts, Cole met with the executive committee in Philadelphia and offered to resign his position as general field agent of the armies operating against Richmond and take the subordinate position of field agent of the Army of the Potomac, apparently to make room for Smith. The executive committee, however, had another way of using the services of Cole and Smith. William E. Boardman had resigned his position as secretary, and the committee voted to elect Smith one of the commission's secretaries. Lemuel Moss, who had come to the commission from the pulpit of the First Baptist Church in Worcester, Massachusetts, would serve as home secretary and Smith as field secretary. Smith was told to report at Philadelphia "as soon as practicable," and Cole, who was recuperating at home, was instructed to return immediately to City Point as general field agent of the armies operating against Richmond. By the end of March, Cole was back at City Point and Smith had returned to Philadelphia. He was at the Philadelphia headquarters in time to participate in the massive movement of supplies and delegates the Christian Commission conducted during the last days of the war.[4]

The headquarters of the Christian Commission was upstairs at 11 Bank Street in Philadelphia, where George Hay Stuart's firm of Stuart & Brother, importer of dry goods, provided free office space in its four-story "neat and substantial brick" building. Bank Street was in the heart of Philadelphia's commercial area. The commission's offices were "surrounded by the clatter of traffic, the fever of greenbacks and gold, the rush of hurrying feet, the din of rattling wheels, the click, click, click of the news, the clangor of the press, [and] the babel of tongues." Hanging from a cord stretched across Bank Street was the Christian Commission's banner.[5]

The visitor who climbed to the top of the stairs at Number 11 found a room 130 feet long and 30 feet wide, with large windows at each end and a skylight in the center. Five or six men used one end of the room as an office. There were sixty pigeonholes in the office, representing sixty newspapers the commission provided with facts and incidents about its work. Another office case held blanks for reports, record books, letterbooks, scrapbooks, and bills. George Stuart worked at a desk there, usually surrounded by people, with whom the energetic Stuart spoke "very fast, scarcely waiting to give each word its full, round pronounciation." One visitor came away wondering why Stuart did not "shut himself up in a private office, like Mr. Secretary Stanton," yet impressed that "everything is done in the most systematic and business-like manner. There is no confusion, no mixing-up, and consequently few mistakes occur, considering the amount of business transacted."[6]

The other end of the commission's room was used for hospital stores and for receiving and shipping supplies for the soldiers. "On the left are library cases and library books. . . . On the right, family papers by thousands. On the left again, note paper and envelopes with printed motto, from the beak of a carrier dove, 'The Christian Commission sends this as the soldier's message, Let it hasten to those who wait for tidings.' . . . On the right again, in boxes piled up, condensed milk, shirts, drawers, socks, condensed beef, farina, cornstarch, dried fruit, pickles, canned fruits, jellies, and jams, and other comforts, and clothing, with blankets, all designed for the field." On another wall a long counter held "knapsack books" and boxes of Bibles from the American Bible Society, "which, though issuing seven thousand copies a day, is unable to keep pace with the demand."[7]

Delegates came to the office daily, volunteers from a variety of denominations, "warm from the fireside, here on their way to the army." Smith was amazed at the number of delegates serving in the East. "Ten delegates are waiting assignment[,]" he wrote while still at City Point, "would they not be good for sore eyes in the Department of the Cumberland?" Transportation for the delegates was also more easily obtained in the East than it had been in Sherman's army. Smith had access to Major General Marsena Patrick, who was provost marshal general, and who, Smith said, considered the Christian Commission his "pet child." Even when the commission brought women delegates to the front without consulting the general, who had been saying that the commission did not assign women, Patrick continued to assist them by passing the delegates to the army.[8]

Even more delegates arrived as Grant's army began its pursuit of Lee's army in early April. More than one hundred delegates went with the advancing army, taking with them new coffee wagons—which the soldiers called the "Christian Light Artillery"—each capable of furnishing ninety gallons of coffee every hour. They fed the Union wounded at Humphrey's Station, Warren Station, Burkesville, and Farmville and Confederate wounded in the commission's chapel at Meade Station. Additional "minute men" were leaving Philadelphia by every train. "The great emergency is now upon us," Stuart announced. Public subscriptions for additional funds were made in Boston, New York, and Philadelphia.[9]

On April 3, news reached Philadelphia that federal troops had occupied Richmond. "Immediately on receipt of the news, all in the [Christian Commission] Rooms engaged in singing the Long Metre Doxology 'Praise God from whom all blessings flow' after which a fervent prayer of thanksgiving for victory" was offered. The commission made plans for a public meeting in Philadelphia that afternoon to solicit aid for the wounded. Posters were put up throughout the jubilant city and a large signboard was carried through the streets, announcing the meeting and saying:

> Brave boys are They
> Gone at their Country's Call
> And yet, and yet we cannot forget
> That many brave boys must fall.[10]

By April 5, more than two hundred delegates were in the field. The commission's office was filled with still more delegates, who had come from as far away as Nevada and San Francisco. Twenty-five or thirty more were on the way to Philadelphia. So great was the response as the war rushed to its end that the commission began to turn delegates away. The demand now was for supplies, including provisions to feed the citizens of Richmond. The public responded so well to the commission's appeals that by April 8 Stuart was able to say, "Money is pouring in like water." On April 9 Lee surrendered.[11]

Shortly after the surrender, Smith spent about a week in Virginia, including Richmond. He returned to Philadelphia convinced that the commission would have to keep up its work for several more months. "The troops are all in the field yet and the hospitals quite full—so that our religious work and the hospital supply goes on for the present as usual. Our future in some respects is uncertain—not whether we shall have one, but [the] form our work for the army will take. We are to have an army and a large one from this time on through all the history of the country—that is one fact. *Another* is, that army will need religious readings . . . and religious effort continually." There would also be educational work among the black soldiers "who are to compose so large a part of the army." The commission opened a new diet kitchen at Wilmington, North Carolina, to serve the returned prisoners and the sick soldiers from Sherman's army who were hospitalized there, and Smith began to recruit new delegates and to order supplies for them.[12]

Among the supplies he ordered were tracts from the American Temperance Union. Smith wrote to the union's secretary, saying, "The soldier's peril is greatest while passing through cities on his way home. Harlots and whiskey dealers beset him on every hand. He is just in the enjoyment of a personal freedom he has not felt for three or four years and he is very likely to 'go in.' Have you a sharp, strong, short, document that will touch the case? We want to put one in the hands of every soldier as he is 'mustered out.' "[13]

In May, George Stuart presided at the presentation of a new house in Philadelphia to General Grant, and Smith wrote a report of the ceremony for the *Congregationalist*. A committee chaired by Stuart had raised some $50,000 to buy and furnish a house for Grant at 2009 Chestnut Street as a way of honoring the general. Grant came to Philadelphia with his family and a military aide, Lieutenant Colonel Ely S. Parker, a Seneca Indian from New York State who was a personal friend of Grant's and one of his military secretaries. After the presentation of the deed and the key to the house, a dinner was served, "on temperance principles," which was "enjoyed all the more," Smith said, "for the prayer of thanksgiving and blessing . . . led by Mr. Stuart." Grant also visited the headquarters of the Christian Commission and showed considerable interest in the supplies gathered there for distribution to the soldiers.[14]

Smith's duties as the commission's field secretary caused him to travel extensively in the months following the war's end. He visited New York in April and Harpers Ferry, Baltimore, and Washington in May. From Washington he wrote about the commission's "glorious last work with our returning heroes. . . . It would do you good to hear these veterans thank the Lord for his goodness in bringing them safe so far and now so near home." On his trips, he communicated constantly with Philadelphia about supplies needed in the field and particularly in the camps where the soldiers were gathered before they were mustered out of the service.[15]

As the army was reduced and the work among the soldiers diminished, the commission put more of its effort into educational work among black soldiers. It had been engaged in that work to some extent before the war's end, notably in the Twenty-fifth Corps in Virginia. In cooperation with the chaplains, educational work had been undertaken in every regiment in that corps, the commission furnishing teachers, books, and other supplies and the government furnishing lumber for school buildings. "Negroes in blue could be seen every where, carrying huge logs upon their shoulders for the schoolhouse, till, as if by magic, thirty neat and commodious edifices attested the eagerness of the colored men to learn to read and write." The men's studying was not confined to the schoolhouses. "It was no uncommon thing for one riding along the line of works held by this corps, to see men, at every stop of his progress, reading or studying in their primers, politely bowing as he passed."[16]

A close relationship developed between the Christian Commission and the American Missionary Association, one of the largest of the many organizations that undertook educational work among the freedmen during the war. The American Missionary Association had been formed in 1846 by evangelical Christians who were radical abolitionists and were determined to conduct missionary work unencumbered by any association with slavery. The organization was "undenominational" and was supported by several denominations, but it received its strongest support from Congregational churches. In September 1861, the association opened its first school for "contrabands" at Fortress Monroe, Virginia. The work grew steadily until, during the last year of the war, the association had more than 250 missionaries and teachers among the freedmen.

The first official contact between the American Missionary Association and the Christian Commission was in December 1863, when George Whipple, the corresponding secretary of the American Missionary Association, asked the Christian Commission for assistance in sending supplies to the freedmen at Vicksburg. Later, Whipple made further requests of the commission: for chapel tents for educational and religious work among black troops at Port Hudson and literature for work with freedmen at Washington.[17]

The Christian Commission had been commissioning some of its delegates to serve as teachers in black army units—in February 1865, it sent out twenty teachers in one day—but two months later Smith was inquiring informally "how far" the American Missionary Association was "prepared to take the business of teaching colored *troops* off our hands if the C.C. decides to relinquish it?" In May, the executive committee of the Christian Commission addressed the question of the commission's future and decided that because it had been created for a specific purpose, it should close its work "as soon as the necessities shall cease which required its organization." At the same meeting, the committee directed Smith to make arrangements for the American Missionary Association to begin to provide the teachers for the black soldiers in the Twenty-fifth Corps. Two days later the arrangements had been made. Teachers would be commissioned by both associations. They would go to the field as delegates of the Christian Commission and would be "grubbed and slept" by the commission, but their salaries would be paid by the American Missionary Association. Smith also made arrangements for some of the Christian Commission property at Point of Rocks—a schoolhouse, church, and dwelling house—to be turned over to the association. Soon plans were made for the association to provide teachers for black soldiers in units other than the Twenty-fifth Corps.[18]

The National Council of Congregational Churches met in Boston in June, and Smith was among those who attended. At the meeting, the council selected the American Missionary Association "from the great number of societies . . . commended to the churches . . . as in all respects best adapted" for work among the freedmen. The association was reported to be "more nearly allied to our own denomination than any other," and the Congregationalists thought it wise to concentrate their efforts on this one association rather than to scatter their resources among the different organizations serving the freedmen. After the meeting, Smith urged the association to take advantage of the offer of support from the Congregationalists. Even though the association thought of itself as "undenominational," Smith thought the endorsement by the Congregational churches would "make all the other denominations shy of [them]" and that the association would be wise to avail itself of the Congregational offer of assistance "in full."[19]

July found Smith in Louisville, Kentucky, where Sherman's army, after rendezvousing in Washington, was transported to be mustered out of the service. The Christian Commission moved with it to work among the soldiers until the army was disbanded, and Smith went along to observe the work. The soldiers were leaving rapidly. "From all appearances," he wrote to Annie Wittenmyer, "C.C. is at the vanishing point. Aug. 1st will close up the Louisville & I think the Nashville Home. . . . We would like to wind up Washington somctime in Aug. [and] all the D[iet] K[itchen]s by Aug. 15. This course becomes a matter of necessity. Funds drying up."[20]

From Louisville, Smith went on to Nashville and a reunion with his family, who had remained in Nashville when Smith went to City Point and Philadelphia six months earlier. Cleavie had continued her work in the commission's home and diet kitchens. T. R. Ewing, who had taken over Smith's duties in the Department of the Cumberland, spoke highly of Cleavie's work.

> Mrs. E. P. Smith . . . most efficiently superintended the diet-kitchens of the department, made our quarters in Nashville a real home to all connected with our work; carried delicacies to the very sick or badly wounded, and distributed reading, and talked of Christ to her "boys in blue," as she called them, wherever she found them. Her presence and attentions, brought a bright ray of home light to many a boy that never would see more of home in this world, and the earnest question from hospital cot and groups of men gathered about her ambulance in the camps, "When will you come again?" will remain with her a more affecting and valued tribute than any that can be written.[21]

John F. Marlay, the secretary of the Cincinnati branch of the commission, also commended Cleavie for her work.

> Mrs. E. P. Smith remained in charge of the "home" in Nashville, performing a service for which few women could have been found equally qualified, with a cheerfulness and a hearty enthusiasm worthy of all honor. Hundreds and thousands of soldiers, who have been in the hospitals of Nashville, will remember Mrs. Smith to their dying day. Not a few will join in gratitude with an Illinois soldier, who said to the friend at his cot, taking his dying message, "Tell Mrs. Smith I shall thank her in heaven for the ice."[22]

Hannah Smith as a Christian Commission delegate.
Courtesy of the National Archives.

Cleavie herself said of her accomplishments simply that "eternity alone can reveal the work done." The commission's task was almost completed in Nashville, and Cleavie was already thinking of the new challenge that presented itself. "There is a great work to be done for freedmen," she wrote. "Blessed is the one that does it." She was also thinking of her family. "I have a growing desire to be once more a united family. My husband writes the separation seems long & tiresome, but he prays for endurance to the end." Smith had written in a similar vein to Mary Ann Ball Bickerdyke, a volunteer who was going to Georgia to assist General Sherman's troops: "The Lord go with you to Georgia & till we come to the world without war & weariness."[23]

From Nashville, Smith made a brief trip to Atlanta. On his return to Nashville, he found a letter from the Reverend Michael E. Strieby, a Congregational minister who was one of the secretaries of the American Missionary Association. Strieby and Smith had spoken earlier about a position for Smith with the association, and in his reply to Strieby's letter Smith said, "I have about two months work in C.C. yet in Phil[a] & then shall be ready to report for duty to the A.M.A. Meanwhile I may possibly be able to do occasional service. . . . I will take any work you assign. My object is *work* & not *place*."[24]

On his tour through Tennessee and Georgia, Smith had already begun to make observations about the association's future work among the freedmen. At Atlanta he found a great need for education; only one school for freedmen had been established. Buildings for schools were scarce, and in the expectation that the association would want to organize schools there, Smith had purchased a portable chapel in Chattanooga, which, he said, the government would ship to Atlanta. He urged the association to send someone to Atlanta "to take hold" no later than the middle of September. "And the sooner a place is secured for the chapel & a home for the preacher & teacher the better."[25]

Smith warned Strieby about the difficulties the association would encounter in its work, one of which was the preference the freedmen were showing for black churches. "This negro problem is full of difficulties. . . . The African Methodists are going to sweep the field. . . . Even the Methodist brethren north cannot hold the churches they have organized, against the tide towards Africa. The ebony preacher who promises perfect independence from white control & direction carries the col[d] heart at once. Our preachers must be wide awake men who will not only allow *fervor* of worship in both expression & form, but will heartily enjoy it." Southern whites, too, presented difficulties. Smith made it clear that the association could expect no cooperation in its religious or educational work from the "old masters. They have a hatred that approaches the perfect for all such movements & workers." Smith thought that Nashville as well as Atlanta offered "an open door for a mission work." "The want now as it seems to me is exploration of *all* this country with a view to plant schools & churches. One of the best men that I know for such work is Jno. A. Cole formerly our Gen[era]l F[iel]d Ag[en]t in the A[rmy] of [the] Potomac. He is at home now in Medway, Mass."[26]

Smith also wrote to General Howard about a plan he and Cole had by which they hoped to "accomplish good for the Freedmen. In order to [do] this it will be necessary for us to explore in one or two Southern States. We have in view Georgia and Alabama. At this point in what we mean to make a life work in some form or other for Freedmen we feel that suggestions from you will be of great value." Howard had been appointed commissioner of the newly formed Bureau of Refugees, Freedmen, and Abandoned Lands, and Smith suggested that his and Cole's observations would be useful to the bureau, "and if our enterprise succeeds it will help solve the greatest problem of the Bureau, full educational and religious privileges for the blacks as the result of their own compensated labor." The exact nature of Smith's plan is not clear. He referred to it elsewhere as a "scheme of 'cotton & negro *elevation*'" and a "*landed* scheme of education & religion." Cole called it "a plan for buying estates in Alabama and farming them for a Stock Company." But whatever the plan was, nothing came of it. Cole soon accepted another position with the Christian Commission in Texas, where large numbers of troops were stationed after the war, and Smith continued to serve as the commission's field secretary, although he was also giving a substantial part of his time to the work of the American Missionary Association.[27]

The Smiths traveled from Nashville to their new home in Philadelphia in July. "Mrs. Smith & Gerty are with me," Smith wrote to a friend. "You can 'guess' whether we are happy." Cleavie and Gerty, however, had a desire to go sightseeing in Washington, and they spent some time in August "looking around" the capital. Cleavie also lent a hand at the "'light' Diet Kitchen" in the commission's Washington headquarters; it was not her nature to be idle for long.[28]

After he returned to Philadelphia, Smith wrote to Michael Strieby about the American Missionary Association and its prospects, a letter so frank that Smith admitted it was "a free way of talking for an outsider." At some previous time he had attended a meeting of the association's executive committee, and he expressed his disappointment in it. "Was that the best showing you have for an Ex. Com[ee][?] I was disappointed in y'r reserve force. I supposed you had men behind you, who were taking hold of the business of the Asso[n] in a business way. Are other religious & benevolent associations in N.Y. merely 'approved' by their Boards & Committees?"[29]

He felt free to pass on to the association criticisms he had received about two of its workers in Washington, and he faulted the association for not placing enough emphasis on organizing churches among the freedmen. "I believe you have lost in not having new [churches], at Rich^d & Norfolk & along the coast, churches organized according to N[ew] Tes[tamen]^t principles[,] & the surest way to do a permanent work will be to aim at making every col^d school the rallying point for a church & to have an eye to that end in the selection of places of opening schools. I think the negroes will take to the Cong[regationa]^l polity, when once they *see it.* They will go for freedom *clear through.*"[30]

Despite his criticisms, Smith was still committed to accepting a position with the American Missionary Association. His responsibilities with the Christian Commission, however, delayed making a change. George Stuart was not well, and Lemuel Moss had left the commission to accept a professorship of systematic theology at the University at Lewisburg, Pennsylvania, which, Smith said, "left me the whole work of closing up."[31]

In addition to closing the commission's stations in the East, disposing of property, and finding delegates for the work that remained in the West and Southwest, Smith was preparing the fourth and final annual report of the commission's work. He was also gathering information for a book about the Christian Commission. In July the executive committee had appointed Lemuel Moss to prepare a history of the commission and had appointed Smith to "prepare a volume of Incidents, such as may be regarded by him fully authentic and most valuable of those which have occurred during the work of the commission." After the commission distributed a circular soliciting information for the two books, Moss began by consulting Philip Schaff, the Swiss-born church historian who had served as a delegate of the commission on at least two occasions. Smith began by writing to former delegates and others who were associated with the commission, asking them to submit incidents from their own experience. He said he did not want an account of the commission's work: "I am not trying now to glorify that Institution but to [give] instances of the power of patriotism, or religion, or both." He asked Chaplain A. H. Quint for any "choice bits that ought to have a permanent record." Anything that would "illustrate Army life, the toils, temptations, failures, or victories, of officers or men is just what we want. . . . Please remember that you first suggested to me the importance of such a book, and told me that I could get it up."[32]

All the delegates had been provided with memorandum books when they went to the field and had been urged to record incidents of their work. With Smith's encouragement, they submitted more than ten thousand accounts of incidents to him for his book. Over the next three years, he selected some five hundred of them, typical of the commission's work in the various fields of the war, and connected them loosely with brief passages from Horace Greeley's *American Conflict* to form his book.[33]

The incidents were full of the sentimentalism the officials of the Sanitary Commission had decried in the Christian Commission's earlier publications. Deathbed scenes, religious conversions, and patriotic sentiments abound: the Christian mother praying for her soldier son, the dying soldier with his "noble brow" and beautiful hair, and the backslider who realizes his mistakes too late. But sentimental or not, the incidents were written with an eye for picturesque detail, and many of them had been honed by frequent repetition with the result that they contain some vivid scenes and some memorable tag lines. "Good-bye, old arm!" a wounded soldier said to his right arm after it was amputated. "We have been a long time together. We must part now. Good-bye old arm! You'll never fire another carbine nor swing another sabre for the government." Then, with tears rolling down his cheeks, he said to the people watching him, "Understand, I don't regret its loss. It has been torn from my body, that not one State should be torn from this glorious Union." In another incident, a delegate passed between two guards after leaving a preaching service in Nashville. " 'Let the Christian Commission man pass,' said one, and there was a tremor in his voice as he added—'*Wherever you find that, you find home.*' " [34]

Smith's book, *Incidents of the United States Christian Commission,* was not completed until 1868. When it was finally published, Smith explained that "entire absorption by the secretary . . . in another labor growing out of the war, and unexpected difficulties in gathering and authenticating so many Incidents, have occasioned a much longer delay than was anticipated in the preparation of the volume." The other labor that absorbed him was his growing involvement in the work done for the freedmen by the American Missionary Association.[35]

11

The American Missionary Association

The American Missionary Association has been working twenty years for
the good of the African race. Since the Rebellion it has turned special attention to the Freedmen, sending teachers and missionaries, and furnishing
clothing to the destitute.

Legend on American Missionary Association letterheads, 1866

Edward Smith's earliest work for the American Missionary Association—
including his part in the founding of Fisk University—was done while
he was still serving as the field secretary of the Christian Commission.

In September and October 1865, his duties with the commission took him
to St. Louis, Missouri; Keokuk, Iowa; and Oberlin and Cincinnati, Ohio. He
wrote to Gerty from Oberlin to describe the college and to tell her about the
many students who were going south to teach the freedmen for the American
Missionary Association. "Some of these teachers are negroes themselves,
going back to the country they ran away from to help teach their brothers and
sisters and other colored children. Many of them are white teachers, who have
learned at Oberlin to pity and love everybody that is poor and wants to learn
how to read and be better: and so they go right away as soon as they hear that
these colored people in Virginia and Georgia want to go to school, and take a
Testament and hymn-book and spelling-book, and find a room, and call the
children in; and sometimes their fathers and mothers and uncles and aunts
and grandfathers come too, and they have a school." [1]

The American Missionary Association (AMA) had proposed to Smith that
he serve as district secretary in Cincinnati, and he used his time in that city to
look for office space. From Cincinnati he went to Camp Nelson, near Lexington, Kentucky. Passing through Lexington, he looked it over as a possible
field of work for the AMA. There were five schools for freedmen in the city
that charged tuition but whose teachers, Smith thought, were "of the crudest
sort &, if the little fellows were not bent on learning *whether or no,* would am^t
to *nothing at all.*" The freedmen themselves were already planning to open a

118

free school in Lexington, and Smith made arrangements to provide a teacher for the school.[2]

The person Smith employed was Belle Mitchell, a black teacher who had earlier been recruited to teach at Camp Nelson by John G. Fee, the founder of Berea College. At the end of the war, Fee was devoting most of his time to work among the many black soldiers and their families at the camp. One Sunday, while worshiping in a nearby black church, he saw "a young woman of light complexion, whose manner . . . favorably impressed" him. He learned that she was a member of the church, "with fair education and good parentage." For years Fee had exhibited his impatience with racial discrimination, and he saw in Mitchell someone he could use to attack the racial barriers he had encountered at Camp Nelson. "Immediately," he said, "it occurred to me that she was the woman with whom to test the caste question among the teachers at Camp Nelson, and set the precedent of giving positions to colored persons as fast as prepared for such." Three days later Mitchell was at Camp Nelson, where Fee gave her a class of students, assigned her to the teachers' dormitory, and gave her a place at his own table in the dining hall, where her presence among the white teachers "produced a sensation." Most of the teachers would not eat with her, and several army officers who were boarding there protested about her presence to Fee, who said dramatically that he would "suffer my right arm torn from my body before I will remove the young woman."[3]

Despite Fee's championship of Mitchell, she was driven away from the camp by what Smith called "a negrophobic combination of officers and teachers," including some of the AMA teachers. When Mitchell left the camp, she went to Danville, Kentucky, and Smith sent there to secure her services for the school at Lexington. Smith advised the AMA secretaries to end the services of Fee at Camp Nelson, saying that "somehow Br. Fee has managed to butt every stump in the clearing. A man in charge with half his zeal & double his discretion would have brought ten times the result. . . . I think Mr. Fee's course of bringing Belle Mitchell here unwise & the opposition to it *shameful*."[4]

From Camp Nelson, Smith went to Louisville and Nashville. At Nashville he visited with old friends and did some preaching. Then he met with Erastus Milo Cravath, who, with Smith, had been commissioned by the AMA to "prospect" for a school in Nashville. Cravath was a Congregational minister who had served as a chaplain in the 101st Ohio Volunteer Infantry in the Army of the Cumberland. When he was mustered out of the service at Nashville in June 1865, he accepted a position as field agent for the AMA. Smith and Cravath spent four days unsuccessfully looking for buildings suitable for schools. Smith said there were from two to three thousand children of freedmen in Nashville who could be gathered into schools, but teachers' homes could not be rented at any reasonable price, and schoolrooms were not available at any price. The government could not provide any facilities, and "from the *citizens* the less you expect the lighter will be y'r disappointment. They will not countenance negro teaching in their present temper. They will not rent for negro schools if they know it. They will not give a home for teachers of col^d schools."[5]

Then, on October 10, Smith and Cravath learned of the proposed sale of the Construction Corps Hospital, near the Chattanooga Depot, "in the center of the thickest negro population." It was composed of buildings equivalent to sixteen or seventeen houses measuring fifty by twenty feet, well suited to be used as homes, schools, or churches. Smith was convinced that it was an ideal site for the AMA to begin its missionary work in Nashville. "A thousand pupils can be accommodated at once. A training school for col^d teachers could be organized next week. A large Sab[bath] School & preaching congregation could be gathered. This 1 ¼ acre would be the acknowledged Hd. Qr's of Miss^y & educational labor for the col^d people of the State." And the work would extend beyond the state, for Smith considered Nashville "the *Gateway* to the Middle South."[6]

The hospital buildings were to be sold by the government at auction two days later. The land on which they were built was owned by a Nashville citizen and though not available for rent was offered for sale for $16,000. Believing that immediate action was necessary to obtain the hospital and that if they owned the land they could control the bidding on the buildings, Smith and Cravath determined to buy the land themselves. They were joined in their plan by John Ogden, a former principal of the Minnesota State Normal School and the author of a well-received text titled *The Science of Education; and Art of Teaching,* who was in Nashville as the regional superintendent of education for the Bureau of Refugees, Freedmen, and Abandoned Lands. The three men "rallied all [their] capital," made the $4,000 down payment on the land, and assumed the obligation to pay the balance in three annual payments of $4,000 each. Smith was sure the three men could get a good return on their investment if they chose to, but he said they had "purchased only in the interests of the Freedmen" and would be willing to rent the land or sell it to the AMA at their cost.[7]

Once the land was obtained, Smith arranged to have the sale of the hospital buildings postponed and then wrote a request to President Andrew Johnson asking that the buildings be turned over to the AMA. Before sending the request, he submitted it to General Clinton B. Fisk for his endorsement. Fisk was a Methodist layman so committed to the church that he liked to say he "had been *reduced* from the rank of Superintendent of the Sunday-school to become a General in the army." He had served as a member of the Christian Commission during most of the war and had recently been elected to the commission's executive committee. When the Bureau of Refugees, Freedmen, and Abandoned Lands was created, George Stuart had recommended Fisk for the position of commissioner of the bureau, but Fisk was instead appointed assistant commissioner for Kentucky, Tennessee, and northern Alabama, with his headquarters in Nashville. As the bureau's assistant commissioner, Fisk endorsed Smith's request for the hospital buildings, saying that "a good school in the hands of practical christian gentlemen will be established at once."[8]

Smith returned to Philadelphia on October 14. Three days later he was in New York consulting with the secretaries of the AMA. At the meeting and in later letters, he urged them to "ground" the association as he and Cravath had done in Nashville, purchasing "buildings & sites wherever there is an advantageous opening with special reference to a building site for a cold ch[urch] at some day not far distant." He also urged the association to establish itself in Nashville "at once," with a headquarters for Cravath and a home for six to ten teachers under Cravath's direction. "We must hold Nashville at all events."[9]

From New York, Smith went to Washington to the office of the assistant secretary of war to press his request that the hospital buildings in Nashville be turned over to the AMA. The War Department, however, declined to give the buildings to the association. Further difficulties arose as the date for the auction of the buildings drew near and Smith and his associates did not have the money to purchase them. The Western Freedmen's Aid Commission had agreed to rent half the buildings, and Smith appealed to the AMA to rent the other half and to advance the money to ensure that the buildings could be bought. The AMA complied, and with additional, borrowed funds, Smith was prepared to buy the buildings and to "trust the Lord" for the next year's payment on the land. In the midst of these arrangements, General Fisk went to Washington to use his influence in the matter, Smith urging him on by paying his fare and expenses for the trip, and on November 16 Fisk telegraphed Smith: "All right. Buildings turned over to me. Sing Long Meter Doxology." "The infant Fisk," Smith said later, "though not yet named, had a cradle." The school, named for Fisk because of his assistance in its founding, was opened January 9, 1866, with John Ogden, sponsored by the Western Freedmen's Aid Commission, serving as principal and Erastus Cravath assuming the general business responsibilities on behalf of the AMA. Later

Fisk University. The Fisk School, begun in these buildings in 1866, became Fisk
University in 1867. Courtesy of Fisk University Library's Special Collections.

that month, Smith wrote to Michael Strieby that "the school at Nashville is
a *great success*. Its fame has gone far & wide over Tenn & attracted the attention of the Legislature. 400 scholars enrolled & the night school for adults
increasing by 15 [every session?]." [10]

In anticipation of his move to Cincinnati as district secretary for the AMA,
Smith visited the city again in late November to secure an office and employ
"a lady clerk," offering the position to Ella Cole of Medway, Massachusetts,
the twenty-three-year-old sister of John A. Cole. Like her brother, Ella Cole
was a veteran of the Christian Commission, having managed the commission's diet kitchen at City Point, Virginia. Smith planned to begin his work
for the AMA in January but offered to take a reduced salary until he had
completed his responsibilities in "closing up" the Christian Commission. [11]

The executive committee of the Christian Commission met on December 1 and set January 1, 1866, as the closing date for the commission's work.
At the committee's final meeting on January 11, the members adopted a resolution recognizing Smith's contribution to the commission and expressing
the committee's "high sense of the zeal, energy, faithfulness, and good judgment, with which you have labored in the offices and in the field, and of the
genial and Christian spirit you have exhibited in all your intercourse with
them. They feel that they are greatly indebted to you under God, for the
success which has crowned their plans. As you enter upon another field of
Christian labor, they trust that you will be so blesst with wisdom and grace

from on high that you may do much to extend the influences of the Gospel in the waste places of our land." That evening Smith left for Cincinnati.[12]

Smith's first month in Cincinnati was devoted largely to completing his work for the Christian Commission, especially to preparing the commission's fourth and last annual report for presentation at the final anniversary celebration in Washington, D.C., in February. He was also responsible for making some of the arrangements for the celebration. George Stuart was eager to have Philip Phillips, "the Singing Pilgrim," sing for the occasion. Phillips lived in Cincinnati, and the arrangements with him fell to Smith. Phillips had sung at the third anniversary the year before. His song "Your Mission" caught the spirit of the occasion and moved the audience.

> If you cannot in the conflict
> > Prove yourself a soldier true,
> If, where fire and smoke are thickest,
> > There's no work for you to do;
> When the battle-field is silent,
> > You can go with careful tread,
> You can bear away the wounded,
> > You can cover up the dead.

Abraham Lincoln was present and wrote a note on his program, which he handed to Stuart: "Near the close let us have 'Your Mission' repeated by Mr. Phil[l]ips. Don[']t say I called for it." Smith secured Phillips's services for the final anniversary and made detailed plans for the music on the occasion. He suggested to Stuart that the most be made of Phillips's singing of "Your Mission." "If there could be an allusion by one of [the speakers] to Pres. Lincoln's love for C.C. & then attention called by the chair[n] to the association of this song it would come in well." [13]

The Christian Commission met at the E Street Baptist Church in Washington on Saturday, February 10, and approved the executive committee's decision to close its work. In the afternoon, a party of about 175, including Smith, went to the White House to pay respects to President Johnson. The delegation gathered in a semicircle in the East Room, where Joseph Patterson, the commission's treasurer, spoke for the group, and Johnson responded. Bishop Matthew Simpson concluded with "an exceedingly fervent" prayer, "closing with the Lord's Prayer, which was repeated in concert by all present." The delegation then paid visits to Secretary of War Edwin Stanton, Secretary of the Navy Gideon Welles, and General Grant, concluding each of the visits with prayer. That evening, Smith presented the fourth and final annual report of the commission's work to the members of the commission.[14]

Those who had worked for the commission gathered at the Baptist Church on Sunday afternoon in a meeting filled "with reminiscence, praise and thanksgiving." Smith was among those who addressed the group. The anniversary exercises were held that evening in the Hall of the House of Representatives, with Schuyler Colfax, the Speaker of the House, presiding. General Grant was present, as were Chief Justice Salmon Chase and Secretary of the Navy Gideon Welles. "A great crowd filled the Hall, overflowing the lobbies outside, and turning thousands away in a disappointed stream." The speakers included Senator James Doolittle, Major General Christopher C. Augur, and Bishop Matthew Simpson. Smith presented an abstract of the annual report he had made to the commission the night before. After reciting the statistics of the commission's work, he concluded by saying: "But these are only figures, which if they cannot lie, neither can tell the truth." Behind the numbers of delegates and dollars was an "unwritten history," a spiritual history of "lives stirred and quickened . . . for which figures have no power." "Finally," he said, "to God, the Giver and Guide of all, we join with each fellow-laborer of the Christian Commission in thanksgiving and praise. The work is his. To him be the glory. We gave the Commission the name of the Master. We sent it forth to speak his words and imitate his deeds. Christ, the Lord, has accepted and honored it; and now, wherever mention shall be made of the work it has accomplished, we desire only that the quick, grateful, adoring response shall be, 'See what the Lord hath wrought!' "[15]

When Smith returned to Cincinnati, there was still work to be done for the Christian Commission in getting the fourth annual report ready for the printer; at one point he said Stuart "is getting *rampant* on Reports." He wrote to Stuart that "compiling this mass of manuscript, cutting down, adding, copying & rewriting is much heavier than I supposed possible. But I am doing *nothing else* at the rate of ten hours per day. Am thinking of availing myself of the eight hour law just passed by the Ohio legislature." The report was not completed until March 7, when he sent the last pages to Stuart and told him that he had done nothing but work on the report since February 1. Then, with the report completed, Smith was ready to begin his work for the American Missionary Association in earnest.[16]

THE AMERICAN MISSIONARY ASSOCIATION was well established as an antislavery association when the Civil War began. Unlike the Garrisonian American Anti-Slavery Society, which had called its members to "come out" of the Christian churches, the members of the AMA were dedicated to remaining in the churches and to spreading an evangelical religion that condemned slaveholding as a sin against God and humanity. It welcomed as members "any person of evangelical sentiments, who professes faith in the Lord Jesus Christ, who is not a slaveholder, or in the practice of other immoralities, and who contributes to the funds." The association defined "evangelical sentiments" as including, "among others, a belief in the guilty and lost condition of all men without a Saviour; the Supreme Deity, Incarnation, and Atoning Sacrifice of Jesus Christ, the only Saviour of the world; the necessity of regeneration by the Holy Spirit, repentance, faith, and holy obedience, in order to salvation; the immortality of the soul; and the retributions of the judgment in the eternal punishment of the wicked, and salvation of the righteous." [17]

Several mission groups had merged to form the AMA in 1846. One of them was the Union Missionary Society, which had grown out of the famous mutiny on the slave ship *Amistad* in 1839. The citizens who defended the African mutineers eventually returned them to Africa and used the occasion to begin a mission to the Mendis in Sierra Leone. By 1860 the AMA had 14 missionaries among the Mendis. Another group that became part of the AMA was the Jamaica–West India Missionary Committee, and because of its interest, the AMA had 25 missionaries in Jamaica in 1860. It also had 2 missionaries in Siam, 2 in Canada, 1 in Haiti, and 1 in the Sandwich Islands. At the same time, the AMA had 112 home missionaries, working chiefly in the settlements of Iowa, Minnesota, and the old Northwest Territory. In the years just before the Civil War, these home missionaries had become increasingly outspoken in their abolitionist views, and a few of them had gone so far as to carry the antislavery message into Kentucky and North Carolina.[18]

The Civil War changed the focus of the AMA's efforts to missionary work among the freed slaves. The association opened its first "contraband" school at Fortress Monroe, Virginia, on September 17, 1861. That school was followed by scores of others as federal troops occupied more and more of the South. By 1863 the AMA had eighty-three teachers among the freedmen; by the end of the war, it had more than three hundred, located in every state of the former Confederacy and in Kentucky, Maryland, and Missouri.[19]

Education had not been a prominent part of the association's work before the war, having been considered secondary to the preaching of the gospel and the crusade against slavery. After the war, education became the center of its work. In focusing its attention on education, the association was responding to a need expressed by the freedmen themselves. During slavery, most of the slaves had been denied an education. It was illegal in every slave state except Kentucky to teach a slave to read and write, though some of them—perhaps 5 percent or more—did manage to learn. When they were freed, blacks of all ages became obsessed with the desire to read and learn, exhibiting what one observer called "a feverish anxiety for initiation into the mysteries of print," and many of them organized schools to make their dream possible.[20]

A young northern journalist who traveled through the South shortly after the war reported that "many of the negroes . . . common plantation negroes, and day laborers in the towns and villages, were supporting little schools themselves. Everywhere, I found among them a disposition to get their children into schools, if possible. I had occasion very frequently to notice that porters in stores and laboring men about cotton warehouses, and cart drivers on the streets, had spelling books with them, and were studying them during the time they were not occupied with their work." Booker T. Washington wrote, out of his own experience, that "it was a whole race trying to go to school. Few were too young, and none too old, to make the attempt to learn. As fast as any kind of teachers could be secured, not only were day-schools filled, but night-schools as well. The great ambition of the older people was to try to learn to read the Bible before they died. With this end in view, men and women who were fifty or seventy-five years old would often be found in the night-school. Sunday-schools were formed soon after freedom, but the principal book studied in the Sunday-school was the spelling-book. Day-school, night-school, Sunday-school, were always crowded, and often many had to be turned away for want of room."[21]

The freedmen recognized that education conferred power—a group of schoolchildren paraded through the streets of Laurens, South Carolina, on one occasion carrying a flag with the motto "Knowledge Is Power"— and the freedmen were willing to make sacrifices to gain an education. A teacher in North Carolina said that the freedmen in Beaufort had contributed $800 toward a new school building, some having gone without meals to save the money. Even in small towns like Cuthbert, Albany, Cave Spring, and Thomasville in Georgia the freedmen raised up to $70 a month for education and as much as $350 for school buildings. But the freedmen often could not provide adequate school buildings and qualified teachers by themselves, and some fifty benevolent societies sprang up in the North to assist them and to organize schools of their own. The AMA, with a missionary organization already in place and a long-standing commitment to the welfare of the blacks, was the first in the field and one of the first to commit its resources to the task.[22]

The end of the Civil War brought increased opportunities for education among the freedmen, and the AMA published an appeal to "the friends of the Sanitary and Christian Commissions" to join them in "the immense work of elevating four millions of Freedmen." The AMA presented itself as "providentially prepared" for the task. It had been the first to begin the work and already had a large force of teachers and missionaries in the field. "Its education and civilization are Christian. It is undenominational but evangelical. . . . As now the Sanitary and Christian Commissions rest from their noble work . . . it is believed that large numbers who have so generously contributed to them will desire some channel or channels for the continued exercise of their benevolence at the South." The AMA presented its work as "cognate to, and as legitimately succeeding, these excellent Commissions" and asked for the support that had previously been given to them.[23]

The AMA also reorganized itself to be better able to take advantage of the new educational opportunities. Three district offices, staffed by three clergymen, were established in Boston, Cincinnati, and Chicago to supplement the work of the AMA's main office in New York City. Edward Smith was employed at a yearly salary of $1,200 and was assigned to the middle district, with his headquarters in Cincinnati. In addition to raising funds and recruiting teachers, he was responsible for supervising the association's work in Kentucky, Tennessee, Alabama, and western Georgia. Smith arranged to board with his family at 191 West Seventh Street in Cincinnati and accepted an invitation to share an office at the corner of Sixth and Vine streets with the Western Freedmen's Aid Commission, the group that shared the administration of the new Fisk School in Nashville with the AMA.

The Western Freedmen's Aid Commission, like the AMA, was dominated by evangelical clergymen, including Methodists, Congregationalists, Presbyterians, Baptists, and "with a small smat[t]ering of Quakerism mixed in." Unlike the AMA, however, it had been formed "for the specific purpose of elevating the millions who have just escaped from the house of bondage." Although it was a much younger organization than the AMA, the commission already had 123 teachers in the field. Its general agent and storekeeper was Levi Coffin, the seventy-six-year-old Quaker sometimes known as the "president" of the underground railroad for his prewar activities. A good relationship soon developed between the two societies. Smith told Michael Strieby that Levi Coffin "thinks about as much of A.M.A. as he does of the Western," and Smith, on his part, was willing to work with any freedmen's society as long as there was "entire agree[t] as to a strictly evangelical sentiment in the schools."[24]

Soon after his arrival in Cincinnati, Smith wrote to George Stuart that the AMA was "working for the negroes in earnest[.] Nearly 300 teachers & missionaries in the South. I am applying C.C. field organization thro' this middle west & find it a great improvement over the former plan pursued by the A.M.A." Drawing on his Christian Commission experience, Smith proposed that the AMA attempt to increase donations by publishing a weekly "acknowledgement column" in two leading Congregational newspapers, the *Congregationalist* and the *Independent*, "with directions about remittances and boxes." He suggested using the word "freedmen" in the newspaper headings and including a note that gifts would be used exclusively for the freedmen, to distinguish the AMA's work from that of the societies that were serving southern whites as well as freedmen. "It is a settled principle in business," he said, "that advertising [pays?] especially where there is competition." He also told the AMA secretaries that the Christian Commission had found it useful to encourage communication between donors and the delegates and soldiers "at the front," and he thought that the students in the South could be encouraged to write to those who sent supplies. "One good letter from the front" to thank donors would, he said, do more good than any appeals from the pulpit for donations. Teachers too, he thought, should be in constant communication with the churches that sponsored them.[25]

Smith also had a definite idea about the strategy the association should adopt for its field work, namely, to establish the association in key locations in the South "by taking position & *entrenching*." Just as Smith and Cravath had "grounded" the work in Nashville, sites should be bought and school buildings and teachers' homes erected in the other major cities of the association's middle district: Atlanta, Macon, Augusta, Montgomery, and Selma. The freedmen should be asked to help with the buildings, and black teachers should be put into twenty other towns. The black teachers, he said, "will be our best investment in many places for the reason that we can send them into a town to be provided for largely by the col[d] people themselves." Smith urged that the work be undertaken quickly. "We must get what we can *now* on the principle that if the churches don[']t give to us they will to some other col[d] operation. The negro is good for so much this year. If we don[']t get it somebody else will." He was also eager to begin work in Kentucky. "Ky is opening now. With a good col[d] corps of teachers we could go all over the state. . . . There is no time to be lost if it is to be done this year." "If you have *any other* col[d] teachers or missionaries male or female, please put me in communication with them."[26]

Another strategy Smith proposed came out of a conversation with a former resident of Cincinnati who was working plantations in Louisiana. The planter asked Smith for a teacher or two and offered to pay their entire expenses. Smith thought the planter had "opened a door which . . . may lead to a wide opening for us." Other men might be found "who want to [do] right by their plantation hands & many others who want to make their col[d] people contented & will be glad to take care of a teacher[,] pay salary, *generally* entire[,] in other cases *in part*." He thought that by advertising for such positions in the southern newspapers the association could get an additional 75 to 150 teachers into the field, "& every one of them would form a nucleus for a future miss.ʸ effort. If we can spread ourselves all over the land in this way, we can go to the ch[urche]s with a strong tug at the heart & purse." Smith began to place advertisements in newspapers both North and South announcing "Plantation Colored Schools" and inviting correspondence from "planters who desire thorough schools and happy Christian influence to help elevate their employes, and make them contented, skillful laborers." "A good plantation school," the advertisements said, "is the best security for a good crop. In most cases the colored people will support it; but it will be well for the employer to assume the general direction and responsibility." Smith's arrangement with the planter from Cincinnati proved unsuccessful, but he was pleased to learn that his agent in Mississippi was beginning to receive applications for teachers from other planters who were willing to support teachers on their plantations.[27]

Little more is known of Smith's "plantation enterprise," but the cities Smith targeted for schools were already receiving teachers. In December 1865, Erastus Cravath had left for Macon with ten teachers. The teachers were accompanied by a matron, Martha Ayers, who was to operate the teachers' home, and a missionary at large, Hiram Eddy. "An apostolic band of twelve," Smith called the group. The freedmen of Macon had organized themselves into an educational association and were prepared to "provide the rooms for schools, furnish fuel, and kindle the fires." The AMA teachers soon organized four schools with a thousand students and a night school with two hundred children and adults. Hiram Eddy, "an old experienced teacher," told a visitor that the black children had made more progress in a given time than the whites in any school he had ever taught. With the schools begun, Smith believed that Eddy would "undoubtedly extend the work in all directions from Macon if we can get the means."[28]

Smith soon asked Eddy for information about the work in Macon to use in his appeals to the public in Ohio. "I am trying to wak[e] up Ohio & find myself all out of sight. With no religious organ & the ground pretty well occupied with the Freedmen[']s Com.ˢ, the recognition by the people is slow." But he was confident from his Christian Commission experience that "Ohio is a good State to give when we get at the hearts of the people."[29]

In addition to visiting various churches and church conferences in Ohio, Smith made his appeal to the public through a circular asking for gifts of money, clothing, stationery, books, and provisions for families. "Clothing, of all kinds—quantity more important than quality, provided the holes are all stopped with substantial patches; five pairs of old shoes—not too old—keep out more frost than two pairs of new. . . . Good books for family reading—not the book on the shelf, high and dry; but the one which has made the round of the family—the one the children say they can't spare, that is the one for them to send." He said that the association in turn would try to do three things for the donors: "1. Send your gifts without delay or loss to those for whom you give them—the suffering colored poor and those who labor among them. 2. Present them in your name. 3. Inform you whom your gifts have relieved and gladdened." The government would furnish transportation for the supplies. (Smith later said to Strieby, "We may as well let 'Uncle Sam' do what he can afford & is willing to do for his poor relatives.") The AMA officials in New York published Smith's circular in their journal, the *American Missionary,* noting that Smith had formerly been field secretary of the Christian Commission and that the circular was "suggested by the experience of that Commission in collecting, transmitting and using money and supplies."[30]

A little more than two weeks after he arrived in Cincinnati, Smith published another circular, describing the work of the AMA in detail. Despite the National Council of Congregational Churches' pledge of $250,000 to the association, Smith insisted that the AMA's work was not sectarian. "It offers to all evangelical denominations its channels for relief, and missionary and educational labors among the colored people, using the funds donated according to the wish of the donor. In our schools are found, working most harmoniously together, Methodists, Baptists, Friends, Episcopalians, Presbyterians and Congregationalists."[31]

He also tried to correct a misapprehension that the association "attempts only a spiritual work." The association's reports, he said,

> show not only a larger working force of missionaries and teachers, but a larger amount of supplies sent for the relief of the destitute, than by any other organization. The Association believes in the Gospel of Jesus as the only hope of man, and that His gospel includes garments for the naked and food for the hungry and schools for the ignorant. . . . Whatever mode of relief, or education, or evangelization, any friend of the colored man can wisely desire a benevolent organization to attempt in his behalf, this Association is now attempting to the extent of the means furnished.
>
> Our "Mission Homes" in the large cities not only furnish quarters for the teachers, but they become centres of happy influences reaching out into the families around. They are the depots of supply to the destitute. Our mission families, thus becoming permanent residents, naturally become the protectors of the colored people and mediators between them and their former masters.

After describing the association's work in Macon and Atlanta and noting its cooperation with the Western Freedmen's Aid Commission, he appealed for aid for "a work which is opening beyond the power of all organizations to fill."

A nation has been born in a day. A whole race asks for the gospel and its elevating influences. It is at our very doors. It will modify our national civilization, religion and history, whether we will or no. Indifference increases alike our guilt and danger. Will not hearts, still throbbing in thanksgiving to God for the great deliverance from rebellion, be ready to make love offerings for these Christ's poor? [32]

12

Secretary for the Middle West

When the coloured people reach the monument-building stage, they should not forget the men and women who went South after the war and founded schools for them.

James Weldon Johnson, *Autobiography of an Ex-Coloured Man*

In March 1866, Smith visited Atlanta, one of the cities he had proposed as a focal point for the work of the AMA. Sherman's army had nearly destroyed the city. Every business block but one had disappeared in flames and explosions. The railroad approaching Atlanta was still lined with burned buildings, twisted rails, and ruined locomotives. Everywhere, a visitor said, were "ruins and rubbish, mud and mortar and misery"—and even piles of bones from the battlefields. Since the war, new buildings had sprung up, but those buildings, in various stages of completion, stood side by side with shanties and ruins of the former buildings. Hundreds of citizens, black and white, were living in makeshift hovels. Social relations too had been profoundly disturbed by the war. One observer spoke of the "alarming insecurity of property and even of life. Passing about the dark, crooked streets of Atlanta after night, unaccompanied and unarmed, was worse than attempting a similar exploration of the Five Points, in New York, ten years ago." The city, nevertheless, hummed with energy and life. The streets were crowded with vehicles, the shops were full of goods, trading was active, and it was clear that Atlanta would soon resume its importance to Georgia and the South in general.[1]

The AMA's schools in Atlanta were also bustling. Smith said that when Cravath and his company of teachers went through Atlanta on their way to Macon in December, they found the two schools established only two months before "full to overflowing," with six teachers serving six hundred pupils and the teachers so overworked that Cravath "was fairly plundered" of one of his teachers. In addition to more teachers, a mission home for teachers like the one established in Macon was needed and after that a chapel and a schoolroom near the contraband camp. In December, Smith had secured four large surplus chapel tents from the Christian Commission and shipped them to Atlanta to provide temporary shelter for the association's activities. He also sent a shipment of woolen garments for distribution among the destitute in the city.[2]

After Smith arrived in Atlanta, he reported to New York that the property for a mission home had already been purchased. He had found, on his arrival, that two adjoining lots were also offered for sale, and he immediately purchased them in his own name. He also found an urgent need for an orphanage to house "100 of the most pitiable little black fellows [you] ever saw or read of," the children of soldiers who had died in the war and of other blacks who had died of smallpox during the winter. Some of the children, he said, had been taken in by freedmen "who have but little more than they." Others wandered the streets or stayed in the buildings at the contraband camp, where the government continued to furnish them with rations even though the camp was officially closed.[3]

Smith described the orphans in the graphic way he had once described the street children of New York City. "I looked in at one of the log shanties—no floor—a few rags and blankets for a bed on the ground, and no other furniture or comfort of any name or kind in the house. 'Who lives here?' I asked. 'We all,' said a little girl seven years old, standing beside her brother, four years old, who was sitting on the ground holding between his feet another brother ten or twelve months old. 'And who is we all?' 'We and brother and baby.' 'Where's your mother?' 'She's done and dead.' 'And your father.' 'Dun no.' "[4]

The AMA had recently opened an orphan asylum in Wilmington, North Carolina, and Smith urged that one be established in Atlanta for the "little fellows from ten months to eight years old living on hard tack and salt pork, and nobody in the wide world to care for them but the Government." When the smallpox had struck, the freedmen formed a relief association that was attempting to raise $200 a month even if it meant borrowing money, but $2,000 was needed to purchase land on which tents for an orphanage could be erected, and Smith appealed through the *American Missionary* for funds to aid the orphans "among a people so poor and so generous."[5]

Shortly after Smith's return from Atlanta, an "unknown friend" of the association, saying that "Smith seemed to be a man that understood himself," offered, on the basis of Smith's word about the need, to provide the entire cost of the purchase of the lot Smith had proposed for the orphanage, a lot on a ridge east of Atlanta, overlooking the city. Smith was always confident that if the needs of the poor were made known, benefactors would arise to meet them. His confidence was rewarded in this case by one whom he called "this good friend of the poor. I wish I knew him. Blessings on him."[6]

The officers in New York had cautioned Smith that their funds were limited, and he admitted to them that his plans did not look much like "retrenchment." But he added that he wished "you could come thro' this country. We have calls repeatedly for teachers." One had just come from the freedmen in Marietta, Georgia, asking for two black teachers for whom the freedmen would provide everything except the salaries. Despite the cautious attitude in New York, Smith told the secretaries that he had "half a mind to send North for the two teachers." He did try to secure them, but two months later he admitted he had failed to find them, not for financial reasons but because of the "scarcity of col[d] teachers. . . . Competent col[d] teachers, such as you would not be ashamed to put into a school, are not to be found."[7]

Financial limitations also dictated that the association's work in Montgomery, Alabama, be deferred until the fall. Smith went as far as he could by offering a commission and a nominal salary to the Reverend John Silsby to open schools in Montgomery if he could raise the remainder of his salary from tuitions or other sources. Smith cautioned Silsby that, if the work was undertaken, he would have to do at Montgomery, "as we must at other points," collect money for school rent and for boarding the teachers from the freedmen, either by contributions or from tuitions to allow the association to "spread wider with the funds at our command."[8]

Smith was also using his own funds to expand the association's work. He purchased three acres of land at Franklin, Tennessee, with the intention of selling two acres to freedmen for building lots. In that way the freedmen would have ready access to land at a cheap price, and the proceeds of the sales would pay for a school, teachers' home, and church. "The only trouble is," he said, "I haven't capital enough of my own to do a business up to the demand." If the AMA could provide $3,000 or $4,000 for this venture, "it would be as good use as A.M.A. [could?] possibly make of its funds. We do the col[d] people a great good & get our foothold in a town without expense."[9]

After his trip to Atlanta, where he had conversations with several young blacks eager to further their education, Smith was convinced of the need for an institution of higher education for the freedmen and convinced that Atlanta was the place for it.

> At all our schools and in many places I have visited South I have found this
> want, a higher grade of education than we are yet offering. There are young men
> who have already mastered the elementary branches and want to take a course of

instruction that shall fit them for teachers and preachers. These two professions seem to cover the whole field of ambition at present. We cannot give such minds proper attention in connection with our elementary schools. Besides they need to be brought together and put under the best *home* influences so as to be trained into a proper conception of true social and domestic life. Such a school must be within the reach of all youths of both sexes, but must not be a charity school[.] Both the expense and the effect upon the scholars make the charity system undesirable[.] The class we wish most to reach cannot afford to pay tuition and the ordinary cost of board[.] If tuition and quarters can be furnished and twenty five acres of land for gardening purposes, by working 4 hours per day and having vacation in the busy season when labor commands the highest prices, the scholars can largely work their own way thro the school year. Many of these young men who are pushing their way into an education have already learned a trade of some sort. They are from the class of the quickest and most enterprising minds, for these the many manufacturing establishments of Atlanta will afford opportunity for good wages in all hours that can be spared from study. . . . I would by all means, open the school to *all* "without distinction of color". Practically the whites will exclude themselves for a while, not long, for I am confident that we can make it such a school as will attract them over the high wall of prejudice, and in course of years will grow to the character and power of a school like Oberlin. We ought to begin next Fall.[10]

A month later, when funding for the school had not yet been found, Smith was concerned that the AMA was "losing by waiting." He had no doubt that "the question of a higher education for col^d people is more or less on the public mind & others will be *liable*, if not *likely*, to get the attention of those who are in their hearts devising liberal things." He thought an appeal for funds ought to be made through the *Independent*. "It will be quite likely to strike some good [man's?] heart somewhere in the land." If $6,000 could be raised, a boarding hall could be built on the lot already obtained for the orphanage, "a beautiful site overlooking the city," and a preparatory department of the college opened in the fall. Plans for the school still had not matured in July, but Smith was determined about the matter. He told George Whipple that "a college at Atlanta ought & s——l be built. I *almost* said it. I have already in my heart, & hope before long to get bold enough to say it in full on paper." [11]

Even without the college, the missionary establishment at Atlanta was expanding. A temporary orphanage was set up in June in tents near the teachers' home, and a two-story building with schoolrooms and an attached chapel was under construction. Smith had pledged to the Congregational Union that, if it would contribute $1,000, a Congregational church would be organized and the chapel would be debt-free in six months. He had also convinced

Storrs School, Atlanta, Georgia. The schoolhouse contained four classrooms,
each large enough for 75 pupils, and an office. The chapel at the rear of the
building, which seated 450 persons, was used both for educational
and religious purposes. From *Harper's Weekly*.
Courtesy of the Cleveland Public Library.

the First Orthodox Congregational Church of Cincinnati to donate $1,000
to the building, which was later named the Storrs School after the church's
pastor, Henry M. Storrs.

Smith had also obtained a building for a chapel in Nashville, a former
Christian Commission chapel seating from seven hundred to nine hundred
persons—"according to size & packing." Smith appealed to New York for
"two good colored pastors" for the chapels at Atlanta and Nashville. "They
ought to be men of character & with a mind to work. They would be in positions to lead off [in?] all questions of education & religious & benevolent
enterprises & of civil rights. . . . I think I shall need in this Depart. four or
five first class col^d *pastors* next Fall[.] Can they be furnished?"[12]

Smith and his associates might propose their plans for the education of
the freedmen, but some angry white southerners did their best to dispose
of them. Smith reported that his agent in Mississippi, the Reverend John P.
Bardwell, was attacked by a "ruffianly crowd" in Grenada, Mississippi, and
was choked and beaten for no other reason, his attackers said, than that "he
was working for the 'niggers.' " The assistant subcommissioner of the Freed-

men's Bureau, Lieutenant J. B. Blanding, "helped [Bardwell] wash the blood from his face and advised a complaint to the Mayor. . . . Three days after, Lieut. Blanding . . . was attacked on the street, shot three times, and died in twenty-four hours." Bardwell said that while Blanding lay dying, a committee of citizens informed Captain Silas May, the subcommissioner of the Freedmen's Bureau, that "the teachers *must leave town*" and threatened to kill May if he did not leave too.[13]

May did not leave, nor was he killed, but the violence continued. While the court of inquest was meeting in the case of Blanding's death, shots were heard, and a black man was seen running for his life, pursued by a white man who repeatedly shot at him. An old resident of the town was knocked down with a chair, stamped on, and given two broken ribs for expressing an opinion on what May called "a reign of terror" by a "gang of *thugs.*" Two attempts were made to find an opportunity to assassinate May, and three weeks after Blanding's death, May reported that "the sound of fire arms is heard nightly on the streets reminding one of being on picket duty."[14]

When accounts of similar violence at Atlanta reached Cincinnati, Smith expressed his confidence in the future of the association's work by saying, "I do not believe the Lord is going to give over the nation to the destruction of madness. . . . The Lord reigns and [from?] any acc^ts that have yet reached us Central Georgia is in His Depart^t."[15]

On May 1 and 2, 1866, whites in Memphis, Tennessee, led by police and firemen, rioted against the freedmen, killing forty-six of them and burning ninety-one houses, twelve schools, and four churches. Smith and the Reverend Richard S. Rust of the Western Freedmen's Aid Commission hurried to Memphis to examine the damage and to file a claim against the city for the association's losses. They found that only one schoolhouse remained in a city where thirty teachers had been teaching some twenty-five hundred students. The Lincoln Chapel, built by the Reverend Ewing Ogden Tade for the AMA and dedicated just four months earlier, was burned to the ground. It had contained both a day school and a Sabbath school. Despite the terror, Smith was convinced that Memphis was a city the association could not abandon. "It is the Gate City to the So. West. . . . What is done here for the colored man, in a very important sense, is done for him all over this territory."[16]

Two months later Smith was back in Memphis to secure a lot for a new building to include a chapel and a high school and another building to serve as a mission home. Thinking it unwise to spend money to rent property, and having a grant from the Freedmen's Bureau in hand, he took it upon himself to exceed the instructions he had from New York and purchased some lots he discovered at a "forced sale." Later he confessed what he called his "malfeasance in office" to George Whipple. He said he knew Whipple would "say at once that you will not do it & then I think you will say it *ought* to be done & *shall* be if it can." Smith added that he had so much confidence in the venture that he had borrowed money and bought an adjacent lot on his own account. The school in Memphis was to be a training school for teachers, and Smith thought that "when others are ready to take up the Normal and High School work, *ours may, and probably will, grow into a College.*" He also proposed to begin a church in Memphis "as soon as 20 reliable christians can be found ready to unite. We shall thro' this graded school get control of the very best negro mind[s] in the city & lay the foundation of a strong healthy church." Smith justified his actions at Memphis by saying he had "consulted freely the friends of the col^d people & of A.M.A. in Memphis" and found them "jublilant" about what he had done.[17]

The expenses Smith had incurred appeared not to daunt him; he was confident that "there must be some good man who means to do a good thing for the colored people before he dies, and who, perhaps, on reading this, will say: 'That is a wise and economical investment—a good thing to do for Christ and His poor. Do it in my name." Nevertheless, Smith admitted to George Whipple that he was aware of the boldness of his actions: "Dear me! I get frightened at my own propositions! But they are not mine. I have only followed God's finger. I have no more doubt that He showed me these lots & at *just the time* when they *must* be sold, than I have that I went to Memphis. Now something will come of it, but only as the lots came, by a vigilant & prompt & full action."[18]

Smith's thoughts were turning more and more to higher education for the freedmen: at least high schools and, where possible, normal schools and colleges. Writing about the school in Macon, Georgia, he said that "at Macon as elsewhere we shall soon get out of the primary instruction altogether & will maintain our hold & do our work by carrying the children up higher. For this a high school is indispensable & for *this* a *building* is indispensable."[19]

In the midst of his travels, Smith had taken time to write an article for the *Congregationalist* about the widespread allegations that without the care of their old masters "the negro race is to die out." Senator James Doolittle was reported to have said in Congress that one-fourth of the blacks had died since the beginning of the war. Smith said that during the war he had been "with the army in its marches into the heart of the Southern country" and had made "extensive tours . . . through the states since reconstruction commenced," and his observations had led him to a different conclusion, "and it is my conviction that the Wisconsin Senator misrepresented facts as badly as he does his constituents."[20]

The opinion was widespread in the South, Smith said, that servitude was the normal condition of the blacks and that, left to their own devices, they "will gradually fade away like the Indians driven from their hunting grounds." Smith had been told in various places that blacks were "getting scarce." He said it was true that there had been migration during the war—owners had run slaves south, and escaped slaves had gone north—but nowhere had anyone been able to show him the graves or the mortality rates to prove that the race was diminishing. Even in the crowded contraband camps, like the one at Nashville, there had been no such death toll. "On the theory of the extinction of one-fourth of the race, there should be a million graves of contrabands somewhere, most of them at these points, and 100,000 of them should be found at Nashville." Yet the government undertaker at Nashville had told him that only a few more than seven thousand blacks had been buried there. "Negro extinction," Smith concluded, "is a favorite topic with many ex-slave owners and their joy in the idea is illy concealed. But I see no prospect of their speedy gratification."[21]

In August 1866, changes in the Western Freedmen's Aid Commission led to a proposal to give Smith a position with that commission as well as with the AMA. The Methodists had been in an uneasy alliance with the Western Freedmen's Aid Commission for some time, and they finally withdrew to form a freedmen's aid society of their own. When they had done so, the Western Commission asked Smith to draw up a proposal for closer cooperation with the AMA district office. Levi Coffin then proposed to George Whipple that Smith be made the corresponding secretary of both bodies. "If our good Brother E P Smith could remain here," Coffin wrote, "I think we could effect some satisfactory arrangement for the preasant & eventually flow together but not at preasant. Friend Smith is a very pleasant Man to work with, and can do more to unite us in labor than any Man you could place here." But by the time Coffin's proposal was made, the AMA had already decided to bring Smith to New York City as its general field agent.[22]

Discussions about Smith's future with the association had begun in May, when Jacob R. Shipherd, the AMA's district secretary at Chicago, suggested to Smith that the entire western work of the association be managed from the Chicago office with one secretary attending to collections and one to field work. Smith agreed that the plan would reduce the association's expenses and increase its efficiency, and he offered to resign his position so that someone else could be appointed to work in Chicago with Shipherd. "I am entirely sincere & frank in this proposition," he wrote to Michael Strieby. "I think that is the way the A.M.A. ought to be worked in the West & know that I could not do it & that some other can be found who can. I came into this work not from any particular taste for it—I love the pastoral better—but I tho[t] perhaps I had a talent somewhat in that direction & that I ought to use it for the Freedmen. I am now satisfied of my mistake, that I overrated my ability in the line I attempted & that men are easily found who can & would like to do this work. You will please consider me then in y'r hands & not allow me to stand in the way of a more perfect union as I am *persuaded* without questioning, Shipherd[']s plan would be."[23]

Smith apparently assumed that the new secretary in Chicago would be responsible for fund-raising, and he admitted that he did not know what he could do to bring in funds and that he was not even sure what funds had been collected by the association's agents in his department. Nor, he confessed, was he entirely sure what the whole scope of the association's work was, which was information he would need if he were to make effective financial appeals to the churches.[24]

When Strieby received Smith's letter, he shared it with George Whipple and asked Whipple's advice about how best to keep Smith in the AMA's service. Whipple told Strieby that "I prize Bro Smith so highly that I am almost ready to offer him anything he will take," but he thought it would be wise for Strieby cautiously to draw Smith out on various plans, "seeking to learn his preferences in order to lay the matter properly before our Ex Committee." Strieby agreed that time was needed to "settle . . . in our own minds what berth we can get ready for him."[25]

The "berth" that emerged from the discussions was the one occupied by Samuel Hunt, the fifty-six-year-old Congregational minister who had served as the association's superintendent of schools since 1864. As the educational work of the association expanded, complaints had arisen about Hunt's management of it. Francis Cardozo, the association's superintendent in Charleston, criticized Hunt for sending him inferior teachers. When Hunt learned about the criticism, he not only refused to withdraw the teachers but also informed them about Cardozo's disappointment in them, much to Cardozo's consternation. Erastus Cravath was also critical of Hunt's work. "Bro. Hunt is not doing for the field work what is required," he wrote. "He seems to me to be a clerk in the educational department of the A.M.A. and nothing more." Cravath thought the position of field secretary should be created and that it required "a man of experience, and great organizing ability" who would personally visit the field and bring efficiency to the association's work. He told Strieby he knew of no better person for the position than Smith.[26]

Smith, too, had been critical of Hunt. Even before he went to Cincinnati, Smith had let Hunt know that his delay in sending teachers to the field was inexcusable. "Delays in the workers when everything else is waiting are very expensive & so far as I can see promise no good." Shortly after Smith arrived in Cincinnati, he requested the services of a teacher he knew personally, only to have Hunt reply that she could not be commissioned until her references had arrived. Sharply, Smith asked Hunt, "Was not my endorsement of her from personal knowledge of her of years standing both as a teacher & a Christian lady sufficient credentials? Do you gain anything by sticking to a form when you have the substance and more?" Smith also criticized other decisions Hunt made in New York that did not fit conditions in the field. Like Cravath, Smith questioned whether the association could conduct its field work without a field superintendent.[27]

Strieby informed Hunt on June 30 that the association was going to bring Smith to New York. After their conversation, Hunt complained bitterly to George Whipple about the way Strieby had treated him. He said Strieby had first broached the subject of calling Smith to New York some two or three months earlier. "After some very uncomplimentary remarks about the present administration of affairs, [Strieby had] added: 'In five years Smith will have the whole concern under his control.'" It appeared to Hunt then that Strieby was thinking of removing him to make room for Smith. Hunt said that in their latest conversation Strieby "added the *invidious* . . . inquiry: *whether I did not think I was better adapted to the pastor's office than to my present position.*"[28]

Stung by Strieby's remarks, Hunt felt free to criticize Strieby's actions and policies and was especially critical of Strieby's plan to bring Smith to New York: "Just as bro. Smith is 'getting warm in his nest' at C[incinnati] overlooking and supervising your great and difficult work in the So. West, when you need your most [eminent?] practical talent and where if ever you need the 'genius' of S[mith] of which bro. Strieby talks . . . it is proposed to transfer him to the East . . . to take my place. . . . Now if this is good generalship or strategy, then my past modes of thinking have been sadly awry."[29]

Hunt defended his own work, saying its success had been "marked, almost wonderful," but he said Strieby could only find fault with it and make comparisons with Smith's work. Hunt said that when he had proposed the appointment of a field superintendent, Strieby, "tho acknowledging he knew nothing about [Smith's] *educational* qualifications," said that Smith, "by holding a Teacher's meeting of three or four days could fit them better for their work, than such a superintendent." "To my New England ears," Hunt said, "such language sounds strangely."[30]

Despite long letters of appeal from Hunt, the secretaries of the AMA decided to go through with their plan to bring Smith to the New York office and to give Hunt's duties to him. The *American Missionary* announced that

Smith had been appointed general field agent and added that "for prudential and economic reasons, as also his necessary connection with the schools, it has been deemed advisable to place under his supervision our educational work, which has been, for the last two years, under the faithful and successful superintend[e]nce of the Rev. Samu[e]l Hunt, who now retires from that department." Hunt found it galling, not only that he was replaced by Smith but that Smith, when he took over the work, did not even ask him what he had done in the position. The notice in the *American Missionary* said that Hunt would "continue to devote his valuable services and give the results of his experience to the extended interests of our work, both North and South," but in fact he submitted his resignation to take effect on January 1, 1867, and left the association bitter toward Strieby and disappointed in Whipple. Leaving the association did not harm Hunt's career. He went on to become clerk of the Committee on Military Affairs of the United States Senate and, later, private secretary to Henry Wilson, vice-president of the United States during Ulysses S. Grant's second administration.[31]

After a brief trip to New York to consult with the AMA secretaries about his new position, Smith returned to Cincinnati to close his work there. Then in late August he turned the Cincinnati office over to Erastus Cravath before moving with his family to New York City.

Cravath was pleased with the state of affairs in the association's middle department as he received it from Smith. The association, he reported, held five "vital points": Nashville, Memphis, Atlanta, Macon, and Lexington. The Fisk School at Nashville he thought "one of the most thoroughly furnished of all the schools in the South." A graded school with a normal class opened in the fall of 1866 with four hundred pupils in attendance. At Memphis, the association was erecting, on the lots Smith had bought, a primary school building and a two-story central schoolhouse with four schoolrooms on the first floor and a chapel on the second. At Atlanta, in addition to the home the AMA had for its teachers, a schoolhouse and chapel that would accommodate three hundred pupils was nearing completion. The five-acre lot for the orphanage and normal school had been fenced, and arrangements were under way to build the orphanage, although funds were still needed for the boardinghouse for the normal school. At Macon, "good colored churches are available for school purposes, so that one thousand colored children can be received to our schools." And at Lexington, the Freedmen's Bureau had secured a large building that the freedmen were furnishing for fall classes.[32]

Normal schools were to be organized in each of the five cities, "and the most thorough drill will be given in order to prepare efficient teachers as rapidly as possible." Schools were planned in smaller communities near these cities, "whenever the circumstances justify," with the expectation that the Freedmen's Bureau would sometimes provide schoolrooms and the freedmen would board the teachers. "We feel," Cravath wrote, "that the great Father's care has been over us continually; that His blessing has rested upon the work of our hands, and He will establish it."[33]

13

The Freedmen's Bureau

I can-not help seeing that Providence has placed me in a peculiar position, with an unusual array of forces, and I trust by the Divine blessing to give some positive, early fruits.

> Oliver Otis Howard, commissioner of the Freedmen's Bureau, to J. T. Backus, July 8, 1868

[I have] always found that people who made loud claims for missionary spirit were the first to stab the cold man. . . . [I] would not trust any dam——d set of [Christians] with money or land without having them under bonds.

> Davis Tillson, assistant commissioner of the Freedmen's Bureau for Georgia

John Cole wrote to Edward Williams on September 1, 1866, that he had met Edward Smith in New York City the day before, "just arrived from Cincinnati, bag and baggage, to enter upon the duties of his new field." Cleavie and Gerty had come East, too, but were planning to spend a month or two in New England before setting up housekeeping in New York. The family eventually moved into a house on Ninth Street between Fourth and Fifth avenues in Brooklyn, a city with which Smith had long been familiar through his uncle Cyrus Porter Smith, a longtime resident and former mayor of Brooklyn. Cyrus Porter Smith had also been for many years the managing director of the Union Ferry Company of Brooklyn; his nephew now joined the crowds of commuters on the company's ferries as he traveled from Brooklyn to his work at the AMA office in Manhattan. Like Walt Whitman, who wrote of his own experiences in "Crossing Brooklyn Ferry," Smith soon became familiar with

> The white sails of schooners and sloops, . . . the ships at anchor,
> The sailors at work in the rigging or out astride the spars,
> The round masts, the swinging motion of the hulls, the slender serpentine
> pennants,

The large and small steamers in motion, the pilots in their pilot-houses,
The white wake left by the passage.

John Cole's sister, Ella, who had been Smith's secretary in Cincinnati, also came to New York to work in the office of the AMA.[1]

The New York offices of the association—or "the Rooms" as they were usually called—were located at 53 John Street. Like the headquarters of the Christian Commission in Philadelphia, the Rooms were often filled with boxes and barrels of supplies for the field: books, desks, slates, maps, report forms, building supplies, clothing, and food. Here too, at the "fountainhead," as Michael Strieby called it, were located the association's national staff and its executive committee, largely Congregationalists.[2]

The two secretaries of the association were George Whipple and Michael Strieby. Whipple, then sixty-one years old, had served as secretary since 1846, when the association was founded. He had been committed to the antislavery cause since his student days at Oneida Institute and was one of a group of students who left Lane Seminary in Cincinnati and went to Oberlin College when the seminary trustees forbade any discussion or practice of the students' antislavery principles. He graduated from Oberlin Seminary and was ordained as a Congregational minister, but rather than serving a church he served as principal of Oberlin's preparatory department and, later, as professor of mathematics in the college until he was elected to his position with the AMA.

Whipple's seniority made him the virtual director of the AMA, and his personality put its stamp on the entire organization. It was said of him that he brought to the AMA "not merely a radical championship of the rights of man and an intense conviction of the sin of slavery, but with it a considerate and irenic spirit, a calm and judicial mind." Even though he was too serious to indulge in humor, his associates found him remarkably kind and thoughtful to those who worked with him (though Samuel Hunt may not have agreed with them). His industry was a legend in the association. In the early days, he had sometimes worked until late at night and then wrapped himself in a blanket and slept on a long table in the outer office, rising by four or five o'clock to begin his work again. A resolution at the time of his death called him "a discreet and sleepless friend of the Freedmen." One who knew Whipple well described "his well-knit form and broad shoulders, gray hair—a silver halo above his face—a fine broad forehead, and kindly eyes looking forth from under Websterian eyebrows."[3]

Michael Epaphras Strieby was also an early abolitionist and a graduate of Oberlin College and Seminary. He had come to the AMA in 1864 at the

George Whipple (1805–76), secretary of   Michael Epaphras Strieby (1815–99).
the American Missionary Association   Courtesy of Plymouth Congregational
for thirty years. Courtesy of the Amistad   Church of the United Church of Christ,
Research Center, New Orleans,   Syracuse, New York.
Louisiana.

age of forty-nine, after serving Congregational churches in Mount Vernon, Ohio, and Syracuse, New York. A man of strong convictions, he was said to be "progressive, even radical, and no less wise when radical." "Often misunderstood and criticized, he was more sorry for his critics than angry with them, and in the stormiest sea his attitude of mind was, 'You may sink me if you will, but I will keep my rudder true.'" Strieby was also admired for his administrative ability, which he had demonstrated in organizing Plymouth Congregational Church at Syracuse and in raising a large endowment for Oberlin College.[4]

When Edward Smith joined Whipple and Strieby in New York, he added both vigor and experience to the staff. At the age of thirty-nine he was twenty-two years younger than Whipple and twelve years younger than Strieby, in good health and full of energy. The English wit Sydney Smith once said that Daniel Webster seemed to him to be "much like a steam-engine in trousers." He might well have said the same of Edward Smith. For the past four years Smith had been in nearly constant motion, traveling widely by steamboat and train both in the North and the South. He could have said of his travels what his contemporary Louis Moreau Gottschalk, the widely traveled pianist, said:

"I live on the railroad—my home is somewhere between the baggage car and the last car of the train. . . . The railroad conductors salute me familiarly as one of the employees." Smith's travels in the South during and after the war and the three years he spent teaching in Alabama before the war had made him familiar with a large part of the territory in which the AMA was working for the freedmen. Like Whipple and Strieby, Smith was a skillful administrator; unlike them, he had a firsthand knowledge of the field in which their work was to be done.[5]

Smith's addition to the AMA's national staff also produced some tensions. Smith was as impetuous as Whipple and Strieby were cautious. Whipple was noted for his good judgment, but he was "not apt to make suggestions of new plans," and he was slow in reaching his conclusions about the plans of others—"cautious in weighing testimony, slow in coming to final decisions and utterly immovable in what he believed to be right." Strieby, too, was a man of "calm, well-balanced judgment." Smith's nature was just the opposite; he was overflowing with new plans and seldom deliberated long before proposing them or acting on them. Smith sometimes found it necessary to keep one step ahead of Whipple and Strieby to maintain the freedom to carry out his plans. His family said that, because Strieby "was always preaching *caution, caution,*" Smith once gave him a southern itinerary slower than his real itinerary to ensure that Strieby's letters would not reach him and the cautious instructions of the secretaries in New York would not stand in the way of the actions he wanted to take.[6]

Within a week of his move from Cincinnati to New York, Smith was in Washington, D.C., at the headquarters of the Freedmen's Bureau, where he was commissioned to visit eleven cities in four southern states as an unpaid agent of the bureau. As a bureau agent, he was "so far deemed in the military service of the United States as to be under the military jurisdiction, and entitled to the military protection of the government." He was also entitled to free government transportation while he was serving as an agent, something that was regularly available to teachers but not to the officials of the associations that sponsored them. Smith's southern trip was only the beginning of his association with the Freedmen's Bureau; over the next four years he would work closely with the officials of the bureau in planning and overseeing the AMA's educational work in the South.[7]

The Freedmen's Bureau was the federal government's answer to the needs of the freed slaves. Both the War Department and the Treasury Department had carried on work among freedmen during the war, and there was some controversy over which department should conduct the work after the war. In the end the Freedmen's Bureau was lodged in the War Department when it was created in March 1865, and many of its officials were blue-coated army officers. The new agency was given the full title of the Bureau of Refugees, Freedmen, and Abandoned Lands and with it broad powers to deal with white Unionists who had been driven from their homes in the South (refugees), the freed slaves (freedmen), and the lands whose owners had voluntarily left to aid the Confederacy (abandoned lands).[8]

Like any new agency, the Freedmen's Bureau was flooded with applications for positions. Some of the applications were from persons who had served in the Christian Commission and were now "out of a place." They were men who had seen the needs of the freedmen and who thought of the bureau's work as an extension of their own work during the war. Bishop Matthew Simpson had prophesied at the commission's final anniversary celebration that its work would go on in other forms. "Beloved workers, as we part we go to other fields. The spirit of the Commission will still live. . . . There are other fields. . . . Freedmen are to be educated. The ignorant everywhere are to be instructed. A great work is before us." At least three men who served as officials of the Christian Commission obtained positions with the Freedmen's Bureau. General Clinton Fisk, who was a member of the commission's executive committee, became the bureau's assistant commissioner in Nashville. Samuel Ashley, the minister Smith had replaced as John Cole's assistant in the Army of the Potomac, became the bureau's unsalaried superintendent of education for the southern district of North Carolina (as well as an agent of the AMA), and the Reverend Thomas K. Noble, the Christian Commission's agent in the cavalry of the Army of the Potomac, became the bureau's superintendent of education in Kentucky.[9]

Educating the freedmen, which attracted men like Ashley and Noble, was but one of the bureau's responsibilities, alongside such duties as locating missing persons, transporting refugees, settling claims, distributing rations, providing medical care, overseeing contracts between freedmen and white planters, and acting as judges where civil courts were either unavailable or unfair. Education was not mentioned in the act that created the bureau. But in one of his earliest statements, the commissioner of the bureau assured the societies working among the freedmen that education would not be neglected. "The utmost facility will be offered to benevolent and religious organizations and State authorities in the maintenance of good schools for refugees and freedmen until a system of free schools can be supported by the reorganized local governments. . . . It is not my purpose to supersede the benevolent agencies already engaged in the work of education, but to systematize and facilitate them." It was not long, too, before the officers of the bureau learned from experience that providing blacks with schools was easier than providing

General Oliver Otis Howard
(1830–1909). Howard met
Edward Smith in Tennessee
during the Civil War. The two
men formed a friendship that
lasted until Smith's death.
Courtesy of the Library of
Congress.

them with land or justice, and the bureau put more and more of its efforts
into schools with good results. Within six years the bureau had furnished
more than $5 million for freedmen's education and could point to eleven
colleges and universities created for blacks, sixty-one normal schools, and
hundreds of elementary and high schools. The financial support given by
the Freedmen's Bureau was a major factor in the success of the AMA in its
educational work among the freedmen.[10]

Some of the societies working among the freedmen complained that the
AMA received more than its share of the bureau's funds, and their complaints had some merit. Everyone recognized that the AMA was one of the
largest benevolent societies at work in the South and deserved a large share
of the bureau's assistance. The association was also willing to invest large
sums of its own money in the work, and the bureau's policy was to match
funds as far as possible. "The society which undertook the most," the bureau's commissioner said, "in that manner received most." But the AMA also
profited by its close ties to key bureau personnel, many of whom, like most
of the officers of the AMA, were Congregationalists.[11]

President Lincoln's choice for commissioner of the bureau was General
Oliver Otis Howard, and after Lincoln's assassination the War Department

assigned Howard to the bureau. The thirty-four-year-old general was not only a Congregationalist but also a committed Christian, known to his soldiers as "Old Prayer Book" and to many others as the "Christian General." Howard's brother Rowland was a Congregational minister, and the general, who had once thought of studying for the ministry, was at ease in the company of the clergy. The friendship he had formed with Smith in the West blossomed as they worked together for the freedmen. At least twice while Smith was in Cincinnati, he had seen Howard, and after Smith's move to New York, he was a frequent visitor in the bureau's headquarters in Washington as Howard was often a visitor in the AMA's Rooms in New York. George Whipple, too, grew close to Howard and had easy access to him when he visited Washington.[12]

Another Congregationalist with a prominent position in the Freedmen's Bureau was the Reverend John Watson Alvord. Alvord was a contemporary of George Whipple, who, like Whipple, had studied at Lane Seminary and then transferred with the other antislavery "Lane Rebels" to Oberlin. After his graduation from Oberlin—in the same class as Whipple—Alvord served as superintendent of six black schools in Cincinnati and boarded with black families because no white families would take him into their homes. He later served Congregational churches in Ohio, Connecticut, and Massachusetts before becoming secretary of the American Tract Society at Boston. During the Civil War, he went to Washington and then to the front to distribute the society's literature to the army, remaining with the men, the society said, "on their marches, in battles, and in retreats, at all seasons of the year, and in all circumstances." He also assisted the freedmen in Savannah, Georgia, in establishing their own school system, with a black board of trustees and black teachers. In 1865 General Howard, who considered Alvord "a great and good man—great because he is good, *and because he is practical*," appointed him the bureau's inspector of finances and schools, and soon after Smith began his work in New York, Alvord became the bureau's general superintendent of schools.[13]

General Howard and John Alvord were the most prominent Congregationalists in the Freedmen's Bureau, but they were not the only ones. Eliphalet Whittlesey, a member of Howard's military staff before becoming the bureau's assistant commissioner in North Carolina and then its acting inspector general in Washington, was a Congregational minister who had once taught at Howard's alma mater, Bowdoin College. Both Whittlesey and George W. Balloch, the bureau's chief disbursing officer, were actively involved in the First Congregational Church in Washington, of which Alvord and Howard were members.[14]

John Watson Alvord (1807–80), superintendent of schools for the Bureau of Refugees, Freedmen, and Abandoned Lands. Courtesy of the Massachusetts Commandery, Military Order of the Loyal Legion and the U.S. Army Military History Institute, Carlisle Barracks, Pennsylvania.

There were still other ties between the Freedmen's Bureau and the AMA. John Mercer Langston, the black lawyer who replaced Alvord as the bureau's inspector of schools, had studied at Oberlin and while there had lived in George Whipple's home. Alexander P. Ketchum, the bureau's adjutant general and Howard's chief of staff in Washington, was the son of Edgar Ketchum, a prominent New York lawyer who was the treasurer of the AMA and who later represented Howard when he was investigated by the House Committee on Education and Labor. The Reverend John P. Bardwell, the AMA's agent in Mississippi, also served as a salaried agent of the bureau, aiding other bureau officials in the establishment of schools. General Howard's brother Charles served in the bureau until 1869, when he became the AMA secretary in Chicago. At the request of the AMA, the bureau continued his service as inspector of schools without pay after he went to Chicago. When

Charles Howard left Washington, he took with him Selden N. Clark, another bureau official, who became an assistant treasurer of the AMA. There were still others who had an allegiance both to the bureau and to the AMA, and the result of all these ties was that the AMA had an unrivaled entrée to the officials and the funds of the Freedmen's Bureau.[15]

The assistance the bureau could give to the AMA and the other benevolent societies was limited at first. The bureau had no appropriated funds during its first year. It gave military protection, provided transportation for teachers and supplies, and permitted teachers to purchase government rations or provided the rations when necessary, but the only buildings it could provide for schools or dwellings were surplus government buildings or buildings obtained with the rent from abandoned lands, and when abandoned property was restored to its owners under President Johnson's direction, that source of assistance diminished rapidly. But in July 1866, Congress directed the bureau to cooperate with the benevolent societies and authorized it to rent or lease school buildings whenever the societies would provide the teachers and the means of instruction.

To fund the bureau's educational activities, Congress gave it the use of all former Confederate property as well as any proceeds from the property's lease or sale. In addition, Congress made an initial appropriation of half a million dollars for the rent and repair of school and asylum buildings. Although Congress restricted the appropriated money to rent and repairs, the bureau also used it to assist with new buildings, simply listing its contributions as "repair" money. No money was available for teachers' salaries; the benevolent societies that supplied the teachers were also expected to pay them.[16]

The price the AMA and the other societies paid for the bureau's assistance was to become part of a vast government bureaucracy that put superintendents in the field to coordinate and standardize freedmen's education and required voluminous reports about schools and funds. John William De Forest, an army officer who served as an agent of the bureau in South Carolina, described the system of army bookkeeping as "a laborious and complicated perfection. . . . As I scribbled over these acres of vouchers . . . I decided that the Romans conquered the world because they had no paper, and I wished that we had one of them at the head of the War Department." But by working with what one of the AMA superintendents called the bureau's "ponderous machinery," the AMA gained at least $213,753 in federal funds for its work during the bureau's brief life.[17]

George Whipple was at first unsure about the wisdom of working with the Freedmen's Bureau. He told his former classmate John Alvord that, although the AMA was not denominational and had every right to share in bureau activities, it was decidedly religious and could not subject its missionary teachers to "any body of men not of a religious character, and we can not separate the educational from the religious element." He was willing to assist the bureau only in ways that did not "diminish the efficiency of our own efforts for the Freedmen or involve our surrender of the control of our missionaries, or of the collecting field thrown open to us by our *Christian* friends." But with sympathetic religious men at the helm of the bureau and government funds available almost for the asking, Whipple's initial concerns quickly vanished, and he was soon cooperating wholeheartedly with the bureau.[18]

SMITH'S SOUTHERN TRIP as an unpaid agent of the Freedmen's Bureau was made in September and October 1866. It took him to Norfolk, Fortress Monroe, and Hampton in Virginia; Beaufort, Wilmington, Raleigh, and Goldsboro in North Carolina; Augusta and Atlanta in Georgia; Charleston, South Carolina; and to other, smaller communities as he made preparations for the new school year and laid plans for the association's future work.

Hampton, Virginia, near Fortress Monroe, was the site of the association's earliest wartime work. When the town was abandoned by its white citizens early in the war, thousands of black "contrabands" settled there. The AMA sent the Reverend Lewis Lockwood to Hampton in September 1861 as its first missionary among the freedmen, and it was at Hampton that Mary Peake, a free black teacher, conducted the AMA's first school for freedmen. More than fifty AMA missionaries served in the area during the war, and by the war's end, the AMA had established six schools among the forty thousand freedmen in and around Hampton and twice as many schools across the Roads in Norfolk.[19]

At Hampton, Smith met with the bureau superintendent, Samuel Chapman Armstrong. Armstrong was twenty-seven years old, the son of missionaries to Hawaii, a graduate of Williams College, and the commander of the Eighth and Ninth regiments of U.S. Colored Troops during the war. The AMA had proposed to establish a normal school at Hampton, a plan with which Armstrong was in agreement. Smith had come to consult with him about the purchase of a large farm, the Wood farm or Little Scotland, the site of Camp Hamilton during the war, that the AMA hoped to obtain at a cost of $20,000. Part of the farm would be sold off to freedmen to help meet the expense of the purchase, but the AMA would keep the "*best half*" with the buildings and the front lots for its school. Smith wrote from Hampton to tell George Whipple that the prospects for getting the farm looked good, but that even if the association did not get that property, "with the help which we can get now from the Bureau, this is undoubtedly *the* time to strike for the Butler *Normal School* & College." [20]

Cleavie Smith said later that when she first visited Hampton, Armstrong told her he would never forget the hour he had spent with her husband on the roof of one of the Hampton buildings, contemplating the future of the school. As Cleavie told the story: "The land was at that date offered for sale; $9,000 must be paid down or the land could not be kept for the General's work. 'Shall we take it?' they asked each other again and again. Then they walked silently on the roof for many minutes, when Mr. Smith broke the silence by saying, 'General, take the land.' The General said, 'Where's the money?' 'Take the land,' said Mr. Smith, 'the money will come.' Before the day for payment arrived," Cleavie said, "a legacy of $10,000 was left to be invested in work for the colored race." The money Cleavie referred to was given in the spring of 1867 when Josiah King, one of the executors of the Avery Fund, visited Hampton and agreed to contribute $10,000 through the AMA toward the purchase of the Wood farm. [21]

Smith suggested to Whipple that the association pay Armstrong something in addition to his bureau salary to serve as the AMA's agent at Hampton, and he spoke enthusiastically about Armstrong's future there.

> I am persuaded that the Gen[l] is the man to make Butler school & college his life work & with God[']s blessing to make it a grand success. His heart is in it. He is thoroughly educated for it[.] Has had a peculiar training in this very direction[.] In fact grew up & was the first graduate in just such a school in the Sandwich Islands. He combines *enthusiasm* & persistency in a wonderful degree. He has had & has now offers, thro' Pres. Hopkins[']s influence, of fine positions in two western colleges. Rightly managed I think he will commit himself to this work, both to raising funds for it & supervising it for the next six months or a year & after that leave every thing for this *one* thing & make it a great thing. [22]

Smith was also making arrangements for the opening of schools in nearby Norfolk and Portsmouth: preparing school buildings and accommodations for the teachers and providing for the superintendence of the schools and the employment of black assistants. About one-fourth of the teaching was to be done by the assistants, who were to be recruited from the pupils in the schools and were to receive at least one hour's "drill in the theory of teaching every day in connection with a Normal class to be gathered out of the High School." In return for their teaching, the assistants would receive $10 a month and free tuition in the normal class. [23]

Smith insisted that the pupils in the schools pay tuition of fifty cents a month. The teachers would be given discretion to waive all or part of the tuition in cases of extreme poverty, but Smith said that both teachers and pupils should understand that "the pay^t of the tuition is the *rule* & the free scholars must be so rare as only to make the exceptions of the rule & those whose tuition is *entirely* free sh^d be very *very* rare. I would bring the tuition down to ten (10) cents a month for the very poor rather than let them feel that they were receiving an *entire gratuity* every month." Smith was not alone in feeling that it was a mistake to give an education to anyone who could pay something toward it; all across the South blacks regularly paid substantial amounts for their education. John Alvord reported about this same time that "15,248 colored pupils pay tuition, the amount of which per month is $11,377.03; and these self-supporting pupils are mainly from the recently emancipated population." [24]

In North Carolina, Smith arranged for the purchase of lots for school buildings in Beaufort and Morehead City and for an outstation "up the Sound." A new lot adjoining the AMA school in Beaufort was for a "white school." "If we can get the poor whites to come into the same yard & to the same teachers with the col^d people it will be a great step ahead & after a while will either compel the Beaufort people to provide public schools or will bring them into our high school." If the white people refused to come into the school, as he feared they would, Smith proposed that the Beaufort building be used to create a freedmen's school to be called the "Washburne Seminary." [25]

A school building in Wilmington was nearing completion, and on the bureau's recommendation, Smith laid plans for a second building. He also rented a house for a teachers' home, arranged for an addition to the orphanage, and investigated the possibility of building schoolhouses at Raleigh, Fayetteville, Smithville, and other outlying locations.

To meet the expenses of these ventures, the AMA would have to advance funds that would later be reimbursed by the Freedmen's Bureau. Smith had an interview with the Reverend F. A. Fiske, the bureau's superintendent of education in North Carolina and found him willing to endorse the association's bills for payment by the bureau, although he expressed surprise "that Genl Howard would authorize that mode of furnishing sch^l Houses." (His surprise was presumably at the promise of payment for new buildings when Congress had authorized money only for rent or repairs.) Smith was eager to move ahead with the buildings and asked George Whipple to respond quickly to his proposals. "It is almost so much money put at our disposal by the bureau," Smith wrote. "What is the limit we can go? . . . Can we put $25,000 into this fund? Will it not be right & best to *borrow* for this purpose?" [26]

Whipple, however, was appalled by the magnitude of Smith's plans. He told Michael Strieby that "if Smith goes on as he has done, he will swamp us inevitably." Letters were arriving one after the other from officials requesting funds to carry out Smith's plans. The letters also revealed some tensions in the wake of Smith's travels. Samuel Ashley, who may still have borne some resentment toward Smith for taking his place at City Point, complained that Smith had acted without consulting him in returning a bureau barracks Ashley had been counting on for a school. "Why was not I consulted before he gave a decision which gives me a heap of hard perplexing work to do over again. M^r. S. says 'buy a lot and build'. Easy to say but hard to do." "M^r. Smith thinks the Bureau will pay. Doubtful but at any rate the expenditure must be authorised by you. Shall I proceed? . . . If you say that these matters are taken out of my hands and given to S., *all right*, his orders shall be executed tho involving more expense & time than my own." Ashley and Whipple both were rapidly learning about the impulsive and determined nature of the man the AMA had made its general field agent.[27]

When Smith reached Augusta, Georgia, he found a circular letter from the secretaries in New York, which he called their "not a dollar" letter, stressing the lack of funds available to the association. He told Whipple that the letter "jumps out at me from every P. O. window where I inquire for letters," but he also insisted that he had not seen the letter until after he finished his work at Wilmington and Raleigh. Fearing that Whipple had already canceled plans he had made for a high school at Raleigh, Smith told him he was convinced from his conversations with bureau officials that the bills the association submitted would be approved in the field and sent to General Howard for final action, "and there is not the least doubt that he will approve & order them paid. . . . Genl Howard distinctly approved of that method. . . . & said if any of the [Assistant] Com^rs refused[,] to let a second application be made direct to him." The only possible hindrance to his plans would be if Howard were removed from office, and that did not seem likely to Smith. "Even A[ndrew] J[ohnson] is not yet demented." Smith was sure that from three-fourths to seven-eighths of the expenditures the association made would be reimbursed by the bureau.[28]

On his way to Augusta, Smith had passed through Charleston, where he met with Francis L. Cardozo, the superintendent of the AMA's Charleston schools. The son of a mother of mixed black and Indian ancestry and a Jewish father, Cardozo was one of the best-educated blacks in the South. After graduating from the University of Glasgow with honors, he studied theology both in Edinburgh and in London and then became the pastor of the Temple Street Congregational Church in New Haven, Connecticut. In July 1865,

Francis L. Cardozo (1837–1903). Edward Smith said of him, "He is quite popular among his own color & is noted for his scholarship, culture & gentlemanly deportment." Courtesy of Margaret Cardozo Holmes.

he had returned to his native Charleston to work in the AMA's schools. "I like *M^r. Cardosa very much*," Smith wrote. "I think such a man is to be congratulated *for his color*. His heart & his ambition are all in the direction of the teaching profession."[29]

Charleston was one of the cities where the AMA planned to establish normal schools, and Smith was enthusiastic about the prospects for such a school.

> "4000 col^d children in Charleston to be educated. The large free col^d element in C. makes it one of the most desirable points for a Normal school. These free col^d men have always maintained schools among themselves. Consequently there are from *one hundred to one hundred & fifty* pupils now in school in C. who are more advanced than our best *ten or fifteen* pupils at other points & are ready to enter upon a higher course of study than our ordinary schools can well furnish. Probably four fifths of these are from the *free* families & are in all respects more promising for teachers than the average of the children of *Freedmen*. The other fifth is of the most promising of the Freedmen. Sixty of these advanced pupils are now under the instruction of Mr. Ca[r]dosa. He is quite popular among his own color & is noted for his scholarship, culture & gentlemanly deportment.[30]

Smith said it was proposed to put "leading col^d men & some one or two white citizens" on the school's board of trustees but to keep the title to the

buildings with the AMA "for the present." He thought a normal school at
Charleston could graduate twenty-five teachers a year and in five years one
hundred a year if that many were willing to become teachers. He admitted
that the school would be expensive, but he said that the officers of the Freedmen's Bureau were willing to help erect a building and that both the white and
the black citizens were willing to help with the finances. Smith told Whipple
that "*it must be done.* I say that much till I get at least *one more* of those letters
from 53 [John Street]." He said the normal school was Cardozo's goal, too,
"& he is willing to make it his life work. I tried to get him to look more to the
ministry, but he is decided in his preference & *taste* to be a teacher & it will
be best I think to work him in his chosen harness." [31]

A black Congregational church had been established in Charleston, and
Smith spoke to the members about their future and asked them to form a
committee to tell him "what they wished us to do for them." The committee reported that it wanted a pastor and that the first choice was Cardozo.
If Cardozo was not willing to take the position, the committee would be
glad to have any other good man, preferably a black, but "a good white man
will do." Smith advised Whipple that "this is the best nucleus for a good
Cong[regationa]l Church that I have seen in the South & I think we are bound
to send them a pastor. . . . We owe it to the Congregationalists to take care
of this their only colored child." But he warned Whipple that they would require a capable minister; "they are a congregation that will ask for something
besides chaff." [32]

Smith concluded his report about Charleston by teasing the overly cautious Whipple, saying that he also had a plan for a high school building in
Augusta. "As usual it is a first class plan[,] indeed the very best . . . I will
write from *Atlanta* tomorrow & by that time I hope to have one or two more
first class projects to lay before you. I am very well & as happy as I can be
with such splendid openings for good work & such piteous calls to which my
heart says yes & when I read the [letter?] from N. York my lips say No." [33]

Detained in Atlanta by illness, which he described as "a five days hauling up for repairs," Smith wrote an appeal to the bureau's superintendent
of education in Georgia for funds for the association's schools in Atlanta:
$2,400 to enlarge and repair a surplus commissary building to serve as a
school for five hundred pupils, $200 rent for a school building the associa-
tion had constructed on the east side of the city, $2,000 for a new school on a
lot the association owned on the west side of the city, and money to purchase
seven hundred school desks. The money was needed, he said, because of the
destruction of suitable buildings during the war. "No colored church in the

City survived the Siege and destruction of Atlanta." The Methodists had re-built their church, and a large school had been held in it during the last year, but the white trustees of the lot on which the church was built had recently taken over the building. "This leaves no *native* School accommodations for Freedmen in Atlanta."[34]

The AMA lot on the west side of the city was one Smith had discovered for sale the same day he appealed for funds to build on it. "Just what we want for a school lot," he said, and bought it. He told Whipple about the purchase, saying, "you must remember that I did not find a *single copy* of that letter at Atlanta," meaning Whipple's "not a dollar" letter. "If Gen. Howard & Gen[l] Tillson say yes to that extra $2000 we can put up quite a snug house for that money. If not, then we have a *lot.* It cost only $750 & will sell for more *any*time."[35]

Smith also sent an appeal directly to Major General Davis Tillson, the bureau's assistant commissioner in Georgia, asking the bureau to rent the land the association had bought in Atlanta for an orphanage. The bureau's rent money would enable the association to replace its tents with permanent buildings and to house fifty or seventy-five orphans at a time while seeking homes for them, in that way saving in a year's time "from five hundred to six hundred children from suffering & put them in a way to be well cared for without further expense to the Government." Smith reported to Whipple from Atlanta that "everything promises well for us here this year[.] Schools open finely. No place in the South so full of life & industry as Atlanta. Everybody is building a house for himself & his neighbor."[36]

On his return trip, Smith met with General Tillson in Augusta. Smith had high hopes for the meeting. He said that Georgia had more Confederate property than all the other states put together, property that Congress had put "at absolute disposal for educational purposes." But the interview was not as successful as Smith hoped. He reported to Whipple:

> There is but *one* school in Georgia that is not ours except those at Savannah & there we hold the ground mainly. At Augusta[,] Atlanta, Milledgeville[,] Macon & Savannah we ought to have school buildings worth not less than six to ten thousand dollars & I hope to accomplish it. With almost any other Ass[t] Com[r] that I have met it could be done. But Gen[l] T. is a *Georgian* by adoption. He goes into cotton raising near Savannah in Dec[r] & has about the same regard for negro elevation that planters generally entertain. In these circumstances I have tho[t] best not to push our requests now for Macon or Savannah or Augusta[,] at least not until I have had an interview with Gen[l] Howard.
>
> Gen[l] T. had not acted on my request for the Orphan Home. . . . He does not

believe in such Asylums. Says he can give away a thousand children in a week to
planters if he had them. We shall probably have to appeal to Gen¹ Howard over
Tillson on this matter of orphans.³⁷

Tillson did endorse Smith's requests for funds for the schools in Atlanta
but asked for pledges that the buildings would be used "perpetually for educational purposes." According to Smith, Tillson said "he had always found
that people who made loud claims for missionary spirit were the first to stab
the cold man & that he would not trust any dam——d set of [Christians] with
money or land without having them under bonds." After meeting with Tillson, Smith decided it would be necessary to stop in Washington on his return
trip "to see the Gen¹." But he was ill again, and on the advice of a physician
he returned by sea directly to New York. His illness proved not to be serious,
and two weeks later he was traveling again, this time to attend the AMA's
annual meeting in Galesburg, Illinois.³⁸

A month after Smith returned from the South, he made his trip to Washington. Despite Smith's optimism about the bureau's willingness to fund his
purchases, there had been difficulty getting money from the bureau both
for buildings and for transportation. Soon after Smith's visit to Washington,
however, the authorizations for payments began to flow from bureau headquarters. It was not long before Smith began to make his requests directly
to Howard rather than going through channels. He wrote to Howard to ask
for funds to complete a schoolhouse in Camden, Delaware, "the first school
house for colored children in Delaware," a request that was approved, and
he asked for rent on the Fisk School property at Nashville, a request that
was referred to the assistant commissioner in Tennessee and denied. Even
though Smith continued to correspond with bureau officials in the field,
his approaches to Howard had ruffled some feathers among them. Samuel
Ashley reported from North Carolina that he had discovered "a good deal
of sensitiveness" among the bureau officials in Raleigh "as to the *manner* in
which requests for appropriations have come from the A.M.A. The officers
at Raleigh feel that instead of coming down from Washington to them [the?]
requests should go up through them. This is the military order." ³⁹

In all these activities, Smith was looking beyond the immediate needs of
the freedmen to their future welfare. In one of his letters to F. A. Fiske, the
bureau superintendent of education in North Carolina, Smith expressed the
goal of his many appeals to the bureau for funds. He said the AMA was
not simply hoping to finance its work among the blacks that year (which in
another place he called "the most important year of their history as a race")
but was "laying foundations and actually establishing an educational work for

all time." On another occasion, Smith wrote to a friend, "I agree with you in the greatness of the work to be done. When the rose color is all out & we settle down really to lift the barbarism that has crushed these poor people the work will assume its proper proportions & we shall find it is not a slight thing to feed our enthusiasm upon for a year or two but a life work for us & an heritage for our children."[40]

14

Teachers Who Dared

Whenever it is written—and I hope it will be—the part that the Yankee teachers played in the education of the Negroes immediately after the war will make one of the most thrilling parts of the history of this country.

Booker T. Washington, *Up from Slavery*

Apart from his work in securing land and buildings for the AMA and funds to pay for them, Smith's duties as general field agent were concerned mainly with the association's teachers. The AMA had 353 missionaries in the South in 1866, most of them teachers. A year later there would be 465 and, by 1870, 525. A circular prepared in New York before Smith arrived described the qualities the AMA sought in its teachers. They should have a "missionary spirit. . . . No one should seek, accept, or be recommended for, an appointment who is not prepared to endure hardness as a good soldier of Jesus Christ. . . . None should go . . . who are influenced by either romantic or mercenary motives; who go for the poetry or the pay; who wish to go South because they have failed at the North." The teachers should be in good health. "This is not a *hygienic* association, to help invalids try a change of air, or travel at others' expense." They should have the energy necessary not only for teaching but for work outside the classroom, "to seek to do good for Christ and his poor, by ministering to the physical wants of the destitute; by family visitation and instruction; in Bible reading and distribution; in Sabbath School teaching and in christian missionary labors generally." Culture was also needed, as were common sense, good personal habits, and successful experience in teaching. No one would be commissioned who was addicted to the use of opium or tobacco or who was "not pledged to total abstinence from intoxicating drinks." Preference was given to applicants whose support was pledged by an individual, a Sabbath school, a church, or some other organization.[1]

Smith was in frequent correspondence with applicants for teaching positions and would ask them in an informal way to provide him with their credentials. He answered an inquiry from two women in Connecticut by writing to one: "Will you please allow me to ask a few questions respecting yourself and your friend. Y'r age. Y'r ex[perience] in teaching. Whether you sing. How much hardship you can endure. Whether you two could go alone into a col^d community [to?] live and labor? Please also give me the name of the pastor of the church or churches to which you both belong."[2]

A variety of motives brought the teachers to the AMA: the need for employment; a longing to escape the limitations of life at home; a fondness for travel; a desire to follow in the steps of their soldier fathers or brothers; a concern for the freed slaves—one teacher confided to Smith, "Father says I have 'negro on the brain.'" A primary motive, however, both of the AMA and of those who became its teachers, was the missionary impulse. At the small salaries the association paid, Smith said, "it is very rarely we secure a teacher . . . who does not go with some sort of a missionary idea, sometimes mistaken, nearly always genuine."[3]

The teachers were earnest Christians, and despite the strong ties between the AMA and Congregationalism, they represented a variety of denominations. On one occasion, Smith told John R. Lewis, the assistant commissioner of the Freedmen's Bureau for Georgia, that even though ten-elevenths of the association's support for its work in that state came from Congregational churches, only half the teachers it had sent to Georgia were Congregationalists. So little attention was paid to denomination, he said, that in some of the teachers' homes "the teachers have not discovered the church relations of one another after a year's companionship in the same family and schoolroom."[4]

Smith spoke to the teachers about their work in religious terms, in language as familiar to most of the teachers as it was to him.

> We feel that your work with all its toil and privation, is a work to be coveted and honored. In your walks among His poor, you surely find the foot-steps of the Master, and not unfrequently, walking by your side, is "the form of one like unto the Son of God." Prayers going up out of such close sympathy of labor and love with Our Lord, will indeed be precious.
>
> At every meeting of the Executive Committee we hold a prayer meeting with special reference to the trials and wants of our fellow laborers in the field. We always remember you at our family altar, in the "still hour," at the church prayer meeting and in the monthly concert, praying always that the work of the Lord may be your joy, and the joy of the Lord your strength.[5]

As important as their missionary zeal was, many of the men and women who went out to teach the freedmen also shared another impelling motive: the desire to "northernize" the South. Union soldiers had often expressed amazement at what they considered the backwardness of the South. "The country is behind the times 100 years," one New York soldier wrote, and a Massachusetts soldier said, "it will probably be more than one generation before any of these slave-cursed states will rival New England." But other soldiers were convinced that the South's deficiencies could easily be overcome by Yankee enterprise. "In the hands of New England people," a soldier from Maine wrote about Virginia, "this country might be converted into a garden." "It is certainly time," an officer stationed in Tennessee concluded, "that something was done to revolutionize this entire country, in fact to teach it all that it needs to make it a civilized, intelligent and enlightened Christian community."[6]

Many northerners, New Englanders particularly, were confident that the cure for the ills the soldiers had discovered in the South was education. The Yankees had long believed in the power of education, and the freedmen's desire for learning confirmed to them that what the South most needed was teachers and schools. The teacher in John Greenleaf Whittier's "Snowbound" was typical of many of the teachers who went south for the AMA.

> Large-brained, clear-eyed, of such as he
> Shall Freedom's young apostles be,
> Who, following in War's bloody trail,
> Shall every lingering wrong assail;
> All chains from limb and spirit strike,
> Uplift the black and white alike;
> Scatter before their swift advance
> The darkness and the ignorance,
> The pride, the lust, the squalid sloth,
> Which nurtured Treason's monstrous growth,
> Made murder pastime, and the hell
> Of prison-torture possible;
> The cruel lie of caste refute,
> Old forms remould, and substitute
> For Slavery's lash the freeman's will,
> For blind routine, wise-handed skill;
> A school-house plant on every hill[.]

One of the AMA teachers expressed the same vision more prosaically when he said, "Now are the golden moments to New Englandize the South by educating and Christianizing the colored people."[7]

The teachers who went south for the AMA were both men and women and both black and white. The majority were white women. They were largely the well-educated daughters of farmers and professionals in New England and the Midwest, most commonly in their late twenties, single, and experienced as teachers in the common schools. W. E. B. Du Bois described them in his eloquent way as "women who dared." "Behind the mists of rain and rapine waved the calico dresses of women who dared, and after the hoarse mouthings of the field guns rang the rhythm of the alphabet. Rich and poor they were, serious and curious. Bereaved now of a father, now of a brother, now of more than these, they came seeking a life work in planting New England schoolhouses among the white and black of the South." The women showed their devotion by working for salaries that rarely exceeded $15 a month; male teachers and missionaries usually received more.[8]

Although the teachers were commonly referred to as "Yankee school-marms," one-sixth of the 399 teachers commissioned during Smith's first seven months in New York were men, and by 1870 nearly one-fourth of those commissioned were men. An official sent by the assistant commissioner of the Freedmen's Bureau in Texas to confer with Whipple, Strieby, and Smith about teachers for Texas reported that the association would attempt to see that one-fourth of the teachers supplied were males, although he added that "the experience of the past has shown great difficulty in obtaining *competent, moral men,* white or black as teachers." (He also offered his opinion that "the officers at New York are pure men, actuated by the most undoubted piety, and love of mission enterprises, and that they possess in the fullest sense, the *confidence and regard of all evangelical christians throughout the country, and good men everywhere.*")[9]

The AMA's first teacher of freedmen had been a free black woman, Mary Peake, and blacks continued to volunteer as teachers. "I have felt a strong conviction of duty," one of them wrote. "I am bound to that ignorant, degraded, long enslaved race, by the ties of love and consanguinity; they are . . . my people." At first the number of blacks commissioned by the AMA was small, but by 1870 nearly one-fourth of the teachers were black, and by 1877 the association had employed at least 467 blacks, 293 of them men and more than a third of them products of AMA normal schools or classes.[10]

The AMA prized black missionaries. Commissioning blacks as teachers and pastors confirmed the association's belief in the abilities of blacks. It was also cheaper to send black men and women to the field, their board often being provided at no cost by the freedmen they served, and it was thought that blacks could be sent more safely than whites to "outposts" away from military protection. But valuable as blacks were, they too had to satisfy the association's stringent religious, moral, and educational requirements. One man with a "great desire to instruct my people" was refused a commission by the AMA because he was not a church member. Another man, capable of doing the work, was not recommended for a commission because he was "too careless and dissolute in his habits. He both *smokes* and *swears*." Lucy Stanton Day, a teacher from Cleveland, Ohio, who had been the first black to graduate from Oberlin College's Ladies' Course, was refused when she applied for a teaching position because she was separated from her husband, William Howard Day. When Robert Harris, the association's superintendent in Fayetteville, North Carolina, and himself black, wanted to employ "a native of this place" as an assistant, he arranged for the assistant's salary to be paid by the local freedmen's aid society and did not request a commission from the AMA because, as he told Smith, "these native teachers can not begin to fulfill the requirements of our Society."[11]

Black, white, male, or female, the teachers were individuals, and Smith accepted them as they were and described them candidly and vividly to their superintendents. "Miss S[tansbury]," he wrote, "is made upon her own pattern, somewhat rigid in her views in life, but full of work & will be unhappy & make you so, unless her hands & heart are kept full." He described a woman at Alexandria, Virginia, as "good in her way but perhaps somewhat peculiar" and a black teacher as "a plucky colored girl, daughter of Rev. Mr. Henson, pastor of [the] Baptist Ch[urch] in Norfolk." He wrote to Edmund A. Ware to say that he had "shipped this day, per Steamer 'Monterey', on Gov't. Transportation, one (1) ex soldier, one armed, in good condition, about twenty five (25) years of age. He was one of our teachers at Hampton last year. He is a good fellow, education fair-to middling, common school. He can make himself useful at almost anything and is ready for it." Smith offered another former soldier to a school in Georgia. "We can send a col'd man to that 'log school house' of yours—a one armed soldier, who writes tolerably well & I suppose is proportionately educated. This is the best we can do for you." He described another man he was sending to Georgia: "W. F. Wentworth, who goes on his own account to Dalton. We commission him and he pays his own way. He is a good little fellow without much weight, more enthusiasm than perseverance but will do some good." (Whatever good he did, Wentworth stayed in Dalton less than six months.)[12]

Smith and his clerks obtained transportation for the teachers at government expense, the Freedmen's Bureau having agreed to provide transportation for teachers of freedmen. The teachers from New England and New York State often passed through the Rooms in New York City on their way to the field to pick up their transportation orders and to receive instructions about their assignments. Smith was willing to make some accommodation for the preferences of the teachers when he assigned them to their posts, but many of them simply accepted their "marching orders" and went wherever they were assigned. "I am ready *now*," one woman wrote, "and willing to go to Wilmington or any other place where God wills and His providences direct me." Another woman said, "I received your letter informing me of my appointment to Beaufort, which I accept as coming from the Lord."[13]

Teachers assigned to cities were usually housed in the association's mission homes, which were operated by matrons under the supervision of the local superintendents. The mission homes were meant to provide companionship for the teachers and a model home for the freedmen, but they were instead often sources of turmoil. The teachers, living in close quarters in a strange environment, irritated one another, quarreled over questions of religion, morality, and social behavior, and struggled over authority within the home. As one woman who was planning to go south to teach told Smith, "I prefer going to a place entirely alone than to go where there are a number of Teachers; for I have observed that w[h]ere a number live together there is more or less trouble." Smith's own observation was that "*Necessarily* life in a Mission home is a perpetual cross bearing."[14]

The difficulties among the teachers frequently required Smith's intervention. In his dealings with them, he followed the scriptural model of "speaking the truth in love." He answered the complaints of one teacher, Frederick Sawtell, about his missionary associates by writing:

> When you say that Miss Hart & Miss Abbott are not worthy of the work they have undertaken you show very plainly that y'r judg^t of persons is very much influenced by *personal* considerations. You are young yet & one of the most important lessons you have to learn is that others may think & feel & act very differently from y'r judg^t of what is expedient or even right and still be very good people and *perhaps* all the better for the peculiar position they seem to you to hold.
>
> This will read a little unkindly perhaps from one who has given you such tokens of estimation & confidence, but I am satisfied to wait y'r more experienced judg^t, say ten years hence, when you will say that I am right and y'r request respecting Mr. S[hepherd] is bordering on the absurd & what you say of these two [Christian] women you ought not to have said.

Smith signed the letter "Very truly & kindly y'r friend and brother."[15]

Such letters were not always appreciated. After receiving a letter of reprimand from Smith, Hattie Foote, a teacher with the AMA for three years, resigned in anger. "I cannot accept a commission for *any* place after receiving the unkind, unjust letter which came from Mr. Smith last week. That letter caused me many bitter tears."[16]

The hostility the teachers sometimes encountered from southern whites was enough in itself to make some of them irritable. A journalist found one southerner in the Carolinas so bitter that he said the Yankees had left him only one privilege: "to hate 'em. I git up at half-past four in the morning and sit up till twelve at night to hate 'em. . . . I'm like a whipped cur; I have to cave in; but that don't say I shall love 'em." The northern teachers became the objects of that hatred. " 'The rebels' great bugbear now is the Northern school-ma'am," a correspondent reported from Charleston. "She occupies the same position in their minds . . . that John Brown and the Abolitionists did previous to the war." [17]

The hatred sometimes led to violence. Edmonia Highgate, a twenty-two-year-old black teacher in Vermillionville, Louisiana, found herself in danger similar to that her brother had faced as a Union soldier before he was killed at Petersburg, Virginia. Highgate, who had once been a member of Michael Strieby's church in Syracuse, New York, wrote to Strieby that "there has been much opposition to the school. Twice I have been shot at in my room. Some of my night school scholars have been shot, but none killed. A week ago an aged freedman just across the way was shot so badly as to break his arm and leg. The rebels here threatened to burn down the school and [the] house in which I board." William L. Coan, who had organized a school for the AMA in Lexington, Virginia, and was expecting teachers from the association, said it was doubtful that there would be overt acts of violence in Lexington "altho there are *threats*, etc. from students and others. It is a *vile hole*, you *better believe*." One of the teachers who went to Lexington said that a group of white students habitually gave her "the polite salutation of 'damned Yankee bitch of a nigger teacher,' with the occasional admonition to take up my abode in the infernal regions." Even when there were no threats, white teachers were sometimes forced to live in complete isolation from the local whites, who would not speak to them, sell to them, or deal with them in any way. The bureau's superintendent of education in Arkansas said that the "estimable Christian ladies" teaching at Pine Bluff were "compelled to live like recluses," and the superintendent in Texas spoke of AMA teachers who had been "placed under the ban" and subjected to "taunts, sneers, and ostracism." [18]

Because of the difficulties the teachers encountered in trying to make purchases from the whites in their communities and because of the high prices or the unavailability of many articles in the South, Smith found himself supplying the teachers not only with teaching materials but with household articles as well: writing paper and envelopes, tablecloths, yard goods, stepping-stones, stencils for marking clothes, sewing machines, and various items of food, including countless barrels of pickles to prevent scurvy.

The cost of supplying the teachers was one of the major costs of the AMA, and with the Freedmen's Bureau providing free transportation for supplies, as it did for the teachers themselves, the association saved both money and problems for the teachers by buying its supplies in the North.

Smith encouraged the teachers to send letters and "pleasing incidents" of their work to churches and other donors in the North to stimulate donations of money and supplies. He recognized that letter writing was an imposition on the overworked teachers, but he said the churches would not contribute unless they heard from the field, and he thought the correspondence absolutely necessary. He also thought letters were necessary to publicize the association where it had competitors. On one occasion Smith told John A. Rockwell, the AMA superintendent in Macon, Georgia, that "there is considerable rivalry between our friends & the friends of the National in B[inghamton] & we must try to give them some interesting letters."[19]

The teachers conducted their classes in whatever buildings were available: a mule stable, a billiard room, cottonhouses, warehouses, churches, and in what was formerly a slave market in New Orleans, where a sign with a thin coat of whitewash over it could still be read: "Negroes for Sale by J. Bruin." But no matter how unfamiliar the settings, the teachers attempted to create in them the familiar common schools of New England and the Midwest, using the textbooks they had used in the North and following the most modern educational techniques. The teachers learned to adapt to new behavior in their students—tardiness, absenteeism, and a limited understanding of the outside world—but they prided themselves on giving their black students the same quality of education they had given their white students in the North. Smith was concerned that the teachers receive the best supervision possible. At Savannah, where the AMA at one time had more children in school than at any other place, Smith insisted on having "a *first class* school sup[t] . . . the very best teacher, a man who is thoroughly posted in his work & all the improved methods of teaching." Both the superintendents and the teachers found their reward when they could report that the black students were doing work that compared favorably with that of white students at home.[20]

The teachers also attempted to teach their students the basics of good citizenship as they understood it: honesty, politeness, obedience, thrift, cleanliness, industry, neatness, self-control, and respect for authority. A series of textbooks published for freedmen's schools by the American Tract Society was available to reinforce the teachers' lessons. The books placed special emphasis on the need to work. "Now that you are free, you have got to take care of yourselves," one of them said. "You have got to *think* and *work* both. . . . Don't fall into the mistake of some, that freedom means idleness." With such virtues, the teachers thought, the freedmen could make an orderly and peaceful transition from slavery to full citizenship.[21]

When they were not in the classroom, the teachers distributed clothing and supplies to the destitute, ministered to the sick, taught Sunday school classes, and organized Bible classes and prayer meetings. A special committee of the AMA, which included Smith, encouraged home visitations to distribute the Bible, to pray, and to engage in religious conversations so that the teachers and missionaries might "lead souls to Christ." "The value of the soul," the committee said, "made most impressive by the sacrifice of the Son of God for its redemption, will so affect you that your preaching, exhortation, personal conversation, and all other means of grace employed, will be adapted to the conversion of men to God. With the Holy Spirit dwelling in you, your loving and earnest Missionary life will be so like that of Jesus, that, in His name you will draw many to Him." [22]

The committee appealed to the association's teachers and missionaries to give particular attention to temperance activities—something also emphasized by the Freedmen's Bureau. "Information received from some districts," the committee said, "causes alarm, in view of the use of intoxicating drinks among Freedmen, a vice from which they were formerly restrained more than others by their poverty and the absolute control of slavery." The AMA officials feared that at election times southern politicians would use strong drink to "steal the brains and votes" of the freedmen as the officials believed they had done with the poor whites. The committee also feared that "the threatening tide of intemperance" might lead to indifference to education, "with disorder, pauperism, pollution, and [crime?], and our high anticipations be blasted." The teachers were encouraged to seek abstinence pledges, organize temperance societies, and distribute tracts and other publications, "with appropriate illustrations, sparing no pains to bring the young and all others into the temperance army." [23]

The committee also encouraged the teachers and missionaries to cooperate in the religious services of the freedmen and their ministers. "Although, from the nature of the circumstances in which the colored people have been placed at the South, especially field hands, there will be more exuberant manifestations of feeling than with others, your frequent presence and earnest yet orderly manner of working, will exert a happy influence, promotive of conversions and of practical godliness." [24]

"What weighty motives command us!" the committee concluded.

Our high mission forbids us to seek, for the subjects of our labors, any form of civilization destitute of pure Christianity. "Christ, and Him crucified," furnishes the only hope for this life, and for that which is to come; and, for society, the basis of a civilization which takes hold upon millennial glory. The millions for whom we labor are posting on with ourselves to death and to judgment. What can we do for them? Day by day, as they are about to pass into the Eternal presence, they beg our prayers for their salvation. . . .

Great will be your joy in the future blessedness of those saved through your instrumentality. In all seasons of trial, with unwonted joy, cling to the "commission promise" of the ascending Saviour, *"Lo, I am with you alway, even unto the end of the world."* [25]

An important part of the Christian civilization the AMA fostered was freedom from racial discrimination, or as they commonly spoke of it, freedom from caste. Lewis Tappan, one of the patriarchs of the AMA, summarized the association's principles in *Caste: A Letter to a Teacher Among the Freedmen,* a letter endorsed by both Whipple and Smith.

> Prejudice against the colored man, which never had any justification either from nature or Scripture, is more wicked and unwise since universal emancipation has been proclaimed, and the colored inhabitants of the land are now entitled to all the privileges of citizenship. The happiness and welfare of the whole people demand that odious distinctions should forever cease. . . . In all positions we should avoid making distinctions on account of color, and absolutely refuse to be a party to the absurd, mean, unchristian customs of those who keep aloof from men because they are colored, and for no other reason. . . . An angry look, a petulant word, a haughty demeanor, acts denoting aversion, affected superiority, or compliance with usages that separate the colored from the white people as a separate class, will be much out of place on the part of instructors. . . . They who can not or will not "conquer their prejudices" in this regard, and eradicate them from their minds and hearts, evince indisputably that they are unfit for the high and responsible office of superintendent or teacher, and should be dismissed from the post they so unworthily fill.[26]

It was, however, easier to preach the association's principles in New York than to practice them in the field. The AMA teachers and officials were constantly forced to decide how far it was practical to push the ideal of racial inclusiveness in the face of opposition from whites, and their differing judgments in the matter resulted in some serious disagreements, including a divisive conflict among the missionaries at Beaufort, North Carolina.

The superintendent at Beaufort had a desire to teach poor whites as well as blacks, and he feared that an insistence on racial integration would alienate the whites and put an end to any opportunity to educate their children. The superintendent, H. S. Beals, a native of Massachusetts then in his early fifties, was an "active and zealous Christian" who had once worked as a colporteur for the American Tract Society and who had "long felt a lively sym-

pathy with the oppressed victims of slavery." After teaching for seventeen
years in Massachusetts and serving as a principal in Angelica, New York—
where he also operated a lumber mill—he had gone with his family to work
among the freedmen. Beals asked the people in the North to "pray for the
white children too. They are poor & weak & ignorant. They have not as many
friends, even here, as the poor col child. They too are Jesus' poor. They are
no way responsible for the wrongs their fathers heaped on the poor Slave, or
their own ignorance." [27]

At first, Beals had encouraged whites to attend the freedmen's school, and
some did, but, he said, "they were subjects of persecution, and ultimately
driven away by the prevailing sentiment among the white people." When the
white citizens of Beaufort later organized a school for white children and
asked Beals to supply a teacher, he did so, and when a black student applied
for admission, neither Beals nor the teacher he had assigned to the school
wanted to admit him, or any other black students, believing that their presence would disrupt the school. Beals urged that the issue of racial inclusiveness be "let entirely alone, and we p[u]rsue our earnest work till God should
convert those, whom *we* cannot." Attempting to enroll blacks in the school
would "doubtless scatter that school in a day. *We* are right, but the prevailing
sentiment of the white people *here*, is *wrong*. Shall we wait to convert them to
our ideas, before we give them what alone will secure that conversion[?] . . .
The whole race of poor white children are crying out for this life giving influence. Is it our policy, or our principle, to hold this multitude, clamoring for
intellectual light, outside the benign influence of schools, till we force them
to adopt our ideas[?]" The missionaries, he said, had access to hundreds of
white families who formerly "were effectually bar[r]icaded against us, and
who will be again, if we allow this school to be scattered, by what seems to
me, an impolitic application of our principles." [28]

Smith himself had once proposed to establish a white school in Beaufort
adjacent to the school for freedmen as a means of encouraging the two races
to interact with each other, but when the white school at Beaufort became an
issue among the blacks in the community and when several northern newspapers reported that the AMA school in Beaufort excluded blacks, Smith
and the other New York officials stated in the *American Missionary* that they
had agreed to provide a teacher to the new school in Beaufort on the express
condition "that no person was to be excluded on account of color, from any
school sustained or aided by us—a rule on which we have always acted, and
on which we shall continue rigidly to insist." [29]

The blacks in Beaufort, however, insisted that the school continued to
exclude them; they reported to George Whipple that "the rebels" openly

Samuel J. Whiton (1839–71).
From Augustus Sherrill
Whiton, comp., *The Whiton
Family in America.* Courtesy of
the Historical Society of
Pennsylvania, Philadelphia,
Pennsylvania.

boasted that "no nigger goes in there." One of the AMA teachers in Beaufort,
Samuel J. Whiton, shared the blacks' indignation at their exclusion and used
his position to stir their discontent. Whiton was a twenty-seven-year-old
Congregational minister from Westford, Connecticut, who had gone to Africa
as a missionary in 1863 and served in the AMA's Mendi mission until the
death of his wife and son and his own illness forced him to return to the
United States. After his return, he wrote a book about his African experiences, *Glimpses of West Africa.* Whiton's personality may have played a part in
his return from Africa; his fellow missionaries had found him "a very difficult
man to get along with." Whiton wrote to Smith to tell him that, regardless of
the AMA's stated policy, citizens of both races in Beaufort understood that
blacks were excluded from the white school. He said that when the *American
Missionary* arrived with its official statement of inclusiveness, the blacks said,
"See there, they *pretend* to make no distinctions, but they *act* directly contrary." The whites, too, he said, noted the inconsistency of the association.
"It pains me, as I visit from house to house, to have the A.M.A. accused of
talking one way and acting another." [30]

After receiving Whiton's letter, Smith wrote to him to reaffirm that the
white school was started "on the distinct understanding that it was open to
any who chose to attend." Whiton, without consulting Beals, quoted Smith's
letter in a public meeting of freedmen and declared that the white school was
open to blacks if any wished to attend, which greatly irritated Beals and those

who supported him. After that, Whiton received another letter from Smith, which has not survived but which Whiton took as a reprimand for "interfering with Mr. Beals' department." "In it," Whiton said to Smith, "you blame me severely, and I think unjustly, for my course concerning the white school, and accuse me of meddling with what was not my business." He said sarcastically that he understood now that the AMA's principles must be "hushed up, and our lips padlocked" so that the white school could continue. "We must talk one way at the North, and act another way at the South for the sake of 'policy.'" Whiton said Smith had written that the AMA regarded "the making of the issue by sending colored children or inducing them to go to the white schools *a very unfortunate and unwise proceeding,*" but Whiton claimed he did not know the students who had applied to the white school and had done nothing more to induce them to apply than to state the policies of the AMA.[31]

Angrily, Whiton resigned his position, saying he had lost confidence in the AMA and could not "consent in any way to sanction distinction on account of color in schools or churches." The teacher of the white school resigned, too, took the school out of the AMA, and continued to teach it under the sponsorship of the county commissioners. Beals was somewhat chastened by the affair, and soon afterward when an outlying school requested a teacher, he told Smith he had replied to the request by saying that he "thought you [Smith] would be more willing to give them a teacher if all the children would attend without distinction of color." Two months later he reported that "in some of our schools to-day, [poor white] children sit side by side with the sons and daughters of Africa." Through the affair, Smith continued to value Beals and his work highly, saying he was "a man we can[']t afford to spare from the work."[32]

The issue of interracial marriages involving the association's teachers was less frequently encountered but just as controversial. One of the teachers in Mobile, Alabama, Sara G. Stanley, informed the AMA superintendent in Mobile of her intention to marry and asked permission to hold the ceremony in the association's home. Stanley, who had studied at Oberlin College and taught in Ohio, once described herself as "a colored woman, having a slight admixture of negro blood in my veins." The man to whom she was engaged was Charles A. Woodward, the white cashier of the Mobile branch of the Freedman's Savings Bank.[33]

On another occasion, when an inquiry about interracial marriages came from a missionary in Africa, Lewis Tappan gave an unequivocal reply: "White or black, whom God puts together let no man put asunder." But Sara Stanley's superintendent in Mobile, George L. Putnam, flatly refused her request to marry a white man in the association's home. Stanley appealed to district secretary Jacob R. Shipherd, saying she was "surprised, indignant and grieved by this manifestation of a spirit of caste and prejudice." Later she told Shipherd that Smith, who was then visiting in Mobile, had told her that he disapproved of Putnam's action and that the association would not support it. "And like a noble and Christian gentleman," she added, "[Smith] tells me that he would himself take pleasure in solemnizing our marriage here." Smith also said, however, that he would not impose his authority on Putnam because the matter was not in Smith's department. Shipherd, in whose department the matter fell, told George Whipple that "Smith would have gotten us in a first class muddle if he had taken the course Miss Stanley intimates he was inclined to take. But my own guess is that she unintentionally over-colored his sympathy." Stanley and Woodward were eventually married, but Shipherd managed to avoid any official connection with the marriage by arbitrarily ruling that "no teacher can be married until her resignation is first accepted at this Office."[34]

Despite all the problems the teachers encountered in their work, including those caused by their own associates and superiors, some of them adjusted well to even the most difficult situations, and those who did so were a joy to Smith. Two women wrote such a cheerful letter from Hilton Head, South Carolina, that Smith forwarded it to the Sabbath school of the Congregational Church in Woodbury, Connecticut, with a note saying:

> Miss Benedict & Miss Summers are laboring among the most destitute & degraded of plantation negroes. I tried to make them feel when they went out that they were going to find a hard field & very hard work. You see how I succeeded.
>
> They are two brave sunny Christian ladies just such as we need at every point. Mr. Wright our Sup^t at Hilton Head has thanked me for them in every letter written since their arrival. He says their cheerful, happy toil is a wonderful encouragement to them all.
>
> Has Woodbury any more such teachers?[35]

15

Colleges for the Freedmen

This was the gift of New England to the freed Negro: not alms, but a friend;
not cash, but character. . . . The colleges they founded were social settlements; homes where the best of the sons of the freedmen came in close and
sympathetic touch with the best traditions of New England. They lived and
ate together, studied and worked, hoped and harkened in the dawning light.
In actual formal content their curriculum was doubtless old-fashioned, but
in educational power it was supreme, for it was the contact of living souls.

W. E. B. Du Bois, *The Souls of Black Folk*

The American Missionary Association held a meeting at the Dutch Reformed Church at Fifth Avenue and Twenty-ninth Street in New York
City on April 14, 1867. The association was $10,000 in debt—one teacher
had not received her salary for four months—and it was taking advantage of
a recent endorsement by the General Synod of the Reformed church to appeal for funds. Edward Smith was among those who spoke about the AMA's
educational work in the South. He said that the success of the teachers had
been "remarkable, changing the aspect of the communities." One-tenth of
the blacks had learned to read in the past eighteen months. "Their cry," he
said, "was for the spelling book," and he illustrated his point by telling of
a man who had traveled forty miles to "learn the alphabet" and who then
returned to his home and organized a school for forty or fifty other students. "The colored people," Smith said, "are willing, anxious to provide the
schoolrooms, the furniture, the accommodations necessary, if we would only
send them teachers." The association had 450 teachers in the field, every one
of whom was a "centre of influence in the South." But it was not possible
to meet all the requests for teachers; the great need now was for "training
schools for teachers."[1]

Smith was clearly concerned for the welfare of the blacks, but he also appealed to other motives in his listeners. "There are ten States to be brought
into the Union, and two-thirds of the inhabitants are to vote on their return,

and it is a question whether they shall come in ignorant or enlightened. The danger of living among the old hot-beds of treason is not over yet. And the danger must be removed by educating the people, that they may see the right way and walk in it."[2]

The training of teachers that Smith emphasized had become a priority of both the AMA and the Freedmen's Bureau. Smith said their goal was to "put the common sch[l] work where it belongs[,] on the state[,] & take up the business of *making teachers.*" In March 1867, Major General Wager Swayne, the bureau's assistant commissioner for Alabama, offered Smith substantial support from the bureau for a new school for training teachers at Talladega, Alabama. The AMA also had promises from the bureau of grants for normal schools at Nashville, Tennessee; Galveston, Texas; and Atlanta, Georgia; and George Whipple was inquiring whether bureau funds would be available not only for a normal school but also for a future college at Beaufort, South Carolina.[3]

Colleges and universities for the freedmen were also on the public mind. A group of concerned citizens, most of them members of the First Congregational Church in Washington, D.C., proposed the creation of a university for freedmen in the nation's capital. On March 2, 1867, Congress passed a bill to establish Howard University in Washington, and on the same day President Johnson signed the university's charter into law. Two months later the Preparatory and Normal Department was opened with five pupils under the direction of Edward Williams, who had once been the Christian Commission's field agent in the Army of the James. The AMA participated in the endeavor by paying Williams's salary.[4]

The AMA, too, organized colleges and universities for the freedmen. None of the AMA's schools was truly a college or a university when it was created. These fledgling institutions were at best normal schools that took the most advanced students from the association's other schools and then engaged in what Smith called "the business of making teachers." But the Freedmen's Bureau insisted on having a corporate body established at each school before it would transfer the money for buildings, and as the AMA incorporated its schools, it looked to the future and organized them as colleges and universities. Years later, Augustus Field Beard, one of the secretaries of the AMA, was asked why these infant schools had been chartered as colleges and universities. He answered: "I was at church yesterday. . . . The minister baptized twenty babies. I noticed that every one of them got an adult name. The colleges and universities were named all right. Now you bring them up."[5]

The Fisk School in Nashville was incorporated as Fisk University on

August 22, 1867, although the school did not even have a normal department until that fall and the first college students were not admitted until 1871. As soon as Smith received the certificate of incorporation, he personally saw General Howard to arrange for the transfer of $7,000 the Freedmen's Bureau had allocated for the university. Fisk University bore another mark of Smith's personal attention. Deacon Charles Crosby, whom Smith had convinced to go from Pepperell, Massachusetts, to Nashville as a delegate of the Christian Commission during the war, was one of the nine original trustees of the university. Crosby reported to Smith on the arrangements made to bring the teachers and students at Fisk together for family worship and meals: "I have enlarged the dining room," Crosby wrote, "and one long table serves for both teachers and students, and even here, no partiality is to be seen for they are mixed in. We hope by this arrangement, if there is any elevating influence to be derived from thus associating, to give the students its benefit."[6]

Atlanta University was approved as a corporation on October 16, 1867, with Smith named as one of the trustees. The new trustee had earlier expressed his concern to Edmund A. Ware, who became the president of the university, "that the controlling men of the Board [be] of the right stamp religiously as well as loyally" and had suggested that both southern whites and blacks be included on the board. Smith assisted the school too by paving the way for a contribution of $10,000 to the university by the Freedmen's Bureau. General Howard said in his autobiography that he remembered how Smith had previously come to his office "and sat down with me to see what could be done to found this institution. I said 'My friend, get your land and your corporation to hold it and I will attend to the erection of your first buildings, and to the transportation thither of your teachers.' " Once the university was incorporated, Howard quickly authorized the funds he had promised. Smith also asked Howard to suggest a name for the new school, but Howard's suggestion, Stanton University, was not accepted. After the organization of the university was completed, a normal department was finally opened in the orphanage building in April 1869, and the cornerstone of the first university building was laid June 1, 1869. Even before that, Smith was convinced about the "great future" of the university. "It *is* a great future[.] Set that down. Every thing points that way & that is a sign of a decree of God."[7]

Berea College in Berea, Kentucky, loosely associated with the AMA, had been organized by John G. Fee before the Civil War as an "antislavery, anticaste, anti-rum, anti-tobacco, anti-sectarian, pious school under Christian influence . . . a college which will be to Kentucky what Oberlin is to Ohio." The school was broken up by mob violence in 1859 but was reopened in 1866. Two years later it had 301 students, one-third of them white and 24 of them in the Normal Department. In 1868 the bureau appropriated $7,000 for the school, and in 1869 the first college class was organized, consisting of five students, all from Kentucky.[8]

The AMA's normal school at Hampton, Virginia, opened in April 1868 with fifteen students and five teachers. The purpose of the school, according to its principal, Samuel Chapman Armstrong, was "the preparing of youth, especially of the South, for the work of instructing the ignorant masses in the South in the branches of a common school education and in the best methods of practical industry." The school applied for incorporation as Hampton Normal and Agricultural Institute, with George Whipple the president of the corporation, Smith the vice-president, and Armstrong the secretary. By January 1869, the school had fifty students, and Smith reported that over $40,000 had been spent on the school, so confident were the officers of its success.[9]

In other places, the association's normal schools evolved more slowly into colleges and universities. A normal school was begun in Talladega, Alabama, in November 1867, when the teacher in the year-old AMA school, the Reverend Henry E. Brown of Oberlin, Ohio, offered to make teachers out of promising students if their families would supply them with provisions. Smith said the first students walked to Talladega with the provisions on their backs and slept at first on cabin floors. They began their studies "in their alphabet," but by the end of the year they were scattered in "bush" schools teaching others for the summer. With the assistance of the Freedmen's Bureau, the school acquired thirty acres of land with a large three-story brick building built before the war for a Baptist academy. The laborers who renovated the building donated a week's work, and northern friends of the AMA invested more than $10,000 in nearby farmland to be used to aid students attending the school. "There is no better place," Smith said, "for a Normal school and ultimately for a College," and he was soon calling the school a college, despite its modest beginnings. Talladega College was incorporated in 1869 with Smith as one of the trustees, but the Normal Department was not organized until 1871, and the first college students were not admitted until 1891.[10]

After the flurry of activity in organizing schools and colleges in 1866 and 1867, Smith's life settled into a routine. He still made occasional trips to Washington to seek funds from the Freedmen's Bureau and devoted time to acquiring lots and buildings, but more of his time was spent with the association's teachers. Most of the correspondence from the teachers was directed to Smith—the letters soon numbered in the thousands—and answering them took a large part of his time. He wrote to recruit teachers, assign them to their posts, and try to settle their disputes. He also sent them supplies: dictionaries,

Bibles, songbooks, textbooks, maps, tracts, building materials, desks, slates, ink, inkwells, garden seeds, flags. He sent constant applications to the Freedmen's Bureau for transportation for teachers and supplies. General Eliphalet Whittlesey complained to Smith that two of his bureau clerks were kept busy just with AMA affairs. Smith's large correspondence had surprisingly little religious content; it often resembled the correspondence of a businessman more than that of a minister. Only an occasional reference to Scripture or the insertion of "D.V." (*Deo volente*, "God willing") when he was discussing his plans revealed that the man writing the letters was a clergyman.[11]

Nevertheless, as his friend Edward Williams put it, he "never forgot that he was a *minister.*" Williams said "he made his life a life of service. . . . He was unhappy if he was not doing something for somebody. His sympathies were the widest. He took an interest in every effort which promised to uplift men. . . . In all that he did, he sought to prepare the way for the Gospel." But even though he was practicing his religion, he missed preaching it. Williams said that "no man ever had a greater love for the regular work of a parish. He has often spoken to me of the loss he was suffering in being deprived of it. For years he cherished the hope that he might take it up again. At length he became convinced that his usefulness was in other directions, and he said to me on one of the journeys we took together, 'Oh, how I long for a parish, and a library, and sermon-writing. But I shall never preach again. I couldn't settle down now.'"[12]

Occasionally, Smith found opportunities for preaching, along with promotional work for the AMA, in local congregations and at church conferences. Although he no longer had many opportunities to speak to children, Smith had not lost his singular ability to communicate with them. On one occasion, after speaking to a Sabbath school at Northampton, Massachusetts, about the work of the AMA, he received a letter from the pastor with a contribution of $16.22. It was the gift of a ten-year-old girl who had sat "in the infant class in the gallery" when Smith spoke and who had come back and listened "with deep interest" when Smith spoke again in the evening. The next day the girl fell ill with "malignant scarlet fever," and on the following day she was dead. Her pastor wrote that "she died peacefully & happily & desired to 'will' her money which had been placed in the savings bank to educate the *colored children.*" The pastor was amazed at what the girl had done because her parents had lived in the South and her mother's relatives were "of Southern tendencies & sympathies" and a contribution to the AMA was "the last object her mother especially would give to."[13]

There were few diversions to Smith's work. He and Cleavie went with Strieby and Whipple and their wives on an Independence Day picnic in New

Jersey one year, but the men also contrived to use the occasion to examine a property they were thinking of buying. Smith was a generous contributor to Park Congregational Church in Brooklyn, giving at one time a fourth of his salary, although he was able to contribute little of his time. His vacations, when he took them, were spent at Marblehead, Massachusetts, or at Pepperell, where his mother and his son were buried, and which he thought of as his hometown. His only other recreation revolved around some mockingbirds he had obtained in the South for his home in Brooklyn.[14]

The Smiths often had visitors at their home, many of them persons connected with the AMA. General Howard and his wife were among the visitors. On one occasion, after the Howards had spent the night with them, Smith told his sister Mary that the general was "wonderfully Christian."[15]

Smith doted on his daughter, Gerty, and boasted about her to his sister. "Gerty goes to school & is the picture of health. She has learned to skate this winter already & we are near enough to the 40 acre lake in Prospect Park for her to walk to it in a pleasant day after school. If I sh^d see such a face & form as hers in a child belonging to anybody else I sh^d say she was a child of rare beauty, but this being a family matter it is hardly worth while to talk about it. Is it a sin to *think* it tho? She takes to drawing quite naturally & is on the whole a promising offshoot of the Smiths."[16]

Late in 1868, Smith's niece Minnie Cook came to New York to work as a clerk in the AMA office. Minnie was the daughter of Smith's sister Martha and her husband, the Reverend Elisha W. Cook. She was twenty years old, a graduate of Ripon College in Ripon, Wisconsin, where her parents were living, and had taught school at Rosendale, Wisconsin, for six months before deciding to join her uncle Edward in the work of the AMA.[17]

Smith's book on the Christian Commission was finally published by the Union Publishing House in New York City in October 1868 with the title *Incidents Among Shot and Shell.* The following year it was republished by J. B. Lippincott in Philadelphia as *Incidents of the United States Christian Commission,* the title by which it is usually known. A trade edition also appeared under the title *Thrilling Incidents of the War.* The book was republished as late as 1888 by Hubbard Brothers in Philadelphia under its original title. It was also published in London in 1870 under the title *Christian Work on the Battlefield,* and selections from the book were published with selections from Lemuel Moss's history of the Christian Commission in a book of the same title in London in 1902. Smith received nothing from the profits of this remarkably successful book, the Christian Commission having pledged to devote the profits to "the spiritual and temporal benefit of those who are, have been, or may be, soldiers or sailors in the service of the United States."[18]

After 1867, Smith's routine was broken only by inspection trips through the South, which he made at least once a year. In January 1868, he went to Washington, where he met with General Howard and received orders to travel through the South as an agent of the bureau to inspect schools and report "upon the existing destitution" in the southern states. Samuel Armstrong was also in Washington, and Smith traveled with him to Richmond, Virginia, to meet with General Orlando Brown, the bureau's assistant commissioner for Virginia. Howard had agreed to provide at least $6,500 for the AMA's school at Hampton but insisted that the application for the money come through Brown. Brown not only approved the funds for Hampton but offered to provide both rations for poor students and cloth for bedding and school uniforms. Having learned something about bureaucracies, Smith advised Whipple that "hereafter I think all our applications for aid at H[ampton] sh^d go direct to O[rlando] B[rown]." At Hampton, Smith reported the need for a "professional truckman" for the farm, and in his usual haste, he told Whipple that "there is no time to be lost, not a day" and said that he had already taken the responsibility of making arrangements for one to be sent from New Jersey.[19]

Smith's trip took him to the AMA's schools in Virginia, North Carolina, South Carolina, Georgia, and Tennessee. After reporting to New York about countless business and educational details, he signed himself on one occasion, "In a tearing hurry & no little fatigue," and on another occasion, "Yours for the generation next coming." A minister living in the association's home in Charleston wrote in flattering terms about Smith's visit to Charleston. "Our 'Home' has been cheered by the genial presence of Bro. Smith for a few days past. . . . A more popular & efficient Field Agt I think it w'd be difficult for the Asso to find. He is . . . justly popular with us, for he brings happiness & blessings in his train. Besides his words of cheer to the Sabbath School concert on Sabbath P.M. & to the church in his evening Sermon, he subscribed $25. out of his own pocket to our building fund." [20]

Smith took his duties as an agent of the bureau seriously and reported on affairs that went beyond the scope of the AMA's work. Bureau assignments in South Carolina had undercut the authority of the bureau's superintendent of education over the schools at Hilton Head and Port Royal, and Smith made recommendations about them that received favorable consideration at bureau headquarters both in South Carolina and in Washington. He also reported that Augusta, Georgia, school officials were discriminating against blacks in the distribution of money from the Peabody Educational Fund, but Major General George Meade refused to take any action against the officials because they were dealing with money from a private charity rather than public funds.[21]

After stops in Cincinnati and Philadelphia, Smith returned home in late February only to go south again in April. He reported from Macon, Georgia, that the work there was "very encouraging. Some forty (40) of our most promising pupils, embracing *all* the Normal scholars—some 20—came forward for prayers & I think there were four or five conversions to-night. This gathering pupils into our mission families is almost a *sure* means of conversion."[22]

Smith also participated in an ecclesiastical council at Macon, called by both blacks and whites who wanted to be organized as a Congregational church. The AMA's fifteen missionaries and teachers in Macon formed the nucleus of the church, and the association's recently completed chapel served as its meeting place. It was the tenth church the Congregationalists had organized in five southern states. The Reverend C. L. Woodworth, the AMA's secretary for New England, who was also present at the council, boasted that blacks who had some education were attracted to Congregationalism. They were "turning away from their ignorant preachers," he said, "and demanding something more rational, and quiet."[23]

With summer approaching, Smith turned his attention to the closing of the association's schools. The usual practice of the teachers was to return north during the summer, but the travel costs were prohibitive unless the Freedmen's Bureau could be persuaded to pay them. Smith asked John R. Lewis, the assistant commissioner for Georgia, for his opinion about the teachers returning to their homes, and Lewis replied that as a rule it was good to send them home because the pupils usually were at work in the summer and the weather was "too oppressive for confinement and study, and many Sections too unhealthy." Before he received Lewis's reply, Smith wrote to Whipple to tell him what he had done, saying he had made his request to Lewis "in such a way as to call out I hope an endorsement that you can take to Gen¹ Howard as a *lever*" to obtain transportation orders. Smith was learning not only how to work with the government's bureaucracy but also how to manipulate it.[24]

From Georgia, Smith went on to Montgomery, Mobile, and New Orleans before returning home. Later he reported on his trip at the AMA's anniversary meeting in Boston. He spoke about "the wonderful eagerness of the colored people to learn" and said he believed the prompt way in which the AMA had responded to their eagerness had "in three years past, given us fifty years of progress." Southern whites, however, were "bitter in the extreme, and since the colored people have dared to vote, the bitterness has been increased. 'Nigger' is the common term, and if a man uses the word 'colored' he is at once known to have come from the North. . . . The feeling is with many that every colored man should be starved or shot." Smith had visited the association's school at Andersonville, Georgia, the site of the notorious

Confederate military prison, and he said that "it will be the old colored men and women and the children who will decorate the patriot graves in the South next Saturday, and no white hand will strew flowers on the 14,000 graves [I] saw at Andersonville last week."[25]

If hostility to the AMA's work presented difficulties in the South, indifference began to present difficulties in the North. Northerners were losing enthusiasm for the work of educating the freedmen, and the AMA's receipts were not adequate for all the association wanted to do. During the previous year, Smith had found it necessary to send a circular to the teachers, asking them to allow the association to delay paying their salaries so it could meet its other obligations. Now Smith told General Howard that the association would no longer be able to send teachers to places where it would have to provide their full support. "Unless local public funds or the Bureau shall come to the aid of our schools, many of them must be given up." To avoid reducing the number of schools, the association appealed to the bureau "for aid directly in the partial support" of the association's teachers.[26]

Like Smith, General Howard had learned to manipulate the bureaucracy he presided over. The Freedmen's Bureau, which had no authority to pay teachers, soon began to provide money for their salaries by paying $10 a month "rent" to each school with an average attendance of thirty or more students. The bureau could not make payments on buildings of its own, but General Howard was eager to transfer ownership of the bureau's buildings to the northern societies or the trustees of the schools for a nominal fee so that "rents" could be paid on them as well. This thinly disguised subsidy for salaries allowed societies like the AMA to continue to provide teachers and even to increase the number, despite declining contributions. When the arrangement for the "rent" was completed, Smith said joyfully, "Great is Genl H[oward] & Alvord is his prophet."[27]

With the help of the Freedmen's Bureau, the AMA had rapidly established a large number of normal schools and colleges. In the opinion of at least one bureau official, however, it had multiplied schools too rapidly. General Eliphalet Whittlesey told Smith frankly that he believed "the A.M.A. has now more colleges and Schools on its hands than it can support *well.*" Whittlesey had recently visited the association's schools in Louisville, Nashville, Mobile, Montgomery, Atlanta, Savannah, Charleston, Wilmington, and Raleigh and said that "with perhaps two exceptions, they are not what I consider first class freedmen's Schools. You have the best buildings, but your teachers (many of them) are not well qualified for their work." He found many of the teachers and principals "dull" persons. In his opinion, good educators had to be well paid, and the association could not afford adequate salaries if it tried to employ too many. The AMA, he said, had done so much that he was "anxious it should not fail to secure the best results; and, this can be done only by making your schools surpass all others." Whittlesey concluded by saying he could not recommend the establishment of any more normal schools by the AMA.[28]

The work of the Freedmen's Bureau, which was so important to the success of the AMA, was gradually coming to an end. By congressional action the bureau was withdrawn from the southern states on January 1, 1869, except for its educational work and its supervision of the claims of black veterans. Smith said that General Howard was opposed to continuing the other activities of the bureau because he was "tired of the thing" and because he wanted to "use all his money for educational purposes."[29]

In January and February 1869, Smith made his annual inspection trip through the South. He visited the association's new school at Talladega, Alabama, and wrote a long description of it for the *American Missionary*. The school was an "outpost" of education in that part of Alabama, he said, there being no other schools for blacks or whites between Talladega and the Tennessee River, "unless it may be a very few of the lowest possible type which they have established among themselves. . . . Up into these dark counties the news of this school has been carried, till it has become the ambition of many young men, one hundred and fifty and two hundred miles away, who have never turned the leaves of a book, to some how make their way to the 'Colored people's College' in Talladega." Smith reported on the progress of the first normal class, which after teaching for the summer was then in its second year of studies.

> The first Normal class and their first schools have helped my misgivings and confirmed my hopes for the race. They have also confirmed my belief that we make our best and most economical expenditures in their behalf when we *take them in hand*, not merely in the school, five hours per day, but when we put them under Christian family influence, and constantly inspire them with a proper idea of true living. Our Normal schools with a home department cost heavily, but they pay well in deep broad foundations for the future. . . .
>
> The school has won its way through the ordinary bitterness and contempt of the white citizens to their confidence and respect. Its influence for good is so marked, and its success so surprising to them, that they now consider it a benefit to their town and for the most part heartily wish it well. . . .
>
> A great work opens for us. We have just secured an incorporation for the college here. We must put up the projected dormitory—Foster Hall—the students will make the brick for it. We must devise other industries that shall give students an opportunity to work their way. More than one hundred are waiting to

come as soon as they can live and study. *We must prepare these young men to preach Christ in these benighted counties. . . .* We are able, and must not fail, to make Talladega felt as a power for good, educationally and religiously, over all Northeast Alabama.[30]

Smith reported progress in the relations between whites and blacks in Alabama. As the blacks were becoming more self-reliant, they were "compelling" the respect of the whites. And the whites were unconsciously taking down the "high wall which they claim God has built around all white men." He attributed the stability and progress of the South to Ulysses Grant's victory in the recent presidential election.

> Humanly speaking, the election of General Grant saved the country. Very few white men voted for him in Talledega, but I believe fewer still of men of influence and property in the town are not glad he is President. Every one admits that all business in town, and in the country around has revived since his election was announced, and the most ardent democrat, if he has any pecuniary interest at stake, will tell you he is glad we are to have a settled government for the next four years.
>
> The truth is this Southern people, to be satisfied, must either govern or be governed. Johnson's mistake was in asking them how the North should govern them. The true way is for those who have the power to determine what is right and then do it. If Grant has a "policy" may it be this.[31]

From Talledega, Smith went to Jackson, Mississippi, to make arrangements with the Freedmen's Bureau for the purchase of land for a "colony scheme with a Normal School." There were no normal schools in Mississippi, and the AMA proposed to buy a farm where it could establish a school similar to the school at Hampton, Virginia. The farm would provide employment for students and would also support a "colony from the North." Smith told General Howard that the AMA hoped "to induce parties to buy lands adjacent & offer them to the right kind of colored men on easy payments, & thus to make an A[f]rica–New England settlement in the heart of Mississippi."[32]

The AMA commissioned one of the bureau officers in Mississippi, Allen P. Huggins, to act as its agent in acquiring land. Despite Eliphalet Whittlesey's unwillingness to recommend the establishment of any more normal schools by the AMA, the bureau assisted the association in acquiring a plantation for a normal school—five hundred acres with an abandoned mansion near the Tougaloo station seven miles from Jackson. In October 1869, H. S. Beals and his family moved to the plantation to prepare the property and open a school. The bureau's state superintendent of education later reported that "under the very efficient management of the present superintendent, Mr. H. S. Beals, the institution bids fair to equal, if not excel, any school of the kind in the United States." Smith had earlier spoken about the school to General Alvan C. Gillem, the bureau's assistant commissioner for Mississippi, who suggested that the school have an industrial department "where the students may learn to labor intelligently as well as to teach from books," and Smith assured Gillem that the association was ready to act on his suggestion. The school was chartered as Tougaloo University on May 13, 1871, and a Normal Department was opened that fall. The first college students, however, were not enrolled until 1897.[33]

After visiting schools in Mobile, Charleston, and Macon, Smith returned to the North in time to witness the inauguration of Ulysses Grant as president. John Cole, who that same month became secretary and treasurer of Howard University, invited the Smiths to come to Washington for the inauguration and promised them they would be "as well provided for as most of the zealous pilgrims who [visit?] the American Mecca for 4th of March." Impressed by the presence of blacks in the inaugural procession, Smith wrote a sketch of the occasion. His sketch has not survived, but a former AMA teacher wrote a poem based on it for the *American Missionary*. Her poem ended with these verses:

O race, by your costly redemption,
     Prove worthy—quit you like men,
Let no chains of sin or folly
     Make slaves of you again!

And thou, chief of this great Republic,
     God grant thee ne'er to forget,
That as it deals with the colored man,
So will God deal with it yet.[34]

Later that month, Smith was back in Washington, lobbying to have General Howard retained as commissioner of the Freedmen's Bureau. Howard had been under investigation for his business dealings with Howard University, and Smith, believing the charges against Howard had been brought out of malice, was doing what he could to keep him in office. He urged George Whipple to prepare a petition to President Grant as an act of "simple justice to the Gen¹." Smith, Whipple, and others had already petitioned Howard to reconsider the resignation he had submitted. The bureau's work would soon end, they said, and "the Benevolent associations that have cooperated with you and have received such constant and cordial support could not expect to become acquainted with and so well adjusted to a new Commissioner in the few months that remain." Smith left Washington convinced that Howard was bearing a "great burden" and wrote to him to say, "May the Master make it light for you." In the end, Howard remained in office, to the relief of the officials of the AMA, who had received substantial benefits by having one so well disposed to them at the head of the bureau.[35]

As new state governments were established in the South, various provisions were made for public education, which affected the work of the AMA, and Smith wrote at length about them in the *American Missionary*. Kentucky, Texas, Mississippi, Georgia, and Virginia still had not created public school systems. Kentucky did have a poll tax to provide for schools and paupers, but Smith said that when blacks applied for tax funds, "the official answer is— the fund is exhausted by the support of the paupers." A fund for "pauper schools" in Georgia was also unavailable to blacks. Mississippi had "*no* fund and *no* legislation"; neither did Texas or Virginia. In these states education for blacks still depended on the blacks' own efforts, the Freedmen's Bureau, and the northern societies.[36]

North Carolina, South Carolina, Florida, and Arkansas had created what Smith considered good school systems but had not yet put them into operation. Men associated with the AMA had played prominent roles in creating the new systems. Samuel Ashley, who had formerly been the AMA's superintendent in North Carolina, had become that state's superintendent of public instruction. Another former AMA agent, C. Thurston Chase, was the superintendent of public education in Florida. Smith said Chase was "working the system vigorously, and unless interfered with, will make it very efficient." The bill that introduced public education into South Carolina had been drawn up by Francis Cardozo, formerly the AMA principal in Charleston. Little, however, had been done to implement the South Carolina law.[37]

Tennessee, Alabama, and Louisiana had not only created systems of public education but were beginning to put them into operation. John Eaton had begun Tennessee's system when he was the superintendent of education in Tennessee, but a new superintendent was, Smith said, "a man notoriously out of sympathy with the idea of public schools," and Smith thought the prospect for public education in that state was "very dark." The state school board in Alabama was composed of "northern and radical men, and a system has been put in force corresponding to their own advanced ideas." Louisiana had created a school system, but Smith admitted he was not well informed about its operation.[38]

Smith thought the public school systems that had been created in the South were "the very best in the country, because they are transcripts of the best systems in the northern states, like those of Michigan and Iowa."

But the new systems would still require northern teachers; "there are very few native teachers competent and willing to instruct colored people." Where invited, the AMA commissioned teachers for service in the state schools and helped pay their expenses. In that way, Smith said, "we . . . secure northern christian teachers, and give not only a good school in itself, but a *model* school for the next ten years."[39]

Smith concluded by questioning whether southerners were willing or able to operate their northern-inspired public schools.

> In estimating the value of these state school systems, we must always keep in mind that they are exotics, carried bodily from the North by northern men, and that they are not yet accepted by the southern people, and that the southern people as a whole are by no means willing to give them a fair trial, even if they were competent to it. But they are not only out of sympathy with them but entirely unable to comprehend and work them, and yet will inevitably have the management before long of their own schools and systems. . . . So that we have this anomaly in the school affairs throughout the south,—a better *system* than *practice*, with the probability, almost certainty, that the system will go down further and more rapidly than the practice will come up.

In that situation, Smith thought the AMA's schools and teachers were needed more than ever to demonstrate the possibilities of the new school systems and to "help stay up the public mind from the impending relapse toward barbarism."[40]

16

"Tell 'Em We're Rising!"

Right in the track where Sherman
   Ploughed his red furrow,
Out of the narrow cabin,
   Up from the cellar's burrow,
Gathered the little black people,
   With freedom newly dowered,
Where, beside their Northern teacher,
   Stood the soldier, Howard.

. . . .

And he said: "Who hears can never
   Fear for or doubt you:
What shall I tell the children
   Up North about you?"
Then ran round a whisper, a murmur,
   Some answer devising;
And a little boy stood up: "General,
   Tell 'em we're rising!"

               John Greenleaf Whittier,
               "Howard at Atlanta"

In January 1870, Edward Smith, whose title had recently been changed from general field agent to field secretary, traveled through the South in the company of John Watson Alvord, the general superintendent of education of the Freedmen's Bureau. When their trip was over, General Howard published Alvord's letters from the South to counteract the persistent accusations made about the freedmen by "those who predict evil, and earnestly desire it" and who said: " 'They are all dying off.' 'They are killing their children.' 'They are guilty of inebriation.' 'They are guilty of infanticide.' 'The whole population is diseased and degraded.' 'They cannot rise.' 'They are thriftless and idle.' 'They will not work,' and so forth." On a visit Howard had made earlier to Atlanta, a young black student, Richard R. Wright, gave him a message for the North: "General, tell 'em we're rising," and Howard was pleased to be able to publish Alvord's evidence for the rise of the freedmen.[1]

Alvord wrote of an entire black population that was rising. At Columbia, South Carolina, Francis Cardozo, who had become South Carolina's secretary of state, and the 125 state legislators who were black were received by the governor in the same manner he received white officials. At Charleston, one of the schools, the Freedmen's Pay School, with 150 pupils, had black teachers and was supported entirely by the freedmen. Large numbers of freedmen were buying land. Half the cotton on the Sea Islands of South Carolina and one-third of the cotton in upper Georgia, he was told, belonged to blacks. Alvord thought that even the clothing of the freedmen demonstrated their progress. "From linsey wolsey, ragged garments, clumsy brogans, or bare feet of former times, we notice the change to clothes of modern material; shoes or gaiters on the feet of boys and girls; whole schools as tidily dressed as most of the common schools at the North."[2]

Alvord was sure that infanticide did not exist. Inebriation, unfortunately, did. "The general admission, however, is that there is not as much drunkenness among the blacks as whites." Crime also existed, but when Alvord compared crimes committed by freedmen with crimes committed by whites, he thought the statistics were "certainly creditable to the colored population." But, in any case, Alvord insisted that the critics of the freedmen had "forgotten the deplorable influences of slavery; the embruted condition from which these people have been so lately taken." Judgments about the freedmen should be suspended for at least a generation to allow them to overcome the effects of slavery. Still, Alvord thought the progress that had already been made was "evidence of a *vitality* prophetic of a rapidly rising people."[3]

Smith, too, was pleased at the condition of the freedmen. One of those who had made accusations about the freedmen was Parker Pillsbury, once a prominent abolitionist. When Smith reported on his trip, he pretended he had expected to learn some unpleasant truths after reading Pillsbury's statement. "I thought," Smith wrote, "if a man so committed to the negro race felt obliged to bear such testimony from actual observation, possibly there was some lower depth of depravity which we had not explored." But, he said, "my tour has repaid a hundred fold in its re-assurance." Pillsbury's brother Gilbert Pillsbury, the mayor of Charleston, had given Smith an entirely different picture. It was true, Smith said, that blacks drank whiskey, "far more than is good for them, but not so much as white people, and they do not behave so badly under its influence. In my tour of a month, passing over three thousand miles . . . visiting negroes in their cabins, watching them in the streets and at the depots as I passed in the cars, making it my business to observe their habits, I have not *seen a single negro intoxicated.* I have perceived the smell of strong drink on some of them, but no drunkenness. This cannot by any means be affirmed of the white people."[4]

Smith reported that he had seen signs of improvement every year in his trips through the South "but never more evidences of increasing industry, thrift and general prosperity than I have observed this winter." There was less poverty, and the suffering he saw among the aged and the sick was "not a tithe of what was to be seen on every hand three years ago. . . . On every hand are tokens of a steady, and by no means gradual, uplifting of the race." It was true that there was still degradation; "the unthrift and deceiving tricks begotten of slavery are on this people and in them. . . . Many of them will go down into a shiftless, idle, trifling life, and be wretched and ignorant till they die. But they represent the sediment of this society just as Water Street and Sixth Ward represent their kind in New York." It was also true that it was difficult to hire laborers, but that was because the freedmen wanted to own land or rent it and would become hired laborers only as a last resort.[5]

John Alvord was the president of the Freedman's Savings Bank, and Smith said they had visited eight of the twenty-five branch banks and that he was "surprised and delighted" to learn how many of the freedmen had used their savings to buy land and homes. (Two months after their trip, John Cole, who was one of the trustees of the Freedman's Bank, recommended Smith as a trustee, and in July he was unanimously elected to the position.) As for the accusation that the black race was dying out, Smith said he had consulted the death records at Savannah, Charleston, and Atlanta and had found the charges untenable. "The truth is," he concluded, "the negro of the South is holding to life with more tenacity than the whites."[6]

At Charleston, Smith found the association's school, the Avery Institute, "in perfect order, few Northern schools will equal it in genuine enthusiasm for study under complete control & discipline." Plymouth Congregational Church was also thriving, and Smith promised it assistance from the AMA in putting up a new building.[7]

Alvord reported from Atlanta that the AMA schools "have their usual excellence," but his greatest praise was reserved for Atlanta University. "The location is beautiful, overlooking the city, on the precise ground where the rebels intrenched in resistance to Sherman's approach. The building is very substantial, economically constructed, and has about one hundred and forty pupils in all, sixty of whom are boarders. . . . Teachers are interspersed at table with the students, and all seem like one great well-bred and happy family." In a conversation Smith had with some of the university teachers, one of them said that the school already needed another building. When Smith asked how they would get the money for a building, the teacher replied, "We own sixty acres of land and we will plant it with onions and raise the money." "After a hearty laugh, Smith answered, 'I think you will get the money.'" When they returned from their trip, Smith and Alvord reported the need to General Howard, and bureau funds were soon allocated for a new building.[8]

Smith and Alvord traveled from Georgia to Tennessee, passing through the places Sherman's army had fought, and Alvord reported to General Howard from Chattanooga that "I came over the 'fighting ground' between here and Atlanta by daylight to see your line of march, entrenched positions, battle-fields, &c. My companion, Rev. [E.] P. Smith, former field agent of the Christian Commission, could point me to each locality of struggle, hospital work, and Christian labor. Thus I spent one of the most interesting days of my life, in this long review of one hundred and thirty miles up to the broader battlegrounds and fastnesses of Chattanooga."[9]

The Tennessee legislature had recently repealed the state's three-year-old free school law, and Alvord was pessimistic about the prospects for public education in Tennessee. Education there was "where all would be throughout the South, if the influence of the General Government should be withdrawn—drooping, discouraged; teachers with blasted hopes, working hard, desperately, but pulling only against the current."[10]

At Berea, Kentucky, Alvord reported that Berea College had some two hundred pupils, nearly equally divided between black and white. "It is a novel sight," Alvord said, "to witness all colors in the same class-room vigorously competing. I could not decide on relative superiority. As a body, these students are more advanced than any I have seen this side of Howard University. Recitations listened to in mathematics, Latin and Greek composition, and other higher branches evinced thorough scholarship and the best instruction."[11]

During their trip, Smith and Alvord were made vividly aware of the activities of the Ku Klux Klan. In Georgia, one of the AMA teachers had recently been driven out of Greensboro, and the man with whom he boarded was taken out of his home at night and "whipped unmercifully." A black member-elect of the state legislature, who supported the teacher, was also taken out of his house and "beaten nearly to death." At Nashville the visitors found state officials discussing measures against "that nuisance now beginning to be universally felt—the 'Ku-Klux,' or, as they are here called, 'masked marauders.'" The Klan was out in force as the men traveled from Berea to Richmond in Kentucky. Three blacks were "cruelly whipped, dragged over the flinty road, until, with bodies lacerated and torn, it is doubtful if they can recover."

At Richmond, where a white man had been hanged a month before and six or seven black men whipped and one killed only weeks before, suspicious persons surrounded the hotel where Smith and Alvord were staying. "Bad men prowled about the premises. They crowded inside to scrutinize and question." Smith and Alvord spoke out against the atrocities they had observed but were careful not to disclose their mission in the South. As the northern visitors were speaking with the crowd, a "fierce yell," directly in Alvord's ear, took him by surprise. He said he had heard the same yell "(multitudinous) on rebel battle-fields. Recovering, I looked the fellow quietly in the face and continued my conversation with bystanders. If this was a *'signal'* it had no effect. Some power held restraint over the crowd, and soon I had numerous apologies for such rudeness. . . . At early dawn, still environed by suspicious men, we entered the stage for Lexington. I may say our courage rose by a number of degrees as we drove rapidly out of this *Kentucky* 'Richmond.' " [12]

From Cincinnati, Alvord summed up his impressions of the trip. "Emancipation has been safe; Freedmen exhibit good conduct; have become industrious; save their earnings; are not 'dying out;' are capable of being educated; are loyal to the government; as free from immorality and intemperance as the whites; schools of all kinds improve rapidly. At the same time, the Freedmen are still, in some quarters, oppressed and ill-treated; a majority are poor and ignorant; many are immoral; intemperance is by far too prevalent; teachers are needed on all subjects, and help from all quarters." But the progress in education and in the financial condition of the freedmen "all show the importance of our work, and that much more should be done for its full accomplishment." [13]

Less than a month after his return to New York, Smith was appointed an "agent at large" of the Freedmen's Bureau, without salary, and was directed to "proceed on public business connected with this Bureau" to thirty-four cities in eleven states and the Indian Territory. He first visited Washington, where he lobbied for further appropriations from the bureau. He obtained a promise of $20,000 for Berea College from Benjamin Runkle, the bureau's assistant commissioner for Kentucky. He also convinced the governor of Georgia and several other Georgia officials to sign a request for $23,000 for Atlanta University, and he attempted to get an appropriation of $20,000 for Talladega College. Altogether, Smith hoped to secure $90,000 from the bureau for the AMA. While he was in Washington, Smith also had an interview with Secretary of the Treasury George Boutwell to request entry for a shipment of Bibles sent to the AMA by students in Scotland. [14]

Smith's trip through the South consisted of his usual flurry of activity: visiting schools, purchasing property, arranging for insurance, assisting in

Edward Smith with a group of black students. After they gained their freedom,
freedmen of all ages were eager to obtain an education. Booker T. Washington said,
"It was a whole race trying to go to school. Few were too young, and none too old,
to make the attempt to learn." Courtesy of Edward Parmelee Smith Papers,
Manuscripts and Archives, Yale University Library, New Haven, Connecticut.

the ordination of a minister and the organization of a new church at Dudley,
North Carolina, helping to design a new church building in Charleston, requesting further funds and transfers of property from the bureau. He spoke
of himself in one of his letters as a "lone pilgrim" and typically signed a letter
from Washington, "In haste & ready to depart." These were "very important
days for A.M.A.," he said, and he wanted to make the most of them.[15]

In New Orleans, Smith visited Straight University, the newest of the
AMA's colleges and universities and the site chosen by the bureau's super-
intendent of education in Louisiana for his office. The university opened in
February 1870 with a faculty of twelve. The principal of the Normal Depart-
ment was Pelleman M. Williams, a black teacher who had studied one year at
Dartmouth College and then had taught both black and white students in the
North for twenty-six years before going to New Orleans as a teacher in 1863.
The school made rapid progress; within a few months nearly nine hundred
students had been taught in day and night schools, and by July 1870, twenty-

five Straight University students had been qualified to go out as teachers. Smith reported to George Whipple that "the University is all right, a fine success."[16]

Smith was troubled, however, by what he saw of the uncontrolled emotionalism of the Congregational churches in New Orleans. "Oh wh[a]ᵗ churches," he wrote to Whipple. He said he had often observed the freedmen's emotional worship but "never with a feeling of much *responsibility* until I saw one of our congregations on the [whirl?] & heard ab[ou]ᵗ 40 men & women praying and singing all at once, everyone his own Hymn & prayer." One of the missionaries told Smith he thought "good faithful *ministers*" could "bring them all right in time," but Smith was not sure. "The experiment may be worth trying, on the whole I think it is—but—yes *but*."[17]

From New Orleans, Smith went to Jackson, Mississippi, to consult with Governor James Alcorn about the future of Tougaloo College. Smith said Alcorn told him that the blacks in the state legislature were going to insist on an "*entree* to the State University at Oxford or a University of *their own,* that there is very little probability that they will at all consent to have A.M.A., or any body but themselves run their machine. Gov. A's idea is that it will be *necessary* in order to satisfy them, to put the management into their hands and appoint colored teachers and managers throughout. That will of course throw us out of the way—we should hardly care to be *connected* even with an Institution under such management as this will be sure to get at so raw hands."[18]

Alcorn thought it would be best if the state owned the property at Tougaloo, and Smith set a price of $22,500 on the school. Smith questioned, however, "whether we shall give up this chance to do a good work at comparatively a small cost, turning over to the State a fine *opportunity* to make a University, or keep on our way without State aid and make the school self supporting as nearly as possible." He thought the college could be made into "a fine school, *the best in the State,*" and that the AMA "might, by a *very vigorous* effort, endow it so as to make it a first Class Normal School and college," even though that would require diverting funds from other places. He feared that if the state had control of the school, it would turn it over to inexperienced black managers, who would prove incompetent, and that years would be lost before the school would be properly organized.

> It is not at all likely that the State effort to establish a Normal School and the higher grades of Education will be at all successful under negro management. The State will vote the money & the Colored Trustees will use [it], but it will go principally for the aggrandizement of some Dinah & Sambo, until they have floundered through two or three years, perhaps five, experience of incompetency

and then new foundations will be laid and a good Institution set up, perhaps as good *educationally* as we can make.[19]

Smith's conclusion was that it would be best for the freedmen for the AMA to hold the school and make it a "model institute," but it would be best for the AMA financially to sell it to the state and use the proceeds for educational work elsewhere. He recommended selling the school unless there were prospects of receiving endowments that would eliminate the need for large annual subsidies from the AMA. The issue was submitted to the association's executive committee, which decided to retain the school at Tougaloo and continued to operate it with assistance from both the Freedmen's Bureau and the state of Mississippi.[20]

Reports reached Smith during his trip about the investigation of General Howard then being conducted by the Committee on Education and Labor of the House of Representatives. Smith was convinced that Howard's "record is perfectly clear so far as personal gain of any kind is concerned," but he feared that "an ugly *look* can be given, for those who prefer it," to some of his financial activities. The rest of the charges against him were "bosh." The investigation was of interest to others in the South too. "The rebels," Smith said, "are delighted here at the charges against the 'praying Brigadier.' " [21]

After he returned from his southern trip, Smith attended the AMA anniversary meeting in Boston and reported that "the South was not completely conquered yet; they required to have more education and Gospel there." He also wrote a long report of his trip for the *American Missionary,* his last account of conditions in the South as field secretary for the AMA. In his report he stressed the improvements he had seen on his tour of five thousand miles through all the southern states except Florida and Arkansas. Material conditions throughout the South were improving rapidly, he said, "but the freedman has the larger share in the improvement, partly because in his very low condition, just out of the poverty of slavery, a slight advance is an immense thing with him; and partly because the poor white has hardly waked up to the openings which freedom has brought to him." The success of the freedmen was due to their own hard work. "Wherever the negro is moderately confident of his pay and fair treatment he labors steadily; and when working land for himself, does an amount of labor which the lash would never inspire." Fair dealing with the black laborer, however, was the exception. "Cases of injustice and outrage are frequent and horrible." [22]

Social changes were as great as material changes, but they had been gained by compulsion, "and this compulsion by no means insures sweetness of temper" among the whites. "Underneath all these rights and privileges conferred, there is the same unmistakeable bitterness, for the expression of which there is but one word—'nigger.' "[23]

"The experiment of the ballot for the freedmen," Smith said, "is a perilous one. There is no doubt that it has been used at times to put unprincipled men in positions of power and harm; and yet without it reconstruction, on the basis of safety and justice to the black man, would have been impossible in half a century." The ballot was possible only because of the recently ratified Fifteenth Amendment; if the amendment had not been ratified, the freedmen would have been disfranchised throughout the South. "Let the friends of the colored people offer one more prayer of thanksgiving for this last enactment, which secures in perpetuity the blessings of those which have gone before."[24]

It would require vigilance, however, to keep black voters from being misled.

> I believe that the solid black vote, which is essential in all the states, to the continuance of the Republican ascendancy, is very sure to be broken up. There are not enough Northern men in the South to manage the negro vote alone, and the dissensions and ambitions of the colored leaders, and the intrigues of their old masters will so divide them into factions that a Democratic victory, which means disloyalty, will be quite easy in most of the states before long. Good men will be pained, but should not be surprised to see the next administration controlled by the enemies of the colored men through the colored vote. I am confident that nothing but their enlarged and continued enlightenment will prevent such a dishonor and calamity.[25]

That enlightenment would come through freedmen's schools, and Smith thought the progress of those schools was remarkable. "The annals of the world may be challenged to show another instance of advancement in letters like that this race has made." The southerners had believed there was a limit to what blacks could learn, but the new high schools, normal schools, and colleges completely refuted the old beliefs. The great enthusiasm for learning evident during and just after the war—"this surprising, unnatural thirst for knowledge"—had abated somewhat among younger students, but those attending the night classes and higher grades still showed a desire for knowledge "rarely if ever seen in our Northern States."[26]

Smith was not as optimistic about the South's public school systems. Black political pressure was strong enough to ensure their creation, but after that "the whole machinery drags," and Smith expected the systems to be "quite generally laid aside as the government shall pass into the hands of the old politicians." Nor was Smith optimistic about the religious condition of the freedmen. They had not advanced religiously as fully as their friends had hoped, which was, Smith said, partly because the northerners had overestimated their religious condition. "The negro piety of the South is the growth of a corrupt Christianity. . . . Their church members need the Gospel as much as the Armenians of Turkey; and the Gospel cannot be brought to them through their old church organizations and ministers." During the first year or two, he said, the missionaries mistakenly tried to work through the black churches, to "enlighten and lift" them. The only thing accomplished was to "inculcate and encourage order and propriety, and an intelligent form of worship," and the missionaries learned that those things could be better accomplished by placing "an orderly Christian church along side of theirs." There the members could be "trained to be Christian in their lives." The missionaries were amazed at the lack of moral discipline in the churches. "It is almost like a new revelation to this people," Smith said, "to see that conversion implies a different life, as well as a profession." In a large church in Georgia, "a man was immersed on Sunday and on Monday was convicted of stealing ten dollars at a Sabbath school picnic. No notice was taken of it by the church or pastor."[27]

Northerners had started new churches, but they had not been successful in attracting the older blacks, and Smith thought he knew why.

> They have a well-defined appetite for the sensuous excitement, which can be easily produced in one of these large gatherings. Their religion is a "power" after which they blindly feel; and for the pleasurable sensations which come from a semi-unconscious dance, or from passing into a swoon, or from the sympathetic throb of a crowd who have excited one another well nigh to delerium, on nothing but the power of sympathy, they find no substitute in a simple meeting of prayer and instruction.
>
> Our churches, therefore, begin small, and mostly with the young.[28]

The growth of the Congregational churches, he said, was slow but satisfactory. At Atlanta, the congregation had eighty members after four years. The church at Macon had grown in two years to become "a recognized power in that city; and so at Chattanooga, Nashville, Memphis, and other centers." Smith said he had once thought that blacks were indifferent to the Congregational churches because they were neither Baptist nor Methodist, the prevailing denominations. But he had since come to believe that the greatest difficulty was "that we have tried to establish a moral and intelligent Christianity!" He warned northerners that when they assisted one of the southern black churches, "they are not necessarily doing any thing to elevate the race, and may be doing the opposite. For these churches, so thoroughly intrenched in absurdity, ignorance, and immorality, will be strongholds of resistance to good influences, when other barriers have given way. The greatest opposition now to our school comes from the ignorant preachers of these churches. They understand that an educated generation will make an end to their occupation, and they do what they can . . . to thwart the teachers and cripple the schools."[29]

About the same time Smith's report on his southern trip was published, the Freedmen's Bureau's appropriations for education expired; on July 1, 1870, the educational work of the bureau came to an end. Smith's appointment as a special agent of the bureau was revoked, and the possibility of receiving federal funds—which had made up nearly one-third of the AMA's receipts— came to an abrupt end. Smith was in Washington on July 1, making a last-minute attempt to arrange for the transfer of unexpended funds to the AMA before the bureau closed its accounts.[30]

The end of funding by the bureau left the future work of the AMA in question, not whether it would go on but what its scope would be. Smith's own future as the association's field secretary was in question too. But within two weeks of the end of the bureau's educational work, an action taken by the United States Congress in an entirely different matter prepared the way for a new stage in Smith's career.

17

Agent for the Chippewas

The proper treatment of the original occupants of this land—the Indians—
is one deserving of careful study. I will favor any course toward them which
tends to their civilization and ultimate citizenship.

Ulysses S. Grant, First Inaugural Address

In his first inaugural address, President Grant had declared his intention
to improve the government's relations with the various Indian tribes. The
former military commander surprised the country by suggesting alternatives
to the extermination of the Indians many of his countrymen were demanding,
and he did it, as he said later, "not only because it is humane, Christianlike,
and economical, but because it is right." One of his first steps was to replace
the men who were serving as Indian agents.[1]

The federal Office of Indian Affairs dealt with the Indian tribes through
agents, and there was considerable evidence of corruption among those politically appointed officials. Shortly before Grant's inauguration, two delegations of Quakers called on the president-elect with suggestions for improving
the situation. One of the delegations brought with it a memorial prepared by
a Quaker conference in Baltimore that urged the administration to "invite
the assistance of the philanthropic and Christian effort which has been so
valuable an aid in the elevation of the freedmen, and render it possible for
justice and good example to restore that confidence which has been lost by
injustice and cruelty." Grant, seeing in the Quakers, with their reputation for
just dealings with the Indians, a source of honest agents, directed his Seneca
aide, Ely S. Parker, to ask the Quakers to nominate Indian agents from their
own members. When the Quakers accepted the proposal, two entire superintendencies, including fourteen agencies, were assigned to them. Grant then
assigned army officers to most of the other agencies, and he and Parker, who
became Grant's commissioner of Indian affairs, believed they had placed the
Indian agencies in the hands of men who would deal with the Indians justly.[2]

The Congress, however, angry at the denial of patronage in the appointment of Indian agents and alarmed by the killing of a group of Piegan Indians by the army, added a provision to the army appropriation bill of July 15, 1870, prohibiting army officers from holding any civil office either by election or appointment. Grant and Parker were bound by the law to reassign the officers they had appointed as Indian agents, but they had no intention of returning to a system of political appointments. Instead, when they became aware of Congress's plans, they decided to expand the Quaker experiment and invited other religious bodies to nominate Indian agents to replace the ineligible officers.[3]

The possibility of expanding the Quaker experiment may have been suggested by a letter George Whipple wrote to Secretary of the Interior Jacob D. Cox, whose department included the Office of Indian Affairs. Whipple wrote in May 1870 to ask whether "the cooperation of the AMA, with the Government, in its educational work among the Indians of the Northwest, would be acceptable." In view of the Quakers' work and the involvement of Catholics in some of the schools for Indians, Whipple saw no reason "why the cooperation of a large organization, representing *various evangelical churches*, and familiar, by long experience, with educational work, should be unacceptable."[4]

Cox replied that "there is nothing I more strongly desire than to meet more than half way such overtures as yours" and asked Whipple to come to Washington to discuss the matter. "If we could agree," Cox wrote, "upon a district of country comprising several tribes, like the districts assigned to the Quakers, that would seem to me a desirable arrangement and one which might lead to similar understanding with other associations." Shortly after writing to Whipple, Cox asked the secretary of the Board of Indian Commissioners, Vincent Colyer, who had also suggested an expansion of the Quaker experiment, to inquire whether other religious bodies would be willing to provide Indian agents. Colyer visited the offices of different denominations and missionary boards and then wrote to them to say that the president had decided to invite their cooperation in Indian affairs and to ask them to name persons who could serve as agents. By the time the army appropriation bill prohibiting the use of army officers was passed, the groundwork for the churches' participation in Indian affairs had been laid, and Cox reported that the government was ready to cooperate with them and to do so quickly to avoid going back to the old system of politically appointed agents. By August 19, Cox had assigned the Indian agencies to the various religious bodies.[5]

President Grant explained the assignments in his annual message to Congress:

The societies selected are allowed to name their own agents, subject to the approval of the Executive, and are expected to watch over them and aid them as missionaries, to Christianize and civilize the Indian, and to train him in the arts of peace. The Government watches over the official acts of these agents, and requires of them as strict an accountability as if they were appointed in any other manner. I entertain the confident hope that the policy now pursued will in a few years bring all the Indians upon reservations, where they will live in houses, and have schoolhouses and churches, and will be pursuing peaceful and self-sustaining avocations.[6]

Because the American Missionary Association had once conducted missionary work among the Chippewa Indians, Secretary Cox offered the agencies among the Chippewas to it. Whipple was hesitant about responding to Cox's offer without consulting Smith, who was vacationing at Marblehead, Massachusetts, and he waited until Smith's return to reply to Cox. Not only did Whipple want Smith's advice, but he also hoped to secure a place for Smith as one of the superintendents the Indian Office employed to oversee its agents. Whipple sent Cox a letter from George Stuart recommending Smith, a letter Whipple described as confirming "the opinion I gave you of [Smith's] eminent adaptedness to the position of Superintendent: and I request you to bear it in mind if any vacancy in that department shall be affected." Smith himself appears to be the one who asked Stuart for a recommendation, which Stuart gave readily, saying to Smith, "You are just the man for the place." Smith at first understood that Cox was thinking only of a "nominal" agency for him, one that would give him time to oversee the work of the other agents supplied by the AMA. But after he returned from Marblehead and had gone to Washington to see Cox, Smith reported that Cox told him "he may be able to prevail on the President to make me Sup^t within a short time."[7]

Cox received another recommendation for Smith from Professor John M. Ellis of Oberlin College, a recommendation that carried extra weight with Cox, who was an Oberlin graduate and the son-in-law of Oberlin's former president, Charles Finney. Ellis said he understood that Cox was planning to appoint four or five general agents or superintendents among the Indians.

> Without any solicitation or his knowledge I want to say a word for Rev. E. P. Smith of the Am Miss Ass N.Y. City[.]
>
> I know him well. He stops at my house often and I have seen him in his house.
> I do not know a man in all my acquaintance better suited for such a position[.]
> He is a graduate of Yale, a strong mind, excellent judgement[,] fine executive power with a wide knowledge of men and the world and good business ability. For the sake of the Indians, for the success of your plan and the reputation of

the country, I should like to see him in this place. I do not believe you can do better if you look the world over[.][8]

As the AMA and the Interior Department sought to find a place for Smith among the Indians, only John Cole questioned the move. He told Smith: "I do hope you will not go. I think it would be a great mistake to have you leave the field work with which you are so well acquainted. The schools and banks of the south need wise and careful inspection. A new man could not for a long time gain that knowledge of the field which you possess." The AMA, however, had already chosen the man who would succeed Smith as field secretary: Erastus Cravath, who had succeeded him at Cincinnati four years before. Smith was given the title of secretary of Indian missions with the expectation that whatever position he received from the Office of Indian Affairs, he would be responsible for supervising the entire Indian work of the AMA.[9]

On Smith's recommendation, Whipple suggested five names to Cox for appointments to Indian agencies in Michigan, Wisconsin, and Minnesota. Two of the men, Selden N. Clark and John P. Bardwell, were known to Smith both from their service with the AMA and as agents of the Freedmen's Bureau. Smith's own name was among the five, and Whipple—probably at Cox's suggestion—proposed that Smith be appointed to a special agency for the "wandering bands" in Wisconsin as well as acting superintendent for the district served by the AMA's agents. Four of the appointments were soon made: Bardwell to the Chippewas of the Mississippi, Clark to the Chippewas of Lake Superior, the Reverend William T. Richardson to the Green Bay Agency in Wisconsin, and Lott Norton Woodruff to the Mackinaw Agency in Michigan. Woodruff's appointment, however, was later revoked, and no action was taken on Smith's appointment. Whipple wrote to Cox that "there seems to be at Washington some interference with the plans for the Indians. . . . In the mean time the Indians are suffering, and some of them are inquiring when we shall enter on the work." Smith and Woodruff were both ready, Whipple said, to leave for the field "and ought not to be kept long in suspense."[10]

Cox assured Whipple that Smith's nomination had not been overlooked and explained why he had not yet been appointed. Cox had learned that the wandering bands in Wisconsin were to be removed to Kansas and that because of their removal no appropriation had been made for an agent for them. Cox thought Smith might still be appointed a "special agent" for those bands, or as an alternative, "the whole of Dakota" might be added to the Wisconsin and Minnesota agencies, making a superintendency to which Smith might be appointed "a little later in the season." "Of course of all the men you have named," Cox said, "he is the one we would prefer to appoint to an agency if it were not probable that we may do better for him." [11]

Whipple was disturbed about the delay in Smith's appointment and in a private letter urged Cox to find a position for him. "We have assigned to this work *that* one of our number from whom, in such a peculiar work, we should hope for the best results. We desire that he should have a prominent place in whatever we may have to do. His talents, his character, his experience, all demand this; hence if we can in some way, secure for him the superintendence of a large work, we shall be glad." [12]

When Cox still did not find a place for Smith, Commissioner Parker suggested to Whipple that the AMA withdraw William Richardson's nomination for the Green Bay Agency and give that agency to Smith. Whipple agreed, but the AMA executive committee decided instead to give Smith the agency for which John P. Bardwell had been nominated and to which Bardwell had already been appointed, the agency for the Chippewas of the Mississippi. Bardwell was a sixty-seven-year-old Congregational minister from Oberlin, Ohio, who had a long association with the Chippewas. When the Western Evangelical Missionary Society, one of the predecessors of the AMA, had established a mission among the Chippewas in Minnesota in 1843, Bardwell became the society's superintendent and financial agent and traveled widely in the 1850s raising money for the mission. Because of Bardwell's experience, Smith had suggested him for one of the AMA agencies, and Bardwell was appointed to the Chippewa agency in September 1870. Barely a month after Bardwell arrived in Minnesota to begin his work, his commission was recalled, and Smith was nominated in his place. Whipple suggested that, if the government agreed, Bardwell would remain in Minnesota as Smith's clerk. [13]

Bardwell was understandably angry when Whipple informed him about the association's action. He was ready to leave for the White Earth Reservation to make annuity payments to the Chippewas when he received Whipple's letter, and surrounded by a train of men and teams, he replied with a "hasty note in the woods." "It seems that I am to serve as a kind of moveable ballast in this Indian business," he wrote, "to be changed at the will of any one who prefers my place. I have gone thro' thick & thin to make these payments & tho' far advanced in years, have made them in less time than any man who has preceded me, & am now in a position to complete them in a short time. . . . I shall cheerfully give place to Bro Smith, but I think these changes will not do credit to A.M.A. either in Washington or in the country as to the individuals concerned." [14]

Bardwell was still angry when he returned from White Earth nearly a month later. "My dear Bro," he wrote to Whipple, "I feel that I have not been fairly dealt with in this matter. I was commissioned on your recommendation and the fact of my appointment was published to the world. One month after the date of my commission, you recommend my removal, & the appointment of another in my place, & that fact will of course be published to the world." The public, he thought, could only conclude that he was either incompetent for the position or untrustworthy. "I don[']t think I am oversensitive about my reputation, but that is about all the Legacy I can leave my children, & I think it an injustice to me & my children for any one to trifle with it. So far as I can see, the only reason for my removal is to make a place for Bro Smith."[15]

Bardwell's complaints were to no avail. Secretary Cox proposed Smith's name to the president, who sent the nomination to the Senate on December 6, 1870. The Senate confirmed his nomination on February 18, 1871. Smith would take Bardwell's place as agent for the Chippewas of the Mississippi, Pillager, and Lake Winnebagoshish bands, and the Indians of Red Lake and Pembina. His appointment was for four years at a salary of $1,500 a year, an amount many considered too low to attract capable, honest agents. Later that year the AMA adopted a resolution asking the government to raise the salaries of agents, saying that $1,500 was "not adequate to command the requisite intelligence, education, and business capacity," but despite many similar requests the salary remained the same.[16]

Smith's friends admired him for his willingness to leave the security of New York City for the frontier of Minnesota, knowing that his labors would be inadequately rewarded. Charles Brace said Smith's "impulse was always to take upon himself the most self-denying part of the labors of humanity. He accordingly left the very responsible, and in many respects comfortable, position in New York, and offered his services as Indian agent to the Government." Edward Williams said that when the AMA desired Smith's services among the Indians "he did not hesitate to give them, though it was a great sacrifice to do so. His field in the South had begun to bear fruit, and it was possible for him, now and then, to spend a few weeks with his wife and child; but as Indian Agent and Field Secretary of the A.M.A., in its Indian work, he must be content with nearly complete exile."[17]

The appointment of an ordained minister to a position in the federal government was not questioned. Once, early in the nation's history, that question had been raised. On July 25, 1778, a motion was made in the Continental Congress "that the sense of the house be taken, whether it is proper that Congress should appoint any person of an ecclesiastical character to any civil office under the United States," but there was so little interest in the question that no vote was taken on it. A decade later James Madison argued that to exclude ministers from civil positions violated "a fundamental principle of liberty by punishing a religious profession with the privation of a civil right," and his argument seemed to settle the matter.[18]

Other ministers had served in federal offices. A previous commissioner of Indian affairs, Nathaniel Green Taylor, was a minister of the Methodist Episcopal church. John Bardwell, who was a Congregational minister, was appointed an agent of both the Freedmen's Bureau and the Indian Office, and Smith himself had served as an unpaid agent of the bureau. Now President Grant was deliberately seeking churchmen to serve as Indian agents; in his administration Smith's ordination was an unquestioned asset.[19]

As he prepared to turn over his responsibilities for the AMA's southern school work to Cravath, Smith could take pride in his accomplishments. Acting decisively at a time when property in the South could be purchased cheaply and taking advantage of all available funds from the Freedmen's Bureau, Smith had played a prominent role in the AMA's acquisition of $555,500 worth of southern property for freedmen's education—not including its property for common schools. During the five years he devoted to educational affairs, the association had established six colleges and universities—Fisk, Atlanta, Hampton, Talladega, Tougaloo, and Straight—and helped to reestablish a seventh, Berea. Sixteen graded and normal schools had been established in key southern cities, and the association's work in common schools had grown until there were 147 schools scattered through fourteen states and the District of Columbia, with nearly twenty-two thousand pupils attending the association's day and night schools. When Smith turned his position over to Cravath, the AMA had a total of 461 teachers in the field.[20]

Officials of the Freedmen's Bureau, who dealt with many societies working among the freedmen, often singled out the AMA for praise. The bureau's superintendent of education in Louisiana reported that "the American Missionary Association has accomplished more, with less Government aid, than many of the other societies." Other bureau officials commended the AMA for the quality of its teachers. The superintendent in Mississippi found them "among the most earnest and competent" and noted their "efficiency, zeal, and success." The superintendent in Texas said the AMA teachers "have proved every way worthy and unexceptionable. Too much praise cannot be bestowed upon them for their zeal and devotion."[21]

Smith received other words of appreciation that may have been even more gratifying. Sarah Nottingham, a student at Capeville, Virginia, wrote to thank him for her teacher.

> It afford me great pleasure to write you these few lines. I am just learning hou to write and it is like a new and a strange thing to me. . . . Feb. last I knew nothing

about a writing but now I thank my God that I can write my own name, Oh! how I thank theA.mA., and the almighty God for this, glorious day of knowledge, I am but alittle girl of 8 years of age[.] we . . . thank you for our teacher oh, how we all love him[.] [22]

Smith's first visit to the AMA's Indian agencies was made before he received his appointment as an agent. Sela Wright, an AMA missionary already serving in Minnesota, had urged George Whipple to visit the agencies assigned to the AMA before the association began its work or, if he could not come himself, to send "a competent man, one of good judgment, a *practical man,* one who has had *experience,* not a *city* man, who does not know how to raise a hill of beans[.]" Whipple gave the assignment to Smith.[23]

Smith's visit opened a new world to him. Widely traveled as he was, he had had little contact with western Indians—although his contacts with educated Indians in the East were as great as or greater than those of most Americans of his time. Dartmouth College was begun as a school for Indians, and Moor's Indian Charity School in Hanover, which served as a preparatory school for the college, had from one to five Indian students each year during the time Smith lived in Hanover. One of his classmates at Union Seminary, Allen Wright, was a Choctaw Indian from the Choctaw Nation in the Indian Territory. After his graduation from Andover Seminary, Smith preached for six months in Pompey, New York, a town only a few miles from the Onondaga Indian Reservation. A Seneca Indian from New York, Hattie Twoguns, taught for the AMA in Monticello, Florida, and George Freeman, a Penobscot Indian from Maine, taught for the Freedmen's Bureau in Corinth, Mississippi; Smith could have met either or both of them while he worked for the AMA. He was present in Philadelphia when Ely Parker, President Grant's commissioner of Indian affairs, visited the city as a member of Grant's military staff shortly after the end of the war. The gifted Seneca, however, who was trained both in engineering and in the law, was hardly typical of the Indians Smith would encounter on the reservations of Minnesota.[24]

If Smith had any knowledge of the Chippewa Indians before his visit to Minnesota, it would have come from Frederick Ayer, who, before going to Atlanta to work in the AMA's mission to the freedmen, had served as a missionary to the Chippewas for more than twenty years, or from John Bardwell, who had superintended the AMA's Chippewa mission, or Sela Wright, who had twenty-five years' experience among the Chippewas. But whether they shared their knowledge with him or not, Smith had not been selected as an agent for what he knew about the Chippewas; it was for the skill he had shown in developing and overseeing mission work among the freedmen, which the AMA and the Indian Office assumed would also serve him well among the Chippewas.[25]

Smith, who was always quick to form his opinions, returned from his initial visit to the AMA agencies with definite conclusions about past and present Indian policies. The old policy was, he said, "merely to keep the Indians quiet and satisfied as Indians. The new policy aims to hasten their civilization and bring them rapidly into the same relations to society and the government as the foreigners sustain when found within our territory." To achieve its goals the Grant administration planned to induce the Indians to settle on reservations and learn agriculture and trades. Smith realized that Grant's policy was not entirely new; for thirty-five years treaties with the Indians had provided for farms, homes, mills, schoolhouses, and all the means of civilization. But despite an abundant supply of money and men, Smith said that "nothing worth naming has been done on any hand, and the Indian has been held responsible for the failure." He said that at one place, where an agent, a carpenter, a farmer, and a miller had been provided by the government, the Indians were still "living on the 'ground' floor in lodges that have a hole in the top for a chimney, and birch bark and matted grass for a covering. With all this government force, they also had one acre of ground plowed last year."[26]

Smith attributed the failure of the old policy to the carelessness with which men were appointed to carry it out. The Indian agents "have not only been greedy of spoil but have been neglectful and sometimes wantonly cruel in their indifference to the welfare of those whom they were sent to befriend and save—men without heart and sometimes without head—only hands and pockets." But in the new policy there was a "new and totally different spirit." The resources of the government would be in the hands of persons "in hearty sympathy with the work to be done." Smith was confident that "more good influences within the next two years can be put in motion for [the Indians'] recovery from barbarism, than have been realized in all the quarter century past."[27]

Smith did not use the word "barbarism" lightly. It described exactly what he thought of Indian ways. "The Indian is pure heathen," he wrote. "He has nothing in common with us as citizens. He is prejudiced against us and with reason; is satisfied as he is; he believes in the Indian; he would not be a white man if he could. He is not anxious to learn, and his children are equally indifferent. He does not like to work, is careless of the future, has no regard for home, and in his estimation the most worthless thing in this world is land. . . . Very few of the Indians attempt to speak English. What the children learn in school they readily forget in the wigwam and on the trail. . . . Among from one half to two-thirds of the Chippewas, and as many of the Menomenees, the Grand Medicine still holds sway, a superstition as absurd and strong as any pagan religion can show." [28]

Even after he began his service in Minnesota, Smith showed no interest in traditional Indian ways. The skills the Chippewas had acquired in hunting and fishing, in harvesting rice, in making maple sugar, or in using birch bark were of no importance to him. Nor were the dances, the costumes, or the crafts. He made no attempt to learn the language of the Chippewas. He was convinced that the salvation of the Indians would come through the ways of the whites, through farms, lumber mills, and churches, and especially through schools. Smith believed that what had succeeded with the freedmen would succeed with the Indians as well; one of his first acts in Minnesota was to begin the construction of a schoolhouse. But he also believed that success would come much more slowly with the Indians. "One cannot look upon the faces of these Indian children," he said, "and go into their schools without appreciating with a new enjoyment the relish with which the negro children take to letters, and half a century cannot do for these Indians by way of schools what has been done for the negroes in five years, and the difference is almost entirely due to this lack of appetite for learning." [29]

Smith left for St. Paul—1,250 miles and sixty-two hours from Washington—on March 22, 1871, leaving Cleavie and Gerty at their home in Brooklyn. On March 31 he reported to Commissioner Parker that he had arrived in St. Paul "& have entered upon the duties of my office as Indian agent in the purchasing and forwarding of supplies of seeds and agricultural implements and searching for proper persons as employees upon the Reservation. I leave on Monday the 3d for Crow Wing." [30]

18

Minnesota

Minnesota is a State where . . . hatred of the Indian is universal and bitter. . . . Agent after agent, many of them men of notorious character, have fattened upon them; their pine has been stolen; their reserve funds have been spirited away; their school-money has been consumed. . . . As a consequence, they have a deep-seated distrust of the whites, and dread a closer contact with them. . . . And the responsibility for the work among these 6,000 Indians scattered over eight reservations, the furthest of which are 350 miles apart, is laid upon one man.

Nation, October 24, 1872

The new agent for the Chippewas spent most of his first six weeks as an Indian agent traveling across the state of Minnesota, acquainting himself with his new field of work or, as he called it, "my great parish." The headquarters of the agency was at Leech Lake, four days' travel from St. Paul and two days from any telegraph station. Leech Lake and Cass Lake were the homes of the Winnebagoshish, the Cass Lake, and the Leech Lake Pillager bands, some two thousand Chippewas who lived in traditional ways and depended on fish, wild game, berries, and rice for their food. The agency property at Leech Lake consisted of a schoolhouse with an old building attached that could be used as a dormitory, a stable, an unfinished dwelling house for the agent, and four other dwellings ("all unfinished and needing repairs") for the agency's physician, blacksmith, farmer, and carpenter. Erecting suitable buildings at Leech Lake was not an easy matter; the nearest sawmill was seventy-five miles away, "over very rough roads." The sawmill was located at Red Lake, among the 1,049 Chippewas of the Red Lake band, but the mill had not seen much use by the government, which had no buildings of any value there. The Red Lake Reservation was large—some 2,250,000 acres— but only about 1,000 acres, along the lakeshore, were suitable for farming. The Red Lake band lived largely on fish from the lake and sugar they made from the abundant maple trees.[1]

The 2,139 Chippewas of the Mississippi were themselves scattered, living at Mille Lacs, Gull Lake, White Oak Point, Snake River, and White Earth. Treaties with the Chippewas of the Mississippi had guaranteed them large tracts of land—at least one hundred townships—but only sixteen townships, located on the White Earth Reservation, were suitable for agriculture, the rest of the land consisting of marshes and timberland. Even though the government saw great potential for agricultural development at White Earth, the agency property there consisted of only two farms, a farmhouse that also served as the office, "a second-hand sawmill entirely broken down," a blacksmith shop, eight or ten houses for Indians, and five to eight yoke of oxen. The Pembina band was the smallest in the agency, fewer than a thousand Indians living on both the Minnesota and the Dakota sides of the Red River. Their condition was said to be "deplorable, and almost hopeless. They are extremely poor, and, owing to the scarcity of game, their means of subsistence are scanty and precarious."[2]

Travel among the reservations was difficult. One of the army officers who had served as agent for the Chippewas had sometimes found it impossible to visit the various bands, "owing to the terrible condition of the roads, having to pass through swamps, rivers, sloughs, and timber" over "vast" distances to reach them. "The distances & roads," Smith told Cravath, "are simply killing." Supplies for the Red Lake Reservation went first by wagon eighty-five miles from Brainerd to Leech Lake, then fifteen miles across the lake on an unsafe and unreliable steamboat, and then by wagon another seventy miles by a road that was often impassable because of water or mud. A complete circuit of the reservations, necessary at least once a year to pay the annuities due the Chippewas by treaty, required 750 miles travel by wagon and an additional 400 by boat. Nine months after he arrived in Minnesota, Smith reported that even though he had spent all but four weeks of his time from the first of April to the middle of November "in passing from point to point in wagon and canoe, stopping at places from two to four days," he was able to see the Red Lake band only once and was not able to see the Pembinas, Mille Lacs, or White Oak Point Indians until the fall annuity visit.[3]

The government bureacracy Smith had become familiar with in his work with the Freedmen's Bureau followed him to Minnesota. Three years after he completed his work in the state, he was still being questioned about the receipts he submitted for payments made on his travels through the wilderness. The auditors questioned a receipt he received from an Indian who operated a ferry across the Mississippi River, another receipt for a dinner at a farmhouse near Crow Wing, and still another for sardines "used for the noon lunch while on journey with the [wagon] train to prevent [the] necessity of halting long enough to cook meals." Smith tried in vain to convince the auditors that proper receipts could not be obtained on the frontier. He said of one claim questioned by the auditors that the person who supplied him "lived 24 miles from Leech Lake on the road to Brainerd. He is an ignorant halfbreed and keeps no accounts but chalk marks on the door." Someone in the accounting office retained his good humor about the matter, noting on the account: "*Door* to be filed in the [account] as sub-voucher." Smith, too, was able to keep his sense of humor, answering questions about a claim for expenses on a trip of "exceeding hardship and away from settlements" by saying that "the expense would have been greater if I could have found more to eat." Smith's difficulties with the bureaucrats were compounded by the actions of his predecessors; no Chippewa agent before John Bardwell had left "any record or paper of any kind" on file at the agency.[4]

Smith was not in Minnesota long before he became aware of the many clashes in the state between the Indians and white settlers. Increased immigration and the extension of the railroads were bringing settlers into parts of northern Minnesota that had long been the home of the Chippewas. The settlers—largely Swedes—were coming "in platoons" and occupying the Indians' hunting grounds and even their reservations, arousing predictable resistance by the Indians. About the time Smith arrived in Minnesota, the settlers appealed to Governor Horace Austin for assistance against "marauding Indians," and Austin, who had once led a company of mounted rangers against the Sioux, responded by telling Major General Winfield Scott Hancock that if the Indian Office or the military did not compel the Indians to return to their reservations he would take it upon himself to furnish the citizens with arms to protect themselves. The War Department did nothing but pass the information on to the Interior Department, suggesting that the Indians were raiding because they were "in a desperate and suffering condition" and that they should be given temporary supplies of food and the means of raising crops.[5]

A serious disturbance occurred at Leech Lake in May among the Bear Island band of Pillagers, better known among whites as the Scalawag band. When Smith heard of the threat of an "outbreak" by fifteen or twenty "of the worst of all the tribe of Chippewas," he asked for troops from Fort Ripley, and a lieutenant and twenty-five men were sent. Smith himself ordered the arrest of six of the Indians, who were known to have committed murder and robbery and who had burned the mill and destroyed farming tools at the agency. The Indians were arrested and put under guard but then managed to escape. During the escape, the guard fired at the Indians, wounding one of them, who was then recaptured. Smith reported that "the arrest caused great excitement & many threats on the part of the rest of this Band which the shooting by the guard greatly increased." He then asked for an additional force of twenty-five soldiers. Smith believed that the majority of the band would "be secretly glad to have these fellows removed, but they have not the courage to stand openly against them."[6]

In an attempt to capture the Indians who had escaped, forty soldiers surrounded their wigwam at daybreak, but the Indians heard their approach and rushed out, firing at the soldiers. When the soldiers returned the fire, another Indian was wounded and captured, while four others escaped again. Smith then met in council with the leading men and chiefs to discuss the matter. After he spoke to them, they brought pressure on the four men who had escaped, and the four came to Smith and "made their confession, said they deserved punishment and asked to be forgiven. . . . The confession is so humble," Smith said, "& the sentiment among the people so healthy that I have thought it entirely safe to let them go on their parole." Two months later the Indians were still quiet, and Smith reported to Washington that he did not believe there were "forty men in all this tribe of Pillagers who will undertake any violence and with so small a minority no serious evil will be undertaken."[7]

Smith had shown himself to be fearless in the presence of the outlaws. Nor did he have any qualms about using force against them. In that respect he fit in well with Grant's Indian policy. Despite their use of churchmen, the authors of what came to be called the "peace policy"—Grant, Cox, and Parker—were military men who were prepared to use force against hostile Indians or Indians who would not remain on their reservations. So was Smith. Edward Williams said that on another occasion he saw Smith end a disturbance among the Pembinas, "which, but for his calmness and boldness, would have proved serious. Drawing his pistol, he threatened to shoot the first man who should venture to dispute his authority. It was amusing to see how soon the crowd dispersed. It was the power of a word and a look." And when the word and the look and his pistol were not enough, Smith was ready to call in the army. During the time army officers had been assigned to the Indian agencies, the public became accustomed to referring to the agents by their military titles. People in Minnesota often referred to Smith as "Major Smith," and the former parish pastor had enough iron in his character to wear the title well.[8]

With many others, Smith was convinced that whiskey was to blame for much of the trouble with the Indians. He said it was brought in "by the two, three and even *ten* gallon cask by the Indians themselves." At first, the whiskey was obtained at Crow Wing, but as the Northern Pacific Railroad extended across the state, more and more "whiskey shops" were established. Because of the Indians' reluctance to testify against whiskey sellers, Smith employed a detective to find the sellers, and he asked for $1,000 from the Indian Office "for detection and arrest of persons committing crimes against Indians," it being illegal to bring liquor into Indian country. "It will involve considerable expense to watch so many points and successfully prosecute these criminals," he wrote to Commissioner Parker. "Yet it must be done." Smith told Cravath that his two "great difficulties" were "whiskey & suspicion. The one I hope to live down, the other dies hard. But I am striking hard at it & expect to have a string of whiskey sellers at the U.S. Court in Winona in June."[9]

Smith had been in Minnesota only three weeks when Columbus Delano, who had succeeded Jacob Cox as secretary of the interior, appointed him to a commission to investigate alleged frauds concerning what was then called "half-breed scrip" issued to the mixed-bloods of the Chippewas of Lake Superior. When a treaty was made with the Chippewas in 1854, a provision was included that granted eighty acres of land to each head of a family or single adult among the mixed-bloods of the Lake Superior band, presumably to gain their help in winning the Indians' approval of the treaty. The Chippewa agent subsequently provided a list of the mixed-bloods, and the Interior Department issued scrip entitling them to land. Although the scrip was not supposed to be transferable, it was traded, and when the scrip was found to be valuable, an appeal was made to Washington to interpret the treaty to allow the same benefits to mixed-bloods of other Chippewa bands, with the justification that all the Chippewas had at one time lived near Lake Superior, and the Indian Office and the Interior Department agreed to the new interpretation.

Hundreds of new applications for scrip were made and approved, but when the Grant administration took office, Commissioner Parker, informed about possible frauds in the issue of the scrip, refused to approve any new applications, and Secretary Cox appointed R. F. Crowell, a resident of St. Paul, to determine who was legally entitled to receive the scrip. Crowell filed a preliminary report, approving some of the new claims, but when Columbus Delano took office, he decided to appoint a full commission to investigate the matter. The commission was chaired by Henry S. Neal, a lawyer from Ironton, Ohio, who had served the Grant administration previously as consul and, later, chargé d'affaires in Lisbon, Portugal. Crowell was appointed to the commission along with Smith and Selden N. Clark, the agent for the Chippewas of Lake Superior.[10]

With the War Department providing transportation, tents, and rations, the commission began its work late in May 1871. Henry Neal was eager to have Smith join the other commissioners, writing to him that "the Secretary of the Interior depends largely upon your judgment. . . . I hear so much of 'Indian Rings' that I am afraid to turn to the right or to the left and should hence be most happy to have your assistance and advice." Smith, too, had heard enough about "rings" that conspired to defraud the Indians to be suspicious even of the new commissioners. He warned Commissioner Parker that Crowell was planning to use the same interpreters that had participated in an earlier, repudiated census of the mixed-bloods. Smith said that frauds in the issue of scrip were "notoriously flagrant, and I fear that the manner of taking this present census will not go far to relieve the suspicion which hangs over the whole matter." He was also suspicious when Crowell and Neal left St. Paul for Leech Lake without waiting for him. "This movement of giving me no proper notice," he said, "and then going around me entirely, could not but have been designed to obviate the necessity of my presence on the commission."[11]

It was weeks before Smith finally caught up with the commission, but when he did, he discovered that his fears were unfounded. He thought Neal had proved himself "fully competent for his duties," and Smith was pleased to find him already aware of the frauds Smith was convinced had been perpetrated on the mixed-bloods. "His apology for leaving me behind," he reported to Parker, "I accept as ample and can confidently endorse what has already been done by the Commission." Smith gained Neal's confidence too. Neal later referred to him as a "most excellent and efficient agent," who "cannot be bribed, or forced to do a wrong."[12]

The mixed-bloods were interviewed "on the prairie and in the woods and wherever the commission came upon them in their journey across the country." The commissioners soon discovered that the applications submitted for scrip were totally unreliable; the mixed-bloods had been persuaded to sign papers without knowing what they were. But when the commissioners talked with the mixed-bloods themselves, they found that "almost without exception, these persons, though ignorant, are truthful, and will not, even to advance their own interests, make false statements." The interviews led the commissioners quickly to the conclusion of fraud. "Of all specimens of fraud, falsehood and perjury," Neal wrote to Washington, "this scrip business caps the climax." The commission determined that the original list of mixed-bloods eligible for scrip had been correct but that none of the 736 persons who had later received scrip were entitled to it. There was no justification, the commission reported, for giving scrip to any Chippewas but those of Lake Superior, who were well-known as a separate band when the treaty of 1854 allowed land for the mixed-bloods of their band. Nor was there any justification for issuing scrip to both husbands and wives as heads of households, as had been done, and surely none for issuing scrip to persons who were dead, as had also been done. In fifty-eight instances, the commissioners found that the same applications for scrip had been submitted twice.[13]

The commission learned that a former Indian agent, Luther E. Webb, had sent mixed-blood employees out to solicit applications for scrip and that the employees paid persons, with money supplied by Webb, to use their names in applications. The work of Webb's employees, the commission reported, had the "proportions of a regular business." Even names of persons they failed to see were used on applications without their permission, as were names of full-blooded Indians who were not eligible under the treaty. Signatures were obtained on blank powers of attorney so the scrip could be sold with some show of legality. Mixed-bloods who were entitled to scrip and had already received it were told it was worthless and were urged to sell it.[14]

The commissioners at first could not understand why the officials in Washington had approved the issue of scrip to mixed-bloods of other bands, but they became convinced it was because at least one of those officials was himself involved in the frauds. The commissioners reported that they had discovered "clear proof of the complicity of William P. Dole," the commissioner of Indian affairs in the Lincoln administration. "A considerable portion of the scrip was given to him as a consideration for issuing it, and where an attorney or agent declined to share it with him, he refused to issue scrip upon the applications filed."[15]

When the commission completed its work, Smith forwarded its report to the Indian Office in Washington. He had been offered bribes to modify the report, and his friend Gustavus Pike said that "so anxious did he become for the safety of the document, that he mailed it at an obscure country Post-office to insure its arrival at Washington." The commission recommended that no more applications for scrip under the treaty of 1854 be received, unless ordered by Congress, and that the practice of issuing scrip under any treaty be discontinued because it "inevitably leads to *fraud* and *corruption*, and brings no help to the half-breed." It also recommended that those responsible for the frauds be prosecuted. Secretary Delano accepted the report and acted on its recommendations, declaring all scrip except the original issue void and all land entries made with scrip canceled. The commission's report received notice far beyond Minnesota. The *New York Times* regarded it as evidence of the Grant administration's determination to expose fraud. "Rarely," its editors said, "has there been a corrupt phase of Indian affairs more thoroughly ventilated."[16]

Suspicions of fraud in dealing with the Indians were widespread. Smith was suspicious of land claims submitted under another treaty made with the Chippewas in 1855. He reported to Commissioner Parker that the claims were already five times what they should be, "and the business of making up claims is just beginning." In Washington, suspicions had led to charges against Parker himself. A congressional committee failed to find evidence of any fraud or corruption on the commissioner's part, but Parker, discouraged by the charges and by increasing restrictions placed on his authority by Congress, resigned his office in the summer of 1871. The new commissioner, thirty-one-year-old Francis A. Walker, "a scholarly, soldierly, gracious gentleman," was given the office to keep him on the federal payroll so he could complete his work on the ninth census of the United States. Walker, however, was respected both for his brilliance and his honesty and was welcomed by those who were hoping to reform Indian affairs.[17]

Clashes between Indians and settlers continued to claim Smith's attention. In August the sheriff of Douglas County arrested six Indians and brought them to Smith along with a statement from the citizens of Alexandria that the six and some twenty other Indians had been committing "petty depredations and annoyances among the settlers." The six, they said, had camped on one settler's land and stolen potatoes and corn from his fields. When they were warned off the land, they attacked the settlers, who shot and killed two of the Indians. The settlers demanded that Smith keep the rest of the Indians on their reservations and threatened to shoot any they found off the reservations.[18]

When Smith investigated the affair, he found that the Indians had in fact been on uncultivated land and that their corn was not stolen but had been bought from another white man. The settlers who came upon them were armed with guns loaded with buckshot. Finding the Indians lying under their blankets, one of the settlers "began to pull off their blankets; struck one young Indian a severe blow on the head with his fist; struck another with his gun; [and] struck a squaw with his gun, when she told him in broken English that she had not stolen corn but had bought it." When the woman's brother approached the settlers, carrying a knife but with no apparent intention of attacking them, he was shot dead, and when the Indians began to defend themselves, another was killed. The community was full of rumors of armed Indians coming for revenge, but Smith said the Indians were "very quiet and seemed to be more grieved than revengeful" and were willing to settle the matter in court. They brought in seven orphaned children of the two murdered Indians, "the oldest about eight years, and the youngest a babe tied to his cradle board. Both mothers," Smith said, "died a short time since, so that these little ones are in utter helplessness." Smith asked that the U.S. district attorney be instructed to prosecute the settlers for murder, and Attorney General Amos Akerman issued the necessary instructions.[19]

When Governor Austin complained to Smith about thefts and assaults by "roving bands" of Indians in Isanti County and asked for the Indians' removal, Smith wrote a careful reply. He said that the Indians involved were the Mille Lacs, whose lands had been "seized by white men and covered with fraudulent scrip and preemption claims equally fraudulent." The citizens' desire to obtain fifty thousand acres of the best pine lands in Minnesota, Smith said, was the real reason they were calling for the Indians' removal. Smith suggested three courses of action Austin might recommend to the residents of Isanti County. First, they could return the lands they had seized, "thus giving to their heathen neighbors a practical lesson in law and order and common justice." Second, the Indians could be held accountable to the laws of the state against trespassing and marauding. "That there is an occasional offender among these Indians I do not doubt, and I have as little doubt that the prompt arrest and punishment of a few of them would restrain the whole Band." Third, the people who were enticing the Indians off the reservation by selling them whiskey could be prosecuted. "If I could state to the Mill[e] Lac Indians in Council," Smith concluded, "that the Minnesota Chief will forbid his men to steal their lands, and will promptly arrest any Indian who trespasses any Minnesota law, I should be ready to guarantee their good behavior in the future."[20]

Treaties with the Chippewas provided for annuities to be paid each year to the various bands and for boards of visitors who were to observe the payments, guarantee their fairness, and then report to Washington on the condition of the agencies. Representatives of the AMA sometimes served on the boards, and the boards that visited the Red Lake and Pembina bands were routinely appointed on the recommendation of the AMA. The members of the board who visited the reservations with Smith in the fall of 1871, Henry M. Tenney, A. J. Pike, and Edward Williams, were impressed by what Smith, with all his other responsibilities, had been able to do for the Indians. At Red Lake, where Sela Wright was the superintendent, the sawmill and gristmill had been repaired and various new buildings erected, including a warehouse with an upper room for a school, a blacksmith shop, and houses for the blacksmith and carpenter. Forty houses for Indians had been built; "nearly half of these Indians," they reported, "are now out of the wigwam." Wright himself reported that, except for hauling the logs, the Chippewas at Red Lake had performed all the labor on the houses themselves. They also had three hundred acres of their land under cultivation. The Indians were much better clothed than ever before and were holding religious meetings in the upper room of the warehouse. Wright said that in his twenty-five years among the Chippewas the great obstacle to their improvement was the unwillingness of the men to labor, but "all this is changing now." "The spirit of improvement is fairly waked up."[21]

The board of visitors gave the credit for the improvements to Smith. "We desire . . . to congratulate the government in securing the services of the present Agent, Major E. P. Smith, a man eminently fitted, in character, education, previous experience and personal sympathy both with the Indians and with the policy of the government toward them, for the post assigned him." Columbus Delano, the secretary of the interior, also expressed his satisfaction with Smith's service, writing to him, "I desire to express my thanks to you for the frequent evidence you have given of your determination to support the Administration in its efforts to deal justly with these wards of the Government." Delano was also reported to have said in a public meeting, "If there is a man living whom not having seen I love, that man is Edward P. Smith."[22]

Smith received another commendation from Henry B. Whipple, the Episcopal bishop of Minnesota. Whipple, a nephew of George Whipple, had long been a champion of the Minnesota Indians. He once said, "I feel deeply for this poor people and sometimes wish I could give up my office as a bishop and go and die with them." Whipple made frequent visits to the Indians and learned about their activities from the missionaries he sent to them, and with that information he defended the Indians' interests both in Minnesota and in Washington. Bishop Whipple was well aware of the qualifications needed in Indian agents. Before Grant became president, Whipple had advised the secretary of the interior that when a change in agent was made, "it must be to appoint some man not of our state, a man of iron will and spotless character. I fear you cannot find a man here, who will ask it, who is not owned body and soul by some Indian ring. . . . I do not know of any one here who would be a good man, that would take it with the present salary." After Grant turned the Minnesota agencies over to the AMA, Whipple expressed his entire satisfaction with the services of Smith and Selden Clark as the new agents. He told the association he had "watched, with a good deal of anxiety, your agents, and I believe you have reason for thankfulness that they have proved themselves so eminently fitted for their place. . . . I do believe that a great door is opened to give a poor suffering heathen race the blessing of a Christian civilization."[23]

After seven months in Minnesota, Smith was sure he knew what was required to bring Christian civilization to the Chippewas. The sale of the Indians' pine timber was a first step. The timber on the Indians' land was a "perpetual object of greed to lumber-dealers," who schemed to take it from the

Edward Smith as U.S. agent for the Chippewas in Minnesota. Henry B. Whipple once said of Minnesota's winters, "When a cold wave strikes northern Minnesota one is never sure where the thermometer will go. The old settlers have a proverb, 'It would have been colder if the thermometer had been longer.'" Courtesy of Edward Parmelee Smith Papers, Manuscripts and Archives, Yale University Library, New Haven, Connecticut.

Indians. Smith urged the Interior Department to sell the timber and use the money for agricultural and educational purposes. He said he was confident that the Indians "will readily acquiesce when they are made to understand their Great Father is exercising his right of guardianship for their good."[24]

With the proceeds from the sale of the timber, some of the bands without agricultural land could be removed to White Earth, where there was good agricultural land in abundance. The sale of timber would also help solve the difficulties with the Pillagers. "For turbulence and general worthlessness of character," Smith reported, "these Pillagers have had a growing reputation for many years. They have burned their saw-mill, broken up farming-tools, killed their oxen, robbed their warehouse, and attacked employes with impunity, and some of them, during the last winter, held councils with other Indians for another raid upon the whites." Smith's firmness with the Pillagers had quieted them, but their prospects at Leech Lake were dismal, the reservation being in a "barren country, with only here and there a patch of ground susceptible of tillage." The sale of their timber would allow the clearing of some land for farming and the erection of a sawmill to enable the Pillagers to build themselves houses.[25]

Smith would also bring civilization to the Chippewas by giving them schools. "A single summer in the school makes a striking change in an Indian boy, and does more to identify him with the customs of civilization than ten years of help from the Government in the ordinary way." Smith said he had placed an orphaned Pillager boy in school four months earlier, "a most unpromising product of the wigwam—filthy, naked, and in primitive ignorance. . . . In one hour Mr. Strong brought him to me with hair cut and neatly dressed. I named him Columbus Delano, and put him in the boarding-school. He had been a pupil but five weeks when, before the board of visitors, he put sentences from his reading book, in a neat hand, upon the blackboard, and read them distinctly." If he had the means, Smith was confident he could put two hundred children into the school "and in a process of training that would prevent their relapse into the wigwam."[26]

Despite the short time he had been in Minnesota, Smith boasted of good results from his policies. "If you could see what has been done at White Earth in the last six months, how steadily and rapidly the Indians come up—how hopeful they are getting to be—how earnest some of them seem to know a better way! If you could have seen those poor Pillagers, the worst and most hopeless of all Minnesota Indians, as they came in to-day for axes and bush scythes to clear away their lands and get ready for next year, you would say there is hope yet. The feeling towards the schools has changed entirely. White Earth school house will be crowded as soon as it is finished. Red Lakers are pressing Mr. Wright on every hand, and these Pillagers are beginning to think it a privilege to have a child at school." On another occasion, Smith told about a visitor who rode into White Earth with him. "Meeting Indians with their ox-wagons, and looking in upon the night-school of young men just beginning to read and write, [he] said, as if he was half talking to himself, 'I don't see that they need shooting.' " [27]

19

Mission to the Apaches

I think it must have been God who sent Gen. Howard out to us, and I only wish he had come years before.

Santos, Pinal Apache chief

At the beginning of the new year, Smith requested permission to return to Washington for consultations about his work in Minnesota. He also wanted to consult with the AMA officials in New York about work in the other agencies he supervised as the association's secretary of Indian missions. With Commissioner Walker's approval, Smith returned to Washington and spent the next two months there and in New York City.[1]

In Washington, Smith assisted the AMA by seeing congressmen about land for Fisk University and making arrangements for the Fisk Jubilee Singers to perform in the capital. But his main concern was the welfare of the Chippewas. Smith appealed to the commissioner of Indian affairs for the authority and the funds to carry out his plans in Minnesota. He wanted to remove several bands of Chippewas to the White Earth Reservation: the Mississippi Chippewas at White Oak Point, the Gull Lakes, the Mille Lacs, the Otter Tail Pillagers, the Pembinas, and the Pillagers at Leech Lake. "A few years of steady prosperity at White Earth," he said, "will make that country attractive to all the Chippewas, until at no distant day it will become the civilized home of the Tribe of this State." The Indians already at White Earth would set a good example for the newcomers; they had "gone steadily to work and are all living in houses & nearly all dress in a civilized way."[2]

Smith was also concerned about the sale of the Indians' timber. He had met the Indians in council and reported that they wanted to have the timber sold, but at that time he did not have any definite proposals from lumbermen. As the proposals came in, he presented them to Commissioner Walker, saying he thought they were fair and that the Indians would agree to them. Walker told Smith to submit the proposals to the Indians and said that if they did agree to them Smith should enter into contracts with the lumbermen.[3]

Smith had still other concerns: a new steamboat for Leech Lake, the construction of a road from White Earth to Red Lake, and funds for houses for the government employees at the White Earth and Red Lake reservations. He also wanted to create a subagency at Leech Lake to provide more supervision for the work among the Indians there.[4]

The Indian Office, however, was not as concerned with the Chippewas as it was with the Apaches. Some of the Apache warriors had refused to stay on their reservations and had engaged in a series of conflicts with the settlers in the Southwest. The most serious engagement resulted in the killing in April 1871 of 118 Indians, most of them women and children, in what came to be known as the Camp Grant Massacre. Following the killings and an outpouring of sympathy for the Indians in the East, Vincent Colyer, the secretary of the Board of Indian Commissioners, was sent to New Mexico and Arizona on a peace mission and succeeded in bringing about half the warring Apaches onto reservations. Colyer, however, had been ridiculed and abused by the settlers for what seemed to them an unrealistic idealism about the Indians. The eastern civilian had also failed to win the confidence of General George Crook, the commander of the Department of Arizona. After Colyer returned home, Indian raids increased under Cochise, the leader of the Chiricahua band of Apaches, and even the Indians Colyer had convinced to go onto reservations began to join in the raids. The army then stepped up its efforts to keep peace. General Crook was ordered to put all the Apaches on reservations and to keep them there by force. Crook let the Apaches know that after February 15, 1872, military action would be taken against any Indians off the reservations.[5]

Felix Brunot, the chairman of the Board of Indian Commissioners, was appalled at the firm stand the military was taking. The Apaches, he told Columbus Delano, should be treated "with judicious kindness and forbearance" to coax them onto the reservations. Delano agreed to send another emissary to the Apaches, "a commissioner with an 'olive branch,'" who would make one more effort for peace, but Delano realized that this time the mission demanded not only someone sympathetic to the administration's peace policy but also someone credible to the settlers and the military authorities. The man he chose for the mission was a military man himself, General Oliver Otis Howard.[6]

Howard was authorized to employ a "clerk" for his trip, but it was not clear who would fill the position. At first, it appeared that his brother Charles would accompany him. Howard's other brother, the Reverend Rowland Howard, was also mentioned. Three days before Howard left Washington, Delano still thought one of his brothers would make the trip. At the last minute, Edward

Smith was given the assignment, probably at General Howard's suggestion, although Delano had enough confidence in Smith to have made the assignment himself. Smith told Gerty that Delano had asked to see him and that he went "supposing it was about my children in Minnesota or the land grabbers, when he surprised me by 'How would you like to go to Arizona with Gen¹ Howard?'" At first Smith did not see how he could go, but "the next day[,] after thinking of it," he agreed to make the trip. When Rowland Howard heard of Smith's selection, he expressed his satisfaction at the choice. He had earlier declined an invitation to accompany his brother, believing that a minister would be held in contempt by the frontiersmen, but he thought Smith was a minister who had demonstrated his fitness for the task. "He is '*Major*' enough not to make his 'Rev' embarrassing in business. His Army & Indian experience, his good health, clear head & kind heart all qualify him admirably for an adviser & a companion."[7]

At General Howard's request, Brevet Captain Melville Cary Wilkinson of Howard's personal staff was also ordered to accompany him. Wilkinson was a thirty-five-year-old veteran of the Civil War who had been wounded at Antietam and had served briefly on the personal staff of Major General Jacob D. Cox. Shortly after Howard University was established, Wilkinson was appointed military instructor and commandant of cadets at the university, where he organized the students into uniformed infantry companies and instructed them in gymnastics, in infantry and artillery tactics, and in the use of the sword, the saber, and the bayonet. It was ironic that Wilkinson was assigned to travel with the agent for the Chippewas. Twenty-six years later he was killed in a battle with the Bear Island Pillagers at Leech Lake in what has been called "the last Indian uprising in the United States."[8]

Smith telegraphed Cravath, asking him to tell Cleavie that he could not meet her for breakfast in New York the next day as planned: "Secretary Delano sends me to Arizona tonight with Gen'l Howard." Smith was not sure how Cleavie would take the news. He told Mrs. Howard that "she has been for a long while accustomed to unexpected movements, but has never before had anything quite so sudden & so far as this." The men planned to travel by train to San Francisco and then by steamship to Arizona to avoid the long ride by stage—six to nine days through dangerous territory—that would be required if they made the trip by land. Smith's niece Minnie Cook was in Washington at the time, and Smith, concerned about affairs in Minnesota during his absence, had her accompany the group on the train to take memos and write letters as they traveled. The group separated at Chicago, Smith and his niece going to Iowa City to visit Smith's sister Mary and her husband George Thacher, who had recently become president of Iowa University.

After their visit, Minnie went on to see her family in Ripon, Wisconsin, and then set out for the Chippewa Agency, where she was to be Smith's clerk. Smith went on to join Howard and Wilkinson in Omaha. From Omaha the three men traveled to San Francisco over the railroad completed just three years earlier, passing the time by singing "every thing we could think of that would sing." [9]

George Thacher had shared his inaugural address with Smith, who read it on the way to Arizona. The nature of his trip led Smith to think about the value of the traditional college education, and he wrote to Mary to say that he liked the address "tho' I don[']t quite believe it on the 'Dead' . . . languages. . . . If [I] had invested in French & German & *Spanish*, and [Engineering?] & Geology and all other 'ologies that lay upon this round world & tell you what's what, wouldn't I have more capital for operations than I have now? Perhaps not; but I would like to trade some of Prof. Hadley's Subjunctive Moods . . . for a few of these hard *real* things that I bump against every day." [10]

Having four days to spend in San Francisco before their ship left, the men visited General John M. Schofield, whose command included General Crook's forces in Arizona. Smith explained Schofield's philosophy about the Apaches in a letter to Gerty. "[Schofield] thinks they are like some naughty children, never will be good till they have been whipped, and that Gen[l] Crook with his cavalrymen can easily whip them if he can get permission & money enough to pay the expenses. It costs a great deal of money to catch an Indian and 'whip' him." The use of childish terms was appropriate with Gerty, but many adults, thinking of the Indians as children, used the same terms among themselves. Commissioner Walker said the Indians were like children who dislike going to school. "I used to have to be whipped myself," he said, "to get me to school and keep me there. . . . I don[']t believe Indians, as a rule, are any more zealous for self-improvement than most children. . . . The precedent condition of doing anything for them is rigidly to control their attention & demand their presence." General Howard agreed but put it more candidly, saying that "whipping" the Indians meant "that you must kill a certain number to make the rest submissive." [11]

Smith was curious about the Chinese he met in San Francisco, "the strangest & most interesting thing" in the city. "The blue tunics, the pig tails, turn up wooden shoes, flat faces & wide open eyes, meet you every where." He visited a "joss house and saw their idols" and attended a historical play at a Chinese theater, but he showed no more sympathy for Chinese culture than he had for the culture of the Chippewas. Their songs "sounded like a crying baby & *Such* an orchestra. A Chinaman's music is *noise*. Their two fiddles sounded like a hundred cornstalks[,] their drum was like the bang of a cracked kettle & their Cymbals like two of the biggest gongs smashed together perpetually." He also visited a Chinese prayer meeting conducted by an AMA missionary and spoke to the members through an interpreter about two Chinese students at Howard University. He found that some of the younger Chinese wanted to join the church but that not everyone welcomed them, and he told Gerty, "I really think if Jesus sh^d come now from his home in Asia, with his olive complexion & his Eastern dress & long hair they would not want him to join their church. Think of it. Not let Jesus Christ join Christ's Church! They might as well, as to refuse to let one of His disciples join His Church." Smith also visited with his uncle Russell Smith, Noah's brother, who was working as an undertaker in San Francisco.[12]

Smith, Howard, and Wilkinson left San Francisco on the steamer *Newbern*, accompanied by fifty soldiers, six officers, and three doctors who were going to join Crook's command, and by four women, including Mrs. Crook. Smith wrote to his sister Mary that "Genl H[oward] is treated with great consideration by all the passengers & I fall in his wake & get on finely." The trip took them along the coast of California and Lower California, around Cape San Lucas into the Gulf of California, and to the mouth of the Colorado River. On one Sunday, the captain in charge of the soldiers brought them on deck and Smith and Howard both preached to a congregation of thirty-three soldiers, the civilian passengers, the ship's crew, and two Cocopah Indians who were returning to their home. Smith said soldiers always liked to hear Howard speak. "It is so strange a thing to find a real live Christian officer & to have him stand up before his men & talk to them about being Christians." On other days the men passed the time fishing, singing, and watching whales, sharks, and pelicans. They also pitched quoits, the one-armed General Howard, Smith said, putting "his left arm at work as skillfully & effectively as any of us." [13]

The ocean voyage gave Smith time to think about his family, and he wrote to his sister Mary that he was "troubled somewhat by the things I have left behind me in Minnesota[,] and then the Brooklyn home gets into my berth sometimes & shortens up the sleeping at both ends & sometimes breaks into the middle, but I have drifted about so much & God has taken so good care of that home without me, that I 'let her drive'." He also used the time aboard ship to write to Gerty about her religious life. "I want to have a good long talk with you about Jesus & what you can do for Him. You don't want to live without him. Everything that you get without Him will be so poor and seem so small that it won't be worth getting, and everything that you have *with* Him will be so rich & large & lasting. So you must take Jesus along with you everywhere. . . . Stick by Him, Gerty. Make Him y'r fast & best Friend. . . . Gerty, dear, love Jesus every day."[14]

When they reached the mouth of the Colorado River, the company transferred to a flat-bottomed steamer, the *Colorado*, which, "with much impatience & much swearing" by the captain, moved slowly up the river to Yuma and what Smith called "the barbarous wilds of Arizona." Along the way they observed the members of the Cocopah tribe, whom Howard described as "entirely friendly to the whites; but . . . very low in the scale of intelligence, living in huts, wearing scarcely any clothing, and cultivating but very little soil." The employees of the Colorado Navigation Company had given them some employment but had also exposed them to the darker side of "civilization." "In morals they have had rough American teaching," Howard said. "Profanity and licentiousness are said to have been brought even to childhood so that little girls from 11 to 15 years of age are corrupted." Howard reported to Secretary Delano that the Cocopahs needed "teaching in everything. . . . Faithful teachers of both sexes, coming to them in the love of the Master and His work, will not fail to find here a missionary field open to them, as promising certainly as that found on the Micronesian Islands." He thought the government's interest in keeping the river open would justify its calling the attention of some missionary body to "this open and inviting field of labor." The *Colorado* eventually stuck fast on a sandbar in the river, and the men left it to complete the last twenty miles of the trip by land. One month after leaving Washington, Howard reported that the men had arrived at Arizona City, "a busy town of some thirty-five hundred inhabitants," and were ready to begin their mission.[15]

Secretary Delano had given Howard "full power and a general discretion" to implement the department's policy in the Southwest, which was to try to induce the Indians to remain on their reservations and, if possible, to accept a reservation farther east, in New Mexico, and to "cease entirely their nomadic habits and their practices of injustice and cruelty toward the whites," while trying to induce the whites "to treat the Indians with humanity, justice, and forbearance." Howard was to confer fully with General Crook and the other military officers and to cooperate with them as far as was practical.[16]

The War Department also ordered Schofield and Crook to cooperate with Howard. The officials in Washington knew how unpopular Vincent Colyer's mission had been with the settlers and the army's field officers, and they realized that the Apaches posed a real threat, but they made it clear that the army did not have funds enough to fight an expensive war in Arizona and that they were supporting Howard's mission, believing that as a military man Howard would be more cooperative with the army than Colyer was. But even though Howard was a military officer, he had no authority to interfere with or control the officers in the field.[17]

Grant himself had written to Schofield to explain that Howard's mission was to avoid Indian warfare and to implement a policy of civilizing the Indians, but he also said that Indians who would not cooperate "will have to be forced, even to the extent of making war upon them," to ensure the security of the settlers. "It is not proposed that all the protection shall be to the Indians, but that, if they will submit to rules and limitations laid down for them, protection by military force shall be mutual." [18]

Finding that General Crook was not in Arizona City to meet them, Smith and Howard used the occasion to speak to the settlers at a public meeting in the city. "A difficult job," Howard said, "to talk to people who do not agree with you. They are all so sore over Indian barbarities & so prejudiced that they are hard to reach." Smith spoke about the administration's peace policy and of its attempt to deal justly with the Indians by giving them agents and employees nominated by religious groups, who also furnished schools and teachers for the Indians. "Thus," he said, "there may be established on every reservation a colony of sober, industrious, honest laborers" who eventually will induce the Indians to labor for themselves and bring them "slowly out of barbarism. If the children can be kept at school, and this process continued two generations, barbarism is cured. . . . Under the new, just, humane and Christian effort, even the wretched, barbarous Indians of Arizona can be reached." [19]

Howard explained that the Interior and the War departments had but one policy, and that was the policy of the president. "They insist on peace if it can be had," but they did not "propose meanwhile to leave the citizens of Arizona in the terror of robbery and murder by savages, but to protect them, and at the same time give the Indians a fair chance under honest agents, and, in security from the attacks of hostile tribes or hostile whites." Howard denied that because he was a Christian he was a "milk and water sort of a man, going round to pat everybody on the back." He was willing to fight at any time for a peace "that insured security and justice." But he wanted to try the peace policy first. "Let us gather these Indians on reservations, and have force enough to keep them and protect them there." He was convinced from what Smith's year of "honest, patient work" had done for the Indians in Minnesota and from his own experiences with the freedmen that once the Apaches were on reservations they could be taught and civilized if the effort was made.[20]

The general made a better impression on the people than did the preacher, who perhaps reminded them too much of Vincent Colyer. The editor of the

Arizona Weekly Citizen believed that Smith was ignoring the plight of the ten thousand whites in Arizona, a majority of whom were "practically imprisoned in villages and settlements" by the Indians. He objected to the "dogmatic way of the reverend man" and said, "with due gratitude, we rejoice that General Howard is the special agent on this occasion, and not Rev. [E.] P. Smith." But two weeks later, after a discussion with Howard and Smith, the editor said he was convinced that Smith had no intention of ignoring "citizen rights and lives in this Indian business, and it was very unfortunate that when talking at Arizona City, he did not say so. But we understand each other now." [21]

From Arizona City, the emissaries went to the camp of "Pascual, the old Yuma chief," whose people, Howard said, "seem quick-witted, laugh heartily, but numbers of them have evidently been poisoned, all through, with the vices and habits of worthless white men." A meeting was held under a brush awning in front of Pasqual's house, and finding the Yumas in need, Howard authorized the issue of supplies that had been promised to them but had not been delivered. He also appointed an army captain temporary agent for the Yumas and the other tribes along the Colorado River. The men then left for Camp McDowell, where they hoped to meet General Crook.[22]

When they finally met Crook, Howard expressed complete satisfaction in his views. Howard wrote directly to President Grant to say that Crook "is industrious, asks for no more force, believes in punishing the guilty, but is far from being sanguinary in his purposes or practice. I would ask for no better officer to work with me in carrying out what I understand to be your Indian policy." Smith, too, was impressed by Crook, calling him "an unusually humane and fair minded officer." Crook, on his part, resented the authority given to Howard and had little good to say about him. Of Howard's two associates, Crook said later, "[Howard] had with him a Rev. Mr. E. P. Smith . . . who was a bright man, and who tried to restrain many of Howard's weaknesses. . . . He also had an aide-de-camp by the name of Wilkinson, whose stock in trade was religion, who acted as capper for the General." Whatever his personal opinions, Crook agreed to suspend active operations against the Indians while Howard was in Arizona to give him the opportunity to make peace, if peace was possible.[23]

At Camp McDowell, the men were joined by Dr. Herman Bendell, the superintendent of Indian affairs in Arizona. Curiously, the superintendent in charge of "civilizing and christianizing" the Indians was a Jew. When Grant first began to assign Indian agencies to religious groups, a delegation of Jewish leaders visited him to ask why no agencies had been assigned to them. "As an evidence of his good will," Grant promised them a superintendency and later appointed Bendell, a physician from Albany, New York, who had served as a surgeon in the Army of the Potomac during the Civil War, as superintendent in Arizona.[24]

Most of the Indian agencies in Bendell's superintendency had recently been assigned to the Dutch Reformed church. Despite the difference in religion, Bendell looked forward to the agents' arrival. He thought the example of "these self-sacrificing and devout people" would make the Indians receptive to "such religious teaching as might be afforded them." The appointment of the new agents, he said, opened "a new field in missionary labor, and will bring the most cruel savage on our continent to the threshold of and face to face with the highest element in our condition of civilization."[25]

The appointments of the Dutch Reformed agents had just been made when Howard and Smith arrived in Arizona, and they found military officers still assigned to the agencies. One of them, Lieutenant Royal E. Whitman, who was serving at Camp Grant, had recently been arrested on orders from General Schofield. Smith reported to Commissioner Walker that there were two distinct opinions of Whitman in Arizona. All the line officers and citizens who had seen his work—even those who hated Indians—admired him for his "tact, integrity, and wonderful sympathetic power over the Indians." The general attitude, however, was that Whitman was an "infamous character. He is constantly classed with Mr. Colyer in infamy by all the papers and in common conversation." Whitman was charged by General Crook with disobedience of orders, orders that Smith said would drive the Indians from the reservations if obeyed. Smith hoped that Whitman, even though confined, would be able to convince the Indians to stay quiet until he and Howard could confer with their chiefs. One of the most important chiefs, Cochise, had left the reservation with a group of warriors, and Smith took it upon himself to send a runner to find him and arrange for a meeting with Howard. Cochise, however, was not yet ready to meet with the general.[26]

Before leaving Camp McDowell, Howard used his authority to increase the rations given to the Indians. Because the temporary reservation at the camp was too small and had been placed too near the Apaches' enemies, Howard thought the increased rations were necessary to keep the Indians on the reservation. Some of the Indians had already left, and Howard tried to meet with them to discuss their grievances but without success. Still, he was able to report that only at Camp McDowell and Verde had Indians left the reservations.[27]

From Camp McDowell, the men traveled to Camp Grant under armed escort, Smith riding on a little horse he had bought at Arizona City. Howard said that Smith, whom he referred to as "Brother E.P.," had proved to be "a diamond in hardness & value" and that both he and Wilkinson were "liked by the officers everywhere." Camp Grant was considered to be the "very center" of the Apache trouble, but the men found few difficulties among the nearly one thousand Indians living there. The Indians, however, were suspicious at the absence of Lieutenant Whitman, and even though a new agent had arrived, Howard asked that Whitman be returned to the agency to calm them. When he came, Howard and Whitman tried to convince the Indians to accept the new agent, but they would not, and Howard finally asked General Crook to allow Whitman to remain at Camp Grant, at least until Howard had finished his work.[28]

Howard reported that he believed Whitman's conduct to be "upright, kind, wise and successful" and his presence necessary to keep the Indians on the reservation. "The hold we have on [the Indians] during this transfer from Lieutenant Whitman is so slight that a slight misunderstanding is liable to scatter them to the mountains." Privately, Howard told his wife (who was a cousin of Whitman's wife) that Whitman had committed mistakes for which he was paying dearly. "I fear drink is at the bottom of all his troubles." "Once he got on a *spree* & I fear more than once. One's mistakes & evil doings find him out." While they were at Camp Grant, the men visited the site of the Camp Grant Massacre, where the bones of the Apache dead, dug up by coyotes, were still visible. Howard noted that Whitman, whatever his faults, had come out boldly in defense of the Indians at the time of the killings.[29]

When Howard met with the Indians at Camp Grant, he carefully noted their grievances. In addition to wanting Whitman as their agent, they wanted a new and better reservation, peace with the Pimas and Papagos, an increase in rations, and the return of twenty-seven children who had been taken from them during the massacre the year before. While they were at Camp Grant, Smith stayed "night and day among the Indians at the agency building," and he and Wilkinson reported that the Indians were determined to remain on the reservation and keep the peace. Believing the Indians would stay at the agency and needing time to locate the missing children, Howard arranged to return to Camp Grant on May 21 for another council. He was optimistic that with "patient and persistent effort" the problems in Arizona could be solved without war.[30]

Smith, Howard, and Wilkinson traveled from Camp Grant to Tucson with Governor Anson Peacely-Killen Safford, who, when they arrived, gave Smith and Howard his own bed and bedroom. They found the people in Tucson, as at other points, in agreement that the president's peace policy was a good one, "*if* it can be carried out." Too many families had been touched by Indian raids to allow the settlers to believe easily in the new policy. "News of depredations is of constant occurrence," Howard reported, "so that the '*if*' is not to be wondered at." Nevertheless, Howard remained convinced about the possibility of peace. The "if," he remarked, "is not said with any more emphasis than it was said in Minnesota a year ago," and the peace policy had already proved itself there.[31]

While they were in Tucson, Governor Safford, who had earned a reputation as an educator, showed Smith and Howard a free school for Mexicans he had organized and a Catholic school for girls. With Howard as a sponsor, Smith baptized the adopted Apache son of the post surgeon in what Howard thought was the first baptism by a Protestant minister in Tucson. On Sunday, Smith preached at the courthouse about the Israelites' journey through the wilderness—a subject prompted perhaps by his own journey through the wilds of Arizona—and Howard spoke about the purpose of their mission. Howard was introduced by Governor Safford, who expressed gratitude that the government had at last sent someone to Arizona who was willing to work with the citizens and not against them.[32]

At Tucson, Captain Wilkinson left the group to accompany Governor Safford to the southern part of the territory, where Indian attacks had been reported. As he traveled, Wilkinson spoke to the settlers about Howard's determination to settle the Indian question, "peacefully if we can, forcibly if we must; *but settled it shall be.*" Smith and Howard visited the Papago Indians and then traveled with Dr. Bendell to the Pima Agency, where they met with the Pima chief, Antonio. From the Pima Agency they went by buckboard through "*deep, deep* dust" that "filled nose, mouth and covered us with thick coatings" to Phoenix. In Phoenix, Smith preached to a group of citizens on "one day in the life of Christ," and Howard spoke about Indian affairs. Those affairs were not improving. Howard reported that robberies and murders still continued among "the incorrigibly hostile," who would not stay on their reservations, and Howard notified General Crook that he was free to take military action against them.[33]

Howard made plans to return to Camp Grant for the council to be held on May 21 with chiefs of the Apaches, Papagos, and Pimas. After the council, Howard and his associates, accompanied by Dr. Bendell, were to take a group of chiefs to Washington in a long-established ritual designed to show the Indians the size and power of the nation and the futility of opposing its wishes.

On May 6 Smith and Howard visited the Apaches at the Date Creek Reservation, and on May 9 they arrived at Fort Whipple, near Prescott, having taken a trail over the mountains to save twenty miles on the trip. Howard said he was glad they took the trail because it showed them the difficulties troops would have in conducting a campaign in that country, "so full of precipices, trackless deserts, and strongholds and hiding-places." At Prescott, Howard and General Crook addressed a large gathering of citizens, and Smith baptized the infant daughter of Captain and Mrs. A. H. Nickerson in the presence of a large company of officers and civilians. It was also at Prescott that Smith received news that convinced him he would have to leave the mission and return to Minnesota.[34]

On the night of April 26, John Cook, who had earlier served as a government employee among the Indians at Leech Lake, had been murdered, along with his wife and three young children, at Oak Lake, Minnesota, some twenty miles south of the White Earth Reservation. After their murders, their house had been burned around them. A report reached Washington that "their bodies were entirely consumed, the charred bones only remaining to mark the spot where their lives were lost." A dozen Pillager Indians had been seen camping and hunting near the Cook home, all of whom left the night of the murders, and moccasin tracks and an Indian knife were found near the ruins of the house. The conviction that the Cooks had been murdered by Indians produced an alarm among the citizens—"almost amounting to a panic"—greater than that caused by any similar incident since the Sioux war of 1862. The disappearance of a white woman, Helen McArthur, near Crow Wing, Minnesota, two days later, and the suspicion that she had been murdered by Indians added to the public's alarm.[35]

Smith reported to Commissioner Walker that because of the unrest in Minnesota he felt compelled to return to his agency and that he had obtained Howard's permission to go. Forced to leave before the council at Camp Grant, he later told Howard that he "felt like a deserter all the way down, and my desolate ride on a buckboard did not improve my state of mind." He said he spent three days and two nights on the buckboard, "alongside of a driver, part of the time asleep and part drunk (I mean the driver,)." He returned by way of San Francisco, where he found the newspapers celebrating Howard's permission to General Crook to resume military action against the Apaches. Smith thought the attitude of the newspapers showed "how greedy they are to the last for blood."[36]

The council at Camp Grant was a success. General Howard obtained pledges of peace from the Apaches and a commitment to assist General Crook in finding the "incorrigible" Indians who remained off the reservation. He also convinced a delegation of chiefs from Camp Grant and from the White Mountain Reservation to accompany him to Washington. On his return to the capital, he reported to the secretary of the interior on the success of his trip. Despite Smith's "desertion," Howard expressed appreciation for his work in Arizona. He reported to Secretary Delano that both Smith and Captain Wilkinson "exhibited during this long and tedious effort at conciliation continued patience and unflagging energy." Four years later, after Smith's death, Howard wrote to Michael Strieby about the Arizona trip and Smith's part in it. "Who can forget his trip with me to Arizona? Multitudes of white people turned out to hear him preach the true Gospel of 'peace and good-will,' and multitudes of Indians then and ever after felt the impulse he gave to their beginnings in the march toward civilization. He preached to tearful listeners. He baptized children. He rode to the front in places of danger with unpretentious and unshrinking courage. He spoke to prejudiced men and women, unpopular and unwelcome truths, succeeding in making 'the peace policy of the President' better understood and more respected in that far off country." [37]

Smith, on his part, thought the trip "quite important and entirely successful." He attributed its success to General Howard's ability to convince the white citizens of Arizona that the peace policy would benefit them as well as the Indians. Smith left Arizona with a new confidence in the administration's policy of "changing the condition of the Indian by treating him as a human being capable of developement and training, rather than feeding him like a caged animal as heretofore. To[o] great stress," he said, "can hardly be laid on the wisdom and duty to provide for schools as well as for honest and competent employees of different kinds." [38]

Smith also left Arizona with a new appreciation for the attitude of the settlers. "On reflection and distance," he told Howard, "I am not so much surprised at the universal feeling against the Indians by citizens. . . . Constant dread of the tomahawk and scalping knife unfits a man for a Christian or even human view of his duty to his neighbor." Reflecting on a massacre reported while they were in Tucson, Smith asked Howard to "multiply the impression which we received at Tucs[o]n on the announcement of that massacre thirty fold every year for ten years, and have no tide of public opinion to correct the wrong feeling, and you can easily imagine where the Com[r] and his 'numerous' staff [Howard, Smith, and Wilkinson] would be at the end of the ten years." After giving Howard his recommendations about the reservations and agents in Arizona, Smith concluded his report with a benediction on the general and the Arizona trip. "May God give you rest and peace and may the Apaches remember their 'Great Father sent from Washington['] with a grateful heart ever more. Now for Grant and Henry Wilson and four years more of humane missionary work." [39]

20

The White Earth Reservation

The Ute and the wandering Crow
Shall know as the white men know,
And fare as the white men fare;
The pale and the red shall be brothers,
One's rights shall be as another's,
Home, School, and House of Prayer!

John Greenleaf Whittier,
"On the Big Horn"

Smith arrived in St. Paul on June 3, 1872, and immediately set out to learn what he could about the Cook murders. Governor Austin had offered a reward for the capture of the murderers and, assuming that they were Indians, issued a proclamation declaring all Indians in the state who were not on their reservations "trespassers and disturbers of the public peace." Public officials were to warn them to return to the reservations, and if they did not, the governor pledged to provide military assistance sufficient to force them to return. He had already furnished arms to the citizens at Oak Lake, the site of the murders. Austin blamed the federal government for the difficulties with the Indians. The government, he said, should keep the Indians on their reservations and maintain them there "and not turn them loose upon unarmed, scattered & poor frontier settlers to gain a precarious subsistence from theft, rapine and murder. The so-called Indian Policy now in vogue is very well in theory, but in results is only less vicious than its predecessor."[1]

James Bean, who was clerk at the Chippewa Agency before Minnie Cook arrived, had feared further Indian attacks and requested that fifteen soldiers be sent to White Earth and that the force at Leech Lake be increased to forty soldiers, and General Winfield Scott Hancock approved his requests. A detachment under the command of Captain William S. McCaskey went to the White Earth Reservation. McCaskey reported that the soldiers would stay there and that sixty Indians with shotguns could be mustered to assist them if necessary. Troops were also sent to Leech Lake, the home of the Pillagers who had been seen at Oak Lake when the Cooks were murdered. Despite all the military precautions, or perhaps because of them, there was no more violence.[2]

Bean had consulted with the governor and then began an investigation of the Pillagers seen at the Cook home. He found a watch and some clothing belonging to the Cooks in the possession of one of the Indians and promptly arrested him, along with an Indian who was accused of another murder the previous year. Bean then went to Leech Lake and met with some 150 Pillagers in council and asked them to arrest the other murderers. Flat Mouth, the head chief of the Pillagers, responded by saying that three Chippewas had been shot by whites during the past year, and nothing had been done about those murders. Flat Mouth said the Pillagers would cooperate in finding the murderers, but he thought white murderers should be punished too.[3]

One of the first things Smith did when he returned to Minnesota was to meet with the Pillagers. The Pillager chiefs sent a petition to Governor Austin, asking him to attend the council, and Smith endorsed the petition, but he did not approve of the Pillagers' request to have the Indian who had been arrested brought to the council. "His presence in irons & under guard," Smith told Austin, "will excite a sympathy among the Indians that will hinder rather than help the full commit[t]al which I hope will be made by the Chiefs of all their influence to help you keep law & order in the State." Nor did Smith approve of Austin's bringing troops with him, as had been rumored. Smith assured the governor that the Indians meant to do no harm and said that the presence of troops would only confirm the fears "which have been so great & wide spread in the western part of the State, but which are now happily subsiding, that a general outbreak is seriously threatened." Smith succeeded in obtaining the council's "strong disapprobation" of the conduct of the murderers and its agreement to assist the government in "putting down any and all enemies of the peace."[4]

Smith did more than talk; he arrested an Indian named Little Snake, who was charged with a murder the previous summer, and sent him to Fort Ripley "in irons." Believing that other Indians who were guilty of murder would visit the prisoner at Fort Ripley, Smith directed Captain McCaskey to arrest any Indian visitors. Smith was convinced that he could obtain the names of the other murderers from the prisoners and that once he had the names, the chiefs would surrender them. If they would not, he thought "the withholding of the annuity payments will be quite certain to bring them to propriety." Smith also went to St. Paul to interview Bobolink, the Indian confined there for the murders of the Cook family. When Bobolink named two accomplices, Smith promptly returned to White Earth and arrested them. To be just to the Indians, Smith also asked Commissioner Walker for authority to provide counsel to prosecute the white murderers Flat Mouth wanted arrested. "A vigorous attempt to see justice done to the Indians in this matter," Smith told Walker, "would have a wholesome effect on both Whites and Indians."[5]

As he pursued his investigation, Smith discovered that the Cook murders were not an isolated incident. A year before, a white man walking on the open prairie had been shot by two Indians. "He was an entire stranger to them, and there seems to have been no motive for it but mischief. His body was plundered, and afterwards covered up by the same Indians." Not long after that a Swedish couple was killed and their bodies and home burned, for no motive except "plunder." Another man had been shot and wounded when he drove an Indian away from his house "for improper conduct." The Indians implicated in these incidents and the Cook murders were all young men, ranging in age from sixteen to twenty-four, who had broken away from tribal restraints and become "vagabonds and outlaws." Smith reported to Commissioner Walker that "there is not, and has not been, the slightest danger of an outbreak by any of the Chippewa Tribes. But this peril of death by marauders will hang over all settlers on the border until this class of Indians are recovered from lawlessness, or placed beyond the power to do harm."[6]

One obvious solution to the conflicts was to force the Indians to remain on their reservations—and Smith thought Austin's proclamation requiring them to stay there "just and proper"—but he also said that at Leech Lake, the source of most of the difficulties, it was a "physical impossibility" for the Indians to live on the reservation. There was not enough game for hunting or enough land suitable for farming. The Otter Tail Pillagers were in an even more desperate situation. Their land had been sold without their consent in 1855, and they had such an aversion to the Leech Lake band that "nothing short of the bayonet will force them to the Leech Lake Reservation." Smith's solution was to ask General Hancock for funds to support both the Leech Lake and the Otter Tail bands as "prisoners of war." He was sure that if he could provide for the Indians for six months and insist on their labor in return for the provisions, he could establish the Otter Tails in new homes at the White Earth Reservation and begin clearing land at Leech Lake so that the Indians there could support themselves by farming. Hancock endorsed Smith's proposal, as did General Philip Sheridan and Secretary Delano, but the secretary of war refused to provide the funds.[7]

As Smith struggled to provide for the Indians and prevent further conflicts, an ugly incident at Brainerd added to the unrest in the state. An Indian woman at Crow Wing accused two Gull Lake Indians of raping and then murdering Helen McArthur, the white woman who had disappeared shortly after the Cook murders. The two Indians were arrested at White Earth and went readily with the sheriff on Smith's assurance of protection and a fair trial. They were imprisoned at Brainerd, where a mob of three hundred men, women, and children battered the jail door down, seized the two, and hanged and shot them. Rumors spread through the town that two hundred Indians were coming to avenge the deaths, and Governor Austin dispatched three companies of militia to Brainerd. At the governor's request, General Hancock ordered the whole garrison of federal troops at Fort Ripley dispatched to White Earth to protect the settlers there. The rumors, however, proved false, and the only fighting occurred when the militia tried to quiet a disturbance at a Swedish boardinghouse in Brainerd. But the incident had already done its damage to the fragile peace in Minnesota.[8]

The constant conflicts between whites and Indians convinced Smith that his previous plan for removing the Chippewas from the scenes of the conflicts had been right, and he increased his efforts to implement it. His plan fit in well with the general policy of the Indian Office, which was to concentrate Indians on reservations where they might be both "christianized and civilized." A treaty made with the Chippewas of the Mississippi in 1867 had set aside thirty-six townships for them at White Earth in northwestern Minnesota. It also provided for allotments of forty-acre tracts to Indians who would move there and put ten acres under cultivation. The Indians were not eager to go, but some five hundred had settled there by the time Smith arrived in Minnesota. Smith, like many others, believed that the White Earth Reservation was an ideal location for the experiment of civilizing the Indians. The soil was "excellent and the country finely diversified by prairie, timber, and lakes." In 1872 Smith moved the agency office from Leech Lake to White Earth, where, on a treeless knoll overlooking twelve lakes and a vast plain, he had arranged for the construction of new government buildings, including a school, a barn, a carpenter's shop, an office, and houses for the agency employees and for himself. He also had fifty houses built for Indians, and with that done he increased his efforts to move the Indians from around the state to the reservation at White Earth.[9]

Smith met in council with the various bands to try to convince them to go to White Earth, and when he received assurances that they would go, he sought funds from Washington to pay for the move. He then negotiated with the Chippewas of the Mississippi, to whom the White Earth Reservation had been given, for reservation land for the other bands. When all parties had agreed to the move, he used the money from Washington to feed the Indians as they arrived at the reservation, requiring them in return to provide the labor for clearing land and building their own houses. Smith used

The office of the U.S. Indian agent at the White Earth Reservation in Minnesota, 1872. Agent Edward Smith and Minnie Cook (1848–1927) are in the doorway. The man leaning on the fence is the issue clerk, Alexander Smith, who was not related to Edward Smith. Photo by Hoard & Tenney, Winona. Courtesy of the Minnesota Historical Society, St. Paul, Minnesota.

every means possible to obtain the removals. The Indians at White Earth were told that any further benefits from the government depended on their giving part of their land to the other bands, and the Indians who were reluctant to move to White Earth were threatened with the withholding of their annuities. The members of the various boards of visitors were generally in agreement with the removals. After visiting the Pembinas, one of the visitors reported that their condition was "SAD!" and their future "yet more DARK." He recommended that "they all, every one, be removed, nolens, volens" to White Earth.[10]

When the Indians were settled at White Earth, Smith insisted that they continue to work. Aaron Murray, who was in charge of the White Earth sawmill, said Smith told him to employ as many Indians as he could, saying, "I wish you would get them from this miserable habit of gambling and try to

The school at the White Earth Reservation in Minnesota. Hattie Cook
is in the front row, left. Photo by Hoard & Tenney, Winona. Courtesy of the
Minnesota Historical Society, St. Paul, Minnesota.

get them to work; get them to put on clothes; have them dig up these stumps
around here . . . ; work every Indian that you can." Smith's rule was that
nothing would be given to an Indian unless he worked for it. Some of the
Indians complained that government supplies were theirs by right—they had
been appropriated for them by Congress—but Smith insisted that work be
performed for anything issued from the warehouse.[11]

Smith's own family also moved to White Earth. Smith's friend from Oberlin, John Ellis, visited White Earth in the fall of 1872 and found Cleavie
Smith busily at work on the reservation. Ellis said that when Smith first came
to Minnesota his wife had stayed in "their beautiful home in Brooklyn," but
that, coming to visit a few months before Ellis's visit, "she became so much
interested in the Indians and the work for them, that she sent back for her
goods, shut up the Brooklyn house and decided to remain at the agency in
the wilderness. There we found her going among the wigwams, caring for the
sick, teaching the women to sew and encouraging old and young to improve
their life and condition." Smith told Cravath that Cleavie was with him at
White Earth, "busy with her work for the Indians. She is giving them the
gospel of soap." Gerty was there, too, but Smith said the young Brooklynite
was already "getting tired of the dull country." Smith's niece Hattie Cook
also came to White Earth to teach the Indian girls "domestic economy." Her

sister Minnie taught with her, in addition to working as her uncle's clerk, cutting and fitting garments, trimming hats, teaching carpet making, giving music lessons, and teaching in the night school.[12]

The presence of his family reminded Smith of the son who was not with them. The Christmas before, Smith had sent a gift to Atlanta University. He enclosed a letter describing the death of his son at Nashville and said he had hoped "the dear boy would live to do good to the poor whom the war was liberating. That could not be, and I want now to connect him with your work in Atlanta. With the enclosed check furnish a room, and over the door, write the name, *Clarke.*" With his family's arrival in Minnesota, Clarke was again on Smith's mind, and when he wrote to Cravath about another family that had lost a child, he said, "May the shadow of a little coffin never fall on your threshold." [13]

John Ellis spoke glowingly of the White Earth Reservation. It was, he said, the "garden of Minnesota—a mixture of woodland, rolling prairie and lakes." The soil was "rich and warm"; for the cultivation of wheat and potatoes "nothing can excel it." Smith, he reported, was attempting to get the Indians "to help themselves, and form the habits of industry and economy." He was using government funds to pay the Indians for building houses and fences and cultivating the land. He said Smith offered a house and ten acres of land to every family that would plant and care for it and forty acres to those who would work a larger farm. "He favors all who will give up their wandering habits, have their hair cut, and give up the blanket for a coat. When they can be induced to do these two things they are fully committed to a civilized life." But Ellis discovered what it cost the Indians to abandon their culture. "An old chief just come to the Reservation, was persuaded after much argument to submit his long locks to the scissors, but as soon as the deed was done, he put his face in his hands and cried like a child." [14]

Ellis was amazed at what Smith had accomplished in a year and a half. A "fine steam saw-mill" was turning out lumber at the rate of ten thousand feet a day, and although the supervisors were whites, all the work was done by Indians. Seventy-five to one hundred Indian children were boarded and taught in two school buildings. Ellis listened to them sing one Sunday, "the same songs which we should have heard in the Oberlin Sunday school." The Episcopal church conducted the mission work on the reservation and had built a chapel and a fine parsonage for the Chippewa minister. Ellis attended a worship service, which three hundred Indians, "well dressed and well mannered," attended and for which Minnie Cook played the organ. Ellis attributed the progress he saw at White Earth to Grant's new Indian policy. "If the present administration had accomplished nothing else, it would deserve the gratitude and support of all good men for its persistent and wise efforts to deal justly with the Red man." [15]

One of the teachers at White Earth, Alice Armor, described the payment of annuities—"that Indian jubilee"—at the reservation that fall. More than a thousand Indians from various bands gathered for the payments. "Wigwams sprang up in the woods and by the wayside, and gay blankets were seen in great abundance." As the Indians' names were called off, the heads of families came forward and received $10 for each member of the family, while traders stood at the door of the office ready to present their bills. Goods were also distributed as specified in various treaties: blankets, coats, and pants; shawls, calico, and linsey; tobacco and beef. "All day long, groups of Indians lay in the grass around the school buildings, some of them flat on their faces sound asleep," while others spent the time gambling. Amid these activities, Armor was pleased to see one man use his money to purchase a cookstove and haul it away with his own team of oxen. Another man, who had been working on the school buildings for several weeks, continued to work through the payments. "It was," Armor said, "as if a boy at home should continue his labor voluntarily in the midst of a fair or a fourth of July celebration." She thought the Indians who had been "under the influence of civilization" at White Earth stood out from the other Indian visitors; Armor noted boys who were "as neatly and tastefully dressed as the average boy at home. These are little things certainly, but they are the straws which we think, show that the wind is blowing in the right direction, and when another autumn brings another pay party we hope they will find that this people have taken another long step toward a Christian civilization." Armor, like Ellis, attributed the progress at White Earth to the president's peace policy and rejoiced that Grant had been elected for another four years.[16]

Methodist bishop Gilbert Haven, who visited White Earth at the time of the annuity payments, also came away praising the president. "The new Indian policy," he wrote, "is all his own. When his place is as remote in history as that of Jefferson and Washington he will shine as bright or brighter for this pre-eminent act of wisdom and righteousness." [17]

Still another visitor to White Earth, writing under the name Kent, noted that the change in the attitude of the Indians was just as remarkable as the physical improvements. The day for the payment of annuities to the Chippewas had long been a day for complaints about their agent; "this year there was an entire absence of anything of the kind." The Indians were pleased at the changes on the reservation. "One has only to see the conscious pride with which men who, a year ago, were worthless savages, drive their oxen, and point to their gardens and houses, to be convinced of the strong hold the new life has upon them." Kent added that the Chippewas were blessed with an agent "not only of irreproachable character" but who also had "much experience" with similar work in the South.[18]

Ellis and Armor published their reports about the White Earth Reservation in the *Lorain County News* at Oberlin, Ohio. Haven published his in the *Independent*. Kent's report was published in the *Nation*, from which it was copied in the *New York Times*. Still other reports about White Earth appeared in the *Advance*, the *American Missionary*, the *Friends' Review*, and the Episcopal *Spirit of Missions*. The White Earth Reservation was becoming a national showpiece for the benefits of Grant's Indian policy, and Smith's name was becoming known far beyond Minnesota.[19]

Half-breed scrip again became a concern of Smith's when Congress passed an act to provide benefits for persons who had come into the possession of fraudulent scrip innocently. After the scrip commission submitted its report, Columbus Delano had asked Smith for his recommendations on implementing it. Smith noted that the scrip had been "freely dealt in by first class banking houses and men of respectable repute in Minnesota," and as a result, the land obtained with it was held by many people "removed from any intent of fraud." Smith suggested, as an act of fairness, that those persons be allowed to buy the land at a reasonable price set by the government. In the summer of 1872 Congress passed an act providing for such purchases, and Delano appointed another commission to determine who the innocent persons were. Smith was appointed to the commission, as were Dana E. King of Minneapolis and Judge Thomas C. Jones of Delaware, Ohio.[20]

When the commission began its work, it discovered that most of the claimants were lumbermen who had obtained valuable pine lands with the scrip, and Smith told Henry Neal that the commission was "inquiring as to who among the pine men of this State are virtuous. They say that there are several such to be found." The commission began its work before the presidential election, and Smith wanted to complete the work as soon as possible in case Grant lost the election and a new administration might revert to the old practices regarding scrip. The commission met in Minneapolis in August 1872 and again in St. Paul in November and, after hearing testimony, reported thirteen individuals and firms that were entitled to the benefits of the act of Congress. The commission also appraised their lands and recommended the prices that should be charged for them. The members of the commission believed the persons involved were innocent of fraud but that they had shown a "reckless carelessness" in their investments and so had become victims of the persons who had "got up the scheme" and had managed it "with wonderful prudence and caution."[21]

Between the two sessions of the commission, the commissioners had visited the White Earth Reservation. Judge Jones was particularly impressed by the church service he attended. He reported to Secretary Delano that when the visitors were asked to address the congregation, he was "so overwhelmed with gratitude to God for the great work He was doing through the President, and your Department, for these poor children of the wilderness, that I could scarcely speak." "The judgment of the whole party" was "that President Grant and those in authority with him were entitled to more credit for the glorious work they are doing for the Indians, than it was possible for any one to conceive who had not witnessed its practical operation." [22]

With the approval of the Office of Indian Affairs, Smith prepared to sell the Indians' timber. Dishonest lumbermen were no longer able to obtain timberlands with fraudulent scrip, but that did not hinder them; they simply invaded the reservations and stole the timber. One man had made a show of legality by calling the Indians together and offering them a contract for their lumber but had done it without Smith's knowledge or approval. Smith appealed to Washington for funds to have the reservations surveyed so as to identify the timber that belonged to the Indians, and then he sought to sell as much of the timber as possible to give the Indians its benefit. After meeting with the Indians and giving notice of the sale, he awarded contracts for the timber on several reservations, subject to the approval of the Indian Office. [23]

The Indian Office, however, soon began to receive complaints from lumbermen that Smith had entered into contracts for the timber without giving adequate notice of the sale. They were joined in their complaints by Cadwallader Washburn, the governor of Wisconsin. Washburn sent a clipping from the *St. Paul Pioneer* that said the notice of the sale was placed in an "obscure corner" of the *Minneapolis Tribune* and did not appear until eighteen days before the bids were due. The affair, Washburn said, had "a bad look, a very bad look. The advertisement shows it to be a job in the interest of rascals who have knowledge that is not in the possession of the general public. A man may have 'Rev.' prefixed to his name and yet be a villain at [best?]." [24]

Bishop Whipple told Commissioner Walker that it would have been better if Smith had given longer notice of the sale, but he also forwarded a letter from C. M. Loring defending Smith. Loring traced the opposition to Smith's actions to Charles A. Ruffee, a trader and an unsuccessful candidate for the Chippewa Agency who had once brought charges against a former agent, Joel Bassett, which the Interior Department investigators were not able to substantiate. According to Loring, Ruffee claimed that Smith had promised one of the timber contracts to him and said he would "break" the agent for not giving it to him. Loring also said that Ruffee tried to learn from Smith what the other bids were "so that he could put in a bid after the regular bids were opened. This the agent refused to do." Loring felt it was his duty "to vindicate the character of a man who I believe to be an honest, sincere and faithful worker." [25]

Smith confirmed that Ruffee had attempted to enter into a "corrupt agreement" with him. Then, in response to the charges made against him, Smith said he had put the advertisement in the principal paper of the principal lumbering town in the state and that before awarding the contract he had consulted with men acquainted with the lumbering business, who assured him that the contract was fair. But one of the men who had not seen the advertisements, Amherst H. Wilder, a businessman from St. Paul with a long history of government contracting, took his appeal directly to Washington. Wilder visited the Office of Indian Affairs, where he told Commissioner Walker that he had not seen the notices of the sale earlier and that he was willing to pay $1.60 per thousand feet for the timber at White Oak Point on Leech Lake. Wilder's bid was higher than any that had been received, and even though the bid was late, Walker's office instructed Smith to cancel the contract he had made earlier and enter into a contract with Wilder. The contract was not made immediately; the Indians at White Oak Point informed Smith that the chief who had given their assent to the sale was not authorized to speak for them, and Smith eventually found it necessary to go to Washington to make the arrangements for the contract. There, at Walker's suggestion, Wilder enlarged his bid to include all the timber at Leech Lake. When the contract with Wilder was finally signed, it became the source of other, more serious charges that would plague Smith nearly a year later.[26]

When Smith visited Washington in late October and early November to settle the timber contracts, he was offered a new position in the Indian service: superintendent of Indian affairs in New Mexico. General Howard was expecting to receive a command that included New Mexico, and if he did, Smith was ready to go with him as superintendent. But Howard did not receive the command, and another man was appointed to the superintendency.[27]

Justice for the Indians was on Smith's mind, and after he returned to Minnesota he wrote an article about it for the *American Missionary*. He told about two contrasting verdicts brought by the same jury at the criminal court in Ottertail County, Minnesota. One case involved two white men who had attempted to arrest an Indian even though they had no authority to do so. When they found him in his home, a third man "put his musket to the Indian's face and shot him dead." The grand jury not only refused to indict the men but refused to have the witnesses called. The jurors did hear the testimony of the man who shot the Indian but dismissed the case against him. A few hours later, the same jury, on hearsay evidence only, voted to indict an Indian for the murder of a white man. Smith said "it was remarked quite freely as a sufficient explantion of this course of justice . . . that several members of the grand jury had lost relatives in the massacre by the Sioux in 1862."[28]

Smith said he found it impossible to explain Ottertail County justice to the Indians, who could not understand "why their Great Father at Washington, or the Minnesota Chief . . . is not able to punish bad white men as well as to catch and punish Indians." Nor could the Chippewas understand why they should be blamed for what their old foes, the Sioux, had done ten years before. The president, Smith concluded, had pledged his support for a humanitarian Indian policy, "but what can the policy of the White Chief, be it ever so kind and true, effect, so long as the practice of his white braves is persistently revengeful, mean and cruel!"[29]

Smith reported the same information to Commissioner Walker and added that he had not been able to obtain any judicial action in the lynchings at Brainerd. None of the more than five hundred persons who witnessed the lynchings would testify about them. "This uneven justice," he told Walker, "has a very depressing effect upon all efforts to induce the Indians to begin to live in an orderly way and to submit their grievances to the cause of law." Walker passed Smith's report on to Secretary Delano, noting that Smith was "a moderate, sensible, and truthful man, whose statements may be accepted with entire confidence." Walker said he passed the letter on only for the record so that if his office was unable to restrain the Indians, "exasperated by such wanton contempt of law, justice, and public decency, neither this office nor the Indians may be unduly blamed for any consequences which may ensue."[30]

At the end of 1872, as he had the year before, Smith returned to Washington to consult with officials in the Indian Office and to visit the AMA secretaries in New York City. This time he remained in the East for ten weeks. His presence in the capital allowed him to attend the annual conference of the religious societies working among the Indians. Each year, in January, representatives of the societies came to Washington to meet with the Board of Indian Commissioners and the commissioner of Indian affairs to report on their activities and to make suggestions for the future. Smith attended the conference and reported on the four agencies assigned to the AMA: the S'Kokomish Agency in Washington Territory, the Green Bay and Lake Superior agencies in Wisconsin, and his own agency in Minnesota.

The Indians at Green Bay, he said, had done their own lumbering during the year and made a profit of $12,000, but such a "great outcry was raised" by the lumbermen in Wisconsin that the secretary of the interior had appointed a commission to investigate the matter. The commission's report that the lumbering was beneficial and "entirely upright" had satisfied the department. Opponents of the lumbering, however, had succeeded in blocking it during the present year, and misrepresentations about the agent had caused the department to ask the association to replace him.[31]

At his own agency, 109 "comfortable log-houses, 18 by 22 feet, with five rooms in each house" had been built during the year, almost all the work having been done by the Indians themselves. The association had no doubt about the "practicality of christianizing" the Chippewas or any of the Indians under its charge. "It is only a question of time and patience, of kind and fair dealing." It was true, Smith said, that the new Indian policy was more expensive than the old one, but the larger expenditures would enable the Indians, in time, to become "self-supporting, valuable citizens" no longer in need of annuities, "and eventually millions of dollars will be saved." He concluded by saying, "I have no question but that a single generation, with the children kept in school, will crush the barbarism in Minnesota."[32]

Bishop Whipple had come from Minnesota to attend the conference and commented on Smith's report. "For the first time in my connection with Indian affairs," he said, "have I found an agent and his employes wholly occupied with their labor for the Indians." Smith had not only been faithful in his duties but had succeeded in doing his work under great opposition. The bishop singled out the agent's wife for special praise for her efforts to "civilize and elevate the Indian women. Mrs. Smith has been teaching these women to make soap, and their households have been entirely renovated; and, so far as I know, every effort which honest, faithful Christian people could make for the safety of these poor people has been made."[33]

The harmony that prevailed among the religious societies at the conference was marred at one point by criticisms of the superintendent of Indian affairs in Arizona. The Reverend John M. Ferris, the representative of the Reformed Church Mission Society, which supplied the agents in Arizona, said that, because of the superintendent's "entire want of training in what we may call Christian benevolent work . . . he utterly fails to cooperate with our agents in regard to education, or in regard to Christian work." Ferris said that a year before, when the society began its work, it had asked the president to replace the superintendent, but he had not done so. Shortly before the conference, a well-qualified man the society wanted to nominate as agent at Camp Apache refused to go if he had to serve under the superintendent. In none of his remarks did Ferris mention the Arizona superintendent's name or acknowledge that the difficulty the mission society had with him was that Dr. Bendell was a Jew.[34]

The Reformed church had also taken its complaints to General Howard and persuaded him to recommend Bendell's replacement by someone "in full sympathy" with the church. Howard recommended that Bendell, whom he had found to be "honest, active, and systematic," be transferred "to a field consonant with his special fitness." Simon Wolf, the Jewish recorder of deeds for the District of Columbia, who had been instrumental in securing Bendell's appointment as superintendent, condemned the missionaries' attempt to replace Bendell, giving them "an exposition of American citizenship" he was sure they would never forget. "But," Wolf said, "it proved ineffectual, the missionary element, dominant and assertive, won the day, and Dr. Bendell shortly after resigned."[35]

After hearing the reports of the various religious societies, the conference also heard reports from two army officers who were present, General Howard and General William Hazen, both of whom expressed satisfaction with the improvements they had seen in the government's Indian policy. Hazen said he had seen more improvement in Indian affairs since the creation of the Board of Indian Commissioners than ever before in his life. At the conclusion of the meetings, a delegation chaired by George Whipple was appointed to report personally to the president. The delegation was also to offer the conference's congratulations on the assurance Grant had recently given that there would be no retreat from his policy toward the Indians. Grant had written to George Stuart, who inquired about rumored changes in the policy, "If any change is made it must be on the side of the civilization and christianization of the Indians. I do not believe our Creator ever placed the different races of men on this earth with the view of having the stronger exert all his energies in exterminating the weaker. If any change takes place in the Indian policy of the Government, while I hold my present office, it will be on the humanitarian side of the question." On behalf of the other representatives, Whipple presented Grant with a written statement to assure the president of the "continued and cordial co-operation of the various bodies represented in the meeting, and implore for you the continued presence and blessing of Almighty God."[36]

21

Commissioner of Indian Affairs

Between the Indian "rings," little and big,—the demand of congressional and local politicians,—the rivalries and jealousies of the army and the civil service . . . between its temptations and difficulties, [the office of commissioner of Indian affairs] is no bed of roses to a man who seeks only to do his duty and contribute to the fair fame and the power of the American government.

Samuel Bowles, *Denver Daily News*, November 24, 1871

After serving only a year as commissioner of Indian affairs, Francis Walker resigned his office to accept a position at the Sheffield Scientific School at Yale University. His resignation led to a good deal of speculation about his successor. Thomas Cree, the former general secretary of the Pittsburgh YMCA who had taken Vincent Colyer's place as secretary of the Board of Indian Commissioners, said there had been "many inquiries as to the Indian Commissionership. It seems to be with many people second only to the President." Cree was sure that the members of the "Indian ring" would name someone for the position and would "leave no stone unturned to have him appointed," and Cree urged the friends of the president's Indian policy to name a candidate of their own and work for his appointment.[1]

Felix Brunot, the chairman of the Board of Indian Commissioners, favored General Howard for the position or, if he was not available, Thomas Cree. George Stuart, who was chairman of the executive committee of the board, inquired about Howard's interest in the position, but Howard told him that the small salary—$3,000 a year—and the limited responsibility given to the commissioner stood in the way of his taking the office. The *New York Times* thought Benjamin Rush Cowen, the assistant secretary of the interior, well qualified for the job. The Board of Indian Commissioners also settled on Cowen and adopted a resolution asking the president to nominate him. Cowen was offered the position, but about the same time, Congress proposed raising his salary as assistant secretary to $6,000, while leaving the salary of the commissioner at $3,000, which made his refusal certain. William Welsh, a prominent Episcopal layman, was also mentioned for the position, as was Smith. The Washington, D.C., *Daily Morning Chronicle* thought Smith had "the best card. His friends urge that his sterling worth as a man, and his popularity with the soldiers during the war," together with his experience as an Indian agent, recommended him to those who favored the president's peace policy.[2]

Smith was still in Washington during these events, trying to secure congressional appropriations for the Chippewas and preparing to return to his agency. Secretary Delano had asked him to go with the governor of Idaho to negotiate with the western Shoshones and Bannocks, but that mission was postponed, and Smith returned to Minnesota early in March 1873. He had been back only a few days when he received a telegram from Benjamin Cowen saying, "You are appointed commissioner of Indian affairs. Return here as soon as possible." The same day Cowen sent the telegram, Grant sent Smith's nomination to the Senate.[3]

Thomas Cree said that Columbus Delano had made Smith's appointment "unsolicited by either Mr. Smith or any body else," although Delano himself said he chose Smith mainly to please George Stuart and Felix Brunot of the Board of Indian Commissioners and William Welsh, who had been the first chairman of the board. Delano's choice pleased some and displeased others. Those who favored Grant's Indian policy saw it as a confirmation that the policy would be continued. Cree thought Smith "an A. 1. good man," "the best man that has been yet named for the position," "an honest man who has done more than any other man to upset land ring manipulation and has saved many thousands to the Indians by his management. The better one knows Secretary Delano the more convinced one must be of his earnest desire to do what is for the successful carrying out of the Indian policy." Eliphalet Whittlesey said later that Grant showed his sincerity "by placing at the head of the Indian Bureau a Christian man, well known, not only in his own Church, but in all the Churches through his connection with the Christian Commission during the war, & freedmen's affairs since."[4]

At the same time, some western senators opposed Smith's nomination. Objections were also received from residents of Minnesota. Despite the objections, the Senate Committee on Indian Affairs recommended the nomination and the Senate quickly confirmed it. But one person who objected to Smith's nomination, Dr. Grenville Mellen Weeks, took his case to the Senate Committee on Indian Affairs and succeeded in forcing a reconsideration of the confirmation. Weeks charged that Smith was the first Indian agent in Minnesota who had not provided a physician for the Red Lake band as guaranteed to them by treaty, that the schoolhouse at Leech Lake, provided by previous agents, had remained unused by Smith, and that Smith had promised protection and a fair trial for the two Indians who were later lynched at Brainerd.[5]

When Delano heard of Weeks's charges, he dismissed him as "a crazy fellow," and the *New York Times* said that Weeks had "latterly given evidences of unsound mind" and had presented "a silly story" about Smith. Weeks, however, was something of a war hero, and he also had enough firsthand acquaintance with Indian affairs in Minnesota to demand a consideration of his charges. Weeks had been acting assistant surgeon on the original ironclad *Monitor* when it sank in heavy seas off Cape Hatteras on December 31, 1862, and was seriously injured during his rescue. He later served as surgeon in the Third Regiment, U.S. Colored Infantry, and was acting medical director of the departments of Florida and South Carolina. After the war, he reentered government service and served as physician for the Red Lake band of Chippewas in Minnesota and acting Indian agent in the agency to which Smith was later assigned. Weeks also served as secretary of a private organization called the United States Indian Commission, whose president was the well-known Peter Cooper.[6]

When Delano realized that Weeks's charges had to be taken seriously, he asked Thomas Cree to intervene with two key senators, one of whom, William Buckingham, chaired the Committee on Indian Affairs. Cree was able to convince the senators that some of Weeks's charges were false and that Smith was not to blame for what truth there was in his other charges. The schoolhouse at Leech Lake was closed for three months only following the resignation of a former teacher; although no physician was assigned to the Red Lake band, the person temporarily filling that position, Sela Wright, had been appointed at the request of the Indians themselves; and the Indians lynched at Brainerd were in the custody of a sheriff at the time—Smith was 150 miles away.

George Stuart also wrote to Buckingham supporting Smith, and Delano himself met with the senator. It was undoubtedly helpful too that Buckingham had been a member of the Christian Commission and the chairman of its Connecticut branch and that he was a vice-president of the American Missionary Association and had every opportunity to know Smith's character and abilities. It could not have been helpful to Weeks's cause that he was himself an applicant for the office of commissioner of Indian affairs. Three days after the original confirmation, the Senate reaffirmed its action, and on March 20, 1873, Smith was appointed commissioner of Indian affairs.[7]

Whatever merit Weeks's charges had, it was good that he was not the one who became commissioner. Long before this controversy, Sela Wright, who had observed Weeks's work in Minnesota, heard that he wanted to reenter the Indian service and said of him that "the Dr. spent a *part* of two years at Red Lake in service of Govt. I feel quite sure that the whole city of New York could hardly furnish a more *thoroughly unfit* man for any such work, a man of *no judgment[,] impracticable, no financial* ability, indeed he knows nothing of what he ought to know to go in such a service. How long will the Govt be *befooled* and the Indian cause [cursed?] by the sending out of *such* men[?]"[8]

Smith was given ten days to finish his work at White Earth before he assumed his new office. As he prepared to leave the reservation, he turned affairs at the agency over to Minnie Cook, who became the acting agent when he left. Letters from Washington soon began to come to her addressed "M. S. Cook, Esq. . . . Sir," showing that apart from the new commissioner the personnel in the Indian Office did not realize that the acting agent at White Earth was a woman—just turned twenty-five years old. Hers was not an easy task. Smith had been gone only a few days when she telegraphed to Washington that an Indian man had tried to kill an Indian woman and the woman's sister and child. "All wounded[,] one skull broken[,] recovery doubtful[.] He is held in custody." The acting agent, who had some of the same firmness as her uncle, had the man taken to Fort Ripley in irons.[9]

When he had made the necessary arrangements in Minnesota, Smith returned to Washington and on April 3, 1873, formally accepted the office of commissioner of Indian affairs. Both General Howard and John Alvord offered Smith the use of their homes in the capital, and he stayed with the Alvords until he could arrange something more permanent. His wife and daughter remained in Minnesota, where Cleavie had "learned to love these children of the forest." She was teaching arithmetic, reading, and writing to three evening classes of young men, "enough to help them in every day life." She told her newest group of students: "Now boys, I want to fit you for Indian clerks. We are going to have Indians for clerks, just as soon as we can make them. . . . I expect to see Indian boys at Washington, before I die." Cleavie was optimistic about the work among the Chippewas. "Everything brightens around us. We are full of hope for the future. We thank God and go forward."[10]

The Office of Indian Affairs over which Smith presided was housed, with the other offices of the Interior Department, in the Patent Office Building, which Walt Whitman, who had visited wounded and dying soldiers hospitalized in it during the Civil War, called the "noblest of Washington buildings." The furnishings of the Indian Office reflected a great concern for paperwork; the rooms contained thirty-four pigeonhole sets, eight hundred files, three hundred "Woodruff patent" files, two file cases, forty-seven desks, and twenty-eight wastebaskets.[11]

The Indian Office was considered by the *New York Times* to be the most responsible federal office below that of a cabinet member, with the possible exception of the office of treasurer of the United States. The commissioner of Indian affairs was responsible for annual expenditures of from $6 to $7 million.[12]

The commissioner also had a sizable staff. At a time when the White House staff consisted of eight people, including a steward and a messenger, Smith's Washington staff consisted of a chief clerk, thirty-one other clerks, and eleven copyists, messengers, and laborers. The new commissioner soon came to regard even that staff as inadequate. He told the House Committee on Indian Affairs, "No man will undertake to do a seven-million [dollar] business on the force that is employed in the Indian Office; he will go to ruin; he will not do it." Nor were the employees of the caliber he needed. "I have not a man in that office," he said, "to whom I can submit one of these important questions, involving thousands of dollars, and get a judgment from him upon which I could rely."[13]

Many of the clerks in the Indian Office were specialists in Indian affairs, attending to land surveys, appropriations, claims for "depredations" by Indians, and the more than $6 million in trust funds held for the various Indian tribes. The clerks produced a voluminous correspondence, all of which went out over the commissioner's signature. It was not long before Smith brought his niece Minnie Cook to Washington as one of the clerks. The policy of the office had been not to employ female clerks, but Smith nevertheless hired her and made her his private secretary.[14]

Smith's chief clerk was Henry R. Clum, a veteran who had been breveted lieutenant colonel at the close of the Civil War and was known in Washington as Colonel Clum. Clum had served as a captain in the Fifth Wisconsin Infantry before becoming a captain in the army Signal Corps. He served as chief signal officer in several departments, including General Benjamin Butler's headquarters, and at the end of the war was adjutant at the Signal Corps headquarters in Washington. Clum had been in the Indian Office since 1865. He became chief clerk in September 1870 and served as acting commissioner after the resignation of Commissioner Walker.[15]

The field work of the Indian Office was performed by agents assigned to the various tribes, as Smith had been to the Chippewas. In 1873 there were seventy-eight Indian agencies. The agents were nominated by the churches and missionary societies that were cooperating with the government in its

Henry R. Clum (1830?–1904).
Courtesy of the Massachusetts
Commandery, Military Order of
the Loyal Legion and the U.S.
Army Military History Institute,
Carlisle Barracks, Pennsylvania.

Indian work. The nominations, however, required confirmation by the Senate, which meant that the political considerations Grant was trying to avoid by using churchmen as agents could not be ignored entirely if the Senate's cooperation was to be ensured. Once confirmed, the agents were appointed by the president. Smith made it clear that although nominated by religious groups, agents were appointed by the government, and "in the administration of the affairs of the Indians and the management of the Agencies under their charge, such Agents are subject to and held responsible by, the Government; through the Department and this office." As he told a newly appointed agent who had been nominated by the AMA, "this appointment is in all respects governmental and in no respect missionary or religious, except that your nomination comes from the American Missionary Association" and that by his nomination the AMA became "morally responsible for the integrity and efficiency" of his administration.[16]

Secretary Delano had also made it clear that nomination by religious societies would not prevent the removal of an agent if the department found that removal necessary: "The Administration will reserve to itself the right to chop off the political heads of your friends whenever occasion may require it, and you must not complain of this."[17]

The church-sponsored agents were sometimes overly zealous in religious matters. Smith had been in office only a short time when he received an inquiry from John B. Monteith, the agent at the Nez Percé Reservation, asking how he should deal with the Catholic Indians on the reservation. Their priest had asked permission to hold services in the schoolhouse and to erect a church some ten or twelve miles from the agency. Monteith had refused his requests, and he wrote to ask Smith, "Have I the right this being a Presbyterian Agency and mission to exercise such control over the morals of this people as will enable me to prohibit the teaching the Catholic faith or the holding Catholic service among them even though the Indians desire it and clamor for it?" Smith told him that the fact that his agency was under the charge of the Presbyterian church did not warrant "any intolerant exercise of power." It was desirable that the mission work be done by the sponsoring church, "yet where there are persons that have another faith and desire religious services of their own it is not in accordance with public policy or the spirit of religious toleration to forbid or hinder such services in any way."[18]

When the Presbyterian Synod of the Pacific objected to Smith's letter, saying it was inconsistent with the original offer of the reservation to the church, Smith refused to change his ruling. The government had no intention, he said, of giving denominations "vested religious rights" on reservations or "any religious control therein the exercise of which outside of a Reserve would justly be considered religious intolerance." Smith did concede that it was desirable for effective work and for harmony among the Indians that other denominations should recognize the prior claim of the denomination that appointed the agent, but that was not a matter for regulation by the government. "How far this precedence will receive recognition among the different religious denominations is a question to be decided by the degree of christian courtesy which will be found . . . to prevail among the denominations themselves, and is in no way within the discretion of this Department."[19]

Encouraged by Smith's ruling, the Catholics later asked the government to build a church and schoolhouse for them with Indian funds, which Smith would not do. Tribal funds could not be used, he said, to build churches or for "strictly denominational" schools. Strictly religious work was to be done at the denomination's own expense. Smith also noted the harm that would result from any "religious contentions for proselytes," especially if there should be any attempt to interfere with the work of the agent in charge of the reservation. But those restrictions did not alter Smith's basic policy about religious freedom, which he stated clearly on another occasion: "No hindrance is placed by this Department to any religious body which desires to undertake missionary work upon any Indian reservation." Columbus

Delano agreed with Smith's position but later cautioned that no denomination was to interfere with the work of another. If difficulties or contentions among denominations arose, his department reserved the right to require a denomination to leave the reservation.[20]

Each Indian agent had a staff employed on his recommendation—usually persons affiliated with the religious society that nominated the agent. Like the agents, Smith expected them to be persons of a "decided religious character," who, in addition to their official duties, would be able to "inspire" the Indians "to earnest efforts for civilization." The work of the agencies themselves required some employees—clerks, interpreters, messengers, teamsters, cooks, storekeepers, mail carriers, laborers—but many more were employed for the "civilization and christianization" of the Indians that was central to the administration's Indian policy: doctors, teachers, farmers, herders, millers, butchers, engineers, masons, sawyers, carpenters, blacksmiths, seamstresses, shoemakers, wagonmakers. Nearly a thousand agency employees were in the field in 1873.[21]

Before Smith became commissioner, most of the Indian agents had reported to superintendents, but Congress had recently acted to reduce the number of superintendents, and most of Smith's agents reported directly to Washington. Notable exceptions were the two superintendencies assigned to the Quakers, whose agents still reported to Quaker superintendents. In place of superintendents, Congress had created the office of inspector, and five inspectors were appointed from over three hundred applicants about the time Smith took office. Religion was an important factor in their appointments; Secretary Delano said that religious considerations were the controlling factor in four of the five appointments. Congress considered the office of inspector so important that it gave the inspectors the same salary as the commissioner to whom they were responsible. To the Indians, the inspectors were "Big Cats"—because they "jumped on people."[22]

Smith's appointment as commissioner came from President Grant, and he had access to the president in urgent matters and when he accompanied delegations of Indians on their visits to the White House, but usually Smith saw Grant only in the company of Columbus Delano, the secretary of the interior, to whom he, as commissioner, was responsible. Smith had a good relationship with the secretary, who respected Smith, considering him "a very estimable gentleman, of experience in business, and with natural aptitude for affairs." Delano was a former congressman from Ohio and a former commissioner of the Bureau of Internal Revenue. He was also a politician who freely used the Interior Department to help his political friends, especially in Ohio—Henry Neal and Thomas Jones, who had been appointed to the scrip commissions in

Columbus Delano (1809–96). Courtesy of the National Archives.

Minnesota, were both Ohioans—but Delano was also fully committed to the president's Indian policy. The secretary took an active part in Indian affairs; by the structure of the department most of Smith's decisions also had to have Delano's approval. The secretary's office had an Indian Division, headed by Ashton S. H. White, a longtime employee of the Interior Department, who was Delano's liaison with Smith. When Delano was away from the office, vacationing or mending political fences in Mount Vernon, Ohio, the assistant secretary, Benjamin Rush Cowen, another Ohioan, acted in his place. Both Delano and Cowen were churchmen, Delano an Episcopalian and Cowen a Methodist.[23]

Alongside the Indian Office and independent from it was another government body concerned with the welfare of the Indians, the Board of Indian Commissioners. Early in the Grant administration, Congress had authorized such a board, and Grant had appointed ten men "eminent for their intelligence and philanthropy" to serve on it. The board, under the president's direction, was to "exercise joint control with the Secretary of the Interior" over the disbursement of funds for the Indians. Congress later made it the board's duty to supervise all expenditures for the Indians and to inspect all goods purchased for them. It was empowered to examine and approve bills, to inspect the records of the Indian Office, to supervise the payment of annuities, and generally to advise the government on its Indian policies.[24]

At first, "joint control" over the disbursement of funds had been a source of conflict between the board and the commissioner of Indian affairs, but by the time Smith became commissioner, the Indian Office had learned to work with the board. By law the board reviewed bills and made recommendations about their payment. But by law the secretary of the interior could overrule its recommendations; as the *American Missionary* commented on the matter, "Ultimate responsibility must rest somewhere, and under the law, this was vested in the Secretary of the Interior." That arrangement did not please the board, but it gave the secretary and the commissioner of Indian affairs both the advice of an independent body and control over their own affairs.[25]

George Stuart, the former chairman of the Christian Commission, was among a group of Philadelphians who, at the beginning of the Grant administration, had expressed their willingness to assist Grant in his Indian policy, and Grant asked Stuart to suggest names for the Board of Indian Commissioners. When Stuart had made his suggestions, Secretary Cox asked the men to serve, telling them that "the design of those who suggested the Commission was that something like a Christian Commission should be established, having the civilization of the Indian in view, and laboring to stimulate public interest in this work, whilst also cooperating with this Department." Stuart himself was placed on the board and became chairman of both the purchasing committee and the executive committee. Four other members of the board had been members of the Christian Commission and would have known Smith at least by reputation. The members of the board generally had a good opinion of Smith, and he and the board began their work in harmony.[26]

The new commissioner had been in office only eight days when the peace policy suffered a severe blow from an Indian attack that shocked the public as nothing had since the assassination of President Lincoln. In November 1872, the Indian Office had ordered the Modoc Indians, who lived on the border of California and Oregon, returned to their reservation, which they had left to go to their old homes. Under the leadership of Keintpoos, or Captain Jack, the Modocs resisted and fled to a stronghold in the lava beds in northern California, where they successfully fought several battles with the army. On Good Friday, April 11, 1873, an unarmed peace commission appointed to negotiate with the Modocs was deliberately and unexpectedly attacked. Two commissioners, General E. R. S. Canby and the Reverend Eleazar Thomas, were killed, and a third, Alfred Meacham, wounded and partially scalped.

The murders of Canby and Thomas resulted in a cry for vengeance not only against the Modocs but against Indians in general, and even though Secretary Delano had given all control of the negotiations with the Modocs to the army—"untrammeled by directions or requests from the Indian Department"—there was also an outcry against the peace policy itself. In Yreka, California, where the bodies of Canby and Thomas were taken, Delano was hanged in effigy. A Colorado newspaper spoke out against "Grant and the preachers." Governor Austin telegraphed from Minnesota that "the present missionary policy" had no advocates on the frontier. Even in the East, support for peaceful dealings with the Indians was at a low ebb. The *New York World* condemned the "canting scoundrels" who had convinced Grant to treat "a pack of outlaws as if they were Sunday-school children."[27]

A meeting on the subject "The Christian Policy of the Government Toward the Indians" had been scheduled at the First Congregational Church in Washington on Easter Sunday evening. The news received from California the night before gave the meeting an unusual interest. General Howard, Commissioner Smith, and Frederick Douglass shared the platform. Howard, after relating his earlier experiences with the Seminoles and the Apaches, explained how the president had broken up the "corrupt ring" and placed "the whole Indian question in Christian hands." He said he had no apology for the Modocs; they had "struck a blow at their own interests" from which he thought they would never recover. The president's policy was peace before war, but the administration believed in punishing lawbreakers, whether white or Indian. Howard said that the Indians could be saved "from the borderers and from themselves" only by extending to them, as to blacks and whites, the "equal protection and punishment of the federal laws."[28]

When Smith spoke, he said he was surprised at the remarks about the Indians he had heard on the Sabbath, on the street and even in the church—the same remarks he had heard about them on the border. But then, he said, if one thought of the murders of Canby and Thomas as of a friend or a relative, one could hardly help feeling like those who were called "border-ruffians." He blamed the Modoc difficulties on the attempt to remove them from a "genial, fruitful country to a bleak and barren" reservation and the fact that the $17,000 promised to them each year was "discernible only by the vouchers filed in the Treasury Department to show the pretended manner of its disbursement." He had no desire to shield the Modocs from punishment, but at the same time he thought that if the government had kept faith with them the murders would not have happened. He told the audience that the actions of the Modocs should not influence people's attitudes toward Indians in general. "Because a man in New York brutally strikes down another with a carhook, that is no reason that in revenge men should go out and strike down unmercifully every drunken man they met."[29]

A reporter said that Smith spoke "strongly for a fair trial of the present Christian policy." The Indians had been treated cruelly in the past, the agents and employees sent to them had not been "representatives of benevolence or Christianity," treaties had not been kept, and money appropriated for them had not been honestly administered. By contrast, the reporter said, Smith gave a "glowing picture" of the Chippewas under the new policy, "reclaimed in a short time by truth and justice from the war to the cow path, and raising the thatch on a comfortable cottage in lieu of lifting the hair of the settler."[30]

Frederick Douglass followed the other two speakers, making the arguments they had made, the reporter thought, "much more eloquently and effectively." Douglass said he had always thought the Indians were doomed to disappear, but the new Indian policy had allowed him to see a new destiny for them. The only salvation for the Indian, he said, was under the protection of the government. "Bibles might be put in their hands, all of them might be converted, but quarrels would be picked with them unless the Government interposed with its strong arm." He was for gathering "the remnants of the once powerful race . . . within the fold of citizenship and equal rights" and assuring them of the government's protection.[31]

In the aftermath of the Canby and Thomas murders, vengeful Oregonians attacked a group of seventeen Modoc prisoners who were being taken to a nearby military camp. Three Modoc men were killed and a woman seriously wounded. Only the arrival of additional troops prevented a greater slaughter. Smith, reacting to the great clamor for punishment of the Indians who killed Canby and Thomas, asked that the whites who killed the Modoc prisoners receive the same punishment. The killing of prisoners in the custody of the army was, he said, as much a violation of the laws of war as the killings of the peace commissioners. Smith asked Delano to have the murderers arrested and tried by the same military commission that tried the Modocs, but Delano, the politician, chose not to pursue the matter. Later, when the public furor had subsided, he turned it over to the Secret Service, but the white murderers were never caught.[32]

The murders of Canby and Thomas also damaged some delicate negotiations the Indian Office was conducting with the governor of Texas about the fate of two Kiowa chiefs, Satanta and Big Tree. The two Kiowas had been arrested with another Kiowa chief, Satank, two years before for leading a raiding party into Texas, where they captured a wagon train, killed seven men, and drove off forty-one mules. Five of the murdered men were found around the wagons, "their heads split open and otherwise mutilated." One was found chained to a wagon, where his body had been burned. When Lawrie Tatum, the Quaker agent of the Kiowas, learned what had been done, he notified the commander at Fort Sill, and General Sherman, who was at Fort Sill to investigate the Indian raids, had the men arrested. Satank attacked a guard and was killed; Satanta and Big Tree were taken to Texas, tried in a civil court, and sentenced to be hanged. Agent Tatum and his superintendent, Enoch Hoag, however, argued that their execution would lead the Kiowas to take revenge, and Texas governor Edmund J. Davis commuted their sentences to life imprisonment at hard labor.[33]

Secretary Delano tried to convince Davis to pardon the chiefs, but when Davis asked army officers for their opinion, General Sheridan objected strenuously, saying, "This chief [Satanta] is well known to me as a shrewd cunning murderer. On two occasions he made the most solemn promises to me without the intention of performance. . . . It will always be a matter of regret to me that I did not hang *Satanta* when I had him a prisoner in the winter of 1868." Commissioner Walker also opposed a pardon. He told Delano that Satanta was "one of the most treacherous and murderous Indians on the Texas frontier" and that he could not be trusted to keep his word. With such objections, Delano did not press for a pardon.[34]

The Quakers, however, who were responsible for the Kiowa Agency, did press for a pardon, and when a delegation of Kiowas went to Washington in August 1872, it was promised that, if the Kiowas ceased raiding, Satanta and Big Tree would be freed. The Kiowas ceased their raiding, and the two chiefs were scheduled to be released about April 15, 1873. After the murders of Canby and Thomas, however, Grant and Delano thought the release politically unwise and considered postponing it. The strong objection of General Sherman to the chiefs' release helped Grant and Delano make their decision. "I believe that Satanta has some fifty murders," Sherman wrote, "and to pardon him, and set him free to renew the same old Game, would to me be worse than murder. . . . I know the man well. With irons on his hand he is humble & harmless enough, but on a horse is the devil incarnate." On April 14, Delano, with Grant's approval, postponed the release.[35]

Enoch Hoag and other leading Quakers would not let the matter lie; they continued to insist that the chiefs should be freed. The Kiowas, Hoag said, had fulfilled their promises; to break faith with them by not releasing Satanta and Big Tree would "furnish them a new excuse for open hostility." Hoag recommended that a council be held at the Kiowa Agency, where the chiefs would be released, while at the same time pledges of peace would be demanded from all the tribes of the Southwest. The council, he said, would be better protection from the Kiowas than a regiment of soldiers.[36]

Smith sided with the Quakers. He recommended calling a "grand council" in the Indian Territory "at which the Indians will be required to enter into a solemn agreement providing for their good behavior in the future. . . . I fully concur with the Superintendent and Agent in the belief that the release of said prisoners will have the effect to pacify the Indians and keep them at peace during the coming summer." Smith recommended bringing Satanta and Big Tree to the council and accompanying them on the journey with an escort sufficient to protect them "from any violence at the hands of the citizens." He also recommended that 130 Comanche women and children, held as prisoners by the army, be freed before the council met. With Delano's approval, the Comanche prisoners were freed and arrangements were made for a council to be held at Fort Sill in October at which Satanta and Big Tree would be released. Under pressure from Grant and Delano, Governor Davis agreed to attend the council, and Smith was to attend to represent the federal government.[37]

In the midst of the Modoc and Kiowa difficulties, Smith left for New York with Benjamin Cowen and Ashton White to meet with the purchasing committee of the Board of Indian Commissioners for the opening of the bids for more than $2 million worth of Indian goods and supplies. When the board was first appointed and George Stuart became the chairman of its purchasing committee, he recommended that the bids for Indian annuity goods and supplies no longer be opened in Washington but rather in New York "as that was the central market of the country." Each spring after that the purchasing committee and the commissioner of Indian affairs spent several weeks in New York opening and awarding bids and doing everything in their power to prevent fraud in the supplying of the Indians. The board members who served with Stuart on the committee—Robert Campbell, John V. Farwell, and William E. Dodge—were all successful businessmen, alert to any sharp practices that might be attempted in the bidding. In the spring of 1873, some one hundred merchants came to New York for the bidding, most of them from the West; altogether 284 bids were submitted by more than two hundred different firms and individuals. Bidders were required to submit samples of their goods, and the large room rented for the occasion was "covered with half emptied boxes of flour, coffee, sugar, tobacco, bacon, soap, saleratus, salt, wheat and other articles."[38]

The awards had barely been made when loud criticisms were voiced about them both by the bidders and the newspapers. The *Washington Daily Morning Chronicle* reported the criticisms and said it was not surprised that attacks had appeared in newspapers opposed to the administration: "The robes of an angel of light would not secure exemption." But it also suggested that the freedom with which the reformers had "indulged in casting indiscriminate reproach on those who have preceded them in the Indian service has invited criticism of their own conduct. . . . *Christian* commissioners will be watched as closely as others."[39]

George Stuart quickly responded to the criticisms. He said that although the commissioner of Indian affairs was the one who made the awards, representatives of the Board of Indian Commissioners and the Interior Department had also been involved. "In no case was an award made without the unanimous approval of these three bodies." Because of the procedures they had adopted, the prices paid by the government were lower than ever before, which, Stuart said, was the real reason for the complaints of the disappointed merchants.[40]

Smith sent Thomas Cree back to Washington to investigate the complaints, but although he found "a great noise, several lawyers pressing cases, newspaper backing and general dissatisfaction," Cree discovered nothing irregular and suggested no changes in the awards. "The ring is hurt," he said, "and they are making their influence felt." Cree found Delano in a good humor about the matter, joking that he was "the head of the new ring," but Smith was "much annoyed" and "worried" by the affair. Delano took the complaints seriously enough to report the matter to the assistant attorney general assigned to his department, who advised that the awards had been made legally, and Delano let them stand.[41]

After six weeks in office, Smith was beginning to understand what Samuel Bowles meant when he said that the office of commissioner of Indian affairs was "no bed of roses."

22

A Guardian and His Wards

The Indian is the ward of the Government. The management and direction of *all* his affairs and relations in a civil capacity has been conferred by the Act of 1832 exclusively upon [the Office of Indian Affairs]. . . . It regulates his estate both real and personal. It supervises his domestic relations. And it exercises all the power over him of guardian and ward.

Ely S. Parker to J. D. Cox, November 27, 1869

Smith was concerned about the medical needs of his Indian wards, as well as their educational needs, and he requested permission to create a new medical and educational division in his office. When Delano approved, Smith appointed a physician, Dr. Josiah Curtis, to take charge of the new division. Curtis had not been in office long when he discovered that one merchant had succeeded in selling fraudulent goods to the new commissioner.[1]

In his first days in office, Smith had been approached by a onetime druggist named Anson Dart, who offered him a "venereal preventive," "which if furnished to the Indians, would protect them from taking the most fatal disorder known to the Indian races." Believing there was a need for such a product and with "a good deal of urging" from Dart, Smith ordered five thousand bottles at one dollar a bottle. The medicine had been delivered and was stored in the Indian Office when Dr. Curtis began his work. Curtis reviewed the information about the medicine and discovered that at least one of the endorsements that accompanied it was fraudulent. An endorsement from the office of the army's chief medical officer said that the venereal preventive had been used successfully at the Ricord Hospital in Washington, but the surgeon general of the army reported that there was no office of chief medical officer and that the Ricord Hospital had been closed at the time the medicine allegedly had been tried. Nor had the person who signed the endorsement ever served in the army's Medical Department. When Dr. Curtis shared the information with Smith, Smith was "astonished," and even though he thought Dart had acted in good faith, he determined not to issue the medicine.[2]

266

Both the Board of Indian Commissioners and the secretary of the interior had approved Smith's purchase of Dart's venereal preventive. When Ashton White, who headed the Indian Division in the secretary's office, heard reports that the product was a fraud, he went to the Patent Office to see if the medicine had been patented as Dart claimed. Indeed it had. The patent Dart received for his "Sanitary Specific" in 1864 said: "The nature of my discovery consists in lubricating the generative organ with an oil of the dwarf olive, combined with an oil extracted from the seeds of a species of the muskmelon not known to grow anywhere except in Hindostan. . . . It is as sure a prevention to taking the venereal diseases as that water will quench fire." Patented or not, Dr. Curtis pronounced the oil worthless. He told Smith it had no more value than common sweet oil. The surgeon general added that it had not been tested as Dart claimed "as it was found impossible to induce men to grease themselves and then have commerce with diseased women, which, in the opinion of medical officers to whom it was referred, was the only manner in which it could be tested."[3]

In fairness to Smith, it should be said that Anson Dart came to him with good credentials. Dart was a brother-in-law of George Catlin, the artist who devoted his talents to preserving Indian life in his paintings, and through Catlin and his own work in the West Dart had acquired some knowledge about Indians. As a wholesale druggist in New York City, he was said to have been among the first persons in America to import quinine. Later he was appointed superintendent for the construction of a large "lunatic asylum" in Utica, New York. At the beginning of Zachary Taylor's administration, Dart came to Washington from Wisconsin, where he was then living, with recommendations from such men as Ninian Edwards and Richard Yates of Illinois, Caleb Smith of Indiana, Henry Sibley of Minnesota, Thomas Corwin of Ohio, and Millard Fillmore of New York and was appointed superintendent of Indian affairs in Oregon, where he served for two years. His Sanitary Specific came with impressive testimonials from medical doctors in New York, Philadelphia, and Washington and with a recommendation from a delegation of Creek Indians that had visited Washington.[4]

Dart, however, had offered his Sanitary Specific to the Indian Office before and had been refused. Commissioner Walker had declined to purchase it on two occasions. Dart had also applied to Commissioner Parker for the position of superintendent of Indian affairs in Arizona, but Parker declined to appoint him. Dart's previous service as superintendent in Oregon had left a bad impression. Senator Joseph Lane of Oregon had said on the Senate floor that Dart had "no honesty, no integrity. . . . He was loathed in Oregon. He was loathed by every honest man and every decent family in the country." When Abraham Lincoln became president, his commissioner of Indian affairs, William P. Dole, had recommended Dart for the superintendency in Washington Territory, but Lincoln refused to appoint him. A member of his cabinet had told Lincoln that Dart had offered him a bribe to obtain a position in the Taylor administration; a Wisconsin representative described Dart to Lincoln as an "immoral and dishonest man"; one of the Oregon senators said Dart had kept a prostitute when he was in Oregon; and the other senator said Dart had recently offered him a bribe to secure the superintendency in Oregon. "Neither you or I could knowingly be for such a man," Lincoln told Dole. Smith, acting on impulse, made a purchase he might not have made if he had asked what others knew about Dart. But Smith readily admitted his mistake, and Dart's medicine remained unused among the stores in the Indian Office the entire time Smith was commissioner.[5]

Three months after he had come to Washington, Smith was still separated from his family. What free time he had from his duties as commissioner he used to teach Sunday afternoon Bible classes for the YMCA, some of which were held in a theater to reach men who might not otherwise have attended religious meetings. Smith's subjects included "The Samaritan Woman," "Scenes and Incidents About the Sea of Galilee," and "The Sermon on the Mount." The new commissioner had also become a trustee of Howard University and was said to be one of the most active members of the board.[6]

Independence Day, the day that for nineteenth-century Americans rose "head and shoulders above its brethren, the holiday of the year," found Smith alone in his office in Washington, writing a letter to his daughter, Gerty. "You see I am spending [the] holiday in the office," he wrote. "It is so hot, and I have nobody to go off with & so many letters to write that I have come down to spend the day all alone in this big building[,] the largest in Washington except the Capital." But he hoped soon to be reunited with his family. He told Gerty about his plans to leave that month for Wisconsin for a council with the Winnebago Indians and then to meet his family at White Earth. From there he had scheduled a trip down the Missouri River, and he was going to invite Cleavie to go with him.[7]

In mid-July Smith left Washington on his trip to the West. It seemed a good time to leave the office in Henry Clum's hands; there was less likelihood of Indian outbreaks in the summer. Smith said that in his experience Indian raids occurred from April to June, after the winter's rest and the resumption of hunting trips. He told a reporter he was confident that the summer and fall would be free of "hostile acts and depredations." When Smith left Washington, Columbus Delano assured the president that the Indian service was in "a favorable and hopeful condition, from Washington Territory to Texas, but, as you know, it is so sensitive a service, that we must not be disappointed at a change in appearance, here and there, at any moment."[8]

The council with the Winnebagos was held at Sparta, Wisconsin, on July 17, 1873. The Indian Office had received a large number of complaints about the Winnebagos from Wisconsin citizens, along with requests that they be removed from the state, and Congress had appropriated the money for their removal to the Indian Territory. A delegation of Winnebagos that went to inspect the territory, however, was dissatisfied, not so much, Smith thought, with the new location as with the idea of moving anywhere. Believing the Winnebagos' presence among the settlers in Wisconsin would lead to "violence and bloodshed," the Indian Office then decided to try to convince them to go to Nebraska, where land had been set aside for them and where part of the tribe was already settled. There teachers, schools, farms, stock, "and all possible civilizing influences" could be provided for them. Smith hoped that with those advantages "some of the present generation will be saved from barbarism" and "most of the children will take to civilized life." Smith's mission in Wisconsin was to try to convince the Winnebagos to go to Nebraska.[9]

At the council, Smith told the Winnebagos that on his travels he had often seen members of their tribe around the railway stations, but no one had ever been able to tell him where they lived. The people he asked had said that "these Indians have no land & no homes. The game is getting scarce & they are getting poorer and poorer every year; while other Indians are living on reservations, & having schools, & wearing clothes like white people." He told them how the Chippewas had gone to farming. "And so all over the country the Indians must begin to live on what grows out of the ground instead of living on what runs over it. So it must be with you." Because they already had good land in Nebraska and plenty of money in Washington to make the move, Smith advised them to go. The money would not be given to them if they stayed in Wisconsin "because you would gamble it away or spend it for whiskey. . . . The government gives money only to those who will make good use of it."[10]

The Winnebagos were not easily convinced. Big Black Hawk told Smith: "All our ancestors lived and died here. One was my father. He died here & I wish to die here too. I do not wish to go away. If I go I shall live no longer. If the Winnebagoes go they will all die off." Little Black Hawk repeated the argument and added, "The Great Spirit put the Winnebagoes in Wisconsin & we wish to stay. We believe God takes care of us here and we want to live."[11]

One of the Nebraska Winnebagos was at the council, and Smith asked him, "Do Indians die there more than here?" to which he answered, "A good many

die." Big Black Hawk asked if the land in Nebraska and the Indian Territory
was good land, and when Smith assured him that it was, he continued:

> It doesn't pay for us to [go to] good land. If we do the government will soon
> remove us again. There is land here that suits us. We will stay here. We will live
> here like white men.
>
> [Smith]. You will live like gophers. No one can live on this land that you roam
> over except gophers. . . . I said before it was better for you to go to Nebraska than
> to stay here. Now I say more, not only is it better for you to go but you must go.
>
> Big Black Hawk. I hear what you say. . . . We wish to remain here & become
> citizens of the United States. If we go away our children will all die off. We all
> have one mind. We do not want to move. Many men come here to talk to us, but
> no one tells us how to live right. We wish to live like white men.
>
> [Smith]. You have been wandering around here for thirty years & have done
> nothing about living right, and you never will. A few may do something, but the
> many will not. The majority will drink whiskey & wander about as you have done.
>
> Big Black Hawk. I do not drink. Our old men do not drink. Some of the young
> men drink. We cannot prevent them. We have no thought of going away. We are
> ready to go to work.
>
> [Smith]. There is no wish on the part of the government to do you any harm at
> all, but to do you good. And a white man can see farther into the future than you
> do. Now you think of living in a country here where a white man would never
> think of living. The blackbirds will fly over this pine brush & never light. . . .
>
> [Little Black Hawk]. You may bring dry grass & pile it up about me & my little
> children & burn us up. You may do this but do not take us away.[12]

Smith asked that a delegation go to look at the land in Nebraska, but there
was little interest in his suggestion, and the Indians ended the council. Smith
was convinced that to leave the Winnebagos in Wisconsin was to leave them
in "degredation of the lowest kind." Some might be able to "eke out a precarious existence" there, but the majority would lead "a vagabond life and be
a growing annoyance to the increasing settlements, and a perpetual barbarism in the heart of Wisconsin." The only serious objection he could see to
the removal was the Indians' attachment to their homes in Wisconsin. "They
cling most tenaciously to the ground over which they have tramped, and to
the place which they have called home, though it be only a tree or a rock." He
was pleasantly surprised to hear a week after the council that one hundred of
the Winnebagos were on their way to Nebraska. The rest of the tribe, however, some six to nine hundred persons, refused to go, and Smith finally had
to resort to a show of force to remove them.[13]

From Wisconsin, Smith went to White Earth and remained at the reservation for nine days. Charles Brace visited White Earth about the time of

Smith's return and wrote a series of articles about the reservation for the *New York Times*. Brace was impressed by the agency employees, who were "performing their quiet, unknown labors in the earnest and honest spirit of a 'friend of the poor.'" He noted that most of them had a good background for the task through their previous work for the Christian and Sanitary commissions or work among the freedmen. They also showed "wisdom and hard sense" in a situation in which "mere sentimentality" would be fatal. He gave special praise to Smith. "I have known him for twenty years," he wrote, "and a man of higher integrity or more adaptation for this especial field of work, it would be difficult to find in the whole Union." He also noted that Smith "never sought or expected" the office he now held.[14]

As others had done, Brace called attention to the work Cleavie Smith was doing among the Chippewas at White Earth. "She instructs them on Sunday in the truths of religion, goes from house to house among them, teaching the practical duties of morality, and sometimes the simplest work of the household. Here she is showing an Indian woman how to milk. There she weeds a bed of beets; in another cabin . . . she reads the Testament by the bedside of the dying, or talks to the ignorant Indian of the love of Christ, and the life which will please Him, on earth."[15]

With the help of a New York merchant, S. N. Goodale, Cleavie had introduced the use of hand looms for weaving, and the Chippewa women had already produced hoopskirts for sale. In place of whalebone or wire, they wove rushes to give the skirts their form. Rushes were also being used to weave mats. Cleavie had taught many of the women how to make "raised bread" and, with the help of a basketmaker, how to weave baskets. She enjoyed showing visitors Indian homes with cookstoves, chairs, bedsteads, crockery, flatirons, and even sewing machines. But as much as she enjoyed her work, when her husband came, she accepted his offer to accompany him on his trip down the Missouri River and to return with him to Washington.[16]

Smith, his family, and Smith's cousin Henry M. Tenney, whom the commissioner had engaged to keep a record of his councils with the Indians, left White Earth on the Northern Pacific Railroad for Bismarck, Dakota Territory, which was as far as the railroad had been completed. Charles Brace had taken the trip to Bismarck two weeks earlier and submitted a vivid description of it to the *New York Times*. One of the cars on his train held seventy carpenters who were going to build winter quarters at Fort Abraham Lincoln, near Bismarck. The carpenters spent the trip "cracking pistols" at the jackrabbits, prairie chickens, ducks, and curlews along the way. The only other passengers were an army officer, "a professional gambler and ruffian," and "a somewhat gaudily-dressed woman" who accompanied the gambler. From his window, Brace watched a procession of whitened bones of buffaloes, piles of firewood brought from one hundred miles away, settlers living in their wagons, houses for the railroad workers "made to put right on the railroad tracks, and move along," and camps of peaceful Yankton Sioux Indians. But not all the Sioux were peaceful. Not long before, one band of the tribe had attacked Fort Abraham Lincoln in retaliation for attacks on them by some of the army's Arikara scouts.[17]

When the Smiths and Tenney reached Bismarck, they hired a team to take them to the fort that had recently been attacked, where they held a council with the Arikaras. Smith urged the tribe to move to the Indian Territory to be free of their enemies, the Sioux, and after some discussion, they agreed to send representatives to examine the land in the Indian Territory. After the council, Smith and his party went by steamboat down the Missouri River 775 miles to Yankton and then traveled to Sioux City and Omaha. Along the way they met with Indians from the Grand River, Brule, Yankton, Santee, and Ponca agencies and paid to have the boat stop for one hour at the Cheyenne River Agency for a brief meeting there.

Smith hoped to encourage stock raising on the reservations where agriculture was not promising, and he purchased stock for the agencies along the way. At the Santee Agency, to encourage the Indians to labor on their farms, Smith offered a yoke of oxen to heads of families who would put up four tons of hay. Most of the Episcopal missionaries to the Indians were also at the Santee Agency for a convocation, and Smith attended an ordination service at the Episcopal Church of the Most Merciful Saviour, where morning prayer was said in Dakota.

As he visited the various agencies, Smith discussed the possibility of requiring the Indians to work for the supplies that had previously been furnished to them free. When he reached the Ponca Agency, he not only discussed the matter but directed the agent, Charles Birkett, to abolish the "free ration system" and "commence a system of universal labor" requiring able-bodied Indians to work for their rations. He thought the Poncas a suitable tribe for testing whether the Indians were capable of sustaining themselves by their own labor. The Indians, however, disliked the requirement, and after Smith left, delegations from other agencies visited the Poncas to try to involve them in "a combination disfavoring and condemning the labor movement." Birkett said that his "abilities as a debater were severely tested, and I was at last brought to see that a dictator was the proper person to cope with the situation." Only two months later, Birkett was able to report a long list of work done at the agency under the new policy and to say that "the feeling is growing that an idle man *is* as much to be scorned as the worker *was*."[18]

At Omaha, Smith called on Barclay White, the Quaker superintendent of Indian affairs. White had just received news of an attack by Sioux warriors on a Pawnee hunting party. Sixty-nine men, women, and children were killed, eleven wounded, and eleven more captured. The Pawnees' agent reported that "the wounded, dead and dying women and helpless children were thrown into a heap and burned in the most barbarous manner possible." The Sioux had a right to hunt in Nebraska, but because of their "wanton and murderous attack" on the Pawnees, Smith later sought to end their hunting there. Even without the violence, he considered the buffalo hunt "a great obstacle to civilization."[19]

Relying on the military to deal with the Sioux, Smith met with Howard White, the agent for the Winnebago Indians, and visited his agency to make arrangements for the arrival of the Winnebagos from Wisconsin. Smith was pleased with what he found at the Winnebago Reservation. Nearly 2,000 acres had been planted in corn and wheat, and all but 350 acres were owned and worked by individual Indians. Seventy-five frame houses had been built, with five rooms each. They were "sided and paper-lined, painted, plastered and wainscoted" and stood on brick foundations. All the other Indians had comfortable log houses, except the Winnebagos who were just beginning to arrive from Wisconsin. Smith said he could not account for the hostility of the Nebraska press to the administration's Indian policy, if the Santee and Winnebago reservations were typical of its accomplishments.[20]

From Omaha, Smith and his family went to St. Paul, where they met Columbus Delano, and then Delano and Smith made a brief visit to the Sisseton Agency in the Dakota Territory, where they found some fifteen hundred Indians who were "engaged in farming; have schools; wear civilized costumes, and live in houses like the whites." When Delano and Smith met with the Sissetons, their discussion revolved around a provision in a treaty of 1867 that specified that $80,000 received for land the Indians had sold would be given to them only in return for work. The Indians claimed not to have understood that they would have to work for the money. "If you had a piece of land and sold it," one of them asked, "would you like to work for the pay[?]" Leaders in nineteenth-century social thought, however, felt strongly about the evils of "pauperism" and opposed supporting anyone in a way that undercut his incentive to earn his own living. Bishop Whipple said on one occasion, "Honest work for wages is the solution of the Indian question. Almshouses make paupers, and Indian almshouses make savage paupers." Smith agreed with that philosophy. He also believed the Indians' survival depended on their learning to support themselves by their own labor, and he spoke to the Indians bluntly about the need to work.

The worst thing to do to an Indian is to shoot him. The next worst thing is to fill their hands, give them all they ask. The white people give this money, and they know that the way to make a man is to make him work. And the big council at Washington won[']t give any more money except for work. A few wild men up the river may have to be fed a little while longer. . . . The land you sold was in dispute. Great father did not consider it wholly yours. He had a right to say what he would do with [the] money. Another right: you are . . . his children, and he must do what is best for you.[21]

Chief Sweetcorn spoke for the others: "We did not suppose we were trading land for chopping wood. We were told that we would be paid for our work, and would get the money for the land extra." He recognized the power of the government to impose its will on them, but he thought the government's power could also be used to change the terms of the treaty. "Great father can do what he wishes, and he can blast rock and smelt iron, and can change this treaty."[22]

Secretary Delano tried to explain that the aim of the government was to teach them how to work so they could become "self-sustaining when the money is gone." Their agent, he said, was distributing the money "just as the Lord does. He who works the hardest gets the most." The sick and the poor who could not work would be cared for by the agent.[23]

The agent, the Reverend Moses N. Adams, had been nominated for the Sisseton Agency by the American Board of Commissioners for Foreign Missions. When he came to the reservation, he found two factions: Christian Indians, nurtured by Presbyterian missionaries, and the "Scout Party," headed by a polygamous chief, Gabriel Renville. Unable to separate his religious leadership from his government responsibilities, Adams had sided with the Christian Indians. He proposed that there would be no business, entertainment, or traveling on the Sabbath, that marriage would be monogamous, that no dances or gambling would be permitted on the reservation, and that a police force would be formed to enforce his rules. He also proposed an elected executive board to govern the Sissetons and recommended that "no Bigamist nor Polygamist be eligible." Predictably, Adams's proposals produced continuous conflict on the reservation.[24]

Smith, who had learned to differentiate his roles as a minister and as a government employee, later found it necessary to caution Adams. "I have noted your remarks that the 'opposition is not against the Agency work alone, but the Gospel of Christ and the best form of civilization.' Care should be used that you do not seem in any way as an officer of the Government, to be a religious champion. The principles of tolerance [are] so fundamental in all the affairs of our Government that official action for the promotion of any form of religion is not expedient even if proper." [25]

When Smith returned from the Sisseton Agency, he and his family visited briefly with Smith's sister Martha Cook in Ripon, Wisconsin, and then went on to Washington, where the family settled into a home on Seventh Street, near Howard University. Altogether, Smith had traveled 5,244 miles in an attempt to acquaint himself with more of the Indian tribes. By his own estimate, he had met with representatives of thirty-five to forty thousand Indians, or about 10 percent of all his Indian wards. [26]

23

Satanta and Big Tree

Satanta . . . was perhaps the most influential of the Kiowa chiefs, a notorious raider and a great lover of whiskey, but not without good qualities and marked ability.

Thomas C. Battey, *The Life and Adventures of a Quaker Among the Indians*

[Big Tree] has no particular force of character and owes his celebrity entirely to the accident of being in company with Satanta on one of his murderous raids.

Edward P. Smith to A. B. Meacham, December 29, 1874

After a month in Washington, Smith set out again for the West, this time to attend the council at Fort Sill called to settle the fate of Satanta and Big Tree. The Quakers had continued to press for the chiefs' release, believing that if they were not released the Kiowas would lose all faith in the government and resume their raiding. Smith assured the Quakers that the Indian Office was doing all it could to secure the release, but he reminded them that the chiefs were still in the custody of the state of Texas and said they needed to "be aware that the Governor of Texas is not under the control of this Department." (He admitted to the Quakers that he did not think the Indians would be able to understand that the "Great Father" in Washington could not control the actions of the Texas governor.) Even after Governor Davis had agreed to release the men at a council in October, Superintendent Hoag informed Washington that the Kiowas could not be controlled until then without some evidence that the men would be released. On his recommendation and with Governor Davis's approval, Satanta and Big Tree were transferred, under military guard, to Fort Sill, where the Kiowas could at least see that the chiefs were still alive. Satanta and Big Tree arrived at Fort Sill on September 4; on September 19, Smith left for the Indian Territory.[1]

Smith had arranged to visit the two Quaker superintendents along the way, Barclay White in Omaha, and Enoch Hoag in Lawrence, Kansas. In both places, he asked the superintendents to call their agents together when he

came. A meeting was held with all the agents of the northern superintendency in White's office in Omaha on September 23, and the next day Smith
went on to Lawrence, where, in addition to meeting with Hoag and six of his
agents, he met with a delegation of Osage Indians from the Indian Territory.
The Osages, he said, "number about 3,000, and are probably, as to physique,
and freedom from white vices, the finest Indians in America. This delegation
of twelve will average over six feet in height, and 200 lb. in weight, and yet the
Agent says they were not picked with any reference to size." The Osages had
sold land in Kansas and moved to the Indian Territory, a move Smith thought
"timely, and in most respects fortunate," although a mistake in drawing the
boundaries of their new reservation had cost them one hundred thousand
acres of the best land. The price they had accepted for their land in Kansas
had also been reduced, a wrong Smith hoped could be corrected.[2]

The Osages were to receive between $5 and $6 million for their land,
and Smith considered the money a "peril" to them and wanted to ensure
that they got the money "without their ruin." The Indian Office had therefore demanded that the Osages work for the money received for their land.
After meeting with the delegation, Smith told Delano that the chiefs "insisted strenuously that they should have their funds in their own hands to use
as they like. It was the same discussion over again, which we had with the
Sissetons, and it was very hard to make them see that the Government has a
right to require them to labor, before they receive their own funds, but they
finally acquiesced in what they could not help, and have gone home more
settled in their minds, than they have ever been before."[3]

Smith and Hoag left Lawrence on September 27 for Wichita, where they
took the stagecoach for Fort Sill. Remote as they were from officialdom, they
were still within reach of the government; a courier managed to deliver a
telegram to them even though he had to overtake the stage from Wichita to
do so. When they arrived at Fort Sill, they found it surprisingly complete and
well arranged. The barracks, officers' quarters, and quartermaster's buildings—all constructed of limestone—surrounded a square parade ground of
nearly ten acres, all of it kept in fine order. Most of the troops, who were
said to be in "excellent drill and condition," were black. Five companies of
the Tenth Cavalry (one of two black cavalry regiments in the army) and two
black infantry companies were stationed at Fort Sill along with one company
of white infantrymen. "Buffalo soldiers" the Comanches called the black
soldiers because of their color and the texture of their hair.[4]

A preliminary council was held on October 4, with Governor Davis, Superintendent Hoag, and Smith on one side and some of the Kiowa chiefs on the
other. The issue was where the council should be held. Davis insisted that it

A delegation of Osage Indians that met with Edward Smith in Lawrence, Kansas, in September 1873. Their agent, Isaac T. Gibson (standing, third from left), said of their visit to Lawrence, "It being the first time many of them had seen the cars and other evidences of advanced civilization, their desire for the improvement of their own people was greatly increased." Smith is the fifth person from the left of those standing. Enoch Hoag is the seventh from the left of those standing. Courtesy of National Anthropological Archives, Smithsonian Institution.

be held in the fort. The Indians protested that some of their friends had been killed there and it was there that Satanta and Big Tree had been arrested, but the governor would not yield. On the advice of Smith and their agent, the Indians finally agreed to meet in the fort.

On October 6, the various parties gathered in front of the office of Lieutenant Colonel John W. Davidson, Fort Sill's commanding officer. A tent fly had been set up and a table and chairs provided for the participants. A guard of black cavalrymen brought Satanta and Big Tree from the guardhouse and sat them on a bench. The other Indians seated themselves on the grass or on their horses around the tent. Colonel Davidson had made sure that the entire garrison was in quarters and the officers on hand. He had one troop of cavalry saddled in the stables and had taken "every precaution to prevent and repress disturbance."[5]

Smith opened the council by stressing its importance and by appealing for truth in the proceedings. Then Governor Davis spoke. He said he had come to make peace for the people of Texas and to tell the Kiowas and the Comanches what the people of Texas wanted them to do to have peace. He pointed out that Satanta and Big Tree were present and gave them an opportunity to talk. Before they could do so, Satanta's old and frail-looking father, Red Tepee, came up and, laying his hand on the governor's head, said, "I am a poor old man. I want you to pity me, and give me my son. You have your wife and your children[;] take pity on me and give me back my son."[6]

When Satanta spoke, he appealed to the Indians to give up their raids into Texas. "Whatever the white men [think] best I want my people to do." Then he told the governor, "Strip off these prison clothes[,] turn me over to my people[,] and they will keep their promise."[7]

Governor Davis, however, was not yet ready to release the chiefs. Although Grant and Delano had convinced him to come to Fort Sill, he was also under considerable pressure from Texans to take a strong stand with the Indians. He carefully recounted the raids the Kiowas and Comanches had made into Texas and then laid out a set of stringent terms for the release of Satanta and Big Tree, making it clear that they were his terms and not those of the commissioner or the Indian agents. The Kiowas and Comanches were to give up their horses and arms at once, settle down to a farming life at Fort Sill, and allow agents among them who would check on them daily to prevent raiding. Rations would be drawn by each man personally and would be given for three days only. The Comanches who had been raiding in Texas would be surrendered, "and those who remain at peace shall put themselves under the direction of the United States troops and aid in arresting the others," who would be turned over to the state of Texas to be tried by law. All captured horses that could be identified would be returned. And Satanta and Big Tree would remain in Colonel Davidson's custody until he was satisfied that all the governor's conditions had been met. Moreover, Satanta and Big Tree were not pardoned; they could be rearrested and punished for their old crimes at any time the governor's conditions were not met. "If these conditions are not complied with," Davis concluded, "it will be better for the people of Texas to resort to open war and settle this matter at once."[8]

When Davis had finished, several chiefs spoke and professed to be pleased with what he had said; they asked only that Satanta and Big Tree be freed. One of them, however, said that Davis was "too particular" to want all the young raiders delivered to him. "They cannot be changed in a day." Some of the chiefs digressed to remind the white officials of various promises the government had not fulfilled. Smith interrupted one of them, Buffalo Good, a

Edmund J. Davis (1827–83). Courtesy of Archives Division, Texas State Library, Austin, Texas.

Below: Satanta (*left*) and Big Tree (*right*), who before their release at Fort Sill, had been imprisoned in Texas for the murders of seven men in a raid on a wagon train. Courtesy of National Anthropological Archives, Smithsonian Institution.

Waco chief, to ask, "Did not the agent send a man to you to show you how to farm?" After Buffalo Good said that he did, Smith asked, "Did you make any use of this man?" Buffalo Good answered that he wanted the man to break up the land first, to which Smith responded, "Exactly. You wanted him to do all the work."[9]

When Enoch Hoag spoke, he said that although Davis claimed he had not made any promises about freeing the chiefs, the president and the secretary of the interior had promised that they would be released. Their only condition was that the Indians keep out of Texas one spring, which they had done. On the basis of the promises made in Washington and the good behavior of the Indians, Hoag appealed to Davis to release the prisoners.

Davis refused to change his terms. He reminded the assembly that he had sole control of the prisoners and the conditions of their release. His main concern was to protect the people of Texas.

Finally, Smith spoke, addressing the interpreter but intending his words for the Comanches, who, unlike the Kiowas, had not stopped their raiding.

> Tell them [that] what the Governor has asked from them today I am here from Washington to demand right now. The Governor told them they had no reasons for doing as they have. . . . He told them that had to stop and I tell them so now. When your captive women and children were given back to you last Spring you gave your solemn pledges not to raid into Texas again but scarcely had these women and children got here when your young men were again down in Texas. Now before the sun is this high[,] have these Comanche murderers right on this spot, and I, and the Governor, will no longer disagree and you will get your captives. Now go home and talk about this and talk about nothing else.[10]

Smith also talked about nothing else. He reported to Delano that the council was "very unsatisfactory." Davis had not shared his terms with Smith before the council but had made them directly to the Indians. Harsh and demanding as Davis's terms were, Smith believed they had to be met if Satanta and Big Tree were to be released, and he believed the men had to be released to keep the peace. He was convinced that the Kiowas had done their part to remain at peace and had done what they could to prevent the Comanches from raiding. Now it was essential for the government to release the chiefs to keep faith with the Kiowas: "it is a great damage to the Agency to have the word of the President forfeited." He told Delano he would ask Davis to turn the chiefs over to him, and he thought Davis would deliver them, "but under protest." Then he would take the responsibility for releasing them.[11]

Smith put his proposal in a long letter to Davis. He said the government had misunderstood Davis's conditions for releasing the chiefs when it promised their release. But the promise had been made, and the Kiowas had kept their pledges of peace. They had returned their captives and the stock they had stolen and had ceased raiding into Texas. "They have also frequently restrained the Comanches and are known to have stopped raiding parties among them by killing their horses, and whipping them, and compelling them to return." Both the Quaker agents and Colonel Davidson had testified that the Kiowas had kept their promises.[12]

The raiding in Texas, Smith said, had been largely by Comanches, and he was prepared to make them surrender the guilty parties. He had hoped the Comanche raiders would already have been brought in, but they had not, and the disappointed Kiowas could not be counted on to compel them. In fact, he feared that the Kiowas would now join the Comanches. "If we are obliged to fight them, it will necessarily be done with the misgiving that the Indians themselves are not altogether in fault."[13]

He asked Davis to give the chiefs to him to be released and in return he agreed to return them, or other chiefs equal to them, if the Kiowas again raided into Texas. Smith also agreed to institute a roll call of all males over sixteen years of age, frequent enough to prevent their absence from the reservation without the agent's knowledge. The Comanches would be put under similar restrictions as soon as possible. In addition, Smith pledged to increase the patrol along the Texas border and to compel the Comanches to surrender not less than five raiders to take the place of Satanta and Big Tree.

If the chiefs were released and resumed their raiding, Smith told Davis, it would add but two fighting men to the Kiowas, but he thought their release would instead keep them all from fighting. "If they are not released, I fear and expect that we shall have to fight all the Kiowas except these two, together with the Comanches." Smith had no doubt that the government could win a war, but a war would mean the "abandonment of property, suffering, pillage and murder" along the border, as well as the sacrifice of many soldiers—"and the country disgraced by an Indian War originating in its own bad faith."[14]

The Indians, knowing nothing of Smith's plans, spent a discouraging day. Thomas Battey, a Quaker teacher who lived among the Kiowas, described their mood.

> The Indians were much excited, though this excitement was not manifested in words or noise; it was of the more deadly kind, which shaded the countenance and gleamed in the eye. The Kiowas were all about, with their bows strung, ready for use at a moment's warning. Kicking Bird said his "heart was a stone; there was no soft spot in it. He had taken the white man by the hand, thinking him to be a friend, but he is not a friend; government has deceived us; Washington is rotten." Lone Wolf said, "I want peace—have worked hard for it—kept

my young men from raiding—followed the instructions Washington gave me to the best of my knowledge and ability. Washington has deceived me,—has failed to keep faith with me and my people,—has broken his promises; and now there is nothing left us but war. I know that war with Washington means the extinction of my people, but we are driven to it; we had rather die than live." [15]

Davis asked Smith to send runners out to call the Indians to another council on October 8. The Indians went to the fort, but they went armed, determined to rescue the prisoners at any price. Battey said they loaded their guns and strung their bows and agreed on a time to free Satanta and Big Tree. Then they placed their men, "as if by accident, in the most favorable position for shooting the governor and the guard" and readied fleet horses for the prisoners' escape. Unknown to the Indians, Colonel Davidson had also prepared his forces; the room directly behind the prisoners was full of soldiers, ready to enforce order whenever necessary. [16]

When the council had assembled, Davis surprised the Indians by reading Smith's letter and then asking Satanta and Big Tree to stand. He told them that since their last meeting Smith, speaking for the government of the United States, had offered to take the responsibility for seeing that the Kiowas and Comanches met his conditions for their release. "Now, Satanta and Big Tree," he said, "when you go to your tribe see that you comply with what is demanded, that they keep good faith with the Government, and it will be well; otherwise the Government will arrest you again and turn you over to me, with other bad Indians. Now remember this and go to your tribes." At that, the two chiefs hugged the governor, and Satanta's father kissed him. Smith then told the Indians: "You see what a load you have put on my back. The Governor of Texas was going to hold Satanta and Big Tree until you do what is right, and I promised him you would do right without his holding them, and now I want you to remember that you have promised me that you will do exactly as he wants you to do. I should be ashamed to go down to Texas a month from now if you don't keep faith." Then he dismissed them, saying he wanted them to bring in the horses they had stolen from Texas. [17]

That afternoon Smith met with the Indians in the agent's office. He demanded that they produce five of the Comanche raiders and gave them until the next morning to tell him whether they would do it. The next morning, the Comanches said they would return the horses and mules they had stolen but they could not give up the five raiders; to attempt to do so could lead to armed resistance in the tribe. They said they would return them only if Smith named them, but Smith had settled on five only as a "convenient number" and could not give them names. Smith would not accept the Comanches' offer, and when the Indians insisted that what he was asking was too hard for them, Battey said Smith was "so indiscreet in his remarks as to affront them, by calling them cowards." They denied it and told Smith if he wanted the five men, there were soldiers at the fort he could use to capture the men himself. Reluctantly, the Comanches finally agreed to send a party of their young men as scouts to help in capturing any raiders that might be found. Smith gave them thirty days to report, telling them that if they did nothing both their rations and their annuities would be cut off.[18]

Smith thought it necessary to use force against Indians who were still raiding. Even before the council was over, he had requested military action against them. Fearing that Cheyennes raiding near Pueblo would unite with the raiding Comanches, Smith asked that the Cheyennes be "struck and destroyed or captured. . . . A blow there will make the solution here much easier, by preventing the tribes above from joining. The Comanche Indians must be kept on reservations by punishment, when other measures have failed." Columbus Delano immediately transmitted Smith's request to the War Department, which gave orders to strike the raiding Cheyennes. When the council at Fort Sill was over, Smith asked Colonel Davidson to place a patrol on the Red River, strong enough to prevent raiders from crossing the river without being observed. He also informed Davidson that the Comanches had agreed to accompany the army into Texas, and he asked that any Comanches found raiding in Texas be struck or intercepted. Smith hoped that with the Comanches' help the raiders could be captured or killed, although he much preferred that they be captured. Davidson took it upon himself to issue the orders Smith requested and then reported them to his superiors. Governor Davis offered ten companies of volunteers if the army did not have sufficient troops available.[19]

When General Sherman learned of Colonel Davidson's orders, he was sure the operation would fail.

> From a personal knowledge and experience, I think the commissioner of Indian affairs has imposed on the military a costly and impossible duty. To chase a small band of raiding Comanches in all Western Texas, a country three or four times as large as the State of Pennsylvania, utterly devoid of supplies, and even grass, will wear down the horses and the men, and result, as hundreds of similar attempts, in failure. The only way to keep the Kioways, Comanches and Cheyennes from raiding is to be sure they stay at home. . . . A needle in a hay-stack would be much easier found than a Comanche on his familiar raid into Texas. These stipulations by Indian Agents and Superintendents are very unreasonable and utterly impracticable.[20]

As Sherman predicted, the expedition to capture the raiders was unsuccessful. The Comanches did go to Texas with Colonel Davidson's soldiers, but no raiders were found. During their absence, a party of Texans made a raid on the Indians and stole some two hundred ponies and mules. Despite the cooperation of all but two bands of the Comanches and their own losses at the hands of the Texans, a telegram from Smith, who had returned to Washington, let them know that they had only ten more days in which to bring in the five raiders. The agent was not to issue any annuities to the Comanches; if the raiders were not brought in, he was to stop issuing rations; and "if they still refuse they will be handed over to the Military." The agent was to assure the Indians that the government was in earnest and was taking steps to "compel the Comanches to do right. . . . General Sheridan will probably make arrangements to move immediately upon these Indians, unless the demands of the government are promptly complied with." When the telegram was read to the Comanches, many of them considered it a declaration of war.[21]

War on the plains seemed inevitable. The clouds were gathering, Thomas Battey said, "which may ere long rain blood upon this land." Warfare was not new to Smith. He had seen hundreds, perhaps thousands of men die and had gone fearlessly into danger himself. What was new was his own responsibility for the killing. He assumed that responsibility easily—almost too easily. There was a grim determination in his actions; the Comanches had promised to behave, and as their guardian he was going to see that they did. If not, they would be "struck," "punished," "whipped"—and Smith knew exactly what those euphemisms meant. Perhaps subconsciously the *Washington Daily Chronicle* had sensed Smith's attitude when it reported earlier that the capital was expecting the return of "General E. P. Smith."[22]

James Haworth, who had replaced Lawrie Tatum as the Indian agent at Fort Sill, reported a great concern among the Comanches after their annuities were cut off. Those who had cooperated with the government resented being punished along with the guilty persons. Haworth, who, despite his Quaker upbringing, had served as a captain in the Fortieth Regiment, Ohio Volunteer Infantry, during the Civil War, appealed to Smith to modify his order. He believed that if the requirement to bring in five raiders was dropped and the offer made to issue annuities when they brought in a certain amount of stolen stock, the Comanches would cooperate. He reminded Smith of the Texans who were conducting raids on the Indians' stock—some of them men who had been with Governor Davis at the council—and said, "When we remember that a large number of the citizens on the Frontier of Texas, are really worse, and meaner than the worst Comanches, we cannot help but feel that the Indian though a great Sinner, is also a great deal sinned against."[23]

Cyrus Beede, Enoch Hoag's chief clerk, also asked Smith to modify his order, and General Sheridan asked him to withdraw it entirely. Sheridan learned of Smith's plans when he, Smith, and the secretaries of war and the interior met with the president to discuss the Indian difficulties. After Sheridan returned to his post at Chicago, General Christopher Augur advised him that Smith's order would only create trouble, and Sheridan suggested that Smith withdraw the directions "for the present." [24]

Felix Brunot, the chairman of the Board of Indian Commissioners, was also critical of Smith's plans. When Brunot inquired about Comanche affairs, Smith told him that the five raiders had still not been surrendered, and he saw "no possible way to protect the Reservation system from the odium that will attach to it, if it continues to provide a refuge to which the guilty may flee, and still continue in favor with the Government and be the recipients of its bounty." He believed that on the approach of a military force the Comanches would surrender the men, and he said he had "asked that special instructions be given the officer in command of the Military to give the Comanches every possible opportunity to do right before any attack is made upon them." [25]

Brunot told Smith he understood that the Indians on the reservations claimed not to be able to stop the raiders. What if the military confronts them, he asked, and they still cannot produce the raiders? Smith had asked that the Comanches have an opportunity to do right before an attack was made upon them. "Upon who?" Brunot asked. "The Indians who are quietly remaining on that reservation in compliance with their treaty agreement. Such a consummation would necessarily rank with the Sand Creek massacre by Chivington, and the murder of Black Kettle and his band. . . . I most sincerely hope that the order may be modified so as to prevent this intended attack upon the reservation Indians, and send the troops against the Indians who are raiding on the Texas border." [26]

The Kiowas also believed Smith had made a mistake. Lone Wolf appealed to Haworth to write to Washington to ask that the issue with the Comanches not be pressed. "I wish Washington would let it pass," he said. "If those foolish young men have killed any of the people of Texas, they are dead. Some of those young men have been killed—they are dead. Let it all pass; do not let it make trouble among the living." Kicking Bird spoke to the Kiowas about Smith, whom he called "Mone-kome-haint," "without a pointing finger," because Smith had at some time lost the forefinger of his right hand.

> The commissioner by making one bad talk has set all this country on fire. He has required a hard thing, which was not in the road our fathers travelled. It is a new road to us, and the Comanches cannot travel it: they cannot bring in the five men. If they attempt it, many women and children will be killed, and many men must die.
>
> It all rests on the commissioner.
>
> This trouble will not affect the Comanches alone: it will spread through all

these tribes, and become general. It is a new road to all the Indians of this country, and they will be affected by it.

I have taken the white people by the hand; they are my friends. The Comanches are my brothers. By and by, when I am riding on these prairies, and see the bones of the Comanches, or the skull of a white man, lying on the ground, my heart will feel very sad, and I shall say, Why is this? It is because *Mone-kome-haint* made a road the Indians could not travel.[27]

On December 2 a delegation of Quakers called on Columbus Delano to appeal for a relaxation of Smith's "rash order." That same day, Smith suspended the order. Agent Haworth was told that he could issue rations, and if the Indians would bring in all the stolen stock, he could also distribute three-fourths of their annuities. When Thomas Battey received the news at the Kiowa Agency, he noted that these new terms were "almost the precise conditions of the offer made by [the Comanches] to the commissioner at the time of the council, and by him utterly refused." Nevertheless, they had now been accepted, and warfare on the plains, if not averted, was at least postponed.[28]

24

"We Are Not Children"

We are not children. We are men. . . . I never thought I would be treated so
when I made the Treaty.

Medicine Horse, Oto chief

On his return from Fort Sill, Smith stopped again in Lawrence, Kansas,
where the Kansas yearly meeting of Friends and the Friends' Associated Executive Committee on Indian Affairs with representatives from several states were meeting. Both he and Enoch Hoag reported on the council
at Fort Sill. Hoag tried to put the council in perspective by pointing out that
of the seventy-five thousand Indians in his superintendency, sixty thousand
dressed in "citizen clothes," lived in houses, and had flourishing schools.
Fifteen thousand Indians still lived in a "wild state," but of those only five
hundred were "savages," and even they were under all possible restraint by
their chiefs. "The papers," he said, "never set forth this side of the Indian
question." [1]

Smith told the Friends that the government was as firm as ever in its support of the peace policy and that policy was "in conformity with the laws of
God and with human nature. We propose," he said, "to help the Indians as
men, no longer, as formerly, to treat them as wild men and leave them such,
keeping him quiet as an Indian, but to approach him as a man." He appealed
to the assembly to send out more people like Thomas Battey, who would
"look through the paint and dirt and see the man that is in him." He admitted
that the five hundred Indians who were savages could be very troublesome
and that it would require "much fortitude, and may be severity, to make them
cease doing wrong." [2]

Several Indian delegations were in Washington or on their way to the city
when Smith returned from the West. From the earliest days of the republic,
Indians had been brought to the capital to impress them with the strength of
the country and the benefits of civilization. The Board of Indian Commissioners thought the visits "one of the most effective peace measures which

the Government has ever adopted." The Indians, eager to gain the prestige of a visit to the "Great Father," prized the visits highly. "It appears to be the Mecca of their hopes," Barclay White told Smith. So common had the visits become that in Plains Indian sign language the name for Washington was "the home of our father, where we go on the puffing wagon to council." Smith's next weeks were busy meeting with the delegations.[3]

Two days after his return, Smith met with a delegation of Crows from Montana. Miners had invaded the Crow reservation, and in March 1873 Congress authorized the secretary of the interior to negotiate with the Crows for the cession of all or part of their reservation, with the provision that the land left for them was to be compact, well-watered and timbered, and useful for farming. The measure had the approval of the Indian Office. It was commonly thought, even by the friends of the Indians, that the Indians had more land than they needed and that if the excess land were sold it would satisfy the miners and settlers and eliminate conflict between them and the Indians. It would also provide a trust fund for the Indians' future and help persuade them to farm their land instead of "roaming" over it.

A commission consisting of Felix Brunot, the chairman of the Board of Indian Commissioners, Eliphalet Whittlesey, and James Wright, with Thomas Cree acting as secretary, met with the Crows in August. They warned the Crows of future trouble with the miners and advised them to yield to the miners' presence. "When a man sees the whirl-wind coming," Brunot asked, "does he tell it to stop? No, he gets out of its way." The commissioners succeeded in convincing the chiefs to give up their reservation on the Yellowstone, which the governor of Montana described as "one of the finest and most extensive valleys in the Rocky mountains," and accept a smaller one in Judith Basin, in return for the annual interest on the sum of $1 million. The commissioners then agreed to the Indians' request to send a delegation of both Mountain Crows and River Crows to Washington to meet the "Great Father." None of the Crows had ever been east or had any conception of the white man's power, and the commission thought it would be useful for them to learn something about it.[4]

Smith's first meeting with the Crow delegation was largely ceremonial. The Indians arrived in blankets and buffalo robes, wearing red paint, feathers, horsehair fringes, beads, and "ponderous brass ear-rings" and carrying fans of light brown feathers. They asked permission to smoke. The pipe was passed around several times, until the room became "blue with smoke." Blackfoot explained that the reason for smoking was "because we want to tell the truth, and we are not going to lie to one another." The Crows had always been friendly to the United States, and the government wanted to keep them friendly. Hearing that the delegates had been uncomfortable in the coaches on their trip east, Smith promised to let them ride on horseback from the train to their homes, "just as you are used to riding." Delano promised to let them see the president before they left. "It is the intention of the Gov^t," he said, "as long as you remain friendly[,] to do all [it] can to make you happy."[5]

Eight days later, as the Crows were about to leave Washington, another council was held with them. They had seen the president, but he had little time for them, and Smith heard their requests and tried to answer them. They wanted the Musselshell River included in their reservation, and Smith promised to take their request to Congress. They also wanted to keep their trader and their agent, whom the government had decided to remove. The agent, Fellows D. Pease, a rancher who had lived in the West nearly twenty years and spoke the Crow language, was well liked by the Crows. Not only did the chiefs want to keep him as their agent, but when Brunot met with the Crows, a large group of children gathered around Pease and held on to him. One of the boys offered the commissioners a horse if Pease could stay, and two girls presented buffalo robes, saying, "We want Pease to stay with the Crow tribe." Smith assured the Crows that they could keep their trader but told them they would be getting a new agent. Finally, the delegates wanted $100 apiece to spend; Smith offered them $50, which they accepted. During the conversations, Long Horse said of Smith, "This white man . . . treat me good. That is what I am looking for. Our tribe are the River Crows. They are waiting to see what news we will bring back, and I wanted to be treated good, and tell them so."[6]

A delegation of Utes was also in the city. Congress had authorized negotiations for the sale of part of their reservation, too. Smith commissioned Felix Brunot to meet with the tribe, noting that if an agreement was made, the Utes should be urged to give up all mining lands and keep enough agricultural land for the entire tribe. Brunot was also instructed to seek an agreement that would give the Interior Department as much discretion as possible in investing or spending the money the Utes would receive for their land. Brunot's commission succeeded in convincing the Utes to give up nearly four million acres of their land.[7]

When the Utes met with Smith and Delano, they wanted to talk about the $25,000 they were to receive each year for their land. The spokesman for the delegation, Chief Ouray, speaking in fluent Spanish, said he had understood from Brunot that the money would be theirs to spend as they saw fit, but now he had heard that only the agent or the government could spend it. Smith told him the money would be spent for them in ways that would benefit them. Ouray said there might be a great difference of opinion about what they needed, and Smith replied, "Yes, you might want horses and we might give you a school house instead." After Brunot told Ouray the government would be likely to grant all his requests, if they were reasonable, Ouray finally agreed to the government's wishes about the money.[8]

Smith told the Utes that he wanted them to live like whites, to plow and sow. When his comments were translated into Spanish, the Indians laughed, and Ouray said they had no desire to live like whites. When Delano spoke to the delegation, he too told them he wanted them to live like whites, "whereupon Ouray made some remark in Spanish, and all the members of the delegation laughed heartily." The interpreter declined to translate Ouray's remark, saying it was only a joke. The delegation, dressed in "citizen clothes" but with ornaments and with feathers in their hats, was then promised a tour of the Navy Yard, a sail down the Potomac River, and a meeting with the president. When they visited the president, he too counseled them to take up the ways of the whites so they would be ready to support themselves by farming when the tide of immigration reached their land.[9]

Delegations of both Northern and Southern Cheyennes and Arapahos also came to the capital. The Northern delegation wanted to talk about the reunion of the Northern and Southern Arapahos and about the boundary line between the Arapahos and the Cheyennes. The Indian Office wanted to talk to them about going to the Indian Territory, and Smith told them bluntly that they had agreed to go there and would be compelled to do so. Smith and Delano went with the delegation to the White House, where Grant told them what Smith had: they would have to move to the Indian Territory. One of the Indians looked defiant when Grant spoke; another said that when he signed the treaty he did not know he was required to go south; still another said he thought it was no use to "buck against the white man"; he proposed to do what the Great Father told him, to "be a white man." Little Robe said only, "I came a good way to see the Great Father; I now see him; I am glad." Delano jokingly suggested that Little Robe had made a speech as terse as many the president had made, and Grant said he hoped he would not lose his reputation for brief speeches. Smith told him he need have no fears on that score.[10]

Smith also brought the Utes and the Arapahos together for a meeting. He thought there had never been a gathering like it in Washington, the best men of enemy tribes, "here in one room to talk with each other." He told the delegates the government not only wanted to be at peace with them but wanted them to be at peace with each other. "I want you to take one another by the hand, and hereafter not fight any more." Smith had brought to the council Friday, an Indian who as a boy had been captured by the Sioux and was now in the hands of the Arapahos and who was thought to be Ouray's son. Smith hoped that his return to Ouray would encourage peaceful relations between the tribes, but Friday said he could not understand the Utes and did not want to go with them, and Ouray was not convinced the young man was his son. Smith still hoped that the tribes could agree on peace, but the Indians wanted to discuss the matter at home, and Smith had to be satisfied with some reluctant handshaking.[11]

The strains between the Indians and their white guardian were nowhere more evident than in a series of councils with a delegation of Otos from Nebraska. At the urging of the Quakers, Congress had authorized the sale of about half the Oto Reservation. The Otos would remain on the other half, and the proceeds of the sale would be used to provide the means of their civilization. The tribe was divided in its own wishes, some wanting to sell the land and remain in Nebraska and others wanting to sell the entire reservation and move to the Indian Territory, where they could live in traditional ways. The leader of the delegation to Washington, Medicine Horse, was also the leader of the "Coyote" faction that opposed the "civilization" the Quakers offered and wanted to go to the Indian Territory. He was accompanied to Washington by four other chiefs: Standby, Little Pipe, Big Bear, and Missouri Chief. Their agent, their trader, and an interpreter were present at the councils as was a delegation of Quakers from Philadelphia.[12]

A large crowd of clerks gathered to see the Otos when they arrived at the Indian Office for their first meeting. A reporter who was present said the Otos were all "of large and compact built forms except 'Little Pipe' . . . whose delicate form appeared in striking contrast to the huge figures of his comrades." The delegates wore colorful blankets, turbans or bead caps, broadcloth breeches, and beaded moccasins and had wide silver bracelets on their arms and wrists. Before each one spoke, he shook hands with Smith and the Quakers, and when he had finished he shook hands again with Smith. The Indians addressed Smith as "Grandfather"; Missouri Chief said he too would call Smith "Grandfather," even though he was as old as the commissioner. A reporter thought the term was suggested by Smith's "bright steel gray hair and dignified manner," but it may have meant more than that. Among the Otos the relationship between a grandfather and a grandson was affectionate and close, with little tension or conflict. The form of address may have been a gentle gesture of goodwill.[13]

Little was done at the first meeting. The Indians were tired and wanted to rest, but Medicine Horse did ask Smith whether their request to go on a buffalo hunt had been granted. Smith said he had thought a long time before

Medicine Horse (*left*) and Standby (*right*), members of an Oto delegation
from Nebraska that visited Washington in the fall of 1873. Courtesy of
National Anthropological Archives, Smithsonian Institution.

making his decision. It was bad, he said, for Indians to go on a hunt "because
we must do one thing or the other. Either let you continue wild as you now
are, or make you like white men; and nothing keeps up this wild living, and
habits like hunting." If he had money to give them he would not allow the
hunt, but because he did not and they were in need of food, they would be
allowed to hunt one last time that year.[14]

When they met the next day, Medicine Horse said they wanted to move
to the Indian Territory. Smith asked him how he wanted to live when he got
there, and he gave the answer he knew was expected: "If I move there I will
live as well as the other Indians there. I can work. I can hang on the plow as
others do." Smith replied: "There are two kinds of Indians there. Some are
good and work, and others are very wild & bad. I should be very sorry to have
Indians go from Nebraska so as to be able to go wild again like some now in
the Territory. . . . If you really want to go to the Indian Territory and commence to live like civilized people, and get your living from the ground, then
we will talk about it, but if you want to go there to get away from the customs

and habits of civilized white people and live wild, I do not want you to go."
Medicine Horse replied: "I have always worked for my living. I have never
lived wild. I am like other people. Always was. I have always raised corn." [15]

The subject of their annuity payments came up, and Smith read from a
treaty with the Otos that said payments could be made to them either in
money or in goods as the president thought best. Up to that time, they had
been paid in money, but, Smith said, they had nothing to show for it, "no
wagons, no houses, no cattle or anything; you certainly need other things
much more than you need money. . . . Is it not better for us to send money to
your Agent to fence your farms than to send it to you to pass over to traders
for trinkets[?] . . . Besides, when you come to have your farms fenced, your
Agent will allow you to do the work and get the pay for it, and then you have
three things, the money, the fence and your farm. . . . You learn to labor and
take care of yourself. That is the only way to be a man." Standby objected,
saying: "We always work. We like to work. I plow the ground and get things
for my children. . . . We always raised something from the ground to support
our families, before we ever saw white men." Nevertheless, Smith said he
would no longer send them money, but a farmer and a miller, "and they will
buy oxen & cows for you." [16]

The discussion came back to the treaty and the right of the government to
pay the annuity in goods rather than in money.

> [Smith]. The money was promised to be spent for your benefit. That is the
> way it reads.
>
> Standby. How would these white men feel to have their property used in
> this way?
>
> [Smith]. If the white men are children and you are their guardian, you can do
> what you please with their money[,] provided you do what is good for them. And
> whenever you send an Agent to take care of a white man you can tell him what
> he shall do with his money.
>
> Medicine Horse. We are not children. We are men.
>
> [Smith]. I take you to be children who cannot take good care of money, and
> that is the reason why you have an Agent. Just as soon as you know how to read
> and write, and go about like white men, you will not need an Agent, but as long
> as you do not know how to make the best use of what is given you, so long you
> will have an Agent, to tell you how to use it.
>
> Medicine Horse. I never thought I would be treated so when I made the
> Treaty.
>
> [Smith] . . . I am satisfied that after 2 or 3 years trial you will see it as I do.
> And the man who cannot see that it is better to use $400.00 for opening a farm,
> than to trade it off for trinkets, ought not to have the $400.00 to spend. . . .
>
> Medicine Horse [no longer using the affectionate term "Grandfather"].

Father, look at me and not at the table. Those black curly haired people I have always heard were made free. I thought I was always a free man. I am free yet.

[Smith]. Why do you have an Agent then?

Medicine Horse. In the old time they always had a white man to stick by and take care of the Indians.

[Smith]. Why? if you were free and took care of yourselves?

Medicine Horse. It hurts me badly what you read in the book. I did not know it was there.

[Smith]. I want you to understand that you are not free in the sense that you can do as you please.

Medicine Horse. What is on the book is our Interpreter's fault[.] Nothing of that kind was talked of.

[Smith]. I have nothing to go by but what is written on that paper.[17]

When the Otos returned for their last meeting with Smith, they were still upset by what he had said to them at the previous meeting.

Medicine Horse. Father, what you said to us the other day hurt our feelings very much, and we could not sleep since. When we made a trade they did not tell us we must use our money as you told us the other day. We all like money as well as any one else. . . . I always thought my money belonged to me. . . . Your talk the other day takes our rights away. Why can't we have rights the same as others[?] . . .

[Smith]. Our Great Father likes his children and does what is best for them. . . . You have received these annuities for nearly twenty years. You have had the best land in Nebraska. . . . Now why is it you have no houses, oxen, cows, horses, and homes like the white men? It is because you do not know how to spend your money as white men do. . . . I do not take your money away, but use it for you. . . . You want to carry good news to those you left behind you[;] now if they have good sense, I will tell you what they will have. I will repair their school house for children this winter. I am going to do it out of other money, not out of theirs. I will fence their farms, not out of their money, but other money. That is good news to carry, unless they think a sack of flour, or piece of bacon better than a good school.[18]

The discussion returned to the sale of half their land, which Smith said they had agreed to and could not be changed. Standby wanted to go home and study the matter, but he felt pressured by Smith. "You want to put it all through at once, like drowning me in the river."

Standby. If you have a piece of land, and I sell it, you would not like it.

[Smith]. If you are my Agent and sell it, it is all right. You must remember there is a difference. You are the child of Government, and it must take care of you.

Standby. If you have children and they want money they have it. They do as they want to.

[Smith]. No, they do not. My child does as I want to have her. If my child wants any thing and I want her to have it she gets it. But if I don't want her to have it she don[']t get it, and she does not turn around and ask me, how I would like it if she had my money, and would not let me have it.

Standby. Well if you treat me as [your] own child, I must have half, once in a while. We could spend half of our annuity for stock and then have half the money left to spend. . . .

Medicine Horse [after learning that Smith had bought cattle and horses for them with money they had received for a railroad right-of-way]. We did not order you to buy any cattle or horses for us.

[Smith]. You did not need to. You are my children, and I had a right to buy what I wanted to for you. It takes you a long time to find out that I am going to do what I think best for you.

Medicine Horse. There is such a thing as children being whipped to death.

Smith finally agreed to use some of the annuity money to pay the tribe's debt to its trader, but then he closed the discussions with an offer to let the chiefs visit the Navy Yard and see the president.[19]

The goodwill the government expected from the visits of the Indian delegations was marred by the accommodations they received. Thomas Cree reported to Smith that at the Washington House the fifteen members of the Crow delegation, men and women, were crowded into one room with "tumble down affairs" for cots and almost no other furniture. "Their provisions," Cree said, "are of the commonest kind. The Indians complain that it is not as good as they had before they left Montana. . . . If the visit East is to give them a taste for civilization they ought to have some attractive surroundings."[20]

The Indian Office had also arranged for the Utes and the Northern Cheyennes and Arapahos to stay at the Washington House, a hotel at Third Street and Pennsylvania Avenue that had hosted Indian delegations for years. When Benjamin F. Beveridge, who with his family operated the Washington House, submitted his bills for the delegations, the Board of Indian Commissioners found that Beveridge had billed the government for $1,338.65 in "extras," including opera and theater tickets, outings to Mount Vernon on an excursion boat, cigars, dates, and figs. The board's examination also revealed that the government had been charged for more tickets and meals than there were Indians in the delegations. When the agents who had accompanied the delegations were questioned, they claimed that Beveridge had presented the bills just as they were leaving the capital and that there had not been time to examine them. Finally, the board found that the extras included hidden charges for prostitutes, which Beveridge in his defense said he had been asked to provide for delegations for more than twelve years. When the board's findings came to Delano's attention, he directed Smith to investigate them. Smith assigned one of his inspectors to the task, who, after his investigation, blamed both Beveridge and the agents for the charges. Smith and Delano refused to pay Beveridge for any of the extras, and because of what Smith called the "surprising depth of low wickedness" at the Washington House, it was declared off-limits to future delegations.[21]

In September 1873, when Smith was preparing to go to Fort Sill, questions were raised about other activities of the Indian Office, questions that tested the integrity of the office—and of the commissioner. Thomas Cree's clerk at the Board of Indian Commissioners, a one-eyed former army sergeant named Samuel Walker, began to write letters pointing to suspicious transactions in the Indian Office. He told Nathan Bishop, a member of the board, that "there is no doubt that hundreds of thousands of dollars have been stolen in Dakotah last year, and that every agent sent there *has been bought.* . . . There is no doubt there was fraud, open and glaring." He later told Cree that "the Indian Office is being 'run' in a perfectly shameless way. I never saw it as bad before." At first Walker said the suspicious activity in the Indian Office "only proves what I am told confidentially, that the Commissioner does not know anything of his business," but then he began to express doubts about the commissioner's own honesty.[22]

Fed by reports from Walker and from suspicious persons in Minnesota, a more influential person began to raise questions. William Welsh, who had been the first chairman of the Board of Indian Commissioners, voiced his suspicions about several actions of the Indian Office, but his concerns soon focused on the contract Smith had made with Amherst Wilder for the sale of the Chippewas' pine timber in Minnesota. Walker provided Welsh with a copy of the contract, which Welsh in turn sent to former senator Henry M. Rice in Minnesota. Rice gave the contract to the *St. Paul Dispatch,* where it appeared under the headline "Robbing the Indians . . . The Greatest Pine Land Grab on Record," along with an editorial asking for an investigation by the Board of Indian Commissioners. "When such robbery as this is conducted in the name of religion," the editorial exclaimed, "honest people may well stand aghast."[23]

Bishop Whipple soon expressed his concern. In addition to what he read in the newspapers, the bishop had been privately informed by Welsh that "there has been and is much corruption in the sale of Indian timber. Wilder is supposed to be the head of the Indian Ring in your region." The chiefs at Leech Lake also told Whipple they had not consented to the sale of their pine, and they found fault with the price paid for it. Whipple shared his concern with Columbus Delano but made no accusations against Smith. He told Delano that from his knowledge of Smith he believed the commissioner had made the Wilder contract in good faith. "[Smith] felt very keenly the need of money for these Indians and saw the opportunity to provide for their wants." "Since Mr. Smith came to the Chippewa agency I have watched his course. No agency in this state was ever managed with greater care. The employees were men of good character, the work well done. I have at times questioned the wisdom of some things he has done as he or you would doubtless question mine, but I have no reason to doubt his integrity." Nevertheless, because of the Indians' complaints and because the sale of the timber was not widely advertised, Whipple advised Delano to appoint a special commission to investigate the contract "so as to place this whole business openly before the world." [24]

Welsh did not have the same confidence in Smith that Whipple had. He sent Delano clippings about the Wilder contract he said he had received from "an intelligent man, who was one of Smith's warmest supporters. He says that every word of the Editorial is true, and he is satisfied that Smith has a pecuniary interest in it." Welsh asked for Smith's removal, but Delano refused to remove him without an investigation. Delano resented the charges, which he assumed had originated with persons disappointed by the reforms made in his department. He told Welsh that "all the bad men, heretofore connected with the Indian Service, are now engaged in seeking to defame and destroy the reputation of those now employed." The charges and the questions about them, however, were serious enough and came from such influential people that Delano felt compelled to have them investigated. To be fair to Smith, Delano waited until the commissioner returned from the council at Fort Sill, and then he appointed a commission to investigate the charges. The commission's appointment set the stage for a widely publicized drama, the chief actors in which were Edward Smith and William Welsh.[25]

25

William Welsh

To no layman in the land is the amelioration of the condition of the Indians, and their progress in Christian civilization in the past twelve years, so largely due as to [William Welsh].

Bishop M. A. DeWolfe Howe, *Memorial of William Welsh*

William Welsh had played a leading role in the formation of Grant's Indian policy. An Episcopal layman who had long been interested in his church's mission to the Sioux, Welsh had lobbied in Washington as early as 1866 for the creation of civilian boards nominated by religious groups to inspect the Indian service. When, in his first inaugural address, Grant made a brief but strong statement of his intention to create a new Indian policy, Welsh invited a group of interested citizens to his Philadelphia home to discuss it. Among them was Welsh's friend and neighbor George Hay Stuart. The group appointed a committee, including Welsh and Stuart, to go to Washington and offer the president their support in carrying out his "noble resolve." One of the suggestions the committee made was that a board of citizens be created to oversee the government's work with Indians. After Grant approved the idea, Welsh worked with his congressman to introduce a bill to provide for what became the Board of Indian Commissioners, while, at Grant's request, Stuart recommended persons to serve on the board.[1]

Welsh became the first chairman of the Board of Indian Commissioners, but his service was brief. Almost immediately, he clashed with Commissioner Parker over control of the expenditures of the Indian Office. Welsh assumed that the board and the Indian Office would have joint control of expenditures, and when he realized that the final word lay with the Indian Office, he promptly resigned, but continued, as he said, "to act in harmony with the President & Secretary[,] paying my own expenses, but conferring freely with them."[2]

Welsh was a man of means, having conducted a successful business in Philadelphia with his brothers, and a man of vigor, despite being in his early

William Welsh (1807–78).
Courtesy of the Peabody
Museum of Natural History,
Yale University, New Haven,
Connecticut.

sixties. He had earlier visited the Sioux Indians and published both a report
on his visit and a book, *Taopi and His Friends,* about Indian missions. After
his resignation from the Board of Indian Commissioners, Welsh continued
to visit Indian tribes in Minnesota, Nebraska, Dakota, and the Indian Territory and published reports of his visits. In addition, he devoted himself to
"ferreting out the thieves" in the Indian service. He brought charges of corruption against Ely Parker, throwing, as he said, "so large a bomb shell into
the Indian Office . . . as to drive out all the vermin." Even though a committee
of Congress found Parker innocent of the charges, the commissioner soon
resigned his office.[3]

Welsh was a familiar and influential figure in Washington. He had access
to the president and frequently visited congressmen, the Board of Indian
Commissioners, the commissioner of Indian affairs, and the secretary of the
interior. The commissioner and the secretary showed him great courtesy and
shared information with him from their correspondence and reports. Welsh's
influence came in part from his friendship with such men as George Stuart
and Bishop Whipple and in part from the knowledge he had accumulated
about the Indians, but even more from his position in the Episcopal church,
one of the leading denominations participating in the president's Indian

policy. Welsh had given long years of service as an Episcopal layman. He was the author of several books, including one entitled *Letters on the Home Missionary Work of the Protestant Episcopal Church,* which stressed the role of the laity in the work of the church and especially in its benevolent work. He was also a member of the denomination's board of missions and a leading member of its Indian commission, the body that nominated the church's Indian agents and oversaw their work. The commission appointed Welsh to its executive committee and gave him responsibility for supervising its missions among the Sioux. That tribe, powerful and resistant to the government, was a major concern of the Indian Office, which often consulted Welsh about them.[4]

At the general convention of the Episcopal church in Baltimore in 1871, Welsh spoke about the government's desire to have the cooperation of the churches in its Indian work and moved that the convention create another body, a standing committee on Indian affairs. The committee was to consist of six laymen who would "operate with the Board of Missions by supervising the secular work of the agencies under their care, by procuring such civilizing agencies as the Government does not provide, and by invoking the aid of the Government, and, if need be, the assistance of the courts, in protecting the rights of the Indians." The motion passed, and a committee, which included a United States senator, John W. Stevenson of Kentucky, was appointed. Welsh was named chairman.[5]

During the next year, Welsh visited most of the Episcopal agencies. They were important agencies: the Yankton Agency, the Ponca Agency, the Upper Missouri Agency, the Whetstone or Spotted Tail Agency, the Cheyenne River Agency, the Red Cloud Agency, and the Shoshone and Bannock Agency. Welsh, whom the Indians called Grey Hat, was an unforgettable figure in his travels through the West. On one occasion he was described as "discoursing from a text in the Psalter" during morning prayer aboard the steamboat *Miner,* while the brass band of the Sixth Infantry assisted with the music. On another occasion, Welsh discovered a whiskey shop "of the worst class" in operation near the Whetstone Agency. Offended by the shop's presence and aware that the chiefs wanted it removed, he bought it (at a price of $1,200), destroyed the stock, and turned it into an inn.[6]

Welsh was also a controversial figure. Many of the people who knew him praised him for his benevolence. One of the Quaker agents called him "a Champion for the right." Others thought him pompous. Smith first met Welsh in Washington, where he found him "very busy . . . but I found it very difficult to prevent him from giving me a full report of his past life to date. . . . Then he proceeded to show me that he had not time to attend to anything outside of his own Ch[urch,] Indian Missions & the running of the Indian

Dep[t] at Washington. Whereupon he proceeded to give a detailed stat[emen][t] of his connection with Girard College, several Reformatory Institutes of Phil[a] & whatever else is important in the world. I barely escaped a full rehearsal of his late expedition & discoveries in [Missouri?]." [7]

Barclay White, the Quaker superintendent of Indian affairs at Omaha, was surprised to find a stranger at his door one day, who greeted him with, "Do you know who *I* am?" When White confessed that he did not, the stranger said, "I will give you three guesses to tell who I am." When White declined to guess, the stranger said, "I am William Welsh of No. 1420 Spruce Street, Philadelphia." Welsh announced to White that he had arranged to meet with the Ponca chiefs at the Omaha Agency in two days to arrange for the Poncas' removal to the Omaha Reservation. Then he asked White to send a note to General Edward Ord, the commander of the Department of the Platte, to ask him to come to White's office for a meeting. White was "surprised at the man's assurance" and told him that no council would be held at the Omaha Agency without his presence as superintendent.[8]

The next day White and Ord both accompanied Welsh to the agency. When they boarded the stage, Ord took the outside seat, and when they arrived at the agency house, the general offered to sleep on the floor. In the morning, Welsh was up early and appeared to be nervous. "He moved up, down and around the room, once or twice stumbling over Ord[']s prostrate and immovable body, reading his lessons and performing his toilet during more than an hour[']s time." When breakfast was announced, Ord "shook himself, passed his fingers through his hair[,] dabbed a little water over his face and hands[,] slid into his coat[,] and said he was ready." All of which White recorded in his journal with astonishment.[9]

Welsh merely annoyed White with his mannerisms, but on another trip Welsh had seriously offended the Quakers in charge of the Santee Agency. After visiting the agency, Welsh wrote to the secretary of the interior that the Santees had unanimously asked him to have their agency placed under the care of the Episcopal church, "that the whole Sioux nation might be bound together in one brotherhood." Welsh's letter was published in a Washington newspaper, and when the Quakers read it, they investigated and found that none of the chiefs had any desire for a change. Seven members of the Committee of Friends on Indian Affairs signed a letter addressed to the president, the secretary of the interior, and the commissioner of Indian affairs, challenging Welsh's statement. "William Welsh," they said, "has evidently been misled, and we regret that he has made public this statement." [10]

On his visits among the Indians, Welsh had become familiar with the Chippewa Agency. Even though the agency was assigned to the American Missionary Association, the mission work at the White Earth Reservation was conducted by the Episcopal church. Shortly before Smith's arrival in Minnesota, Welsh had gone to Crow Wing with Selden Clark, Bishop Whipple, and former Minnesota senator Henry Rice to attend a large council with the Chippewas. At the council, he learned about the potential of the reservation at White Earth, and when he returned from his trip, he urged the Indian Office to proceed with the surveys necessary for establishing the Chippewas on the reservation. Then he urged that the supplies promised the Chippewas be sent to them; he was told at the council that the Indians at White Earth had for a time been forced to live on acorns and roots. Welsh also solicited the cooperation of the board of directors of the Northern Pacific Railroad in the work at the White Earth Reservation. The directors assured him of their cooperation if the Indians would not interfere with the railroad or its employees. Welsh was in frequent correspondence with Bishop Whipple and Henry Rice, and through his correspondence he gained full knowledge of Smith's activities in Minnesota.[11]

When Welsh first learned of Smith's appointment to the Chippewa Agency, he wrote to him cordially, telling him he hoped and believed "that all danger from the political, the whiskey & the Indian Rings will be averted by a higher power, operating through some very earnest & influential men." He told Smith that "the most powerful influences, even beyond what you dream of, were brought to bear upon the powers that be, to prevent Major Clark's appointment. Fortunately or providentially the machinations of politicians, thieves & the whiskey Ring did not prevail. . . . I have full faith that God is with us in this movement." [12]

So pleased had Welsh been with Smith's performance in Minnesota that he recommended him for one of the Indian inspectorships when they were created. Welsh was also pleased when Smith was appointed commissioner of Indian affairs. When the appointment was announced, Welsh wrote to Smith to congratulate him.

We are enjoined in everything with prayers, intercession, and thanksgiving, *to make our requests known unto God.* When we began to obey this command, thanking God for every ray of light, then the windows of heaven were opened, and a copious blessing descended upon our Indian work, *culminating in your being settled in the Indian office. As the office sought you, the assurance that it is a call of God,* is more manifest. I send a copy of the prayer that aided in drawing you there, and that will assist in giving you wisdom and strength. You may rest assured of my hearty cooperation. . . . All that I ask is that you will never believe any report of my saying anything against you, until I have first said it to you. When I give confidence, it is full.[13]

Welsh's confidence in Smith rapidly disappeared. The Wilder contract aroused his suspicions about the commissioner. Welsh had a suspicious nature, so suspicious that his statements sometimes left other people astounded. Early in 1870 Welsh told Bishop Whipple that he had had a long conversation with President Grant and Secretary Cox. "They seemed amazed," Welsh said, "at my assertion that Washington was in the possession of a few adroit men, who manipulated the Departments through clerks." Even Bishop Whipple did not escape Welsh's suspicions. On another occasion, Welsh asked Whipple whether Wilder had ever contributed to his schools, and the bishop bristled at the hint of accusation. "The question can have only one meaning[,] that I am guilty of having my eyes blinded by a gift & that my love to the poor & helpless is such a cheap thing it can be bought by a gift. Had a man of the world written me I could not have answered that letter. . . . Had you stopped to think you would never have written those words."[14]

After Welsh sent the Wilder contract to Henry Rice in Minnesota and charges were made about Smith's part in it, Welsh brought them to Delano's attention, noting that Bishop Whipple had asked for an investigation. The secretary, however, said flatly, "I don't believe a word of it." Before Delano had recommended Smith as commissioner, he had consulted with Welsh, Felix Brunot, and George Stuart, and Delano reminded Welsh that Smith held his office because they had recommended him.

> I selected Mr. Smith as Commissioner mainly to gratify Mr. Brunot, Mr. Stuart and yourself. My fear when I selected him was that his strength was not equal to the work; but my confidence in his capacity has grown upon acquaintance, and my confidence in his integrity is as good today as it was the day that you[,] Mr. Brunot and Mr. Stuart endorsed him. . . .
>
> There is one clause in your letter to which I wish to invite your attention particularly[,] it is this: "I had been more than once credibly informed that indiscreet and perhaps convivial members of the existing ring, had revealed secrets as to the influence they had acquired over nearly every one under you." If you have such *credible* information it ought not be to withheld from me any longer. If such a ring exists, and it has acquired such influence as you suggest, it is certainly not very creditable to my capacity for administration to say the least, and if you have information to this effect, and believe me to be an honest man, I think it is your duty as a Christian brother to furnish me that information immediately.

In his reply to Delano's letter, Welsh asked if the contract with Wilder had been entered into with Delano's "knowledge and consent." Delano explained that he had been out canvassing for Grant at the time the contract was made and that he had not been aware of it. Then, suspecting that Welsh was trying to implicate him in the charges against Smith, he asked, "Now tell me candidly why you asked whether the contract had been approved by me or not."[15]

Delano wrote privately to the Reverend Heman Dyer, the secretary of the Episcopal missionary society, that his office was open to investigation at any time, and he was willing to assume that Welsh's purposes in his investigations were "pure and good." Nevertheless, he told Dyer he was compelled to say "in all candor" that Welsh was "often indiscreet and injudicious, and I do think needlessly suspicious and sometimes imprudently so."[16]

After Smith returned from Fort Sill and learned about the charges against him, he requested the appointment of a commission to investigate them. Then, with Amherst Wilder, Smith called on Welsh at his home in Philadelphia to talk to him face to face about the charges. The full conversation they had is not known, but Edward Williams reported that when Smith reminded Welsh that he held his office in part because of Welsh's support, Welsh replied: "No, sir! I never wanted you! I was opposed to you. You were Cowen's man, and I have long *known of your dishonest transactions at White Earth.*"[17]

They continued their discussion by letter. Welsh wrote to Smith asking him not to "lose sight of the fact that in my efforts to do justly for the Indian I have no personal animosities," to which Smith replied:

If you could have added, "I have no personal animosities and will also do justly by others," it would have been much more satisfactory to myself.

I think I have reason to complain that you have not dealt justly by me. Let me specify. You forward a contract to Mr. Rice which he publishes in a blackguard St. Paul paper. . . . That paper makes charges that I have given away a large quantity of pine on Leech Lake Reservation. Mr. Rice returns the newspaper article to you. You carry it in your pocket; you enquire of my friends whether they have lost confidence in me, and in other ways insinuate that I have entered into a fraudulent transaction, when the fact is as you yourself acknowledged the other evening that the contract itself provides that not a stick of pine is given away. . . . And even now neither you nor Mr. Rice ask that paper to take back those charges which you acknowledge were false. On the contrary that same paper publishes other articles which are forwarded to you by Mr. Rice, and which you carry round in your pocket and show to my friends and the Board of Commissioners. In other words you deal with my reputation as an honest man as if it was not of the slightest account to me or to anyone else. When you spoke the other day of your reputation and that of your family being at stake I wanted to say to you, what I did not, that I also had a family and a reputation.[18]

Smith went on to cite contracts from the Indian Office which he said showed that Welsh's accomplice in the charges, Henry Rice, had been for years a "principal actor" in the Indian frauds in Minnesota, "sometimes in his own name but oftener behind the scenes." "And yet," Smith continued, "this is the man whom you allow to use your influence and good name to persecute me." He concluded: "In all these matters I have never for a moment doubted your purpose to defend the Indians from wrong. I have only been trying to show you that your methods are not the proper ones. And I am sure if you had known as much as I now know about Mr. Rice you would never have taken the course you have." Smith sent copies of his letter to George Stuart, George Whipple, and Secretary Delano—and also to Henry Rice.[19]

When George Whipple received his copy of Smith's letter to Welsh, he wrote to tell Smith that after he saw the clippings from the St. Paul papers he had pointed out to Welsh that the content of the published contract did not justify the interpretation the newspapers placed on it. He also told Smith that his confidence in the commissioner's integrity was "not impaired" and that he would be "very slow to believe anything concerning you, unworthy of the character of a Christian gentleman." Smith kept Whipple's reassuring letter on his desk for months.[20]

The commission appointed by Delano to investigate the charges against Smith convened in St. Paul on November 30, 1873. It consisted of Nelson J. Turney of Circleville, Ohio, who was a member of the Board of Indian Commissioners, James Smith, Jr., of St. Paul, William K. Jennings of Pittsburgh, and Thomas C. Jones, the Ohioan who had served on the second scrip commission with Smith. Smith believed that the charges against him had been instigated by persons involved in scrip fraud in retaliation for his part in its investigation, and he had requested that someone familiar with the scrip investigation be added to the commission.[21]

Delano instructed the commission to investigate the charges about the Wilder contract, and if it found that the charges had been made without sufficient cause, it was to "inquire into the authorship of the charges" and the reasons behind them. Smith had also asked that the commission inquire into any other matters "touching my actions as Indian agent in Minnesota, concerning which any respectable man is found to make any complaint," and Delano passed his request on to the commission. Welsh engaged attorneys to represent him but did not appear before the commission himself. Instead, he submitted his charges in an informal letter from Philadelphia. His attorneys, after considerable delay, announced that since the commission did not have the power to compel witnesses to testify or produce evidence "the investigation can result in little more than a farce," and they refused to appear before the commission.[22]

The commissioners, puzzled by the position of Welsh's attorneys, decided to go ahead with their work so as to provide the "full and fair investigation" requested by Delano and out of "justice to the party accused." Because Welsh had indicated that Henry Rice had information about the case, a subpoena was issued for Rice's appearance and served by a United States marshal, but Rice also refused to appear. He said he had in his possession "important documentary evidence" and that he could provide the names of people who could give other evidence, but he declined to appear unless the commission had "full power and authority" to compel witnesses to testify. Smith, desiring a full investigation of the charges, asked that one of the Indian inspectors be added to the commission to give it the power to compel the attendance of witnesses. The Interior Department, however, informed him that the inspectors had the authority only to administer oaths and not to compel the attendance of witnesses.[23]

With the hearings barely under way, Welsh sent a telegram to Delano, saying, "Please postpone consideration . . . commission may arrange amicably." Delano replied that he did not want to suspend the hearings without good reasons. "The commission was organized at your suggestion, and injustice to Mr. Smith might result from abruptly terminating." Welsh telegraphed again: "As Minnesota commission cannot enforce witnesses, please suspend it formally, and let us confer privately, or I will be compelled to ask congressional investigation."[24]

Despite Welsh's appeals, the commission proceeded with its investigation, taking testimony in St. Paul and later in Washington. Welsh was again invited to appear before it, but he refused. He said he had in his possession evidence "that if placed before you will oblige you to criminate Agent Smith, but under the circumstances I am not willing to make him the scape-goat, over whom others far more guilty may secretly confess their sins. Whenever an investigation of the whole case is made by those who are authorized to convict the men who lured Mr. Smith on to his ruin, I will promptly attend and produce papers in my possession." But at the same time Welsh had not hesitated to publish a lengthy open letter to President Grant titled "Indian Office—Wrongs Doing and Reforms Needed," which he shared with the commission.[25]

In his letter, Welsh said he was appealing to the president because his efforts to work with Delano to reform the Indian Office had failed. He repeated his charges against Smith and quoted letters from former commissioner Walker that seemed to blame Smith for the Wilder contract, saying he had simply followed Smith's advice in the matter. Welsh said he was ready to verify every charge he had made against Smith "before a competent tribunal" and to add other charges against his conduct as commissioner, some of which he listed. Among them was the money Smith had spent for "a quack nostrum of doubtful morality"—Anson Dart's Sanitary Specific—and a charge that since the last public awards of contracts for Indian supplies, "the contractors have combined, and seem to possess greater practical influence in the Interior Department than the board of Indian commissioners." He said Cowen and Smith had both urged that large contracts for cattle and freight be given to Amherst Wilder. Welsh appealed to Grant to reform the Indian Office so that the president's "humane policy" could be continued. He wanted Grant to know that he faulted "no well-intentioned person because of improper appointments to office, but only when such officers are allowed to remain after their incompetency could and should be known." [26]

Smith testified before the commission that the contract with Wilder, for which he was blamed, had in fact been made in Washington by Commissioner Walker. After Wilder presented his bid at the Indian Office, Walker had directed Smith to negotiate with him, and it was Walker who completed the negotiations and who suggested expanding the original contract for timber at White Oak Point to include the entire Leech Lake Reservation. The testimony Walker gave showed that in making the contract he had placed great reliance on Smith's advice and that he had confidence in Smith's integrity. "I was very largely influenced," he said, "by the high reputation which Mr. Smith had sustained as an Indian agent, unsurpassed by that of any officer in that branch of the service, and by the confidence which I had acquired through consultation and correspondence with him, in his good judgment and practical wisdom as well as in his official integrity. . . . I have always believed, and still believe, Mr. Smith to be an honest, conscientious, and capable public officer. So believing, I was glad . . . to have him for a subordinate. So believing, I shall, as a private citizen, cheerfully lend him the support of my voice." [27]

The commission heard testimony from Amherst Wilder, Benjamin Cowen, several Minnesota lumbermen, and a delegation of Chippewas from the White Earth Reservation. Wilder's testimony was consistent with that of Smith, Walker, and Cowen. He said that although Smith had given his advice, it was Walker who, with Cowen's consent, had made the contract. The lumbermen were questioned in detail about the terms of the contract and generally agreed that it was fair to the Indians involved and that the terms were as good as Smith could have obtained. The Indians agreed that it was an advantageous contract, although they believed it would have been better if their consent had been obtained before making it. Smith said he had always assumed that the Indians' consent was necessary for such contracts and that he had raised the issue with Commissioner Walker before the contract was made, but that Walker, as the Indians' guardian, had decided on his own authority and with Assistant Secretary Cowen's approval to make the contract without the Indians' consent.[28]

The work of the commission was prominently reported in the Minnesota newspapers. Many of the reports were sensational, with headlines such as "Pine Land Steal," "Delano and Gang," "A Chapter of Rascality," and "Smith's Fraud, The Proof Positive." In the midst of the newspaper attacks, Welsh asked the Indian Office for copies of Smith's personal financial accounts. When Henry Clum telegraphed Smith in St. Paul for his advice, Smith told him to discontinue Welsh's access to government documents. The Indian Office had been accustomed to giving Welsh any documents he requested, but now Smith directed Clum that "all communications with Mr. Welsh should be official and written. Office documents heretofore furnished him have been represented and used by parties here for malicious purposes." Welsh, on his part, wrote to Edward Williams, "Towards the Rev. Mr. Smith I have not an unkind feeling, but unless I have lost all intelligence he must be brought to repentance for his fearful wrongs." As the commission was concluding its work in St. Paul, Welsh told Bishop Whipple: "The comedy of whitewashing Smith was appropriately closed in St. Paul by the farce of Indian testimony. Not having a prompter present some of the red men were too honest only to repeat what had been told them. . . . E. P. Smith's disease seems to be deep seated . . . I am satisfied that he is thoroughly guilty." [29]

In one last attempt to obtain testimony from Welsh, commissioners Thomas Jones and James Smith went to Philadelphia to see him, but Welsh still refused to testify. Nor was he willing to testify as long as the commission did not have the authority to compel the attendance of witnesses. Welsh, the commissioners said, "seemed incapable of appreciating the gross injustice he was doing by this wholesale allegation of crime, while refusing to furnish the evidence upon which it is based." [30]

The commission submitted its report on February 2, 1874. It determined that the contract with Wilder had been a "project" of Commissioner Walker's "own conception," not Smith's, "and was entered into, on consultation with Assistant Secretary Cowen, upon [Walker's] own judgment." Smith's only contribution had been an opinion about the reasonableness of the price to be paid for the timber. The commission concluded that "no fraud was practiced in making this contract, either by Mr. Smith or Mr. Wilder; and that, so far as we have been able to see, the agreement is in all respects a fair one, and will, if honestly carried out, prove highly advantageous to the Indians." Not only did the commission declare Smith innocent of the charges, but the commissioners unanimously agreed that the testimony showed he had "as to all things connected therewith been actuated by the purest motives, and the most commendable zeal for the promotion of the welfare of the Indians." It was true that the consent of the Indians had not been obtained before the contract with Wilder was made, but, the commission thought, with so many bands of Indians involved and so many persons competing for the timber, the only practical way for the government to proceed was to make the contract for them. And the commission agreed that the sale of the timber was appropriate in view of the destitution of the Chippewas. "Indeed," the commissioners said, "unless Congress will provide by special appropriations for the pressing necessities of these people, it is obvious that any delay in realizing from the sale of their timber, will prove disastrous to them." Several other charges Welsh had made were dismissed as groundless, including his claim that Smith had conspired with Charles Howard, Selden Clark, and Edward Williams to enter into another fraudulent timber contract with Williams's brother-in-law.[31]

The commission expressed its bewilderment at the actions of Rice and Welsh, who were the only witnesses who objected to the subpoenas of the commission. Why they refused to present their information, "impartial men will find it difficult to conjecture, unless it was intended by such intimation to create a prejudice in the public mind against the accused." It seemed obvious to the commission "that Mr. Rice had some interest in this matter beyond that of an ordinary witness." What that interest was or why it would cause him to withhold testimony, the commission did not attempt to discover.[32]

The commissioners were harsh with Welsh. He had broadcast his charges all over the land in his printed pamphlet, they said, making charges against others as well as Smith, "with as little reluctance or hesitation as if he were circulating the ordinary incidents connected with the public service." He accused the commission of acting without a prosecutor when his own attorneys, who might have filled that role, would not appear before the commission. "Mr. Welsh's reasoning faculties are peculiar," the commissioners said, "and therefore we cannot always account for his deductions." If Welsh had the confidence he professed in the president, why did he not lay the evidence before him? "Why this ostentatious publication of a letter containing . . . such reckless aspersions and false insinuations?" Among Welsh's "many strange and unaccountable assumptions" was his insistence that the commission could not reach the truth, while he, entirely on his own, had obtained the evidence that would compel Smith's conviction. The commission said that none of its members knew Welsh before the investigation; they had known of him only as someone distinguished for his contributions to charity. They therefore limited their comments about him to what was strictly necessary "in the proper discharge of a painful duty."[33]

26

Accusations

Oh Lord, our God, we come in this place to deplore before Thee the spirit
of lying which is abroad, and we beseech Thee to rebuke the giant demon
of slander that stalks forth casting upon all the earth a fearful shadow; para-
lyse the hand that writes the willful detraction; palsy the tongue that utters
wanton calumny. . . . Let Thy flaming spirit take vengeance upon the false
accuser and consume this spirit of ruin from all the land.

> Byron Sunderland, chaplain of the U.S. Senate, opening prayer
> in the Senate, March 3, 1874

Shortly after the commission appointed to investigate Welsh's charges
published its report, President Grant engaged in a long interview in
which he expressed himself freely about Indian affairs. He spoke "with considerable severity" about the way some of the press dealt with Indian affairs,
repeating stories of corruption without acknowledging the reforms that had
been made during his administration.

He cited, as an illustration of this systematic purpose of misrepresentation,
the case of Indian Commissioner Smith. This officer, he said, had for months
rested under a load of vindictive charges, never uttering a word of complaint,
but inviting the most searching investigation, and giving his accusers a free field.
Many of the newspapers had assailed him most virulently before trial, and now
that he was not only exonerated but the integrity of his action completely vin-
dicated these same papers were absolutely silent, ignoring the facts, while the
Commissioner himself could contemplate the result with only such gratification
as could be given by the personal misfortune of a wife driven to an insane asylum by the assaults of personal and political enemies upon the good name and
fame of her husband.

The president believed there should be a new statute "for the punishment
of lying."[1]

Cleavie Smith was indeed mentally ill and was confined to an "insane asylum" in Massachusetts. Whatever caused her illness, those who spoke about it

Hannah Smith. Courtesy of the
Amistad Research Center, New
Orleans, Louisiana.

believed, as Grant did, that it was the result of the attacks of Smith's enemies.
Bishop Whipple noted that charges had been made, not only about Smith
but about his wife as well, alleging that she had been placed on the payroll
"to connive with her husband to defraud the Indians." Whipple quoted both
friends and enemies of Smith who believed that Cleavie's illness was related
to the charges made against the Smiths. One person who believed Smith dishonest told Whipple, "I pity Smith deeply, the more because his wife has
been taken to an insane hospital. She must have known that all was not right."
Another person who believed Smith honest told Whipple, "Worn out with
labor, and in the absence of her husband, the myriad of slanders against him
fell like molten lead on her quivering nerves, and she succumbed." Charles
Brace said, "So bitter were these calumnies, that his wife, whose nervous system was already overstrained by her self-denying labors, broke down under
them and became insane."[2]

A *New York Times* editorial lashed out at the Democratic newspapers that
had abused Smith and caricatured his family. The editorial said that Smith's
wife "could not bear this storm of scandal. . . . Her high-spirited and sensitive nature broke under it, and she became a lunatic, and was taken to an
insane aslylum." Yet, the *Times* noted, none of the newspapers that had con-

demned Smith had expressed any regret or even mentioned that he had been acquitted of the charges.[3]

Seven months later, Smith told General Howard that Cleavie was still hospitalized but had improved, and he was hopeful that in a few more months she would be able to return home. She was "much less depressed & fearful," he said, and was quiet most of the time and sometimes even appeared cheerful, "tho' she is still firmly convinced that she shall live but a few days."[4]

Smith served in the Indian Office during a time of wholesale public charges —some of them well-founded but many of them indiscriminate and unbridled—not only about the Indian Office but about public affairs in general. The commissioner of pensions was charged with wrongdoing. The governor of South Carolina was tried for larceny. General Howard was under investigation by a court of inquiry, which later acquitted him. The superintendent of Indian affairs in Washington Territory was suspended and then, after an investigation, reinstated, whereupon he charged the inspector who had suspended him with libel. The air was filled with a jangle of accusations about "Washington rings," "police rings," "customhouse rings," "street cleaning bureau frauds," "courthouse frauds." Thomas Nast pictured a dejected Grant surrounded by newspapers with titles such as *The Truthful Liar*, *The Black-Mailer*, and *The Slanderer*. "There was always some exciting topic at the Capitol," Mark Twain and Charles Dudley Warner wrote in *The Gilded Age*, "or some huge slander was rising up like a miasmatic exhalation from the Potomac, threatening to settle no one knew exactly where." The slander, however, was not bred in the Potomac but in a dark corner of the American spirit. Thirty years earlier, Charles Dickens had commented on the "Universal Distrust" he found in America. "Any man who attains a high place among you, from the President downwards, may date his downfall from that moment; for any printed lie that any notorious villain pens, although it militate directly against the character and conduct of a life, appeals at once to your distrust, and is believed. You will strain at a gnat in the way of trustfulness and confidence, . . . but you will swallow a whole caravan of camels, if they be laden with unworthy doubts and mean suspicions."[5]

A New York commissioner of charities and corrections said he was tired of the investigations that resulted from the suspicions. They seemed to him to be "the order of the day, without any defined reasons for inquiry." A newspaper editorial decried "the reckless manner in which charges are preferred against officials. . . . There is a growing license indulged in by gentlemen desiring to attract public attention of recklessly charging the gravest crimes against an officer that they would not dare utter against a private citizen. . . . If any man can set in motion the machinery of Congress and entail the vast expense absolutely required, and consume valuable time in investigation, on his mere statement that he believes certain reports to be true against a public officer, there can be no limit." Yet the investigations multiplied in an attempt to find the truth among the charges and countercharges of an era too simply labeled corrupt.[6]

Smith, too, made charges. He accused Henry Rice of defrauding the Indians by taking bribes for securing the passage of bills relating to Indian affairs and by dealing in Chippewa half-breed scrip. Smith told Bishop Whipple that "the course which that gentleman has pursued for the last twenty-five years in Indian affairs in Minnesota if fairly exposed to the light I believe would make any honorable man recoil from having any associations with him." Smith was sure that Rice was behind Welsh's charges against him. He thought Rice wanted to put himself in a position with the Indians so as to "compel somebody to buy him off before he will let go." Amherst Wilder also made charges against Rice although without naming him. He published a letter to Welsh in which he said, "It has been intimated to me on several distinct occasions that if I would 'divide' with a particular bosom friend of yours, the name of whom was given to me, either in the profits of the contract or otherwise, there would be no opposition on your part, and everything would be lovely and serene." Delano thought there was enough truth in the charges about Rice to join Smith in advising Bishop Whipple not to take Rice with him to a council with the Chippewas.[7]

Wilder also brought charges against Welsh in a court of law, suing him for $100,000 in damages for "contriving and maliciously intending to injure" him by a "false, scandalous, malicious and defamatory libel" in another one of Welsh's accusations. About the time Welsh made his charges about the timber contract, George Stuart gave him a voucher from the Ponca Agency to review, the Ponca Agency being one of those assigned to the Episcopal church. Welsh had questions about the voucher and brought it to Smith, who determined that although the voucher was submitted improperly, there was no fraud or intention of fraud. But after their conversation, Welsh declared the voucher fraudulent and demanded immediate prosecution of the guilty parties.[8]

The voucher was for farm animals and supplies furnished by Wilder, who conducted a large business in supplies for the Indian Office and the War Department. Wilder was known as a businessman of considerable wealth, who could "raise sums of money from fifty to one hundred thousand dollars in a day" and was able to "fulfill large contracts without delay and to wait for compensation for unusually long periods of time." Smith had authorized purchases from Wilder for the Ponca Agency when he visited the agency on his trip down the Missouri River. When the voucher for the purchases came to Welsh's attention, he said: "It appears that Agent Birkett was induced to sign a voucher without filling up the prices, leaving that to the person with whom the Commissioner of Indian Affairs had privately bargained to furnish certain supplies. The prices were filled up by A. H. Wilder & by him presented for payment." Smith had tried to explain to Welsh that Birkett did not know the prices of the supplies and that he issued a voucher without the prices when he should have issued only a receipt for the goods received—an innocent mistake. A clerk in Smith's office had then entered the prices on Birkett's voucher when he should have treated it only as the receipt it was. Although the paperwork for the purchase was improper, Smith believed no fraud was intended or committed. Smith resented Welsh's accusation and said, "That Mr. Welsh seeks to promote justice for the Indians no one doubts; but how to account for the unjust, flippant, and reckless dealing with the reputation of others, passes my comprehension." Wilder then took the matter to court, where, after the charges were filed, the case rested for two full years.[9]

Charges were also made about the private conduct of the secretary of the interior. When Delano had ordered an investigation of Benjamin Beveridge's bills for housing Indian delegations at the Washington House, Thomas Cree asked the inspector to include an investigation of purchases Delano had made from one of the merchants suspected of conspiring with Beveridge to defraud the government. After Delano learned about Cree's action, he told a friend that he had purchased only a few articles from the merchant, "and those at prices so high that I had resolved never to trade with him again. . . . Perhaps Mr. Cree is kept here as a spy, complainer and informer and I do not know but he volunteers insinuations for the purpose of making mischief, because I did not make him a member of the Board as Mr. Brunot wished me to. . . . I certainly do not feel disposed to hold official intercourse with men who are capable of entertaining such suspicions in regard to me as these charges seem to indicate."[10]

Without Delano's knowledge, the Board of Indian Commissioners had authorized another investigation of Indian affairs. Just at the time the commission to investigate Welsh's charges against Smith was gathering in St. Paul to begin its work, the board had secretly dispatched its clerk, Samuel Walker, to examine conditions at the Red Cloud and Whetstone agencies in Dakota Territory. On December 6, 1873, Walker reported to Felix Brunot, the chairman of the board, that he had found a large number of questionable activities at both agencies. The flour provided to the Indians appeared to be "very inferior." The price of corn was far above the market price. The distance supplies were freighted had been inflated, as had the number of Indians at the agencies. No records were kept of the receipt of beef except the receipts given by the contractor who supplied the beef, John H. Bosler. The agent at the Red Cloud Agency, Dr. John J. Saville, gave receipts for cattle "he never saw." Walker declared Saville's receipts "false and fraudulent" and was sure there was collusion between Saville and Bosler "to obtain payment from the Government for beef not delivered."[11]

Delano learned about Walker's report for the first time "through an un-official channel" two months later. He was furious that the Board of Indian Commissioners had authorized an investigation of his department without his knowledge and then had withheld the report from him, and he requested a copy of the report from Brunot. The board at first sent only extracts from Walker's report, and only at Delano's insistence did he receive a full copy.[12]

Felix Brunot, who had not sent a copy of Walker's report to Delano when it was first available, had, however, shared the report with the Board of Indian Commissioners and had sent a copy to the mission board of the Episcopal church. Copies were also sent to "other persons not connected with the Board of Indian Commissioners." If those "other persons" did not include William Welsh, he soon obtained a copy of the report from them and published in-formation from it in a public letter *To the Members of the Forty-Third Congress.* Welsh told the congressmen that the country was threatened with two wars by Indians who had been "wronged and irritated by Government officials." There was danger of "serious trouble" with the Chippewas, whose timber had been sold without their consent. There was also "imminent danger" of a war with the Sioux.[13]

The source of the trouble with the Sioux was the infrequency of beef rations caused by the frauds of cattle contractors. Welsh said he had evidence that "frauds have been practised at the Red Cloud and Whetstone or Spotted Tail Agencies, with a boldness and a persistency that are wholly inexplicable, except by those who are familiar with the intimate relations of the cattle con-tractors to the Interior Department." He said that in ten months the Board of Indian Commissioners had disapproved thirty-nine vouchers for Indian sup-plies totaling $426,909.96 but Delano had overruled them in eighteen cases representing $369,520.97. Nearly $200,000 of the questionable vouchers he approved was paid to cattle contractors.[14]

On February 23, 1874, Delano appointed a commission to investigate Samuel Walker's charges about corruption at the Red Cloud and Whetstone agencies. On March 10, the House of Representatives, spurred on by Welsh's charges, authorized an investigation of its own into charges of fraud in Indian contracts and the transportation of Indian supplies. The House investigation was conducted by the Committee on Indian Affairs behind closed doors, and the testimony was kept secret pending the committee's report.[15]

While the two investigations were being conducted, Welsh continued to write letters and make charges. He published an open letter to Columbus Delano about the sales of Indians' pine timber. In it he made the charges he was unwilling to make before the commission appointed to investigate the Wilder contract. Commissioner Walker, he said, was "deceived into the approval of the contract, which it is alleged and believed had been previously prepared in Minnesota with the utmost care." The "immense sale" of timber, Welsh charged, was made without a thorough investigation of the extent of the timber, "without advertising, without any competition, without notice to the owners of the timber, and against their wishes." He referred to Henry Rice as one of his authorities for charging Smith with fraud and said that "no Indian ever had a better, a more disinterested, or a more self-sacrificing friend than the Hon. Henry M. Rice." Welsh also mentioned that the Minnesota state senate had made its own investigation of the timber sales, and he drew on its report for further charges against Smith.[16]

Welsh noted that the commission appointed by Delano had asked why he did not lay the evidence for his charges before the president or the head of the department. He said that three years earlier, when he preferred charges against Commissioner Parker, he had taken them to the president, but "owing to implicit confidence in his friends, [the president] is too often blind to their wrong doings." Only when Congress investigated the matter was the "neglectful, incompetent, and lawless" Parker forced out of office. In the same way, Welsh had discovered evidence of "stupendous frauds" to the Teton Sioux and at the Grand River Agency and laid his evidence before Delano and Cowen, but he "never heard of any effort made to investigate these frauds, or to punish the offenders." In the present case, he said he had sought an interview with the president, and for months he had been pleading with Delano for a remedy, but all in vain.[17]

Welsh also made accusations about Smith in a letter to General Howard, marking the letter "confidential" so that Howard did not feel free to share it with Smith. Smith, however, when he learned about the letter, appealed to Welsh, who authorized Howard to let Smith see it. Smith was blunt in telling Welsh how he felt about the accusations.

> I have read the correspondence and am constrained to express my surprise at your statements and the spirit which animates the letter. I had never supposed it possible for any respectable person, for whose judgment I had any regard, to express or entertain any such views about myself, and being conscious that they are without any foundation, and feeling confident that they are without grounds for suspicion even, I write now to ask if you are not prepared to withdraw the charges and insinuations contained in this correspondence and also other charges and insinuations of a very damaging character which you have

made against me through the press and through documents which you have scattered broad-cast over the country. . . .

You certainly are aware that you have damaged me beyond reparation. To many people in all parts of the country my good name is destroyed. When you have done your best to withdraw these charges you cannot leave me where your attack found me, but that I shall have to bear during the rest of my life. I only ask now that you will do what you can to make me whole.

Welsh, however, found it easier to make charges than to withdraw them, and he took back nothing of what he had said.[18]

The commission appointed to investigate Samuel Walker's charges submitted its report on April 22, 1874. Because the Red Cloud and Whetstone agencies were assigned to the Episcopal church, Delano had appointed Bishop William H. Hare and the Reverend Samuel D. Hinman to the commission. Hare was the Episcopal bishop of Niobrara, the church's missionary bishop to the Indians. Hinman had been an Episcopal missionary to the Santee Sioux for fifteen years and had frequently served the government as an interpreter. The other two members of the commission were J. D. Bevier, one of the five Indian inspectors, and Francis H. Smith, one of the official reporters of the House of Representatives and the president of the Washington YMCA who had recently been appointed to the Board of Indian Commissioners. The commission, with Bishop Hare as chairman, visited the two agencies, interviewed agency employees under oath, and shared Walker's report with the agents, asking for their responses to his charges.[19]

The Hare Commission reported that some of the most damaging affidavits Walker had presented about the character of the agents were clearly partial and that one of his principal witnesses about the administration of the agencies was "a well-known deserter and thief." The agents gave satisfactory explanations for the matters in Walker's report, and the commission was satisfied that the irregular practices that were found were unavoidable in agencies to which thousands of Indians from northern tribes periodically came and demanded to be fed ("a turbulent party," Bishop Hare called them, "which for the time rules the Agencies with a high hand"). "Transactions which at first sight seemed suspicious and to which a criminal intent had been imputed, were shown to have been characterized by entire good faith, to have been carried on in broad daylight, and, where not justifiable, to have been not wrong-doing, but the mistakes of men new in an office where, peculiarly, the incumbent can learn only from experience." The commission relieved the agents of all suspicion and expressed its belief that the men had performed their duties "during a time of great trial and in the midst of great embarrassments with energy, honesty, and entire fidelity . . . and that they deserve the confidence and commendation of the Department."[20]

If anyone suffered from the investigation, it was Walker himself. Two of the cattle contractors denied they had made the statements he attributed to them. The storekeeper at the Red Cloud Agency said he thought Walker "wanted to find out that the agent was wrong. . . . I thought at first he came to find out the truth, but I afterward thought from his talk that he was not quite right. I thought his examination not fair." Another man, who had spoken to both Walker and Welsh in Philadelphia, said that Walker had taken part of his testimony but not all of it. "He did not take the part where I spoke of the herd being a fine herd. I told him he had not taken all and he said he had all he wanted." J. D. Bevier later spoke for the Hare Commission when he said it had concluded that Walker "went there to find fault, right or wrong; that his charges were unfounded and unjust." Bishop Hare called Walker's method of inquiry "contemptible" and his report "unfair." [21]

Before the commission's report was printed, Welsh obtained a copy of it and furnished it to Walker. Walker regarded the report as a "disgraceful attack" on him by the commission, "who appear to have taken to investigating me . . . rather than investigating the truth of my statements." He told Thomas Cree that the commission had attacked him "in order to break the force of evidence which remained uncontradicted. . . . It is a bad day for the public morals when churchmen recognize one code of morals for Government transactions such as calling 'fraud and theft' 'excusable irregularities,' and another for private dealings." [22]

Welsh was mentioned only briefly in the commission's report, but Bishop Hare was aware of Welsh's role in spreading Walker's charges. Hare, who respected Welsh for his efforts on behalf of the Indians, told Bishop Whipple, "Our investigations have not sustained [Welsh's] assertions. Unfortunately he *suspects* all who differ from him. I feel sad enough about it." [23]

Shortly after the Hare Commission's report reached the Board of Indian Commissioners, six members of the board submitted their resignations. The six—Felix Brunot, Robert Campbell, Nathan Bishop, William E. Dodge, John V. Farwell, and George Stuart—were the remaining members from the original board appointed at the beginning of Grant's presidency. Soon after, Thomas Jones, who had been appointed on Delano's recommendation, also resigned, as did Thomas Cree, the board's secretary. Samuel Walker also left his position with the board.

The resignations culminated the board's five years of frustration in trying to exercise "joint control" over Indian expenditures with the Department of the Interior. The members of the board devoted large amounts of time to reviewing vouchers from the Indian Office only to have their objections to vouchers frequently overruled by the secretary of the interior. Moreover, Secretary Delano had requested that the board be required to conduct its business in the city of Washington, and it appeared that that requirement would be included in the new Indian appropriation bill. None of the members was in a position to move to Washington, and in any case, they said, Delano's overrulings "would frequently render the labor of examining and deciding upon the accounts and vouchers as useless as it is arduous and vexatious." The board had also recommended that the Indian Office become independent from the Interior Department "with an officer of high ability at its head," but Delano was not ready to make such a recommendation to Congress. The resigning board members did not mention fraud, but they had clearly lost confidence in Delano and no longer cared to see their efforts thwarted by him.[24]

A Washington correspondent said the members of the board were not entirely candid about their resignations. The correspondent thought the real reason for the resignations was the doubt the Hare Commission had thrown on the charges of the board's clerk, Samuel Walker, and the rumored inability of the House investigation to substantiate other charges of fraud in the Indian service.[25]

Smith did not speculate about the matter, although he did say he regarded Nathan Bishop as the one who "broke up the old Board," but he was obviously pleased at the new appointments to the board, which were made after consultations with the missionary societies. Clinton Fisk, who was nominated by the Methodists, became the new chairman, and Eliphalet Whittlesey replaced Samuel Walker as the board's clerk. Smith told General Howard that "Genl Whittlesey is really the Board of Com^s now so far as acc^{ts} go, & of course they go straight & without any captious opposing." After six months in office, the new board acknowledged "with pleasure the promptness of the Department in the correction of every error and abuse to which their attention has been called, and their gratification in the improvement, which is manifest from year to year, in the honesty and efficiency with which the difficult business transactions for the Indian service are conducted." The *New York Tribune*, however, dismissed the new board as Delano's "tools, who were always ready to do his bidding."[26]

The House Committee on Indian Affairs made its report on June 22, 1874. The committee was charged with investigating "all frauds, unfairness, or irregularity, if any," connected with the making or execution of contracts for Indian supplies or their transportation during the two prior fiscal years. The committee heard testimony from Smith, Wilder, Welsh, members of the Board of Indian Commissioners, disappointed bidders for government contracts, and agency employees.[27]

This committee had the "power to send for persons and papers," and

Welsh agreed to appear before it. He was asked if he knew of any "fraud, un-fairness, or irregularity" in the making or execution of contracts for Indian supplies or transportation. At first he said he had knowledge of contracts for supplies irregularly made, but he knew of contracts for transportation only through the Board of Indian Commissioners, "not personally." "By irregu-larity," he said, "I mean without notice to the Board of Indian Commis-sioners, without advertising, or the other public notice that is indicated in the law. I mean that kind of irregularity." The question was then put to him more precisely.

By Mr. Harris: The question is whether you know of any fraud, unfairness, or irregularity in the execution of contracts, tending to show fraud, unfairness, or irregularity in the making of them?—A[nswer]. I answer, that outside of that derived from the Board of Indian Commissioners, I have no knowledge on that subject.

By Mr. Richmond: Do you know of any irregularities or frauds in the making of contracts for supplies and transportation between the Government or its agents and the contracting parties?—A[nswer]. No, sir; I have no knowledge.

With that, Welsh was dismissed.[28]

Two weeks after Welsh testified, the House of Representatives broadened its investigation to include not only frauds in the making and execution of contracts but "frauds, unfairness or irregularity" of any kind connected with the Indian service. When Benjamin Cowen later accused Welsh of obstruct-ing the investigation by not presenting his charges to the committee, Welsh replied that he had not been asked to testify under the broader resolution and implied that if he had been he would then have presented the charges.[29]

A great many subjects were discussed with the other witnesses. Corn was one of them. At Thomas Cree's suggestion, Smith had changed a contract for Indian supplies to substitute corn for flour. Testimony showed that the Board of Indian Commissioners had challenged Smith's action but also that the assistant attorney general assigned to the Interior Department had rec-ommended that his action be approved. The committee called the change "ir-regular" but said that it was made "with no corrupt or improper motives, was satisfactory and beneficial to the Indians, and not detrimental to the Govern-ment." Beef was also discussed. At the Red Cloud and Whetstone agencies, beef had been issued in excessive amounts, but the committee was satis-fied that when various northern bands of Sioux came onto the reservations and demanded supplies, the agents would have been in danger if they had not made the issues. Disappointed merchants testified that the low bids they made in New York had been rejected in favor of higher bids, but the assistant attorney general had ruled that the commissioner had every right to reject bids for good reason, and it was shown that his rejections had been made with the full concurrence of the Board of Indian Commissioners and the assistant secretary of the interior. Smith's purchase of Anson Dart's Sanitary Specific was brought up, and Smith spoke candidly about it. The Board of Indian Commissioners, he said, had approved the purchase, and such a medicine, if effective, would be useful, but he had learned "that there was some humbug about this certificate and about the man himself, and I concluded there is about the medicine." And he had not issued it.[30]

When the testimony was complete, Benjamin Cowen summed up the evidence that had been submitted. He reminded the committee of the charges Welsh had published before the investigation began and noted Welsh's unwillingness to make any charges under oath. "Mr. Welsh," Cowen said, "finds it one thing to write in the quiet seclusion of his sumptuous residence the charges which may destroy the fair name of a Christian gentleman of high character, and quite another thing to meet the man whom he has maligned face to face upon the witness-stand, and there make good his charges. If Mr. Welsh's statements in his published letters were true, then is his testimony before your committee false, and *vice versa*. Let him choose whichever of the propositions he may."[31]

Cowen admitted that the recommendations of the Board of Indian Commissioners about the payment of bills had sometimes been overruled by the secretary of the interior. But he cited the statute that gave the secretary the express authority to do so, and he noted that Nathan Bishop had testified that he understood the law and said that the board did not mean to imply that there was anything fraudulent in the secretary's overruling its recommendations.

Cowen also cited the statutes that allowed government officers to reject low bids if it was in the interest of the government to do so and to make purchases without advertising or bids in emergencies—statutes that gave Smith the authority to take the actions some witnesses had questioned.

He concluded:

> For the last twelve months disappointed bidders, combining with other parties, who from various causes have been thwarted in their designs by the officials in control of the Indian service, have sought to intimidate and black-mail the Office under threats of some wonderful disclosures of fraud which were to shock the country and destroy the reputation of high officials.
>
> These threats have frightened no one, they have influenced no one, in the Indian service; but they have produced this investigation which you have been prosecuting for the past four months. The black-mailers and their abettors have had every opportunity to make good their charges upon the witness-stand, with what result you know. . . .

Four months have been thus consumed, and I submit that not a solitary item of evidence has been produced going to show any criminality, fraud, irregularity, or unfairness, in the conduct of business by the [Interior] Department, the Indian Office, or any of its subordinates.

Cowen appealed to the committee to make its report before Congress adjourned, fearing that a delay in reporting would be "misconstrued by a press, eager for damaging and libelous reports relative to public officials."[32]

The committee then submitted a report that was concise and conclusive.

From the testimony herewith reported, transactions which seemed suspicious, and to which bad faith had been imputed, have been shown before the committee to be characterized by honesty of purpose and entire good faith to the Government and the Indian service. Practices which were deemed irregular appear to have been justifiable under the peculiar circumstances of the case, and incidental and almost unavoidable in a service of this character and magnitude. . . .

It does not appear that the Commissioner of Indian Affairs, or any other officer of the Government, or any one connected with the Indian service, has sought or derived any profit or personal advantage whatever, in any of the transactions which have come within this inquiry.[33]

27

Helping the Indians

The best way to help a poor man is to lead him or compel him to help himself.

> Edward P. Smith to Taylor Bradley, May 28, 1874

Whatever you do for an Indian which he can do for himself . . . is a damage to him and a wrong to the government.

> Edward P. Smith to J. G. Hamilton, March 29, 1875

Whenever you make it easy or possible [for an Indian] to get his living from charity or from the Government without labor, you defeat your end and injure your ward.

> Edward P. Smith to L. Stowe, July 10, 1874

No other blessing can come to an Indian so great as that of industry.

> Edward P. Smith to L. S. Dyar, September 27, 1875

The purchases of Indian goods and supplies in New York City required Smith's presence again in late June and early July 1874. Minnie Cook had represented him in New York during the hearings by the House Committee on Indian Affairs; his only absence from Washington during the hearings was a brief trip to Hampton Institute, for which he was a trustee, to attend the commencement exercises and the dedication of a new college building, Virginia Hall. The day after the House committee submitted its report, Smith left Washington for New Haven to celebrate the twenty-fifth anniversary of his graduation from Yale, and from there he went to New York City. This time the awards of contracts for Indian goods and supplies were made without the controversy that met them the year before.[1]

General Howard had also attended the commencement exercises at Hampton Institute, but shortly afterward he accepted the command of the Department of the Columbia and moved to Portland, Oregon. Howard, too, had been under investigation, in his case by a military court of inquiry. The court found him innocent of the charges brought against him, but Howard had had enough of Washington and applied for active duty in the army. Smith and Howard had grown close, and after Howard left for Oregon, Smith carried on a warm correspondence with the general, sending him chatty letters full of Washington gossip. Howard relied on Smith to help look after his affairs in Washington. On one occasion he asked Smith to take a letter about a West Point appointment to the president. "Do not let my letter go in by usual official routine, please," Howard asked, "but let the President see your pleasant face and oblige a worthy young man, who will repay you by a memorable life."[2]

With Howard gone and Cleavie hospitalized, Smith looked for friendship to the First Congregational Church in Washington. Many of the church members were known to Smith from his work with the Freedmen's Bureau. The Alvords were members, as the Howards and Charles Howard had been before they left the capital. General George Balloch and General Eliphalet Whittlesey were on the board of trustees and both taught Sunday school classes. Smith too became a teacher in the Sunday school; one of his pupils was his niece Minnie Cook.

The pastor of the church was Jeremiah Eames Rankin, the author of over two hundred hymns, including the popular "God Be with You Till We Meet Again." After a severe conflict and the resignation of Rankin's predecessor, the church was racially integrated, and there were at any one time from thirty to fifty black members, including Francis Cardozo, whom Smith had known from his work with the freedmen. Frederick Douglass, John Mercer Langston, and Senator Blanche K. Bruce often attended services as did faculty members and students from Howard University. So notable was the participation of blacks that the church was commonly known in Washington as "the nigger church."[3]

Indian delegations continued to demand Smith's attention. Delegations of Delawares, Peorias, Cherokees, Loyal Creeks, Mandans, Arikaras, Onondagas, and Osages came to Washington in the spring of 1874. A new subject was introduced into the discussions with the delegations when Congress passed the Indian appropriation act in June. The act required Indians to work for their supplies. "For the purpose of inducing Indians to labor and become self-supporting," Indian agents were to require all able-bodied male Indians between the ages of eighteen and forty-five "to perform service upon the reservation, for the benefit of themselves or of the tribe, at a reasonable rate . . . to an amount equal in value to the supplies to be delivered." Allowances for the Indians were to be distributed "only upon condition of the performance of such labor," the only exception being that the secretary of the interior could exempt a particular tribe if he deemed it "proper and expedient." Congress later strengthened the law by applying it to annuities as well as supplies.[4]

The law had Smith's unqualified support. One of his agents wondered about the value of requiring work on rented land, which would give the Indians no permanent return for their labor. Smith told him that if he was obliged to feed the Indians there was no reason why "they should not be made to labor in return, even though the labor itself brought no other result than a tendency to cultivate industry and self reliance. Better employ them in digging ditches one day and filling them up the next, than feed them in idleness."[5]

The law proved impossible to enforce on many reservations, and letters began to arrive in Washington from agents asking to be exempted from its provisions. Smith passed them on to Delano, noting that some of the tribes were not "sufficiently advanced in civilization to comply with the requirement of the law" and asking exemptions. At many other agencies, however, the law was implemented with little difficulty.

After Congress applied the requirement to annuities as well as supplies, George Whipple questioned Smith about the law's fairness. He said that if the annuities were gifts, he could understand the requirement to labor for them. But if the annuities were payments owed to the Indians, Whipple thought it "would be difficult to convince the Indian that a promise to pay for value received can be set aside by any subsequent, arbitrary condition, desired by the promisor. I don't know but some of the Indians' friends may be as blind as the Indians in being able to see any justice in such mode of procedure."[6]

Smith replied that he thought the new regulation was in "the best interests of the Indians as well as of the Government." The Indians were wards of the nation, he said, and the government as their guardian had a duty to seek their "elevation out of barbarism," and that meant teaching them to work. "Nothing tends more strongly to perpetuate barbarism among the Indians than the indisposition to toil. . . . So long as they can procure sufficient food and clothing by any means in idleness or by the chase there can be no sufficient motive brought to bear upon them to induce labor."[7]

Smith told Whipple that five-sixths of the goods and supplies furnished to the Indians was indeed "a gratuity to them, not being based upon treaty obligation," and he thought no one would object to the government's requiring labor for gratuities given to the Indians. But the acts of Congress went further in requiring labor by the few tribes to whom annuities were owed. It was in these cases, Smith said, that Whipple's question might be asked.

Can the Government rightfully compel an Indian to labor for what the Government owes him without labor? To the question, in such unqualified form, of course there is but one answer. It cannot. But if you will put the question so as to cover the facts in the case the answer may be different. The Government has agreed to give a certain tribe of Indians an annuity of from $10 to $50 per capita, amounting to from $50 to $300 annually to each Indian family of the tribe. This money if received in cash by the Indians will be of little if any value to them. It is certain to be of some injury, tending, as all gifts do, to pauperism and idleness, and may be of material damage in inducing intemperance on their part, and intrigue on the part of the miserable set of white men who always hang around an Indian reservation.

On the other hand, let these Indians be first given to distinctly understand that the money is their own, and that the Government proposes to give them every dollar of it; but that they being wards of the Government, for whom it is bound to provide, not only during the few years for which this annuity money has been pledged, but for all the future, until they come to citizenship, it must insist that they shall get the most good out of their funds; that it will be greatly for their good to learn to labor, and that therefore the Government will insist that they shall labor, as a condition of getting this money. Would not the moral sense of mankind indorse this position and action of the Government?[8]

Smith thought it would, especially when it was realized that the labor was not for the government, but for the Indian's own benefit, labor on his own house and farm, which would bring him "from ten to twenty-fold the amount of his money annuity" in crops and improvements, while at the same time teaching "habits of industry" and "the first lessons in self-support." The method of "forced industry" had been in effect, he said, among several tribes over the past two years with good results. One tribe had received cash annuities for twenty years, while "occupying one of the richest tracts of land in the United States, and yet had every year become more squalid and wretched." They were "very much aggrieved and angered" when Smith ordered their agent to require them to work for their money. "They [pleaded] their rights and the faith of the Government. I [pleaded] in answer their necessities and the purpose of the Government to benefit them, and held them to it." The result was "a complete transformation" of the tribe, which now had good crops, schools, houses, and stock.

I think you will agree with me, not only that the Government had the right to so use the annuities of this tribe as to inforce this industry, but also that in humanity and kind dealing it had *not* the right, as their guardian, and bound to do the best thing for them, longer to give them their annuities in any other way. After a few years of such treatment, if the treaty obligations still continue and the Indians have acquired habits of industry, it may be safe and advantageous to again give them a part or the whole of their annuities in cash.[9]

Smith set priorities for his agents in putting the Indians to work. The most needy were to be employed first, and full-blooded Indians were to be given preference over mixed-bloods, "especially if they are comparatively wild Indians who can thus be induced to take their first lessons in industry." Indians who had received previous help with things like houses and cattle were to be left as much as possible to their own devices, and the agents were to help those "who are beginning to help themselves, and to induce others to make a beginning in the way of self support by farming."[10]

Smith took a special interest in teaching the Indians how to work. He frequently wrote letters about such matters as the care of sheep and soap- and basketmaking. Perhaps because of Cleavie's activities at White Earth, he was particularly interested in weaving. He provided for the erection of a large industrial hall at White Earth, where weaving and basketmaking were taught to the Chippewa women, and then he encouraged his agents in other places to promote the weaving of mats, carpets, and blankets that had been successfully begun among the Chippewas. Smith's twenty-four-year-old niece Hattie Cook was in charge of the industrial department at White Earth, and he sent her to the Yankton and Santee agencies to set up looms and teach weaving to the Indian women there.[11]

Smith also sent Hattie to Fort Defiance, New Mexico, to teach the Navajo women to weave flannel on hand looms. She traveled to St. Louis, where she met the Navajo agent, W. F. M. Arny ("Alphabetical Arny" some called him), and then went with him by train to Pueblo, Colorado. From Pueblo they took a stagecoach 325 miles to Santa Fe, then a wagon 170 miles to Fort Wingate, and finally they traveled with the agency teamsters the last 40 miles to Fort Defiance. Hattie found the Navajo women already skilled at blanketmaking and not interested in what she had to teach them. They made fun of her flannel, saying they could see through it, and insisted on being well paid to do any work on her looms.

Hattie also found the fort a dangerous place. From her bedroom window, she could see the graves of three agents who had been killed by Indians. When Agent Arny was called to Washington, the Indians took advantage of his absence and raided the warehouse. Even though the threat of troops caused the Indians to return the goods they had stolen, the women were advised to leave the agency. They left in three vehicles, one of them driven by Hattie. Nine days later they arrived in Santa Fe, where Hattie boarded a stage, unaccompanied but with a Smith and Wesson revolver in her belt, to begin a memorable trip through rain and quicksand to Pueblo and then home. For all its excitement, Hattie thought her trip had accomplished nothing; Arny, however, was pleased with the looms whose construction Hattie had supervised before she left the agency and with the good example Hattie had set for his other employees. If they would imitate her good example, he said, he would consider himself "the happiest Indian agent on this continent."[12]

THE PEACE SO DILIGENTLY SOUGHT at Fort Sill in the fall of 1873 was broken in the spring of 1874, when the Kiowas, Comanches, and Cheyennes resumed their raiding in Texas and Kansas. The raiding was in part the result of a culture that glorified war and the warrior, but the Indians were also angered by the massive slaughter of buffaloes and the theft of horses by whites, and they were seeking revenge for Indians killed on previous raids. By summer the violence had grown into what came to be called the Red River War.[13]

In May 1874, after Indians attacked the Tenth Cavalry near Fort Sill, Colonel Davidson asked for authority to follow the warriors onto the reservation to "punish" them. Earlier in the year, Smith had rejected a proposal similar to Davidson's, fearing that it would lead to "indiscriminate slaughter" on the reservation, but when he received Davidson's request, Smith gave his approval. He said he deemed it a "special hindrance" to the civilization of the Indians that they should be allowed to break their pledges against raiding and then make their reservation "a refuge for crime." Indians along the Red River were there "only for mischief," he said, and if they could be followed "upon a hot trail and struck by the military before reaching the camp of other Indians," Davidson "should not be restrained from so doing by the reservation line. Of course great care and vigilance should be exercised to strike only those who are on a marauding expedition and before they reach the camps of the tribe."[14]

Two months later, the secretary of war forwarded requests from Generals Sheridan and Sherman for the same permission, and Smith again gave his approval. He asked, however, that care be taken to separate the friendly Indians from those who were hostile. Most of the Indians, including Satanta, were cooperating with the government; "no military movement rendering these friends of the Government liable to attack and massacre by our soldiers could be justified." In fairness to the Indians, Smith noted that among the causes of the difficulties on the plains was the failure of the government to protect the Indians from buffalo hunters, horse thieves, and whiskey traders. "I only wish it were possible under law for the Honorable Secretary of War to send his forces to the homes of these marauders and compel justice from them as well as from the Indians."[15]

After Smith approved the plan to pursue the raiding Indians onto the reservations, the orders were issued to the army. The hostile Kiowas, Comanches, and Cheyennes then fled west, but by early 1875 the army gained control of them. During the fighting, Satanta left his reservation to visit the Wichita Agency—without intending to join in the fighting, Smith thought—but was considered hostile and was forced to surrender. Jonathan Richards, one of the Quaker agents, also doubted that Satanta was engaged in the fighting, but if he was, Richards thought it was while he was under the influence of liquor. The chief told Richards he had been drinking "and hardly knew what he had done." Satanta was returned to prison in Texas, where it appeared he would be executed. President Grant, however, appealed for a delay until it could be determined whether Satanta had violated his parole, and the governor of Texas eventually commuted his sentence to life imprisonment. Four years later, still a prisoner in Texas, Satanta committed suicide.[16]

Large numbers of Indians who had been off the reservations began to come in to make peace, and the Quaker agents asked for advice in dealing with them. Smith told the agents to examine the Indians to determine their guilt or innocence. The guilty were to be turned over to the army. "If there is doubt let firmness and protection have the benefit of it for the present"; there would be time for leniency later. The agents were to make sure the Indians knew they must submit to the authority of the government "and that the Government will no longer consult their notions and superstitions, or the wishes and follies of their young men, at the expense of the life and property of citizens of the Government."[17]

Warriors who were convicted of crimes by a military commission were to be imprisoned, and Smith agreed with the policy. The imprisonment of the leaders, he thought, would have a better effect on the discipline of the tribe than executions, "and the more complete the separation of the prisoners from the tribe . . . , the more effectual will be the punishment." He said the Indians should be made to understand that the length of the imprisonment was entirely up to the War Department and depended on the good behavior of the tribe.[18]

The prisoners were to be taken to Fort Marion at St. Augustine, Florida, and General Sheridan had proposed that their immediate families be allowed to accompany them, "not as an indulgence to [the] men themselves, but as a matter of humanity to the family," but Smith disagreed. He thought that in addition to the extra expense of sending the families and the demoralizing effects of life at a military post, allowing the families to accompany the prisoners "would be no inconsiderable mitigation of deserved punishment, and would be so regarded by the tribes." He recommended that the families be left with the tribes, where they would serve as a "constant reminder" of the punishment of the warriors.[19]

Smith demonstrated the same sternness in regard to the army's efforts to prevent fighting between Ute and Sioux warriors. He recommended that, if necessary, some of their chiefs or principal men be seized and held "as hostages, for the good behavior of their people."[20]

To everyone's surprise, one of the Quaker agents, John D. Miles, the agent at the Upper Arkansas Agency, exhibited a similar sternness in requesting military assistance against Indian raiders. Hostile Cheyennes, Kiowas, and Comanches had appeared near the agency, killing and scalping one man only thirty miles away. Miles immediately sent a courier to Fort Sill to request troops to protect the agency, and the troops were sent on a temporary basis. Miles also mustered a small party of employees to escort him to Caldwell, Kansas. Along the way, they found ranches that had been attacked and at one place four men who had been delivering Indian supplies lying murdered in the road. All four had been scalped; one had been tied to his wagon and burned—the fire was still burning when Miles arrived. Miles telegraphed to Smith for two or three companies of cavalry for protection at the agency and on the road to it. "Let the hostile element be struck from every point," he wrote, "at once & with such power as shall make the work quick & effectual."[21]

Smith approved Miles's request, but the agent's Quaker superiors did not. After meeting with Miles, the Friends' Committee on Indian Affairs reported that it recognized the seriousness of the situation that prompted his request for troops; nevertheless, "some of his actions and the warlike tenor" of his request to Smith showed that he was not "sufficiently in harmony" with the Quakers' pacifist principles. The committee asked for his resignation. Miles, however, refused to resign, saying that "it will not do for us to remain quiet and permit the horrid butchery of innocent persons—this would have been criminal negligence."[22]

Smith spoke out against the request for Miles's resignation. He told a leading Quaker that it was an injustice to Miles "and if insisted upon will work great harm to the peace policy." If an agent takes a stand "in favor of law and order" and then loses his position "in a kind of disgrace with the Society of Friends, it will be impossible to administer affairs through the Society of Friends in the Indian Territory. I regard Agent Miles as the best Agent, with possibly one exception, that the Friends have in the field and he has done nothing more than ordinary prudence required him to do, and certainly nothing that the Government does not thank him for doing." Smith told Miles that he hoped good sense would prevail with the Friends and that they would be able to see that what they would do in a city by calling for police protection against murder and theft "is reasonable and right and [a] duty that you should do in the Indian country, in calling for the military, when the property of the Government and the lives of the employees are in peril. . . . One thing is certain, that any peace policy that purposes to use only memorials as a restraint for murdering and thieving Indians is an unmitigated farce."[23]

Smith told General Howard that Agent Miles, "the fighting Quaker," had lost favor with the Friends and that he probably would, too, for backing Miles. He said that at least one Quaker, Lawrie Tatum, had already appealed to Delano in the matter. "Between the War Dep[t] & Ultra peace men like Tatum there ought to be a golden mean but whether I shall be allowed to pursue it will depend on several things the principal of which is official back bone." But Smith's actions were approved, and John Miles continued to serve as the agent for the Cheyennes and Arapahos, even though many of the Quakers continued to oppose any cooperation with the army in Indian affairs.[24]

Miles not only asked Smith for troops, he also asked for arms, and Smith provided fifteen Springfield rifles and two thousand cartridges for the agency. Smith frequently received requests for arms from his agents, both to protect the agencies and to equip the Indians for hunting. The commissioner's correspondence was filled with requests for powder and balls, needle guns, muzzle-loading rifles, and carbines, along with requests for permits for traders to sell guns and ammunition to the agencies and the Indians. A request was even received from the Fort Belknap Agency for a Gatling gun or a twelve-pound howitzer "for any emergencies that may arise," but even though the Indian Office provided many of the arms requested, it did not see fit to fill that request. Nor would it permit the sale of pistols to Indians.[25]

The War Department questioned the wisdom of providing arms to the agencies, and Smith said there was a general "hue and cry" whenever there was talk of arming any Indians, "however friendly." Nevertheless, he thought it more economical to provide arms to agency employees than to rely solely on troops for protection, and he favored arming the Indians themselves where they were peaceful and in danger from other tribes. Arms for hunting, he said, would help the Indians supply their own needs when government funds for food and clothing were not sufficient. Smith made it clear, however, that his office would revoke the license of any trader who sold arms or ammunition to hostile Indians. Arms and ammunition were to be furnished only to "friendly and peaceable" Indians and then only in the smallest possible quantities and for the shortest possible times. Smith recommended that "wild tribes" like the Comanches be "disarmed completely, even to their side arms, bows and arrows," and that they be provided only with a few guns on loan to kill the cattle issued to them by the government.[26]

In mid-August 1874, Smith accompanied Columbus Delano to Long Branch, New Jersey, to meet with Grant at his summer home, presumably to discuss the Red River War. They also attended a church service with the president at the Methodist Church, where Bishop Matthew Simpson was preaching. From Long Branch, Smith went on to Marblehead, Massachusetts, to begin a month's vacation at the shore. Groups of vacationers from Nashua, New Hampshire, and Lowell, Massachusetts, were accustomed to summering on Marblehead Neck. Both towns were near Pepperell, Massachusetts, and Nashua was the home of Roswell Smith, which made it natural for Smith to make the Nashua camp his own camping place. Marblehead Neck was crowded each summer with tents and small cottages; the several hundred campers who stayed in them spent their days on the rocks, roaming in the fields, or rowing in the harbor. Gerty went with her father to the shore, and two of General Howard's children, Grace and Guy, joined them there, where the three young people enjoyed themselves boating, sailing, swimming, and riding. Smith was still within reach of Washington. Telegrams about matters that needed his attention were received at Marblehead and carried by messenger to Marblehead Neck.[27]

One of the telegrams that arrived in Marblehead reported the murder of five Osage Indians, reportedly by members of the Kansas militia. The Indians were among a group of twenty-nine Osages, including ten women and children, who were off their reservation with permission to hunt buffaloes when they were attacked without provocation. Smith, fearing further violence against the Osages, telegraphed former Kansas senator Samuel Pomeroy: "Kansas citizens have treacherously and wantonly murdered five Osage Indians in the Indian Territory. Is it possible that the State authorities instead of sending to punish this atrocity prepare to endorse it and exceed its barbarism by sending the militiamen to pillage and massacre the Osages in their own homes[?]"[28]

When he returned to Washington, Smith ordered an investigation of the murders. The investigation revealed that a party of forty whites had captured, disarmed, and then murdered four Osages, two of whom were scalped or otherwise mutilated. Fifty-four ponies, colts, and mules were stolen from the hunting party, and their other property was either stolen or destroyed. Ten days later the governor of Kansas had called the murderers into the service of the state, backdating their orders to include the time of the killings. When the governor questioned the report of the investigators, Smith submitted additional evidence that the Osages were murdered without provocation.

The evidence included a statement the leader of the whites had made before the killings: "There," he said, "was a chance for some fun." [29]

Smith said the testimony "exhibits in all its nakedness the cool premeditated and atrocious character of the motives that inspirited this so-called Militia Captain to the commission of a wanton barbarity that will bring the blush of shame for our white race whenever the tale is told." Although Smith did not hope to see the murderers prosecuted, he did try to recover the Osages' stolen property. But nearly a year after the murders, the governor was still resisting all pleas for restitution, and Smith reported that the Osages were "still deeply grieved and incensed. The customary morning and evening wail of the orphans and widows is still kept up in the Osage villages, and it is with the utmost difficulty that they are daily restrained from going out in what are called mourning parties to assuage their grief in the blood of white men." [30]

The Black Hills were in the news in the fall of 1874. The Hare Commission had described the Black Hills as "the hive of the hostile Sioux, their retreat in times of danger, their place of council when marauding parties are being organized." Bishop Hare himself called them "the kernel of their nut, the yoke of their egg," and said that the Indians' attachment to them was "a passion." "Medicine-place" the Sioux called the Black Hills, a place sacred to them. The War Department had decided to send a military expedition under General George Armstrong Custer into the Black Hills to explore them with the purpose of locating a site for a military post from which the army could control the hostile Sioux. By summer the Custer expedition was reporting the presence of abundant game in the Black Hills and, more newsworthy, gold. [31]

Bishop Hare expressed his doubts about the expedition to Columbus Delano, who passed them on to William Belknap, the secretary of war. Delano told Belknap he was aware of the "misconduct of the wild tribes" among the Sioux but said he was concerned that an attempt to "punish" them might provoke general hostilities. Delano said on another occasion that he "deplored the Custer expedition from the first, and have done everything in my power to prevent it and mitigate its effects." But the expedition continued, even after Bishop Hare appealed directly to the president. [32]

Custer's reports of gold in the Black Hills loosed a stream of adventurers and prospectors toward land that was reserved by treaty for the Sioux. The government made every effort to expel the whites from the Indians' land. Just as the Indian Office freely used military force to keep Indians on the reservations, it also used force to keep whites off the reservations. To make sure of the office's authority to do so, the attorney general was asked for a legal opinion. He ruled that the commissioner, with the secretary of the interior's approval, had ample power to remove unauthorized whites from Indian reservations and that the president was authorized to employ military force to assist him. Smith recommended that force be used in the Black Hills. "It will be a shameful record for the country," he said, "if it shall be found hereafter that it was impossible for the United States Government to carry out so plain and simple an obligation as to protect Indians from intrusion in a country which they hold, and which the Government has repeatedly declared to be, sacredly their own." At the request of the Indian Office, the army was ordered to keep whites out of the Black Hills, and the government said it would protect the Indian lands if it took the whole army to do it, but as wagon trains assembled in nearby cities and thousands of adventurers prepared to invade the hills, the army found it increasingly difficult to stop them.[33]

In October 1874, Smith and Eliphalet Whittlesey, accompanied by Daniel Sherman, the agent for the New York Indians, paid a brief visit to two of the Seneca reservations in New York State. The Senecas, who had been adapting to the ways of the whites for many years, were proof that Indians could become what Smith wanted them to be. Whittlesey reported that the Senecas at the Allegany Reservation lived in "small one-story frame or log houses, are decently clad, and some have made a good beginning at farming." Others made their living by renting land to the railroaders and settlers who had crowded onto the reservation. Thirty Seneca children attended a boarding school the Society of Friends had founded sixty years earlier. At the Cattaraugus Reservation, the visitors rode through "a good farming country, well cultivated," where they counted seventy-five farmhouses, all but one of them frame houses, "some of two stories and well painted. The farms are fenced, have good barns, orchards of fruit, cattle, horses, hogs, poultry, and all the appearance of comfort and thrift that is seen in any average farming district." The Cattaraugus Reservation also had three churches, two public schools, and a large asylum for orphan and destitute children.[34]

The Senecas had already begun to take their place in American society. Maris Bryant Pierce had studied at Thetford Academy and then graduated from Dartmouth College in 1840, four years before Smith entered Dartmouth. Ely Parker had become commissioner of Indian affairs. Parker's brother Nicholson, who was serving as the interpreter for the New York Agency, had studied at the Albany State Normal School, as had another brother, Newton, and their sister, Caroline. Hattie Twoguns, a Seneca from the Cattaraugus Reservation, had also studied at Albany and then had gone south to teach the freedmen.[35]

Smith and Whittlesey held councils with the Senecas at both the Allegany and Cattaraugus reservations. At each place the Indians were divided into two parties, one content with the progress that had been made, the other eager to have their land deeded to individuals and to become American citizens—"to be men among men." In his report of the trip, Whittlesey supported those who desired citizenship. He described the New York Indians as "well able to take care of themselves, and fully competent to discharge their duties as citizens. No good reason can be given for treating them longer as aliens and foreigners, or as wards and children." The next year, Smith proposed that the New York Indians be placed under the care of the state of New York and that steps be taken to given them citizenship.[36]

That fall, Cleavie was finally well enough to return home and even to do some visiting in Philadelphia and New Jersey. Her husband said, however, that she was "not at all cured of her delusion, only relieved from its intensity so as to be able to be diverted for a time, and so as not to suffer such agony of terror as she did last winter." Her doctor was hopeful but concerned that the length of her illness might be a sign that it was chronic. Five months later, she had shown some small improvement. Smith said she was "slowly, *very* slowly improving. Sleeps & eats pretty well, but keeps her delusion perfect yet, [but] not so intense as formerly. Indeed some hours & almost days she is quite natural in her bearing & conversation."[37]

In the fall of 1874, too, Gerty left home to study in the Preparatory Department at Vassar College. Grace Howard was also a student at Vassar, and Gerty profited by Grace's help and friendship, even though she became known at the school as "Gracie[']s Infant."[38]

The year 1874 ended with an attempt by one of Smith's clerks to blackmail him. In March 1874, a third-class clerk in the Indian Office, John H. Smoot, submitted his resignation, which Smith accepted. In November, Smoot asked to be reinstated. He said it was probable that parties hostile to Smith would return to Washington when Congress reassembled, "with a view of instigating further trouble." He asked Smith for a substantial raise and a two-month leave of absence with pay, "with a view of absenting myself and avoiding any of the subjects that have become hateful to me." Smoot's letter implied that if Smith did not meet his demands he would disclose to Smith's enemies the "many material facts" he had gathered during his service in the Indian Office.[39]

Smith replied to Smoot's letter by saying that Smoot's "course of life for some time past" had been "entirely unworthy of a clerkship." When the former clerk had demonstrated that he could "abandon licentiousness and intemperance," Smith said he would be compelled to listen to his appeal to be reinstated. But Smith was not interested in what Smoot proposed to do for his "protection."

I neither seek nor desire any such protection for myself, or the Indian Office, or anyone connected therewith.

If you have in your possession, or within your knowledge, facts showing, or tending to show, that wrong practices exist in this Office, and if you believe an adequate remedy will not be promptly found upon my attention being called thereto, or if you believe them to be so gross that . . . an exposure should be made as well as a remedy found, then there is but one honorable course open to you, viz. to proceed upon your own motion, without fear or favor, and lay the whole matter before someone, or some body of men, in authority, who can procure redress and punishment.

If, on the other hand, the "many material facts" which you claim to have gathered are not facts, but a mass of distorted statements and inferences drawn by yourself from hearsay information and from inspection of accounts, all of which, on proper enquiry, might be found to be entirely consistent with right and propriety, but which, nevertheless, have been gathered for the purpose of compelling action in your favor, I have no suggestion to make as to the disposition of these papers except to request that you will make me no more propositions to buy you off, and to frankly tell you that if a Comanche Indian were to undertake an impudent villainy equal to what this would show you to have in hand[,] I should forever despair of his civilization.[40]

28

The Sioux

You have spoken to me about another country, but this does not concern me. That is south of the Republican [River]. I was not born there, and I do not know anything about it. If that is such a nice country, you ought to put the white men there who invade our country.

Spotted Tail, 1875

The constant attacks on his character, along with Cleavie's illness, were beginning to take their toll on Smith. He increasingly found fault with the Indians. He told a prospective agent that the Indians were "sharp and full of complaint & the more faithful an agent is to them the more they don't like him." Smith seldom corresponded directly with Indians—usually he communicated with them through their agents—but on one occasion, he vented his frustration in a sharp letter to a Chippewa chief named Ah-bun-way, who had asked to come to Washington to settle some difficulties facing the Snake River band in Minnesota.

I have no doubt you are in trouble, and all of the Snake River Indians also, and the trouble is a great deal deeper than you think, and is going to grow still worse from this time on, but it does not arise from the fact that you only got five dollars this year instead of ten. . . . The trouble is that every thing around you has changed since you were a boy, and yet you go on with your eyes shut as if you did not see anything. Now open your eyes and see if the country around Snake River is not a different country from what it was twenty years ago, and if you are going to live in that country you will have to live in a different way. . . . You must get your living no longer by trapping and begging, but go to work like an honest man. I was ready to give you oxen and help you in building houses, and clearing land and furnish you some cattle, and axes and hoes, and saws, and was ready to do everything for you but the work[,] *that* I wanted you to do. And *that* is exactly what you did not want to do, because of your old habits which you were not ready to change.

If the Agent only paid you five dollars, of course there is more that belongs to you, but it is not well for you that you should have it in money. Money means to most of you whiskey, and that means fighting and mischief generally. . . .

Now if you were to come to Washington and stay with me "three moons" I could not tell you any more than I have in this letter, and you can see it is hardly worth while to spend your time and mine in coming to Washington, besides that[,] I have no money I could spend if I wanted to, so you must stay at home and get some one to read this letter to you once a week.[1]

Smith also became critical of his agents, finding fault with their absences from their posts, with the information they provided, and with their inability to follow his instructions. He told one agent who had filled out a form incorrectly that "the manifest inattention of Agents to plain directions and the carelessness with which many of the returns are made up are not encouraging." To another, who had failed to furnish certain statistics, he said sharply, "This inattention to plain directions seems to be inexcusable." Some of his criticisms, however, were well deserved. He learned from J. L. Burchard, the Methodist minister who was the agent at the Round Valley Agency in California, that discipline there was enforced by whipping. "This demoralizing and detestable custom of *whipping* men or women," Smith told him, "is a relic of barbarism, and as a means of correction for offences committed against the United States, was by statutory law abolished more than thirty five years ago. It meets with my unqualified disapproval and must never be repeated. . . . Cut down your whipping post, and use your lash hereafter only on oxen and mules."[2]

The whipping of Indians at Round Valley was one of the topics when the Indian appropriation bill for nearly $5 million was debated in the House of Representatives in January 1875. The debates also produced a commendation for Smith from a Democratic member of the House. John K. Luttrell, a Democrat from California, said that when he learned of frauds in the Indian service in his district, he took them directly to Smith, "and I found him to be a good, honest man, and willing to do what he could in the premises. Consequently I have submitted all my complaints to him, and the agents were removed. . . . He has acted the part of a true, honest, and faithful official."[3]

That same month, representatives of the religious societies working among the Indians gathered for their annual meeting with Smith and the Board of Indian Commissioners. The representatives reported on their work and shared information about their common problems. The presence of soldiers at the agencies was one difficulty. Although the representatives recognized that the army was needed to keep the Indians on the reservations, they said the soldiers also introduced liquor and prostitution and sometimes interfered with the agents in their duties. Detectives Smith had appointed to stop the sale of liquor were also seen by some of the representatives as interfering with the work of the agents. Disputes between Protestants and Catholics over the right to work on various agencies was another subject of discussion, although no Catholic representative was present to speak to the issue.

Appropriations were on Smith's mind when he addressed the group. He lamented that Congress did not plan more than one year in advance when it appropriated money for the Indians, and he decried the inadequate salary, "the miserable pittance," the government provided for the agents to whom it entrusted great responsibility. He also spoke to the concerns of one representative who thought the abandonment of cash annuities was a violation of Indian treaties. Smith argued that cash payments were not in the best interest of the Indians. "If, some years ago, under some mistaken notion, we made such an arrangement with these tribes," he asked, "are we forever to continue to indulge them at the expense of the Government, at the expense of all reformatory efforts; thus destroying all hope of ever civilizing or Christianizing these people to any considerable extent? Are we under any such bond as that with these people who are our wards? I think not. It seems to me, that if I made a will for my child, and I found afterward that that child was going to the bad by reason of that will, I think I have a right to alter it. . . . [The Indians] are not foreign powers. They are wards of the Government, and ought to be so treated."[4]

Smith appealed to the religious societies to take more seriously the "wonderful power" of nominating Indian agents that had been given to them. That power, he said, ought not to be used to provide places for men "who have broken down in the church and are on their hands, or somebody for whom they must find a place of retirement or support in old age or in some other kind of infirmity." The power to nominate agents was the key to the solution of the entire Indian problem. Christian agents could provide what the "mere machinery" of government could not. "It takes the hand and the heart of the live and philanthropic man to lift up this fallen creature from his degraded condition. . . . When you are seeking to lift up a barbarian you must go to him with a full heart, and you must make him see that you mean his good." He also asked the societies to attempt to curb the attacks on agents that appeared in religious publications—the "innuendo about fraudulent transactions; vague and pointless, but full of harm"—remembering that the quality of the agents was their own responsibility. And he encouraged them to stand behind the agents with their prayers and moral support.[5]

The meeting concluded with the unanimous adoption of a resolution saying that "on the review of the labors of the year past revealing the great positive advance in civilizing and Christianizing these wards of the nation, our confidence in the wise and humane Indian policy of our honored Chief Magistrate is unabated." When one of the representatives proposed that the resolution be amended to include a commendation of Smith and Delano, Smith spoke against the proposal. The credit for the new Indian policy, he said, "rests with the President himself" and the president's persistence in carrying it out.[6]

Smith seldom made suggestions about the nominations of agents, but shortly after the Washington conference, he did suggest to the Dutch Reformed Home Missionary Society that George Clum, the brother of John P. Clum, the agent at the San Carlos Agency, be considered for an agency of his own. Smith said he knew nothing of the brother except the good impression he made when they met, "and the fact that he is the brother of one of the best agents I have. If he has anything of the pluck and sagacity and devotion of his brother John P. I hope you will secure him for the Apache Agency." But Smith made it clear that he was willing to leave the nomination entirely to the society. On another occasion, he told the same society he had reports that a man it had nominated as agent was "not a total abstinence man." If the reports were true, he said, "neither your church nor the Indian Office can afford to think of having him go to Arizona. No man who is not a total abstinence man on principle is safe for an hour in that country; and I should be as unwilling to have your church represented by such a man, as I should to entrust the very delicate affairs of that agency in his charge." He asked the society to investigate the reports he had received about its nominee.[7]

A group of Modoc and Klamath Indians on a lecture tour had recently visited the White House and the Indian Office, and a speech one of them gave at Independence Hall in Philadelphia painted a vivid picture of his impressions of both the president and the commissioner of Indian affairs. After the Modoc War, 153 Modoc prisoners had been taken to Fort McPherson, Nebraska, and then, under the custody of Captain Melville Wilkinson, were removed to the Indian Territory. After their arrival there, Alfred B. Meacham, who had been the chairman of the peace commission sent to deal with the Modocs, asked permission to take some of the captives on a lecture tour. With both Grant's and Delano's approval, Smith gave his permission. (Meacham had also asked to take Satanta and Big Tree with him, and Smith was willing to permit it if the imprisoned Satanta was found innocent, but Satanta remained in prison, and Smith did not think Big Tree important enough for Meacham's purpose without Satanta.)[8]

When the group reached Philadelphia, the Indians were invited to speak at Independence Hall. Wal-aiks-ski-dat, one of two Klamath Indians who accompanied the Modocs, was among the speakers. He used the occasion to reflect on freedom and slavery. The blacks, he said, had been freed, and a black was "all the same as a white man now." So were Irishmen, Englishmen, Spaniards, Portuguese, "and some Chinamen too; all these men are just the same as the white men." But, he said,

> an Indian cannot go anywhere without his agent gives him a paper. He is just the same as a slave. He is not free. . . . Men look at me as though I was a mountain lion. They seem to think that I am a wild man. I am not wild. *I am a man.* . . . I went to see the President. He looks just like any other man. I was not afraid of him. I intended to tell him what my people wanted, but his ear was to[o] small, he could not hear me. I brought all the things in my heart away.
>
> Then I went to see the Commissioner. He had large ears. He *seemed* to listen to what I had to tell him, but I looked him in the eye. He did not put the things I told him in his heart. My heart got sick, because I had came a long way with Colonel Meacham to see these men, but they would not take the words I gave them. I saw a colored man talking to the Commissioner, and he listened to all the colored man said. I have got my heart full of the things I have seen. Some things make me feel *sick*. . . . When the Indian tries to stand by the side of the white man, he pushes him away. He does not push the Negro away, nor the Spaniard.[9]

The Black Hills were in the news again in the spring of 1875. Delano had despaired of keeping the miners out of the Black Hills and thought it best to try to convince the Sioux to cede the land to the United States. "Their title to the Black Hills country," he said, "while of no essential value to them, is giving constant anxiety to the Department" because of the minerals found there. He asked Congress to appropriate money to bring a delegation of Sioux chiefs to Washington to negotiate for the land. He also authorized a geological survey of the Black Hills, under the direction of Walter P. Jenney, to learn just what the mineral value of the land was. In the meantime, he told inquirers that until the treaty with the Sioux was modified, it was illegal for whites to go into the Black Hills. He also thought the presence of whites there would add to the difficulties of the negotiations with the Sioux.[10]

Smith expressed strong doubts that the Sioux would agree to give up the Black Hills, but he agreed that the government should attempt to convince them. He made the necessary arrangements for Jenney's expedition and for a delegation of Sioux to come to Washington, and then he prepared to leave for New York City to attend to the annual purchase of Indian goods and supplies.

Just before Smith left Washington, he was visited by Professor Othniel Charles Marsh of Yale University, a nephew of George Peabody, the philanthropist whose benevolence in support of education in the South was well known to Smith. Marsh was a prominent paleontologist who had recently returned from a trip to the fossil fields on Indian lands south of the Black Hills, where he had added to the collection of fossil vertebrates—horses, pterodactyls, and mosasaurs or "sea serpents"—for which he was becoming famous.

When Marsh had gone west on an earlier trip, Smith wrote to Spotted Tail to introduce Marsh, telling the chief about Marsh's work and saying that the Great Father "would not have told this teacher to come to you, if he didn't know that he was a good man, who won[']t steal your ponies, or harm you or your lands in any way." The Indians not only gave their permission for Marsh's work but assisted him in it. They called him "the man that picked bones" and "Heap-Whoa-Man" because of his nervous habit of continually jerking his horse and trying to restrain it. Marsh's white associates called him "the bone-sharp." [11]

To obtain Red Cloud's permission to work on land near the Red Cloud Agency during his latest trip, Marsh had promised the chief he would carry his complaints about inferior Indian supplies back to Washington. Marsh visited Smith to show him samples of the flour, sugar, coffee, and tobacco Red Cloud had given him. Smith agreed that the samples were inferior but suggested to Marsh that they might not be fair samples of the supplies issued. When Marsh reported that Dr. John J. Saville, the agent at the Red Cloud Agency, was not a proper man for such an agency, Smith wearily replied that qualified men were hard to obtain for a salary of $1,500 a year. Marsh was not satisfied with Smith's responses. He said he left Smith's office feeling that Smith "had told me in plain terms that Red Cloud had deceived me, and that I really knew nothing about the agency, and for that very reason I did not give him one-twentieth part of the information I had about it." The next day Marsh carried his samples to the president and repeated his story to him. [12]

The Board of Indian Commissioners had gathered in New York City for the awards of contracts, and when the commissioners read the newspaper accounts of Marsh's visits to Smith and Grant, they asked him to present his information to them. Marsh met with the board at the Fifth Avenue Hotel, and when the commissioners saw his samples, they agreed that they were indeed inferior in quality. Marsh also repeated his criticisms of Indian agents, saying that the agents were not necessarily dishonest, but that the religious men working for such small salaries were "likely to be lacking in the business capacity for such a trust." Marsh took a newsman, William Wyckoff, with him to the hotel, and Wyckoff's report of Marsh's meeting with the board was published in the *New York Tribune*, a paper so strongly opposed to the Grant administration that Henry Adams called it "one of the most criminal" in its attacks. The *Tribune* had recently accused Delano's son, John Delano, who was his father's chief clerk, of corruption and had reported that the president had asked the secretary to resign. Now the newspaper underscored Marsh's charges in several editorials and ended with the statement, "Under such circumstances the saving of Mr. Delano's character is quite out of the question." [13]

Professor Marsh's charges did not go unchallenged. William R. Steele, a Democratic member of Congress from Wyoming, also met with the Board of Indian Commissioners. He contradicted Marsh's statements and suggested that in fairness, Marsh should have looked into the warehouse at the agency to see if the samples Red Cloud gave him were representative of the supplies issued to the Indians. He also said that Marsh had told him privately that "he did not know but Red Cloud had put up a job upon him" and that he did not know for a fact that the supplies were bad when they were issued to the Indians. Steele said he was not entirely in favor of the administration's Indian policy, but he thought it only fair "to thoroughly examine and establish any allegations of wrong before making them the basis of wholesale charges." Dr. Christopher Cox, who had recently served on a special commission to the Sioux, also challenged Marsh. Marsh, he said, had no previous experience with Indians and had "neither time nor opportunity by actual investigation to test the truthfulness of their declarations. . . . A little better acquaintance with Indian character would have very materially weakened his confidence in the numerous complaints persistently forced upon his attention. More resolute, chronic grumblers than these same Indians do not breathe." [14]

Secretary Delano, stung by Marsh's charges and by the unfavorable publicity his department was receiving, asked Clinton Fisk, the chairman of the Board of Indian Commissioners, to suggest members of the board or other suitable persons to serve on a commission to investigate the charges. In his letter to Fisk, Delano made the mistake of referring to "certain reports put in circulation by a Mr. Marsh," a statement that led the opposition newspapers to attack Delano for what appeared to be an insult to a man of Professor Marsh's reputation. The *Tribune* began to call for Delano's resignation. [15]

In the midst of the controversy over Marsh's charges, the Sioux delegations from the Red Cloud, Spotted Tail, and Cheyenne River agencies arrived in Washington. Senators from Kansas and Nebraska and representatives from several western states and territories as well as other interested whites also gathered to use their influence in urging the Sioux to give up the Black Hills. When the delegations arrived at the Indian Office and were introduced to Smith, he told them he had sent for his own interpreter (Samuel Hinman) so there would be no misunderstandings in their talks. He wanted all the other interpreters to "keep their ears open" and if they did not understand something to say so "on the spot." He did not want the delegates to find fault with their agents without good reason, but if they had something to say, they were to speak their mind. Red Cloud, Spotted Tail, and White Swan spoke briefly. Spotted Tail said he had one friend in Washington he wanted to see; "he treated me good when I was here before, and I want to go to him again." The friend was Benjamin Beveridge, the proprietor of the Washington House, whose questionable practices with previous delegations had earned him the disfavor of the Indian Office. Smith had already arranged for the delegates to stay at the Tremont House, and he told them their accommodations could not be changed. After the introductions, the Indians were sent off to visit the model room of the Patent Office.[16]

The following day Smith and Cowen took the delegations to the White House and introduced them to the president. Some of the Indians arrived carrying tomahawks decorated with colored ribbons; others carried long ornamental pipes. One, who carried his pipe in the position of "shoulder arms," had inserted a small campaign flag in the pipestem. On the flag were the words "Grant and Wilson." Standing in the center of a circle of Indians, Grant told the delegations he had two great chiefs, the secretary of the interior and the commissioner of Indian affairs, with whom he wanted them to speak freely and to settle all their business. If there was any misunderstanding, it would be referred to him. "We have the interests of the Indians at heart," Grant said, "and in view of the great growth of the population among the white people, we know better what is for your interests than you can know yourselves; and it is your interests we are looking after." When the Indians spoke, Spotted Tail said he had dealt with the two great chiefs before, and they had made promises that were not kept. He did not want to talk with them but with the Great Father himself. Red Cloud, too, said he did not want to talk with anyone but the president.[17]

Two days later, Spotted Tail and Red Cloud visited Smith's office with their interpreters to demand that they be moved from the Tremont House, where they said their rooms were too small, to the Washington House, where they had been housed before. Smith, still angry at the proprietor of the Washington House for his dealings with previous delegations, refused their request and offered them instead tents and provisions for camping if they insisted on leaving the Tremont House, an offer they refused. The Indians then defiantly made the move themselves, even though the Washington House had been declared off-limits to Indian delegations. But when the Indians learned that the government would not pay their expenses at the Washington House and that Grant would not see them if they stayed there, most of them moved back.[18]

Sioux delegations from the Red Cloud, Spotted Tail, and Cheyenne River agencies that were brought to Washington in the spring of 1875 to discuss the cession of the

The chiefs of the Cheyenne River Sioux also came to talk with Smith and Cowen. The principal speaker, Long Mandan, an old man wearing green goggles, complained of short rations and annuities. He also asked for mechanics, blacksmiths, and traders, a mowing machine, cloth for tents, horses for the members of the delegation, and guns for hunting. Smith told him that the shortages in their rations were the result of the large numbers of Sioux who came to the reservations from the Black Hills. As long as they had to be fed, there would not be enough food for everyone. The difficulty with giving them guns, he said, was that the guns might fall into the hands of "wild Indians." He asked whether muzzle-loaders would be suitable for hunting game, but the Indians preferred shotguns and Winchester rifles.

Charger asked Smith why he did not deal with Indians equally. Some had too much to eat, and some did not have enough. "Do you think it a good plan to feed Indians who are the ugliest and to lessen the rations each year of those who do the best? I think these are the people you ought to treat very

Black Hills and the Sioux hunting rights in Nebraska. Courtesy of National Anthropological Archives, Smithsonian Institution.

well, those who are quiet, peaceable and getting along. . . . Red Cloud and Spotted Tail have always been disaffected and they seem to get more than the Indians on the Missouri where you never hear any bad news."[19]

Smith said he realized that Spotted Tail and Red Cloud had "demanded a great many things and have got them. They refused to be counted and asked for every thing they wanted, and they got it with their guns. But we have now got some other guns up there with some blue coats and we give them now only what they ought to have."[20]

Charger also complained about broken wagons the government had furnished them and said their agent told them they had to do their own plowing, and he wanted to know if that was true. Smith replied that the agent was correct. Congress had told the president that

what the Indians have they must labor for, and that he must not do any thing to help an Indian when the Indian can do it himself. Now you will never learn to plow by looking on and seeing some one else have hold of the handles. Your little boy would never learn to walk if you should put him in a chair and only let him see other people walking. . . .

I used to live among the Indians and I used to give them a good many wagons and I noticed that the first time I gave an Indian a wagon it was very easily broken. . . . But after a while when the Indian had learned to drive his oxen he did not break his wagon so much. And I began to think that the trouble was not so much in the wagon as in the people who did not know how to drive. And yet it was better for them to have the wagons and break them than not to learn to drive.[21]

When he was asked about provisions for the mixed-bloods, Smith replied that a mixed-blood was "half a white man" and ought to be able to take care of himself. "They know how to work and if they won[']t work they ought to go hungry. . . . That is the way God has made us all. 'If a man will not work, neither shall he eat.' And the reason why we feed the Indians and give them something to wear is because they don[']t know how to work."[22]

Smith told Charger he liked the way he talked. "You talk like a man who knows what things he needs and asks for them." He also commended the delegation, saying it had done more toward "getting into the white man's ways" than any of the Sioux except perhaps those at the Yankton Agency. He assured the Indians that the president would do all he could for them. "But," he said, "you must remember that the president does not make the money and he does not carry the key of the big boxes where the money is kept." He could not give them any more money than Congress allowed.[23]

The three delegations returned to the White House, where Grant spoke briefly about the Sioux treaty of 1868. He explained that the treaty had provided for issues of food for only five years. The five years had passed; the last two years, food had been issued gratuitously. Grant suggested that the Sioux consider moving to the Indian Territory, where they could support themselves. He also introduced the subject of the Black Hills and said that if the Sioux did not give them up, the presence of whites there might lead to hostilities.[24]

Smith and Delano then met with the three delegations in Cowen's office in the Interior Department. Delano recited the changes in the West since the treaty of 1868. Buffalo no longer roamed in the lands reserved for the Sioux, and whites were pressing onto the lands. "Now you see the government has more children than you; you are the government's children, the children of the Great Father; so are the white people; and the Great Father has to do what is best for all." The government would not force them to give up their lands, but it wanted them, too, to consider what was best for all. Their land was said to contain silver and gold, and the whites were eager to mine them. "You do not know how much trouble the president and the commissioner of Indian affairs, and I, have had to keep the white people away from there." But it was impossible to keep them away. "What we fear is, that this anxiety of the white people to get into your country for gold and silver, will increase, and that the trouble to keep out white people will increase until there will be war and bloodshed about a country which is too cold and barren for agricultural purposes."[25]

Delano repeated what Grant had said: provisions had been furnished the Sioux beyond what the treaty required. He feared now that if they did not give up their lands, Congress would no longer give the provisions. Like Grant, he urged the Indians to move to the Indian Territory, where their children could "learn to be like white men." "In this way we shall avoid all this trouble about the Black Hills country. . . . And you will get a country in place of it a great deal better than you have now, and where you and your children will be a great deal happier than up in this cold country."[26]

Spotted Tail said he had no interest in going to the Indian Territory. "You have spoken to me about another country, but this does not concern me. . . . If that is such a nice country, you ought to put the white men there who invade our country." He said he was satisfied with the lands he had and shrewdly asked for agricultural implements, churches, and schools to develop those lands.[27]

Smith then raised another issue with the delegations. After the Sioux murders of Pawnee hunters in Nebraska, the Indian Office had recommended that Congress end the right of the Sioux to hunt there. Smith reminded the Sioux that Congress had appropriated $25,000 for them if they would give up that right. The money would be available only one more month, and Smith told them he needed to know if they would accept it. Spotted Tail said their right to hunt was guaranteed by treaty, but if the government would add $100,000 to the $25,000, they would give the land up before the month was out "and give you all the buffalo in it." Nor would he be rushed into making any decision about the Black Hills. He suggested that a commission be appointed to go out to their country and that the Sioux would talk with them there.[28]

The next day the Spotted Tail and Red Cloud delegations met again, this time with Cowen and Smith. At Cowen's invitation, Professor Marsh was also present, and Cowen asked Red Cloud to repeat the complaints about rations he had made to Marsh. Red Cloud told about supplies that were spoiled, but he admitted they might have been rained on while they were being transported to the agency. Professor Marsh asked Red Cloud whether the samples given him were representative of the supplies issued at the agency. Red Cloud replied that he merely meant to say they were taken from food issued: "I do not mean to say that it was all like that." When questioned, he said that five wagonloads were like the samples and again said they might have gotten wet on the way to the agency. He also said there had been a delay in providing rations during the winter but admitted it had occurred because the man who was delivering them "was frozen." Marsh was embarrassed by Red Cloud's evasiveness, which Red Cloud blamed on the interpreters. A newspaper reporter who was present thought from Red Cloud's statements "that he had formerly deceived Mr. Marsh, or he was not then telling the truth." Undeterred, Marsh called on the president several days later, carrying with him statements from army officers that supported his charges about the poor quality of Indian supplies. Grant assured Marsh of his determination to correct any abuses found in the Indian service.[29]

The meetings with the Sioux delegations continued into early June. Red Cloud stated clearly that he would not move to the Indian Territory. He asked for better rations, agricultural implements, and the guns he said Felix Brunot ("the man who closed his eyes and prayed to the Great Father") had promised him. As for the $25,000 for their hunting rights, "that is so little I can hold it in my two hands." Like Spotted Tail, he asked for a commission to meet with them in the West about the Black Hills.[30]

Once again, Grant met with the delegations, this time at the Interior Department in a meeting from which the press was excluded. He urged the delegates to give up both their hunting rights in Nebraska and their rights to the Black Hills. Grant was willing to send a commission to treat with them later about the Black Hills, "but it is important to you that while you are here, you settle the question of the limits of your hunting grounds, and make preliminary arrangements to allow white persons to go into the Black Hills."

> One word more that has nothing to do with this. I have always felt ever since I was a young officer of the army, a great interest in the welfare of the Indians. I know that formerly they [have] been abused and their rights not properly respected. Since it has been in my power to have any control over Indian affairs I have endeavored to adopt a policy which should be for your future good, and calculated to preserve peace between the whites and Indians for the present; and it is my great desire now while I retain some control over the matter, that the initiatory steps should be taken to secure you and your children hereafter. If you will co-operate with me I shall look always to what I believe is for your best interests. Many of the Indians who accepted [at] an early day, what we propose to you to-day, are now living in houses, have fences around their farms; have school houses, and their children are reading and writing as we do here.[31]

The desire of white settlers for more land, Grant said, could not be denied, but he was hoping to prepare the Sioux for the changes new settlements would make in their lives.

> Where there is a population of industrious people, who understand how to work, they cannot let their population be pent up and be destroyed while there is territory where they can go, and get a subsistence. And what I want to do, is to prepare the Indian for a contingency that will be sure to arise; so that he will be able to live upon the ground and get a support from it, the same as white people. . . . [The Indian's sentiment] will have to give way before the growth of numbers who are not going to starve, merely out of a sentimental consideration of a title that others may have.[32]

The chiefs were reluctant to make any decisions without consulting their people first. Grant and Delano both tried to convince them that they had to act soon or they would lose the $25,000 Congress had appropriated for their hunting rights and that they needed to make other decisions about their future before Grant left office. Delano told them that Grant's term of office would end in a little less than two years. "It is not certain that the next Great Father will be as good a friend to the Indians, as the present one is; but what treaties and agreements the present Great Father makes, he will be bound by." The chiefs, however, were still reluctant to sign any agreements, and Delano assured them that he would have no "angry feelings" if they did not. But, he said, "I shall be sorry for you. I shall still be your friend, and will keep on trying as heretofore, to do the best I can for you."[33]

The following day, Smith met with the Red Cloud and Spotted Tail delegations at the Tremont House. He had learned that they were preparing to go home without making any agreements, and he consented to their offer to sign the agreement for the $25,000 after they returned home and then telegraph a list of purchases they wanted made with the money. He told them there was a risk of not completing the purchases before the appropriation expired (just twenty-seven days later), but, he said, "that risk you take yourselves." He urged them to give up the hunting rights because the buffalo were almost gone and the lands were of little use to them. Both Red Cloud and Spotted Tail indicated their belief that the agreement could be signed after they had consulted with their people.[34]

Smith and Delano held a final council with all three delegations on June 4. Delano had agreed to ask Congress for an additional $25,000 if the Indians would give up their hunting rights in Nebraska. Now he told them that whether they signed the agreement or not, he and the president would be compelled "for the peace and safety of the country" to refuse them the right to hunt any longer on the Smoky Hill Fork. He told them again of the government's desire to buy the Black Hills and said that a commission would be sent to treat with the Sioux for the purchase, if they were willing to meet with the commissioners.[35]

Before leaving Washington, Red Cloud's delegation met one more time with Smith in his office. Red Cloud raised the question of pay for the men who had accompanied the delegation as interpreters. The government had authorized three interpreters, but three others came as well. Smith was blunt in his reply.

> There are some things to be said about those men who have come along, that I would rather not be obliged to say to you. They have not come by the wish of any body but themselves, so far as I know. And they have been sources of mischief and trouble, ever since they came here. They got you to insist on going to the Washington House; and they got some of you to go there, after I had told you that it was not a proper place for you. They have led you into bad practices since you have been here. They have taken you with Beveridge the proprietor of the Washington House, at night into bad places; and now they have the impudence to come and ask me to pay them for that sort of service.[36]

Little Wound too spoke about pay for the men they had brought as interpreters. Smith denied that the men who had accompanied them were interpreters. He said one of them failed when he tried to interpret, and another "likes whisky so well, that he broke down. . . . He got so drunk that I could not see him for several days." Smith said he would pay two of the men, who did interpret, but not the others. "Those other men who have deceived you, who have kept you from doing your duty, and have led you into bad houses, have no claim for anything; and they may be thankful that they are not driven out of the country. . . . Now this is plain talk to you, but I may just as well talk of things as they are, rather than we should deceive one another."[37]

When Red Cloud mentioned the bills for six of his men who had stayed four days at the Washington House and for one man who had stayed there the whole time, Smith replied in anger.

> The proprietor of that house knew very well that I did not want you to go there. And he knew very well why I did not want you to go there. Yet he has tried from the day you came, to get you there. Some of you he has actually forced to go; and others of you who did go there, and some of you who remained at the Tremont, he has taken out himself at midnight, to some of the worst places in this city. I do not think he will have the face, and I give him credit for a great deal of cheek, but I do not think he will have the face to present me any bill for

the board of Indians this year; and he has got you to do it, because he is ashamed to present it himself.

Red Cloud replied that he had merely been given a bill to bring to Smith. "I am not a relative of that man you speak of, I have never spoken any evil against any white man; I think you are prejudiced against that man." To which Smith replied, "Well I am, slightly."[38]

The Cheyenne River Sioux also met with Smith before their departure. Long Mandan asked for $300 for each member of the delegation to buy presents, but Smith told him he could only give them $25. Their final discussion was about the Black Hills. Smith said philosophically:

> The trouble with most of us in this world, is that we cannot always have what we want. If you and I could have exactly what we wanted in regard to the Black Hills, they would be yours forever; but that we cannot have, and it is only a question as to what is the next best thing to do. I think now if you should balance that question of having the Black Hills forever, against having something to eat, you would probably give up the hills. The gold, if there is any gold, and the pine trees there, will not feed you at all. You had better sell that, and get something that you can eat.
>
> Lone Horn. You have asked us for something that is very important to us. We have asked you for $300, and you will not give it to us.
>
> [Smith]. I asked you for something you had; what you ask of me, is not mine to give.
>
> Spotted Elk. . . . I was in hopes that we would get some presents to take back to show how we have been treated. . . . You have not granted a thing they have asked you.[39]

Long before the Sioux delegations came to Washington, Smith told Delano he did not believe negotiations with them could be completed in the capital. "Individual Indians," he said, "are very slow to take responsibility for any matter affecting the whole body without a full understanding with the mass of the tribe." He thought it would be necessary after their talks in Washington to send a commission to meet with them in their own country, where definite results might be achieved. When the delegations left Washington without making any agreements, the president, on Smith's recommendation, appointed a commission to follow them west and treat with them there for the purchase of the Black Hills.

The commission met with the Sioux in a grand council in late September. The commissioners offered what they thought was a liberal price for the mining rights to the Black Hills, or, alternatively, $6 million to purchase the hills, but the offers were met with "derisive laughter" from the Indians. Red Cloud declared that the $6 million was "a little bit of a thing . . . just a little spit out of my mouth." The Indians demanded a price far higher than the commissioners would consider, and the council ended in failure. The matter of the Sioux hunting rights in Nebraska also required discussions with the rest of the Indians, but they quickly agreed to take the money offered for their rights, and a formal agreement was signed on June 23, seven days before the appropriation expired.[40]

29

Professor Marsh

I have no confidence whatever in the sincerity of the Secretary of the Interior or the Commissioner of Indian Affairs, when they publicly announce their wish and determination to correct the present abuses in Indian management, because I have reason to know that they have long been aware of these abuses, and have made no sincere effort to reform them. . . . The evidence now in my possession reflects unfavorably on both Secretary Delano and Commissioner Smith.

Professor O. C. Marsh to President Grant, July 10, 1875

When the Sioux delegations left Washington, Smith turned his attention to Professor Marsh. Smith had suggested to Dr. Saville, the agent at the Red Cloud Agency, that in view of Marsh's charges it would be best for him to resign, but Saville thought it an injustice to him to resign while the charges were still pending against him. Smith obtained his agreement, however, to submit his resignation immediately, to take effect after a thorough investigation of the charges.

Smith also asked Marsh to submit his charges in written form so they could be investigated. "As yet," he told Bishop Hare, "they seem to be nothing but the complaints of Red Cloud and the statements of the military gentlemen with whom Professor Marsh was in close sympathy while in that vicinity." Clinton Fisk also asked for "specific written charges" from Marsh so that a commission could investigate them. Then, as Delano had requested, Fisk suggested names of persons who might be appointed to the commission.[1]

As Smith and Delano made arrangements for the commission, they thought it wise to consult Grant, who was staying at Long Branch. In late June, Smith and Delano went there to review the appointments to the commission and the instructions for the commissioners. Three times in July Smith returned to Long Branch for consultations with the president.[2]

Professor Marsh quietly prepared his case against the Interior Department and the Indian Office. As he did so, he took advantage of an offer from Smith to provide him with any information he needed from the government's files. He also corresponded with Felix Brunot, the former chairman of the Board of Indian Commissioners, who told Marsh he had no doubt that affairs at both the Red Cloud and Spotted Tail agencies had been "*greedily* misman-aged" for the past two years. Brunot also told Marsh about the investigation Samuel Walker had made and provided Marsh with a copy of Walker's re-port and his address in Washington. Walker, Brunot said, had gone to the agencies "unheralded and alone" and had seen things as they were; Bishop Hare, whose commission contradicted Walker's findings, had gone "without experience[,] [duly?] heralded, and accompanied by the agent and an attorney of the contractors and saw things as the ring wished him to see them."[3]

Marsh also corresponded with William Welsh. Even though Marsh's charges concerned the Red Cloud Agency, one of the agencies assigned to the Episcopal Indian Commission of which Welsh was a member and Welsh himself had recommended Dr. Saville for the agency, Welsh expressed his belief in the frauds. He said he believed "the Indian Ring of contractors and the Interior Department are leagued together for defensive and offen-sive measures. Poor agents cannot do what they know to be right against the known wishes of officers of the government." Welsh too referred Marsh to Samuel Walker as someone who could give him valuable information.[4]

Samuel Walker soon began to provide Marsh with ammunition for his campaign and advice for waging it. He told Marsh that Dr. Saville had given a contract for lumber to his own father-in-law, paying four to six times the value of the lumber. "Saville is *in* the ring," he wrote, "and they handle him carefully." Walker also told Marsh about the men Clinton Fisk had recom-mended for the commission to investigate Marsh's charges. "They will be as infants in the hands of the Ring." "They are totally unacquainted with the nature of the manipulations they are to investigate. In view of this fact it might be advisable for you *not* to make known *all* your facts until they report, when you can upset any theoretical evidence they present. The whole thing is arranged, and the gentlemen of the commission will, no doubt[,] have plenty of evidence furnished them that you were mistaken." Walker thought that if he were appointed secretary of the commission, "without letting the Dep't know," they could "get the facts," but he thought there was little chance of his appointment.[5]

Delano was angry that Marsh had at no time come to him with his charges and still had not provided the charges in writing. Delano first met Marsh at one of the councils with the Sioux delegations, and since Marsh had been in the city and had attended councils with the Sioux for several days with-out calling on him, Delano invited Marsh to come to his office. According to

Professor O. C. Marsh (1831–99) and the Sioux chief Red Cloud (1822–1909), New Haven, Connecticut, 1883. Red Cloud said of Marsh, "He told the Great Father everything just as he promised he would, and I think he is the best white man I ever saw." Courtesy of the Peabody Museum of Natural History, Yale University, New Haven, Connecticut.

Marsh, when he went to the office Delano proclaimed himself "a christian gentleman and not a thief" and said that Marsh should have come to him with his charges before going to the president. Marsh said Delano also objected to his "running around attending councils etc. as though I was at the head of the Department." Delano appealed to Marsh to present him with his evidence of corruption so he could take steps to stop it, but Marsh refused to do so. Marsh said that he intended no discourtesy to the secretary but that as a citizen he had every right to go to the president as he had. He believed he had discovered "great mismanagement" and "great fraud," and he was prepared to substantiate every statement he had made when the commission requested his proof. Marsh returned to Delano's office three days later, but he continued to refuse to share his information with Delano, telling him that he reserved the right to share it with the president, the press, or the Congress as he thought best.[6]

After the Red Cloud Commission was appointed and Smith had informed Marsh about its appointment, Marsh finally presented his charges in a lengthy publication entitled *A Statement of Affairs at Red Cloud Agency, Made to the President of the United States.* Marsh sent his statement not only to the president and the members of the commission but also to the president's cabinet and then released it to the press and sent copies to some fifteen hundred prominent persons around the country. In the statement, Marsh expressed his willingness to present his facts to the commission but not to the Interior Department alone. He said he had no confidence in the sincerity of the secretary of the interior or the commissioner of Indian affairs when they expressed their determination to correct abuses in the Indian service because he had "reason to know that they have long been aware of these abuses, and have made no sincere effort to reform them." He believed their interest was merely in preventing "all publicity or exposure" of the abuses.[7]

Marsh's charges were specific and damaging. Agent Saville, he said, was "wholly unfitted" for his position and was guilty of "gross frauds." Saville had issued goods in "a loose and unbusinesslike way"; on one occasion he had issued a whole year's supply of goods in a few hours on a single day. He had also defrauded the Indians by withholding supplies he claimed had been issued. The number of Indians at the agency had been "systematically overstated, for purposes which can only contemplate fraud." The distribution of annuity goods Marsh had witnessed at the agency was "a suspicious transaction, and, in part, at least, fraudulent"; Saville had been sent thirty-seven bales of blankets and had issued only eighteen.[8]

The cattle contractor at the agency, Marsh said, was "the well known Bosler, notorious for frauds in previous contracts," and the cattle issued were inferior "owing to systematic frauds practiced by the agent and beef contractors." Marsh had himself observed seven head of cattle at the agency that were certified by several army officers as "undersize and puny." Marsh said Saville had certified that another herd of cattle issued during Marsh's visit averaged 1,043 pounds, but according to Marsh, Saville had admitted that they averaged only 850 pounds—and Marsh thought the average was really closer to 750. The pork issued was not fit for human food, and the flour was inferior. The coffee, sugar, and tobacco were also substandard, and there was evidence of fraud in the transportation of the supplies. As a consequence of all these manipulations, the Indians had suffered greatly during the past winter. Marsh accompanied his charges with a mass of printed evidence that he said indicated both mismanagement and fraud at the Red Cloud Agency, and he said he had only "faintly indicated the corruption pervading Indian affairs." "You alone," Marsh told the president, "have the will and the power to destroy that combination of bad men, known as the Indian Ring, who are debasing this service and thwarting the efforts of all who endeavor to bring to a full consummation your noble policy of peace."[9]

When Marsh was criticized for releasing his statement to the press before he had presented it to the president, he visited Grant at Long Branch to explain what he had done and to elaborate on his evidence. Wayne MacVeagh, a Pennsylvania lawyer who was also at Long Branch and who spent a long evening with Grant after Marsh left, later wrote to the professor to report the president's remarks about the affair. He said Grant believed

it to be his duty to probe the matter to the bottom and said he would not lose a day in doing so. . . . He spoke very kindly of Mr Delano and Mr Smith and seemed to think it improbable to the last degree that either of them was open to censure to the extent you supposed. He said Mr Smith's appointment was asked and made distinctly upon the ground that he was not at all a politician but a clergyman and of such high character as [was] sure to protect his administration from any suspicion of [connivance?] with fraud in this long-suspected branch of the public service. At the same time he did not seek to "whittle away" the force of your statement in the least or to evade the need of thorough and radical investigation which it created. . . . Is it possible that you may misunderstand Smith? Can he be of such crooked and perverse intelligence as to look on you as an enemy of the human race for speaking disrespectfully of the department over which his virtue keeps guard? I have known such men who gave all the signs of dishonesty but after all were not dishonest.[10]

Grant himself wrote to Marsh to say that he was taking steps to "verify or refute" Marsh's statements. "The charges and statements you make are sufficiently explicit either to be substantiated or refuted—to prove fraud and bad management, or incompetent observation. Assuring you of my earnest desire for an honest administration in every department of the Government, and [my] willingness to ferret out and punish fraud wherever found." Grant passed Marsh's charges on to Columbus Delano for use in the investigation, saying he was convinced that either Agent Saville was "wholly incompetent and unfit for his position or that Prof. Marsh is an incompetent observer, easily led without his knowledge to work the designs of bad and unscrupulous men." To make sure Delano could not be accused of appointing a commission to investigate himself, Grant personally appointed two additional members to serve on the Red Cloud Commission.[11]

Smith expressed his opinion about Marsh's charges to his friend General Howard. "The young Professor seems to have been in quite close correspondence with Wm Welch and Welch's henchman, Sam Walker, and to be made up generally after the Wm Welch pattern in vanity and [egotism?] with money. He is more fortunate however than his prototype in having an 'organ.' One of the editors of the New York T[r]ibune is a personal friend; and another editor being personally bitter to the Secretary, they are able to give the Indian Bureau a scoring daily." Smith signed his letter to Howard, "Yr's in love & *some* hope." He then went to Marblehead for a vacation.[12]

Cleavie had continued to be seriously ill, and Smith hoped the sea air might bring her some relief. "But," he told Bishop Whipple, "my fears are daily increasing that my Heavenly Father has other plans for her & me than that she shall be long spared to earth. The pain which this slowly growing conviction gives is beyond description. I had no conception of the strength of the tie that holds me to her, but I am trying to be ready for the will of God, but I find as the parting comes on I have done nothing by way of its anticipation."[13]

The American Missionary Association declared its belief in Smith's innocence of Professor Marsh's charges. An editorial in the *American Missionary* admitted that "the temptations and complications of Indian affairs are very great, but we do not believe [Smith] has been party to a single fraud. Our faith in his integrity is unshaken. He is a clear-headed man, and we are not prepared to believe that he has been hoodwinked or intimidated by the Indian rings." Nevertheless, the editorial writer could not deny that the charges against Smith were strong and that his past record and the good opinion of his friends were not a sufficient defense against them. Even though the writer said he expected Smith's "complete vindication," he could not disguise his fear that Smith might be found guilty. "Should he be found guilty, we should be greatly disappointed. We should see more clearly than ever the weakness of human nature, and the strength of ring temptations, but we should not lose faith in man nor in the Christian religion. There *are* honest Christian men, whom all the rings in the world cannot seduce from their integrity."[14]

As the Red Cloud Commission was gathering to begin its work, the Board of Indian Commissioners met with the president at Long Branch and then issued a letter "To the Christian Public." The commissioners described the government's Indian policy as "eminently humane and Christian" and said it should have the support of "all religious bodies, and all Christian men." The commissioners were confident that the accusation that an Indian "ring" controlled the Indian service was unfounded. "We are not aware of the existence of any 'rings', in connection with the Indian service, differing at all from the 'rings' or combinations, which are seen by all shrewd men, in connection with the letting of all large contracts, in other public or in private service. Where there is a carcass, the vultures will gather."[15]

The commissioners reminded the churches that the entire Board of Indian Commissioners and nearly all the Indian agents had been nominated for their appointments by missionary societies. With the small salaries paid to Indian agents, the commissioners said, it was not surprising that "now and then" one should prove incompetent or corrupt, "but we feel confident, that in this department, the government was never so honestly served, as at the present time." The board made it clear that there was "no hesitation on the part of the Government to remove Agents on our recommendation, who are proved to be incompetent or corrupt." But the board's letter also added a note of caution.

> Neither this Board nor the Government would be justified in accepting loud mouthed accusation for proof of guilt, especially in view of the fact that most of the charges of fraud and incompetency come from disappointed contractors and traders, whose hope of gains under the more careful lettings of contracts, and rigid inspection of supplies, is gone. Nor on the other hand, would they be justified, in withholding the most rigid investigation, when, as in some cases, charges are made by respectable and responsible parties. . . .
>
> There is required on the part of all good men a comprehension of the difficulties of this work, a fair amount of patience with those who administer it, and a disposition to wait for proof of corruption, before they withdraw confidence from those who have deservedly enjoyed it.[16]

William Welsh had long since withdrawn his confidence from the Interior Department and had no confidence in the commission appointed to investigate Marsh's charges. He told Marsh, "If they sustain you I will be agreeably surprised." He believed Bishop Hare's commission had been "hoodwinked" and that this commission would be too unless Samuel Walker went along "as a Detective."

> Allow a veteran to caution you against underestimating the resources of an enemy. The patronage of the Interior Department enabled it to control the last Congress completely or I would have had an investigating committee to examine Secretary Delano's doings. The appointment of three additional commissioners selected with great care by Delano & Cowen means a union between Grant & Delano to wage a war of extermination against you. . . . I pity President Grant as Delano canvassed for him & therefore has claims that cannot be set aside.

The cattle thieves, Welsh said, were well-known by Delano, Cowen, and Smith, "who are in harmony with them." He warned Marsh that he could expect to be abused because Bosler, the cattle contractor, could control the witnesses called by the commission. "I hope you care as little about abuse as I do."[17]

Despite Welsh's doubts about it, the Red Cloud Commission that gathered in New York City to begin its work was an able group, chaired by Thomas C. Fletcher, a former Republican governor of Missouri. The other members nominated by the Board of Indian Commissioners were both members of Congress: Benjamin W. Harris, a Republican from Massachusetts, and Charles J. Faulkner, a Democrat from West Virginia who had once served on Stonewall Jackson's personal military staff. (Faulkner let Marsh know that the professor's activities had "excited" his "approbation and admiration" and asked for any "hint or suggestion" to guide him in the investigation.) One of the men Grant appointed to the commission was a United States senator, Timothy O. Howe, a Republican from Wisconsin. Grant's other appointee was George Washington Atherton, professor of political economy and constitutional law at Rutgers College.[18]

The commission interviewed Professor Marsh in New York City in July and then set out for the West, taking testimony at Omaha, Cheyenne, Denver, Kansas City, Fort Laramie, the Spotted Tail and Red Cloud agencies, and the military forts near the agencies, and then concluded its work in Washington in September. Testimony was obtained from the agents and employees at the two agencies, from businessmen with beef and transportation contracts, from other businessmen knowledgeable about supplies but not themselves contractors, from inspectors, from army officers, and from the Indians. The commissioners, four of whom were lawyers, questioned the witnesses closely, brushing aside what the witnesses presented as common knowledge or their own conclusions and aggressively probing for facts and for personal knowledge of frauds—"worming the truth out of them," as Benjamin Harris put it.[19]

The investigation was widely reported, and Marsh received letters of support from all over the country. Former commissioner of Indian affairs Francis Walker wrote to wish him "great success" with his statement of frauds. Nathan Bishop, a former member of the Board of Indian Commissioners, wrote, saying, "I sincerely hope you will be able to fasten some of the many frauds in [the] Indian Department upon the perpetrators." Persons familiar with Indian affairs throughout the West described frauds alleged to have taken place at various agencies over many years. A curious letter came from the former druggist Anson Dart, who wrote to Marsh to thank him for his work in exposing frauds. "All that you are now engaged in doing," Dart wrote, "is, (I am sorry to say) but a drop in the bucket, when compared with frauds in other sections of our country. . . . I could give you facts that would [a]stonish you, had I an opportunity. You are at work at the heads of the *ring,* and I am very glad to believe they will not dare to attempt to *buy,* or sell, you." There is no doubt that Anson Dart could indeed have told Professor Marsh a good deal about frauds in the Indian service.[20]

As the commission gathered its evidence, Samuel Walker continued to stir the controversy from his home in Washington: "I am keeping the cauldron bubbling here," he told Marsh. Walker submitted material about Delano, Cowen, and Smith to the *New York Tribune,* the *Philadelphia Times,* and the *Washington Capital* and wrote an article under the name "Fidelis" for the *New York Herald,* which, he said, "has created a furor and has, I think, accomplished my object, namely, to fix the responsibility on Delano, Cowen and the Smith family" (meaning three unrelated Smiths involved in the controversy, Edward P. Smith, Francis H. Smith, the secretary of the Board of Indian Commissioners, and Walter H. Smith, the assistant attorney general assigned to the Interior Department). "Believe me," Walker assured Marsh, "I am not idle."[21]

In his letters to the newspapers Walker said he had evidence to prove that during Delano's administration "more than two millions of dollars have been stolen by the Indian ring in the one article of beef alone at the Sioux agencies" and that these were not the only frauds at the agencies. He also cited documents which he said showed that Delano had spent more than $10,000 a year on carriages, horses, and drivers and that one of the carriages was kept at the secretary's home in Mount Vernon, Ohio, for his own personal use. He accused Delano of spending public money on a "geranium and bouquet nursery" with gardeners and laborers at a cost of $10,000 a year. Messengers were taken on trips as body servants. "Private houses," he said, "are fitted up by mechanics paid by government. Furniture is procured and carpets supplied which are charged to the contingent fund." Walker also brought up the old issue of Delano's paying vouchers that had been rejected by the

Board of Indian Commissioners and of purchases made without advertising. He recognized that Assistant Attorney General Walter H. Smith had declared these actions legal, but, he said, "Of course the 'opinion' could not be adverse." Walker was sure the officers of the Interior Department were in collusion with the beef contractors, and he implied that the "pliant" representative of the attorney general's department was part of the collusion.[22]

Someone in the administration responded to Walker's attacks by attacking him, accusing him of drunkenness. Walker thought Benjamin Cowen was responsible for the attacks and turned his guns on him, accusing him and John Delano, the secretary's son, of making purchases for the Indians in their own names from a store that was "the headquarters of the Indian Ring."[23]

Walker was also corresponding with William Welsh, and he reported to Marsh that "Mr. Welsh is at work" and that Welsh's "manly aid came at the right time and now I [overtop?] the thieves." Welsh was indeed at work. He published an open letter to President Grant defending Walker against his attackers. Welsh believed the attacks had come from Cowen with the approval of Delano and that they were made because Walker had exposed frauds in their department. Welsh said that he himself had suggested Walker's appointment as clerk of the Board of Indian Commissioners, and he described Walker as "a soldier who served this country faithfully, and who has a certificate of meritorious conduct from his commander." Welsh told Grant bluntly that "every suggestion I ever made to you was promptly responded to, save only the investigation of frauds allowed by your appointees. Even this lamentable trait I believe springs from a distorted virtue. Your protection of Gen. Parker when he was convicted of misfeasance or malfeasance as commissioner of Indian affairs, and of those who had control of that office, seems wholly unaccountable except on the hypothesis that love in you is blind." He told Grant he had found it necessary to write publicly because "you have in every instance closed your mind to evidence that must have convinced any other man."[24]

Welsh also published a series of six long letters addressed to Professor Marsh. He repeated the allegations he had made earlier: Delano had paid vouchers the Board of Indian Commissioners had rejected as "illegal or tainted with fraud"; the commissions appointed by Delano had no power to compel witnesses; Delano did not act on frauds when they were brought to his attention; Smith made contracts with Wilder "without competition, without advertising, and without notice to the Board of Indian Commissioners, therefore violating three of the laws of the United States." Welsh also mentioned his previous charge that Amherst Wilder had been guilty of fraud in the sale of supplies to the Ponca Agency, and he told how Wilder had sued him over the matter. The suit had not yet been tried, and Welsh said that if Wilder had only pressed the suit and could have been put on the witness stand, "there would have been revelations of such a character as to render these letters unnecessary." In the same way, Welsh said that if the commission that investigated Smith's pine sales had investigated his other activities as agent, there would be "revelations more humiliating than anything yet published." Welsh said that Smith was also guilty in giving contracts for transportation to Dwight J. McCann; according to Welsh, the government had lost $44,000 on a single operation of McCann's. In addition to his letters to Marsh, Welsh exchanged public letters with Benjamin Cowen, debating Samuel Walker's character and Welsh's unwillingness to present his charges to previous investigators. After the publication of Welsh's letters, Bishop Hare announced that neither he nor the other Episcopal officials involved in Indian affairs agreed with Welsh and that their confidence in the integrity of Secretary Delano and Commissioner Smith was unbroken.[25]

Another series of letters appeared in the *St. Louis Globe-Democrat* over the signature "Pi-Ute." The letters pretended to be the observations of an Indian on the investigations of the Red Cloud Commission. At first they appeared to be a harmless burlesque of the proceedings. An old gentleman was said to have reported to Chairman Fletcher that "some beans and other things" promised to the Indians at the time of the Black Hawk War (forty-three years earlier) had not been delivered. The commission was also said to have received a suggestion that the whites solve the Indian problem by building a railroad to the "happy hunting grounds" and sending all the Indians there. Other letters in the series, however, seemed to be directed against Professor Marsh and his case. In one, Pi-Ute depicted "another peculiarity of the whites. If one of them does not understand what another is doing, he at once accuses him of rascality. The great defect in the white man's law is that there is no provision made for requiring every one to mind his own business." In another letter, Pi-Ute suggested that the next delegation that went to Washington should have Fletcher's "wages docked, unless he reports in favor of Mocha or Java coffee instead of Rio, and white sugar instead of brown." The *New York Tribune* gleefully revealed that the author of the letters was Thomas Fletcher, the chairman of the Red Cloud Commission. Fletcher did not deny that he wrote the letters, but he did deny that they showed any prejudice in his handling of the investigation.[26]

In September the Red Cloud Commission traveled to Washington to complete its investigation. Chairman Fletcher asked Welsh to testify before the commission, but Welsh refused. Instead he sent Fletcher a pamphlet about frauds he had published in 1871 and said that since Delano had done nothing about the frauds charged in the pamphlet he was an accomplice in them. The commission met again with Marsh, who complained about the newspaper attacks made on him by the Interior Department, saying they included "gross and willful falsehoods" about him. The intent of the department, he said, was to mislead the commission and the public and to turn them against him "for having made known matters unfavorable to the Indian service." He continued to assert that there was abundant evidence to show the department's knowledge of fraud and mismanagement at the Red Cloud Agency.[27]

The commissioners examined Marsh closely, his charges being at the heart of the investigation. Marsh was forced to make some admissions that hurt his case. He admitted that Red Cloud could have selected bad coffee to give him: "I don't think at that time I had considered the matter very carefully," Marsh said, "because I was very busy." When he said he "believed" there was collusion to commit fraud on the part of the cattle contractor and the agent, Thomas Fletcher asked if he charged that there was, and he replied, "Not on facts within my own knowledge; but from the information I have—" Fletcher interrupted him to say, "I did not ask you about your knowledge or information now, or anything of that kind. . . . I want to know now if that is the charge we are investigating, and if you make it?" Marsh replied, "I do not make the charge directly, of my own knowledge." Nor could he say of his own knowledge that there were frauds in stampeding cattle for which the government had been charged and then charging for them again, as he had asserted previously.[28]

Samuel Walker appeared before the commission and was also examined closely. He repeated his charges, including the charge that the Indian Office knew that the mileage paid to Dwight McCann was incorrect but did nothing about it. The commissioners asked him about the letters he had published. He acknowledged writing the letters that had appeared over his name in the *Washington Capital* as well as other letters that were spread "all over"; he was not sure how many there had been. When asked directly whether he had written the "Fidelis" letter he had boasted about to Marsh, he refused to answer.[29]

Smith, too, met with the commission in Washington. He admitted that he had not showed much interest in the information Marsh originally presented to him. "[Marsh's] statements and complaints were so much after the old stereotyped form, with which I had become familiar, and which every new man seems to learn by heart the first day out of Cheyenne, that I did not attach much value to them, and it is not unlikely that I showed the feelings which would be natural when I thought Professor Marsh had volunteered to be the bearer of complaints which were not well founded, and when I more than half suspected that the Indian had gotten the better of the Professor." [30]

Marsh, Smith said, had not claimed to be a philanthropist or reformer; he told Smith he had come to the Indian Office only to fulfill his bargain with Red Cloud and that he had "no time or inclination to meddle with the Indian question, though he did not believe in the present Indian policy; but that having been crowded into this question he must go through. His reputation for good sense was at stake, and he would show that he was right." Smith said Marsh had admitted to him that he had no great confidence in Red Cloud's statements, and Smith believed Marsh's actions proved it. "The fact that Mr. Marsh, at no greater distance than New Haven, kept these dreadful tales of wrong and suffering, intrusted to him by the Sioux chief for safe conveyance to his Great Father, during all the biting cold of an unusually severe winter, from November to the last of April, without in any way endeavoring to call the attention of those who he must have supposed could right these wrongs, tends to show that he did not himself attach very much importance to [them]." Smith found it remarkable that Marsh did not even write to him about Red Cloud's complaints until his scientific work brought him to Washington and he "incidentally" fulfilled his pledge to the chief. [31]

Smith claimed he had said nothing to Marsh in their meetings to indicate a desire to prevent the exposure of frauds, but he admitted that he had objected to Marsh's allowing the press to use his name "in connection with statements, which were not true, and especially to parade the samples which he had taken from Red Cloud's hands as evidence of great fraud and corruption . . . when he had not at any time tested the fairness of those samples." [32]

There was no doubt in Smith's mind that the supplies furnished to the Indians were of good quality. He pointed out that the contracts for them had been publicly awarded with the consent of the Board of Indian Commissioners and that the supplies had been inspected by reputable merchants. The supplies, he said, were equal to those used by a majority of the working people of the country "and are of a quality which ought to be satisfactory to the Indians." [33]

Marsh had asserted that Smith was aware of frauds at the Red Cloud Agency and had done nothing about them, but Smith maintained that all reports of irregularities and wrongs had been given "timely, full, and proper consideration by the Indian Office" during his administration. Samuel Walker's report had been fully investigated by the Hare Commission. A later report by Inspector J. D. Bevier critical of Agent Saville had also been investigated, and although Bevier's report gave Smith "uneasiness and apprehension," it did not destroy his confidence in Saville. Smith also refuted the allegation of payments for exaggerated mileage in the transportation contracts given to Dwight McCann. Because of repeated difficulties in measuring the actual distance between Cheyenne and the Red Cloud Agency, the Interior Department had withheld a portion of the funds due McCann until the measurement was made; the government lost nothing under the contracts. Finally, Smith called the commission's attention to the investigation made by the House Committee on Indian Affairs, which had satisfactorily explained other charges that were still being made against the Indian Office. Smith also made a personal appeal to the commission.

> I have had but one desire or ambition as Commissioner of Indian Affairs, and that is to do something to lift 275,000 people out of a barbarous and semi-barbarous condition into Christian civilization and American citizenship. It was for this purpose alone, at a sacrifice of personal comfort and inclination, that I accepted and have consented to try to fill the very difficult, embarrassing, often discouraging, and always thankless office of Commissioner of Indian Affairs. I know that I despise wrong and meanness, and that in my estimation there is nothing meaner than to defraud an ignorant, helpless, barbarian; and that no inducement could be offered to make me desire to shield from exposure and punishment any man guilty of such a crime. Up to the present time I have enjoyed the reputation among a large circle of acquaintances of being an honest man; that reputation is all that I have which is of any value to me. Professor Marsh has, in fact, though probably without intention, done all that a man in his high position could do to destroy my name and take from me that which I prize above all earthly things, the good opinion of good men. He has done this by sweeping assertions, which have been made without any proper inquiry as to the facts, and which by free expenditure of money and use of the press have been scattered over the wide world.
>
> I ask you to find the *facts* in this case, nothing more. If they condemn me, if they throw a shadow of suspicion upon me, by all means declare it, and give the declaration full emphasis. If on the other hand the author of these charges is mistaken and has made the venture of this assault without proper inquiry, then that fact requires to be so stated that the wide spread suspicion and distrust which have been created by the action of Professor Marsh, respecting the honest, hearty, effective, and hopeful effort for the elevation of the Indians, which the President and his officers and agents, with the cordial co-operation of the religious people of the country, are now making, may be remedied as far as possible.[34]

The newspaper controversy continued while the commission obtained testimony in Washington and after it retired to write its report. Walker published more accusations, and newspapers around the country commented on the claims and counterclaims, some defending the administration but many taking the position that there must be some truth in the allegations. During the controversy, Marsh and Delano happened to meet at breakfast in a Washington hotel. After some pleasantries, Delano asked Marsh when he was going to stop assaulting him, to which Marsh replied, "Probably when you stop attacking me." When Marsh continued to speak of the attacks on him, Delano repeatedly called him a "liar" and a "poltroon" and said angrily, "You have set Welsh[,] Walker and other hounds on me." Marsh said that during the exchange Delano was "pale and quivering with rage." Twelve days later, President Grant announced Delano's resignation.[35]

The president said Delano had submitted his resignation earlier, but he had held the letter "because of the continuous persecution which I believed, and believe, was being unjustly heaped on you through the public press." In accepting the resignation, Grant said he believed the secretary had "filled every public trust confided to you with ability and integrity." When John M. Ferris, the secretary of the mission board of the Dutch Reformed church, learned of Delano's resignation, he expressed his regret and said, "We have always and do still regard him as an unusually capable and honest officer of the government," to which Smith remarked, "When the rattle of a few noisy men has ceased to be heard, there will be more voices of this tenor in all parts of the country."[36]

Three weeks after Delano's resignation, the Red Cloud Commission published its report.

30

"Out from Under
This Terrible Burden"

That there have been mistakes, now and then, in [Smith's] decisions, that in dealing with 70 or 80 different agents, representing the interests of nearly 300,000 Indians, he may sometimes have relied too implicitly on the testimony of men presumed to be honest and wise, rather than found to be so, may be admitted. But he has infused the spirit of honesty into the Department; has been a thorn in the side of the Indian Ring; [and] is thoroughly hated by all those who seek to grow rich at the Indian's expense.

Edward F. Williams, *Advance*, November 11, 1875

The report of the Red Cloud Commission was comprehensive; with transcripts of the testimony given to the commission, the report covered 929 printed pages. The commissioners fully agreed with Professor Marsh that Agent Saville was "incompetent and unfit" for his position at the Red Cloud Agency and recommended that he be removed at once. "His striking deficiencies," they reported, were "a nervous and irritable temperament, inordinate loquacity, undignified bearing and manners, a want of coolness and collectedness of mind, and of firmness and decision of character." But the commission found no proof that he was in collusion with the contractors to defraud the Indians. "We see nothing in the evidence to satisfy us that Dr. Saville is either a grasping, covetous, or corrupt man. His tastes are rather literary and scientific, and the love of money seems to form no part of his character."[1]

In two matters, the contract he had given to his father-in-law and a certificate given to Dwight McCann, the commission thought Saville showed "an unpardonable disregard of the moneyed interests of the Government" and should have been removed because of his actions. Saville was blamed, not for greed but for weakness: "As it does not appear that he was to derive any personal benefit from these transactions, his errors may be explained by that want of firmness, which caused him to yield to the importunities of the selfish and unprincipled." The commissioners concluded that Dr. Saville had not profited by any of his official actions. "He may certainly be referred to as an example of at least one Indian agent who goes out of office a poorer man than when he entered it." [2]

The general condition of affairs at the Red Cloud Agency left an unfavorable impression on the commissioners. They found one of the employees drunk when they arrived, they thought the clerk was incompetent, and they were appalled by the "low and inferior character" of the employees generally. (In his defense, Saville said that because of the "wild disposition" of the Indians he "cared more for a man that could stand by me and handle a pistol than I cared about his morals.") The commissioners also found a lack of order in the supplies kept at the agency, and everything they saw indicated "a looseness of management and a lack of administrative capacity which were in keeping with the characteristics of the agent." Saville's lack of system invited fraud and left him open to the accusation of theft, "not because he has stolen, but because it was thought that he had the opportunity to steal." The report did concede that the difficulties at the agency had been very great—especially the threats of the tribes that periodically came in from the north—and that affairs at the agency were better than they had been two years before.[3]

The Indian Office was made to share the blame for the poor accounting at the agency. The 1868 treaty with the Sioux had provided for the presence of an army officer to supervise the distribution of supplies to them but none had been assigned to the duty, and no one in office was even aware of the provision in the treaty. Nevertheless, the commissioners did not agree with Marsh's charges about the distribution of supplies. Despite the professor's claim that Saville had not issued all the blankets sent to him, the commissioners were convinced that Saville had issued them. Marsh had also faulted Saville's distribution of all the supplies in a single day, but the commission thought that rather a merit than a fault because the Indians were in need of the food.

The commissioners found much of Marsh's argument about the issue of beef "in the nature of argument upon assumed facts, rather than a statement of facts within the writer's personal knowledge." Marsh, they said, had relied too much on the opinions and conclusions of others. It was true that the beef contractor had combined with others to furnish the beef, but that in itself was not fraudulent as Marsh had claimed. Marsh's charges against the contractor they found "wholly unsupported," nothing having been presented to them that called his honesty into question. Marsh had entirely misunderstood the seven "undersize and puny" cattle he had seen; Saville had never receipted for them nor did he ever issue them. From their observations, the commissioners believed the cattle he did issue could have weighed what Saville said they weighed, and the prices paid for them were the accepted prices that year. In fact, the Indian Office was paying less for beef than the army was. And whatever suffering there was at the agency (the commission found the stories of suffering hard to substantiate), there was no evidence that it was caused by fraud.[4]

The commissioners believed Marsh had been misled by his witnesses. One of them, a mixed-blood named Louis Reshaw, was found to be "capable of gross misrepresentation and falsehood." It appeared to the commissioners, too, that Red Cloud himself had misled the professor. From testimony they had heard, they had no doubt that the chief had picked out the coffee he gave to Marsh "grain by grain, to serve his own purpose." They had obtained a chemical analysis of the sample of flour Red Cloud gave Marsh to take to the president. Eight percent of it was sand, and no flour like it was found at the agency. "That wily chief," the commissioners said of Red Cloud, "is as distinguished for low artifice as he is for brute courage, and the opportunity which the Professor had for learning his true character should have made him cautious in accepting too implicitly his statements, especially as he availed himself of no opportunity when he was at the agency to compare that sample with even the worst specimens of the flour he saw there. . . . We are forced to the conclusion that Red Cloud is responsible for this imposture practiced upon the learned Professor."[5]

Although the flour supplied to the agency was generally good, the commissioners criticized Smith for some of the arrangements in furnishing and inspecting it. But, they said, "His prompt and energetic action . . . in repairing his previous errors and omissions, when awakened to the conduct" of the other parties involved, "evinced an honest purpose to protect the interests of the Government." They also criticized Smith for the McCann transportation contract. Despite the evidence that Smith had tried to learn the distance from Cheyenne to the agency and that he had ensured that McCann would not be overpaid if the distance was less than estimated, the commissioners thought it inexcusable that he had allowed the route to go unmeasured as long as he had. They thought he should also have ascertained whether an alternate route would have been shorter, as one of his inspectors had recommended. The arrangements Smith had made for the transportation were found to be "irregular and pernicious as precedents." Nevertheless, the commissioners believed Smith had acted in good faith and that "no loss will probably result to the Government" from the contract with McCann.[6]

"We have seen nothing in the course of our investigations," the commissioners concluded, "that would lead us to any other conclusion than that the present Commissioner earnestly and sincerely desires to perform his duty faithfully to the country."

> We have encountered no transaction which casts the least shadow upon his personal or official integrity; but we have met with many marked by the want of that vigilance, astuteness, and decision of character which should belong to the head of that important Bureau. We have already had occasion ... to comment upon acts of the Commissioner which exhibit a want of due diligence and a liability to be deceived and imposed upon by cunning and unprincipled men. ... In addition ... the forms of contracts, as prepared in the Indian Office, do not seem to us to be marked by that clearness and precision, those carefully-guarded provisions, minute specifications of terms of performance which should distinguish contracts of such magnitude and interest to the public. ...
>
> It is not to be denied that there has been improvement in the Indian service under Commissioner Smith's administration. Whether this is due exclusively to him or conjointly to him and the Board of Indian Commissioners we need not attempt to determine. Each is, no doubt, entitled to a proper share of credit for this gratifying result. The contracts are now more faithfully executed, and, so far as our visit afforded us the opportunity of observation, the recent supplies have been of an unexceptionable character.
>
> It is equally apparent that the temper and feelings of the Indians have undergone a very favorable change toward our people and Government. ... We believe the day has gone by when a formidable Indian war can ever again occur in this country.[7]

Because Delano was out of office, the commission's report dealt briefly with him. The report said simply that there was no evidence to support Marsh's charge that the secretary and the commissioner had long been aware of frauds without making a sincere effort to investigate and stop them. The commission had been convinced by witnesses like Bishop Hare, who testified that he had never brought what he thought to be a "suspicious proceeding" to the department's attention, "that it was not immediately noticed and attended to. ... I can say perfectly fully and freely ... that all my intercourse with the Secretary of the Interior, the Assistant Secretary, and the Commissioner of Indian Affairs has tended but to win for them my respect and regard."[8]

Samuel Walker pronounced himself completely satisfied with the results of the investigation. He told Marsh: "Now that the smoke and dust of the battle have all blown away, I suppose it is quite clear to you that you have won a very complete victory over the Indian Ring. The members of the Red Cloud Commission have gone to their homes with a very keen sense of the loss of character which they have sustained. ... [The report's] value in whitewash is so small that nobody wants it." Walker said that Smith was "fearfully excited" about the report. "[Smith] says he would rather be 'called knave than fool' any time. The Commission almost said he is the latter! You have ample revenge so far as *he* is concerned." [9]

If Smith was "fearfully excited," it was because he feared that the criticisms of the Indian Office loosed by the Marsh investigation would lead to the abandonment of Grant's peace policy. He said people were telling the president that he had given the Indian Office to the religious people for five years "& they do not seem to care for it—some of the worst abuse of the Indian Office has been in the religious papers. They don't seem to know what to do with the medicine you gave them. Now give it back to us." Grant, however, assured a delegation of ministers with the same concern that he did not regard his Indian policy as a failure, and not only would he not abandon it but he hoped to establish it so firmly that it would be the "necessary policy" of his successors.[10]

Smith realized that no matter what the commission had reported, after all the charges and the wide publicity given to them, his usefulness as commissioner had come to an end. He told his cousin Henry Tenney that "when it came over me yesterday at my desk that I sh^d probably be out from under this terrible burden within a few weeks you can have no idea of the sense of relief I felt. I could have walked on eggs without breaking them. What next? I don't know, but *something*." Then, stung by the charges made against him, he added bitterly, "I find that I have made such poor use of the $500,000 which I have stolen, that I shall be obliged to borrow about $500 to pay my debts & get out of town." [11]

President Grant had already appointed Zachariah Chandler of Michigan to replace Delano as secretary of the interior, and both the president and the new secretary had come to the conclusion that Smith too had to be replaced. Grant wrote to Oliver Hoyt, a leather merchant and Methodist layman of Stamford, Connecticut, to say that "both the new Secretary of the Interior and myself believe that public opinion demands a change of the present Commissioner of Indian Affairs. And I feel disposed in this instance to listen to its demand. I will state however that my confidence in the integrity and zeal of the present incumbent is not in the least degree shaken. But I think a change will answer (insure) the public interest." [12]

Grant asked Hoyt to serve in Smith's place, and when Hoyt declined, he offered the position to Edward S. Tobey, the president of the American Missionary Association and a former member of the Board of Indian Commissioners, who also declined, and then to Marcus L. Ward, a former New Jersey governor and United States congressman, and William H. Upson, a former congressman from Ohio, but they too declined. Smith told General Howard he had the unenviable position of keeping an office because nobody could be found "low down enough to take it off my hands. How long the good of the service will require that kind of self abnegation I can't tell but I hope not long." He said he was "glad to go the first moment any body will [consent?] to take up the work . . . & yet willing to stay & be abused until such a man can be looked up. I would not have supposed I could stand it but somehow you learn to do wh[a]ᵗ you thoᵗ you couldn't[.] Is it grace or a thickening of the epidermis?" The position was finally accepted by John Quincy Smith, a Republican from Ohio who had lost his bid for reelection to the United States Congress.[13]

One of Chandler's first acts as secretary was, on Smith's recommendation, to make a "clean sweep" of the clerks in the Indian Office. Chief Clerk Clum, three heads of divisions, and seven other principal clerks with long service in the office were abruptly dismissed. Smith said he had been at a disadvantage when he became commissioner by "being put into a machine with all the old force still in operation." He hoped to spare his successor that disadvantage by "a thorough and almost *complete* weeding out of the old brood." When Chandler acted on his recommendation, Smith expressed his satisfaction to General Howard, saying that he

> swept the decks a week ago of a crowd of bummers who have dragged me down from the beginning. If I could have got my superiors to send them off two years ago, the whole front would have changed. As it is I have the credit of all that I have failed to do because of being obliged to work thro a force of men who had no possible sympathy with wh[a]ᵗ I was trying to accomplish, and also the credit of all which was wrong that my clerks have led me to do. This latter, however, so far as I can see, is not anything of moment if indeed there is anything at all, but the miserable hounds whom I have kicked out at last are now trying to sell their "papers" to newspaper men[.] These consist of memoranda made up from the office records of any irregularities or regular [transactions?] upon which side lights can be thrown so as to give them a bad look. Fortunately I don't know of anything to fear so that I don't scare very well. . . .
>
> Well, Genˡ, this is a funny world. The Jubilees sing it[,] "I'm sometimes up & sometimes down" & it is about as funny being down as up if you don't take [it] to heart too much. I know I have done a good work for the Indians. This is the way I put it to myself & there is no use of modesty when you are only talking to y'rself. I know that I have done it without wrong doing being mixed with it, so far as I am concerned.

Chandler showed his confidence in Smith not only by following his advice in the dismissals but by asking Smith to take the place of Ashton White, who had been removed from his position as head of the Indian Division in the Interior Department, the secretary's liaison with the Indian Office. Smith did not accept that position but did agree to stay on as commissioner until his successor arrived.[14]

Constant controversies occupied Smith in his last weeks in office. General John Pope and other military officers in the West had published statements critical of the Indian Office's slowness in supplying the western agencies, which they thought could lead to hostilities. President Grant had been informed that during two months that summer "not one pound of supplies of any description" except beef had been received at Fort Sill, and he asked for an explanation. The explanation given by the Interior Department was that the delivery of the supplies had been impossible because a bridge was under construction at that time, but it was also respectfully reported to the president that army officers were inclined to "magnify and exaggerate" the faults of the Indian Office. Smith said that the Indians were well supplied with beef and in no danger of starvation: "I submit . . . that the alarm raised as to the danger of war, if these Indians do not receive coffee and sugar, is without sufficient basis." (On another occasion, Smith had told Annie Wittenmyer that there was "a grand effort all along the line to break down the attempt to civilize Indians by any other power or means than such as gentlemen with the belt & bayonet are prepared to prescribe.")[15]

A controversy had also erupted at the White Earth Reservation, where Catholic and Protestant missionaries were quarreling, and Smith asked the cooperation of the Board of Indian Commissioners in investigating the complaints he had received from the reservation. The Osages had brought charges against their agent, Isaac Gibson, which resulted in an investigation of his conduct. Gibson was found innocent of the charges, but Smith thought the conflicts they caused required a change of agents. The new agent, Smith said, should have the "ability to manage unreasonable men without provoking personal animosities." An attorney recently nominated by the Methodists for the Fort Peck Agency was indicted for forgery and suspended from practicing law for receiving illegal fees. Smith learned about the agent's legal difficulties after his appointment, while he was on his way to his agency, and suspended him from his duties. The *New York Herald* was also publishing sensational stories about Indian frauds at the Fort Berthold Agency.[16]

In the latter part of his service as commissioner, Smith uncharacteristically showed an interest in Indian culture. As preparations were made for the celebration of the nation's centennial in 1876, Spencer F. Baird, the assistant secretary of the Smithsonian Institution, obtained Smith's cooperation in gathering artifacts for an Indian exhibit at the Centennial Exhibition in Philadelphia. Several expeditions were sent out to gather materials, and Smith directed his agents to gather additional materials. He asked for "implements and utensils, the weapons of war and the chase, articles used in the preparation of food, for locomotion, for dress and ornament, and in religious and funeral ceremonies, plays, games, amusements and in short everything in use among the Indians at the present time." Relics of former times found in graves, mounds, or heaps of shells were also wanted. The completeness of the exhibit was, Smith said, a matter of great importance to the Indian Office.[17]

Shortly before he left office, Smith reported that Indian burial places in southern California had already yielded three tons of materials for the exhibit. A fifty-foot canoe had been obtained from Washington Territory and also materials for the erection of a large Indian residence on the exhibition grounds, to be furnished with the furniture of the northwest Indians. Smith also proposed a living exhibit of twelve Indian families. "Such a display," he said, "representing the American Indian in his appropriate surroundings, dwelling in his particular residence, practising his own arts, and illustrating the different habits of such extremes as the Seminoles on one hand and the Aleutian Islanders or Esquimaux on the other, would be most interesting to our own citizens, and very attractive to the European visitors, and would I believe, leave a record of more permanent value to scientists and scholars, than any other feature of the centennial exposition." [18]

As he was preparing to leave office, Smith published his third and last annual report as commissioner. He called attention to the "encouraging tenor" of the reports of his agents, "conveying unmistakable evidence of a year of advance in the civilization of Indians." Although public attention had been focused on the Sioux in their "disturbed condition," encouraging reports had been received from a large proportion of the remaining 225,000 Indians; 42,638 male Indians had begun to support themselves "by labor with their own hands" and had raised a considerable crop. Lands cultivated by Indians had increased 149 percent since 1871. The number of Indian families living in houses had nearly doubled in the same period.[19]

The commissioner pronounced his office's cooperation with religious bodies a success. That cooperation had provided a better class of officers than political appointments could provide, and it brought "to the aid of the Government the sympathies and co-operation of a large number of the best citizens of the country." With years of experience behind him, he said that "no movements for changing the character and habits and prevailing condition of a people or a class can attain anything worthy the name of success without calling for the help which a volunteer benevolent or religious organization outside of the Government alone can give." And he cited the work of the Sanitary and Christian commissions, the prison associations, the Children's Aid Society, and other relief societies to prove his point. The cooperation of the religious groups had, he said, been marred only by some interference by Catholics in agencies assigned to other denominations (a statement that was immediately objected to by Father J. B. A. Brouillet of the Office of the Catholic Commissioner for Indian Missions, who pointed out that eighty thousand Catholic Indians lived at thirty agencies controlled by Protestants and that the Catholic church had every right to protect their interests).[20]

The year before, Smith had reported that "a general Indian war can never again occur in the United States," and he said in his final report that since that time there had been less conflict with the Indians than for many years. Even the Sioux, who were reported by the critics of the Indian Office to be hungry and desperate, had not proved hostile. But the commissioner did note the probability of having to force the "non-treaty Sioux, under the leadership of Sitting Bull, . . . to cease marauding and settle down."[21]

On November 3, Smith attended a meeting at the White House that included the president, Secretary Chandler, Assistant Secretary Cowen, Secretary of War William Belknap, General Philip Sheridan, and General George Crook. A decision was made at the meeting to drop any further resistance to miners entering the Black Hills. The president did not want to rescind the order forbidding their entry, but he had decided that the use of troops was only making matters worse. He later reported to Congress that because gold was found in paying quantities in the Black Hills, any further attempt to remove the miners would only result in the desertion of the troops sent to remove them.

A decision was also made to use force against the nontreaty Sioux. These were the Indians most opposed to giving up the Black Hills, and Grant and his advisers thought their submission would settle the vexed question of the Indians' cession of the Black Hills. Six days after the meeting at the White House, Inspector E. C. Watkins, who had just completed an inspection of the Sioux country, provided additional justification for the decision when he reported on the "wild and hostile bands" under Sitting Bull and other chiefs. He described their repeated raids against settlers and other Indian tribes and concluded: "The true policy, in my judgment, is to send troops against them in the winter, the sooner the better, and *whip* them into subjection." On December 6, at Chandler's direction, Smith instructed the Sioux agents to notify all the roaming tribes to move onto the reservations by January 31, 1876. If they did not, they would be declared hostile and would be subject to military force. With this directive, given in his last week in office, Smith set in motion the series of events that ended with Custer's defeat on the Little Big Horn six months later.[22]

The following day, Smith issued a circular to several agencies, including the Red Cloud and Spotted Tail agencies, on which the government was under no legal obligation to issue supplies to the Indians. Because the supplies were a "pure gratuity," Smith thought their issue was subject to whatever conditions the government saw fit to impose, and he directed his agents to use the supplies to "promote discipline and civilization." "The whole tendency of tribal control," he said, "is against the policy of civilization. Any method which tends to bring the individual Indian to assert himself is desirable." The agents, therefore, were no longer to issue supplies to chiefs for their bands but rather to families and individuals. They were also to make "good behavior" on the part of the Indians a condition for receiving supplies, and they were authorized to use luxuries like coffee, sugar, and tobacco to enforce good behavior and particularly to enforce "regular and punctual school attendance." The agents were no longer to issue cloth for tepees but were to inform the Indians that they were expected to build houses "by their own labor." Smith told the agents they could use the leverage of supplies to promote any plans they had for the benefit of the Indians.[23]

Before he left office, Smith wanted to dispose of the five thousand bottles of Anson Dart's Sanitary Specific he had bought shortly after he became commissioner and which had been stored in the office ever since. He asked Dr. Josiah Curtis, the head of the Medical and Educational Division of the Office of Indian Affairs, what he should do with the medicine. Curtis convened an official board, which declared the Sanitary Specific "utterly useless." Then Curtis told Smith that if he made any attempt to issue it, "its use would attach an odor to him as long as he lived." "If you must do something with it," Curtis said, "my advice is to pitch it into the Potomac River."[24]

Smith turned his office over to John Q. Smith on December 11, 1875. Secretary Chandler, however, asked him to stay on for a short time to acquaint the new commissioner with his duties, and Smith agreed to do so "for his sake & for the sake of the work." He confided to George Whipple that he was not sure what he would do when he finally left the Indian Office. "About the future I don't know. If Mrs. S. were well & A.M.A. was not crippled with debt I sh[d] like of all things just now to strike out for the continent of Africa, back from Liberia among the Mohammedan negroes. That is the next great work to start, but A.M.A. is staggering & my poor wife is still ill."[25]

Smith thanked Whipple for the "kindness & faith" he had shown toward him. "There have been times in the last two years when I have looked over the list of my friends to see who of them could not be made to believe that I was a thief & a hypocrite & among them I have had no difficulty in locating you. You have not known how much such consciousness respecting you has been worth to me & you never *can* know it." [26]

Smith could also be grateful for the confidence Whipple's nephew, Bishop Henry Whipple, declared in the peace policy Smith had administered. The bishop wrote to President Grant to assure him that despite the public fault-finding his peace policy had been a "marked success. No act of any President will stand out in brighter relief on the pages of history than your kindness to a perishing race." He said that when Grant took office an honest agent was "a rare exception," and the Indians were "almost universally hostile" and "almost at the last stage of degradation." Now a dishonest agent was the exception, and thousands of Indians were "learning to live as civilized men and among them are many as true Christians as can be found among the whites. For all this you are held in esteem by thousands of the best men in America. I cannot find words to express my own deep sense of obligation for your perseverance when a less brave man would have faltered." Whipple's commendation of the president's Indian policy was something in which the retiring commissioner of Indian affairs could take some small pride. [27]

31

Howard University

Reared against the eastern sky
Proudly there on hilltop high,
Far above the lake so blue
Stands old Howard firm and true.
There she stands for truth and right,
Sending forth her rays of light,
Clad in robes of majesty;
O Howard, we sing of thee.

> J. H. Brooks,
> Howard University's Alma Mater

Five days after Smith turned his office over to the new commissioner of Indian affairs, the board of trustees of Howard University in Washington, D.C., unanimously elected him president of the university. The presidency, however, had been embroiled in controversy, in which Smith as a university trustee and a member of the executive committee was involved, and he looked on the position as an unpleasant duty. Shortly before his election, he shared his feelings with George Whipple, who had also been involved in the controversy. "Howard University trustees are talking about me for president & I am afraid they will elect me. Somehow I lose my courage for fighting as I grow older & would gladly be let off for a little while at least. Well I can't begin now to run away from duty if [it] is hard[,] & if I am chosen & God gives me to see that I ought to try I shall do it[,] just as I left A.M.A. for the woods of Minnesota."[1]

The controversy about the presidency dated from the time of General Howard's resignation as president. Two other men had served as president before Howard—both of them white ministers—but it was under Howard's leadership that the school had prospered. He had taken an active role in the founding of the university and then as commissioner of the Bureau of Refugees, Freedmen, and Abandoned Lands had provided the school with over half a million dollars in public funds. He had also solicited other donations,

John Mercer Langston (1829–97).
Courtesy of the Library of Congress.

had participated in the selection of the site of the university, and had helped
organize the university's Military, Theological, Law, Music, and Commercial departments. Then, at the end of 1873, Howard submitted his resignation, suggesting that an acting president be appointed to take his place.
The man he suggested for the position was John Mercer Langston, the black
lawyer from Ohio who had once served as inspector of schools for the Freedmen's Bureau and who had become dean of the university's Law Department. The trustees did not accept Howard's resignation for another year,
granting him a leave of absence in the meantime, but they did follow his
suggestion and elected Langston both vice-president and acting president.[2]

When Howard's resignation was finally accepted, the trustees had to decide whether to give Langston the presidency. His credentials for the position were excellent. After graduating from Oberlin College, he returned to
obtain a degree in theology, and then read law and was admitted to the Ohio
bar. He had been dean of Howard's Law Department since 1870. For those
trustees concerned about religious affiliation, Langston attended the First
Congregational Church in Washington and paid pew rent to the church, even
though he was never a member of it or any other church. But during his service as acting president, the university had experienced financial difficulties.
The Panic of 1873, the end of aid from the Freedmen's Bureau, and the
loss of General Howard's leadership all played a part in the difficulties, but
Langston received some of the blame. At one point Smith said the trustees

had to "push" Langston into "the collection field." Langston's personality also hampered his candidacy; those who worked with him found him vain, overly precise about details, "as proud as Lucifer," extremely sensitive to criticism, and somewhat arrogant. In November 1874, Smith told General Howard that "the feeling is . . . getting very decided that there must be a change in the control" of the university, and he himself spoke of "disposing" of Langston. The trustees, however, were not agreed on the matter, and it soon appeared that their difference of opinion about Langston was influenced by racial considerations.[3]

General Howard's resignation was accepted at a meeting of the trustees on Christmas Day 1874. In anticipation of the election of a new president, twenty students from Langston's Law Department submitted a petition asking that "Langston's color will not operate as an 'invidious bar' " to his election. Other petitions "numerously signed" were submitted urging Langston's election, "mainly, on the ground that it was due to the race that the organization should be in the hands of a colored man." At the meeting, five persons were nominated for the presidency. Three of them were black: Langston, Frederick Douglass, who was also a trustee, and Charles H. Thompson of Straight University. The other two nominees were white: Erastus Cravath and George W. Atherton, who would later serve on the Red Cloud Commission. Smith was one of three trustees appointed to confer with the candidates, and he reported in January that he favored Atherton. Smith said later, however, that Atherton had decided that "to govern the University, endow the Professorships, & fight Langston, is a good deal bigger job than he wants to contract." When the election was finally held in June 1875, there were only two candidates, George Whipple and Langston. The fifteen trustees present (eleven of whom were white and four black) gave Whipple ten votes, Langston four, and Frederick Douglass one.[4]

Langston said later that the trustees voted along racial lines; every black trustee voted for him and every white trustee for Whipple (which, even if essentially true, was a slight exaggeration; only ten trustees voted for Whipple, and someone voted for Douglass). Langston angrily said a black official at Howard was considered "of small account, indeed rather a pest only as he serves to give color to the enterprise." Frederick Douglass said that Whipple was elected "in the face of the earnestly expressed desire of the colored members of the Board that the position should be given to a colored man." He and Langston both intimated that by electing Whipple the white trustees were attempting to place the university under the control of the American Missionary Association and the Congregationalists. Charles B. Purvis, a black physician who taught in the university's medical department, called their charge a "pure invention." He said that Langston's defeat had in fact been caused by the black trustees, who had been severely critical of Langston and one of whom had been pleading with the white trustees for some time not to elect him. Langston then charged that Purvis was being used by the white trustees.[5]

But even the editor of the *Christian Recorder,* the newspaper of the African Methodist Episcopal church, supported the action of the trustees, calling it an economic necessity. "While the election of the Acting President would have been a conceded honor to the race with which he is identified, that it would have replenished the coffers—replenished them sooner and fuller than will the election of Rev. Geo. Whipple is to be doubted." The money the university needed, he said, would have to come "from the pockets of the whites," and he believed Whipple's election was "best for the Institution and best for the race." In the end, Langston resigned from his posts at the university, and George Whipple, probably because of the controversy and the low morale it caused in the school, declined the presidency. Six months after Whipple's election, on December 16, 1875, Smith was elected president by a unanimous vote.[6]

Smith had no hesitation about taking the place some thought belonged to Langston. He clearly did not care for Langston, perhaps because of the professor's personality. Smith thought too that Langston's religious views were not suited to the university; he said Langston had instilled a spirit of skepticism in the upper classes and that he sneered at missionaries. But Smith also had reservations about black leadership in such an important position. Earlier he had told General Howard that the black commissioner of the Freedman's Bank (Robert Purvis) had scuttled a bill for the relief of the bank when he discovered "it would likely deprive him of his $3,000 dollar Office. . . . It is only another instance," Smith said, "of [the] peril of colored manipulation. If Howard U. is stranded it will be on that African beach."[7]

Smith reported to General Howard that Langston was "very bitter" and was threatening the trustees with the loss of the university's Miner Fund of $31,000 and with the possibility of opening a rival law school. But, Smith said, "the University on the whole is doing much better since he was sloughed off. Scholars not so many nor teachers, but harmony & industry abound, both among Professors[,] pupils & trustees."[8]

Except for its finances, the university was indeed doing well. The Academical Branch had grown to include Preparatory and College departments as well as a Normal Department with a model school. The Professional Branch consisted of departments of medicine, law, and theology. There were 309 students in the university—white as well as black—21 faculty members, with both black and white teachers in each of the school's departments, a general library of some seven thousand volumes, additional libraries in the professional departments, and a budget of more than $70,000. The university was located on "a commanding and beautiful site just outside of the city proper, on the north, at the head of Seventh Street." The location was considered "one of the most desirable and healthy on the outskirts of the city" and had the advantage of easy access by the city's streetcars. The main building, four stories high, contained lecture rooms, the library, a chapel, "philosophical rooms, museum, and offices." Two other buildings provided accommodations for the students and teachers, and separate buildings housed the Medical Department.[9]

Smith's election to the presidency came just at the end of the autumn term, and with winter vacation approaching, he accepted an invitation to attend the dedication of a new building, Jubilee Hall, at Fisk University in Nashville, Tennessee. Fisk had outgrown the buildings Smith, Erastus Cravath, and John Eaton had obtained a decade before, and a new location for the university was needed. George L. White, the school's music teacher, thought of creating a singing group to raise money for a new building and a new site, and the famed Jubilee Singers had begun their concert tours in 1871. Cleavie Smith was one of those who assisted the singers when they came to New York on tour. It was said that when the singers began their "hazardous experiment" Cleavie welcomed them to her Brooklyn home, "almost gave it up to their service, enlisted her Christian neighbors in their behalf, and thus for many weeks provided for them until they had sung themselves into favor in the churches of New York and vicinity."[10]

The Fisk Jubilee Singers were successful in their efforts, and the new university building, Jubilee Hall, built with the proceeds of their concerts, was dedicated on New Year's Day 1876. It stood in marked contrast to the abandoned construction corps hospital that was the university's first home. Jubilee Hall was made of "the best pressed brick, with stone trimmings," at a cost of $120,000. It contained 120 rooms and was "supplied with all the conveniences of water, steam and gas." The front halls and stairways were wainscoted with wood brought from the American Missionary Association's Mendi mission in Sierra Leone. Michael Strieby quoted Madame de Staël's remark that "architecture is frozen music" as being particularly appropriate to the occasion; the music of the Jubilee Singers, he said, "has by a magic touch been solidified into this beautiful specimen of architecture."[11]

General Fisk, the president of the university's board of trustees, was present for the dedication, as were Tennessee governor James D. Porter, AMA secretary Michael Strieby, a large number of visitors, black and white, and the Sixteenth Infantry Band, which played both "Yankee Doodle" and "Dixie" for the occasion. General Fisk praised George White for his efforts. With

Jubilee Hall, Fisk University. Funds for building the hall were raised in concert
tours by the Fisk Jubilee Singers. W. E. B. Du Bois said that "Jubilee Hall seemed
ever made of the songs themselves, and its bricks were red with the blood and dust
of toil. Out of them rose for me morning, noon, and night, bursts of wonderful
melody, full of the voices of my brothers and sisters, full of the voices of the past."
Courtesy of Fisk University Library's Special Collections.

good grace, Fisk confessed that when White had proposed the singing tours
and asked for support, he had told him "not to think of such a thing; that he
would bring disgrace upon us all, and [I] told him to stay at home and do his
work." Fisk said White had replied that he trusted in God and not in General
Fisk, and then he went ahead with the tours that proved so successful.[12]

When Smith spoke, he recited the story of the school's founding and gave
credit for the school's success to its teachers.

> What it cost then and costs now to be identified with and responsible for such
> a school, none of us who have not tried it can know. The world has its roll of
> honor, and sometimes the names and deeds inscribed thereon get intermingled
> with a strange incongruity; but even now as the years go by, those who have

lived and died unselfishly for others, are steadily pushed towards the top, and when that which is in part has passed, and we know as we are known, high up among those who followed most closely in the foot steps of their Great Master, and are best fitted for the purest joy and highest duty of heaven, will be found the names of the young men who left business and professional prospects, and cultured Christian women who gave up home and consented to be outcasts in this city from society, ay, what is called Christian society, and toiled and prayed and hoped through those early years in the old barrack buildings. My friends, when hereafter the question is asked, Who originated Fisk University? let the answer be, It was founded in the loving patient toil of its first teachers.[13]

After brief visits to Chattanooga and Atlanta, Smith returned to Washington and then shared his experiences in the South and his plans for the future with General Howard, writing from the general's desk in the president's office at Howard University. "The first non business letter written at the old table & before the pen rack & ink stand & paper weight which used to serve in rotation for a right arm to Gen[l] Howard shall be to him, my very dear, I almost said, best friend." He described his trip to Nashville, Chattanooga, and Atlanta to "look at the old places of first things in the F[reedmen's] B[ureau] & A.M.A. work."

It is worth going a long way to see the improvement manifest on every side. Y'r white [aproned?] boy in Atlanta who was confident that the people were rising was not mistaken. He is himself an example in part. He has pushed his way steadily through until he is in the *Senior* class in Atlanta, a bright true young man about 23 y'rs old. He wants to come to Howard to study *law* next fall. I get great encouragement by a trip through the South, not from any marked changes in the prevailing sentiment of the [white] people. . . . My hope is in the [freedmen's] inevitable "rising as a people." They do come up in spite of all difficulties & will keep coming and after awhile take their proper place. . . .

"What am I going to do?" Who knows? I wish you would tell me. I had made up my mind to put the next ten years of a declining life, with wh[a]t "decision of character" I have left, into this University and perhaps I will yet, but just as I had said so the A.M.A. comes in and asks me to consider the question of going to Africa to explore for a mission field until next October. There is really not much work for me to do here just now. The teaching is already laid out & provided for pretty much. To beg for funds in these times is absolutely futile. So it looks now as if I might get a *leave* from Howard without pay & go for A.M.A. with payment of expenses. I will give the year's work for the travel & the cause. So if you see that I have gone you will know what is the matter & if you see that I don[']t come back from Africa you will believe that it is not because I was running away from duty but because I wanted to find some way by which the cold people of the South could be bound more closely in their idea of duty & sacrifice to their fatherland & its benighted millions.

In fact, his mind was already made up. The same day he wrote to Howard, Smith had an interview with President Grant to ask him for an introduction to the khedive of Egypt.[14]

Africa was on the minds of many Americans. The newspapers regularly reported the European exploration of Africa, and American Christians saw the continent as a new and promising mission field. They repeatedly quoted the psalm that said, "Ethiopia shall soon stretch out her hands unto God" (Ps. 68:31), and they were sure it was meant as an invitation to send Africans the gospel. They were equally convinced that the mission to Africa was a work for which black Americans were uniquely suited. Africa had proved a graveyard for too many white missionaries, and it seemed to many whites that black Americans would be better able to adjust to the climate and that with their newly acquired education they were providentially prepared for the task. Many blacks agreed and were eager to carry Christianity to the land of their ancestors. The students at Fisk University had formed a Society for the Evangelization of Africa, whose members pledged themselves to do what they could in the cause, "to pray, give, or go, as God shall call."[15]

When Michael Strieby spoke at the dedication of Jubilee Hall, he lifted up the freedmen's call from Africa. "Has not God a great work for them in Africa? Will not their color win a welcome for them in the land of their fathers? Will not the climate be less fatal to them? . . . These Freedmen have a grand duty to perform for themselves in this land, but how much deeper will their souls be stirred if they can be aroused by the grander impulse to carry Christianity, civilization and empire to the benighted millions of Africa?" Gustavus Pike, the business manager of the Jubilee Singers, spoke on the same theme, stressing the openings created by the work of the khedive of Egypt, who, Pike said, was attempting to "Americanize" Egypt. "The Mohammedans call the Khedive an infidel—and perhaps he is—for he believes the steamboat and steam engine the best missionaries at present for Africa." With the way prepared by the khedive's modernizations, Pike challenged his audience to "let Fisk University be the grand missionary college of the South for the promotion of African evangelization."[16]

Led by Strieby and Pike, the AMA invited Smith to explore Africa "with a view to the strengthening and enlarging of the work of this Association in that dark land." Those who knew Smith had high expectations of his trip. Edward Williams said his "judgment was so ripe, his knowledge of men so wide, his piety so fervent, his experience in mission work so great," that his advice on African missions would be accepted "almost without a question." The *American Missionary* reported on Smith's assignment and said that those who were intimate with him knew that "it is the impulse of his heart and the aim of his life to undertake the difficult tasks of the Christian soldier—to go into battles that others shrink from, where duty and not human glory calls." The magazine's readers were asked to "remember him at the throne of grace as he goes on this important and perhaps dangerous enterprise." The danger was not exaggerated; of the forty-nine missionaries the AMA had sent to Africa, sixteen had died in the field and thirteen had returned within a year because of ill health.[17]

After his interview with Grant, Smith put his African plans and his request to the president in writing. He described the educational and industrial work the AMA was conducting in the South and then told of the association's plans for a similar work

> in some portion of Africa and their attention has been especially directed to the negroes of the Soudan in the region of the upper Nile within the kingdom of the Khedive of Egypt. The base idea of the proposed work is Christian civilization to be inaugurated largely through the means of industrial schools similar to that established by the Association at Hampton, Virginia. . . .
>
> The Association has honored me with a commission of inquiry and report upon the feasibility of such an enterprise and if possible not only to procure permission for the experiment from the Khedive, but to enlist his interest in it and secure his endorsement of it as a [promoter?] of civilization among his subjects.

Smith asked Grant for a letter of introduction to the khedive "commendatory of the proposed object of my visit; and, so far as the facts and your acquaintance will warrant, of myself as a reliable representative of such an enterprise."[18]

The president's secretary, Levi Luckey, passed Smith's request on to Hamilton Fish, the secretary of state, asking for the letter Smith requested and noting that Smith was the former commissioner of Indian affairs "and a gentleman the President esteems very highly." He also noted that Smith intended to sail the following Saturday, January 29. The secretary of state did not reply to Luckey's request until after Smith had left the country, and when he did, it was to say that it would be improper to give such a letter to a private citizen. He did send a letter addressed to the American agent and general consul at Cairo, assuring Smith that that letter and his passport would give him all the "aid and protection" he needed.[19]

Clinton Fisk, who was a member of the executive committee of the AMA, also asked General Sherman for a letter introducing Smith to the khedive. Sherman had visited Egypt four years before and had recommended a number of former Union and Confederate officers for service in the khedive's army. Sherman provided a letter of introduction, not to the khedive but to

General Charles P. Stone, a former Union general Sherman had recommended as the Egyptian ruler's chief of staff and confidential military adviser, asking Stone to introduce Smith to the khedive. Smith noted with amusement that Sherman did not mention in his letter that he had once had Smith arrested for ringing a church bell at Kingston, Georgia.[20]

Four days before he was to sail for Africa, Smith was in New York City applying for a passport. On his application he described himself as forty-eight years old and five feet, ten and a half inches tall. His eyes were brown; his forehead, "high & wide"; nose, "straight Roman"; mouth, "close & medium"; chin, "medium[,] not prominent"; complexion, "dark"; face, "round"; hair, "grey & thin, inclined to curl."[21]

On the eve of his departure for Africa, Smith was unexpectedly subpoenaed to testify before the House Committee on Indian Affairs, which had been presented with charges of fraud in the awards of contracts the year before. One sensational report even had Smith under arrest on the charges. With mock indignation, the *Washington Star* called his detention "an outrage" and said everyone who knew Smith wanted him to "go and be a missionary," preferably in "some cannibal region where the old-fashioned hospitality of keeping cold missionary on the side-board is kept up with rigor. But that fond hope is dashed, and Smith remains at home, a jugged, inglorious missionary, un-eat, unhonored, and unsung." Though not jailed, Smith was compelled to give up his reservations and return to Washington to appear before the House committee.[22]

The House of Representatives in the new Forty-fourth Congress was controlled by the Democrats for the first time during the Grant administration and was eager to investigate the administration's conduct of Indian affairs. The House had referred the report of the Red Cloud Commission to its Committee on Indian Affairs and had also directed the committee to conduct a general investigation of the Indian service. Then, in response to charges by a Pennsylvania contractor, William J. Kountz, that his low bid for the transportation of Indian supplies had been fraudulently rejected, the committee was also authorized to investigate Kountz's charges. It was those charges that brought Smith back from New York.[23]

Kountz, the president of Kountz Line Steamers, had complained to Ezra Hayt, the chairman of the Board of Indian Commissioners' purchasing committee, that his low bids for transportation were passed over and the contracts given to persons who had submitted much higher bids. Hayt told him that his bid had been ruled out because of reports about Kountz's "very tardy delivery" of supplies under a previous contract. Kountz replied that the complaints against him and his company were "concocted by a pack of thieves and scoundrels connected with the Indian Ring. . . . I have always carried out all my contracts with the Government promptly and to the letter, and the man who reported to the contrary is a liar, thief, and scoundrel, and if he had his just dues would be in the penitentiary." When Kountz brought his complaint to Clinton Fisk, Fisk told him that the members of the Board of Indian Commissioners had been new at the time of the awards and that they had relied on reports from the Indian Office about Kountz's poor performance on other contracts. Kountz told Fisk that if there was any commissioner so new "as to not fully understand that Delano, Cowen, and Smith are at the head of the Indian ring, they are entirely too new to belong to such an important commission." Kountz also appealed to Secretary Delano, telling him that "this thing shall be sifted to the bottom" and that "the scoundrels who threw the bid out should be brought to justice." When Kountz received no satisfaction from the board or from Delano, he called for a congressional investigation.[24]

When Smith appeared before the House committee, he testified that the reports of Kountz's unsatisfactory performance had come from Benjamin Cowen, from the Pacific Railroad Company, and from merchants in Montana. He said he had never had "a greater accumulation of testimony" about a matter in his life. And it was understood that the government reserved the right to reject any bid for good cause. The testimony of other witnesses about Kountz differed, but there was considerable evidence from railroad officials, merchants, and army quartermaster officers that Kountz's boats were unreliable. One of them called his line "a total failure" and his boats "utterly worthless." Because of the complaints about Kountz's boats, General Benjamin C. Card, the chief quartermaster of the Department of Dakota, had ordered an investigation of the Kountz line, which showed that all his boats were in bad condition at the time his bid was rejected. Card testified that he would not have given Kountz any contracts for transportation at that time. The testimony before the committee revealed that this was not the first time Kountz had been involved in a controversy over his activities; some of the witnesses had themselves been subjected to Kountz's charges. One said he had had "the honor of being blackguarded in [Kountz's] paper"; another had a libel suit pending against Kountz.[25]

The committee also heard testimony on a variety of other subjects, including alleged frauds on the Kaw Reservation and accusations about the misuse of funds for the relief of the Pawnees. Charges were made about a contract Amherst Wilder had to remove the Winnegabos from Wisconsin, and a Wisconsin lawyer challenged Smith's right to use force in their removal. Several witnesses—including Anson Dart—were questioned about Smith's purchase of Dart's Sanitary Specific. Smith made no excuse for the purchase, saying simply, "I admit that the purchase was clearly a mistake on my part—that I acted hastily."[26]

James Eby, one of the clerks who had been dismissed from the Indian Office and who Smith thought had been looking "to see what lies can be manufactured about me for the benefit of an investigating Com^ee," appeared before the committee and accused Smith of fraud in the payment of a temporary employee, a black man named Boston. Smith said in his defense that he had simply changed his order about how Boston should be paid to ensure that the man would earn enough to repay an advance Smith had given him on his earnings. Smith believed Eby was bringing charges against him because he had asked for Eby's discharge from the Indian Office after Benjamin Cowen accused him of taking bribes for approving accounts and of "acting as a spy and informer to outside parties." Smith told the committee he was aware of Eby's "bitter denunciation of me, and his determination to pursue me." Eby in turn said Smith was hostile toward him because he believed Eby had furnished information to Samuel Walker. He denied that he had given information to Walker but said he had talked to "men like William W[e]lsh and others."[27]

John Smoot, whom Smith had also dismissed from the Indian Office and who had tried to blackmail Smith earlier, also appeared before the committee. He said that Amherst Wilder had given him $300 to leave Washington, and he implied that it was because of his knowledge about frauds in the Indian Office. Smoot also said he had seen Smith leaving Wilder's room just before Wilder paid him the money. Wilder and other persons from Minnesota, however, testified that after Smoot's dismissal he had been almost constantly drunk and, being from their state, had come to them for help. Wilder said the money he gave Smoot was a loan to enable him to return to his family in Minnesota. Smoot also testified that Smith was $300,000 behind in his accounts from his service as the agent for the Chippewas, "for which he has not accounted for a cent." While Smith was commissioner, Smoot said, he was adjusting those accounts; he had sent his niece to White Earth to settle them. "In other words he manipulated the whole thing, and arranged it and fixed it to suit himself."[28]

Smith's accounts from Minnesota were in fact unsettled. He told the committee they had been presented to the Treasury Department, but because the accounts of several agents who preceded him in Minnesota had not been settled, his were still awaiting review by the auditors. Minnie Cook testified that Smith had sent her back to White Earth not to help with his own accounts but to help with the accounts of his successor and that most of her work on Smith's accounts in Washington was simply transferring to government forms accounts that had already been prepared.[29]

The committee continued to take testimony after Smith finally left for Africa. C. H. Beaulieu, a mixed-blood clerk at the store on the White Earth Reservation, accused Smith of dealing in half-breed scrip while he was an agent, a charge that Charles Ruffee had also made in an official report on the Chippewas of Minnesota a year before. Minnie Cook and several agency employees testified that Smith had helped various mixed-bloods sell their scrip to other parties but only to ensure that they received a good price for it; Smith himself, they said, received nothing from the sales.[30]

When the Committee on Indian Affairs reported on its investigation— the first report of its kind by a Democratic-controlled committee during the Grant administration—it was harsh in its judgment of Grant's Indian policy. The president's policy had not shown good results, it said, either in civilizing the Indians or in curbing expenditures. The allotment of agencies to religious bodies did not seem to the committee to be "expedient under our system of government." And whatever value the Board of Indian Commissioners had was undercut when Congress gave the secretary of the interior the authority to overrule the board's recommendations about expenditures.[31]

The committee was also harsh in its judgment of Smith, calling his appointment "peculiarly unfortunate." His entering another office when his accounts as an Indian agent remained unsettled was said to be in violation of federal law and gave him the opportunity to "cover up by mal-administration" any previous irregularity in his accounts.[32]

Nor did the committee think Smith qualified for the office of commissioner. During his testimony, Smith had illustrated the complexity of Indian accounts by saying that "he could not take the place of one of his clerks in the Indian Office and perform its duties satisfactorily," and the committee took his statement as an admission of his unsuitability for his office. The committee dismissed the charges about Smith's conduct as the Chippewa agent as "indirect" and "hearsay," but it had no hesitation about condemning one of his acts as commissioner: his purchase of Anson Dart's Sanitary Specific, a medicine it declared "wholly worthless in itself, and for an object almost without excuse." Smith's credulity in making the purchase was, the committee said, either "that of an incompetent or unfaithful officer. For the very purpose for which the article purchased was to be used, was sufficient to condemn it. That to Christianize the Indian and lead him away from immoral practices, he should be provided with the means of avoiding the evil results of the immorality, would seem to contradict accepted theories of morals and sound policy. . . . While there is no evidence to satisfy [the committee] that the Commissioner received any part of the proceeds of this sale, yet it was so clearly wrong, so immoral in its tendencies and so highly descreditable to the department, that in the opinion of the committee, it deserves the severest censure." [33]

The committee also censured Smith for rejecting William Kountz's bid for transportation. The evidence of Kountz's inability to provide the service he bid for was, in the committee's judgment, "meagre[,] and aside from the opinions of certain army officers[,] whose knowledge extended to army transportation only [and] who had been personally dissatisfied with Mr[.] Kountz[,] was vague and insufficient." The committee thought the government's rejection of Kountz's bid showed "favoritism and partiality towards its preferred friends at the expense of the government and in violation of fair dealing." [34]

The testimony convinced the committee that the "management of our Indian Affairs has been very unsatisfactory and in many instances disgracefully corrupt." The members of the committee found the management of John Q. Smith a decided improvement and expressed their belief "that much more may be hoped for, from the present Commissioner in the way of enlightened and honest management than was realized from the administration of his immediate predecessors." [35]

There was, however, not as clean a break in the management of Indian affairs as the committee thought. Barclay White, the Quaker superintendent of Indian affairs, visited Washington in February and was surprised to see Edward Smith, who had been out of office for two months, in John Q. Smith's private office. The new commissioner had kept Minnie Cook as his confidential clerk with a desk in his own office, and White observed that when John Q. Smith left the room, Edward Smith came in and told Minnie to drop the appropriation for the salary of a matron at the Santee Agency, an item the Quakers had specifically asked to have included in the appropriations. White found the episode "very discouraging." [36]

The former commissioner also used Minnie's services to reply to objections the Treasury Department auditor had to his accounts as Indian agent. The auditor had finally reviewed the accounts and listed his objections to them. Shortly before he left the country, Smith dictated his replies to the objections to Minnie for transmittal to the auditor.

Smith expressed his hope that the auditor would "make due allowance for the fact that in my two years service in Minnesota I performed more than six years of ordinary agency labor and that in keeping my accounts I had but one clerk" (alluding to the fact that after he left Minnesota three agents were assigned to do the work he had done himself). Smith also said he had not been aware of the need for certain receipts when he began his duties as agent and that five years later it was impossible to obtain them, but he assured the auditor that in no case was the government the loser for not having them. He added a personal appeal: "I entered upon the work of elevating the Mississippi Chippewas with the enthusiasm of zeal and hope. I labored most diligently night and day. I succeeded beyond the expectations of the friends of the Chippewas and accomplished more within the two years of my administration than had ever been done before in all the years and with all the money expended in Minnesota. I do not say this boastfully but as an apology for not presenting my accounts in all respects conformed to the requirements of the Treasury." [37]

Almost to the day of his departure for Africa, Smith was defending the expenditures he had made in Minnesota: payments for horses, oxen, meals, telegrams, salaries, repairing wagons, shoeing horses, and the like. The auditor continued to dispute the accounts, saying that some of the expenditures were in "utter violation" of laws and treaties. There was no accusation of fraud; the dispute was simply a case of an administrator in the field interpreting the rules liberally and an auditor in Washington trying to enforce the letter of the law. The auditor was not satisfied with Smith's explanations, but by the time his review was completed, Smith was dead, and the auditor finally agreed to drop most of his objections.[38]

32

Old Calabar

Abasi (God) sends man to market; when you have made your market, you must lift your basket and [be] off. [Meaning, when God's purpose with you is served, you must die.]

Old Calabar proverb

Edward Smith sailed for Liverpool on the White Star steamship *Germanic* on March 11, 1876. Cleavie and Gerty were with him. Cleavie's health was good enough for her to make the trip—better than it had been for some time—and she was looking forward to working with the Howard University students on their return. The Smiths took Gerty out of Vassar so she could stay with her mother in Germany while Smith explored in Africa.[1]

The country the Smiths left behind them was full of accusations and investigations of all kinds. William Belknap, the secretary of war, had just resigned after the disclosure of his role in selling post traderships. President Grant's brother Orvil was being questioned about his activities as a post trader. The president's private secretary, Orville Babcock, had recently resigned his position because of charges of his involvement in the "whiskey ring," even though he had been tried and acquitted of the charges. The House Committee on Ways and Means was investigating the affairs of the Alaska Seal Fur Company. The Senate Committee on Privileges and Elections was investigating charges against Senator George E. Spencer. Charges against Henry Ward Beecher were being discussed in the nation's churches. The newspapers reported about "the Tweed Cases," "the Adulterated Milk Cases," "the Naval Investigation," and "the Post Office Investigation." Looking ahead to the nation's centennial that summer, James Russell Lowell imagined Columbia asking Brother Jonathan "what she should display / Of true home-make on her Centennial Day" and Jonathan replying,

> Show your State Legislatures; show your Rings;
> And challenge Europe to produce such things
> As high officials sitting half in sight

To share the plunder and to fix things right;
If that don't fetch her, why, you only need
To show your latest style in martyrs—Tweed:
She'll find it hard to hide her spiteful tears
At such advance in one poor hundred years.[2]

Amherst Wilder's libel suit against William Welsh had finally come to trial in Washington, and the trial ended shortly before the Smiths' departure. Welsh had accused Wilder of fraud in the sale of supplies at the Ponca agency, and Wilder sued Welsh for $100,000 in damages for "false, scandalous, malicious and defamatory libel." Welsh appeared at the trial and presented his charges against Wilder, but he failed to convince the members of the jury, who agreed unanimously that Wilder had neither intended nor committed any fraud, and they found no evidence of fraud by any officer of the government. Like many of their contemporaries, the jurors were baffled by Welsh's actions and could not agree about his motivation in making the charges. The judge had instructed the jurors that for Welsh to be held liable for damages, they would have to prove malice in his actions. But the jury could not agree whether Welsh had acted with malice or whether he had acted "with pure motives, and from a sense of public duty."[3]

The Belknap and Babcock affairs in particular were on Smith's mind as he crossed the Atlantic. He wrote to General Howard that there had been "no sadder day of mortification in Washington since Bull Run" than the day Belknap's activities became known. The corruption in his own office was also on his mind. The recent congressional investigation had given Smith a new awareness of the low character of some of his former clerks. He had also become disillusioned with Benjamin Cowen, whom he had found two-faced and "capable of deceit & fraud & treachery" beyond his conception. He said he had trusted Cowen as his "best friend" until the previous summer. But now he was sure that Cowen had "played false all thro, false to Delano & false to me," and Smith noted with satisfaction that Cowen had been "obliged to resign to save disgrace." Smith wrote to General Howard that "I look back now on my Bureau life with horror & disgust. Below me a set of clerks full of tricks & fraud[,] above me the superior officer with whom I had much to do entirely without principle & daily taking bribes. . . . I am glad to get away from the fearful fight of personal & political bitterness. . . . Wh[a]ᵗ a paradise the upper Nile will be!"[4]

The Smiths planned to meet Erastus Cravath and the Jubilee Singers in London and to consult with other persons in England who were familiar with African missions. Then Smith planned to "deposit" Cleavie and Gerty in Germany. He told General Howard that he expected then to go on to Cairo

"& up the Nile perhaps to the desert of Nubia, seeking a black country in which a white man can live long enough to raise up a native Christian to take the work he leaves. . . . I do not know that anything will come of this African trip, but I hope that a way is to [be] found for carrying the Gospel into the heart of that black continent."[5]

Smith did accompany his family to Germany, but then he returned to London. He had decided to spend two months visiting mission stations on the west coast of Africa before going to Egypt. On April 21 he was aboard a ship off the Madeira Islands, writing a formal letter of acceptance of the presidency of Howard University. On April 29 he was at the mouth of the Gambia River, hoping to travel up the river to explore for a mission field, but the only available steamer was out of commission and would not be repaired for weeks. He considered the possibility of sailing in a trader's cutter, but he discovered that the slower trip would bring him into the rainy season "and thus cause unusual danger of fever." He also heard tales of physical danger—the governor had narrowly avoided being taken captive on a recent trip up the river—and Smith decided that "an essential element of an enlarged mission to Africa, viz. a protecting government, native or otherwise, is wanting for the present on the Gambia."[6]

Smith went on to Sierra Leone, arriving on the coast on May 1. The next day he took a steamer to Sherbro Island, where he visited the Good Hope mission station, one of the stations of the American Missionary Association's Mendi Mission. He was pleased at the church and schools he found at the mission but appalled at the language spoken on the island, "that most wretched nondescript of a language, Sierra Leone English, which is neither African nor European, but consists of such English words, and put into such forms and combinations as a savage, or a 'Heathen Chinee' is most likely to use when he first begins to attempt the Anglo-Saxon tongue. How such language came to be brought into use as a vehicle of thought for educated men is one of the wonders of this wonderfully dark country. No heathen language can be so utterly poor and barren."[7]

He had a "hot fever" when he reached the wharf at Good Hope, but it soon left him, and after staying at the mission one day, he boarded the mission boat, the *Olive Branch*, an open boat with eight oars, two masts with large sails, and an African crew, to sail to the Avery station about forty miles away. The Avery station was in a more healthful location, and Smith wrote to Cleavie to assure her that "my little fever from which I was down when I wrote just as I was leaving Sherbro last Friday has all disappeared. I am very careful about exposure to the sun & to the rain & am quite well[.]"[8]

The missionary at the Avery station, Daniel Burton, had erected a sawmill, which pleased his visitor. Smith reported that the mill "furnishes the natives useful employment—gives them new ideas of life and gathers a little community around, who are closely allied to the mission, and can be brought much more easily than any others under educational and religious influences." Smith found the Avery station a promising place for mission work, hampered only by the "want of an adequate missionary force." [9]

Burton offered to take Smith on a "little exploration," and Smith wrote to Cleavie to say he was looking forward to a "pleasant & profitable trip into the country. If I can keep the fever off I am sure I shall enjoy it." Burton took Smith in the *Olive Branch* some thirty miles up one of the rivers to visit a walled town. They left the boat and walked another twelve or fifteen miles to the town, which they were permitted to enter through a gate in the wall. Smith wrote to Cleavie about his trip, which she in turn described to a friend. "After sending the Heathen King, one bushel of Rice[,] a Sheep & six chickens they were admitted to the court to see the King. Such is Heathendom, & you must submit to such ceremonies or not be able to get at them at first[.] Edward has found places where teachers are wanted. The field is white, & now are we ready to help." Cleavie said that Smith planned to go on to Liberia, but she did not expect him to go farther south because "the rainy season has commenced & then great care has to be taken or people fall sick with fever." [10]

Cleavie's health had improved dramatically in Germany. She said her friend would hardly know her. "My heart goes up in joy that I am now on the road to health. Not a *chill!!* or headache, & my accustomed cheerfulness coming back. I now feel as if I could accomplish almost anything. Last summer everything looked like a mountain, . . . but God has taken off my fetters and I want to serve him more closely than ever. I don[']t feel as if I was in the same world as last year at this time. . . . I hope to go back to America well, & ready to help make missionaries at Howard University for African work. I find this work growing on me, & I long to get hold of the oars & help pull." [11]

Her husband sailed from the Avery station to Freetown, where on May 23 he took a steamer to Monrovia, Liberia. At Monrovia he boarded the African Steam Ship Company's *Ambriz*, a screw-propelled schooner named for the port of Ambriz in Angola and bound for Accra. It was a comfortable, two-deck vessel, 324.6 feet in length and 35.2 feet in breadth, built in Liverpool only five years before and powered with a 250-horsepower engine. A few days later Smith celebrated his forty-ninth birthday on board the *Ambriz*. He was but one year from what he called the "dead line of fifty," which he dreaded, fearing he would lose his physical strength and become "a burden and a drag," unable to continue life "with the harness on." [12]

When he left Sierra Leone, Smith was in good health, but after going ashore at Cape Coast Castle, he became "very dangerously ill" with "African fever"—undoubtedly malaria—and was unable to land at Accra. He recovered before the ship reached Bonny and was planning to leave the ship there and board another ship going back to Accra, but on June 13 "he was taken with very alarming brain symptoms, and from the first was confident that he would not live." He called for the ship's purser and dictated a message to Dr. O. H. White, an American minister serving as an agent of the American Missionary Association in London, for White to send to his family.

> Telegraph from Madeira asking Dr. White to tell my wife that I am dying with the saddest, saddest regret that I cannot see her and my dear child once more. Good bye, good bye. Jesus, His blessing is gracious, is wonderfully gracious to me. Dear Gerty, love thy Saviour every day in finding somebody to make better and happier, and you will find this the most glorious, blessed of all services, my daughter, to love Jesus.

After dictating that much of the message, "he seemed to lose himself." About a half hour later, he asked the ship's doctor to take down the rest of the message, which he dictated, his mind sometimes wandering.

> My dear Wife and Daughter, I would not suppose it possible to go to Heaven so blessedly, and certainly nothing but the love of the dear Saviour could carry me so easily across the river. You are the first and the last on my heart, next to Him whom I am going to meet so blessedly. My sisters and their dear, dear children come next in my thoughts; then the dear people in Washington, especially the students of the Howard University and General Howard; my dear friends in Brooklyn, New York; then Alex'r Thompson, Dr. Rankin's family, and General Howard and his delightful family of children, dear boys and girls, Gracie and Harry and dear little Bessie; then to the dear brothers and sisters of the church in Washington. I could not die happier, easier, more hopefully and blessedly than I am now passing away. I wish I could see you all again, and if God be gracious to me, as I trust most joyously He will, we shall live together again and do service with unspeakable joy under a weight, even a burden of glory. Oh! Who would not have such a Saviour! I am passing away to him now, quietly, peacefully; and it is scarcely a step to the very banquet of his love. I would like to live for more service for Him, but there is nothing else worth talking about to keep me here. Come my friends, come oh! beloved friends come, we will have better service, more glorious, in the life above. Hold on straight to the end. How glorious—how joyous—how blessed! It could not be possible for me to set out on an excursion so triumphantly, transcendently, magnificently, as I now pass away to join Him whom we love, and shall yet serve in magnificent glory. My dear daughter Gerty, love Jesus; oh! I want to see you and mother once more.

Dear Cleavie, oh! how I want to see you! I trust I am going to my Saviour; and Gerty, you cannot, you must not, you shall not, by the Lord Jesus, the prayers of your father and your dear mother, fail—Jesus loves you—to meet mamma, to meet Jesus, dear Jesus—to meet Jesus—He loves you, oh! how He loves you and how many, many poor people there are who need to be told how to love Him! Get ready, Gerty, to tell them in the best way possible and above all by your own loving, winning way tell them how to love Him.[13]

Smith died on the night of June 15, 1876, aboard the *Ambriz*, which was then off the coast of Fernando Po on its way to the port of Old Calabar in the Bight of Biafra. The next day the ship landed at Old Calabar, and the ship's officers removed Smith's body and took it to the Presbyterian mission station for burial. The Reverend Alexander Ross and the other missionaries at the mission church conducted the services at the European Cemetery, on a hillside on the west bank of the Calabar River, overlooking Duke Town, "the river with its steamers, vessels and hulks," and the beach where slaves had once been sold. The services were attended by a large number of Africans and Europeans, including the officers and crew of the *Ambriz*. [14]

When the *Ambriz* returned from Old Calabar and Daniel Burton learned about Smith's death, he boarded the ship to return with it to Liverpool. When he reached Madeira, six weeks after Smith died, he telegraphed the news to O. H. White in London. White in turn sent an eight-word telegram to Cleavie to inform her, although when he learned later about Cleavie's history of mental illness, he wished he had communicated with Gerty instead. Cleavie's health, however, was good enough to allow her to accept the news, and she returned to Liverpool, expecting to accompany her husband's body back to America. When she learned that he had been buried in Africa, she and Gerty returned to Germany and remained there, where she had been so happy and so well, for several years.[15]

Smith's death cast a shadow over the future of Howard University. The university had just published a circular with Smith's name as president, listing the entrance requirements for the coming year, when it was compelled to send out another circular announcing his death. John Alvord told George Whipple that the news of Smith's death made him so sad he could hardly write. "What shall we do here at the University? . . . We shall go forward. But who is our man now? We *must* have one of similar spirit. '*Africa evangelized*' must be our watchword. . . . This was Smith[']s ambition I know, while he shrunk somewhat before the obstacles environing, for the time being, this institution. Mrs Smith had the faith of it, & I had believed our dear brother would return with strength & hard earned prestige to move him triumphantly forward. . . . My secret thought for this school has been that I could influence pious students, *some,* if not many, to adopt this plan, *Africa* is *to be opened to Christ.* That grave of Bro Smith is a beacon light upon that shore telling those who dare follow him how they can labor, & *how they can die*[.]" Knowing Cleavie's interest in the university and her enthusiasm "in regard to enlisting Christians in Europe & England for us" and that she had already done some fund-raising for the school, Alvord proposed that she be appointed matron of the university, but nothing came of his proposal.[16]

A memorial service was held in September at the Congregational Church in Pepperell, Massachusetts, the site of Smith's only pastorate. The American Missionary Association memorialized its former field secretary, saying he "exhibited in all his perplexing and exhaustive duties a sweet and attractive Christian spirit. The wounded soldier, the degraded freedman, the outcast Indian and the heathen African were alike the objects of his tenderest pity and most devoted service." General Howard summed up his career for a memorial service at the annual meeting of the American Missionary Association.

> I knew Brother Smith first when he joined us in the field in the Tennessee and Georgia campaign of 1863 and 1864. He was then a fearless and faithful worker in the Christian Commission. His unflagging vigor, his perennial flow of spirit, his tenderness and strong sympathy that always ended in doing something for the relief of the wounded and suffering, are still fresh in my memory. *Then came* that arduous, thankless work of a field Secretary to your Association. He went from place to place establishing schools for the freedmen. He always cooperated with me as the head of the Bureau, and I enjoyed his eminent practical ability and his uniform unselfish, unprejudiced efforts to give system and permanency to our work of education.
>
> After this you transferred him to the Indians. His successful labors in the Northwest, establishing schools and industries, causing the building of houses and the cultivation of farms, where these things had hitherto been a fiction, have become historic. . . .
>
> The remainder of his labors, the endurance of contumely in that thankless Bureau, the prolonged opposition of good men who misunderstood him, these, and the like, you know better than I. He labored hard. He suffered greatly, but silently, by public persecution and private affliction. At last, [he served] in the missionary field where he was always ambitious to be, looking for the interests of the American Missionary Association, and studying the welfare of the African people, with the education given at Howard University as part of his future plan of campaign.

Howard thought Smith's last message to his family epitomized his life work and character and gave "a true consolation to his friends as, bidding us a tender and regretful farewell, he bounds forward through the gateway of eternity." [17]

Even more meaningful than the tributes of Smith's friends was that given by the *New York Tribune*, which had been bitterly opposed to Smith's administration of the Office of Indian Affairs. When it reported Smith's death, the *Tribune* charitably noted that none of the investigations of his office led to any charges against him and that the Red Cloud Commission said it had seen nothing "that would lead to any other conclusion than that he earnestly and sincerely desired to perform his duty faithfully to the country." [18]

Epilogue

A Friend to God's Poor

Love your friend with his fault.

Italian proverb

Three years after Smith's death, the executive committee of the American Missionary Association allocated $100 to purchase a monument to mark his grave. With the money, a monument of gray sandstone, five feet ten inches tall, was erected at Old Calabar and inscribed with Smith's name and the dates of his birth and death. Smith had often told Cleavie that if it could truthfully be said of him that he was "a friend to God's poor" that is what he would like as his epitaph, and that too was inscribed on his monument.[1]

Smith's contemporaries, too, generally thought of him as a friend to the poor and admired his devotion to their needs, but as some of his contemporaries pointed out, Smith was a friend with faults, a friend who almost brought on a war with the Kiowas and Comanches because of his uncompromising attitude toward them, a friend who wasted $5,000 of the Indians' appropriations on a useless patent medicine. Smith's contemporaries, however, when they found fault with people, carefully distinguished between different faults and judged them differently, as did Smith himself. When he was general field agent for the American Missionary Association, Smith received complaints about the activities of Mrs. R. C. Mather, one of the AMA's missionaries at Beaufort, South Carolina. Moved by the suffering of the freedmen, Mather had tried to help them by giving away the association's supplies "without discrimination" to anyone who asked for them. As a result, men and women were soon leaving their work for days at a time to seek out Mather and her free corn. Conditions became so bad that soldiers were sent to disperse "the crowd that trooped after Mrs. M. clamoring for corn." The other missionaries, the military authorities, and most of the citizens considered her actions not only unwise but injurious, and Smith concluded that the AMA could no longer sanction her work. Nevertheless, when he reported the matter to Michael Strieby, Smith said he was "more than glad to add that my confidence in Mrs. M's piety & genuine Christian character is entire. Her difficulty is with her head & not her heart."[2]

Those who knew Smith best said the same thing about him. When Smith's sale of the Chippewas' timber was questioned, Bishop Whipple made it clear that he did not agree with the sale, but even though he questioned Smith's judgment, he did not question his motives. He told Columbus Delano he had "at times questioned the wisdom of some things [Smith] has done as he or you would doubtless question mine, but I have no reason to doubt his integrity. If he has made mistakes I believe they are of the head and not of the heart." Later, when Professor Marsh brought charges against Smith and Agent Saville, Clinton Fisk defended them both. He said he had known Smith for fifteen years, and he did not believe Smith could be guilty of fraud. If Smith had made mistakes, Fisk was sure they were "mistakes of judgment, and not of intention."[3]

Despite his good intentions, Smith did make mistakes of judgment, and the cause was usually his impulsiveness. When he was a young pastor in Pepperell, one of the townsmen described him as "a man of remarkable executive ability; with him to think was to act; so much so that he was liable to hastily follow his first impulse, rather than wait for the sober second thought." That quality served him well in many cases; the impulsive Smith acquired property and built schools for the American Missionary Association on a scale the deliberate secretaries of the AMA, George Whipple and Michael Strieby, would never have attempted by themselves. But it was also Smith's impulsiveness that led to the purchase of Anson Dart's Sanitary Specific, which he came to recognize and regret.[4]

Smith made still other judgments our generation would consider mistakes but which Smith's contemporaries did not because most of them agreed with him. The offhand rejection of black and Indian culture—of such things as the freedmen's forms of worship and the Indians' reliance on the chase—seems to us mistaken, but that rejection was typical of the time and was not peculiar to Smith. Smith's paternalism toward the Indians—an attitude that seems inappropriate to us—was little different from the paternalism of the many other Christians who supported President Grant's Indian policy. Smith's implementation of policies designed to control the poor—the removal of vagrant children from the city to rural homes and his plantation schools designed to make black workers "content"—would not be acceptable to us, but they were to the social theorists of his generation. In its blindness

The monument erected to Edward Parmelee Smith in the European Cemetery at Old Calabar, West Africa. The date of Smith's death on the stone is incorrect. Courtesy of the Amistad Research Center, New Orleans, Louisiana.

to the value of other cultures, in its glaring paternalism, and in its policies of social control, a large part of an entire generation seems to us to have been mistaken.[5]

One could go further and ask whether those faults were simply mistaken judgments—faults of the head—or whether they were not also, at least subconsciously, wrong intentions—faults of the heart. Smith and his contemporaries would not have recognized terms like "rationalization" or "subconscious motivation" if those terms were used to explain their actions, but they would have recognized the biblical text that said, "The heart is deceitful above all things, and desperately wicked: who can know it?" (Jer. 17:9). With the deceitfulness of the human heart in mind, one might ask, When the Christian men who made Indian policy convinced the Indians to give up the chase, and along with it millions of acres of their land, were they simply mistaken in their judgment about how the Indians might best use the land or was there an unacknowledged self-interest at work, which, though not benefiting them directly, benefited the culture and the people of which they were a part?

Was the paternalism of Smith's generation merely a mistaken judgment about the ability of blacks or Indians to make decisions for themselves or were the hearts of that generation deceived about their own need to direct and control people of different cultures? Was the removal of homeless New York children to the West only for the children's benefit or was it designed just as much to protect the city from what Charles Brace unashamedly called "the dangerous classes"? Was only the head mistaken in these matters, or was the heart also at fault? But then, if asked that question, Smith's generation, who knew the Bible thoroughly, might well have responded with the rest of Jeremiah's words, "I the Lord search the heart . . . to give every man according to his ways" (Jer. 17:10), and they might have reminded us that final judgment in matters of the heart has not been delegated to our generation.

Whatever his faults, Smith was a man whose conscious intentions were honest and good. Few people in public life have had their actions investigated more closely than Smith, and the conclusion of most of those who conducted the investigations and those who knew him best was that he had tried to do what was right. He sincerely sought the welfare of blacks and Indians as he had earlier sought the welfare of homeless children and warring soldiers, and he did it at no small cost to his family and himself. The ills he bore—the loss of his son at Nashville, the repeated defamation of his character, the illness of his wife, which many thought had been caused by the defamation, and his early death a continent away from his family and friends—are ample witnesses to the depth of his devotion to those he called "God's poor." He *was* a friend to them and one worthy of respect—even with his faults.[6]

Abbreviations

AMA   American Missionary Association
ARC   Amistad Research Center, New Orleans, Louisiana
BIC   Board of Indian Commissioners
BRFAL   Bureau of Refugees, Freedmen, and Abandoned Lands
CD   Columbus Delano (1809–96)
EPS   Edward Parmelee Smith (1827–76)
GHS   George Hay Stuart (1816–90)
GW   George Whipple (1805–76)
LC   Library of Congress, Washington, D.C.
LR   Letters Received
LS   Letters Sent
NA   National Archives, Washington, D.C.
OCM   Othniel Charles Marsh (1831–99)
OIA   Office of Indian Affairs
OOH   Oliver Otis Howard (1830–1909)
OR   *The War of the Rebellion: A Compilation of the Official Records of the Union and Confederate Armies*
RG   Record Group (of documents in the National Archives, Washington, D.C.)
USCC   United States Christian Commission
USG   Ulysses S. Grant (1822–85)

Notes

Works that appear in the Bibliography are given in short form throughout the notes. Works that do not appear in the Bibliography are cited in full at first mention in each chapter and in short form in subsequent notes within the chapter.

Preface

1. Oliver H. Orr, Jr., has written an interesting and relevant article, "The Trials of Minor Biography," *Quarterly Journal of the Library of Congress* 24 (Oct. 1967): 249–59. Jean Strouse has also written about the study of what she calls "uncelebrated" or "obscure" lives in an article entitled "Semiprivate Lives" in Daniel Aaron, ed., *Studies in Biography* (Cambridge, Mass.: Harvard University Press, 1978), pp. 113–29.

1. A Stammering Priest

1. *Religious Intelligencer*, Nov. 6, 1830.

2. Report of Moor's Indian Charity School for the Year 1813–14, Dartmouth College Archives, Hanover, N.H.; Chapman, *Sketches of the Alumni of Dartmouth College*, p. 195.

3. The two essays by Noah Smith are in Andover Newton Theological School Archives, Newton Centre, Mass. His marriage is discussed in Harriet Woodbridge Cook Gilfillan, "The Smith Genealogy," EPS Papers, ARC, and in Noah Smith to Samuel Fletcher, Sept. 9, 1820, and Wm. Graham to Samuel Fletcher, Sept. 10, 1822, both in Dartmouth College Archives.

4. Noah Smith to Samuel Fletcher, Apr. 29 and Dec. 11, 1820, Dartmouth College Archives; *Religious Intelligencer*, Nov. 6, 1830; Missionary Society of Connecticut, *Twenty-Third Annual Narrative of Missions . . . for the Year 1821* (n.d.), and *Twenty-Fourth Annual Narrative* (1822). The revivals were part of the Second Great Awakening, a movement described in William G. McLoughlin, *Revivals, Awakenings, and Reform:*

An Essay on Religion and Social Change in America, 1607–1977 (Chicago: University of Chicago Press, 1978), pp. 98–140.

5. Noah Smith to Abel Flint, Feb. 4, 1822, Records of the Missionary Society of Connecticut (microfilm), Hartford, Conn.

6. Records of the Committee of Missions, Oct. 3 and Dec. 3, 1821; Letter 1013 to Noah Smith, Dec. 18, 1821; Christopher Walker to Abel Flint, Aug. 28, 1821; Noah Smith to Abel Flint, Nov. 8, 1821, Feb. 4 and May 16, 1822, ibid.

7. South Britain Congregational Church Records, 5:11, 51, and miscellaneous records, Southbury, Conn.; John King Lord, *A History of Dartmouth College, 1815–1909* (Concord, N.H.: Rumford Press, 1913), pp. 198–99.

8. William Cothren, *History of Ancient Woodbury, Connecticut*, 3 vols. (Waterbury, Conn.: William R. Seeley, 1871), 1:235–36; Sharpe, *South Britain*, p. 7; South Britain Congregational Church Records, 2:7.

9. Sharpe, *South Britain*, p. 7; Genealogical materials headed "Facts Relating to Samuel Smith, Sen." in EPS Papers, ARC; South Britain Congregational Church Records, 5:70.

10. South Britain Congregational Church, *Sesquicentennial Celebration of the Construction of the Present Meetinghouse* (N.p.: N.p., 1975); Edmund W. Sinnott, *Meeting House and Church in Early New England* (New York: McGraw-Hill, 1963), pp. 102–6, 215; J. Frederick Kelly, *Early Connecticut Meetinghouses*, 2 vols. (New York: Columbia University Press, 1948), 2:201–7; South Britain Congregational Church miscellaneous records.

11. South Britain Congregational Church Records, 5:4a–f.

12. South Britain Congregational Church, *Sesquicentennial Celebration of the Construction of the Present Meetinghouse;* Southbury Town Records, Southbury, Conn.; 2:124.

13. Hannah Canfield to "Dear Sister and Brother" [Mr. and Mrs. John Wright], May 2, 1829, copy, and Gilfillan, "Smith Genealogy," p. 79, EPS Papers, ARC.

14. Noah Smith and Hannah Canfield to Edward Smith, May 19 and 21, 1830, EPS Papers, ARC; *Religious Intelligencer*, Nov. 6, 1830.

15. Gilfillan, "Smith Genealogy," pp. 79–80. The records of Noah Smith's estate are in the Connecticut State Library, Hartford (#4090), and in the probate records, Book 16, District of Woodbury, Woodbury, Conn.

16. Gilfillan, "Smith Genealogy," pp. 72–75; Hamilton Child, *Gazetteer of Grafton County, N.H., 1709–1886*, Part First (Syracuse, N.Y.: Syracuse Journal Co., 1886), pp. 316–17; Roswell T. Smith, "History of Hanover, N.H.," EPS Papers, ARC.

17. Ruth Crawford Mitchell, "EPS: Biographical Chronology," and Gilfillan, "Smith Genealogy", pp. 78, 87, 90, EPS Papers, ARC; *American Missionary,* Oct. 1876, p. 235.

18. EPS to S. C. Armstrong, Apr. 1, 1867, AMA Archives, ARC; EPS to Mary S. Smith, Feb. 12, 1846, EPS Papers, ARC. Roswell T. Smith's recollections are in "The Life Experience of a Cripple" and "History of Hanover, N.H.," ibid.

19. Smith, "Life Experience of a Cripple."

20. Smith, "History of Hanover, N.H."

21. Ibid.; EPS to "My Dear Child Gerty," Mar. 23–24, 1872, EPS Papers, Manuscripts and Archives, Yale University Library, New Haven, Conn.

22. Smith, "Life Experience of a Cripple"; *American Missionary*, Oct. 1876, p. 235.

23. Smith, "Life Experience of a Cripple"; John Eaton, ed., *Seventy-Fifth Anniversary and Reunion . . . Thetford Academy, Thetford, Vermont* (Concord, N.H.: Republican Press, 1895), p. 168. See also Allen C. Cummings, *An Account of the Observance of the Centennial of Thetford Academy, June 27, 1919* (N.p.: N.p., n.d.).

24. Henry Adams, *The Education of Henry Adams* (Boston: Houghton Mifflin, 1918), p. 33; Whittier, "Snow-bound," in *Complete Poetical Works*, pp. 398–406; Smith, "History of Hanover, N.H."; Stowe, *Oldtown Folks*, 1:304.

25. Smith, "History of Hanover, N.H."

26. Hale, *New England Boyhood*, p. 129; Larcom, *New England Girlhood*, p. 74; Adams, *Education of Henry Adams*, p. 7.

27. Hanover [Center] Church of Christ Records, Dartmouth College Archives; Stowe, *Oldtown Folks*, 2:77, 94; South Britain Congregational Church Records, 5:4c; EPS to "Gerty dear," [Mar.] 28–Apr. 3, 1872, EPS Papers, Manuscripts and Archives, Yale University Library.

28. Stowe, *Poganuc People*, pp. 121, 250; Larcom, *New England Girlhood*, pp. 53–55.

29. Larcom, *New England Girlhood*, p. 9; Stowe, *Oldtown Folks*, 1:36–37.

30. Smith, "History of Hanover, N.H."; Richard B. Sewall, *The Life of Emily Dickinson* (1974; rpt. New York: Farrar, Straus and Giroux, 1980), p. 730; Hale, *New England Boyhood*, pp. 185–86.

31. Smith, "History of Hanover, N.H."; Stowe, *Poganuc People*, pp. 42, 184, 209, 239; Stowe, *Oldtown Folks*, pp. 379, 386; Larcom, *New England Girlhood*, p. 22.

2. Cleavie

1. EPS, "Memorandum of a straggling life," John Eaton Papers, University of Tennessee Library, Knoxville; Chapman, *Sketches of the Alumni of Dartmouth College*, pp. 195, 223; *Dartmouth College . . . General Catalogue, 1769–1940* (Hanover, N.H.: Dartmouth College Publications, 1940), pp. 111, 118, 845. The *New York Daily Tribune* and the *New York Times* for Feb. 14, 1877, have obituaries of Cyrus Porter Smith.

2. EPS to Mary S. Smith, Feb. 12, 1846, EPS Papers, ARC. Roswell T. Smith's portrait painting is discussed in Clara Endicott Sears, *Some American Primitives: A Study of New England Faces and Folk Portraits* (Boston: Houghton Mifflin, 1941), pp. 91–109.

3. Richardson, *History of Dartmouth College*, 2:429–33, 440, 445, 456–57.

4. EPS to Mary S. Smith, Feb. 12, 1846, EPS Papers, ARC; EPS, "Memorandum of a straggling life"; *The Works of Walt Whitman*, 2 vols. (New York: Funk and Wagnalls, 1968), 2:11; Whittier, "To My Old Schoolmaster," in *Complete Poetical Works*, pp. 190–92; Elisabeth and David Bradley, "Schools in Town and Village," in Francis

Lane Childs, ed., *Hanover, New Hampshire: A Bicentennial Book, Essays in Celebration of the Town's 200th Anniversary* (Hanover: N.p., 1961), pp. 222–33; Richardson, *History of Dartmouth College,* 1:244–46, 393, 2:452–53.

5. "Facts Relating to Samuel Smith, Sen." in EPS Papers, ARC. The sister is identified there as Sarah. It is more likely that it was Mary, although both were teachers. See also EPS to Mary Shipman Smith, Derby, Conn., n.d., and Hattie C. Gilfillan to "My dear Ruth [Crawford Mitchell]," n.d., ibid.

6. Timothy Dwight, *Memories of Yale Life and Men, 1845–1899* (New York: Dodd, Mead, 1903), pp. 22, 61, 72, 89–91, 96.

7. EPS autograph album, esp. pp. 13, 18, 21, 26, and 78, EPS Papers, Manuscripts and Archives, Yale University Library.

8. Ibid., p. 95; EPS, "Memorandum of a straggling life"; EPS to "My dear Sister," Nov. 5 and 6, 1849, and undated note ("Wed. morn."), EPS Papers, ARC.

9. EPS to "My dear Sister," Nov. 5 and 6, 1849, and undated note ("Wed. morn."), EPS Papers, ARC.

10. Thompson, "Mobile, Alabama," pp. 14, 16, 27, 36, 39, 125, 131, 155; *American Missionary,* Oct. 1876, p. 235.

11. Thompson, "Mobile, Alabama," pp. 59, 161–65; information with letter from Caldwell Delaney, Museum Department, City of Mobile, Alabama, to the author, Apr. 15, 1983; Mrs. Jo Peary, Board of School Commissioners of Mobile County, Alabama, to the author, May 17, 1983; EPS to Mary [Smith Thacher], Oct. 13 [1851], EPS Papers, ARC.

12. Session Minute Books, Second Presbyterian Church (now Central Presbyterian Church) Archives, Mobile, Ala.

13. *Minutes of the Synod of Alabama convened in the Town of Selma, Oct. 9–13, 1851* (Mobile: Strickland & Benjamin, 1851); EPS to Mary [Smith Thacher], Oct. 13, [1851], EPS Papers, ARC.

14. EPS to Mary [Smith Thacher], Oct. 13, [1851], EPS Papers, ARC.

15. EPS to "My dear brother" [George Thacher], July 30, 1851, and EPS to Mary [Smith Thacher], Dec. 5, 1851 (continued on Feb. 23, 1852), ibid.

16. EPS to Mary [Smith Thacher], Dec. 5, 1851 (continued on Feb. 23, 1852), ibid.

17. *History of the Town of Whately, Mass. . . . 1661–1899,* rev. and enlarged by James M. Crafts (Orange, Mass.: D. L. Crandall, 1899), pp. 80, 316, 318, 411; Whately, Mass., cemetery inscription; Levi Bush obituary (two notices), *Westfield* [Mass.] *Western Hampden Times,* Aug. 15, 1877.

18. Ruth Crawford Mitchell to Registrar, Mt. Holyoke College, Oct. 9, 1947, EPS Papers, ARC; H. Cleaveland Bush to Parker Cleaveland, Dec. [2?], 1844, Mount Holyoke College Library/Archives, South Hadley, Mass.

19. *Congregationalist,* Dec. 24, 1858; Henry Wadsworth Longfellow, "Parker Cleaveland," in *The Complete Poetical Works of Henry Wadsworth Longfellow,* Cambridge ed. (Boston: Houghton Mifflin, 1903), p. 319; H. Cleaveland Bush to Parker Cleaveland, June 4, 1845, Mount Holyoke College Library/Archives, South Hadley, Mass.

20. Mrs. Jo Peary, Board of School Commissioners of Mobile County, Alabama,

to the author, May 17, 1983. For the Presbyterian Female Seminary, see the Records of the Presbytery of South Alabama, vol. 6, Oct. 12, 1848, Apr. 6 and Oct. 18, 1849, and Apr. 4, 1850 in Presbyterian Church (U.S.A.) Department of History (Montreat), Montreat, N.C. For the Uniontown church, see First Presbyterian Church Archives, Uniontown, Ala.

21. EPS to Mary [Smith Thacher], Dec. 5, 1851 (continued on Feb. 23, 1852), EPS Papers, ARC.

22. Ibid.

23. *American Congregational Year-Book for the Year 1854* (New York: American Congregational Union, 1854), pp. 128–38.

24. Bruce Kuklick, *Churchmen and Philosophers: From Jonathan Edwards to John Dewey* (New Haven: Yale University Press, 1985), pp. 94–111; Roland H. Bainton, *Yale and the Ministry* (New York: Harper & Brothers, 1957), pp. 81–83, 96–101; Sydney E. Ahlstrom, *A Religious History of the American People* (New Haven: Yale University Press, 1972), pp. 415–22; Sidney Earl Mead, *Nathaniel William Taylor, 1786–1858: A Connecticut Liberal* (Chicago: University of Chicago Press, 1942), pp. 190, 235–36. An engraving of Taylor still among Smith's papers at the Amistad Research Center attests to his affection for his teacher.

25. Henry Sloane Coffin, *A Half Century of Union Theological Seminary, 1896–1945: An Informal History* (New York: Charles Scribner's Sons, 1954), pp. 12–13; *Catalogue of the Officers and Students of the Union Theological Seminary, New-York, November, 1853* (New York: John A. Gray, 1853); Robert T. Handy, *A History of Union Theological Seminary in New York* (New York: Columbia University Press, 1987), pp. 1–9.

26. Coffin, *Half Century*, p. 12; *Catalogue of the Officers and Students of the Union Theological Seminary*, p. 16.

3. The Children's Aid Society

1. Gene Schermerhorn, *Letters to Phil: Memories of a New York Boyhood, 1848–1856* (New York: New York Bound, 1982), pp. 4, 35–38, 70; Children's Aid Society, *First Annual Report* (1854), p. 4; Nevins and Thomas, eds., *Diary of George Templeton Strong*, 2:57, 341. See also Smith Rosenberg, *Religion and the Rise of the American City*, pp. 163–85.

2. Charles Dickens, *American Notes* (New York: Oxford University Press, 1957), p. 90; Ladies of the Mission, *The Old Brewery and the New Mission House at the Five Points* (New York: Stringer & Townsend, 1854), p. 33.

3. Ladies of the Mission, *Old Brewery*, pp. 36–39, 45, 62, 68–80; "Five Points Mission," *Encyclopedia of World Methodism* (Nashville: United Methodist Publishing House, 1974), p. 850; Smith, *Revivalism and Social Reform*, pp. 170–71; Carroll Smith Rosenberg, "Protestants and Five Pointers: The Five Points House of Industry, 1850–1870," *New-York Historical Society Quarterly* 48 (Oct. 1964): 327–47.

4. Brace, *Dangerous Classes of New York*, p. 78; Ernest Sutherland Bates, "Charles

Loring Brace," in Allen Johnson, ed., *Dictionary of American Biography,* vol. 2 (New York: Charles Scribner's Sons, 1929), pp. 539–40; [Brace], *Life of Charles Loring Brace,* pp. 489–92.

5. [Brace], *Life of Charles Loring Brace,* p. 490.

6. James Russell Lowell, "The Present Crisis," in *The Complete Poetical Works of James Russell Lowell,* Cambridge ed. (Boston: Houghton Mifflin, 1925), pp. 67–68; Brace, *Dangerous Classes of New York,* pp. 75–76. The context in which Brace began his work is well-described in Smith Rosenberg's *Religion and the Rise of the American City.*

7. Children's Aid Society, *Second Annual Report* (1855), p. 8.

8. [Brace], *Life of Charles Loring Brace,* p. 491; Children's Aid Society, *First Annual Report* (1854), p. 10, and *Second Annual Report* (1855), pp. 8–9; Larcom, *New England Girlhood,* p. 118; Children's Aid Society, *Annual Report* (1876), p. 53, written by Brace, although unsigned.

9. [Brace], *Life of Charles Loring Brace,* p. 164; Brace, *Dangerous Classes of New York,* p. 282; Children's Aid Society, *First Annual Report* (1854), pp. 33–34. The *Third Annual Report* (1856), p. 48, indicates that the description of the incident was written by Smith.

10. [Brace], *Life of Charles Loring Brace,* p. 491.

11. Children's Aid Society, *Annual Report* (1876), p. 53; *New York Times,* Sept. 21, 1854; Children's Aid Society, *Third Annual Report* (1856), pp. 54–60. The placing-out system is also described in Brace, *Dangerous Classes of New York,* pp. 223–33, Miriam Z. Langsam, *Children West: A History of the Placing-Out System of the New York Children's Aid Society, 1853–1890* (Madison: State Historical Society of Wisconsin, 1964), Annette Riley Fry, "The Children's Migration," *American Heritage* 26 (Dec. 1974): 4–10, 79–81, and Donald Dale Jackson, "It Took Trains to Put Street Kids on the Right Track Out of the Slums," *Smithsonian* 17 (Aug. 1986): 94–103. Other New York agencies also placed children in rural homes; see Smith Rosenberg, *Religion and the Rise of the American City,* pp. 210–18, 235–36.

12. EPS to Cleavie [Bush], July 12, 1854, EPS Papers, Manuscripts and Archives, Yale University Library, New Haven, Conn.

13. Ibid.

14. Ibid.

15. [Brace], *Life of Charles Loring Brace,* pp. 197–98; Children's Aid Society, *Annual Report* (1876), p. 53.

16. Dunning, *Congregationalists in America,* pp. 287–90.

17. *American Congregational Year-Book for the Year 1854* (New York: American Congregational Union, 1854), pp. 70–73, and *American Congregational Year-Book for the Year 1855* (New York: American Congregational Union, 1855), pp. 121–25; Walker, *History of the Congregational Churches in the United States,* pp. 352–53; Bruce Kuklick, *Churchmen and Philosophers: From Jonathan Edwards to John Dewey* (New Haven: Yale University Press, 1985), pp. 85–87.

18. EPS to Cleavie [Bush], Nov. 11 and 16, 1854, EPS Papers, Manuscripts and Archives, Yale University Library.

19. Smith's license to preach, dated Feb. 13, 1855, ibid.; *Report of the Secretary of the Class of 1849 of Yale College* . . . (New Haven: N.p., 1859), p. 40; George S. Brookes, *Cascades and Courage: A History of the Town of Vernon and the City of Rockville, Connecticut* (1955), pp. 139–40; Joan D. Apel, Union Congregational Church, Rockville, Conn., to the author, May 3, 1983; *Pompey Centennial Addresses, 1896* (Cazenovia, N.Y.: N.p., 1896), p. 8; *Congregationalist*, Apr. 4, 1856 (which refers to the Pompey church as the First Presbyterian Church).

4. Pepperell

1. C. Harvey Gardiner, ed., *The Literary Memoranda of William Hickling Prescott*, 2 vols. (Norman: University of Oklahoma Press, 1961), 1:62 (n. 17), 93 (n. 10), and 2:60, 95, 182, and passim.

2. Hamilton, *Twelve Miles from a Lemon*, p. 7.

3. Eighth Census of the United States, 1860, for Pepperell, Mass.; *Pepperell Reader*, pp. 65–66, 81–82, 98.

4. Hurd, *History of Middlesex County*, 3:224, 226; Records of the Evangelical Congregational Society, Community Church, Pepperell, Mass., 1:204; Records of the Church of Christ in Pepperell, Mass., ibid., 3:171–72; *American Missionary*, Oct. 1876, pp. 235–36.

5. Certificate of marriage from city clerk, Westfield, Mass., Sept. 8, 1981; Records of the Church of Christ in Pepperell, Mass., 3:176–78; certificate of Laura Parmelee Smith's death from town clerk, Pepperell, Mass., Aug. 5, 1981.

6. Records of the Church of Christ in Pepperell, Mass., 3:282, 4:115.

7. Ibid., 3:255, 283, 4:101, 142; Hattie G. Gilfillan to Ruth [Crawford Mitchell], [1927?], EPS Papers, ARC; *Congregationalist*, Nov. 6, 1857, June 25, 1858, June 24, 1859.

8. Records of the Church of Christ in Pepperell, Mass., 3:282 and 4:3–4; *Congregationalist*, Oct. 28, 1859.

9. Walker, *History of the Congregational Churches in the United States*, pp. 220–22; Anson Phelps Stokes, *Church and State in the United States*, 3 vols. (New York: Harper & Brothers, 1950), 1:418–27.

10. Records of the Church of Christ in Pepperell, Mass., 3:186; Whittier, "Among the Hills," in *Complete Poetical Works*, pp. 83–89.

11. Records of the Church of Christ in Pepperell, Mass., 3:187–88, 190–91, 193–94.

12. Ibid., p. 197.

13. Ibid., pp. 212, 216, 220–21, 228.

14. Records of the Evangelical Congregational Society, Pepperell, Mass., 2:16–20, 24. Originally, the pews had been owned by church members, but after the building burned in 1859, the society agreed that the pews in the new building would not be sold but owned by the parish "*forever*."

15. Ibid., pp. 28–31, 34.

16. Records of the Church of Christ in Pepperell, Mass., 3:179–80, 184, 227, and 4:102–3.

17. Certificate of birth from town clerk, Pepperell, Mass., Aug. 5, 1981.

18. *Record of the Graduated Members of the Class of 1849 of Yale College* . . . (New Haven: N.p., 1895), p. 118; *Report of the Secretary of the Class of 1849 of Yale College* . . . (New Haven: N.p., 1859); *Congregationalist,* Aug. 5, 1859; Hurd, *History of Middlesex County,* 3:226.

19. Records of the Evangelical Congregational Society, Pepperell, Mass., 1:212, 219–20; Records of the Church of Christ in Pepperell, Mass., 3:234–35.

20. Hurd, *History of Middlesex County,* 3:226; Records of the Evangelical Congregational Society, Pepperell, Mass., 1:226–41.

21. Certificate of birth from town clerk, Pepperell, Mass., Aug. 5, 1981; EPS to Martha [Cook], Sept. 8, 1860, EPS Papers, ARC.

22. *Congregationalist,* Jan. 25 and Feb. 8, 1861.

23. Records of the Church of Christ in Pepperell, Mass., 3:253–55.

24. Stowe, *Poganuc People,* p. 197; S. C. Foster, "There's a Good Time Coming," in *Songs, Compositions, and Arrangements,* Foster Hall Reproductions, compiled by J. K. Lilly, 1933; Tyler, *Freedom's Ferment,* pp. 477, 493. Timothy L. Smith's *Revivalism and Social Reform* provides a good analysis of these expectations and organizations.

25. Records of the Church of Christ in Pepperell, Mass., 3:215, 218, and 4:80; Hamilton, *Twelve Miles from a Lemon,* pp. 30–32; Martha D. Ayers to EPS, Sept. 25, 1867, AMA Archives, ARC; *Congregationalist,* May 27, June 3, 24, and Oct. 28, 1859.

26. Hurd, *History of Middlesex County,* 3:222–36; Shattuck, *Military Record of Pepperell; Pepperell Reader,* pp. 29, 115.

27. *Congregationalist,* July 5, 1861.

28. Records of the Church of Christ in Pepperell, Mass., 4:78.

29. *Congregationalist,* Aug. 9, 23, and 30, 1861.

30. EPS to John A. Andrews [sic], Sept. 14, 1861, Governor's Series, Executive Letters, vol. 174, no. 47, Massachusetts State Archives, Boston.

31. EPS to John A. Andrews [sic], Sept. 20, 1861, Governor's Series, Executive Letters, vol. 28A, no. 38, and Thomas Drew to EPS, Oct. 22, [186]1, Governor's Series, Letters Official, vol. 6, p. 379, ibid.; EPS to John Andrew, Oct. 14, 1861, John Andrew Papers, Massachusetts Historical Society, Boston.

32. Shattuck, *Military Record of Pepperell,* p. 30.

5. The Christian Commission

1. Thompson, ed., *Life of George H. Stuart,* pp. 128–34; James O. Henry, "The United States Christian Commission in the Civil War," *Civil War History* 6 (1960): 374–75; M. Hamlin Cannon, "The United States Christian Commission," *Missis-*

sippi Valley Historical Review 38 (June 1951): 61–64; Moss, *Annals*, pp. 63–108. The navy was served primarily by the New York auxiliary and was not an important part of the national commission's work.

2. Grant, "The Flag and the Cross," pp. 13–14, LC; Moss, *Annals*, pp. 110–21, 168–69.

3. *Life and Labours of the Rev. W. E. Boardman by Mrs. Boardman* (New York: D. Appleton and Co., 1887); W. E. Boardman, *The Higher Christian Life* (Boston: Henry Hoyt, 1858).

4. Moss, *Annals*, pp. 108–9; Basler, ed., *Collected Works of Abraham Lincoln*, 5:67.

5. USCC, *Facts, Principles and Progress, Oct. 1863* (Philadelphia: C. Sherman, Son & Co.), pp. 14, 19.

6. Grant, "The Flag and the Cross," pp. 20, 24; Lowenfels, ed., *Walt Whitman's Civil War*, pp. 103–4. For Whitman's association with the Christian Commission, see Glicksberg, ed., *Walt Whitman and the Civil War*, pp. 3–6. Whitman's commission as a Christian Commission delegate is reproduced in Justin Kaplan, *Walt Whitman: A Life* (New York: Simon and Schuster, 1980), illus. no. 37, following p. 320.

7. Grant, "The Flag and the Cross," p. 20; USCC, *Information for Army Meetings*, Oct. 1864, p. 27; EPS, *Incidents*, pp. 195–96; USCC, *Fourth Annual Report*, p. 192; Basler, ed., *Collected Works of Abraham Lincoln*, 5:497–98. A Confederate surgeon described the same circumstances on the other side of the war: "There is no Sunday in the army when a fight is expected" (Nancy D. Baird, "There Is No Sunday in the Army: Civil War Letters of Lunsford P. Yandell, 1861–62," *Filson Club History Quarterly* 53 [1979]: 325).

8. *Congregationalist*, Sept. 12, 1862.

9. Edward Franklin Williams Diary, Apr. 8, 1863, Williams Papers, ARC; EPS, *Incidents*, pp. 110–12.

10. EPS, *Incidents*, pp. 88–90.

11. Moss, *Annals*, pp. 305–8.

12. Records of the Church of Christ in Pepperell, Mass., Community Church, Pepperell, Mass., 4:94–95.

13. Records of the USCC, Scrapbooks: Documents and Circulars, 1:17, RG 94, Entry 791, NA; Moss, *Annals*, p. 611.

14. Johnson, *Preliminary Historic Resource Study*, pp. 149–53; Stephen Vincent Benét, *John Brown's Body* (Garden City, N.Y.: Doubleday, Doran, 1928), p. 235.

15. Johnson, *Preliminary Historic Resource Study*, pp. 153–56; Lowenfels, ed., *Walt Whitman's Civil War*, pp. 29, 35–36; Glicksberg, ed., *Walt Whitman and the Civil War*, pp. 69–70.

16. Moss, *Annals*, pp. 372–74; Loomis, *Christian Work Among Soldiers*, pp. 1–2; Herbert A. Wisbey, Jr., ed., "Civil War Letters of Gorham Coffin," *Essex Institute Historical Collections* 93 (Jan. 1957): 89–90.

17. Moss, *Annals*, pp. 369–72; *Bible Society Record* 8 (Apr. 1863): 54; *Congregationalist*, Apr. 3 and 24, 1863; EPS, *Incidents*, pp. 138–39.

18. Moss, *Annals*, pp. 375–76. The phrase "to see the elephant" is discussed in the

Ohio Repository (Canton, Ohio), June 6, 1866, and in John Russell Bartlett, *Dictionary of Americanisms*, 2d ed. (Boston: Little, Brown, 1859), pp. 136, 392.

19. EPS, *Incidents*, pp. 129–30.

20. Mark DeWolfe Howe, ed., *Touched with Fire: Civil War Letters and Diary of Oliver Wendell Holmes, Jr., 1861–1864* (Cambridge, Mass.: Harvard University Press, 1946), p. 91; Alfred S. Roe, *The Thirty-Ninth Regiment Massachusetts Volunteers, 1862–1865* (Worcester, Mass.: Regimental Veteran Assoc., 1914), p. 247; George R. Agassiz, ed., *Meade's Headquarters, 1863–1865: Letters of Colonel Theodore Lyman from the Wilderness to Appomattox* (Boston: Atlantic Monthly Press, 1922), p. 232; W. Springer Menge and J. August Shimrak, eds., *The Civil War Notebook of Daniel Chisholm* (New York: Orion Books, 1989), p. 12. See also Gerald F. Linderman, *Embattled Courage: The Experience of Combat in the American Civil War* (New York: Free Press, 1987), pp. 217–18.

21. USCC, *Information for Army Meetings*, Dec. 1864, p. 20; Moss, *Annals*, pp. 209, 570–71, n. 1. For a strong statement of appreciation for the Christian Commission from a Union soldier, see Emil Rosenblatt and Ruth Rosenblatt, eds., *Hard Marching Every Day: The Civil War Letters of Private Wilbur Fisk, 1861–1865* (Lawrence: University Press of Kansas, 1992), pp. 166–67, 200–201, 211–14, 315–16.

22. Stillé, *History of the United States Sanitary Commission*, p. 464; Thoburn, ed., *My Experiences During the Civil War*, pp. 50, 99; Edward M. Greene, "The Huntingdon Bible Company," *Civil War Times Illustrated* 3 (Apr. 1964): 22–24; B. W. Chidlaw, *The Story of My Life* (Philadelphia: William H. Hirst, 1890), p. 202; Lowenfels, ed., *Walt Whitman's Civil War*, p. 123; H. Wayne Morgan, ed., "A Civil War Diary of William McKinley," *Ohio Historical Quarterly* 69 (Jan. 1960): 283; USCC, *Information for Army Meetings*, Jan. 1865, p. 15. The Christian Commission furnished the "men in their graveclothes" with oiled linen "identifiers"—predecessors of modern dogtags—to identify them in case of injury or death; see Harold M. Hyman, "A Devildog's Dogtag of the Civil War," *Lincoln Herald*, 62, no. 3 (1960):99–100.

23. *Well-Spring* 20 (July 3, 1863): 108. The letter was reprinted in the *Youth's Companion* 37 (July 23, 1863): 119.

24. *Well-Spring* 22 (Jan. 20, 1865): 10.

25. I have collected Smith's letters to Gerty and edited them as a book for children. They have been published as *Gerty's Papa's Civil War* (New York: Pilgrim Press, 1984).

26. *Well-Spring* 20 (Apr. 10, 1863): 58; Reynolds, "Benevolence on the Home Front in Massachusetts During the Civil War," p. 92 and passim; USCC, *Fourth Annual Report*, exhibit G; Moss, *Annals*, pp. 519–40.

27. Moss, *Annals*, pp. 144–47.

6. The Army of the Cumberland

1. Hurd, *History of Middlesex County*, 3:226.

2. EPS's Christian Commission memorandum book, EPS Papers, ARC; EPS to

S.W. [sic] Boardman, [Mar.] 30, 1863, and EPS to GHS, Apr. 2 and 8, 1863, Records of the USCC, RG 94, Entry 740, NA; EPS to Hodges and Parkhill, Apr. 2, 1863, U.S. Sanitary Commission Records, Western Department Records, LR, Rare Books and Manuscripts Division, New York Public Library, Astor, Lenox and Tilden Foundations; USCC, *Second Annual Report,* p. 95; Moss, *Annals,* pp. 147–48.

3. Summary of EPS letter of Apr. 13, 1863, Department of the Cumberland, Register of LR, vol. 16, and Special Field Order No. 101, Apr. 14, 1863, (vol. 51), Department of the Cumberland, RG 393, NA; EPS to Dr. Perrin, Apr. 27 and May 1, 1863, U.S. Sanitary Commission Records, Western Department Records, LR, Rare Books and Manuscripts Division, New York Public Library, Astor, Lenox and Tilden Foundations; *Nashville Daily Union,* May 10, 1863; Moss, *Annals,* pp. 147–48.

4. EPS to Charles Demond, Apr. 13, 1863, clipping from the *Boston Traveller,* Apr. 22, 1863, in Records of the USCC, Scrapbooks, RG 94, Entry 791, NA.

5. Moss, *Annals,* p. 142, n. 1; *Philadelphia Bulletin,* Feb. 24, 1863, and *Washington Chronicle,* Feb. 25, 1863, clippings in Records of the USCC, Scrapbooks, RG 94, Entry 791, NA; *Major General Howard's Address at the Second Anniversary of the USCC* (Philadelphia: Caxton Press of C. Sherman, Son & Co., 1864), pp. 11–14.

6. USCC, *First Annual Report,* pp. 77–78, 115; Thoburn, ed., *My Experiences During the Civil War,* pp. 6, 130; Wiley, *Life of Billy Yank,* p. 264.

7. *Mahoning Register* (Youngstown, Ohio), Dec. 11, 1862; Alvin Duane Smith, ed., "Two Civil War Notebooks of James Russell Miller," *Journal of the Presbyterian Historical Society* 37 (June 1959): 73–74; Edwin S. Redkey, "Black Chaplains in the Union Army," *Civil War History* 33 (Dec. 1987): 332–33. For a sympathetic contemporary view of the chaplains, see [John Fitch], *Annals of the Army of the Cumberland* (Philadelphia: J. B. Lippincott, 1863), pp. 320–26.

8. Moss, *Annals,* pp. 111, 211, 337, 423, 425, 544; USCC, *Information for Army Meetings,* Jan. 1865, pp. 12–13; USCC, *Christ in the Army,* p. 105; EPS to American Tract Society, Dec. 1, 1865, Records of the USCC, LS, RG 94, Entry 739, NA; *Presbyterian Banner,* May 27, 1863, and *Congregationalist,* Sept. 25, 1863, in Records of the USCC, Scrapbooks, RG 94, entry 791, NA; *Congregationalist,* Mar. 25 and Dec. 16, 1864.

9. Moss, *Annals,* pp. 272–73; Redkey, "Black Chaplains in the Union Army," p. 344; USCC, *Fourth Annual Report,* p. 21.

10. Cist, *Army of the Cumberland,* pp. 96–97, 127, 136.

11. Moss, *Annals,* pp. 455–60.

12. Ibid.; USCC, *Second Annual Report,* pp. 93–99; *Sunday School Times,* June 27, 1863, and *Boston Recorder,* July 10, 1863, in Records of the USCC, Scrapbooks, RG 94, Entry 791, NA.

13. EPS, *Incidents,* pp. 97–99.

14. *Pittsburgh Evening Chronicle,* July 27, 1864, in Records of the USCC, Scrapbooks, RG 94, Entry 791, NA; USCC, *Third Annual Report,* p. 140.

15. *Pittsburgh Christian Advocate,* Sept. 26, 1863, in Records of the USCC, Scrapbooks, RG 94, Entry 791, NA.

16. Records of the Church of Christ in Pepperell, Community Church, Pepperell, Mass., 4:112–16; *Congregationalist,* May 8, 1863.

17. Draft letter, GHS to USG, June 6, 1863, in Records of the USCC, RG 94, Entry 740, NA.

18. Moss, *Annals,* p. 122, n. 1; USG to James E. Yeatman, Apr. 7, 1863, in John Y. Simon, ed., *The Papers of Ulysses S. Grant,* 18 vols. to date (Carbondale: Southern Illinois University Press, 1967–91), 8:33–35; Special Orders No. 88, Mar. 29, 1863, *OR,* Ser. I, vol. 24, pt. 3, pp. 153–54; Laura Wood Roper, *FLO: A Biography of Frederick Law Olmsted* (Baltimore: Johns Hopkins University Press, 1973), pp. 222–23. Grant later amended the steamboat order to allow travel also by officials of the Western Sanitary Commission, an independent organization that operated west of the Mississippi River.

19. EPS to W. E. Boardman, May 29, 1863, Records of the USCC, RG 94, Entry 740, NA.

20. EPS to "My Dear Sabbath-School Children," Aug. 11, 1863, *Well-Spring* 20 (Sept. 25, 1863): 155; USCC, *Second Annual Report,* p. 129.

21. EPS, *Incidents,* pp. 119–20.

22. EPS to Dr. J. S. Newberry, July 23 [1863], in *Presbyterian,* Aug. 29, 1863, Records of the USCC, Scrapbooks, RG 94, Entry 791, NA.

7. The Two Commissions

1. Stillé, *History of the United States Sanitary Commission,* is still useful. The Auxiliary Relief Corps is described on pp. 272–86. See also Maxwell, *Lincoln's Fifth Wheel,* and Laura Wood Roper, *FLO: A Biography of Frederick Law Olmsted* (Baltimore: Johns Hopkins University Press, 1973), pp. 156–232.

2. Stillé, *History of the United States Sanitary Commission,* pp. 80–81, 295, 481–82; Reynolds, "Benevolence on the Home Front in Massachusetts," pp. 194–97, 205–7. As the war progressed, some "sanitary fairs" were held jointly by the Sanitary and Christian commissions. See William Y. Thompson, "Sanitary Fairs of the Civil War," *Civil War History* 4 (Mar. 1958): 51–67, and Moss, *Annals,* pp. 520–21. On the rivalry between the two commissions, see Robert H. Bremner, "The Prelude: Philanthropic Rivalries in the Civil War," *Social Casework* 49 (Feb. 1968): 77–81.

3. Henry Warner Bowden, ed., *Dictionary of American Religious Biography* (Westport, Conn.: Greenwood Press, 1977), pp. 441–42; draft letter, GHS to USG, June 6, 1863, Records of the USCC, RG 94, Entry 740, NA; *Presbyterian Standard,* Sept. 24, 1863, Records of the USCC, Scrapbooks, RG 94, Entry 791, NA.

4. John W. Chadwick, *Henry W. Bellows: His Life and Character* (New York: S. W. Green's Son, 1882), pp. 11, 13, 26–27; Henry W. Bellows, *Essential Goodness the Reality of Religion* (Concord, N.H.; N.p., 1873), pp. 8–9; Walter Donald Kring, *Henry Whitney Bellows* (Boston: Skinner House, 1979), pp. 116, 174–76.

5. Nevins and Thomas, eds., *Diary of George Templeton Strong,* 3:311.

6. Ibid., p. 589.

7. Edwin Haviland Miller, *Walt Whitman: The Correspondence*, vol. 1 (1842–67) (New York: New York University Press, 1961), pp. 110–11. Elias Hicks was a liberal Quaker of an earlier generation.

8. EPS to Dr. J. S. Newberry, Aug. 24, 1863, U.S. Sanitary Commission Records, Western Department Records, LR, Rare Books and Manuscripts Division, New York Public Library, Astor, Lenox and Tilden Foundations.

9. Robt. T. Thorne to J. S. Newberry, Aug. 27, 1863, EPS to "My dear brother," Sept. 4, 1863, ibid.

10. EPS to "My dear brother," Sept. 4, 1863, J. S. Newberry to EPS, Sept. 8, [186]4, and W. A. Lawrence to J. S. Newberry, Sept. 27, 1864, ibid.; *Congregationalist*, June 10, 1864. On the relations between the two commissions, see also *Sanitary Commission Bulletin* 1 (Nov. 15, 1863): 52, and 1 (Dec. 1, 1863): 87–90.

11. Cist, *Army of the Cumberland*, pp. 153–55; Stillé, *History of the United States Sanitary Commission*, pp. 342–43.

12. Moss, *Annals*, pp. 461–66; USCC, *Second Annual Report*, pp. 99–104.

13. *New York Observer*, Sept. 3, 1863, and unidentified clipping with letter from Samuel A. Cushing dated Sept. 5, 1863, in Records of the USCC, Scrapbooks, RG 94, Entry 791, NA.

14. EPS to GHS, Aug. 31, 1863, in the *Press*, Sept. 8, 1863, ibid.; *Well-Spring* 20 (June 5, 1863): 92, and (June 12, 1863): 96.

15. *Bible Society Record* 8 (Sept. 1863): 137–38.

16. Records of the Church of Christ in Pepperell, Community Church, Pepperell, Mass., 4:118, 166; *Congregationalist*, Sept. 11, 1863.

17. Wm. L. Perkins to GHS, Sept. 22, 1863, Records of the USCC, RG 94, Entry 740, NA; *Congregationalist*, Sept. 25, 1863.

18. Records of the Church of Christ in Pepperell, Mass., 4:121–23; Records of the Evangelical Congregational Society, Community Church, Pepperell, Mass., 2:42.

19. EPS to "The Tuesday Evening Prayer Meeting at Home," Oct. 17, 1863, loose letter in Records of the Evangelical Congregational Society, Pepperell, Mass., vol. 2.

20. EPS to "The Prayer Meeting Tuesday Eve'g in Pepperell," Nov. 18, 1863, ibid.

21. J. S. Newberry to EPS, Sept. 27, 1863, U.S. Sanitary Commission Records, Western Department Records, LR, Rare Books and Manuscripts Division, New York Public Library, Astor, Lenox and Tilden Foundations; Jas. A. Hardie to GHS, Aug. 18, 1863 (with annotations by EPS), and Sept. 22, 1863, Records of the USCC, RG 94, Entry 740, NA; Moss, *Annals*, p. 140.

22. A. M. Read to "My Dear Doctor" [J. S. Newberry], Nov. 9, 1863, U.S. Sanitary Commission Records, Western Department Records, LR, Rare Books and Manuscripts Division, New York Public Library, Astor, Lenox and Tilden Foundations.

23. David L. Wilson and John Y. Simon, eds., *Ulysses S. Grant: Essays and Documents* (Carbondale: Southern Illinois University Press, 1981), pp. 110–11; EPS to USG, Nov. 17, 1863, Records of U.S. Army Continental Commands, 1821–1920,

Military Division of the Mississippi, misc. LR, RG 393, NA; Moss, *Annals*, pp. 148–49; John Y. Simon, ed., *The Papers of Ulysses S. Grant*, 18 vols. to date (Carbondale: Southern Illinois University Press, 1967–91), 16:10.

24. Special Field Orders No. 32, Records of U.S. Army Continental Commands, 1821–1920, Military Division of the Mississippi, Special Orders, Vol. 15, RG 393, NA; Moss, *Annals*, pp. 136–41, 148–49.

25. Bruce Catton, *Grant Takes Command* (Boston: Little, Brown, 1968, 1969), pp. 63–85; EPS, *Incidents*, p. 232.

26. EPS, *Incidents*, pp. 233–34. Because of Smith's practice of speaking of himself in the third person in his book (ibid., p. 7), it is not clear from his account that he was the one who spoke to the soldier who was "almost up," but General O. O. Howard said that it was Smith (*Autobiography*, 1:487).

27. EPS, *Incidents*, pp. 235–37; Moss, *Annals*, p. 480.

28. Records of the Church of Christ in Pepperell, Mass., 4:165–66; commission issued to Mrs. E. P. Smith, EPS Papers, ARC.

8. Nashville

1. The description of wartime Nashville is drawn from Maslowski, *Treason Must Be Made Odious*, Durham, *Nashville* and *Reluctant Partners*, Hoobler, *Cities Under the Gun*, and the files of the *Nashville Daily Union* and the *Congregationalist*.

2. *Nashville Daily Union*, June 17, Nov. 26, and Dec. 3, 1864; David Coe, ed., *Mine Eyes Have Seen the Glory: Combat Diaries of Union Sergeant Hamlin Alexander Coe* (Rutherford, N.J.: Fairleigh Dickinson University Press, 1975), p. 212.

3. "Sanitary Report of the Condition of the Prostitutes of Nashville, Tennessee," Jan. 31, 1865, William P. Palmer Collection, Western Reserve Historical Society, Cleveland, Ohio; James Boyd Jones, Jr., "A Tale of Two Cities: The Hidden Battle Against Venereal Disease in Civil War Nashville and Memphis," *Civil War History* 31 (Sept. 1985): 270–76; Charles Smart, ed., *The Medical and Surgical History of the War of the Rebellion*, 3 vols. (Washington, D.C.: U.S. Government Printing Office, 1888), vol. 1, pt. 3, pp. 893–94; Durham, *Nashville*, pp. 184–86, 268–69, and *Reluctant Partners*, pp. 46–49, 112–15, and 203–4; Mary Elizabeth Massey, *Bonnet Brigades* (New York: Knopf, 1966), pp. 76–78.

4. *Nashville Daily Union*, Oct. 6 and 16, 1864, Feb. 17, 1865; Aloysius F. Plaisance and Leo F. Schelver III, "Federal Military Hospitals in Nashville, May and June, 1863," *Tennessee Historical Quarterly* 29 (Summer 1970): 166–75; R. Wallace, "United States Hospitals at Nashville," *Cincinnati Lancet & Observer* 7 (Oct. 1864): 587–92; Nixon B. Stewart, *Dan McCook's Regiment, 52nd O.V.I.* (Claysville, Ohio: The Author, 1900), p. 42.

5. *Nashville Daily Union*, Oct. 10, 11, 17, and 18, 1863, Dec. 31, 1864.

6. *Nashville City and Business Directory for 1860–61;* USCC, *Information for Army Meetings*, Sept. 1864, pp. 4–5.

7. *Presbyterian Banner*, Feb. 17, 1864, and *Cincinnati Journal Messenger*, Aug. 26,

1864, both in Records of the USCC, Scrapbooks, RG 94, Entry 791, NA; *Pittsburgh Christian Advocate,* May 7, 1864.

8. Alvin Duane Smith, ed., "Two Civil War Notebooks of James Russell Miller," *Journal of the Presbyterian Historical Society* 37 (Sept. 1959): 165.

9. Durham, *Reluctant Partners,* pp. 28, 141; Leroy P. Graf and Ralph W. Haskins, eds., *The Papers of Andrew Johnson,* 9 vols. to date (Knoxville: University of Tennessee Press, 1967–91), 6:430; *Western Christian Advocate,* Mar. 30, 1864, and *Presbyterian Banner,* Apr. 20, 1864, Records of the USCC, Scrapbooks, RG 94, Entry 791, NA.

10. Moss, *Annals,* pp. 483–84; unidentified article by Mrs. W. A. Ranney, Records of the USCC, Scrapbooks, RG 94, Entry 791, NA.

11. *Pittsburgh Christian Advocate,* Apr. 16 and July 30, 1864.

12. Moss, *Annals,* pp. 483–84.

13. Ibid., pp. 663–65.

14. USCC, *Christ in the Army,* pp. 84–88; USCC, *Information for Army Meetings,* Aug. 1864, pp. 25–26; Wallace, "United States Hospitals at Nashville," p. 590; Moss, *Annals,* p. 666.

15. Moss, *Annals,* pp. 663–84; *Sunday-School Times,* Aug. 13, 1864; W. E. Boardman to EPS, Aug. 31, 1864, Records of the USCC, LS, RG 94, Entry 739, NA; EPS to GHS, Jan. 6, 1864, Wittenmyer Papers, State Historical Society of Iowa, Des Moines. Annie Wittenmyer's own account of her diet kitchen work is in her book *Under the Guns* (Boston: E. B. Stillings, 1895), pp. 217–18, 259–67.

16. EPS to Annie Wittenmyer, Nov. 18, 1864, and Jan. [4?], 1865, Wittenmyer Papers, State Historical Society of Iowa.

17. EPS to Rev. V. Hickey, June 29, 1865, and EPS to Joseph C. Thomas, Feb. 21, 1866, Thomas Papers, LC.

18. Moss, *Annals,* pp. 714–24; Carrol H. Quenzel, "Books for the Boys in Blue," *Journal of the Illinois State Historical Society* 44 (1951): 218–30; Charles F. Cooney, "Turn Rakes into Readers," *Civil War Times Illustrated* 23 (Jan. 1985): 22–24; David M. Hovde, "The U.S. Christian Commission's Library and Literacy Programs for the Union Military Forces in the Civil War," *Libraries and Culture* 24 (Summer 1989): 305–10; USG to GHS, Feb. 26, 1864, in *Philadelphia Inquirer,* Mar. 12, 1864; Thoburn, ed., *My Experiences During the War,* pp. 70–71.

19. *Nashville Daily Union,* Apr. 13, 1864; Lewis, *Sherman,* p. 351; D. W. Whittle Diary, p. 86, in Moody Papers, LC; Angle, ed., *Three Years in the Army of the Cumberland,* p. 168.

20. Angle, ed., *Three Years in the Army of the Cumberland,* pp. 177–78; Moss, *Annals,* pp. 489–91; EPS to "My dear Mollie," May 4, 1864, EPS Papers, ARC; EPS, *Incidents,* pp. 276–81.

21. *Congregationalist,* Mar. 4, 1864.

22. General Orders No. 6, Military Division of the Mississippi, Apr. 6, 1864, *OR,* Ser. I, vol. 32, pt. 3, pp. 279–80.

23. EPS to OOH, Apr. 13, 1864, OOH to W. T. Sherman, Apr. 16, 1864, and OOH to EPS, Apr. 16, 1864, OOH Papers, Bowdoin College Library, Brunswick, Maine.

24. Lewis, *Sherman*, p. 352; Joseph H. Ewing, "The New Sherman Letters," *American Heritage* 38 (July–Aug. 1987): 34.

25. *Nashville Daily Union*, Mar. 17, 22, and 30, Apr. 5, and May 7–8, 1864; Coe, ed., *Mine Eyes Have Seen the Glory*, p. 105.

26. EPS to Annie Wittenmyer, Mar. 5, 1864, Wittenmyer Papers, State Historical Society of Iowa; EPS to "My dear Mollie," May 4, 1864, EPS Papers, ARC.

27. Moss, *Annals*, p. 484; *American Missionary*, Feb. 1872, pp. 27–28.

9. Marching Through Georgia

1. Moss, *Annals*, p. 496.

2. Ibid., pp. 492–96.

3. EPS, *Incidents*, p. 283.

4. Moss, *Annals*, p. 497; J. F. Marly to GHS, Sept. 17, 1864, and A. E. Chamberlain to GHS, Aug. 12, 1864, Records of the USCC, LR, RG 94, Entry 740, NA.

5. W. T. Sherman to H. W. Halleck, July 14, 1864, *OR*, Ser. I, vol. 38, pt. 5, p. 137.

6. W. T. Sherman to GHS, Jan. 19, 1866, GHS Papers, LC. See also Sherman's comments about sanitary commissions in *New York Times*, Sept. 26, 1874.

7. Moss, *Annals*, pp. 497–500; Howard, *Autobiography*, 1:535–36. D. W. Whittle also recorded this incident but dated it November 10, 1864, and said that Corse had ordered the bell-ringer "tied up." "Some time after[,] a gentleman wished to see Gen. Corse very much and General C.—— stepping out finds a person in citizens dress tied to a tree. 'Who be you?' he asked. 'An Agent of the Christian Commission tied up for ringing a Church bell on Sabbath morning' was the reply. 'I declare I had forgotten it was Sunday,' says the General and sincerely apologizing he released the unhappy Agent. General Sherman was of course much amused at the incident" (D. W. Whittle Diary, pp. 147–49, Moody Papers, LC).

8. Moss, *Annals*, pp. 500–501.

9. EPS, *Incidents*, pp. 289–91.

10. USCC, *Information for Army Meetings*, Nov. 1864, p. 36.

11. Edwin R. Hodgman, *A Brief Memoir of Rev. Joseph Bancroft Hill . . .* (Boston: A. Mudge & Son, 1868), pp. 99–102; Moss, *Annals*, p. 739.

12. USCC, *Information for Army Meetings*, Aug. 1864, pp. 28–35. Captain John William De Forest also noted the demoralization of the soldiers he commanded (though without noting any openness among them to religious influences). "The men are not so *good* as they were once; they drink harder and swear more and gamble deeper. De Quincy is right in his statement that if homicide is habitually indulged in, it leads to immorality" (*A Volunteer's Adventures: A Union Captain's Record of the Civil War* [New Haven: Yale University Press, 1946], p. 80).

13. Records of the Evangelical Congregational Society, Community Church, Pepperell, Mass., 2:51, 54; Records of the Church of Christ, ibid., 4:137–45; *Congregationalist*, Dec. 2 and 30, 1864.

14. USCC, *Information for Army Meetings*, Aug. 1864, pp. 24–25, and Sept. 1864, pp. 2–9, 28–31; EPS to Joseph C. Thomas, July 11, 1864, Thomas Papers, LC; Moss, *Annals*, pp. 504–7.

15. Records of the USCC, Minutes of the Executive Committee, Oct. 12 and November 4, 1864, Entry 753; Register of Delegates, City Point, Va., Entry 759; EPS to "My dear brother," and EPS to W. E. Boardman, both Nov. 11, 1864, Entry 740, all in RG 94, NA.

16. Records of the USCC, W. E. Boardman to EPS, Nov. 18, 1864, LS, Entry 739; Minutes of the Executive Committee, Nov. 18, 1864, Entry 753, both in RG 94, NA.

17. Moss, *Annals*, p. 507.

18. EPS, "The Battle of Nashville," in USCC, *Third Annual Report*, pp. 147–50; Moss, *Annals*, p. 596.

19. EPS, "Battle of Nashville," in USCC, *Third Annual Report*, pp. 147–50; Moss, *Annals*, pp. 507–12.

20. EPS, *Incidents*, p. 430; Bell Irvin Wiley, *Southern Negroes, 1861–1865* (1938; rpt. New Haven: Yale University Press, 1965), pp. 332–33; *Nashville Daily Union*, Dec. 16, 1864; Durham, *Reluctant Partners*, p. 261.

21. EPS to Annie Wittenmyer, Jan. [4?], 1865, Wittenmyer Papers, State Historical Society of Iowa, Des Moines; A. E. Chamberlain to GHS, Nov. 17, 1864, Records of the USCC, LR, RG 94, Entry 740, NA.

22. GHS to John A. Cole, Feb. 3, 1865, LS, Entry 739, Records of the USCC, RG 94, NA; *Sunday-School Times*, Mar. 4, 1865.

23. GHS to John A. Cole, Feb. 3, 1865, LS, Entry 739, and Minutes of the Executive Committee, Feb. 3, 1865, Entry 753, both in Records of the USCC, RG 94, NA; USCC, *Fourth Annual Report*, p. 30.

24. GHS to Generals Ord, Meade, Patrick, and Grant, Feb. 8, 1865, GHS to Charles Demond, [Feb. 8?], 1865, and W. E. Boardman to John A. Cole, Feb. 13, 1865, LS, Entry 739; Minutes of the Executive Committee, Feb. 11, 1865, Entry 753; Register of Delegates, City Point, Va., Entry 759, all in Records of the USCC, RG 94, NA.

25. Moss, *Annals*, pp. 146–47; E. F. Williams Diary, p. 59, Williams Papers, ARC.

26. Williams Diary, p. 62, Williams Papers, ARC; "John Adams Cole," *The National Cyclopaedia of American Biography* (New York: James T. White & Co., 1948), 34:334–35; Loomis, *Christian Work Among Soldiers*, pp. 2–3.

27. Moss, *Annals*, p. 514.

10. Field Secretary

1. Moss, *Annals*, pp. 322–23, 420–22, 440–42, 661–63; USCC, *Information for Army Meetings*, June and July 1864, pp. 21–22; USCC, *Third Annual Report*, pp. 75–78; USCC, *Fourth Annual Report*, pp. 101–11; W. Springer Menge and J. August Shimrak, eds., *The Civil War Notebook of Daniel Chisholm* (New York: Orion Books, 1989), p. 120.

2. EPS to GHS, Feb. 13, 1865, in USCC, *Information for Army Meetings*, Mar. 1865, pp. 24–28.

3. Ibid., pp. 27–28.

4. Moss, *Annals*, pp. 442–43; C. C. Carpenter to E. F. Williams, Mar. 8, 1865, Williams Papers, ARC; Minutes of the Executive Committee, Mar. 18, 1865, Records of the USCC, RG 94, Entry 753, NA; GHS to J. A. Cole and L. Moss to J. A. Cole, both Mar. 18, 1865, LS, Records of the USCC, RG 94, Entry 739, NA. Smith's title was originally secretary of field organization. It was soon changed to field secretary.

5. Moss, *Annals*, p. 129, n. 2; USCC, *Second Annual Report*, pp. 238–42.

6. USCC, *Second Annual Report*, pp. 238–42; "A Visit to the Rooms of the Christian Commission," *Christian Instructor*, Oct. 11, 1863, Records of the USCC, Scrapbooks, RG 94, Entry 791, NA.

7. USCC, *Second Annual Report*, pp. 238–42.

8. *Presbyterian Banner*, Apr. 5, 1865, Records of the USCC, Scrapbooks, RG 94, Entry 791, NA; EPS to Annie Wittenmyer, Mar. 14, 1865, Wittenmyer Papers, State Historical Society of Iowa, Des Moines; Moss, *Annals*, pp. 139–40.

9. GHS to E. S. Tobey, Apr. 3, 1865, GHS to Dr. Franklin Rising, Apr. 5, 1865, and GHS to R. H. McDonald, Apr. 5, 1865, Records of the USCC, LS, RG 94, Entry 739, NA; Moss, *Annals*, pp. 443–47; Loomis, *Christian Work Among Soldiers*, p. 16.

10. Records of the USCC, Apr. 3, 1865, Scrapbooks, RG 94, Entry 791, NA.

11. GHS to B. F. Jacobs, Apr. 8, 1865, and passim, Apr. 1–12, 1865, Records of the USCC, LS, RG 94, Entry 739, NA.

12. EPS to L. Moss, Apr. 22, 1865, EPS to A. E. Chamberlain, Apr. 24, 1865, and EPS to Rev. D. [Dyer?], Apr. 25, 1865, Records of the USCC, LS, RG 94, Entry 739, NA.

13. EPS to Rev. John Marsh, May 1, 1865, ibid.

14. *Congregationalist*, May 12, 1865; Thompson, ed., *Life of George H. Stuart*, pp. 180–84.

15. EPS to Rev. George A. [?], May 17, 1865, Records of the USCC, LS, RG 94, Entry 739, NA.

16. USCC, *Fourth Annual Report*, pp. 118–20.

17. Johnson, "American Missionary Association," pp. 5–40; *American Missionary*, July 1865, p. 146; G. Whipple to GHS, Dec. 10, 1863, Aug. 1, and Sept. 21, 1864, Records of the USCC, LR, RG 94, Entry 740, NA; GHS to G. Whipple, Aug. 13, 1864, Records of the USCC, LS, RG 94, Entry 739, NA.

18. David Henry White to Simeon S. Joscelyn [sic], Feb. 25, 1865, and EPS to M. E. Strieby, Apr. 25, 1865, AMA Archives, ARC; Minutes of the Executive Committee, May 18, 1865, Records of the USCC, RG 94, Entry 753, NA; Moss, *Annals*, pp. 225–27; S. Hunt to EPS, May 20, and 30, 1865, Records of the USCC, LR, RG 94, Entry 740, NA; EPS to W. N. [Kirkby?], May 22, 1865, EPS to E. F. Williams, June 2, 1865, and EPS to F. A. [?], June 5, 1865, Records of the USCC, LS, RG 94, Entry 739, NA.

19. *Congregationalist,* Aug. 4, 1865; EPS to M. E. Strieby, Aug. 10, 1865, AMA Archives, ARC.

20. EPS to Annie Wittenmyer, July [10?], 1865, Wittenmyer Papers, State Historical Society of Iowa.

21. USCC, *Fourth Annual Report,* pp. 151–52.

22. Ibid., pp. 30–31.

23. Mrs. E. P. Smith to Annie Wittenmyer, May 26 and June 1, 1865, Wittenmyer Papers, State Historical Society of Iowa; EPS to Mary Ann Ball Bickerdyke, Jan. 20, 1865, Bickerdyke Papers, LC.

24. EPS to M. E. Strieby, July 21, 1865, AMA Archives, ARC.

25. Ibid.

26. Ibid. Smith's statement about "hatred" is an allusion to the "perfect hatred" of Ps. 139:22.

27. EPS to OOH, undated but received Aug. 28, 1865, BRFAL, LR by the Commissioner, RG 105, M-752, NA; EPS to M. E. Strieby, Sept. 11 and 20, 1865, AMA Archives, ARC; J. A. Cole to E. F. Williams, Aug. 25, 1865, Williams Papers, ARC.

28. EPS to Wm. A. [Lawrence], July 31, 1865, and Wm. [Lawrence?] to EPS, two letters dated Aug. 17, 1865, Records of the USCC, LR, Entry 740, RG 94, NA; EPS to "Mrs. C.," Aug. 14, 1865, Records of the USCC, LS, Entry 739, RG 94, NA.

29. EPS to M. E. Strieby, Aug. 10, 1865, AMA Archives, ARC.

30. Ibid.; EPS to Geo. Whipple, Aug. 1865 (No. 16452), AMA Archives, ARC.

31. EPS to M. E. Strieby, Sept. 11, 1865, ibid.; *The Seventy-Seventh Anniversary of the Pennsylvania Baptist State Mission Society* . . . (Philadelphia: Craven-Doan, 1904), pp. 12–13.

32. Records of the USCC, Minutes of the Executive Committee, July 6, 1865, Entry 753, RG 94, NA; L. Moss to Rev. Dr. [P.] Schaff, July 18, 1865, EPS to "My dear Bro. Q[uint]," Aug. 17, 1865, and L. Moss to "Bro. Parsons," Sept. 9, 1865, Records of the USCC, LS, Entry 739, RG 94, NA; EPS to E. F. Williams, Nov. 3, 1865, Williams Papers, ARC; *USCC, To All Who Have Participated in Its Work,* GHS Papers, LC.

33. *Christian Commission for the Army and Navy,* p. 26; EPS, *Incidents,* pp. 5–8.

34. EPS, *Incidents,* pp. 86, 422.

35. Ibid., p. 6.

11. The American Missionary Association

1. *Well-Spring* 22 (Dec. 15, 1865): 199.

2. EPS to M. E. Strieby, Oct. 4, 1865, AMA Archives, ARC.

3. Ibid.; *Autobiography of John G. Fee, Berea, Kentucky* (Chicago: National Christian Association, 1891), pp. 180–82.

4. EPS to M. E. Strieby, Oct. 4, 1865, AMA Archives, ARC. See also EPS to John Ogden, May 2, 1866, ibid., and Richard Sears, "John G. Fee, Camp Nelson, and

Kentucky Blacks, 1864–1865," *Register of the Kentucky Historical Society* 85 (Winter 1987): 29–45.

5. "Erastus Milo Cravath" in Rossiter Johnson, ed., *The Twentieth Century Biographical Dictionary of Notable Americans* (1904; rpt. Detroit: Gale Research Co., 1968), 3 (n.p.); *The National Cyclopaedia of American Biography* (New York: James T. White, 1932), 22:300–301; Allen Johnson and Dumas Malone, eds., *Dictionary of American Biography*, vol. 4 (New York: Charles Scribner's Sons, 1930), p. 516; EPS to M. E. Strieby, Oct. 11, 1865, AMA Archives, ARC.

6. EPS to M. E. Strieby, Oct. 11, 1865, and EPS to GW, Nov. 10, 1865, AMA Archives, ARC.

7. EPS to M. E. Strieby, Oct. 11, 1865, ibid.

8. Ibid.; EPS, *Incidents*, p. 105; GHS to E. M. Stanton, May 1, 1865, Records of the BRFAL, LR, RG 105, M-752, NA; Records of the Assistant Commissioner for the State of Tennessee, BRFAL, RG 105, M-999, Reel 4, p. 133, NA. See also Hopkins, *Life [of] Clinton Bowen Fisk*, and *Fisk University*.

9. EPS to M. E. Strieby, Oct. 18, 19, and Nov. 2 [mailed Nov. 28], 1865, AMA Archives, ARC.

10. EPS to assistant secretary of war, Oct. 23, 1865, LR by the Secretary of War, Registered Series, S 2853/154, and Thomas T. Eckert to EPS, Oct. 26, 1865, LS by the Secretary of War Relating to Military Affairs, both in RG 107, NA; EPS to GW, Nov. 10, 13, 16, and 21, 1865, and EPS to M. E. Strieby, Jan. 20, 1866, AMA Archives, ARC; *Fisk University*, pp. 38–41. For the founding of Fisk University, see also Richardson, *History of Fisk University*, and Alrutheus Ambush Taylor, "Fisk University, 1866–1951: A Constructive Influence in American Life," typescript, ARC.

11. EPS to E. M. [sic] Strieby, Nov. 24, 1865, and Jan. 1, 1866, AMA Archives, ARC; Moss, *Annals*, p. 682.

12. Minutes of the executive committee, Jan. 11, 1866, Records of the USCC, RG 94, Entry 753, NA; EPS to Joseph C. Thomas, Jan. 11, 1866, Thomas Papers, LC. The term "waste places" comes from Isa. 51:3.

13. Moss, *Annals*, pp. 256–57; Basler, ed., *Collected Works of Abraham Lincoln*, 8:245–46; Kenneth A. Bernard, "Lincoln and the Music of the Civil War," *Civil War History* 4 (1958): 269–83; EPS to GHS, Jan. 22 and Feb. 3, 1866, Records of the USCC, LR, RG 94, Entry 740, NA.

14. Moss, *Annals*, pp. 230–79; Program for the Fourth and Last Anniversary Meeting, Feb. 11, 1866, in GHS Papers, LC; *Presbyterian*, Feb. 24, 1866, Records of the USCC, Scrapbooks, RG 94, Entry 791, NA.

15. *Sunday School Times*, Feb. 24, 1866, Records of the USCC, Scrapbooks, RG 94, Entry 791, NA. "See what the Lord hath wrought!" is a reference to Num. 23:23.

16. EPS to J. C. Thomas, Feb. 21, 1866, Thomas Papers, LC; EPS to GHS, Feb. 21 and Mar. 7, 1866, Records of the USCC, LR, RG 94, Entry 740, NA.

17. Constitution of the AMA, printed periodically in *American Missionary*. See also Johnson, "The American Missionary Association: A Short History," and Johnson, "The American Missionary Association, 1846–1861."

18. Johnson, "The American Missionary Association, 1846–1861," pp. 93, 310, 426, 466, and passim.

19. Johnson, "The American Missionary Association: A Short History," pp. 33–34.

20. Johnson, "The American Missionary Association, 1846–1861," pp. 414–15; Thomas L. Webber, *Deep Like the Rivers: Education in the Slave Quarter Community, 1831–1865* (New York: Norton, 1978), pp. 29, 131; Reid, *After the War*, p. 511.

21. Sidney Andrews, quoted in Harding, *There Is a River*, p. 308; Booker T. Washington, *Up from Slavery*, in Louis R. Harlan, ed., *The Booker T. Washington Papers*, 14 vols. (Urbana: University of Illinois Press, 1972–89), 1:229–30.

22. S. J. Whiton to EPS, Jan. 1, 1867, AMA Archives, ARC; Jones, *Soldiers of Light and Love*, p. 62; Butchart, *Northern Schools, Southern Blacks, and Reconstruction*, p. 4; Williamson, *After Slavery*, pp. 213–24.

23. *Boston Recorder*, Aug. 11, 1865, Records of the USCC, Scrapbooks, RG 94, Entry 791, NA.

24. *American Missionary*, Feb. 1866, p. 34, and May 1866, p. 108; Joseph E. Holliday, "Freedmen's Aid Societies in Cincinnati, 1862–1870," *Cincinnati Historical Society Bulletin* 22 (July 1964): 169–85; *Western Freedmen's Aid Commission*, Mar. 1, 1866, EPS to GW, Dec. 1, 1865, EPS to M. E. Strieby, Jan. 8 and May 25, 1866, and Levi Coffin to GW, Aug. 16, 1866, AMA Archives, ARC.

25. EPS to GHS, Feb. 21, 1866, Records of the USCC, LR, RG 94, Entry 740, NA; EPS to M. E. Strieby, two letters dated Jan. 1, 1866, and letters dated Jan. 8 and 20, 1866, AMA Archives, ARC.

26. EPS to GW, Dec. 1, 1865, EPS to Strieby, Oct. 18, Nov. 2 [mailed Nov. 28], 1865, and Jan. 20, 1866, and EPS to S. Hunt, Jan. 20, 1866, AMA Archives, ARC.

27. EPS to M. E. Strieby, Feb. 17 and 27, 1866 (with attached clipping), EPS to GW, Apr. 20, 1866, and EPS to Wm. E. Whiting, May 5, 1866, ibid.

28. *American Missionary*, Feb. 1866, p. 33; Trowbridge, *Desolate South*, pp. 245–46; EPS to E. M. [sic] Strieby, Dec. 19, 1865, AMA Archives, ARC.

29. EPS to H. Eddy, Jan. 27, 1866, Rockwell Papers, ARC.

30. *American Missionary*, Feb. 1866, pp. 35–36; EPS to M. E. Strieby, Feb. 1, 1866, AMA Archives, ARC.

31. EPS, *Work for the Freedmen by the American Missionary Association*, Jan. 30, 1866, pamphlet in AMA Archives, ARC.

32. Ibid. Smith's statement "A nation has been born in a day" is an allusion to Isa. 66:8 ("Shall the earth be made to bring forth in one day? or shall a nation be born at once?").

12. Secretary for the Middle West

1. Trowbridge, *Desolate South*, pp. 237–38, 242; John Richard Dennett, *The South as It Is, 1865–66* (New York: Viking Press, 1965), pp. 266–68; Reid, *After the War*, pp. 355–56.

2. EPS to E. M. [sic] Strieby, Dec. 19, 1865, AMA Archives, ARC; *American Missionary*, Feb. 1866, p. 33, May 1866, pp. 114–15, and Feb. 1867, pp. 28–29; Jerry Thornbery, "Northerners and the Atlanta Freedmen, 1865–69," *Prologue* 6 (Winter 1974): 236–54.

3. EPS to M. E. Strieby, Mar. 14, 1866, AMA Archives, ARC; *American Missionary*, May 1866, pp. 97–98.

4. *American Missionary*, May 1866, pp. 97–98.

5. Ibid.

6. GW to M. E. Strieby, May 3, 1866, EPS to W. E. Whiting, May 8, 1866, and EPS to GW, May 22, 1866, AMA Archives, ARC. See also Thornbery, "Northerners and the Atlanta Freedmen," pp. 242–44.

7. EPS to M. E. Strieby, Mar. 14, 1866, EPS to John Ogden, May 2, 1866, AMA Archives, ARC.

8. EPS to J. Silsby, Mar. 30, 1866, ibid.

9. EPS to M. E. Strieby, Apr. 27, 1866, ibid.

10. Copy of EPS to M. E. Strieby, Apr. 27 and 28, 1866, ibid.

11. EPS to GW, May 28, July 9 and 14, 1866, ibid.

12. EPS to M. E. Strieby, Apr. 27 and May 22, 1866, ibid.; *American Missionary*, Feb. 1867, pp. 28–29, and Mar. 1867, pp. 60–61.

13. *American Missionary*, June 1866, p. 138; *New York Times*, July 2, 1866; John Y. Simon, ed., *The Papers of Ulysses S. Grant*, 18 vols. to date (Carbondale: Southern Illinois University Press, 1967–91), 16:228–29.

14. Silas May to Lt. Stuart Eldridge, Apr. 30 and May 3, 1866, and May to M. P. Bestow, May 21, 1866, Records of the Assistant Commissioner for Mississippi, BRFAL, RG 105, M-826, NA.

15. EPS to F. Ayer, Aug. 4, 1866, Ayer Papers, Atlanta University Center, Atlanta, Ga.

16. EPS to M. E. Strieby, May 8, 1866, and Ellen A. Cole to GW, May 10, 1866, AMA Archives, ARC; *Well-Spring* 23 (June 22, 1866): 98–99; *Congregationalist*, Jan. 19, 1866; August Meier and Elliott Rudwick, *From Plantation to Ghetto*, rev. ed. (New York: Hill and Wang, 1970), pp. 173–74; Joe M. Richardson, ed., "The Memphis Race Riot and Its Aftermath: Report by a Northern Missionary," *Tennessee Historical Quarterly* 24 (Spring 1965): 63–69; Bobby L. Lovett, "Memphis Riots: White Reaction to Blacks in Memphis, May 1865–July 1866," *Tennessee Historical Quarterly* 38 (Spring 1979): 9–33; James Gilbert Ryan, "The Memphis Riots of 1866: Terror in a Black Community During Reconstruction," *Journal of Negro History* 62 (July 1977): 243–57; *American Missionary*, Mar. 1866, pp. 61–62, and Aug. 1866, pp. 171–72.

17. *American Missionary*, Aug. 1866, pp. 171–72; EPS to GW, July 5, 1866, AMA Archives, ARC.

18. *American Missionary*, Aug. 1866, pp. 171–72; EPS to GW, July 11, 1866, AMA Archives, ARC.

19. EPS to GW, July 14, 1866, AMA Archives, ARC.

20. *Congregationalist*, May 11, 1866.

21. Ibid. On the southern anticipation of the "black demise" see Carter, *When the*

War Was Over, pp. 166–68, and Joel Williamson, *The Crucible of Race: Black-White Relations in the American South Since Emancipation* (New York: Oxford University Press, 1984), pp. 84–85.

22. Joseph E. Holliday, "Freedmen's Aid Societies in Cincinnati, 1862–1870," *Cincinnati Historical Society Bulletin* 22 (July 1964): 183–85; EPS to GW, Aug. 9, 1866, EPS to M. E. Strieby, Aug. 15, 1866, and Levi Coffin to GW, Aug. 16, 1866, AMA Archives, ARC.

23. EPS to M. E. Strieby, May 25, 1866, AMA Archives, ARC.

24. Ibid.

25. M. E. Strieby to GW, June 4 and 11, 1866, GW to M. E. Strieby, June 8, 1866, ibid.

26. Richard Bryant Drake, "The American Missionary Association and the Southern Negro, 1861–1888" (Ph.D. dissertation, Emory University, 1957), pp. 87–90; Joe M. Richardson, "Francis L. Cardozo: Black Educator During Reconstruction," *Journal of Negro Education* 48 (Winter 1979): 76–77; E. M. Cravath to M. E. Strieby, July 16, 1866, AMA Archives, ARC.

27. EPS to S. Hunt, Dec. 1, 1865, Jan. [?], 1866 (with Hunt to Smith, Jan. 10, 1866), Jan. 25, 1866 (with Hunt to Smith, Jan. 22, 1866), and Mar. 17, 1866, EPS to M. E. Strieby, Jan. 30, 1866, and an incomplete, undated EPS memo (No. H2550), AMA Archives, ARC.

28. S. Hunt to GW, July 2, 1866, AMA Archives, ARC.

29. Ibid.

30. Ibid.; S. Hunt, "To the Secretaries," July 4 and 25, 1866, and S. Hunt to GW, July 24, 1866, AMA Archives, ARC.

31. *American Missionary,* Jan. 1867, p. 10; S. Hunt to M. E. Strieby, Dec. 7, 1866, AMA Archives, ARC; Drake, "The American Missionary Association and the Southern Negro," p. 90; "Samuel Hunt," *Appletons' Cyclopaedia of American Biography,* 6 vols. (New York: D. Appleton, 1888–89), 3:318.

32. *American Missionary,* Oct. 1866, pp. 217–18.

33. Ibid.

13. The Freedmen's Bureau

1. John A. Cole to E. F. Williams, Sept. 1, 1866, Williams Papers, ARC; EPS to M. E. Strieby, Apr. 21, 1869, AMA Archives, ARC; obituaries of Cyrus Porter Smith in *New York Daily Tribune* and *New York Times,* Feb. 14, 1877; Walt Whitman, "Crossing Brooklyn Ferry," in *The Works of Walt Whitman,* 2 vols. (1948; rpt. New York: Funk and Wagnalls, 1968), 1:168.

2. M. E. Strieby to GW, June 11, 1866, AMA Archives, ARC.

3. Johnson, "The American Missionary Association: A Short History," p. 22; Swint, *Northern Teacher in the South,* p. 169; Beard, *Crusade of Brotherhood,* pp. 207–10; *American Missionary,* Nov. 1876, pp. 241–43, and Dec. 1876, p. 280; *New York*

Times, Oct. 8, 1876. The incident that led Whipple and the other "Lane Rebels" to leave Lane Seminary for Oberlin College is described in Lawrence Thomas Lesick, *The Lane Rebels: Evangelicalism and Antislavery in Antebellum America* (Metuchen, N.J.: Scarecrow Press, 1980).

4. Beard, *Crusade of Brotherhood*, pp. 267–69; *Congregationalist*, Mar. 25, 1864; *American Missionary*, Apr. 1899, pp. 1–6; Joseph E. Roy, *Pilgrim's Letters* (Boston: Congregational Sunday-School and Publishing Society, 1888), p. 55.

5. Hesketh Pearson, *The Smith of Smiths* (New York: Harper and Brothers, 1934), p. 271; Louis Moreau Gottschalk, *Notes of a Pianist*, ed. Jeanne Behrend (New York: Knopf, 1964), pp. 99, 116.

6. *American Missionary*, Nov. 1876, p. 242, Dec. 1876, p. 280, and Apr. 1899, pp. 1–6; Coz. Hattie [Harriet Cook Gilfillan] to Ruth [Crawford Mitchell], Dec. 9, 1928, EPS Papers, ARC.

7. Special Orders No. 134, Sept. 5, 1866, BRFAL, in AMA Archives, ARC; *U.S. Statutes at Large*, 14:174, sec. 3; EPS to OOH, Nov. 21, 1866 (with endorsements), AMA Archives, ARC.

8. *U.S. Statutes at Large*, 13:507–9.

9. See letters from A. K. Moulton and J. R. Miller, May 24, 1865, R. Parkinson, June 6, 1865, Henry M. Holmes, June 19, 1865, and George Hitchen, June 30, 1865, LR by the Commissioner, BRFAL, RG 105, M-752, NA; W. W. Belden to EPS, Nov. 15, 1865, Records of the USCC, RG 94, Entry 740, NA; Moss, *Annals*, pp. 277, 279, 436–37; Alvord, *Fourth Semi-Annual Report on Schools for Freedmen*, p. 55; *Wilmington* (N.C.) *Daily Post*, May 3, 1868.

10. Alvord, *Fifth Semi-Annual Report on Schools for Freedmen*, pp. 5–6; Peirce, *Freedmen's Bureau*, pp. 58, 82; Bentley, *History of the Freedmen's Bureau*, p. 176.

11. Howard, *Autobiography*, 2:271.

12. Bentley, *History of the Freedmen's Bureau*, pp. 51–52; Oscar Osburn Winther, ed., *With Sherman to the Sea: The Civil War Letters, Diaries and Reminiscences of Theodore F. Upson* (Baton Rouge: Louisiana State University Press, 1943), p. 97; Howard, *Autobiography*, 1:91, 93, 119; EPS to J. A. Rockwell, July 25, 1866, Rockwell Papers, ARC. Rowland Howard served as a Christian Commission delegate in 1863 (Moss, *Annals*, p. 608).

13. *Congregational Year-Book* (1881), p. 16; Osthaus, *Freedmen, Philanthropy, and Fraud*, pp. 12–13; American Tract Society, *The Rev. J. W. Alvord's Work in the Army* (1863), pamphlet in AMA Archives, ARC; Morris, *Reading, 'Riting, and Reconstruction*, pp. 36–38; Robert C. Morris, introduction to AMS Press reprint of John W. Alvord's *Semi-Annual Reports on Schools for Freedmen; Congregationalist*, Aug. 8, 1862, and June 8, 1866; *Oberlin Review*, Feb. 19, 1880, p. 149.

14. Bentley, *History of the Freedmen's Bureau*, pp. 58, 215; Records of First Congregational Church, Washington, D.C.

15. John Mercer Langston, *From the Virginia Plantation to the National Capitol* (Hartford, Conn.: American Publishing Co., 1894), pp. 80–81; U.S. Congress, *House Report No. 121*, 41st Cong., 2d sess., pp. 50, 320, 333, 364; "Alexander P. Ketchum,"

National Cyclopaedia of American Biography, 63 vols. (New York: James T. White, 1898–1984), 2:351; EPS to E. A. Ware, Aug. 8, 1867, Ware Papers, Atlanta University Center, Atlanta, Ga.; *Register of Officers and Agents . . . in the Service of the U.S. on the Thirtieth Sept., 1867* (Washington, D.C.: U.S. Government Printing Office, 1868), pp. 199–202; GW to OOH, May 5, 1869, with endorsement by E. Whittlesey, AMA Archives, ARC. See also Osthaus, *Freedmen, Philanthropy, and Fraud,* pp. 60–61.

16. Howard, *Autobiography,* 2:271, 257–58, 584–85; Peirce, *Freedmen's Bureau,* pp. 75–76; Bentley, *History of the Freedmen's Bureau,* pp. 74–75, 134, 171–72; Alvord, *Third Semi-Annual Report on Schools for Freedmen,* p. 32, and *Fourth Semi-Annual Report,* p. 12; *U.S. Statutes at Large,* 14:92, 173–77; Carpenter, *Sword and Olive Branch,* p. 155.

17. John William De Forest, *A Union Officer in the Reconstruction* (New Haven: Yale University Press, 1948), pp. 40, 87–88; H. S. Beals to EPS, Dec. 31, 1866, AMA Archives, ARC; U.S. Congress, *House Report No. 121,* 41st Cong., 2d sess., pp. 369–72.

18. GW to J. W. Alvord, Sept. 5, 1865, LR by the Educational Division, BRFAL, RG 105, M-803, NA.

19. Engs, *Freedom's First Generation,* pp. xviii, 3, 29, 45–46; L. P. Jackson, "The Origin of Hampton Institute," *Journal of Negro History* 10 (Apr. 1925): 131–49.

20. Armstrong, *Founding of the Hampton Institute,* p. 3; Engs, *Freedom's First Generation,* pp. 111, 143; Armstrong and Ludlow, *Hampton and Its Students,* p. 27; EPS to GW, Sept. 10 and 11 (No. HI-9226), 1866, AMA Archives, ARC.

21. *Memories of Old Hampton* (Hampton, Va.: [Hampton] Institute Press, 1909), pp. 103–4; Armstrong and Ludlow, *Hampton and Its Students,* pp. 27, 165.

22. EPS to GW, Sept. 11 (No. HI-9226), 1866, AMA Archives, ARC. It is not clear to what extent Smith understood Armstrong's philosophy of education, the industrial education described and criticized in Spivey's *Schooling for the New Slavery,* pp. ix–44. Smith's own philosophy of education went far beyond Armstrong's. He acceded to a bureau request for an "industrial department" at Tougaloo College, but he also envisioned Atlanta University as growing "to the character and power of a school like Oberlin." J. M. Stephen Peeps describes the transition in black higher education from its "egalitarian beginnings" under leaders like Smith through the "great detour" of industrial education under leaders like Armstrong in "Northern Philanthropy and the Emergence of Black Higher Education—Do-Gooders, Compromisers, or Co-Conspirators?" *Journal of Negro Education* 50 (Summer 1981): 251–69.

23. EPS to GW, Sept. 11, 1866 (No. HI-9224), AMA Archives, ARC.

24. Ibid.; Alvord, *Third Semi-Annual Report on Schools for Freedmen,* p. 3.

25. EPS to GW, Sept. 17, 1866, AMA Archives, ARC.

26. Ibid.; EPS to GW, Sept. 20, 1866, ibid.

27. GW to "Bro. Strieby," Sept. 24, 1866, ibid.

28. EPS to GW, Sept. 26, 1866, ibid.

29. Joe M. Richardson, "Francis L. Cardozo: Black Educator During Reconstruction," *Journal of Negro Education* 48 (Winter 1979): 73–83; Clifton H. John-

son, "Francis Cardoza [sic]: Black Carpetbagger," *Crisis* 78 (Sept. 1971): 226–28; Edward F. Sweet, "Francis L. Cardoza [sic]—Profile of Integrity in Reconstruction Politics," *Journal of Negro History* 46 (Oct. 1961): 217–32; Morris, *Reading, 'Riting, and Reconstruction*, p. 86; EPS to GW, Sept. 26, 1866, AMA Archives, ARC.

30. Undated EPS memo (No. HI-9575), AMA Archives, ARC.

31. Ibid.; EPS to GW, Sept. 26, 1866, ibid. Smith later obtained funding from the Avery Fund for the construction of the school that became Avery Normal Institute. See Edmund L. Drago, *Initiative, Paternalism, and Race Relations: Charleston's Avery Normal Institute* (Athens: University of Georgia Press, 1990), p. 50.

32. EPS to GW, Sept. 26, 1866, AMA Archives, ARC.

33. Ibid.

34. Draft letter, EPS to G. L. Eberhart, Oct. 3, 1866, and EPS to GW, Oct. 3, 1866, ibid.; EPS to G. L. Eberhart, Oct. 3, 1866, with endorsements, Records of the Assistant Commissioner for the State of Georgia, BRFAL, RG 105, M-798, NA.

35. EPS to GW, Oct. 3, 1866, AMA Archives, ARC.

36. EPS to Maj. Gen. Tillson, Oct. 3, 1866, and EPS to GW, Oct. 3, 1866, ibid.

37. EPS to GW, Oct. 11, 1866, ibid.

38. Tillson endorsement on EPS to G. L. Eberhart, Oct. 3, 1866, and AMA certificate dated Dec. 15, 1866, pledging that the school buildings in Atlanta would be used "perpetually for the educational interests of the citizens of Atlanta without distinction of color," in Records of the Assistant Commissioner for Georgia, BRFAL, RG 105, M-798, NA; EPS to GW, Oct. 11 and 15, 1866, AMA Archives, ARC; *American Missionary*, Dec. 1866, pp. 265, 268. A more favorable assessment than Smith's of Tillson's policies in Georgia is given in Paul A. Cimbala, "The 'Talisman Power': Davis Tillson, the Freedmen's Bureau, and Free Labor in Reconstruction Georgia, 1865–1866," *Civil War History* 28 (June 1982): 153–71.

39. EPS to G. L. Eberhart, Nov. 19, 1866, Records of the Superintendent of Education for Georgia, BRFAL, RG 105, M-799, NA; GW to M. E. Strieby, Nov. 22, 1866, OOH to EPS, Dec. 1, 1866, and S. S. Ashley to EPS, Feb. 25, 1867, AMA Archives, ARC; EPS to F. Ayer, Dec. 16, 1866, Ayer Papers, Atlanta University Center; EPS to OOH, Nov. 22, 1866 (with reply), and Dec. 8, 1866, LR by the Commissioner, BRFAL, RG 105, M-752, NA; EPS to F. A. Fiske, Dec. 20, 1866, and Jan. 4, 11, and 29, 1867 (among others), Records of the Superintendent of Education for North Carolina, BRFAL, RG 105, M-844, NA.

40. EPS to F. A. Fiske, Jan. 29, 1867, Records of the Superintendent of Education for North Carolina, BRFAL, RG 105, M-844, NA; EPS to J. A. Rockwell, Feb. 21, 1867, Rockwell Papers, ARC; EPS to "My dear Prof" [John Ogden?], May 13, 1867, AMA Archives, ARC.

14. Teachers Who Dared

1. Drake, "The American Missionary Association and the Southern Negro," p. 284; *American Missionary*, July 1866, pp. 151–53.

2. EPS to E. A. Hunt, draft reply with E. A. Hunt to EPS, Oct. 1, 1867, AMA Archives, ARC.

3. Mary N. Whittington to EPS, Sept. 26, 1868, ibid.; EPS to E. A. Ware, July 22, 1868, Ware Papers, Atlanta University Center, Atlanta, Ga.

4. EPS to Col. J. R. Lewis, May 17, 1869, Records of the Superintendent of Education for Georgia, BRFAL, RG 105, M-799, NA.

5. *American Missionary*, Feb. 1868, pp. 35–36. "The form of one like unto the Son of God" is a reference to Dan. 3:25.

6. Wiley, *Life of Billy Yank*, pp. 96–97; Thoburn, ed., *My Experiences During the Civil War*, p. 79. See also Current, *Northernizing the South*.

7. Whittier, "Snow-bound," in *Complete Poetical Works*, pp. 398–406; Alva A. Hunt to EPS, Feb. 27, 1868, AMA Archives, ARC.

8. Jones, *Soldiers of Light and Love*, pp. 15, 30–31; Du Bois, *Souls of Black Folk*, p. 65; Jones, " 'A Glorious Work,' " p. 176. Jacqueline Jones describes the difficulties the women teachers faced in the male-dominated AMA in "Women Who Were More Than Men: Sex and Status in Freedmen's Teaching," *History of Education Quarterly* 19 (Spring 1979): 47–59.

9. *American Missionary*, Apr. 1867, pp. 73–78, and June 1870, pp. 121–28; A. H. M. Taylor to Maj. Gen. Griffin, Aug. 1, 1867, AMA Archives, ARC.

10. DeBoer, "The Role of Afro-Americans in the Origin and Work of the American Missionary Association," pp. 491–93; Linda M. Perkins, "The Black Female American Missionary Association Teacher in the South, 1861–1870," in Jeffrey J. Crow and Flora J. Hatley, eds., *Black Americans in North Carolina and the South* (Chapel Hill: University of North Carolina Press, 1984), pp. 122–36; Earle H. West, "The Harris Brothers: Black Northern Teachers in the Reconstruction South," *Journal of Negro Education* 48 (Spring 1979): 126–38; U.S. Congress, *House Report No. 121*, 41st Cong., 2d sess., p. 373.

11. M. E. Perry to EPS, Sept. 25, 1868, and Robert Harris to EPS, Feb. 27, 1867, AMA Archives, ARC; Ellen N. Lawson, "Lucy Stanton: Life on the Cutting Edge," *Western Reserve Magazine* 10 (Jan.–Feb. 1983): 9–12; Robert Samuel Fletcher, *A History of Oberlin College*, 2 vols. (Oberlin, 1943), 2:534; Sterling, ed., *We Are Your Sisters*, pp. 266–67; Morris, *Reading, 'Riting, and Reconstruction*, p. 99.

12. EPS to W. L. Clark, Dec. 14, 1868, and EPS to S. C. Armstrong, Nov. 13, 1868, AMA Archives, ARC; EPS to E. F. Williams, Aug. 14, 1867, Williams Papers, ARC; EPS to E. A. Ware, Sept. 17, 1868, Ware Papers, Atlanta University Center; EPS to E. A. Ware, Sept. 23, 1867, and W. F. Wentworth to E. A. Ware, Mar. 8, 1868, Records of the Superintendent of Education for Georgia, BRFAL, RG 105, M-799, NA.

13. Ellen E. Adlington to EPS, Mar. 4, 1867, and R. C. Mather to EPS, Oct. 18, 1867, AMA Archives, ARC.

14. Sarah H. Champney to EPS, Aug. 11, 1868, and EPS to H. W. Goodman, draft reply with Goodman to EPS, June 22, 1868, ibid.

15. EPS to Fred^k A. Sawtell, Mar. 31, 1870, draft reply with Sawtell to EPS, Mar. 24, 1870, ibid.

16. Hattie C. Foote to E. M. Cravath, Oct. 10, 1870, ibid.

17. Trowbridge, *Desolate South*, p. 311; Current, *Northernizing the South*, p. 72. Not all white southerners were opposed to educating the freedmen, but there was a general hostility to northerners as their teachers. See Carter, *When the War Was Over*, pp. 185–86, and Vaughn, *Schools for All*, pp. 38–43.

18. Edmonia Highgate to M. E. Strieby, Dec. 17, 1866, quoted in Haywood, "The American Missionary Association in Louisiana During Reconstruction," pp. 103–4; Sterling, ed., *We Are Your Sisters*, pp. 271–73, 294–304; DeBoer, "The Role of Afro-Americans in the Origin and Work of the American Missionary Association," p. 270; W. L. Coan to R. M. Manly, Dec. 12, 1865, Records of the Superintendent of Education for Virginia, BRFAL, RG 105, M-1053, NA; Swint, *Northern Teacher in the South*, pp. 95–96; Larry Gara, "Teaching Freedmen in the Post-War South: A Document," *Journal of Negro History* 40 (July 1955): 274–76; Alvord, *Eighth Semi-Annual Report on Schools for Freedmen*, p. 57, and *Tenth Semi-Annual Report*, p. 36; Vaughn, *Schools for All*, pp. 31–36, 44–48; Mary Elizabeth Massey, *Bonnet Brigades* (New York: Knopf, 1966), pp. 125–26. The notorious murder of a teacher originally recruited for the AMA school at Talladega, Alabama, is described in Gene L. Howard, *Death at Cross Plains: An Alabama Reconstruction Tragedy* (University, Ala.: University of Alabama Press, 1984).

19. *American Missionary*, Feb. 1866, p. 36; EPS to W. E. Whiting, Mar. 30, 1866, EPS to "per R[eeves]," Jan. 24, 1868, and EPS undated circular about teachers' correspondence (No. H9300), AMA Archives, ARC; EPS to E. A. Ware, July 22, 1868, Ware Papers, Atlanta University Center; EPS to J. A. Rockwell, Dec. 13 and 17, 1866, Rockwell Papers, ARC.

20. Litwack, *Been in the Storm So Long*, pp. 474–75; *Congregationalist*, Feb. 9, 1866; EPS to GW, Oct. 11, 1866, AMA Archives, ARC.

21. Litwack, *Been in the Storm So Long*, pp. 479–80; Jones, *Soldiers of Light and Love*, pp. 109–24; Rev. J. B. Waterbury's *Friendly Counsels* quoted in Morris, *Reading, 'Riting, and Reconstruction*, p. 191.

22. GW, J. M. Holmes, Wm. B. Brown, EPS, and S. S. Jocelyn, "To the Missionaries and Teachers of the American Missionary Association in the South," Mar. 1867, printed letter in AMA Archives, ARC.

23. Ibid.

24. Ibid.

25. Ibid. "Christ, and Him crucified" is a reference to 1 Cor. 2:2. The "commission promise" is quoted from Matt. 28:20.

26. Lewis Tappan, *Caste: A Letter to a Teacher Among the Freedmen* (New York: William E. Whiting [Oct. 1867]), pp. 6–7, 9, 10–11.

27. William J. Niles to Lewis Tappan, Jan. 25, 1862, H. S. Beals to S. S. Jocelyn, Feb. 19, 1862, and H. S. Beals to EPS, Apr. 30, 1867, AMA Archives, ARC; Singnan Fen, "Notes on the Education of Negroes at Norfolk and Portsmouth, Virginia, During the Civil War," *Phylon* 28 (Summer 1967): 200 (n. 19), 202–3. Additional information about Beals is from the 1860 U.S. Census of Angelica, New York.

28. H. S. Beals to EPS, Feb. 15 and Mar. 12, 1867, and Amy L. Chapman to EPS, Apr. 5, 1867, AMA Archives, ARC; *American Missionary*, Apr. 1866, pp. 78–79.

29. *New York Tribune*, Mar. 26, 1867; *American Missionary*, May 1867, pp. 109–10. The Beaufort schools are discussed in Litwack, *Been in the Storm So Long*, pp. 489–90, Richardson, *Christian Reconstruction*, pp. 230–31, Jones, " 'A Glorious Work,' " pp. 232–40; Maxine D. Jones, "The American Missionary Association and the Beaufort, North Carolina, School Controversy, 1866–67," *Phylon* 48 (Summer 1987): 103–11; and Maxine D. Jones, " 'They Too Are Jesus' Poor': The American Missionary Association and the White Community in North Carolina," *Southern Studies* 23 (Winter 1984): 386–96.

30. Hyman Thompson to GW, Mar. 1867, AMA Archives, ARC; Augustus Sherrill Whiton, comp., *The Whiton Family in America* . . . (New London, Conn.: Whiton Family Assoc., 1932), pp. 110–11; Samuel J. Whiton, *Glimpses of West Africa, with Sketches of Missionary Labor* (Boston: American Tract Society, 1866); *American Missionary*, Oct. 1863, p. 220, and Jan. 1867, p. 4; unsigned endorsement on Geo. W. Wood to GW, Nov. 21, 1865, S. J. Whiton to EPS, Feb. 16, 1867, and S. J. Whiton to GW, Feb. 28, 1867, AMA Archives, ARC.

31. John Scott to EPS, Mar. 6, 1867, S. J. Whiton to EPS, Mar. 4, 1867, Amy L. Chapman to EPS, Mar. 16, 1867, and H. S. Beals to EPS, Feb. 15, 1867, AMA Archives, ARC.

32. S. J. Whiton to EPS, Mar. 4, 1867, Amy L. Chapman to EPS, Apr. 2, 1867, and H. S. Beals to EPS, [Apr. 19?], 1867 (No. 101134), ibid.; *American Missionary*, Aug. 1867, p. 173; EPS to E. A. Ware, July 30 and Sept. 4 and 11, 1868, Ware Papers, Atlanta University Center.

33. Sterling, ed., *We Are Your Sisters*, pp. 265, 269, 271–73, 277–79; Osthaus, *Freedmen, Philanthropy, and Fraud*, p. 232; Ellen NicKenzie Lawson with Marlene D. Merrill, *The Three Sarahs: Documents of Antebellum Black College Women* (New York: Edwin Mellen Press, 1984), pp. 47–64, 143–47; Morris, *Reading, 'Riting, and Reconstruction*, p. 231. Morris mistakenly assumed that Stanley was white and Woodward black.

34. Clara Merritt DeBoer, "Blacks and the American Missionary Association," in Barbara Brown Zikmund, ed., *Hidden Histories in the United Church of Christ* (New York: United Church Press, 1984), p. 85; Sara G. Stanley to J. R. Shipherd, Apr. 6 and May 2, 1868, J. R. Shipherd to GW, May 6, 1868, and [J. R. Shipherd] to Geo. L. Putnam, May 7, 1868, AMA Archives, ARC.

35. EPS to Sab[bath] School of Con[gregation]l Ch[urch] in Woodbury, Conn., Mar. 6, 1867, with J. E. Benedict to EPS, Feb. 5, 1867, AMA Archives, ARC.

15. Colleges for the Freedmen

1. EPS to G. L. Eberhart, Apr. 3, 1867, Records of the Superintendent of Education for Georgia, BRFAL, RG 105, M-799, NA; Martha [Ayers] to EPS, May 7, 1867, AMA Archives, ARC; *American Missionary*, June 1867, p. 124.

2. *American Missionary*, June 1867, p. 124.

3. Unsigned letter from "Major General" [presumably Wager Swayne] to EPS, Mar. 23, 1867, EPS to "My dear Prof" [John Ogden?], May 13, 1867, and EPS to GW, June 3, 1867, AMA Archives, ARC; GW to OOH, Apr. 20 and July 2, 1867, and EPS to OOH, Aug. 26, 1867, LR by the Commissioner, BRFAL, RG 105, M-752, NA.

4. Logan, *Howard University*, pp. 12–23, 33, 35; Alvord, *Fourth Semi-Annual Report on Schools for Freedmen*, p. 6; DeBoer, "The Role of Afro-Americans in the Origin and Work of the American Missionary Association," p. 436; *Annual Catalogue of the Normal and Preparatory Department of Howard University, Washington, 1867* (N.p.: N.p., n.d.).

5. EPS to GW, June 3, 1867, AMA Archives, ARC; Alvord, *Fifth Semi-Annual Report on Schools for Freedmen*, p. 52; Brownlee, *New Day Ascending*, p. 178.

6. Richardson, *History of Fisk University*, pp. 13–15; EPS to A. P. Ketchum, Sept. 3, 1867, and EPS to Geo. H. Balloch, Sept. 25, 1867, LR by the Commissioner, BRFAL, RG 105, M-752, NA; C. Crosby to EPS, Jan. 12, 1867, AMA Archives, ARC.

7. EPS to E. A. Ware, Aug. 8 and 24 and Dec. 18, 1867, and Mar. 24, 1868, Ware Papers, Atlanta University Center, Atlanta, Ga.; EPS to OOH, Aug. 6, 1867, and J. A. Sladen to EPS, Aug. 13, 1867, OOH Papers, Bowdoin College Library, Brunswick, Maine; Howard, *Autobiography*, 2:402–3; Bacote, *Story of Atlanta University*, pp. 14–25.

8. Alvord, *Sixth Semi-Annual Report on Schools for Freedmen*, p. 61; *History of the Educational Institutions of the American Missionary Association in the South* (N.p.: N.p., 1884), pp. 1–2; Brownlee, *Heritage of Freedom*, pp. 21–24; Elisabeth S. Peck, *Berea's First Century, 1855–1955* (Lexington: University of Kentucky Press, 1955), pp. 23–24, 42–44; *Literary Institution, Berea, Kentucky*, Apr. 2, 1866, AMA Archives, ARC.

9. Engs, *Freedom's First Generation*, pp. 147–48; Armstrong and Ludlow, *Hampton and Its Students*, p. 40; *Act of Incorporation . . . Hampton Normal & Agricultural Institute* (Hampton, Va., 1883), p. 4; S. C. Armstrong to O. Brown, Aug. 25, 1868, and EPS to GW, Jan. 9, 1869, AMA Archives, ARC; GW to OOH, Feb. 11, 1870, LR by the Commissioner, BRFAL, RG 105, M-752, NA.

10. Alvord, *Sixth Semi-Annual Report on Schools for Freedmen*, pp. 64–65; *American Missionary*, Oct. 1868, pp. 217–18; EPS to OOH, Nov. 1, 1869, LR by the Commissioner, BRFAL, RG 105, M-752, NA; Brownlee, *Heritage of Freedom*, p. 32, and *New Day Ascending*, pp. 194–97; *History of the Educational Institutions of the American Missionary Association in the South*, pp. 5–6; Gene L. Howard, *Death at Cross Plains: An Alabama Reconstruction Tragedy* (University, Ala.: University of Alabama Press, 1984), pp. 7–13, 18–21; Joe M. Richardson, " 'To Help a Brother On': The First Decade of Talledega College," *Alabama Historical Quarterly* 37 (Spring 1975): 19–37; Jones and Richardson, *Talladega College*, pp. 1–9, 49–50; Loren Schweninger, "The American Missionary Association and Northern Philanthropy in Reconstruction Alabama," *Alabama Historical Quarterly* 32 (Fall and Winter 1970): 147–48.

11. EPS to "per R[eeves]," Jan. 24, 1868, AMA Archives, ARC.

12. *Advance*, Sept. 7, 1876.

13. S. E. Bridgman to EPS, Jan. 12, 1867, AMA Archives, ARC.

14. M. E. Strieby to GW, July 1, 1869, EPS to "Dr Pike," Aug. 5, 1871, ibid.; *American Missionary*, Oct. 1876, p. 237.

15. EPS to Mollie [Mary Thacher], Dec. 22, 1868, EPS Papers, ARC.

16. Ibid.

17. E. W. Cook to Bro. Coe, Nov. 12, 1868, American Home Missionary Society Archives, ARC; Pedrick Notebook Collection, Ripon College Archives, Ripon, Wisc.; Official Personnel Folder for Emily Smith Cook, U.S. Office of Personnel Management, Washington, D.C.

18. EPS, *Incidents*, pp. 4, 8.

19. EPS to GW, Jan. 19, 23, and 24, 1868, AMA Archives, ARC; Special Orders No. 8, Jan. 17, 1868, Records of the BRFAL, RG 105, NA.

20. EPS to Reeves, Feb. 1, 1868, EPS to Miss Thayer, Feb. 10, 1868, and Benj. F. Jackson to M. E. Strieby, Feb. 12, 1868, AMA Archives, ARC.

21. EPS to OOH, Apr. 3, 1868, Records of the Assistant Commissioner for South Carolina, BRFAL, RG 105, M-869, NA; EPS to Gen¹ J. R. Lewis, Apr. 10, 1868, with endorsements, Records of the Superintendent of Education for Georgia, BRFAL, RG 105, M-799, NA.

22. EPS to GW, Apr. 16, 1868, AMA Archives, ARC.

23. *Congregationalist*, Apr. 30 and May 7, 1868. The AMA's ultimate failure with its southern churches is discussed in Joe M. Richardson, "The Failure of the American Missionary Association to Expand Congregationalism Among Southern Blacks," *Southern Studies* 18 (Spring 1979): 51–73.

24. EPS to Gen¹ Lewis, Apr. 14, 1868, with Lewis's endorsement, Apr. 16, 1868, and EPS to GW, Apr. 16, 1868, AMA Archives, ARC.

25. *American Missionary*, July 1868, p. 158.

26. EPS to M. Y. Porter, Apr. 25, 1867, AMA Archives, ARC; EPS to OOH, July 28, 1868, LR by the Commissioner, BRFAL, RG 105, M-752, NA.

27. Alvord, *Eighth Semi-Annual Report on Schools for Freedmen*, p. 10; EPS to E. A. Ware, Oct. 16 and Nov. 5, 1868, Ware Papers, Atlanta University Center. See also Bentley, *History of the Freedmen's Bureau*, pp. 173–74.

28. E. Whittlesey to EPS, Dec. 10, 1868, AMA Archives, ARC.

29. Alvord, *Seventh Semi-Annual Report on Schools for Freedmen*, p. 3; Bentley, *History of the Freedmen's Bureau*, p. 202; EPS to S. C. Armstrong, Nov. 30, 1868, courtesy of Hampton University Archives; *U.S. Statutes at Large*, 15:193–94.

30. *American Missionary*, Mar. 1869, pp. 61–63.

31. Ibid.

32. EPS to GW, Feb. 2 and 4, 1869, AMA Archives, ARC; EPS to OOH, Nov. 11, 1868, LR by the Commissioner (M-752), BRFAL, RG 105; NA.

33. EPS to Gen. Gillem, Nov. 30, 1868, Records of the Assistant Commissioner for Mississippi (M-826), BRFAL, RG 105, NA; Campbell and Rogers, *Mississippi*, pp. 6–14; McPherson, *Abolitionist Legacy*, p. 205; Alvord, *Ninth Semi-Annual Report on Schools for Freedmen*, p. 36.

34. J. A. Cole to EPS, Mar. 1, 1869, AMA Archives, ARC; *American Missionary,* June 1869, p. 139.

35. EPS to GW, Mar. 30 and 31, 1869, AMA Archives, ARC; GW, EPS, et al. to OOH, Mar. 24, 1869, LR by the Commissioner, BRFAL, RG 105, M-752, NA; EPS to OOH, Apr. 3, 1869, OOH Papers, Bowdoin College Library; *Congregationalist,* Apr. 8, 1869.

36. *American Missionary,* Nov. 1869, pp. 241–43.

37. Ibid.

38. Ibid.

39. Ibid.

40. Ibid.

16. *"Tell 'Em We're Rising!"*

1. OOH introduction to Alvord, *Letters from the South.* For the incident at Atlanta, see *Atlantic Monthly* 23 (Mar. 1869); 367–68; *American Missionary,* Apr. 1869, p. 90, and June 1869, p. 134; *Complete Poetical Works of John Greenleaf Whittier,* pp. 348–49; OOH to James T. McCleary, Dec. 5, 1903, OOH Papers, Bowdoin College Library, Brunswick, Maine. A song popular at the time, "We Are Rising as a People," included the lines, "We are rising, we are rising, / 'Mid the changes in our land." See USCC, *Fourth and Last Anniversary Meeting,* Feb. 11, 1866, program in GHS Papers, LC.

2. Alvord, *Letters from the South,* pp. 5–7, 9–10, 18–19, and passim.

3. Ibid., pp. 8–12, 17–18.

4. *American Missionary,* Mar. 1870, pp. 59–62.

5. Ibid.

6. Ibid.; Journal of the Board of Trustees, Freedman's Saving and Trust Company, Apr. 15 and July 7, 1870, and Feb. 12, 1874, RG 101, M-874, NA. During the three and a half years Smith was a trustee of the Freedman's Bank, he attended only three meetings of the board, having served as U.S. Indian agent in Minnesota two of those years. Smith's resignation from the board was presented on Feb. 12, 1874. For the history of the Freedman's Bank, see Osthaus, *Freedmen, Philanthropy, and Fraud.*

7. EPS to GW, Jan. 12, 1870, AMA Archives, ARC.

8. Alvord, *Letters from the South,* p. 21; Bacote, *Story of Atlanta University,* pp. 26–27.

9. Alvord, *Letters from the South,* p. 28.

10. Ibid., pp. 30–32; Alvord, *Ninth Semi-Annual Report on Schools for Freedmen,* pp. 48–49. On the short-lived public school system in Tennessee, see Paul David Phillips, "Education of Blacks in Tennessee During Reconstruction, 1865–1870," *Tennessee Historical Quarterly* 46 (Summer 1987): 104–5.

11. Alvord, *Letters from the South,* p. 38.

12. Ibid., pp. 22, 30, 35, 39–40; Alvord, *Ninth Semi-Annual Report on Schools for Freedmen,* p. 28.

13. Alvord, *Letters from the South*, pp. 41–42.

14. Appointment Books, Feb. 26, 1870, and Special Orders No. 21, Mar. 1, 1870, BRFAL, RG 105, NA; EPS to GW, Mar. 1 and 2, 1870, AMA Archives, ARC.

15. EPS to GW, Mar. 2 and 23, 1870, and EPS to "Bro Pike," Mar. 12, 1870, AMA Archives, ARC; *Congregationalist*, Mar. 24, 1870.

16. EPS to Geo. L. White, Mar. 25, 1870, and EPS to GW, Apr. 11, 1870, AMA Archives, ARC; Alvord, *Ninth Semi-Annual Report on Schools for Freedmen*, p. 40, and *Tenth Semi-Annual Report*, p. 31; Morris, *Reading, 'Riting, and Reconstruction*, pp. 23, 107, 111–12, and 278–79, n. 120.

17. EPS to GW, Apr. 11, 1870, AMA Archives, ARC.

18. EPS to "Dear Genl," [C. H. Howard], Apr. 2, 1870, ibid.

19. Ibid.

20. Ibid.; Campbell and Rogers, *Mississippi*, pp. 12–13.

21. EPS to GW, Apr. 11, 1870, AMA Archives, ARC.

22. *American Missionary*, July 1870, pp. 156–61, 164.

23. Ibid., p. 157.

24. Ibid., pp. 157–58.

25. Ibid., p. 158.

26. Ibid., pp. 158–59.

27. Ibid., pp. 159–60.

28. Ibid., p. 160.

29. Ibid., pp. 160–61.

30. Revocation of Smith's appointment as special agent, July 15, 1870, Appointment Books, BRFAL, RG 105, NA; EPS to C. E. Compton, July 1, 1870, Records of the Superintendent of Education for Tennessee, RG 105, M-1000, NA; *Congregationalist*, Aug. 25, 1870.

17. *Agent for the Chippewas*

1. Richardson, ed., *Compilation of the Messages and Papers of the Presidents*, 9:4106.

2. Armstrong, *Warrior in Two Camps*, pp. 140–41; Fritz, *Movement for Indian Assimilation*, p. 72; Kelsey, *Friends and the Indians*, pp. 166–70.

3. Armstrong, *Warrior in Two Camps*, p. 150; *U.S. Statutes at Large*, 16:319; Prucha, *Great Father*, 1:514.

4. GW to Jacob D. Cox, May 26, 1870, Selected Classes of LR, Indian Division, Records of the Office of the Secretary of the Interior, RG 48, M-825, NA.

5. J. D. Cox to GW, June 1, 1870, AMA Archives, ARC; S. B. Treat to J. D. Cox, June 28 and July 6, 1870, Selected Classes of LR, Indian Division, Records of the Office of the Secretary of the Interior, RG 48, M-825, NA; J. D. Cox to S. B. Treat, July 19 and Aug. 19, 1870, and J. D. Cox to William Welsh, Aug. 23, 1870, LS, Indian Division, Records of the Office of the Secretary of the Interior, RG 48, M-606, NA; *Second Annual Report of the BIC*, p. 4; Bender, "*New Hope for the Indians*," pp. 27–28.

Responsibility for soliciting Catholic participation in the plan was given to William F. Cady, the chief clerk of the Indian Office, who was himself a Catholic (Rahill, *Catholic Indian Missions*, p. 35).

6. Richardson, ed., *Compilation of the Messages and Papers of the Presidents*, 9:4063–64.

7. GW to J. D. Cox, Aug. 30, 1870, and GHS to "My Dear Bro." [presumably EPS], Aug. 29, 1870, Selected Classes of LR, Indian Division, Records of the Office of the Secretary of Interior, RG 48, M-825, NA; EPS to GW, Aug. 24 and 30, 1870, AMA Archives, ARC.

8. John M. Ellis to J. D. Cox, Aug. 24, 1870, Appointments Division, Central Office Appointment Papers Indian Agents (no agency) S-V, Records of the Office of the Secretary of the Interior, RG 48, NA.

9. John A. Cole to EPS, Aug. 29, 1870, AMA Archives, ARC; *American Missionary*, Oct. 1870, facing p. 217, p. 226, and Jan. 1871, facing p. 1.

10. Wm. F. Cady to GW, Sept. 9 and 23, 1870, AMA Archives, ARC; GW to J. D. Cox, Aug. 25, Sept. 3 and 13, and Oct. 3, 1870, Appointments Division, Letters of Application and Recommendation, Records Relating to Church Appointments, Records of the Office of the Secretary of the Interior, RG 48, NA. Later, the S'Kokomish Agency in Washington Territory was also assigned to the AMA, but Smith had little relationship to it.

11. J. D. Cox to GW, Sept. 14 and Oct. 12, 1870, AMA Archives, ARC.

12. GW to J. D. Cox, Oct. 14, 1870, Cox Papers, Oberlin College Archives, Oberlin, Ohio.

13. Geoffrey Blodgett, *Oberlin Architecture, College and Town: A Guide to Its Social History* (Oberlin, Ohio: Oberlin College, 1985), pp. 60–61; J. P. Bardwell, *Ojibue Missions*, AMA Archives, ARC; Wm. F. Cady to GW, Sept. 23, 1870, and Wm. F. Cady to EPS, Sept. 24, 1870, ibid.; GW to E. S. Parker, Nov. 2, 1870, LR, Records of the OIA, Green Bay Agency, RG 75, M-234, NA; GW to E. S. Parker, Nov. 12, 1870, Records of the Office of the Secretary of the Interior, Appointments Division, Letters of Recommendation and Application, RG 48, NA.

14. J. P. Bardwell to GW, Nov. 18 and Dec. 29, 1870, AMA Archives, ARC.

15. J. P. Bardwell to GW, Dec. 29, 1870, ibid.

16. EPS appointment as agent, Feb. 27, 1871, EPS Papers, ARC; E. S. Parker to GW, Nov. 28, 1870, and H. R. Clum to EPS, Mar. 6, 1871, AMA Archives, ARC; *New York Times*, Feb. 19, 1871; *American Missionary*, Dec. 1871, pp. 273–74. Bardwell served briefly as Smith's clerk and died July 28, 1871, at Leech Lake, Minnesota (*American Missionary*, Oct. 1871, p. 235).

17. Children's Aid Society, *Annual Report* (1876), p. 54, written by Brace, although unsigned; *Advance*, Sept. 7, 1876, p. 4.

18. *Journals of the Continental Congress*, 34 vols. (Washington, D.C.: U.S. Government Printing Office, 1904–37), 11:717–18; William O. Douglas, *An Almanac of Liberty* (Garden City, N.Y.: Doubleday, 1954), p. 23.

19. Kvasnicka and Viola, *Commissioners of Indian Affairs*, p. 115.

20. *American Missionary,* June 1870, p. 128, and Jan. 1871, pp. 1–3.

21. Alvord, *Seventh Semi-Annual Report on Schools for Freedmen,* p. 29, *Eighth Semi-Annual Report,* p. 44, and *Tenth Semi-Annual Report,* pp. 31, 36.

22. Sarah Nottingham to EPS, July 1, 1869, AMA Archives, ARC.

23. S. G. Wright to GW, June 27, 1870, ibid.

24. Richardson, *History of Dartmouth College,* 1:417–20; Leon B. Richardson, "The Dartmouth Indians, 1800–1893," *Dartmouth Alumni Magazine* 22 (June 1930); 524–27; W. David Baird, "Cyrus Byington and the Presbyterian Choctaw Mission," in Milner and O'Neil, eds., *Churchmen and the Western Indians,* p. 36; *Catalogue of the Officers and Students of the Union Theological Seminary, New-York, November, 1853* (New York: John A. Gray, 1853), p. 8; *American Missionary,* May 1869, p. 102; Hattie S. Clark to C. L. Woodworth, Oct. 11, 1867, AMA Archives, ARC; J. P. Bardwell to A. W. Preston, Mar. 31, 1867, Records of the Assistant Commissioner for Mississippi, BRFAL, RG 105, M-826, NA; *Congregationalist,* May 12, 1865.

25. Morris, *Reading, 'Riting, and Reconstruction,* pp. 65–66; "Frederick Ayer, Teacher and Missionary to the Ojibway Indians 1829 to 1850," *Collections of the Minnesota Historical Society,* 6:429–37; William E. Bigglestone, "Oberlin College and the Beginning of the Red Lake Mission," *Minnesota History* 45 (Spring 1976): 21–31; *Missionary Herald,* 63:373; Letter from S. G. Wright, Nov. 9, 1871, in *New York Times,* Dec. 4, 1871.

26. *Advance,* Feb. 2, 1871.

27. Ibid.

28. *American Missionary,* Mar. 1871, pp. 58–59.

29. Ibid.; EPS to E. M. Cravath, Apr. 22, 1871, AMA Archives, ARC. Smith's lack of interest in Indian culture was typical of the people who sought to reform Indian affairs. See Linda K. Kerber, "The Abolitionist Perception of the Indian," *Journal of American History* 62 (Sept. 1975): 288–89.

30. *Detroit* (Minnesota) *Record,* Feb. 8, 1873; Records of the U.S. General Accounting Office, Indian Claims Accounts, May 24, 1871, RG 217, File No. 1690, NA; EPS to E. S. Parker, Mar. 31, 1871, LR, Records of the OIA, Chippewa Agency, RG 75, M-234, NA.

18. Minnesota

1. Records of the U.S. General Accounting Office, Indian Claims Accounts, May 24, 1871, RG 217, File No. 1690, NA; EPS to A. H. Clapp, Apr. 9, 1871, American Home Missionary Society Archives, ARC; J. P. Bardwell to E. S. Parker, Feb. 4, 1871, EPS to E. S. Parker, May 30, 1871, E. Douglass to EPS, Sept. 1, 1873, LR, Records of the OIA, Chippewa Agency, RG 75, M-234, NA; *Annual Report of the Commissioner of Indian Affairs* (1871), p. 588, and (1875), pp. 295–96. Other Pillager bands lived at Otter Tail and White Earth.

2. *Annual Report of the Commissioner of Indian Affairs* (1871), p. 588; J. P. Bardwell

to E. S. Parker, Feb. 4, 1871, EPS to E. S. Parker, Feb. 5 and May 3, 1871, and Report of Board of Visitors, Oct. 20, 1871, LR, Records of the OIA, Chippewa Agency, RG 75, M-234, NA; *Report of Commission Appointed . . . to Investigate Charges Against Hon. E. P. Smith . . . Feb. 2, 1874*, p. 85.

3. EPS to E. M. Cravath, Apr. 22, 1871, AMA Archives, ARC; EPS to commissioner of Indian affairs, Jan. 15 and Nov. 16, 1872, and GW to CD, July 31, 1871, LR, Records of the OIA, Chippewa Agency, RG 75, M-234, NA; *Annual Report of the Commissioner of Indian Affairs* (1869), Serial 1414, p. 867.

4. Records of the U.S. General Accounting Office, Indian Claims Accounts, RG 217, File No. 8088, NA; EPS to E. S. Parker, May 19, 1871, LR, Records of the OIA, Chippewa Agency, RG 75, M-234, NA.

5. EPS to E. M. Cravath, Apr. 22, 1871, AMA Archives, ARC; H. Austin to Maj. Gen. W. S. Hancock, Feb. 14, 1871, and W. Belknap to Secretary of the Interior, Mar. 6, 1871, LR, Records of the OIA, Chippewa Agency, RG 75, M-234, NA; Folwell, *History of Minnesota*, 3:18.

6. EPS to [?], May 16, 1871, LR, Records of the OIA, Chippewa Agency, RG 75, M-234, NA.

7. EPS to E. S. Parker, May 22 and 26 and Aug. 4, 1871, LR, Records of the OIA, Chippewa Agency, RG 75, M-234, NA.

8. *Advance*, Sept. 7, 1876.

9. EPS to E. S. Parker, Apr. 10 and May 26, 1871, LR, Records of the OIA, Chippewa Agency, RG 75, M-234, NA; EPS to E. M. Cravath, Apr. 22, 1871, AMA Archives, ARC.

10. U.S. Congress, *House Executive Document No. 193*, 42d Cong., 2d sess.; William Watts Folwell, *Minnesota: The North Star State* (Boston: Houghton Mifflin, 1908), pp. 112–16; CD to commissioner of Indian affairs, Apr. 21, 1871, copy in Records of the U.S. General Accounting Office, Indian Claims Accounts, RG 217, File No. 8088, NA; CD to W. Welsh, Mar. 3, 1871, CD Letterbooks, Illinois Historical Survey, University of Illinois Library, Urbana-Champaign; *Biographical Directory of the American Congress, 1774–1971* (Washington, D.C.: U.S. Government Printing Office, 1971), p. 1461.

11. W. Belknap to secretary of the interior, May 23, 1871, Henry Neal to EPS, May 22, 1871, EPS to E. S. Parker, May 30, 1871, LR, Records of the OIA, Chippewa Agency, RG 75, M-234, NA.

12. EPS to E. S. Parker, June 28, 1871, and Henry S. Neal to CD, Aug. 22, 1872, ibid.

13. Records of the U.S. General Accounting Office, Indian Claims Accounts, RG 217, File No. 8088, NA; Henry S. Neal to CD, June 8, 187[1], LR, Records of the OIA, Chippewa Agency, RG 75, M-234, NA; U.S. Congress, *House Executive Document No. 193*, 42d Cong., 2d sess., pp. 12–16, 53–64.

14. U.S. Congress, *House Executive Document No. 193*, 42d Cong., 2d sess., pp. 12–16, 53–64.

15. Ibid.

16. *American Missionary*, Oct. 1876, p. 236; U.S. Congress, *House Executive Document No. 193*, 42d Cong., 2d sess., p. 65; CD to commissioner of Indian affairs, Mar. 19, 1872, LR, Records of the OIA, Chippewa Agency, RG 75, M-234, NA; *New York Times*, Oct. 7, 1871. The report was signed by Neal, Smith, and Clark; Crowell submitted a minority report.

17. EPS to E. S. Parker, May 29 and June 28, 1871, LR, Records of the OIA, Chippewa Agency, RG 75, M-234, NA; Armstrong, *Warrior in Two Camps*, pp. 152–60; H. Craig Miner, "Francis A. Walker," in Kvasnicka and Viola, eds., *Commissioners of Indian Affairs*, pp. 135–40; *New York Times*, Jan. 11, 1873.

18. EPS to H. R. Clum, Aug. 23, 1871, LR, Records of the OIA, Chippewa Agency, RG 75, M234, NA.

19. Ibid.; A. T. Akerman to C. K. Davis, Sept. 12, 1871, ibid.

20. H. Austin to EPS, Sept. 2, 1871, and EPS to H. Austin, Sept. 3, 1871, LR, Records of the OIA, Chippewa Agency, RG 75, M-234, NA; *American Missionary*, Nov. 1871, pp. 249–51.

21. Report of Board of Visitors, Oct. 20, 1871, and S. G. Wright to EPS, Nov. 9, 1871, LR, Records of the OIA, Chippewa Agency, RG 75, M-234, NA; CD to GW, Aug. 1, 1871, LS, Indian Division, Records of the Office of the Secretary of the Interior, RG 48, M-606, NA;

22. Report of Board of Visitors, Oct. 20, 1871, LR, Records of the OIA, Chippewa Agency, RG 75, M-234, NA; CD to EPS, Oct. 16, 1871, LS, Indian Division, Records of the Secretary of the Interior, RG 48, M-606, NA; *Nation*, Nov. 26, 1874, p. 341. Delano's statement, "If there is a man living whom not having seen I love," is an allusion to 1 Pet. 1:8.

Robert Keller sees evidence of "favoritism to his friends in the ministry" in Smith's offer to put Erastus Cravath and Gustavus Pike on the boards of visitors, but the AMA was authorized to suggest persons for the boards. Smith may, however, have stretched a point when he wrote to Pike about one of the boards: "Sorry you can't come too. I can work you in to something that will pay y'r expenses. Make you money guard, [illegible] teamster, asst cook. Come if you can with Mr. Whipple" (EPS to Dr. Pike, Aug. 5, 1871, AMA Archives, ARC). See Keller, *American Protestantism and United States Indian Policy*, pp. 121 and 284, n. 44.

23. H. B. Whipple to J. D. Cox, Aug. 26, 1870, Cox Papers, Oberlin College Archives, Oberlin, Ohio; H. B. Whipple to O. H. Browning, Jan. 26, 1869, Selected Classes of LR, Indian Division, Records of the Office of the Secretary of the Interior, RG 48, M-825, NA; *American Missionary*, Dec. 1871, p. 273. Bishop Whipple's activities in Minnesota are described in Martin N. Zanger, "'Straight Tongue's Heathen Wards': Bishop Whipple and the Episcopal Mission to the Chippewas," in Milner and O'Neil, eds., *Churchmen and the Western Indians*, pp. 177–214.

24. EPS to H. R. Clum, Nov. 8, 1871, in *Annual Report of the Commissioner of Indian Affairs* (1871), p. 593.

25. Ibid., p. 591.

26. Ibid., pp. 591–92.

27. *American Missionary*, Sept. 1871, p. 208, and Sept. 1872, p. 209.

19. Mission to the Apaches

1. EPS to F. A. Walker, Jan. 3, 1872, LR, Records of the OIA, Chippewa Agency, RG 75, M-234, NA; F. A. Walker to EPS, Jan. 9, 1872, Records of the U.S. General Accounting Office, Indian Claims Accounts, RG 217, File No. 8088, NA.

2. EPS to F. A. Walker, Dec. 30, 1871 [incorrectly dated 1872], and Jan. 16, 1872, LR, Records of the OIA, Chippewa Agency, RG 75, M-234, NA; E. M. Cravath to EPS, Jan. 22, 1872, and EPS to Cravath, Feb. 24 and 27, 1872, AMA Archives, ARC.

3. EPS to F. A. Walker, Feb. 5, 1872, and Walker to EPS, Feb. 14, 1872, Indian Division, Records of the Office of Secretary of the Interior, RG 48, Special File 17, NA.

4. EPS to F. A. Walker, Jan. 15 and 16, 1872, LR, Records of the OIA, Chippewa Agency, RG 75, M-234, NA.

5. Carpenter, *Sword and Olive Branch*, pp. 210–11; Dan L. Thrapp, *The Conquest of Apacheria* (Norman: University of Oklahoma Press, 1967), pp. 79–112. The exact number of Indians killed at Camp Grant is not certain. See ibid., p. 90, n. 17.

6. F. Brunot to CD, Jan. 27, 1872, Selected Classes of LR, Indian Division, Records of the Office of the Secretary of the Interior, RG 48, M-825, NA. Delano referred to Howard as "a commissioner with an 'olive branch' " in CD to E. J. Davis, June 14, 1872, LS, Indian Division, Records of the Office of the Secretary of the Interior, RG 48, M-606, NA.

7. *Annual Report of the Commissioner of Indian Affairs* (1872), p. 159; CD to secretary of war, Feb. 29, 1872, CD to F. Brunot, Mar. 4, 1872, and CD to OOH, Mar. 4, 1872, LS, Indian Division, Records of the Office of the Secretary of the Interior, RG 48, M-606, NA; *New York Times*, Mar. 4, 1872; EPS to "My Dear Child Gerty," Mar. 23–24, 1872, EPS Papers, Manuscripts and Archives, Yale University Library, New Haven, Conn.; Rowland Howard to OOH, Mar. 11, 1872, OOH Papers, Bowdoin College Library, Brunswick, Maine.

8. CD to secretary of war, Feb. 29, 1872, LS, Indian Division, Records of the Office of the Secretary of the Interior, RG 48, M-606, NA. Biographical information about Wilkinson is from his Loyal Legion Record in the Civil War Library and Museum, Philadelphia. See also Louis H. Roddis, "The Last Indian Uprising in the United States," *Minnesota History Bulletin* 3 (Feb. 1920): 273–90, and 7 (Sept. 1926): 372; Logan, *Howard University*, pp. 53–54; *Catalogue of the Officers and Students of Howard University, 1869–70, District of Columbia* (N.p.: N.p., n.d.), pp. 6, 68–69.

9. EPS to E. M. Cravath, Mar. 7, 1872, and Minnie S. Cook to W. E. Whiting, Apr. 8, 1872, AMA Archives, ARC; EPS to E. M. Cravath, Mar. 7, 1872, and EPS memo about M. S. Cook's services, Mar. 30, 1872, Records of the U.S. General

Accounting Office, Indian Claims Accounts, RG 217, File No. 1690-B, NA; EPS to Mrs. [O. O.] Howard, Mar. 18, 1872, OOH Papers, Bowdoin College Library, Brunswick, Maine; EPS to "My Dear Child Gerty," Mar. 23–24, 1872, EPS Papers, Manuscripts and Archives, Yale University Library.

10. EPS to Mollie [Thacher], Mar. 27, 1872, EPS Papers, ARC. Professor Hadley was James Hadley (1821–72), professor of Greek at Yale College.

11. EPS to "My Dear Child Gerty," Mar. 23–24, 1872, EPS Papers, Manuscripts and Archives, Yale University Library; Munroe, *Life of Francis Amasa Walker*, p. 135; *American Missionary*, June 1872, p. 130.

12. EPS to "My Dear Child Gerty," Mar. 23–24, 1872, EPS Papers, Manuscripts and Archives, Yale University Library.

13. EPS to "Dear Mollie," Mar. 27, 1872, EPS Papers, ARC; EPS to "My Dear Child Gerty," Mar. 23–24, 1872, and EPS to "Gerty dear," [Mar.] 28–Apr. 3, 1872, EPS Papers, Manuscripts and Archives, Yale University Library; OOH to Mrs. Howard, Mar. 27, 1872, OOH Papers, Bowdoin College Library.

14. EPS to "Dear Mollie," Mar. 27, 1872, EPS Papers, ARC; EPS to "My Dear Child Gerty," Mar. 23–24, 1872, EPS Papers, Manuscripts and Archives, Yale University Library.

15. EPS to "Gerty dear," [Mar.] 28–Apr. 3, 1872, EPS Papers, Manuscripts and Archives, Yale University Library; OOH to Mrs. Howard, Apr. 3 and 7, 1872, OOH Papers, Bowdoin College Library; OOH to CD, Apr. 4, 1872, Selected Classes of LR, Indian Division, Records of the Office of the Secretary of Interior, RG 48, M-825, NA; OOH to CD, Apr. 7, 1872, LR, Records of the OIA, Arizona Superintendency, RG 75, M-234, NA; *Annual Report of the Commissioner of Indian Affairs* (1872), pp. 149–50.

16. *Annual Report of the Commissioner of Indian Affairs* (1872), p. 159.

17. E. D. Townsend to J. M. Schofield, Mar. 6, 1872 (two items), LR, Records of the OIA, Arizona Superintendency, RG 75, M-234, NA.

18. USG to Gen. J. M. Schofield, Mar. 6, 1872, in *Annual Report of the Commissioner of Indian Affairs* (1872), p. 160.

19. OOH to Mrs. Howard, Apr. 9, 1872, OOH Papers, Bowdoin College Library; *American Missionary*, June 1872, pp. 128–29.

20. *American Missionary*, June 1872, pp. 129–31.

21. *Arizona Weekly Citizen*, Apr. 20 and May 4, 1872.

22. *Annual Report of the Commissioner of Indian Affairs* (1872), pp. 150–51.

23. Ibid., pp. 163–65; EPS to OOH, June 12, 1872, OOH Papers, Bowdoin College Library; Carpenter, *Sword and Olive Branch*, p. 212; Martin F. Schmitt, ed., *General George Crook: His Autobiography*, rev. ed. (Norman: University of Oklahoma Press, 1960), p. 169.

24. *New York Times*, Dec. 9, 1870; *New York Herald*, Nov. 1 and Dec. 9, 1870; *Albany Times Union*, Nov. 14, 1932; *Albany Evening News*, Nov. 14 and 16, 1932; *The American Jewish Year Book, 5694*, vol. 35 (Philadelphia: Jewish Publication Society of America, 1933), p. 122.

25. *Annual Report of the Commissioner of Indian Affairs* (1872), Serial 1560, p. 699; Norton B. Stern, "Herman Bendell: Superintendent of Indian Affairs, Arizona Territory, 1871–1873," *Western States Jewish Historical Quarterly* 8 (Apr. 1976): 265–82; St. Pierre, "General O. O. Howard and Grant's Peace Policy," pp. 238–40, 277.

26. EPS to F. A. Walker, Apr. 8, 1872, LR, Records of the OIA, Arizona Superintendency, RG 75, M-234, NA.

27. OOH to J. M. Schofield, Apr. 18, 1872, Selected Classes of LR (misc.), Indian Division, Records of the Office of the Secretary of the Interior, RG 48, NA.

28. OOH to Mrs. Howard, Apr. 18, 1872, OOH Papers, Bowdoin College Library; OOH to CD, Apr. 27, 1872, LR, Records of the OIA, Arizona Superintendency, RG 75, M-234, NA.

29. OOH to Mrs. Howard, Apr. 25 and May 9, 1872, and undated letter (No. 293–94), OOH Papers, Bowdoin College Library; OOH to CD, Apr. 27, 1872, and OOH to F. A. Walker, Apr. 27, 1872, LR, Records of the OIA, Arizona Superintendency, RG 75, M-234, NA; *Annual Report of the Commissioner of Indian Affairs* (1872), pp. 151–52.

30. *Annual Report of the Commissioner of Indian Affairs* (1872), pp. 152, 168; OOH to Mrs. Howard, Apr. 25, 1872, OOH Papers, Bowdoin College Library; OOH to CD, Apr. 27, 1872, LR, Records of the OIA, Arizona Superintendency, RG 75, M-234, NA.

31. *Annual Report of the Commissioner of Indian Affairs* (1872), pp. 152–53; OOH to Mrs. Howard, Apr. 30, 1872, OOH Papers, Bowdoin College Library.

32. OOH to Mrs. Howard, Apr. 30, 1872, OOH Papers, Bowdoin College Library; *Arizona Weekly Citizen,* May 4, 1872.

33. *Annual Report of the Commissioner of Indian Affairs* (1872), pp. 154–55, 168–70; OOH to Mrs. Howard, May 5 and 9, 1872, OOH Papers, Bowdoin College Library; OOH to CD, May 10, 1872, and OOH to George Crook, May 9, 1872, Selected Classes of LR, Indian Division, Records of the Office of the Secretary of the Interior, RG 48, M-825, NA.

34. OOH to CD, May 8, 1872, Selected Classes of LR, Indian Division, Records of the Office of the Secretary of the Interior, RG 48, M-825, NA; *Arizona Weekly Citizen,* June 8, 1872; *Annual Report of the Commissioner of Indian Affairs* (1872), pp. 154–55; OOH, *Famous Indian Chiefs I Have Known* (New York: Century, 1908), pp. 54–71.

35. James Bean to F. A. Walker, May 7, 1872, LR, Records of the OIA, Chippewa Agency, RG 75, M-234, NA; *Detroit* (Minnesota) *Record,* June 29 and July 7 and 20, 1872.

36. EPS to F. A. Walker, May 13, 1872, LR, Records of the OIA, Chippewa Agency, RG 75, M-234, NA; EPS to OOH, May 15 and June 12, 1872, OOH Papers, Bowdoin College Library.

37. *Annual Report of the Commissioner of Indian Affairs* (1872), pp. 155–58 (Howard's entire report is on pp. 148–75); *American Missionary,* Dec. 1876, pp. 281–82. See also

Howard's account of his trip in his book *My Life and Experiences Among Our Hostile Indians* (Hartford: A. D. Worthington, 1907), pp. 120–76. The trip is also discussed in St. Pierre, "General O. O. Howard and Grant's Peace Policy," pp. 190–245.

38. EPS to OOH, June 12, 1872, OOH Papers, Bowdoin College Library; *New York Times*, June 10, 1872.

39. EPS to OOH, June 12, 1872, OOH Papers, Bowdoin College Library.

20. The White Earth Reservation

1. Notice of Austin reward, May 11, 1872, and Austin proclamation, May 13, 1872, LR, Records of the OIA, Chippewa Agency, RG 75, M-234, NA; Austin's undated notes on Indian affairs (56.A.2.8F) in Horace Austin and Family Papers, Minnesota Historical Society, St. Paul, Minn.

2. James Bean to commanding officer, Fort Ripley, May 24, 1872, Capt. Wm. S. McCaskey to AAG, St. Paul, May 25, 27, and 30, and June 3, 1872, W. S. Hancock to W. S. McCaskey, May 26, 1872, and Hancock order, June 3, 1872, J. A. Manley to AAG, St. Paul, June 3, 1872, and EPS to F. A. Walker, June 4, 1872, LR, Records of the OIA, Chippewa Agency, RG 75, M-234, NA.

3. James Bean to F. A. Walker, May 16 and [23?], and June 7, 1872, ibid.

4. EPS to Gov. Austin, June 5, 1872, Horace Austin and Family Papers, Minnesota Historical Society; Walker, *Indian Question*, pp. 166–69.

5. EPS to W. S. McCaskey, June 12 and 20, 1872, EPS to Horace Austin, Mar. 28, 1873, and [W. H. Hammer?] to [A. Manly?], June 13, 1872, Horace Austin and Family Papers, Minnesota Historical Society; EPS to F. A. Walker, June 20 and 27, 1872, LR, Records of the OIA, Chippewa Agency, RG 75, M-234, NA; *Detroit* (Minnesota) *Record*, June 22 and 29, 1872.

6. EPS to F. A. Walker, June 20, 1872, LR, Records of the OIA, Chippewa Agency, RG 75, M-234, NA.

7. EPS to F. A. Walker, June 20 and July 4, 1872, EPS to W. S. Hancock, June 20, 1872, with Hancock and Sheridan endorsements, and Wm. W. Belknap to the secretary of the interior, July 30, 1872, ibid.

8. *Detroit* (Minnesota) *Record*, July 20 and 27, and Aug. 3, 1872; *Annual Report of the Commissioner of Indian Affairs* (1872), p. 208 [EPS report of Oct. 1, 1872]; Folwell, *History of Minnesota*, 3:79–80.

9. Folwell, *History of Minnesota*, 4:195–96; Report of Board of Visitors to White Earth and Leech Lake, received Nov. 29, 1872, EPS to F. A. Walker, Oct. 23, 1872, and various contracts for buildings in LR, Records of the OIA, Chippewa Agency, RG 75, M-234, NA; *Independent*, Nov. 7, 1872; *Advance*, Sept. 19, 1872.

10. *Annual Report of the Commissioner of Indian Affairs* (1873), p. 12; EPS to E. S. Parker, May 16, 1871, EPS to F. A. Walker, Dec. 30, 1871, and June 20, 21, July 4, Dec. 17 and 31, 1872, and Prescott Fay to commissioner of Indian affairs, Oct. 18,

1872, LR, Records of the OIA, Chippewa Agency, RG 75, M-234, NA. See also U.S. Congress, *House Executive Document No. 83,* 42d Cong., 2d sess., on the removal of the Chippewas.

11. U.S. Congress, *House Miscellaneous Document No. 167,* 44th Cong., 1st sess., pp. 414–21.

12. *Lorain County* (Ohio) *News,* Oct. 10, 1872; EPS to E. M. Cravath, Aug. 15, 1872, AMA Archives, ARC; Records of the U.S. General Accounting Office, Indian Claims Accounts, Dec. 31, 1872, File No. 1690-C, and memo about Minnie's work, Jan. 15, 1879, in File No. 8088, RG 217, NA. The easy manner in which Cleavie Smith and her nieces adapted to life among the Indians was hardly typical of white women generally. See Glenda Riley, *Women and Indians on the Frontier, 1825–1915* (Albuquerque: University of New Mexico Press, 1984).

13. *American Missionary,* Feb. 1872, pp. 27–28; EPS to E. M. Cravath, Sept. 2, 1872, AMA Archives, ARC.

14. *Lorain County* (Ohio) *News,* Oct. 10, 1872.

15. Ibid.; *Advance,* Sept. 19, 1872.

16. *Lorain County* (Ohio) *News,* Oct. 17 and Dec. 19, 1872.

17. *Independent,* Nov. 7, 1872.

18. *Nation,* Oct. 24, 1872, pp. 264–65; *New York Times,* Nov. 2, 1872.

19. In addition to the notes above, see *American Missionary,* May 1872, pp. 113–15, and Nov. 1872, p. 258 (the latter copied from the *Friends' Review*), and *Spirit of Missions,* Oct. 1872, pp. 616–21. The *Fourth Annual Report of the BIC* (1872), pp. 161–64, contains the report of a visit to White Earth by Charles Howard.

20. EPS to CD, Jan. 25, 1872, and CD to F. A. Walker, July 8 and 30, 1872, with a copy of "An Act to Perfect Certain Land Titles . . . ," dated June 8, 1872, LR, Records of the OIA, Chippewa Agency, RG 75, M-234, NA; William Watts Folwell, *Minnesota: The North Star State* (Boston: Houghton Mifflin, 1908), pp. 115–16.

21. EPS to H. S. Neal, Aug. 16, 1872, EPS and T. C. Jones to F. A. Walker, Nov. 25, 1872, and a minority report by Dana E. King, Dec. 13, 1872, LR, Records of the OIA, Chippewa Agency, RG 75, M-234, NA.

22. *American Missionary,* Nov. 1872, p. 258.

23. EPS to F. A. Walker, Dec. 30, 1871, Jan. 1, Feb. 5, and Aug. 7, 1872, LR, Records of the OIA, Chippewa Agency, RG 75, M-234, NA.

24. Gov. C. C. Washburn to CD, Aug. 24, 1872, Houlton and Nickerson to CD, Aug. 28, 1872, N. P. Clark to commissioner of Indian affairs, Oct. 19, 1872, ibid.

25. H. B. Whipple to F. A. Walker, Aug. 25, 1872, with C. M. Loring to H. B. Whipple, Aug. 17, 1872, ibid.; Fritz, *Movement for Indian Assimilation,* pp. 50–51.

26. EPS to F. A. Walker, Aug. 15 and Oct. 25, 1872, A. H. Wilder to F. A. Walker, Sept. 16, 1872, and Walker to Wilder, Sept. 19 and 24, 1872, H. R. Clum to EPS, Sept. 18, 1872, and John T. Averill to commissioner of Indian affairs, Oct. 29, 1872, LR, Records of the OIA, Chippewa Agency, RG 75, M-234, NA; Jarchow, *Amherst H. Wilder,* pp. 56–59.

27. Samuel Walker to Felix R. Brunot, Nov. 9, 1872, and Thomas K. Cree to Felix R. Brunot, Dec. 18, 1872, Records of the OIA, LS, BIC, RG 75, NA; *Annual Report of the Commissioner of Indian Affairs* (1873), p. 263; St. Pierre, "General O. O. Howard and Grant's Peace Policy," p. 288.

28. *American Missionary,* Feb. 1873, pp. 33–34.

29. Ibid.

30. EPS to F. A. Walker, Dec. 10, 1872, LR, Records of the OIA, Chippewa Agency, RG 75, M-234, NA; *Washington Daily Morning Chronicle,* Jan. 15, 1873.

31. *Journal of the Second Annual Conference of the Board of Indian Commissioners with the Representatives of the Religious Societies Co-operating with the Government,* pp. 5–6.

32. Ibid.

33. Ibid., pp. 6–7.

34. Ibid., pp. 28–29.

35. H. R. Clum to H. Bendell, Mar. 26, 1873, LS, Records of the OIA, RG 75, M-21, NA; *Annual Report of the Commissioner of Indian Affairs* (1872), p. 177; Norton B. Stern, "Herman Bendell: Superintendent of Indian Affairs, Arizona Territory, 1871–1873," *Western States Jewish Historical Quarterly* 8 (Apr. 1976): 266–68, 279–80. Bendell's resignation may also have been prompted by suggestions that his superintendency would be discontinued and by his own plans to return to Albany to be married.

36. *Journal of the Second Annual Conference,* pp. 45–46, 64.

21. Commissioner of Indian Affairs

1. Munroe, *Life of Francis Amasa Walker,* p. 149; Thomas K. Cree to William Welsh, Oct. 26, 1872, Cree to F. Brunot, Dec. 16, 1872, Records of the OIA, LS, BIC, RG 75, NA.

2. Cree to GHS, Jan. 31 and Mar. 8, 1873, Cree to [N. J. Turney?], Feb. 4, 1873, minutes of BIC meeting, Jan. 16, 1873, Records of the OIA, LS, BIC, RG 75, NA; OOH to GHS, Nov. 23, 1872, GHS Papers, LC; Cyrus Beede to E. Hoag, Jan. 17 and 28, 1873, Hoag Indian Papers, Quaker Collection, Haverford College Library, Haverford, Pa.; W. Welsh to H. B. Whipple, Mar. 1, 1873, Whipple Papers, Minnesota Historical Society, St. Paul, Minn.; *New York Times,* Oct. 23, 1872; Slattery, *Felix Reville Brunot,* pp. 197–98; *Washington Daily Morning Chronicle,* Jan. 17, 1873.

3. Thomas K. Cree to F. Brunot, Mar. 5 and 7, 1873, B. R. Cowen to EPS, Mar. 12, 1873, misc. LR, Records of the OIA, RG 75, M-234, NA; *New York Times,* Mar. 13, 1873.

4. Thomas K. Cree to GHS, Mar. 13, 1873, Cree to Felix Brunot, Mar. 12, 1873, Cree to Nathan Bishop, Mar. 12 and 15, 1873, Cree to John D. Lang, Mar. 22, 1873, Cree to N. J. Turney, Mar. 22, 1873, Records of the OIA, LS, BIC, RG 75, NA; CD to A. T. Torbert, Mar. 24, 1873, and CD to W. Welsh, Sept. 25, 1873, CD Letter-

books, Illinois Historical Survey, University of Illinois Library, Urbana-Champaign; E. Whittlesey to Rev. H. M. Dexter, n.d., Records of the OIA, LR, BIC, RG 75, Entry 1384, NA.

5. Thomas K. Cree to Nathan Bishop, Mar. 15, 1873, Cree to William Welsh, Mar. 18, 1873, and Cree to GHS, Mar. 18, 1873, Records of the OIA, LS, BIC, RG 75, NA; *New York Times,* Mar. 17 and 22, 1873; *Springfield* (Mass.) *Weekly Republican,* Apr. 11, 1873.

6. *New York Times,* Jan. 11 and Mar. 17, 1873; *Washington Daily Morning Chronicle,* Jan. 14, 1873; *Who Was Who in America* (Chicago: A. N. Marquis, 1943), 1316; Robert W. Daly, ed., *Aboard the USS Monitor, 1862: The Letters of Acting Paymaster William Frederick Keeler, U.S. Navy to His Wife, Anna* (Annapolis: U.S. Naval Institute, 1964), 231, 232, 236, 248, 259; William C. Davis, *Duel Between the First Ironclads* (Garden City, N.Y.: Doubleday, 1975), pp. 160–64; Grenville M. Weeks, "The Last Cruise of the Monitor," *Atlantic Monthly* 11 (Mar. 1863): 366–72; *Annual Report of the Commissioner of Indian Affairs* (1867), Serial 1326, p. 342 (1869), Serial 1414, p. 865; G. M. Weeks to J. D. Cox, June 15 and July 22, 1870 (with printed information about the U.S. Indian Commission), Selected Classes of LR, Indian Division, Records of the Office of the Secretary of the Interior, RG 48, M-825, NA; Prucha, *Great Father,* 1:498–99. Further information about Weeks is from the Civil War Library and Museum, Philadelphia, and from his U.S. pension application file (No. XC 2 721 847), Veterans Administration Regional Office, Cleveland, Ohio.

7. Thomas K. Cree to William Welsh, Mar. 18, 1872, Cree to GHS, Mar. 18, 1873, and Cree to F. R. Brunot, Mar. 18, 1873, Records of the OIA, LS, BIC, RG 75, NA; *Springfield* (Mass.) *Weekly Republican,* Apr. 11, 1873; Moss, *Annals,* pp. 169, 351; *New York Times,* Mar. 18 and 22, 1873; *Washington Daily Morning Chronicle,* Mar. 16, 1873; notice of appointment as commissioner of Indian affairs, Mar. 20, 1873, EPS Papers, ARC.

8. S. G. Wright to GW, June 27, 1870, AMA Archives, ARC.

9. B. R. Cowen to EPS, [Mar.] 13, 1873, Records of the U.S. General Accounting Office, Indian Claims Accounts, RG 217, File No. 8088, NA; M. S. Cook to EPS, Apr. 14, 1873, LR, Records of the OIA, Chippewa Agency, RG 75, M-234, NA; *Detroit* (Minnesota) *Record,* Apr. 19, 1873.

10. EPS to CD, Apr. 3, 1873, Records of the Office of the Secretary of the Interior, Appointments Division, Letters of Application and Recommendation, Commissioner of Indian Affairs, RG 48, NA; EPS to "My dear Gerty," May 12, 1873, EPS Papers, Manuscripts and Archives, Yale University Library, New Haven, Conn.; *American Missionary,* May 1873, p. 107.

11. Inventory of property, Oct. 31, 1871, Records of the OIA, LS by the Chief Clerk and the Assistant Commissioner, RG 75, Entry 181, NA; Lowenfels, ed., *Walt Whitman's Civil War,* pp. 87, 173–74; Marc Pachter, ed., *Telling Lives: The Biographer's Art* (Washington, D.C.: New Republic Books/National Portrait Gallery, 1979), p. 43.

12. *New York Times,* Oct. 28, 1872.

13. *Register of Officers and Agents . . . in the Service of the United States, on the Thirtieth*

of September, 1873 . . . (Washington, D.C.: U.S. Government Printing Office, 1874), p. 314; U.S. Congress, *House Report No. 778*, 43d Cong., 1st sess., p. 221.

14. H. R. Clum to M. S. Cook, Aug. 4, 1873, Records of the OIA, LS, RG 75, M-21, NA; H. R. Clum to Louise F. Hopkins, May 21, 1873 (saying "this office does not employ female clerks"), Records of the OIA, LS by the Chief Clerk and the Assistant Commissioner, RG 75, Entry 181, NA; *Annual Report of the Commissioner of Indian Affairs* (1873), p. 386. The clerks in the Indian Office made a note of the person who drafted each of the letters sent from the office, which makes it possible to identify the letters Smith wrote himself.

15. J. Willard Brown, *The Signal Corps, U.S.A., in the War of the Rebellion* (Boston: U.S. Veteran Signal Corps Association, 1896), pp. 86, 745, and passim; Clum obituaries in the *Washington Post* and *Evening Star*, both Apr. 15, 1904; *New York Herald*, Oct. 5, 1870; U.S. Congress, *House Miscellaneous Document No. 167*, 44th Cong., 1st sess., p. 279; Henry R. Clum pension file and military service record, NA.

16. EPS to [?] Springer, May 31, 1873, Records of the OIA, Outgoing Letterpress Correspondence of the Commissioner of Indian Affairs, RG 75, Entry 165, NA; *Register of Officers and Agents, 1873*, pp. 314–31; EPS to A. E. Rogers, Nov. 28, 1874, and EPS to J. G. Hamilton, Mar. 29, 1875, LS, Records of the OIA, RG 75, M-21, NA.

17. *New York Times*, Jan. 14, 1871. Robert H. Keller, Jr., describes the political pressures brought to bear on the appointment of Indian agents (*American Protestantism and United States Indian Policy*, pp. 92–97). Keller asserts that Grant and Delano were among those bringing political pressure.

18. EPS to J. B. Monteith, May 24, 1873, LS, Records of the OIA, RG 75, M-21, NA. See also EPS to J. B. Monteith, Oct. 28, 1875, ibid., Rahill, *The Catholic Indian Missions and Grant's Peace Policy*, pp. 112–17, and Robert C. Carriker, "Joseph M. Cataldo, S.J.: Courier of Catholicism to the Nez Percés," in Milner and O'Neil, eds., *Churchmen and the Western Indians*, pp. 119–21. A year and a half later, Delano withdrew permission for the Catholics to establish churches and schools on the reservation after discovering that a treaty with the Nez Percé required the tribe's permission for any whites except those in the Indian service to reside on the reservation. See CD to EPS, Nov. 23, 1874, LS, Indian Division, Records of the Office of the Secretary of the Interior, RG 48, M-606, NA.

19. EPS to CD, Dec. 30, 1873, Records of the OIA, Report Books, RG 75, M-348, NA.

20. EPS to CD, Jan. 4, 1874, ibid.; EPS to W. P. Adair, Sept. 23, 1874, LS, Records of the OIA, RG 75, M-21, NA; CD to EPS, Nov. 23, 1874, LS, Indian Division, Records of the Office of the Secretary of the Interior, RG 48, M-606, NA. See also EPS to I. L. Mahan, Nov. 6, 1874, and EPS to J. B. Monteith, Oct. 28, 1875, LS, Records of the OIA, RG 75, M-21, NA.

21. *Register of Officers and Agents, 1873*, pp. 314–31; EPS to GW, May 28, 1873, Records of the OIA, LS, RG 75, M-21, NA.

22. *Register of Officers and Agents, 1873*, pp. 314–31; Stuart, *Indian Office*, pp. 73–85; *U.S. Statutes at Large*, 17:463; CD to GW, June 5, 1873, CD Letterbooks, Illinois

Historical Survey, University of Illinois Library; Julia B. McGillycuddy, *McGilly-cuddy Agent: A Biography of Dr. Valentine T. McGillycuddy* (Stanford: Stanford University Press, 1941), p. 228.

23. CD to Alfred H. Love, Mar. 13, 1873, CD Letterbooks, Illinois Historical Survey, University of Illinois Library; Trani, *Secretaries of the Department of the Interior*, pp. 108–14.

24. Stuart, *Indian Office*, pp. 55–71; Marshall Dwight Moody, "A History of the Board of Indian Commissioners and Its Relationship to the Administration of Indian Affairs, 1869–1900" (Master's thesis, American University, [1951?]).

25. *American Missionary*, July 1874, p. 156.

26. J. D. Cox to Eli K. Price et al., Mar. 25, 1869, Cox to William Welsh, Apr. 14, 1869, and Cox to John V. Farwell, Apr. 15, 1869, Cox Papers, Oberlin College Archives, Oberlin, Ohio; J. D. Cox to GHS, Apr. 13, 1869 (two items), GHS Papers, LC; Thompson, ed., *Life of George H. Stuart*, pp. 239, 242; Prucha, *Great Father*, 1:505–7, and *American Indian Policy in Crisis*, pp. 34–35.

27. Keith A. Murray, *The Modocs and Their War* (Norman: University of Oklahoma Press, 1959); Mardock, *Reformers and the American Indian*, pp. 115–28; Prucha, *American Indian Policy in Crisis*, pp. 85–88; *New York Times*, Apr. 14, 1873; *New York World* quoted in *Washington Daily Morning Chronicle*, Apr. 17, 1873; *New York Herald*, Apr. 18, 1873; CD to William Welsh, Apr. 16, 1873, CD Letterbooks, Illinois Historical Survey, University of Illinois Library; *Annual Report of the Commissioner of Indian Affairs* (1873), pp. 12–14, 16–17, 74–82.

28. *New York Herald*, Apr. 14, 1873; *Washington Daily Morning Chronicle*, Apr. 13–14, 1873; *New York Times*, Apr. 14–15, 1873.

29. *Washington Daily Morning Chronicle*, Apr. 13–14, 1873; *New York Herald*, Apr. 14, 1873.

30. *New York Herald*, Apr. 14, 1873.

31. *Washington Daily Morning Chronicle*, Apr. 13–14, 1873; *New York Herald*, Apr. 14, 1873.

32. Mardock, *Reformers and the American Indian*, pp. 121–22; EPS to CD, Sept. 4, 1873, Records of the OIA, Report Books, RG 75, M-348, NA.

33. Benjamin Capps, *The Warren Wagontrain Raid* (New York: Dial Press, 1974); Nye, *Carbine and Lance*, pp. 124–47; J'Nell Pate, "Kiowa Defiance: Chiefs Satanta and Satank and the War on the Southern Plains," in Glenn H. Jordan and Thomas M. Holm, eds., *Indian Leaders: Oklahoma's First Statesmen* (Oklahoma City: Oklahoma Historical Society, 1979), pp. 126–40; Donald Worcester, "Satanta," in David R. Edmunds, ed., *American Indian Leaders: Studies in Diversity* (Lincoln: University of Nebraska Press, 1980), pp. 107–30; Hagan, *United States–Comanche Relations*, pp. 76–96; Allen Lee Hamilton, "The Warren Wagontrain Raid: Frontier Indian Policy at the Crossroads," *Arizona and the West* 28 (Autumn 1986): 201–24.

34. Edmund J. Davis to C. C. Augur, Apr. 11, 1872, with endorsements (including that of P. H. Sheridan), and F. A. Walker to CD, June 5, 1872, in Records of the Office of the Secretary of the Interior, Special File No. 8 on Satanta and Big Tree, RG 48, NA.

35. W. T. Sherman to CD, Apr. 16, 1873, ibid. For the negotiations about the release of Satanta and Big Tree, see also Lawrie Tatum to Jonathan Richards, May 30, 1871, Kiowa Agency Records, Microcopy KA 37, Archives and Manuscript Division, Oklahoma Historical Society, Oklahoma City; H. R. Clum to secretary of the interior, Mar. 19, 1873, Edmund J. Davis to CD, Apr. 1, 1873, and Enoch Hoag to CD, Apr. 29, 1873, Records of the Office of the Secretary of the Interior, Special File No. 8 on Satanta and Big Tree, RG 48, NA; CD to Edmund J. Davis, June 14, 1872, Mar. 22, Apr. 14 and 18, 1873, LS, Indian Division, Records of the Office of the Secretary of the Interior, RG 48, M-606, NA; EPS to Henry E. Alvord, Sept. 18, 1873, LS, Records of the OIA, RG 75, M-21, NA; CD to Edmund J. Davis, Mar. 22, May 27, and June 5, 1873, LR, Records of the OIA, Kiowa Agency, RG 75, M-234, NA. Lawrie Tatum did not agree with the Quakers who wanted Satanta and Big Tree released and resigned his position on Mar. 31, 1873. See his *Our Red Brothers*, pp. 131–33.

36. Enoch Hoag to CD, Apr. 29, 1873, Enoch Hoag to EPS, Apr. 9, 1873, Records of the Office of the Secretary of the Interior, Special File No. 8, Satanta and Big Tree, RG 48, NA.

37. EPS to the secretary of the interior, Apr. 18, 1873, ibid.; EPS to CD, May 22, 1873, Records of the OIA, Report Books, RG 75, M-348, NA.

38. Thompson, ed., *Life of George H. Stuart*, pp. 242–43; two undated items about bidding in BIC Newspaper Clippings, RG 75, Entry 1396, NA; *Washington Daily Morning Chronicle*, May 17, 1873; *New York Times*, May 1, 1873.

39. *Washington Daily Morning Chronicle*, May 14, 17, and 29, 1873.

40. *New York Times*, May 17, 1873; see also May 3, 16, 21, 29, and 31, 1873.

41. EPS to CD, May 20, 1873, Records of the OIA, Report Books, RG 75, M-348, NA; CD to EPS, May 27, 1873, LS, Indian Division, Records of the Office of the Secretary of the Interior, RG 75, M-606, NA. See also several letters from Thomas K. Cree dated May 17, 1873, Records of the OIA, LS, BIC, RG 75, NA.

22. A Guardian and His Wards

1. EPS to secretary of the interior, June 26, 1873, Records of the OIA, Outgoing Letterpress Correspondence of the Commissioner of Indian Affairs, RG 75, Entry 165, NA; CD to EPS, July 9, 1873, misc. LR, Records of the OIA, RG 75, M-234, NA.

2. Anson Dart to secretary of the interior, Dec. 14, 1871, and Anson Dart to EPS, Apr. 21, 187[3] (with Smith endorsement), misc. LR, Records of the OIA, RG 75, M-234, NA; H. R. Clum to Dr. A. Dart, Apr. 21 and 23, 1873, LS, Records of the OIA, RG 75, M-21, NA. For the Anson Dart affair, see U.S. Congress, *House Miscellaneous Document No. 167*, 44th Cong., 1st sess., pp. 116–19, 141–42, 198–99, 279–80, 287, 351, 398–401, 411–12, and *House Report No. 778*, 43d Cong., 1st sess., pp. 217–18.

3. U.S. Patent No. 45,028 for "Improved Compound Oil," Nov. 15, 1864; *House Miscellaneous Document No. 167*, pp. 351, 398–401.

4. Oregon Appointment Papers Re: Anson Dart, Records of the Office of the Secretary of the Interior, RG 48, NA; Anson Dart to secretary of the interior, Apr. 10, 1872, with enclosures, Selected Classes of LR (misc.), Indian Division, ibid. Marjorie Catlin Roehm, *The Letters of George Catlin and His Family: A Chronicle of the American West* (Berkeley: University of California Press, 1966), contains considerable information about Dart. Additional information can be found in Thaddeus Lincoln Bolton, *Genealogy of the Dart Family in America* (Philadelphia: Cooper Printing Co., 1927).

5. Anson Dart to E. S. Parker, Aug. 1, 1870, Anson Dart to commissioner of Indian affairs, Apr. 1, 1872, and Anson Dart to secretary of the interior, Dec. 14, 1871, misc. LR, Records of the OIA, RG 75, M-234, NA; F. A. Walker to Anson Dart, Dec. 19, 1871, and Apr. 4, 1872, copies with Anson Dart to secretary of the interior, Apr. 10, 1872, Selected Classes of LR (misc.), Indian Division, Records of the Office of the Secretary of the Interior, RG 48, NA; Roehm, *Letters of George Catlin and His Family*, p. 325; Keller, *American Protestantism and United States Indian Policy*, pp. 121, 284 n. 45; Basler, ed., *Collected Works of Abraham Lincoln*, 4:403–4.

6. The YMCA Bible classes are noted in the *Washington Daily Morning Chronicle*, Apr.–June 1873. Information about Howard University is from the *New York Herald*, July 5, 1873.

7. Hamilton, *Twelve Miles from a Lemon*, p. 171; EPS to "My dear Gerty," July 4, 1873, EPS Papers, Manuscripts and Archives, Yale University Library, New Haven, Conn.

8. *Washington Daily Morning Chronicle*, June 9, 1873; CD to USG, July 18, 1873, CD Letterbooks, Ohio Historical Society, Columbus, Ohio.

9. EPS to CD, June 13 and July 3, 1873, Records of the OIA, Report Books, RG 75, M-348, NA; EPS to Byron H. Kilbourn, July 25, 1873, Selected Classes of LR (misc.), Indian Division, Records of the Office of the Secretary of the Interior, RG 48, NA; *New York Times*, July 4, 1873.

10. Proceedings of Council with the Winnebagoes, July 17, 1873, with H. R. Clum to secretary of the interior, Aug. 7, 1873, and EPS to H. R. Clum, July 24, 1873, LR, Indian Division, Records of the Office of the Secretary of the Interior, RG 48, NA.

11. Proceedings of Council with the Winnebagoes, July 17, 1873, ibid.

12. Ibid.

13. EPS to Byron H. Kilbourn, July 25, 1873, Selected Classes of LR (misc.), ibid.; EPS to CD, Nov. 4 and 26, 1873, and Jan. 10, 1874, Records of the OIA, Report Books, RG 75, M-348, NA; EPS to CD, July 26, 1873, Selected Classes of LR, Indian Division, Records of the Office of the Secretary of the Interior, RG 48, M-825, NA. Smith later made remarks similar to those he had made to the Winnebagos at a council with Sac and Fox Indians from Kansas. See Joseph B. Herring, "Indian Intransigency in Kansas: Government Bureaucracy vs. Mokohoko's Sacs and Foxes," *Western Historical Quarterly* 17 (Apr. 1986): 196.

14. *New York Times*, July 28, 31, Aug. 3, 5, 6, 9, and Nov. 22, 1873; see also ibid., July 14, 1873.

15. Ibid., Nov. 22, 1873.

16. Ibid.; *American Missionary*, Sept. 1873, pp. 211–12; *Advance*, July 24, 1873. Goodale's work is described in *American Missionary*, Aug. 1873, p. 179, and EPS to CD, Jan. 3, 1874, Records of the OIA, Report Books, RG 75, M-348, NA. For a negative view of the services of S. N. Goodale, see Priest, *Uncle Sam's Stepchildren*, pp. 63–64 and p. 265, n. 23.

17. Records of the U.S. General Accounting Office, Indian Claims Accounts, RG 217, File No. 1530, NA; *New York Times*, Aug. 5, 1873; EPS to CD, July 3, 1873, Records of the OIA, Report Books, RG 75, M-348, NA; *Fifth Annual Report of the BIC* (1873), p. 26.

18. Records of the U.S. General Accounting Office, Indian Claims Accounts, RG 217, File No. 1530, NA; EPS to Joseph Webster, Nov. 12, 1873, LS, Records of the OIA, RG 75, M-21, NA; *What the Government and the Churches Are Doing for the Indians*, p. 12; *New York Times*, Aug. 13, 1873; *Friends Intelligencer*, Oct. 25, 1873; *Spirit of Missions*, Oct. 1873, pp. 624–27; *Annual Report of the Commissioner of Indian Affairs* (1873), pp. 242–43.

19. *Omaha Daily Herald*, Aug. 12, 1873; *New York Times*, Aug. 28, 1873; EPS to CD, Sept. 18, 1873, Records of the OIA, Report Books, RG 75, M-348, NA; *Annual Report of the Commissioner of Indian Affairs* (1873), p. 186.

20. Journal of Barclay White, 1:374–75 (Aug. 12, 1873), Friends Historical Library of Swarthmore College, Swarthmore, Pa.; *Friends Intelligencer*, Sept. 13, 1873. The operation of Grant's peace policy in Nebraska is analyzed in Milner, *With Good Intentions*.

21. *New York Times*, Aug. 28, 1873; Everett W. Sterling, "Moses N. Adams: A Missionary as Indian Agent," *Minnesota History* 35 (Dec. 1956): 167–77; Minutes of Council, Aug. 18, 1873, Adams Papers, Minnesota Historical Society, St. Paul; Whipple, *Lights and Shadows of a Long Episcopate*, p. 288.

22. Minutes of Council, Aug. 18, 1873, Adams Papers, Minnesota Historical Society, St. Paul.

23. Ibid.

24. Sterling, "Moses N. Adams," pp. 167–77.

25. EPS to M. N. Adams, Jan. 22, 1874, LS, Records of the OIA, RG 75, M-21, NA.

26. Records of the U.S. General Accounting Office, Indian Claims Accounts, RG 217, File No. 1530, NA; *New York Times*, Aug. 28, 1873. The U.S. census reported 383,712 Indians in the United States (*New York Times*, May 17, 1873).

23. Satanta and Big Tree

1. EPS to E. Hoag, May 21, 24, and June 24, 1873, LS, Records of the OIA, RG 75, M-21, NA; E. Hoag to EPS, July 17, 1873, and H. R. Clum to secretary of the

interior, July 21, 1873, Records of the Office of the Secretary of the Interior, Special File No. 8 on Satanta and Big Tree, RG 48, NA; *New York Times*, Sept. 9 and 21, 1873.

2. Journal of Barclay White, 1:375 (Sept. 23, 1873), Friends Historical Library of Swarthmore College, Swarthmore, Pa.; EPS to CD, Sept. 27, 1873, Records of the OIA, Report Books, RG 75, M-348, NA.

3. EPS to CD, Sept. 27, 1873, Records of the OIA, Report Books, RG 75, M-348, NA.

4. Edward F. Hoag to EPS, Sept. 13, 1873, LR, Records of the OIA, Kiowa Agency, RG 75, M-234, NA; copy of telegram, Sept. 30, 1873, in Hoag Indian Papers, Quaker Collection, Haverford College Library, Haverford, Pa.; *Nation*, Oct. 30, 1873, pp. 286–87; William H. Leckie, *The Buffalo Soldiers: A Narrative of the Negro Cavalry in the West* (Norman: University of Oklahoma Press, 1967), pp. vii–viii, 25–26.

5. J. W. Davidson to AAG, Dept. of Texas, Oct. 8, 1873, LR, Records of the OIA, Kiowa Agency, RG 75, NA; Battey, *Life and Adventures of a Quaker Among the Indians*, pp. 199–200. See also William H. Leckie, *The Military Conquest of the Southern Plains* (Norman: University of Oklahoma Press, 1963), pp. 176–81.

6. Record of the Indian Council of Oct. 6, 1873, at Fort Sill (with J. W. Davidson to AAG, Dept. of Texas, Oct. 8, 1873), LR, Records of the OIA, Kiowa Agency, RG 75, NA; report of council in clipping from *National Republican*, Oct. 15, 1873, Records of the OIA, BIC Newspaper Clippings, RG 75, Entry 1396, NA. See also Vail, *Memorial of James M. Haworth*, pp. 38–46, Tatum, *Our Red Brothers*, pp. 173–77, Nye, *Carbine and Lance*, pp. 164–82, and Hagan, *United States–Comanche Relations*, pp. 97–100.

7. Record of the Indian Council of Oct. 6, 1873.

8. Ibid.

9. Report of council in *National Republican*, Oct. 15, 1873; Record of the Indian Council of Oct. 6, 1873.

10. Record of the Indian Council of Oct. 6, 1873.

11. EPS to CD, Oct. 7, 1873, LR, Records of the OIA, Kiowa Agency, RG 75, M-234, NA.

12. EPS to E. J. Davis, Oct. 7, 1873, ibid.

13. Ibid.

14. Ibid.

15. Battey, *Life and Adventures of a Quaker Among the Indians*, pp. 202–3.

16. Ibid.; Vail, *Memorial of James M. Haworth*, pp. 42–43.

17. E. J. Davis to EPS, Oct. 7, 1873, and EPS to CD, Oct. 8, 1873, LR, Records of the OIA, Kiowa Agency, RG 75, M-234, NA; clipping from *National Republican*, Oct. 15, 1873, Records of the OIA, BIC Newspaper Clippings, RG 75, Entry 1396, NA.

18. Battey, *Life and Adventures of a Quaker Among the Indians*, pp. 205–6; EPS to F. Brunot, Nov. 28, 1873, LS, Records of the OIA, RG 75, M-21, NA; *New York Times*, Oct. 14 and 21, 1873.

19. CD to secretary of war, Oct. 7, 1873, CD to EPS, Oct. 8, 1873, and W. H. Smith to secretary of war, Oct. 13, 1873, LS, Indian Division, Records of the Office

of the Secretary of the Interior, RG 48, M-606, NA; EPS to J. W. Davidson, Oct. 9, 1873, LR, Records of the OIA, Kiowa Agency, RG 75, M-234, NA; E. J. Davis to secretary of the interior, Oct. 13, 1873, Selected Classes of LR, Indian Division, Records of the Office of the Secretary of the Interior, RG 48, M-825, NA; *New York Times*, Oct. 9, 1873.

20. W. T. Sherman endorsement on J. W. Davidson's orders, Nov. 3, 1873, LR, Records of the OIA, Kiowa Agency, RG 75, M-234, NA.

21. Battey, *Life and Adventures of a Quaker Among the Indians*, pp. 206, 211–13; Hagan, *United States–Comanche Relations*, pp. 100–102; EPS to E. Hoag, Nov. 24, 1873, LS, Records of the OIA, RG 75, M-21, NA; J. Haworth to EPS, Dec. 2, 1873, LR, Records of the OIA, Kiowa Agency, RG 75, M-234, NA.

22. Battey, *Life and Adventures of a Quaker Among the Indians*, p. 212; *Washington Daily Chronicle*, Oct. 18, 1873, clipping in Records of the OIA, BIC Newspaper Clippings, RG 75, Entry 1396, NA.

23. J. Haworth to EPS, Nov. 14 and 24, 1873, LR, Records of the OIA, Kiowa Agency, RG 75, M-234, NA; on "James Mahlon Haworth," in "Dictionary of Quaker Biography," typescript in Quaker Collection, Haverford College Library; Vail, *Memorial of James M. Haworth*, pp. 13–14.

24. Cyrus Beede to EPS, Nov. 22, 1873, and P. H. Sheridan to EPS, Dec. 2, 1873, LR, Records of the OIA, Kiowa Agency, RG 75, M-234, NA; *New York Times*, Nov. 26 and 30, 1873.

25. EPS to F. Brunot, Nov. 28 and Dec. 23, 1873, LS, Records of the OIA, RG 75, M-21, NA.

26. F. Brunot to EPS, Dec. 1, 1873, LR, Records of the OIA, Kiowa Agency, RG 75, M-234, NA.

27. Vail, *Memorial of James M. Haworth*, pp. 47–48; Battey, *Life and Adventures of a Quaker Among the Indians*, pp. 225–26.

28. Battey, *Life and Adventures of a Quaker Among the Indians*, p. 230; Vail, *Memorial of James M. Haworth*, pp. 73–74; Hagan, *United States–Comanche Relations*, p. 103; H. R. Clum to J. M. Haworth, two telegrams dated Dec. 2, 1873, LS, Records of the OIA, RG 75, M-21, NA. The telegrams were signed by Clum but drafted by Smith.

24. *"We Are Not Children"*

1. *Friends' Review*, Nov. 1 and 8, 1873.

2. Ibid.

3. *Fourth Annual Report of the BIC* (1872), p. 125; Garrick Mallery, "Sign Language Among North American Indians. . . ." *First Annual Report of the Bureau of Ethnology* (Washington, D.C.: U.S. Government Printing Office, 1881), p. 476; Milner, *With Good Intentions*, p. 127. See also Viola, *Diplomats in Buckskins*.

4. *U.S. Statutes at Large*, 17:626; Report of Council Held with the Crows by the Special Commission Appointed to Negotiate with the Crow Indians, Sept. 8, 1873

(C-533), LR, Records of the OIA, RG 75, NA; *Annual Report of the Commissioner of Indian Affairs* (1873), pp. 19, 23, 113–43; *Washington Daily Chronicle*, Oct. 22, 1873, clipping in Records of the OIA, BIC Newspaper Clippings, RG 75, Entry 1396, NA.

5. Report of council with Crow delegation, Oct. 21, 1873, (I-824), LR, OIA, RG 75, NA; *Washington Evening Star*, Oct. 21, 1873, clipping in Records of the OIA, BIC Newspaper Clippings, RG 75, Entry 1396, NA.

6. Report of Council Held with the Crows, Sept. 8, 1873 (C-533), and Report of Council with Crow Delegation, Oct. 29, 1873 (I-905), LR, Records of the OIA, RG 75, NA; *Annual Report of the Commissioner of Indian Affairs* (1873), p. 131; U.S. Congress, *House Miscellaneous Document No. 167*, 44th Cong., 1st sess., pp. 201–4.

7. *U.S. Statutes at Large*, 17:55 and 18 (pt. 3):36–41; EPS to F. Brunot, July 2 and Sept. 5, 1873, LS, Records of the OIA, RG 75, M-21, NA; *Annual Report of the Commissioner of Indian Affairs* (1873), pp. 16, 83–113.

8. *New York Times*, Oct. 23, 1873; *Washington Evening Star*, Oct. 22, 1873, clipping in Records of the OIA, BIC Newspaper Clippings, RG 75, Entry 1396, NA.

9. *New York Times*, Oct. 25, 1873; *Washington Evening Star*, Oct. 22, 1873, clipping in Records of the OIA, BIC Newspaper Clippings, RG 75, Entry 1396, NA.

10. *Washington Daily Chronicle*, Nov. 3, 1873, and unidentified clipping about the White House visit, Records of the OIA, BIC Newspaper Clippings, RG 75, Entry 1396, NA; Stan Hoig, *The Peace Chiefs of the Cheyennes* (Norman: University of Oklahoma Press, 1980), pp. 128–30.

11. Report of Council Between Arapahos and Utes, Nov. 3, 1873 (I-840), LR, Records of the OIA, RG 75, NA; *Washington Daily Chronicle*, Nov. 4, 1873, clipping in Records of the OIA, BIC Newspaper Clippings, RG 75, Entry 1396, NA; *Annual Report of the Commissioner of Indian Affairs* (1873), pp. 111–13; Ann Woodbury Hafen, "Efforts to Recover the Stolen Son of Chief Ouray," *Colorado Magazine* 16 (Mar. 1939): 53–62.

12. The reports of the councils are in LR, Records of the OIA, RG 75, NA: Oct. 31, 1873 (I-907), Nov. 1, 1873 (I-908), and Nov. 4, 1873 (I-850). See also *Annual Report of the Commissioner of Indian Affairs* (1873), pp. 19–21, 196–98; *Friends' Intelligencer*, Nov. 22, 1873, and June 6, 1874; Milner, *With Good Intentions*, pp. 123–34 and passim; and Peter Nabokov, ed., *Native American Testimony: An Anthology of Indian and White Relations* (New York: Thomas Y. Crowell, 1978), pp. 168–76.

13. Report of Interview with Otoes of Nebraska, Oct. 31, 1873 (I-907), LR, Records of the OIA, RG 75, NA; Milner, *With Good Intentions*, p. 128; *Washington Daily Morning Chronicle*, Nov. 1, 1873.

14. Report of Interview with Otoes of Nebraska, Oct. 31, 1873 (I-907), LR, Records of the OIA, RG 75, NA.

15. Report of Council with Otoes of Nebraska, Nov. 1, 1873 (I-908), LR, Records of the OIA, RG 75, NA.

16. Ibid.

17. Ibid.

18. Report of Council with Otoes of Nebraska, Nov. 4, 1873 (I-850), ibid.

19. Ibid.

20. Thomas K. Cree to EPS, Oct. 25, 1873, Records of the OIA, LS, BIC, RG 75, NA.

21. Viola, *Diplomats in Buckskins*, pp. 64–68; CD to EPS, Dec. 19 and 26, 1874, LS, Indian Division, Records of the Office of the Secretary of the Interior, RG 48, M-606, NA; EPS to CD, Dec. 24, 1874, Records of the OIA, Report Books, RG 75, M-348, NA.

22. Samuel Walker to N. Bishop, Sept. 9, 12, 18, 19, and [25?], 1873, and Samuel Walker to Thomas K. Cree, Oct. 2, 1873, Records of the OIA, LS, BIC, RG 75, NA; *New York Herald*, Aug. 13, 1875.

23. Samuel Walker to W. Welsh, Sept. 6, 1873, Records of the OIA, LS, BIC, RG 75, NA; clipping from *St. Paul Dispatch*, Sept. 18, 1873, with H. B. Whipple to secretary of the interior, Sept. 20, 1873, Selected Classes of LR (misc.), Indian Division, Records of the Office of the Secretary of the Interior, RG 48, M-825, NA; CD to W. Welsh, Sept. 25, 1873, CD Letterbooks, Ohio Historical Society, Columbus, Ohio; W. Welsh to H. B. Whipple, Sept. 11, 1873, Whipple Papers, Minnesota Historical Society, St. Paul.

24. W. Welsh to H. B. Whipple, Sept. 11, 1873, Whipple Papers, Minnesota Historical Society; H. B. Whipple to CD, Sept. 4, 18, 20, and Oct. 3, 1873, Selected Classes of LR (misc.), Indian Division, Records of the Office of the Secretary of the Interior, RG 48, M-825, NA. Bishop Whipple said in his autobiography that the last time he and Smith met, Smith "burst into tears as he grasped my hand and said: 'I am so grateful Bishop, for your kind words. You believe me honest. God knows I have tried to do my duty' " (Whipple, *Lights and Shadows of a Long Episcopate*, pp. 49–50).

25. W. Welsh to CD, Sept. 23, 1873 in extracts from letters of Wm. Welsh, Esq. and Mr. Delano, in Special File No. 17, Report of Commission to Investigate Charges Against Commissioner of Indian Affairs, Indian Division, Records of the Office of the Secretary of the Interior, RG 48, NA; CD to W. Welsh, Sept. 25, 1873, CD Letterbooks, Ohio Historical Society; CD to H. B. Whipple, Sept. 27, 1873, LS, Indian Division, Records of the Office of the Secretary of the Interior, RG 48, M-606, NA; *New York Times*, Sept. 18, 1875.

25. William Welsh

1. Whipple, *Lights and Shadows of a Long Episcopate*, pp. 262–64; Mardock, *Reformers and the American Indian*, pp. 50–51, 57–58; Thompson, ed., *Life of George H. Stuart*, p. 239; Beaver, *Church, State, and the American Indians*, p. 131; Welsh, comp., *Taopi and His Friends*, pp. 73–84.

2. Armstrong, *Warrior in Two Camps*, pp. 143–45; Keller, *American Protestantism and United States Indian Policy*, pp. 73–77, 81–84; W. Welsh to EPS, Oct. [7?] 1870 (H-3467), AMA Archives, ARC.

3. Armstrong, *Warrior in Two Camps*, pp. 151–60; W. Welsh to H. B. Whipple, Apr. 15 and Dec. 10, 1870, Whipple Papers, Minnesota Historical Society, St. Paul.

4. Welsh, *Letters on the Home Missionary Work of the Protestant Episcopal Church;*

Welsh, *Letter to J. D. Cox*, p. 5; Welsh, *Visit to the Sioux Indians*, p. 1; Minutes of the Indian Commission and Minutes of the Executive Committee of the Indian Commission, Archives of the Episcopal Church, U.S.A., Austin, Texas.

5. *Journal of the Proceedings of the General Convention of the Protestant Episcopal Church . . . 1871* (N.p.: N.p., n.d.), pp. viii, 177, 233–34, 254, 528, *1874*, pp. v–viii, 126–28, 504–5, 510–11, 514, and *1877*, pp. viii, 144–45; Minutes of the Episcopal Indian Commission, 1870–78, Archives of the Episcopal Church, U.S.A.

6. Welsh, *Report of a Visit to the Sioux and Ponka Indians; Spirit of Missions*, Aug. 1872, pp. 471–74, and Oct. 1872, p. 606; *New York Times*, Oct. 27, 1874; Poole, *Among the Sioux of Dakota*, pp. 210–12.

7. Jonathan Richards Letterbooks, 2:114–16, Quaker Collection, Haverford College Library, Haverford, Pa.; EPS to GW, Dec. 15, 1870, AMA Archives, ARC.

8. Journal of Barclay White, 1:321–26 (June 26–27, 1872), Friends Historical Library of Swarthmore College, Swarthmore, Pa.

9. Ibid.

10. Dillwyn Parrish et al. to the President of the U.S., etc., Jan. 11, 1871, Friends Historical Library of Swarthmore College; Keller, *American Protestantism and United States Indian Policy*, p. 41; Fritz, *Movement for Indian Assimilation*, pp. 152–53.

11. Welsh, *Report and Supplementary Report of a Visit to Spotted Tail's Tribe*, pp. 1–4, 21–22; W. Welsh to H. B. Whipple, Oct. 4, 1870, Whipple Papers, Minnesota Historical Society; W. Welsh to J. D. Cox, Sept. 3, 1870, LR, Records of the OIA, Chippewa Agency, RG 75, M-234, NA; W. Welsh to E. S. Parker, Oct. 22 and 29, 1870, misc. LR, Records of the OIA, RG 75, M-234, NA.

12. W. Welsh to EPS, Oct. 6, 1870, AMA Archives, ARC.

13. William Welsh to H. B. Whipple, Mar. 6, 1873 (filed as Mar. 1), Whipple Papers, Minnesota Historical Society; William Welsh to EPS, Apr. 5, 1873, quoted by Edward F. Williams in *Advance*, Nov. 11, 1875.

14. W. Welsh to H. B. Whipple, Apr. 15, 1870, and H. B. Whipple to W. Welsh, Jan. 19, 1874, Whipple Papers, Minnesota Historical Society. Welsh's suspicious nature had many of the characteristics described in Richard Hofstadter, "The Paranoid Style in American Politics," in *The Paranoid Style in American Politics and Other Essays* (New York: Knopf, 1965), pp. 3–40.

15. W. Welsh to H. B. Whipple, Dec. 6, 1872, Whipple Papers, Minnesota Historical Society; extracts from letters of Wm. Welsh, Esq., and Mr. Delano in Special File No. 17, Report of Commission to Investigate Charges Against Commissioner of Indian Affairs, Indian Division, Records of the Office of the Secretary of the Interior, RG 48, NA; CD to W. Welsh, Sept. 25, 27, and Nov. 10, 1873, CD Letterbooks, Ohio Historical Society, Columbus.

16. CD to H. Dyer, Nov. 19, 1873, CD Letterbooks, Ohio Historical Society.

17. Thomas K. Cree to John V. Farwell, Nov. 6, 1873, and Cree to F. Brunot, Nov. 6, 1873, Records of the OIA, LS, BIC, RG 75, NA; *Advance*, Nov. 11, 1875.

18. EPS to W. Welsh, Nov. 26, 1873, Records of the OIA, Outgoing Letterpress Correspondence of the Commissioner of Indian Affairs, RG 75, Entry 165, NA.

19. Ibid.

20. GW to EPS, Nov. 28, 1873 (with undated and unsigned endorsement: "This paper has been on the Commissioner's table since last year."), misc. LR, Records of the OIA, RG 75, M-234, NA.

21. EPS to CD, Nov. 22, 1873, Records of the OIA, Outgoing Letterpress Correspondence of the Commissioner of Indian Affairs, RG 75, Entry 165, NA. For the commission, see *Report of Commission Appointed . . . to Investigate Certain Charges Against Hon. E. P. Smith,* and Special File No. 17, Report of Commission to Investigate Charges, Indian Division, Records of the Office of the Secretary of the Interior, RG 48, NA. The commission and its investigation are discussed in Keller, *American Protestantism and United States Indian Policy,* pp. 116–22, Jarchow, *Amherst H. Wilder,* pp. 54–64, and Fritz, *Movement for Indian Assimilation,* pp. 153–55.

22. *Report of Commission Appointed . . . to Investigate Certain Charges Against Hon. E. P. Smith,* pp. 24–25, 28–30.

23. Ibid., pp. 4, 33; unidentified clipping about the U.S. marshal in Records of the OIA, BIC Newspaper Clippings, RG 75, Entry 1396, NA; *New York Times,* Dec. 10, 1873, and Jan. 12, 1874.

24. *Report of Commission Appointed . . . to Investigate Certain Charges Against Hon. E. P. Smith,* p. 33.

25. Ibid., pp. 36–43.

26. William Welsh, "Indian Office—Wrongs Doing and Reforms Needed," printed in full, ibid., pp. 37–43.

27. Ibid., pp. 30–32, 80–100, 142–45.

28. Ibid., pp. 45–81, 85, 87–89, 100–119, 124–26.

29. Jarchow, *Amherst H. Wilder,* p. 63; H. R. Clum to EPS, Dec. 15, 1873, LS, Records of the OIA, RG 75, M-21, NA; W. Welsh to H. R. Clum, Dec. 6, [1873], and EPS to H. R. Clum, Dec. 17, 1873, LR, Records of the OIA, Chippewa Agency, RG 75, M-234, NA; W. Welsh to E. F. Williams, Dec. 15, 1873, quoted in *Advance,* Nov. 11, 1875; W. Welsh to H. B. Whipple, Dec. 22, 1873, Whipple Papers, Minnesota Historical Society.

30. *New York Times,* Jan. 26, 1874; *Report of Commission Appointed . . . to Investigate Certain Charges Against Hon. E. P. Smith,* p. 20; Welsh, *Sales of Indians' Pine Timber,* p. 2.

31. *Report of Commission Appointed . . . to Investigate Certain Charges Against Hon. E. P. Smith,* pp. 8–18.

32. Ibid., pp. 19–20.

33. Ibid., pp. 10, 20–22. Because of the controversy over the Wilder contract, Columbus Delano suspended all contracts for the sale of Indian timber and asked the attorney general for an opinion on their validity. The attorney general delayed giving an opinion until the U.S. Supreme Court ruled on a related case, *U.S.* v. *Cook,* which dealt with timber cut by Oneidas on their lands in Wisconsin. The court ruled that Indians had only the right of occupancy on their reservations. As occupants they could clear the land and sell the timber cut during the clearing, but any cutting of

timber beyond that was unauthorized, and the timber so cut became the property of the United States. "The timber while standing is a part of the realty, and it can only be sold as the land could be. The land cannot be sold by the Indians, and consequently the timber, until rightfully severed, cannot be." The result of the Court's decision was to invalidate the contract with Wilder. See CD to H. B. Whipple, Mar. 31, 1874, Whipple Papers, Minnesota Historical Society; *U.S.* v. *Cook*, 86 U.S. (19 Wall.), 591 (1873); *New York Times*, Nov. 28 and Dec. 24, 1874; and Keller, *American Protestantism and United States Indian Policy*, p. 282, n. 29.

26. Accusations

1. *New York Times*, Feb. 21, 1874.

2. *New York Times*, Apr. 1, 1874, and Sept. 24, 1876; Children's Aid Society, *Annual Report* (1876), p. 54, written by Brace, although unsigned.

3. *New York Times*, Feb. 26, 1874.

4. EPS to OOH, Sept. 20, 1874, OOH Papers, Bowdoin College Library, Brunswick, Maine.

5. *New York Times*, Jan. 21, Feb. 14, Mar. 9 and 20, May 10 and 12, June 1 and 3, 1874; *Harper's Weekly*, Feb. 27, 1875; Mark Twain with Charles Dudley Warner, *The Gilded Age*, 2 vols. (New York: Harper & Brothers, 1873), 2:125–26; Charles Dickens, *American Notes* (1842; rpt. New York: Oxford University Press, 1957), pp. 244–45.

6. Unidentified clipping (about Feb. 1874) in Records of the OIA, BIC Newspaper Clippings, RG 75, Entry 1396, NA.

7. EPS to H. B. Whipple, Feb. 27, 1874, LS, Records of the OIA, RG 75, M-21, NA; *Advance*, Nov. 11, 1875; CD to H. B. Whipple, Feb. 26, 1874, CD Letterbooks, Ohio Historical Society, Columbus.

8. Declaration of the Case, Apr. 2, 1874, in Records in Law Case 12.261, Supreme Court of the District of Columbia, *Wilder* v. *Welsh*, RG 21, NA.

9. Jarchow, *Amherst H. Wilder*, pp. 78–80, 96; W. Welsh to GHS, Nov. 17, 1873, and EPS to CD, Nov. 28, 1873. See also *Washington Star*, Mar. 6, 1876.

10. CD to T. C. Jones, Mar. 13, 1874, CD Letterbooks, Ohio Historical Society.

11. *Report of the Special Commission Appointed to Investigate the Affairs of the Red Cloud Indian Agency, July, 1875*, pp. 801–6.

12. CD to H. Dyer, Jan. 26, 1874, CD Letterbooks, Ohio Historical Society; CD to Thomas K. Cree, Feb. 4 and 9, 1874, CD to F. Brunot, Feb. 9, 1874, and CD to T. C. Fletcher, Aug. 2, 1875, LS, Indian Division, Records of the Office of the Secretary of the Interior, RG 48, M-606, NA; F. Brunot to CD, Feb. 6 and 12, 1874, Selected Classes of LR (misc.), ibid. In his letter to Delano of February 12, Brunot claimed he had informed Delano about sending Walker to the agencies. Whether he had or not, he had not shared Walker's report with the secretary.

13. CD to F. Brunot, Feb. 9, 1874, LS, Indian Division, Records of the Office of the Secretary of the Interior, RG 48, M-606, NA; W. Welsh, *To the Members of the*

Forty-Third Congress, Feb. 17, 1874, in Whipple Papers, Minnesota Historical Society, St. Paul, Minn.

14. Welsh, *To the Members of the Forty-Third Congress.*

15. *New York Times,* Mar. 30 and June 6, 1874.

16. Welsh, *Sales of Indians' Pine Timber.*

17. Ibid. The Minnesota state senate authorized an investigation of the timber sale as it related to certain school and swamp lands on the Indian reservations that the state claimed as its own. As a result of the investigation, Wilder withdrew his claim to any timber that belonged to the state. See "Report of the Pine Land Committee" in *Journal of the Senate of the Sixteenth Session of the Legislature of the State of Minnesota (1874),* pp. 426–27, 541–52, and Jarchow, *Amherst H. Wilder,* pp. 64–67.

18. EPS to W. Welsh, Mar. 28 and Apr. 1, 1874, Records of the OIA, Outgoing Letterpress Correspondence of the Commissioner of Indian Affairs, RG 75, Entry 165, NA.

19. *Report of the Commissioners Appointed by the Secretary of the Interior to Examine the Red Cloud and Whetstone Indian Agencies; New York Times,* Feb. 23, 1874. Bishop Hare's life story is told in Howe, *Life and Labors of Bishop Hare.*

20. *Report of the Commissioners Appointed by the Secretary of the Interior to Examine the Red Cloud and Whetstone Indian Agencies,* pp. 15–16; Howe, *Life and Labors of Bishop Hare,* pp. 111–20.

21. *Report of the Commissioners Appointed by the Secretary of the Interior to Examine the Red Cloud and Whetstone Indian Agencies,* pp. 25, 27–28, 35; *Report of the Special Commission Appointed to Investigate the Affairs of the Red Cloud Indian Agency, July, 1875,* pp. 603–17, 728–40.

22. Samuel Walker to F. Brunot, May 5, 1874, and Walker to Thomas K. Cree, May 19, 1874, Records of the OIA, LS, BIC, RG 75, NA.

23. Howe, *Life and Labors of Bishop Hare,* p. 48; W. H. Hare to H. B. Whipple, May 3, 1874, Whipple Papers, Minnesota Historical Society.

24. Felix R. Brunot et al. to the president, May 27, 1874, Records of the OIA, LR, BIC, RG 75, Entry 1384, NA; CD to the president, Feb. 5, 1874, LS, Indian Division, Records of the Office of the Secretary of the Interior, RG 48, M-606, NA; *New York Times,* Feb. 26 and June 15, 1874; Slattery, *Felix Reville Brunot,* pp. 219–24.

25. *New York Times,* June 8, 1874.

26. EPS to OOH, Sept. 20, 1874, OOH Papers, Bowdoin College Library; *New York Times,* June 23 and 24, July 3 and 4, 1874; *Sixth Annual Report of the BIC,* p. 5; CD to Benjamin Tatham, June 25, 1874, and Misc. Correspondence, pp. 438ff., CD Letterbooks, Ohio Historical Society; *New York Tribune,* July 14, 1875.

27. U.S. Congress, *House Report No. 778,* 43d Cong., 1st sess., "Investigation on the Conduct of Indian Affairs."

28. Ibid., pp. 1, 27.

29. Ibid., p. 5; *New York Herald,* Aug. 25, 1875, clipping in OCM Papers, Manuscripts and Archives, Yale University Library, New Haven, Conn.

30. *House Report No. 778.* See especially Smith's testimony, pp. 175–221.

31. Ibid., p. 277.

32. Ibid., pp. 275–83.

33. Ibid., pp. 1–2.

27. Helping the Indians

1. Records of the U.S. General Accounting Office, Indian Claims Accounts, RG 217, File No. 3051, NA; *Record of the Graduated Members of the Class of 1849 of Yale College* . . . (New Haven, 1875), p. 118; *New York Times*, June 11 and 13, 1874. A useful perspective for understanding Smith's philosophy of helping the Indians can be found in Bremner, *American Philanthropy*, pp. 89–104.

2. Carpenter, *Sword and Olive Branch*, pp. 232–33, 242–43; OOH to EPS, Nov. 14, [1874], OOH Papers, Bowdoin College Library, Brunswick, Maine.

3. Records of First Congregational Church and Society, Washington, D.C.; Everett O. Alldredge, *Centennial History of First Congregational United Church of Christ, Washington, D.C., 1865–1965* (Baltimore: Port City Press, Inc., [1965]).

4. *U.S. Statutes at Large*, 18:176, 449. Smith had made it his policy to require labor for annuities even before the law was passed. See EPS to the agent at Grand Ronde, Oregon, Apr. 9, 1874, LS, Records of the OIA, RG 75, M-21, NA.

5. EPS to J. B. Vosburgh, May 15, 1875, ibid.

6. EPS to CD, Sept. 19, 1874, Records of the OIA, Report Books, RG 75, M-348, NA; GW to EPS, Sept. 29, 1875, LR, Records of the OIA (misc. W1530/76), RG 75, NA.

7. EPS to GW, Oct. 2, 1875, printed copy in LR, Records of the OIA (misc. W1530/76), RG 75, NA. See also EPS to Wm. Windom, May 21, 1874, LS, Records of the OIA, RG 75, M-21, NA.

8. EPS to GW, Oct. 2, 1875; printed copy in LR, Records of the OIA (misc. W1530/76), RG 75, NA.

9. Ibid.

10. EPS circular, Aug. 7, 1874, LS, Records of the OIA, RG 75, M-21, NA.

11. EPS to E. Douglas, June 27, July 9 and 12, 1873, EPS to M. N. Adams, June 27, 1873, EPS to S. N. Goodale, Dec. 29, 1873, and Feb. 19, 1874, EPS to Jos. Webster, Apr. 14 and May 2 and 6, 1874, EPS to J. G. Gasmann, Feb. 23 and May 7 and Nov. 12, 1874, and EPS to H. W. Cook, June 20, 1874, LS, Records of the OIA, RG 75, M-21, NA; *Annual Report of the Commissioner of Indian Affairs* (1873), pp. 11, 181. An editorial in the *New York Times*, Aug. 14, 1876, discusses Smith's contribution to industrial training for the Indians.

12. Harriet Woodbridge Gilfillan, "Stage Coaching in New Mexico Fifty Years Ago," typescript in EPS Papers, ARC; Lawrence R. Murphy, *Frontier Crusader: William F. M. Arny* (Tucson: University of Arizona Press, 1972), pp. 78, 230–31; EPS to W. F. M. Arny, Jan. 14 and June 12, 1875, and EPS to Hattie W. Cook, Jan. 16, 1875, LS, Records of the OIA, RG 75, M-21, NA; *Annual Report of the Commissioner*

of Indian Affairs (1875), pp. 71, 330–32; Bender, *"New Hope for the Indians,"* pp. 132, 134, 141–42, 154. Hattie Cook's experience with Indians extended long beyond the time her uncle was commissioner of Indian affairs. She was married to Joseph Gilfillan, the Episcopal missionary at White Earth, and made her home with him among the Chippewas until 1898. See *The Story of Harriet Woodbridge Gilfillan Told by Her Children,* pamphlet in EPS Papers, ARC.

13. Utley, *Frontier Regulars,* pp. 219–21, and *The Indian Frontier of the American West,* pp. 173–78; Hagan, *United States–Comanche Relations,* pp. 105–19.

14. EPS to CD, Jan. 21 and May 14, 1874, Records of the OIA, Report Books, RG 75, M-348, NA.

15. EPS to CD, July 18, 1874, ibid.

16. *New York Times,* July 22 and Nov. 19, 1874; Donald Worcester, "Satanta," in David R. Edmunds, ed., *American Indian Leaders: Studies in Diversity* (Lincoln: University of Nebraska Press, 1980), pp. 107–30 (see pp. 126–29); CD to Richard Coke, Nov. 13, 1874, LS, Indian Division, Records of the Office of the Secretary of the Interior, RG 48, M-606, NA; *Friends' Review,* Nov. 7, 1874.

17. EPS to Enoch Hoag, Aug. 15, 1874, LS, Records of the OIA, RG 75, M-21, NA.

18. EPS to CD, Nov. 20, 1874, Records of the OIA, Report Books, RG 75, M-348, NA.

19. EPS to CD, Nov. 20, 1874, and Feb. 21, July 12 and 14, 1875, ibid.

20. EPS to CD, Dec. 12, 1874, ibid.

21. John D. Miles to EPS, July 7, 1874, LR, Indian Division, Records of the Office of the Secretary of the Interior, RG 48, NA.

22. *Friends' Review,* July 25, 1874; "John D. Miles," in "Dictionary of Quaker Biography," typescript in Quaker Collection, Haverford College Library; *New York Times,* Aug. 22, 1874.

23. EPS to Zadok Street, July 20, 1874, and EPS to John D. Miles, July 20, 1874, LS, Records of the OIA, RG 75, M-21, NA; EPS to John D. Miles, July 20, 1874, Records of the OIA, Outgoing Letterpress Correspondence of the Commissioner of Indian Affairs, RG 75, Entry 165, NA.

24. EPS to OOH, Sept. 20, 1874, OOH Papers, Bowdoin College Library. For the Miles incident, see Keller, *American Protestantism and United States Indian Policy,* pp. 139–46.

25. B. R. Cowen to EPS, Sept. 17, 1874, LS, Indian Division, Records of the Office of the Secretary of the Interior, RG 48, M-606, NA; EPS to John D. Miles, Sept. 18, 1874, and H. R. Clum to W. H. Fanton, Dec. 3, 1873, LS, Records of the OIA, RG 75, M-21, NA; EPS to CD, Sept. 16, 1874, Records of the OIA, Report Books, RG 75, M-348, NA.

26. EPS to B. F. Potts, July 22, 1874, and EPS circular, Mar. 31, 1874, LS, Records of the OIA, RG 75, M-21, NA; EPS to CD, Apr. 23, 1875, Records of the OIA, Report Books, RG 75, M-348, NA. See also EPS to C. Birkett, July 7, 1873, EPS to James Irwin, Sept. 2, 1873, EPS to W. F. Ensign, Nov. 5, 1873, EPS to W. W. Alder-

son, Mar. 30, 1874, EPS to J. M. Haworth, May 4, [1874], LS, Records of the OIA, RG 75, M-21, NA; EPS to CD, May 24, 1873, Mar. 19, and Apr. 30, 1874, Records of the OIA, Report Books, RG 75, M-348, NA; *Annual Report of the Commissioner of Indian Affairs* (1873), p. 8.

27. *New York Times*, Aug. 9–10, 1874; F. R. Kimball, *Handbook of Marblehead Neck* (Boston, 1882), pp. 10–15; receipt for carrying telegrams, Sept. 6, 1875, Records of the U.S. General Accounting Office, Indian Claims Accounts, RG 217, File No. 3051, NA; EPS to OOH, Sept. 20 and Nov. 7, 1874, OOH Papers, Bowdoin College Library; EPS to GW, n.d. (No. 99535), AMA Archives, ARC.

28. EPS to S. C. Pomeroy, Aug. 26, 1874, Records of the U.S. General Accounting Office, Indian Claims Accounts, RG 217, File No. 3051, NA.

29. *Friends' Review*, Oct. 17, 1874; EPS to CD, Oct. 13, 1874, and Feb. 24, 1875, Records of the OIA, Report Books, RG 75, M-348, NA.

30. EPS to CD, Dec. 15, 1874, Feb. 24, and July 3, 1875, Records of the OIA, Report Books, RG 75, M-348, NA; *Annual Report of the Commissioner of Indian Affairs* (1874), pp. 67–68, 215, 226–27.

31. *Report of the Commissioners Appointed by the Secretary of the Interior to Examine the Red Cloud and Whetstone Indian Agencies*, p. 8; *New York Times*, June 21, 1875; *Report of the Special Commission Appointed to Investigate the Affairs of the Red Cloud Indian Agency, July, 1875*, p. 260.

32. CD to W. W. Belknap, June 9, 1874, and CD to H. B. Whipple, July 3, 1874, LS, Indian Division, Records of the Office of the Secretary of the Interior, RG 48, M-606, NA; CD to H. [Glascke?], Aug. 27, 1874, CD Letterbooks, Ohio Historical Society; *Friends' Review*, Aug. 1, 1874; Hyde, *Red Cloud's Folk*, pp. 217–19; Howe, *Life and Labors of Bishop Hare*, pp. 124–29.

33. *New York Times*, Sept. 13, 1874, and Mar. 17, 1875; EPS to CD, Dec. 24, 1874, Records of the OIA, Report Books, RG 75, M-348, NA; *Annual Report of the Commissioner of Indian Affairs* (1874), pp. 7–8. The 1868 treaty with the Sioux explicitly prohibited white intrusion on Sioux lands. See Lazarus, *Black Hills/White Justice*, pp. 434–35, 441.

34. *Sixth Annual Report of the BIC*, pp. 72–74.

35. H. A. Vernon, "Maria Bryant Pierce: The Making of a Seneca Leader," in L. G. Moses and Raymond Wilson, eds., *Indian Lives: Essays on Nineteenth- and Twentieth-Century Native American Leaders* (Albuquerque: University of New Mexico Press, 1985), pp. 19–42; Armstrong, *Warrior in Two Camps*, pp. 47–48; Hattie S. Clark to C. L. Woodworth, Oct. 11, 1867, AMA Archives, ARC.

36. *Sixth Annual Report of the BIC*, p. 74; *Annual Report of the Commissioner of Indian Affairs* (1875), pp. 16–18.

37. EPS to OOH, Nov. 23, 1874, and Apr. 13, 1875, OOH Papers, Bowdoin College Library.

38. EPS to OOH, Apr. 13, 1875, ibid.; Frances Goudy, Vassar College Library, to the author, Aug. 4, 1980.

39. EPS to John H. Smoot, Mar. 6, 1874, Records of the OIA, LS by the Chief

Clerk and the Assistant Commissioner, RG 75, Entry 181, NA; U.S. Congress, *House Miscellaneous Document No. 167,* 44th Cong., 1st sess., pp. 302–3.

40. EPS to John Smoot, Dec. 12, 1874, Records of the OIA, Outgoing Letterpress Correspondence of the Commissioner of Indian Affairs, RG 75, Entry 165, NA.

28. The Sioux

1. EPS to OOH, Nov. 23, 1874, OOH Papers, Bowdoin College Library, Brunswick, Maine; EPS to Ah-bun-way, Feb. 6, 1875, LS, Records of the OIA, RG 75, M-21, NA.

2. EPS to Geo. I. Betts, Oct. 23, 1874, EPS to J. E. Roberts, Oct. 27, 1874, and EPS to J. L. Burchard, Feb. 19, 1875, LS, Records of the OIA, RG 75, M-21, NA; *Congressional Record,* 43d Cong., 2d sess., pp. 470–71.

3. *New York Times,* Jan. 14–15, 21–22, 1875; *Congressional Record,* 43d Cong., 2d sess., p. 464.

4. *Sixth Annual Report of the BIC,* pp. 146–48.

5. Ibid., pp. 147–48.

6. Ibid., pp. 150–51.

7. EPS to J. M. Ferris, Jan. [25?] and May 20, 1875, Records of the OIA, Outgoing Letterpress Correspondence of the Commissioner of Indian Affairs, RG 75, Entry 165, NA; EPS to J. M. Ferris, Apr. 10, 1875, LS, Records of the OIA, RG 75, M-21, NA.

8. EPS to M. C. Wilkinson, Nov. 4, 1873, and EPS to A. B. Meacham, Nov. 6, 18, and Dec. 29, 1874, LS, Records of the OIA, RG 75, M-21, NA; CD to EPS, Nov. 6, 1874, LS, Indian Division, Records of the Office of the Secretary of the Interior, RG 48, M-606, NA.

9. A. B. Meacham, *Wi-ne-ma (The Woman-Chief) and Her People* (Hartford, Conn.: American Publishing Co., 1876), pp. 12–13, 74, 94–95, 103–7; *New York Times,* Mar. 12, 1875. See also Theodore Stern, *The Klamath Tribe: A People and Their Reservation* (Seattle: University of Washington Press, 1965), pp. 87–88.

10. CD to USG, Mar. 17, 1875, CD to W. B. Allison, Mar. 18, 1875, CD to secretary of war, Mar. 22, 1875, CD to EPS, Mar. 26 and 30, 1875, LS, Indian Division, Records of the Office of the Secretary of the Interior, RG 48, M-606, NA. The preliminary report of the Jenney survey is in *Annual Report of the Commissioner of Indian Affairs* (1875), pp. 181–83.

11. EPS to CD, Mar. 26, 1875, Records of the OIA, Report Books, RG 75, M-348, NA; Schuchert and LeVene, *O. C. Marsh,* pp. 139–46; EPS to Spotted Tail, June 9, 1873, and Erwin H. Barbour to Ernest Howe, Apr. 20, 1931, OCM Papers, Manuscripts and Archives, Yale University Library, New Haven, Conn.; *New York Times,* Oct. 4, Nov. 18, and Dec. 4, 1874; *Report of the Special Commission Appointed to Investigate the Affairs of the Red Cloud Indian Agency, July, 1875,* pp. 162, 336–37.

12. *New York Tribune,* Apr. 26, 1875; *Report of the Special Commission,* p. 52.

13. Schuchert and LeVene, *O. C. Marsh*, pp. 147–48; *New York Tribune*, Apr. 20–21, 30, 1875; Henry Adams, *The Education of Henry Adams* (Boston: Houghton Mifflin, 1918), p. 278.

14. Schuchert and LeVene, *O. C. Marsh*, pp. 148–49; *New York Tribune*, May 15, 1875, and other unidentified clippings in Records of the OIA, BIC Newspaper Clippings, RG 75, Entry 1396, NA; *New York Times*, May 3, 5, 7, and 11, 1875.

15. Schuchert and LeVene, *O. C. Marsh*, pp. 149–50; CD to Clinton Fisk, May 10, 1875, LS, Indian Division, Records of the Office of the Secretary of the Interior, RG 48, M-606, NA; *New York Tribune*, May 12, 1875.

16. *New York Times*, May 10, 17–19, 1875; reports of interviews from the *Washington Daily Tribune* (C-700), LR, Records of the OIA, RG 75, NA.

17. *New York Times*, May 20, 1875; Report of Interview Between the President and Sioux Delegations, May 19, 1875 (C-713), LR, Records of the OIA, RG 75, NA.

18. *New York Times*, May 22, 23, 25, and 26, 1875.

19. *New York Times*, May 22, 1875; Interview Between the [Assistant] Secretary of the Interior, Commissioner of Indian Affairs, and the Cheyenne River Delegation, May 21, 1875, (C-700), LR, Records of the OIA, RG 75, NA.

20. Interview Between the [Assistant] Secretary of the Interior, Commissioner of Indian Affairs, and the Cheyenne River Delegation, May 21, 1875 (C-700), LR, Records of the OIA, RG 75, NA.

21. Ibid.

22. Ibid. The quotation "If a man will not work, neither shall he eat" is from 2 Thess. 3:10.

23. Ibid.

24. Reports of interviews with Sioux delegations in the *Washington Daily Tribune* (C-700), LR, Records of the OIA, RG 75, NA.

25. Report of Interview with Sioux Delegations, May 27, 1875 (C-728), ibid.

26. Ibid.

27. Ibid.

28. Ibid.; EPS to P. W. Hitchcock, Jan. 31, 1874, LS, Records of the OIA, RG 75, M-21, NA; *U.S. Statutes at Large*, 18:224; *Annual Report of the Commissioner of Indian Affairs* (1873), p. 8, (1874), p. 9.

29. Report of Interview with Sioux Delegations, May 28, 1875 (C-728), LR, Records of the OIA, RG 75, NA; Schuchert and LeVene, *O. C. Marsh*, pp. 151–52; *New York Times*, May 31 and June 1, 1875; reports of interviews with the Sioux delegations in the *Washington Daily Tribune* (C-700), LR, Records of the OIA, RG 75, NA; B. R. Cowen to OCM, May 28, 1875, OCM Papers, Manuscripts and Archives, Yale University Library.

30. Report of Council with Sioux Delegations, June 1, 1875 (C-751), LR, Records of the OIA, RG 75, NA.

31. Report of Council with the Sioux Delegations, June 3, 1875 (C-761), ibid.

32. Ibid.

33. Ibid.

34. Council with Sioux Indians at Tremont House, June 3, 1875 (C-752), ibid.

35. Report of Council with Delegations of Sioux, June 4, 1875 (C-765), ibid.

36. Report of Interview with Sioux Delegation, June 5, 1875 (C-765 [C-753?]), ibid.

37. Ibid.

38. Ibid.; Viola, *Diplomats in Buckskins*, pp. 78, 123–26.

39. Report of Two Indian Talks, June 5, 1875 (C-753), LR, Records of the OIA, RG 75, NA.

40. EPS to CD, Mar. 26 and June 5, 1875, Records of the OIA, Report Books, RG 75, M-348, NA; *New York Times*, June 16, 1875; *Annual Report of the Commissioner of Indian Affairs* (1875), pp. 179–80, 184–201; Lazarus, *Black Hills/White Justice*, p. 121.

29. Professor Marsh

1. EPS to W. H. Hare, June 12, 1875, Records of the OIA, Outgoing Letterpress Correspondence of the Commissioner of Indian Affairs, RG 75, Entry 165, NA; EPS to CD, June 24, 1875, Records of the OIA, Report Books, RG 75, M-348, NA; F. H. Smith to CD, June 22 and 24, 1875, Records of the OIA, LS, BIC, RG 75, NA; *New York Times*, June 19, 1875.

2. Records of the U.S. General Accounting Office, Indian Claims Accounts, RG 217, File No. 3051, NA.

3. F. Brunot to OCM, May 17 and June 4, 1875, OCM Papers, Manuscripts and Archives, Yale University Library, New Haven, Conn.; OCM to EPS, May 31 (with reply), June 1, 18, 25, 1875, ibid.

4. William Welsh to OCM, May 24, 1875, ibid.; CD to H. Dyer, Jan. 26, 1874, CD Letterbooks, Ohio Historical Society, Columbus, Ohio.

5. Samuel Walker to OCM, June 12, 27, and July 2, 1875, OCM Papers, Manuscripts and Archives, Yale University Library.

6. OCM memorandum of conversations held with CD on June 5 and 8, 1875, ibid.; CD to USG, July 20, 1875, and statement of John Eaton with CD to Fletcher, Harris, and Faulkner, July 28, 1875, LS, Indian Division, Records of the Office of the Secretary of the Interior, RG 48, M-606, NA; *New York Times*, July 15, 1875.

7. EPS to OCM, July 1, 1875, OCM Papers, Manuscripts and Archives, Yale University Library; Schuchert and LeVene, *O. C. Marsh*, pp. 152–55; Marsh, *Statement of Affairs at Red Cloud Agency*.

8. Marsh, *Statement of Affairs at Red Cloud Agency*.

9. Ibid.

10. Schuchert and LeVene, *O. C. Marsh*, p. 156; Wayne MacVeagh to OCM, July 20, 1875, OCM Papers, Manuscripts and Archives, Yale University Library.

11. USG to OCM, July 16, 1875, OCM Papers, Manuscripts and Archives, Yale University Library; USG to CD, July 16, 1875, USG Papers, LC; CD to T. O. Howe

and G. W. Atherton, July 30, 1875, LS, Indian Division, Records of the Office of the Secretary of the Interior, RG 48, M-606, NA; Schuchert and LeVene, *O. C. Marsh*, p. 159.

12. EPS to OOH, July 16, 1875, OOH Papers, Bowdoin College Library, Brunswick, Maine. "Yr's in love & faith & *some* hope" is an allusion to 1 Cor. 13:13.

13. EPS to H. B. Whipple, Aug. 23, 1875, Whipple Papers, Minnesota Historical Society, St. Paul, Minn.

14. *American Missionary*, Sept. 1875, pp. 198–99.

15. BIC, "To the Christian Public," July 29, 1875, Records of the OIA, LR, BIC, RG 75, Entry 1384, NA. "Where there is a carcass, the vultures will gather" is a reference to Matt. 24:28.

16. Ibid.

17. W. Welsh to OCM, July 19, 23, and 24, 1875, OCM Papers, Manuscripts and Archives, Yale University Library. Grant intended to appoint three additional commissioners, but only two accepted appointments; see *New York Times*, July 24, 1875.

18. Charles J. Faulkner to OCM, July 14, 1875, OCM Papers, Manuscripts and Archives, Yale University Library. Biographical information about the members of the commission was obtained from the *Dictionary of American Biography* and the *Biographical Directory of the American Congress, 1774–1971* (Washington, D.C.: U.S. Government Printing Office, 1971). Atherton joined the other commissioners in Cheyenne after they had begun their investigation. Howe was present during only a small part of the investigation and did not sign the commission's report (*Report of the Special Commission Appointed to Investigate the Affairs of the Red Cloud Indian Agency, July 1875*, p. lxxvii). Opponents of the administration were disappointed in Faulkner's role in the investigation. The *New York Tribune* said that although he was a Democrat, Faulkner "rarely interposed an inquiry, and seems to be little interested in the proceedings" (*New York Tribune*, Sept. 14, 1875).

19. *Report of the Special Commission Appointed to Investigate the Affairs of the Red Cloud Indian Agency, July, 1875*.

20. F. A. Walker to OCM, July 8, 1875, N. Bishop to OCM, July 2, 1875, and Anson Dart to OCM, July 22, 1875, OCM Papers, Manuscripts and Archives, Yale University Library.

21. Samuel Walker to OCM, July 27 and Aug. 2, 23, 28, 1875, ibid. The *New York Tribune* reprinted some of Walker's letters in its attempt to discredit Delano and Smith. On one occasion, it attributed a Walker letter to *General* Walker, leaving the impression that it had been written by former commissioner of Indian affairs Francis Walker. On another occasion, the *Tribune* stated that E. P. Smith's son was a clerk in the commissioner's office. The *Tribune* was not careful with its facts. See the *Tribune* for May 14 and Sept. 6, 1875.

22. *Washington Capital*, Aug. 22 and Sept. 12, 1875; *New York Herald*, July 31, 1875; *Washington Daily Tribune*, Aug. 30, 1875, clippings in OCM Papers, Manuscripts and Archives, Yale University Library.

23. *Washington Tribune*, Sept. 21, 1875, and *New York Tribune*, Aug. 13, 1875, clippings in OCM Papers, Manuscripts and Archives, Yale University Library.

24. Samuel Walker to OCM, July 31, Aug. 19, 28, 1875, OCM Papers, Manuscripts and Archives, Yale University Library; William Welsh to the President of the U.S., Aug. 11, 1875, in *New York Herald*, Aug. 13, 1875.

25. Clippings containing Welsh's letters to Marsh are in the OCM Papers, Manuscripts and Archives, Yale University Library. See also *New York Herald*, Aug. 16, 17, 23, 25, 30, and Sept. 8, 20, 1875. Bishop Hare's comments are in *New York Tribune*, Sept. 8, 1875.

26. *Nation*, Nov. 11, 1875, p. 300, Dec. 23, 1875, p. 400, and Dec. 30, 1875, pp. 414–15.

27. Unidentified clipping citing W. Welsh letter to T. C. Fletcher, Sept. 10, 1875, in OCM Papers, Manuscripts and Archives, Yale University Library; *Report of the Special Commission Appointed to Investigate the Affairs of the Red Cloud Indian Agency, July, 1875*, pp. 57–110.

28. *Report of the Special Commission*, pp. 57–110.

29. Ibid., pp. 618–53.

30. Ibid., pp. 663–64.

31. Ibid., p. 664.

32. Ibid.

33. Ibid., p. 659.

34. Ibid., pp. 661–63, 665.

35. Three OCM memorandums of the incident, Sept. 10, 1875, OCM Papers, Manuscripts and Archives, Yale University Library; *New York Herald*, Sept. 14, 1875.

36. *New York Times*, Sept. 27, 1875; EPS to "Dear Mr. Secretary," Sept. 29, 1875, Records of the OIA, Outgoing Letterpress Correspondence of the Commissioner of Indian Affairs, RG 75, Entry 165, NA.

30. *"Out from Under This Terrible Burden"*

1. *Report of the Special Commission Appointed to Investigate the Affairs of the Red Cloud Indian Agency, July, 1875*, p. xvii.

2. Ibid., p. xvii.

3. Ibid., pp. xvii–xviii, xlvi, 416.

4. Ibid., pp. xx–xlii, xliv, lx.

5. Ibid., pp. xliii, lv–lix.

6. Ibid., pp. lvi–lviii, lxii, lxix–lxx, 49–50, 786–90, 819–21.

7. Ibid., pp. lxix–lxx.

8. Ibid., pp. lxv–lxix, 603–17.

9. Samuel Walker to OCM, Oct. 26 and Nov. 6, 1875, OCM Papers, Manuscripts and Archives, Yale University Library, New Haven, Conn.

10. EPS to H. M. Tenney, Oct. 29, 1875, EPS Papers, Manuscripts and Archives, Yale University Library, New Haven, Conn.; *New York Times*, Nov. 2, 1875.

11. EPS to H. M. Tenney, Oct. 29, 1875, EPS Papers, Manuscripts and Archives, Yale University Library.

12. USG to Oliver Hoyt, Nov. 4, 1875, USG Papers, LC.

13. *New York Times,* Nov. 28, 30, and Dec. 1 and 3, 1875; *Washington Star,* Dec. 1 and 4, 1875; *Washington National Republican,* Dec. 1, 1875; *New York Tribune,* Dec. 1, 6, 8, 1875; EPS to OOH, Dec. [?], 1875, OOH Papers, Bowdoin College Library, Brunswick, Maine.

14. *New York Times,* Nov. 28, 30, 1875; *Washington National Republican,* Nov. 29–30, 1875; *Washington Star,* Nov. 30, 1875; *Friends' Review,* Dec. 4, 1875, EPS to GW, Dec. 11, 1875, AMA Archives, ARC; EPS to OOH, Dec. [?], 1875, OOH Papers, Bowdoin College Library.

15. USG to CD, Sept. 9, 1875, USG Papers, LC; CD to USG, Sept. 14, 1875, LS, Indian Division, Records of the Office of the Secretary of the Interior, RG 48, M-606, NA; EPS to secretary of the interior, Sept. 11 and 27, 1875, Records of the OIA, Report Books, RG 75, M-348, NA; Richard N. Ellis, *General Pope and U.S. Indian Policy* (Albuquerque: University of New Mexico Press, 1970), pp. 196–201; EPS to Annie Wittenmyer, July 14, 1875, Records of the OIA, Outgoing Letterpress Correspondence of the Commissioner of Indian Affairs, RG 75, Entry 165, NA.

16. EPS to secretary of the interior, Oct. 23 and Nov. 22, 1875, Records of the OIA, Report Books, RG 75, M-348, NA; F. H. Smith to C. B. Fisk, Oct. 1, 1875, and E. Whittlesey to EPS, Nov. 15, 1875, Records of the OIA, LS, BIC, RG 75, NA. The *New York Herald* articles on the Fort Berthold Agency were published frequently during the fall of 1875.

17. Robert A. Trennert, Jr., "A Grand Failure: The Centennial Indian Exhibition of 1876," *Prologue* 6 (Summer 1974): 118–29: H. Craig Miner, "The United States Government Building at the Centennial Exhibition, 1874–77," *Prologue* 4 (Winter 1972): 202–18; *Ethnological Directions Relative to the Indian Tribes of the United States,* Prepared under the Direction of [the] Indian Bureau by Otis T. Mason (Washington, D.C.: U.S. Government Printing Office, 1875); Indian office circular, Apr. 3, 1875, LS, Records of the OIA, RG 75, M-21, NA; EPS to CD, Jan. 8, Mar. 25, and Sept. 22, 1875, Records of the OIA, Report Books, RG 75, M-348, NA.

18. EPS to secretary of the interior, Nov. 15, 1875, Records of the OIA, Report Books, RG 75, M-348, NA.

19. *Annual Report of the Commissioner of Indian Affairs* (1875), pp. 3–4.

20. Ibid., pp. 22–23, 26–27; J. B. A. Brouillet to Z. Chandler, Dec. 24, 1875, LR, Records of the OIA, RG 75 (Misc. B1934/75), NA.

21. *Annual Report of the Commissioner of Indian Affairs* (1875), pp. 4–5.

22. James D. Richardson, ed., *A Compilation of the Messages and Papers of the Presidents,* 9:4355; Harry H. Anderson, "A Challenge to Brown's Sioux Indian Wars Thesis," *Montana: The Magazine of Western History* 12 (Jan. 1962): 40–49; Utley, *Frontier Regulars,* pp. 252–54, and *Cavalier in Buckskin: George Armstrong Custer and the Western Military Frontier* (Norman: University of Oklahoma Press, 1988), pp. 145–47, 155–56; Hyde, *Red Cloud's Folk,* pp. 249–51; *New York Times,* Nov. 4, 1875; Lazarus, *Black Hills/White Justice,* pp. 83–85, 342–43; Philip H. Sheridan to Alfred H. Terry, Nov. 9, 1875, Sheridan Papers, LC; EPS to E. A. Howard (and identical letters to other agents), Dec. 6, 1875, LS, Records of the OIA, RG 75, M-21, NA.

23. EPS to H. F. Livingstone (and similar letters to other agents), Dec. 7, 1875, LS, Records of the OIA, RG 75, M-21, NA.

24. U.S. Congress, *House Miscellaneous Document No. 167*, 44th Cong., 1st sess., pp. 398–401.

25. *Washington Star*, Dec. 11, 1875; EPS to GW, Dec. 11, 1875, AMA Archives, ARC.

26. EPS to GW, Dec. 11, 1875, AMA Archives, ARC.

27. H. B. Whipple to USG, Nov. 11, 1875, misc. LR, Records of the OIA, RG 75, M-234, NA.

31. Howard University

1. *New York Times*, Dec. 18, 1875; *Washington Star*, Dec. 17, 1875; EPS to GW, Dec. 11, 1875, AMA Archives, ARC.

2. Logan, *Howard University*, pp. 59–64; Carpenter, *Sword and Olive Branch*, pp. 169–84.

3. Records of First Congregational Church, Washington, D.C. (G-1, Treasurer's Record); Logan, *Howard University*, pp. 49, 70–75; Maxwell Bloomfield, "John Mercer Langston and the Rise of Howard Law School," in Francis Coleman Rosenberger, ed., *Records of the Columbia Historical Society of Washington, D.C., 1971–72* (Washington, D.C.: Published by the Society, 1973), pp. 421–38; Cheek and Cheek, *John Mercer Langston and the Fight for Black Freedom*, pp. 92, 223–25, 435; EPS to OOH, Nov. 23, 1874, and Apr. 13, 1875, OOH Papers, Bowdoin College Library, Brunswick, Maine.

4. Logan, *Howard University*, pp. 75–81; Petition to the Board of Trustees of Howard University, Dec. 31, 1874, in Records of the Moorland-Spingarn Research Center, RG 1, Box HRC-2506, Howard University Archives, Howard University, Washington, D.C.; EPS to OOH, Apr. 13, 1875, OOH Papers, Bowdoin College Library; *New York Times*, June 24, 1875.

5. William Francis Cheek III, "Forgotten Prophet: The Life of John Mercer Langston," pp. 140–49; Logan, *Howard University*, p. 77; Charles B. Purvis letter of July 8, 1875, published in the *New York Evening Post*, July 10, 1875, in Records of the Moorland-Spingarn Research Center, RG 1, Box HRC-2506, Howard University Archives.

6. *Christian Recorder*, July 1, 1875; EPS to OOH, Jan. 14, 1876, OOH Papers, Bowdoin College Library. Clara Merritt DeBoer characterizes Langston as "an example of a black man charging prejudice when the real culprit was the shortage of funds." Like the editor of the *Christian Recorder*, DeBoer believes that the need for a white president who would be in a better position to raise funds outweighed the desirability of giving the presidency to a black man. See DeBoer, "The Role of Afro-Americans in the Origin and Work of the American Missionary Association," pp. 544–53.

7. EPS to OOH, Apr. 13, 1875, and Mar. 18, 1876, OOH Papers, Bowdoin College Library; Osthaus, *Freedmen, Philanthropy, and Fraud*, pp. 208–13.

8. EPS to OOH, Dec. [?], 1875, OOH Papers, Bowdoin College Library.

9. *Catalogue of the Officers and Students of Howard University from June 1874 to February 1876* (Washington, D.C.: O. H. Reed, 1876); *Boyd's Directory of the District of Columbia* (1873). See also Charles B. Purvis letter, July 8, 1875, in *New York Evening Post*, July 10, 1875.

10. Obituary of Hannah Cle[a]veland Smith, Nov. 24, 1898, in Harriet Woodbridge Cook Gilfillan, "The Smith Genealogy," p. 38, EPS Papers, ARC; DeBoer, "The Role of Afro-Americans in the Origin and Work of the American Missionary Association," p. 528.

11. *Fisk University; New York Times*, Dec. 13 and 23, 1875, and Jan. 2, 1876; *American Missionary*, Feb. 1876, pp. 32–37.

12. *American Missionary*, Feb. 1876, p. 34.

13. *Fisk University*, pp. 40–41. "When that which is in part has passed, and we know as we are known" is an allusion to 1 Cor. 13: 9–12.

14. EPS to OOH, Jan. 14, 1876, OOH Papers, Bowdoin College Library; EPS to USG, Jan. 24, 1876, Misc. Letters of the Department of State, 1789–1906, RG 59, M-179, NA. The student who was confident that the black people were rising, Richard Robert Wright, was valedictorian of Atlanta University's first graduating class in 1876. See John A. Garraty and Edward T. James, eds., *Dictionary of American Biography*, Supplement 4 (New York: Charles Scribner's Sons, 1974), pp. 915–16.

15. *Fisk University*, pp. 47–48. See Walter L. Williams, *Black Americans and the Evangelization of Africa, 1877–1900* (Madison: University of Wisconsin Press, 1982).

16. *Fisk University*, pp. 34–35, 48–62.

17. *American Missionary*, Feb. 1876, p. 26, and Nov. 1876, p. 243; *Advance*, Sept. 7, 1876.

18. EPS to USG, Jan. 24, 1876, Misc. Letters of the Department of State, 1789–1906, M-179, NA. The history of industrial education in Africa after Smith's abortive attempt to establish it there is described in Spivey, *Schooling for the New Slavery*, pp. 109–34.

19. Levi Luckey endorsement on EPS to USG, Jan. 24, 1876, Misc. Letters of the Department of State, 1789–1906, RG 59, M-179, NA; EPS to Secretary of State, n.d., but received Mar. 13, 1876, Misc. Letters of the Department of State, RG 59, NA; Hamilton Fish to EPS, Mar. 14, 1876, Domestic Letters of the Department of State, 1784–1906, RG 59, M-40, NA.

20. Clinton B. Fisk to William T. Sherman, Jan. 22, 1876, Sherman Papers, LC; EPS to OOH, Mar. 18, 1876, OOH Papers, Bowdoin College Library. See also William B. Hesseltine and Hazel C. Wolf, *The Blue and the Gray on the Nile* (Chicago: University of Chicago Press, 1961).

21. Passport application No. 48523, Edward P. Smith, Jan. 25, 1876 (issued Jan. 26), NA. The passport is in EPS Papers, Manuscripts and Archives, Yale University Library, New Haven, Conn.

22. *New York Times*, Feb. 1, 1876; *Washington Star*, Jan. 25, 1876.

23. *Congressional Record*, 44th Cong., 1st sess., pp. 250, 294, 402, and 2561; U.S.

Congress, *House Miscellaneous Document No. 167*, 44th Cong., 1st sess.; undated manuscript report of House Committee on Indian Affairs, Indians (Misc.) file in Box 21, Accompanying Papers File, House of Representatives, 44th Cong., RG 233, NA.

24. *House Miscellaneous Document No. 167*, pp. 1–25. See also Kountz's letter to the editor in *New York Tribune*, Aug. 28, 1875.

25. *House Miscellaneous Document No. 167*, pp. 27–52, 127–35, 199–200, 211–14, 412–14.

26. Ibid., passim. For testimony on Dart's Sanitary Specific, see pp. 116–19, 141–42, 198–99, 279–80, 287, 351, 398–401, and 411–12.

27. Ibid., pp. 133–36, 154–59; EPS to OOH, Jan. 14, 1876, OOH Papers, Bowdoin College Library.

28. *House Miscellaneous Document No. 167*, pp. 264–75, 281–312, 335–40, 352–55.

29. Ibid., pp. 127–45, 384–99.

30. Ibid., pp. 355–64, 265–75, 365–80, 384–99, 414–23; C. A. Ruffee, *Report on the Condition of the Chippewas of Minnesota, Jan. 1875* (St. Paul: Pioneer Co. Print., 1875), pp. 14–15.

31. Undated manuscript report of House Committee on Indian Affairs, Indians (Misc.) file in Box 21, Accompanying Papers File, House of Representatives, 44th Cong., RG 233, NA.

32. Ibid.

33. Ibid.

34. Ibid.

35. Ibid.

36. Journal of Barclay White, 2:209–13, Friends Historical Library of Swarthmore College, Swarthmore, Pa. Minnie Cook continued to work for the Office of Indian Affairs until 1918, a continuous service of forty-six years. See the official personnel folder of Emily Smith Cook, U.S. Office of Personnel Management, Washington, D.C.

37. M. S. Cook to Second Auditor of the Treasury, Mar. 15, 1878, with accompanying papers, Records of the U.S. General Accounting Office, Indian Claims Accounts, RG 217, File No. 8088, NA.

38. Ibid. The cumbersome procedures for settling accounts are described in Viola, *Diplomats in Buckskins*, pp. 61–63.

32. Old Calabar

1. *New York Times*, Mar. 11 and 12, 1876; EPS to OOH, Mar. 18, 1876, OOH Papers, Bowdoin College Library, Brunswick, Maine.

2. J[ames] R[ussell] L[owell], "The World's Fair, 1876," *Nation*, Aug. 5, 1875, p. 82.

3. Records in Law Case 12.261, Supreme Court of the District of Columbia, *Wilder* v. *Welsh*, RG 21, NA; Jarchow, *Amherst H. Wilder*, pp. 78–80; *New York Times*,

Feb. 29, 1876; *Washington Star,* Mar. 6, 1876; U.S. Congress, *House Miscellaneous Document No. 167,* 44th Cong., 1st sess., pp. 305–6; "The Wilder-Welsh Libel Suit . . . A Card from the Jury," clipping dated Mar. 10, 1876 in Records of the OIA, BIC Newspaper Clippings, RG 75, Entry 1396, NA.

4. EPS to OOH, Dec. [?], 1875, and Mar. 18, 1876, OOH Papers, Bowdoin College Library.

5. EPS to OOH, Mar. 18, 1876, ibid.; *Advance,* Jan. 27, 1876.

6. [Hannah Cleaveland Smith] to "My dear Bessie," June 11, 1876, and Mordecai W. Johnson to Ruth Crawford Mitchell, Nov. 9, 1950, EPS Papers, ARC; *American Missionary,* Aug. 1876, pp. 177–79.

7. *American Missionary,* Aug. 1876, pp. 177–79.

8. Ibid.; EPS to "My dear wife," May 9, 1876, EPS Papers, Manuscripts and Archives, Yale University Library, New Haven, Conn.

9. *American Missionary,* Aug. 1876, pp. 177–79.

10. EPS to "My dear wife," May 9, 1876, EPS Papers, Manuscripts and Archives, Yale University Library; [Hannah Cleaveland Smith] to "My dear Bessie," June 11, 1876, EPS Papers, ARC. "The field is white" is a reference to John 4:35: "Lift up your eyes, and look on the fields; for they are white already to harvest."

11. [Hannah Cleaveland Smith] to "My dear Bessie," June 11, 1876. EPS Papers, ARC.

12. Michael Taylor, National Maritime Museum, London, England, to the author, Sept. 29, 1981; D. H. Hazlehurst, Ocean Transport & Trading Limited, Liverpool, England, to the author, Dec. 2, 1981; M. V. Roberts, Guildhall Library, London, England, to the author, Dec. 15, 1981; *Advance,* Sept. 7, 1876. In most of the notices of Smith's death, the *Ambriz* was incorrectly identified as the *Ambrig.*

13. *American Missionary,* Sept. 1876, p. 193; D. W. Burton to "Dear Bro. Whipple," July 25, 1876, printed letter in EPS Papers, ARC. A slightly different handwritten copy of Smith's last message is in EPS Papers, Manuscripts and Archives, Yale University Library. The Reverend Doctor Alexander Thompson was an official of the Dutch Reformed Home Missionary Society. The Reverend Doctor Jeremiah Eames Rankin was the pastor of the First Congregational Church in Washington, D.C.

14. D. W. Burton to "Dear Bro. Whipple," July 25, 1876, printed letter in EPS Papers, ARC; *American Missionary,* Nov. 1876, pp. 244–45; Ruth Crawford Mitchell to J. Fletcher Smith, Oct. 30, 1973, and Ruth Crawford Mitchell to Lawrence C. Howard, Sept. 4, 1981, EPS Papers, ARC.

15. O. H. White to M. Strieby, July 31, 1876, AMA Archives, ARC; unidentified obituary of EPS in Harriet Woodbridge Cook Gilfillan, "The Smith Genealogy," and Henry [Tenney] to "My dear Bess," Aug. 18, 1876, EPS Papers, ARC. After they returned to America, Gerty taught school for a time, while maintaining a close relationship with General Howard, who considered her a daughter; she called him her "Papa General." Their correspondence—some of it in French—is in the OOH Papers, Bowdoin College Library. Gerty married Hanford Crawford of New York City in 1886. Their only child was Ruth Crawford Mitchell (1890–1984). Cleavie

Smith accepted a position as superintendent of a training school for nurses in Brooklyn. After Gerty's marriage she left the school and lived with Gerty and her family in New York City. Cleavie Smith died in 1898; Gerty Smith Crawford in 1930.

16. Howard University circular, Aug. 1, 1876, on reverse of J. B. Johnson to M. E. Strieby, Aug. 26, 1876, and J. W. Alvord to GW, Aug. 23, 1876, AMA Archives, ARC.

17. "Lines Suggested by the Death of Rev. E. P. Smith," loose printed document in vol. 2 of Records of the Evangelical Congregational Society, Community Church, Pepperell, Mass.; *American Missionary*, Dec. 1876, pp. 280–82.

18. *New York Tribune*, Aug. 16, 1876.

Epilogue

1. AMA, Executive Committee Minutes, Oct. 6, 1879, AMA Archives, ARC; A. G. Boorman to Ruth Crawford Mitchell, Nov. 5, 1947, and Harriet Woodbridge Cook Gilfillan, "The Smith Genealogy," pp. 91–92, EPS Papers, ARC.

2. EPS to "Dr. Bro Strieby," Oct. 6, 1868, AMA Archives, ARC.

3. H. B. Whipple to CD, Oct. 3, 1873, Selected Classes of LR, Indian Division, Records of the Office of the Secretary of the Interior, RG 48, M-825, NA; *New York Tribune*, July 15 and 19, 1875.

4. Hurd, *History of Middlesex County*, 3:226.

5. Francis Paul Prucha describes the deep-seated paternalism of U.S. Indian policy in *The Indians in American Society* (Berkeley: University of California Press, 1985).

6. Another Indian agent rivaled Smith in the number of investigations he endured. One newspaper called Dr. Valentine T. McGillycuddy, the agent at the Pine Ridge Agency, "the most investigated man of the age." See Julia B. McGillycuddy, *McGillycuddy Agent: A Biography of Dr. Valentine T. McGillycuddy* (Stanford: Stanford University Press, 1941), p. 247.

Bibliography

Manuscripts

Atlanta, Georgia. Atlanta University Center
   Frederick Ayer Papers
   Edmund A. Ware Papers
Austin, Texas. Archives of the Episcopal Church, U.S.A.
   Minutes of the Indian Commission
   Minutes of the Executive Committee of the Indian Commission
Berea, Kentucky. Berea College
   Berea College Archives
Boston, Massachusetts. Massachusetts Historical Society
   John Andrew Papers
Boston, Massachusetts. Massachusetts State Archives
   Governor's Series (Executive Letters and Letters Official)
Brunswick, Maine. Bowdoin College Library
   Oliver Otis Howard Papers
Cambridge, Massachusetts. Houghton Library, Harvard University
   Three EPS letters in bMS Am (1838) (591,900)
Carlisle Barracks, Pennsylvania. U.S. Army Military History Institute
   Sladen Family Papers
Cleveland, Ohio. Western Reserve Historical Society
   William P. Palmer Collection
Columbus, Ohio. Ohio Historical Society
   Columbus Delano Letterbooks
Des Moines, Iowa. State Historical Society of Iowa
   Annie Wittenmyer Papers
Hampton, Virginia. Hampton University
   Hampton University Archives
Hanover, New Hampshire. Dartmouth College
   Dartmouth College Archives

Doctor Gilman Frost Genealogical Records
Hanover [Center] Church of Christ Records
Harrogate, Tennessee. Lincoln Memorial University
    Oliver Otis Howard Papers (microfilm)
Hartford, Connecticut. Connecticut State Library
    Records of the estate of Noah Smith, 1831 (No. 4090)
Hartford, Connecticut. Connecticut Conference of the United Church of Christ
    Records of the Missionary Society of Connecticut (microfilm)
Haverford, Pennsylvania. Quaker Collection, Haverford College Library
    Hoag Indian Papers
    Jonathan Richards Letterbooks
    Thomas Wistar Journal and Letterbooks
Knoxville, Tennessee. University of Tennessee
    John Eaton Papers
Mobile, Alabama. Central Presbyterian Church
    Second Presbyterian Church Archives
Montreat, North Carolina. Presbyterian Church (U.S.A.) Department of History
(Montreat)
    Records of the Presbytery of South Alabama, vol. 6
New Haven, Connecticut. Manuscripts and Archives, Yale University Library
    Othniel Charles Marsh Papers (microfilm)
    Edward Parmelee Smith Papers
    Yale University Archives
New Orleans, Louisiana. Amistad Research Center
    American Home Missionary Society Archives
    American Missionary Association Archives
    John A. Rockwell Papers
    Edward Parmelee Smith Papers
    Edward Franklin Williams Papers
Newton Centre, Massachusetts. Andover Newton Theological School
    Andover Newton Theological School Archives
New York, New York. American Bible Society
    American Bible Society Archives
New York, New York. Children's Aid Society
    Children's Aid Society Archives
New York, New York. Rare Books and Manuscripts Division, New York Public
Library, Astor, Lenox and Tilden Foundations
    United States Sanitary Commission Records (Western Department)
Oberlin, Ohio. Oberlin College Archives
    Jacob Dolson Cox Papers
Oklahoma City, Oklahoma. Oklahoma Historical Society
    Kiowa Agency Records (microfilm)

Pepperell, Massachusetts. Community Church
  Records of the Evangelical Congregational Society
  Records of the Church of Christ in Pepperell
Pepperell, Massachusetts. Office of the Town Clerk
  Pepperell Town Records
Philadelphia, Pennsylvania. Civil War Library and Museum
  Loyal Legion Record of Melville Cary Wilkinson
Philadelphia, Pennsylvania. Historical Society of Pennsylvania
  Lewis-Neilson Collection
Pittsburgh, Pennsylvania. Historical Society of Western Pennsylvania
  Brunot Family Papers
Ripon, Wisconsin. Ripon College Archives
  Pedrick Notebook Collection
Saint Paul, Minnesota. Minnesota Historical Society
  Moses N. Adams Papers
  Horace Austin and Family Papers
  William Watts Folwell and Family Papers
  Joseph Alexander Gilfillan and Family Papers
  Henry Hastings Sibley Papers
  Henry B. Whipple Papers
  Amherst Holcomb Wilder and Family Papers
Southbury, Connecticut. Southbury Town Hall
  South Britain Congregational Church Records
Southbury, Connecticut. Town Clerk's Office
  Southbury Town Records
South Hadley, Massachusetts. Mount Holyoke College
  Mount Holyoke College Library/Archives
Swarthmore, Pennsylvania. Friends Historical Library of Swarthmore College
  Journal of Barclay White
Uniontown, Alabama. First Presbyterian Church
  First Presbyterian Church Archives
Urbana-Champaign, Illinois. Illinois Historical Survey, University of Illinois Library
  Columbus Delano Letterbooks
Washington, D.C. First Congregational Church
  Records of the First Congregational Church and Society
Washington, D.C. Library of Congress
  Mary Ann Ball Bickerdyke Papers
  James A. Garfield Papers (microfilm)
  James Grant manuscript, "The Flag and the Cross: A History
    of the United States Christian Commission, Dated Feb., 1894."
  Ulysses S. Grant Papers (microfilm)
  Dwight L. Moody Papers
  Philip H. Sheridan Papers

William T. Sherman Papers (microfilm)
Matthew Simpson Papers
George Hay Stuart Papers
Joseph Conable Thomas Papers
Washington, D.C. Moorland-Spingarn Research Center, Howard University
University Archives: Walter Dyson Papers
Manuscript Division: John Mercer Langston Scrapbooks
Washington, D.C. National Archives
RG 21 Supreme Court of the District of Columbia
Law Case 12.261 (*Wilder* v. *Welsh*)
RG 48 Records of the Office of the Secretary of the Interior
Appointments Division
M-606. Letters Sent, Indian Division
M-825. Selected Classes of Letters Received, Indian Division
Special File 8 (Satanta and Big Tree)
Special File 17 (Report of Commission to Investigate Charges Against Commissioner of Indian Affairs)
RG 59 General Records of the Department of State
M-40. Domestic Letters of the Department of State
M-179. Miscellaneous Letters of the Department of State
RG 75 Records of the Office of Indian Affairs
M-21. Letters Sent
M-234. Letters Received
M-348. Report Books
M-734. Records of the Arizona Superintendency
M-1121. Procedural Issuances: Orders and Circulars
Entry 165. Outgoing Letterpress Correspondence
of the Commissioner of Indian Affairs
Entry 181. Letters Sent by the Chief Clerk and
the Assistant Commissioner
Records of the Board of Indian Commissioners
Letters Sent
Entry 1384. Letters Received
Entry 1396. Newspaper Clippings
Record of Contingency Accounts
RG 94 Records of the United States Christian Commission
Entry 739. Letters Sent, Central Office
Entry 740. Communications Received, Central Office
Entry 753. Minutes of the Executive Committee
Entry 758. Registers of Delegates
Entry 759. Register of Delegates
Entry 791. Scrapbooks
RG 101 Records of the Freedman's Savings and Trust Company
M-874. Journal of the Board of Trustees

RG 105 Records of the Bureau of Refugees, Freedmen, and Abandoned Lands
  M-752. Letters Received by the Commissioner
  M-798. Records of the Assistant Commissioner for Georgia
  M-799. Records of the Superintendent of Education for Georgia
  M-803. Letters Received by the Educational Division
  M-826. Records of the Assistant Commissioner for Mississippi
  M-843. Records of the Assistant Commissioner for North Carolina
  M-844. Records of the Superintendent of Education for North Carolina
  M-869. Records of the Assistant Commissioner for South Carolina
  M-999. Records of the Assistant Commissioner for Tennessee
  M-1000. Records of the Superintendent of Education for Tennessee
  M-1053. Records of the Superintendent of Education for Virginia
RG 107 Records of the Office of the Secretary of War
  Letters Received by the Secretary of War, Registered Series
  Letters Sent by the Secretary of War Relating to Military Affairs
RG 217 Records of the U.S. General Accounting Office.
  Indian Claims Accounts
RG 233 Records of the United States House of Representatives
  House of Representatives, 44th Congress, Accompanying Papers File
RG 393 Records of the U.S. Army Continental Commands
  Department of the Cumberland
  Military Division of the Mississippi
Washington, D.C. U.S. Office of Personnel Management
  Emily Smith Cook Official Personnel Folder
Westfield, Massachusetts. Office of the City Clerk
  City of Westfield Records
Williamstown, Massachusetts. Williams College
  Samuel Chapman Armstrong Papers
Woodbury, Connecticut. District of Woodbury
  Noah Smith Probate Records (Bk. 16)

Newspapers

Arizona Weekly Citizen, Jan.–July 1872
Detroit (Minnesota) *Record*, May 1872–June 1875
Lorain County (Ohio) *News*, Sept. 1872–May 1873
Nashville Daily Union, 1863–65
New York Herald, 1873, 1875
New York Times, 1871–76
New York Tribune, 1875–76
Washington Daily Morning Chronicle, 1873, 1875–76
Washington Evening Star, 1873
Washington Star, 1875–76

Significant clippings from many other newspapers are contained in the United States
   Christian Commission scrapbooks (RG 94, Entry 791, NA), the Board of Indian
   Commissioners scrapbooks (RG 75, Entry 1396, NA), and the collection of clip-
   pings in the Othniel Charles Marsh Papers (Yale University Library).

Periodicals

Advance, 1868–76
American Congregational Year-Book, 1854–59, 1881
American Missionary, 1857–76
Bible Society Record, 1862–67
Congregationalist, 1855–71
Congregational Quarterly, 1859–77
Friends' Intelligencer, 1873–76
Friends' Review, 1873–76
Nation, 1870–76
Pittsburgh Christian Advocate, 1863–64
Religious Intelligencer, 1822–30
Spirit of Missions, 1868–78
Sunday-School Times, 1863–65
USCC. *Information for Army Meetings*, June and July 1864–Mar. 1865
Well-Spring, 1861–76

United States Public Documents

Acts of Congress Relating to the Board of Indian Commissioners, and By-Laws of the Board.
   Washington, D.C.: U.S. Government Printing Office, 1875.
Annual Reports of the Board of Indian Commissioners, 1872–76.
Annual Reports of the Commissioner of Indian Affairs, 1867, 1869, 1871–75.
*Journal of the Second Annual Conference of the Board of Indian Commissioners with the Rep-
   resentatives of the Religious Societies Co-operating with the Government, and Reports
   of Their Work Among the Indians.* Washington, D.C.: U.S. Government Printing
   Office, 1873.
*Report of Commission Appointed by the Secretary of the Interior to Investigate Certain
   Charges Against Hon. E. P. Smith, the Commissioner of Indian Affairs.* 1874.
*Report of the Commissioners Appointed by the Secretary of the Interior to Examine the Red
   Cloud and Whetstone Indian Agencies* [Hare Commission]. Washington, D.C.: U.S.
   Government Printing Office, 1874.
*Report of the Special Commission Appointed to Investigate the Affairs of the Red Cloud Indian
   Agency, July, 1875.* Washington, D.C.: U.S. Government Printing Office, 1875.
U.S. Congress, *House Report No. 121*, 41st Cong., 2d sess. Howard Investigation.
   1870.

————, *House Executive Document No. 83,* 42d Cong., 2d sess. Removal of the Chippewa Indians. 1872.

————, *House Executive Document No. 193,* 42d Cong., 2d sess. Chippewa Half-Breeds of Lake Superior. 1872.

————, *House Report No. 778,* 43d Cong., 1st sess. Investigation on the Conduct of Indian Affairs. 1874.

————, *House Miscellaneous Document No. 167,* 44th Cong., 1st sess. Testimony Taken Before the Committee on Indian Affairs Concerning the Management of the Indian Department. 1876.

United States Statutes at Large, vols. 13–18.

The War of the Rebellion: A Compilation of the Official Records of the Union and Confederate Armies. 128 vols. Washington, D.C.: U.S. Government Printing Office, 1880–1901.

What the Government and the Churches Are Doing for the Indians. Washington, D.C.: U.S. Government Printing Office, 1874.

Books, Articles, and Dissertations

Alcott, Louisa May. *Hospital Sketches.* Edited by Bessie Z. Jones. Cambridge, Mass.: Belknap Press of Harvard University Press, 1960.

Alvord, J. W. *Letters from the South, Relating to the Condition of Freedmen. . . .* Washington, D.C.: Howard University Press, 1870.

————. *Semi-Annual Reports on Schools for Freedmen,* vols. 1–10 (1866–70).

American Missionary Association. *Annual Reports,* 1871–74, 1876.

Angle, Paul M., ed. *Three Years in the Army of the Cumberland: The Letters and Diary of Major James A. Connolly.* Bloomington: Indiana University Press, 1959.

Armstrong, Mrs. M. F., and Helen W. Ludlow. *Hampton and Its Students.* 1874. Chicago: Afro-Am Press, 1969.

Armstrong, Samuel C. *The Founding of the Hampton Institute.* Old South Leaflets 149. Boston: Old South Association, n.d.

Armstrong, William H. *Warrior in Two Camps: Ely S. Parker, Union General and Seneca Chief.* Syracuse: Syracuse University Press, 1978.

Bacote, Clarence A. *The Story of Atlanta University: A Century of Service, 1865–1965.* Atlanta: Atlanta University Press, 1969.

Barclay, James J. *An Address Delivered on the 13th of January, 1879 . . . in Commemoration of William Welsh. . . .* Pennsylvania Institute for the Deaf and Dumb.

Basler, Roy P., ed. *The Collected Works of Abraham Lincoln.* 9 vols. New Brunswick, N.J.: Rutgers University Press, 1953.

Battey, Thomas C. *The Life and Adventures of a Quaker Among the Indians.* 1875. Reprint. Norman: University of Oklahoma Press, 1968.

Beard, Augustus Field. *A Crusade of Brotherhood: A History of the American Missionary Association.* Boston: Pilgrim Press, 1909.

Beaver, R. Pierce. *Church, State, and the American Indians: Two and a Half Centuries of Partnership in Missions Between Protestant Churches and Government.* St. Louis: Concordia Publishing House, 1966.

Bender, Norman J. *"New Hope for the Indians": The Grant Peace Policy and the Navajos in the 1870s.* Albuquerque: University of New Mexico Press, 1989.

Bentley, George R. *A History of the Freedmen's Bureau.* Philadelphia: University of Pennsylvania Press, 1955.

Berkhofer, Robert F., Jr. *Salvation and the Savage: An Analysis of Protestant Missions and American Indian Response, 1787–1862.* Lexington: University of Kentucky Press, 1965.

Bowden, Henry Warner. *American Indians and Christian Missions: Studies in Cultural Conflict.* Chicago: University of Chicago Press, 1981.

Brace, Charles Loring. *The Dangerous Classes of New York, and Twenty Years' Work Among Them.* New York: Wynkoop & Hallenbeck, 1872.

———. *The Life of Charles Loring Brace, Chiefly Told in His Own Letters.* Edited by his daughter. New York: Charles Scribner's Sons, 1894.

Bremner, Robert H. *American Philanthropy.* Chicago: University of Chicago Press, 1960.

———. "The Impact of the Civil War on Philanthropy and Social Welfare." *Civil War History* 12 (Dec. 1966): 293–303.

———. *The Public Good: Philanthropy and Welfare in the Civil War Era.* New York: Knopf, 1980.

Brownlee, Frederick L. *Heritage of Freedom.* Philadelphia: United Church Press, 1963.

———. *New Day Ascending.* Boston: Pilgrim Press, 1946.

Bryan, Charles F., Jr. "Nashville Under Federal Occupation." *Civil War Times Illustrated* 13 (Jan. 1975): 4–11, 40–47.

Butchart, Ronald E. *Northern Schools, Southern Blacks, and Reconstruction: Freedmen's Education, 1862–1875.* Westport, Conn.: Greenwood Press, 1980.

Campbell, Clarice T., and Oscar Allan Rogers, Jr. *Mississippi: The View from Tougaloo.* Jackson: University Press of Mississippi, 1979.

Cannon, M. Hamlin. "The United States Christian Commission." *Mississippi Valley Historical Review* 38 (June 1951): 61–80.

Carpenter, John A. *Sword and Olive Branch: Oliver Otis Howard.* Pittsburgh: University of Pittsburgh Press, 1964.

Carter, Dan T. *When the War Was Over: The Failure of Self-Reconstruction in the South, 1865–1867.* Baton Rouge: Louisiana State University Press, 1985.

Chapman, George T. *Sketches of the Alumni of Dartmouth College.* Cambridge, Mass.: Riverside Press, 1867.

Cheek, William Francis III. "Forgotten Prophet: The Life of John Mercer Langston." Ph.D. dissertation, University of Virginia, 1961.

Cheek, William, and Aimee Lee Cheek. *John Mercer Langston and the Fight for Black Freedom, 1829–65.* Urbana: University of Illinois Press, 1989.

Children's Aid Society, *Annual Reports*, 1854–58, 1876.

Christian Commission for the Army and Navy of the United States of America. Philadelphia: Ringwalt & Brown, 1862.

Cist, Henry M. *The Army of the Cumberland*. New York: Charles Scribner's Sons, 1882.

Current, Richard N. *Northernizing the South*. Athens: University of Georgia Press, 1983.

DeBoer, Clara Merritt. "The Role of Afro-Americans in the Origin and Work of the American Missionary Association, 1839–1877." Ph.D. dissertation, Rutgers University, State University of New Jersey, 1973.

Douglass, H. Paul. *Christian Reconstruction in the South*. Boston: Pilgrim Press, 1909.

Drake, Richard Bryant. "The American Missionary Association and the Southern Negro, 1861–1888." Ph.D. dissertation, Emory University, 1957.

Du Bois, W. E. Burghardt. *The Souls of Black Folk*. 1903. Reprint. New York: New American Library, 1969.

Dunning, Albert E. *Congregationalists in America*. New York: J. A. Hill, 1894.

Durham, Walter T. *Nashville: The Occupied City, the First Seventeen Months, February 16, 1862, to June 30, 1863*. Nashville: Tennessee Historical Society, 1985.

————. *Reluctant Partners: Nashville and the Union, July 1, 1863, to June 30, 1865*. Nashville: Tennessee Historical Society, 1987.

Engs, Robert Francis. *Freedom's First Generation: Black Hampton, Virginia, 1861–1890*. Philadelphia: University of Pennsylvania Press, 1979.

Fisk University: History, Building and Site, and Services of Dedication, at Nashville, Tennessee, Jan. 1st, 1876. New York: Trustees of Fisk University, n.d.

Folwell, William Watts. *A History of Minnesota*. 4 vols. St. Paul: Minnesota Historical Society, 1926.

Fritz, Henry E. *The Movement for Indian Assimilation, 1860–1890*. Philadelphia: University of Pennsylvania Press, 1963.

Glicksberg, Charles I., ed. *Walt Whitman and the Civil War*. Philadelphia: University of Pennsylvania Press, 1933.

Hagan, William T. *United States–Comanche Relations: The Reservation Years*. New Haven: Yale University Press, 1976.

Hale, Edward Everett. *A New England Boyhood*. 1893. Reprint. New York: MSS Information Corp., 1970.

Hamilton, Gail. *Twelve Miles from a Lemon*. 1873. Reprint. Freeport, N.Y.: Books for Libraries Press, 1972.

Handy, Robert T. *A Christian America: Protestant Hopes and Historical Realities*. New York: Oxford University Press, 1971.

————. *A History of the Churches in the United States and Canada*. New York: Oxford University Press, 1977.

Harding, Vincent. *There Is a River: The Black Struggle for Freedom in America*. New York: Vintage Books, 1981.

Haywood, Jacquelyn Slaughter. "The American Missionary Association in Louisiana During Reconstruction." Ph.D. dissertation, University of California, Los Angeles, 1974.

Henry, James O. "History of the United States Christian Commission." Ph.D. dissertation, University of Maryland, 1959.

———. "The United States Christian Commission in the Civil War." *Civil War History* 6 (1960): 374–88.

History of the Educational Institutions of the American Missionary Association in the South. 1884.

Hoobler, James A. *Cities Under the Gun: Images of Occupied Nashville and Chattanooga.* Nashville: Rutledge Hill Press, 1986.

Hopkins, Alphonso A. *The Life [of] Clinton Bowen Fisk.* 1888. Reprint. N.p.: Negro Universities Press, 1969.

Hotchkiss, Wesley A. "Congregationalists and Negro Education." *Journal of Negro Education* 29 (Summer 1960): 289–98.

Hovde, David M. "The U.S. Christian Commission's Library and Literacy Programs for the Union Military Forces in the Civil War." *Libraries and Culture* 24 (Summer 1989): 295–316.

Howard, Oliver Otis. *Autobiography of Oliver Otis Howard, Major General United States Army.* 2 vols. New York: Baker & Taylor, 1907.

Howe, M. A. DeWolfe. *The Life and Labors of Bishop Hare: Apostle to the Sioux.* New York: Sturgis & Walton, 1911.

———. *Memorial of William Welsh.* Reading, Pa.: Owen, 1878.

Hurd, D. Hamilton. *History of Middlesex County, Massachusetts . . . ,* vol. 3. Philadelphia: J. W. Lewis, 1890.

Hyde, George E. *Red Cloud's Folk: A History of the Oglala Sioux Indians.* Norman: University of Oklahoma Press, 1937.

Jaquette, Henrietta Stratton, ed. *South After Gettysburg: Letters of Cornelia Hancock from the Army of the Potomac, 1863–1865.* Philadelphia: University of Pennsylvania Press, 1937.

Jarchow, Merrill E. *Amherst H. Wilder and His Enduring Legacy to St. Paul.* St. Paul: Amherst H. Wilder Foundation, 1981.

Johnson, Clifton H. "The American Missionary Association: A Short History." In *Our American Missionary Association Heritage.* [Memphis, Tenn.: LeMoyne College, 1966].

———. "The American Missionary Association, 1846–1861: A Study of Christian Abolitionism." Ph.D. dissertation, University of North Carolina, 1958.

Johnson, Ronald W. *Preliminary Historic Resource Study—Chatham—Fredericksburg and Spotsylvania County Battlefields Memorial National Military Park, Virginia.* Edited by Harlan D. Unrau. Denver: National Park Service, 1981.

Jones, Jacqueline. *Soldiers of Light and Love: Northern Teachers and Georgia Blacks, 1865–1873.* Chapel Hill: University of North Carolina Press, 1980.

Jones, Maxine Deloris. "'A Glorious Work': The American Missionary Association and Black North Carolinians, 1863–1880." Ph.D. dissertation, Florida State University, 1982.

Jones, Maxine D., and Joe M. Richardson. *Talladega College: The First Century.* Tuscaloosa: University of Alabama Press, 1990.

Kaser, David. *Books and Libraries in Camp and Battle: The Civil War Experience.* Westport, Conn.: Greenwood Press, 1984.

Keller, Robert H., Jr. *American Protestantism and United States Indian Policy, 1869–82.* Lincoln: University of Nebraska Press, 1983.

———. "Episcopal Reformers and Affairs at Red Cloud Agency, 1870–1876." *Nebraska History* 68 (Fall 1987): 116–26.

Kelsey, Rayner Wickersham. *Friends and the Indians, 1655–1917.* Philadelphia: Associated Executive Committee of Friends on Indian Affairs, 1917.

Kvasnicka, Robert M., and Herman J. Viola, eds. *The Commissioners of Indian Affairs, 1824–1977.* Lincoln: University of Nebraska Press, 1979.

Larcom, Lucy. *A New England Girlhood: Outlined from Memory.* Boston and New York: Houghton Mifflin and Riverside Press, Cambridge, 1892.

Lazarus, Edward. *Black Hills/White Justice: The Sioux Nation Versus the United States, 1775 to the Present.* New York: HarperCollins, 1991.

Levine, Richard R. "Indian Fighters and Indian Reformers: Grant's Indian Peace Policy and the Conservative Consensus." *Civil War History* 31 (Dec. 1985): 329–52.

Lewis, Lloyd. *Sherman: Fighting Prophet.* 1932. Reprint. New York: Harcourt, Brace, 1958.

Litwack, Leon F. *Been in the Storm So Long: The Aftermath of Slavery.* 1979. Reprint. New York: Vintage Books, 1980.

Logan, Rayford W. *Howard University: The First Hundred Years, 1867–1967.* New York: New York University Press, 1969.

Loomis, Rev. H. *Christian Work Among Soldiers.* Yokohama, Japan: Fukuin Printing Co., n.d.

Lowenfels, Walter, ed. *Walt Whitman's Civil War.* New York: Knopf, 1960.

McFeely, William S. *Grant: A Biography.* New York: Norton, 1981.

———. *Yankee Stepfather: General O. O. Howard and the Freedmen.* New York: Norton, 1970.

McPherson, James M. *The Abolitionist Legacy: From Reconstruction to the NAACP.* Princeton: Princeton University Press, 1975.

———. *The Struggle for Equality: Abolitionists and the Negro in the Civil War and Reconstruction.* Princeton: Princeton University Press, 1964.

Mardock, Robert Winston. *The Reformers and the American Indian.* Columbia: University of Missouri Press, 1971.

Marsh, O. C. *A Statement of Affairs at Red Cloud Agency, Made to the President of the United States, by Professor O. C. Marsh.* July 10, 1875.

Maslowski, Peter. *Treason Must Be Made Odious: Military Occupation and Wartime Reconstruction in Nashville, Tennessee, 1862–65.* Millwood, N.Y.: KTO Press, 1978.

Maxwell, William Quentin. *Lincoln's Fifth Wheel: The Political History of the United States Sanitary Commission.* New York: Longmans, Green, 1956.

Milner, Clyde A. II. *With Good Intentions: Quaker Work Among the Pawnees, Otos, and Omahas in the 1870s.* Lincoln: University of Nebraska Press, 1982.

Milner, Clyde A. II, and Floyd A. O'Neil, eds. *Churchmen and the Western Indians, 1820–1920.* Norman: University of Oklahoma Press, 1985.

Moody, Marshall Dwight. "A History of the Board of Indian Commissioners and Its Relationship to the Administration of Indian Affairs, 1869–1900." Master's thesis, American University, [1951?].

Morgan, H. Wayne, ed. *The Gilded Age: A Reappraisal.* Syracuse: Syracuse University Press, 1963.

Morris, Charles, ed. *Makers of Philadelphia.* Philadelphia: L. R. Hamersly, 1894.

Morris, Robert C. *Reading, 'Riting, and Reconstruction: The Education of Freedmen in the South, 1861–1870.* 1976. Reprint. Chicago: University of Chicago Press, 1981.

Moss, Lemuel. *Annals of the United States Christian Commission.* Philadelphia: J. B. Lippincott, 1868.

Munroe, James Phinney. *A Life of Francis Amasa Walker.* New York: Henry Holt, 1923.

Nevins, Allan, and Milton Halsey Thomas, eds. *The Diary of George Templeton Strong.* 4 vols. New York: Macmillan, 1952.

Nye, W. S. *Carbine and Lance: The Story of Old Fort Sill.* Norman: University of Oklahoma Press, 1943.

Osthaus, Carl R. *Freedmen, Philanthropy, and Fraud: A History of the Freedman's Savings Bank.* Urbana: University of Illinois Press, 1976.

Peirce, Paul Skeels. *The Freedmen's Bureau: A Chapter in The History of Reconstruction.* 1904. Reprint. New York: Haskell House Publishers, 1971.

A Pepperell Reader. [Pepperell, Mass.: N.p., ca. 1975].

Phisterer, Frederick. *Statistical Record of the Armies of the United States.* New York: Charles Scribner's Sons, 1883.

Poole, D. C. *Among the Sioux of Dakota: Eighteen Months' Experience as an Indian Agent, 1869–70.* 1881. Reprint. St. Paul: Minnesota Historical Society Press, 1988.

Priest, Loring Benson. *Uncle Sam's Stepchildren: The Reformation of United States Indian Policy, 1865–1887.* New Brunswick: Rutgers University Press, 1942.

Prucha, Francis Paul. *American Indian Policy in Crisis: Christian Reformers and the Indian, 1865–1900.* Norman: University of Oklahoma Press, 1976.

———. *The Great Father: The United States Government and the American Indians.* Vol. 1. Lincoln: University of Nebraska Press, 1984.

Quenzel, Carrol H. "Books for the Boys in Blue." *Journal of the Illinois State Historical Society* 44 (1951): 218–30.

Quimby, Rollin W. "The Chaplain's Predicament." *Civil War History* 8 (1962): 25–37.

———. "Congress and the Civil War Chaplaincy." *Civil War History* 10 (1964): 246–59.

Rahill, Peter J. *The Catholic Indian Missions and Grant's Peace Policy, 1870–1884.* Washington, D.C.: Catholic University of America Press, 1953.

Reid, Whitelaw. *After the War: A Tour of the Southern States, 1865–1866.* 1866. Reprint. Edited by C. Vann Woodward. New York: Harper & Row, 1965.

Reynolds, Robert Lester. "Benevolence on the Home Front in Massachusetts During the Civil War." Ph.D. dissertation, Boston University, 1970.

Richardson, James D., ed. *A Compilation of the Messages and Papers of the Presidents.* Vol. 9. New York: Bureau of National Literature, 1897.

Richardson, Joe M. *Christian Reconstruction: The American Missionary Association and Southern Blacks, 1861–1890.* Athens: University of Georgia Press, 1986.

———. *A History of Fisk University, 1865–1946.* University, Ala.: University of Alabama Press, 1980.

Richardson, Leon Burr. *History of Dartmouth College.* 2 vols. Hanover, N.H.: Dartmouth College Publications, 1932.

Round, Harold F. "Federal Supply Bases on the Potomac." *Civil War Times Illustrated* 5 (Nov. 1966): 20–26.

Rushmore, Elsie Mitchell. *The Indian Policy During Grant's Administrations.* Jamaica, N.Y.: Marion Press, 1914.

Sabine, David B. "The Fifth Wheel: The Troubled Origins of the Chaplaincy." *Civil War Times Illustrated* 19 (May 1980): 14–23.

St. Pierre, Judith. "General O. O. Howard and Grant's Peace Policy." Ph.D. dissertation, University of North Carolina at Chapel Hill, 1990.

Schaff, Philip. *Der Buergerkrieg and das christliche Leben in Nord-Amerika.* 3d ed. Berlin: Wiegandt u. Greben, 1866.

Schuchert, Charles, and Clara Mae LeVene. *O. C. Marsh: Pioneer in Paleontology.* New Haven: Yale University Press, 1940.

Sharpe, W. C. *South Britain: Sketches and Records.* Seymour, Conn.: Record Print, 1898.

Shattuck, C. P. *Military Record of Pepperell, Massachusetts: Historical Address Given in Prescott Hall, June 18, 1877.* Nashua, N.H.: H. R. Wheeler, 1877.

Shattuck, Gardiner H., Jr. *A Shield and Hiding Place: The Religious Life of the Civil War Armies.* Macon, Ga.: Mercer University Press, 1987.

Slattery, Charles Lewis. *Felix Reville Brunot, 1820–1898: A Civilian in the War for the Union, President of the First Board of Indian Commissioners.* New York: Longmans, Green, 1901.

Smith, Alvin Duane, ed. "Two Civil War Notebooks of James Russell Miller." *Journal of the Presbyterian Historical Society* 37 (June 1959): 65–90, and (Sept. 1959): 155–76.

Smith, Edward Parmelee. *Gerty's Papa's Civil War.* Edited by William H. Armstrong. New York: Pilgrim Press, 1984.

———. *Incidents of the United States Christian Commission.* Philadelphia: J. B. Lippincott, 1869.

Smith, Jane F., and Robert M. Kvasnicka. *Indian-White Relations: A Persistent Paradox.* Washington, D.C.: Howard University Press, 1976.

Smith, Timothy L. *Revivalism and Social Reform in Mid-Nineteenth-Century America.* New York: Abingdon Press, 1957.

Smith Rosenberg, Carroll. *Religion and the Rise of the American City: The New York City Mission Movement, 1812–1870.* Ithaca: Cornell University Press, 1971.

Spivey, Donald. *Schooling for the New Slavery: Black Industrial Education, 1868–1915.* Westport, Conn.: Greenwood Press, 1978.

Stanley, A. Knighton. *The Children Is Crying: Congregationalism Among Black People.* New York: Pilgrim Press, 1979.

Sterling, Dorothy, ed. *We Are Your Sisters: Black Women in the Nineteenth Century.* New York: Norton, 1984.

Stillé, Charles J. *History of the United States Sanitary Commission.* Philadelphia: J. B. Lippincott, 1866.

Stowe, Harriet Beecher. *Oldtown Folks.* Boston: Houghton Mifflin, 1911.

————. *Poganuc People: Their Loves and Lives.* 1878. Reprint. Hartford, Conn.: Stowe-Day Foundation, 1977.

Stuart, Paul. *The Indian Office: Growth and Development of an American Institution, 1865–1900.* Ann Arbor: UMI Research Press, 1979.

Swint, Henry Lee. *The Northern Teacher in the South, 1862–1870.* New York: Octagon Books, 1967.

Tatum, Lawrie. *Our Red Brothers and the Peace Policy of President Ulysses S. Grant.* 1899. Reprint. Lincoln: University of Nebraska Press, 1970.

Thoburn, Lyle, ed. *My Experiences During the Civil War by Major Thomas C. Thoburn.* Cleveland, Ohio: N.p., 1963.

Thompson, Alan Smith. "Mobile, Alabama, 1850–1861: Economic, Political, Physical, and Population Characteristics." Ph.D. dissertation, University of Alabama, 1979.

Thompson, Gregory Coyne. "The Origins and Implementation of the American Indian Reform Movement, 1867–1912." Ph.D. dissertation, University of Utah, 1981.

Thompson, Robert Ellis, ed. *The Life of George H. Stuart Written by Himself.* Philadelphia: J. M. Stoddart, 1890.

Thompson, William Y. "The U.S. Sanitary Commission." *Civil War History* 2 (1956): 41–64.

Trani, Eugene P. *The Secretaries of the Department of the Interior, 1849–1969.* [Washington, D.C.]: National Anthropological Archives, 1975.

Trennert, Robert A. "John H. Stout and the Grant Peace Policy Among the Pimas." *Arizona and the West* 28 (Spring 1986): 45–68.

Trowbridge, John T. *The Desolate South, 1865–1866: A Picture of the Battlefields and of the Devastated Confederacy.* Edited by Gordon Carroll. Boston: Little, Brown, 1958.

Tyler, Alice Felt. *Freedom's Ferment: Phases of American Social History from the Colonial Period to the Outbreak of the Civil War.* 1944. Reprint. New York: Harper Torchbooks, 1962.

USCC. *Annual Reports*, 1–4 (for the years 1862–65).

———. *Christ in the Army: A Selection of Sketches of the Work of the United States Christian Commission by Various Writers.* N.p.: Printed for the Ladies' Christian Commission, 1865.

Utley, Robert M. "The Celebrated Peace Policy of General Grant." *North Dakota History* 20 (July 1953): 121–42.

———. *Frontier Regulars: The United States Army and the Indian, 1866–1891.* New York: Macmillan, 1973.

———. *The Indian Frontier of the American West, 1846–1890.* Albuquerque: University of New Mexico Press, 1984.

Vail, A. L. *A Memorial of James M. Haworth, Superintendent of United States Indian Schools.* Kansas City: H. N. Farey, 1886.

Vaughn, William Preston. *Schools for All: The Blacks and Public Education in the South, 1865–1877.* Lexington: University Press of Kentucky, 1974.

Viola, Herman J. *Diplomats in Buckskins: A History of Indian Delegations in Washington City.* Washington, D.C.: Smithsonian Institution Press, 1981.

Walker, Francis Amasa. *The Indian Question.* Boston: James R. Osgood, 1874.

Walker, Williston. *A History of the Congregational Churches in the United States.* New York: Charles Scribner's Sons, 1916.

Waltmann, Henry G. "Circumstantial Reformer: President Grant and the Indian Problem." *Arizona and the West* 13 (Winter 1971): 323–42.

———. "John C. Lowrie and Presbyterian Indian Administration, 1870–1882." *Journal of Presbyterian History* 54 (Summer 1976): 259–76.

Welsh, William. *Indian Office—Wrongs Doing and Reforms Needed.* Philadelphia, Jan. 8, 1874.

———. *Letters on the Home Missionary Work of the Protestant Episcopal Church and the Report of the Lay Committee to the House of Clerical and Lay Deputies, on the Same Subject.* Philadelphia, 1863.

———. *Letter to J. D. Cox, Sept. 23, 1870.*

———. *Report and Supplementary Report of a Visit to Spotted Tail's Tribe of Brule Sioux Indians, the Yankton and Santee Sioux, Ponkas and the Chippewas of Minnesota, Oct. 1870.* Philadelphia, 1870.

———. *Report of a Visit to the Sioux and Ponka Indians on the Missouri River, Made by William Welsh, July, 1872.* Philadelphia: McCulla & Stavely, 1872.

———. *Sales of Indians' Pine Timber, Mar. 13, 1874, William Welsh to Columbus Delano.*

———. *To the Members of the Forty-Third Congress.* Feb. 17, 1874.

———. *A Visit to the Sioux Indians.* New York: American Church Press, 1869.

———, comp. *Taopi and His Friends, or the Indians' Wrongs and Rights.* Philadelphia: Claxton, Remsen & Haffelfinger, 1869.

———, ed. *Women Helpers in the Church: Their Sayings and Doings.* Philadelphia: J. B. Lippincott, 1872.

Whipple, Henry Benjamin. *Lights and Shadows of a Long Episcopate.* New York: Macmillan, 1899.

Whitner, Robert Lee. "The Methodist Episcopal Church and Grant's Peace Policy: A Study of the Methodist Agencies, 1870–1882." Ph.D. dissertation, University of Minnesota, 1959.

Whittier, John Greenleaf. *The Complete Poetical Works of John Greenleaf Whittier.* Cambridge Edition. Boston: Houghton Mifflin, 1894.

Wiley, Bell Irvin. *The Life of Billy Yank: The Common Soldier of the Union.* Indianapolis: Bobbs-Merrill, 1951, 1952.

Williamson, Joel. *After Slavery: The Negro in South Carolina During Reconstruction, 1861–1877.* New York: Norton, 1975.

Winfrey, Dorman H., and James M. Day, eds. *The Indian Papers of Texas and the Southwest, 1825–1916.* Vol. 4. Austin: Pemberton Press, 1966.

Wolfe, Allis. "Women Who Dared: Northern Teachers of the Southern Freedmen, 1862–1872." Ph.D. dissertation, City University of New York, 1982.

Index

499